D0154614

Inclusive Education

Practical Implementation of the Least Restrictive Environment

Lissa A. Power-deFur, PhD
Policy Analyst
Virginia Department of Education
Richmond, Virginia

Fred P. Orelove, PhD
Executive Director
Virginia Institute for
Developmental Disabilities
Virginia Commonwealth University
Richmond, Virginia

AN ASPEN PUBLICATION®
Aspen Publishers, Inc.
Gaithersburg, Maryland
1997

Library of Congress Cataloging-in-Publication Data

Inclusive education: practical implementation
of the least restrictive environment/
Lissa A. Power-deFur, Fred P. Orelove [editors].
p.   cm.
Includes bibliographical references and index.
ISBN 0-8342-0806-7
1. Mainstreaming in education—United States.
2. Handicapped children—Education—United States.
I. Power-deFur, Lissa A.
II. Orelove, Fred P.
LC4031.I523 1997
371.9'046'0973—dc20
96-31327
CIP

Copyright © 1997 by Aspen Publishers, Inc.
All rights reserved.

Aspen Publishers, Inc., grants permission for photocopying for limited personal or internal use.
This consent does not extend to other kinds of copying, such as copying for general distribution,
for advertising or promotional purposes, for creating new collective works, or for resale.
For information, address Aspen Publishers, Inc., Permissions Department,
200 Orchard Ridge Drive, Suite 200, Gaithersburg, Maryland 20878.

Orders: (800) 638-8437
Customer Service: (800) 234-1660

About Aspen Publishers • For more than 35 years, Aspen has been a leading professional publisher in a variety of disciplines. Aspen's vast information resources are available in both print and electronic formats. We are committed to providing the highest quality information available in the most appropriate format for our customers. Visit Aspen's Internet site for more information resources, directories, articles, and a searchable version of Aspen's full catalog, including the most recent publications: **http://www.aspenpub.com**
Aspen Publishers, Inc. • The hallmark of quality in publishing
Member of the worldwide Wolters Kluwer group.

Editorial Resources: Jane Colilla
Library of Congress Catalog Card Number: 96-31327
ISBN: 0-8342-0806-7

Printed in the United States of America

1 2 3 4 5

This book is dedicated to our families—Patrick deFur,
Johanna Cluver, Irene Carney, Emma and Sam Orelove,
and Harriet Power—for their patience and love.

Table of Contents

Chapter 19—Staff-Development Activities **289**
Susan Mongold

Contributors

Carol S. Beers, EdD
Assistant Superintendent
Academic Services
Williamsburg–James City County Schools
Williamsburg, Virginia

Sharon H. deFur, EdD
Educational Specialist
Office of Special Education and Student Services
Virginia Department of Education
Richmond, Virginia

Diane C. Elliott, MS
Community-Based Coordinator
Spotsylvania Special Services
Spotsylvania, Virginia

Johnna R. Elliott, MEd
Consulting Teacher
Blacksburg High School
Montgomery County Public Schools
Blacksburg, Virginia

K. Brigid Flannery, PhD
Assistant Professor
Specialized Training Program
University of Oregon
Eugene, Oregon

Christina Thomasson Gilley, MA
Special Education Consulting Teacher
Belview Elementary School
Christiansburg, Virginia

Patrick H. Haley, MBA
Administrator
Juvenile Services
Department of Human Services
Lynchburg, Virginia

Jaye Harvey, EdD
Interim Assistant Professor
Early Childhood Special Education
Virginia Commonwealth University
Richmond, Virginia

Kathleen Jamison, MS
Consulting Teacher
Christiansburg Middle School
Christiansburg, Virginia

Leslie W. Jones, EdD
Director of Special Services
Spotsylvania County Schools
Spotsylvania, Virginia

Kathe Klare, MSN, JD
Director
Mental Disabilities Law Clinic
Assistant Clinical Professor of Law
University of Richmond School of Law
Richmond, Virginia

Ramona D. Kroll
Special Education Teacher
Christiansburg Middle School
Christiansburg, Virginia

Tracy Landon, EdD
Director
Westminster Child Care Center
Charlottesville, Virginia

Dianne Koontz Lowman, EdD
Assistant Professor
Department of Occupational Therapy
Virginia Commonwealth University
Richmond, Virginia

Pamelia Luttrull, MS
Educational Diagnostician
Big Thicket Special Education Cooperation
Lumberton, Texas

Anne Malatchi, MA
Director
Together We Can Project
Virginia Institute for Developmental Disabilities
Virginia Commonwealth University
Richmond, Virginia

Gail McGregor, EdD
Project Director
Montana Statewide Systems Change Project
Adjunct Associate Professor
Rural Institute on Disabilities
University of Montana
Missoula, Montana

Virginia L. McLaughlin, EdD
Dean and Chancellor Professor
School of Education
College of William and Mary
Williamsburg, Virginia

Susan Mongold, MEd
Director of Continuing Education
School of Dentistry
Virginia Commonwealth University
Richmond, Virginia

Judy K. Montgomery, PhD
Associate Professor
School of Education
Chapman University
Orange, California

Fred P. Orelove, PhD
Executive Director
Virginia Institute for Developmental Disabilities
Virginia Commonwealth University
Richmond, Virginia

Cynthia R. Pitonyak
Special Education Consulting Teacher
Beeks Elementary School
Blacksburg, Virginia

Lissa A. Power-deFur, PhD
Policy Analyst
Virginia Department of Education
Richmond, Virginia

Douglas L. Russell, MEd
Regional Transition Specialist
Educational Services Unit
Virginia Department of Rehabilitative Services
Richmond, Virginia

Melody A. Nay Schaff, MS
Inclusion Specialist
Eastern Instructional Support Center
Instructional Support System of Pennsylvania
Pennsylvania Department of Education
King of Prussia, Pennsylvania

Brenda Chafin Seal, PhD
Associate Professor
Department of Communication Sciences and Disorders
James Madison University
Harrisonburg, Virginia

Janet R. Shelburne
Language Arts and Social Studies Teacher
Christiansburg Middle School
Christiansburg, Virginia

Jeffrey R. Sprague, PhD
Assistant Professor
Specialized Training Program
University of Oregon
Eugene, Oregon

Anne W. Todd, BEd
Specialized Training Program
University of Oregon
Eugene, Oregon

Alice Udvari-Solner, PhD
Assistant Professor
Department of Curriculum and Instruction
Department of Rehabilitation Psychology and
  Special Education
University of Wisconsin, Madison
Madison, Wisconsin

Wyllys D. VanDerwerker
Director for Special Education
Lynchburg City Schools
Lynchburg, Virginia

Ray E. Van Dyke, MA
Principal
Kipps Elementary School
Blacksburg, Virginia

Joyce L. Videlock, PhD, CCC-SP
Supervisor of Special Education
West Chester Area School District
West Chester, Pennsylvania

Mary Dunkle Voorhees, PhD
Early Childhood Special Education Consultant
Charlottesville, Virginia

Preface

We designed this book to be a guide for school personnel who want to provide an inclusive education program for students with disabilities. Our goal is to benefit readers who are just beginning to plan for inclusive education and those who are looking for resources to make improvements. The book's opening chapters provide background information, while subsequent chapters deal with more specific school settings and situations. However, readers should not feel they need to read from start to finish, but rather are encouraged to turn to the particular chapter most relevant to their own situations. Chapters are cross-referenced to help the reader identify other chapters that may be of interest.

Chapter 1 sets forth the philosophy of inclusive education and information regarding the emergence of inclusion as an educational approach. The chapter presents the contrast between successful and unsuccessful education programs and the contrast in the policy and position papers of key educational associations. (Complete texts of policy and position papers are provided in Appendix A.) The remaining chapters are written by contributors who have current experience providing inclusive education opportunities for students with disabilities. The contributors bring experiences from many professions—teacher, speech-language pathologist, principal, special education administrator, social service director, attorney—to provide a rich discussion of the essential elements of a successful approach to inclusive education.

Joyce L. Videlock, Melody A. Nay Schaff, and Gail McGregor (Chapter 2) discuss inclusive education efforts within the overall concept of school reform. Their experience in assisting school divisions combine their inclusion efforts with existing reforms is evident.

Ray E. Van Dyke, Cynthia R. Pitonyak, and Christina Thomasson Gilley (Chapter 3) draw on their successful experience in Montgomery County, Virginia, to provide guidance regarding planning, implementing, and evaluating a successful inclusive education program. The next two chapters provide legal and fiscal background material that many readers should find valuable. In Chapter 4, Kathe Klare, an attorney with over a decade of experience in special education law, gives the reader an overview of federal law, case law, and federal policy decisions that influence the programs our schools offer. (Appendix B includes federal statutes, regulations, and summary of relevant case law.) Leslie W. Jones (Chapter 5) relies on his experience as a state and local special education administrator in his discussion of funding sources and costs of inclusive education.

The success of the student's inclusion into a regular classroom frequently rests on the nature of the adaptations made to the general education curriculum. Alice Udvari-Solner, with extensive public school and university teaching experience, provides practical information in Chapter 6 to assist teachers make these adaptations without feeling that they are compromising the content area. Anne Malatchi, a teacher and advocate, discusses in Chapter 7 the role of dreams in the lives of all students, especially students with disabilities. Her commonsense suggestions will enable educators truly to be partners with the child's family in planning for the child's future.

Patrick H. Haley, a local social services director, and Wyllys D. VanDerwerker, a local special education director, share their experiences working with one another and with other agency representatives to provide coordinated services for students. Their chapter gives the reader information on how interagency planning and services can support local school divisions trying to provide an education for students in the community.

The next section of the book offers a discussion of issues associated with inclusive education from all grade levels—early childhood through secondary school. In Chapter

9, Mary Dunkle Voorhees, Tracy Landon, and Jaye Harvey draw on their successful experiences in developing inclusive educational opportunities for preschool-aged children with disabilities. Johnna R. Elliott builds on her many years of experience as a consulting teacher and statewide special education consultant to create a rich discussion of the elementary years (Chapter 10).

For some educators, the middle school years are the most challenging years. The ideas and information provided by teachers Kathleen Jamison, Ramona D. Kroll, and Janet R. Shelburne will help any middle school teacher or principal. Building on the principles discussed in Chapter 2, Jamison et al. illustrate how inclusive education complements the implementation of middle school reform initiatives.

Judy K. Montgomery's experience as a speech-language pathologist, principal, and special education director in the California public schools are evident in her discussion of an inclusive high school (Chapter 12). Diane C. Elliott, Pamelia Luttrull, and Sharon H. deFur apply their experience working in vocational special needs to Chapter 13, which is a practical guide to working with vocational educators to include students with disabilities. deFur then teams with Douglas L. Russell in Chapter 14 to discuss how the philosophies of inclusive education and transition complement each other for students of transition ages. They point out how the transition process required by the Individuals with Disabilities Education Act is really a bridge to the student's inclusion in life.

Often, educators encounter difficulties providing an inclusive education program in certain challenging situations. Chapters 15 through 18 are designed to assist educators address these situations successfully. The recent focus on safe schools and discipline is often perceived to be at odds with the inclusion of students with challenging behavior. In Chapter 15, K. Brigid Flannery, Jeffrey R. Sprague, and Anne W. Todd discuss methods they have implemented in Oregon and elsewhere to determine the type of programming needed to address challenging behavior and successful implementation strategies. They conclude the chapter with a discussion of situations that become violent or dangerous. Their frank discussion enables educators to meet the rights of a student with disabilities without infringing on the rights of other students.

Dianne Koontz Lowman's chapter (16) addresses children with special health care needs. Lowman's own experience is apparent in the practical suggestions offered. The unique educational needs of children who are deaf are described in Chapter 17 by Brenda Chafin Seal. Seal's 25 years of experience with children and adults who are deaf or hard of hearing is evident in her commonsense discussion of addressing students who may communicate in a different language (American Sign Language) or choose to associate with a distinct social group (Deaf culture). Virginia L. McLaughlin paired her experience in special education with Carol S. Beers's experience as a reading specialist to address the concerns many teachers and families have regarding including students with dyslexia (Chapter 18).

The book concludes (Chapter 19) with a compilation of staff development activities, designed to assist personnel provide inservice training programs in their schools or divisions. Susan Mongold has tailored the inservice materials to reflect the information presented in each of the preceding chapters. In this manner, the readers can focus their staff development on the needs of their school.

We hope readers will come away from this book with some practical ideas that will enrich their schools and classrooms. We also hope that readers will finish this book believing, as we do, that all children are important and are capable of learning and thriving in inclusive educational programs. Finally, we hope that this combination of information and philosophy will inspire readers in their important work in the schools.

The editors gratefully acknowledge the support and assistance provided by their colleagues. We especially want to acknowledge the extraordinary support Elaine Ferrell provided throughout the development of the book.

Lissa A. Power-deFur
Fred P. Orelove

CHAPTER 1

Inclusive Education: The Past, Present, and Future

Lissa A. Power-deFur and Fred P. Orelove

INTRODUCTION

Special issues of academic journals are devoted to intense debates on the merits of inclusive education. Parents of children with disabilities are advocating to have school districts serve their children in general education classrooms. Federal courts are issuing an increasing number of decisions to determine the extent to which schools are required to include learners. National and local print and electronic media are replete with stories about inclusive education.

Public education in the United States has always been an intensely personal issue that is closely scrutinized by its citizens. There is never a shortage of controversial topics—from racial desegregation, to family life education, to violence in the schools. Similarly, controversy is no stranger to the narrower field of special education. There has long been heated discussion around concerns such as labeling, testing, and preparation for adult life. In spite of this history, it is fair to say that the debate over inclusive education has been unusually passionate—and, at times, highly personal. Underneath this passion lie personal values about children and youths with disabilities, and beliefs about the function of education and the role of schools and teachers.

Although it is important to recognize that not all educators and parents are in agreement on inclusive education, this chapter is not designed to analyze the two sides of the inclusion debate. There are many sources to which interested readers can turn.* Rather, this chapter is based on the

*See, for example, the December 1994/January 1995 issue of *Educational Leadership*, the December 1995 issue of *Phi Delta Kappan*, or the Spring-Summer 1995 issue of *The Link*, published by the Appalachian Educational Laboratory.

authors' belief that inclusive education is a philosophy and practice that, when planned and implemented properly, is beneficial for all children and professionals alike. Thus, the chapter is devoted primarily to describing successful inclusion (i.e., what it is and what makes it work). The chapter also explores the historical precedents to inclusive education and examines the foundation for objections to inclusion. Finally, the authors suggest several trends in the provision of inclusive education.

HISTORICAL PRECEDENTS TO INCLUSIVE EDUCATION

Law and Public Policy

Until fairly recently, the issue for students with disabilities was not *where* they would be taught, but *whether* they would be taught. The last group of citizens to be afforded the right to a public education, children with disabilities were guaranteed this right only with the passage of the Education for All Handicapped Children's Act (now the Individuals with Disabilities Education Act, or IDEA) in 1975. Many students with mild disabilities entered general education programs with their peers and succeeded. School districts created separate schools and classes for other students, frequently those with more severe disabilities, for whom there had previously been no educational services.

Both IDEA itself and the regulations that govern the statute provide a legislative basis for inclusion, although the term is not part of the law. The statute speaks to the states' responsibility for placing students with disabilities in the least restrictive environment (LRE). The regulations describe required procedures for educating children with disabilities "with children who are not disabled" and further stipulate that children be removed from the "regular educational environment" only when such education "cannot be achieved satisfactorily." (Chapter 4 describes IDEA and other legislative mandates in greater detail.)

Increasingly, case law has used the LRE standard to require school districts to exhaust attempts to serve children with disabilities in the general education classroom ("Regular classroom placement," 1993). As Osborne and Dimattia (1994) note, these LRE decisions "do not mandate that all students with disabilities must be educated in general education classrooms" (p. 12). They do state, however, that the fact that students with disabilities "may require a different curriculum or may not easily keep up with the rest of the class is not sufficient cause for exclusion" (p. 12). Moreover, schools must consider the nonacademic benefits of inclusion, as well as the academic gains.

Curiously, however, the legal decision that may have provided the most significant impetus to the modern practice of inclusive education came not from special education legislation or disability case law, but from the landmark school desegregation case, *Brown v. Board of Education* (1954). One can appreciate the import of this case for special education by substituting "children with disabilities" for "Negro children" in Chief Justice Earl Warren's comments:

> To separate [children with disabilities] from others of similar age and qualifications solely because of their [disability] generates a feeling of inferiority as to their status in the community that may affect their hearts and minds in a way unlikely ever to be undone. . . . We conclude that in the field of public education, the doctrine of "separate but equal" has no place. Separate educational facilities are inherently unequal. (p. 493)

The education of students with disabilities can be viewed from the same democratic perspective that guided the integration of African-American children—by the belief that every child has a right to a public education with his or her age peers.

Educational Practice and Philosophy

Federal legislation and case law have made it easier for families and advocates to seek placements and supports for students with disabilities in general education classrooms. In addition, many professionals in special education were expressing their growing unrest about the status of learners with special needs. Fueled by shifting philosophical and social values, particularly normalization (Wolfensberger, 1972), educators and parents began to question the usefulness of special education classification, labeling, and placement practices (Stainback, Stainback, & Bunch, 1989). Consequently, there was a shift in the late 1970s and early 1980s to begin integrating students with mild disabilities in

general education class placements on at least a part-time basis. This practice, called *mainstreaming*, was based on the assumption that students must "earn" their opportunity through their ability to keep up with the work assigned by the teacher (Rogers, 1993). For many students, mainstreaming was limited to nonacademic activities (e.g., physical education, art, music, lunch, recess, and assemblies).

In the early to mid-1980s, the mainstreaming concept expanded and assumed a new name: the regular education initiative (REI). The REI movement had as a goal "to increase dramatically the number of children with disabilities in mainstream classrooms by use of large-scale, full-time mainstreaming" (Fuchs & Fuchs, 1994, p. 297). This goal was to be achieved through individualized instruction and cooperative learning (e.g., Slavin & Stevens, 1991). Other major goals were to merge special and general education into one system and to strengthen the academic achievement of students with mild and moderate disabilities (Fuchs & Fuchs, 1994). Madeleine Will, assistant secretary of special education and rehabilitative services, in her report to the secretary of education, offered support for these goals:

> The Office . . . is committed to increasing the educational success of children with learning problems. [The Office of Special Education and Rehabilitation Services] OSERS challenges States to renew their commitment to serve these children effectively. The heart of this commitment is the search for ways to serve as many of these children as possible in the regular classroom by encouraging special education and other special programs to form a partnership with regular education. The objective of the partnership for special education and the other special programs is to use their knowledge and expertise to support regular education in educating children with learning problems. (Will, 1986, p. 20)

In the late 1980s, the U.S. Office of Special Education Programs invited proposals for Statewide Systems Change Grants. These grants were designed to encourage states to change the delivery of educational services for students with severe disabilities from segregated to integrated environments. Some states, particularly in the first several years in which grants were awarded, concentrated primarily on moving learners from segregated schools to regular educational facilities. As the systems change projects evolved, the efforts became increasingly focused on serving children in general education classrooms.

Inclusion, or inclusive education, became a logical extension of the ideas, practices, and beliefs described to this point. The inclusive schools movement, which has its origins in the late 1980s, and which has gained significant strength and visibility in the 1990s, was started principally by advocates for learners with severe disabilities, who were not an essential part of the regular education initiative. Inclusive education also gained significant momentum as a result of public debate around educational reform. In particular, the effectiveness of a segregated special education system was being called into question (e.g., Gartner & Lipsky, 1987; Lipsky & Gartner, 1989; "Separate and unequal," 1993). Researchers found that, compared to students without disabilities, students with disabilities graduated at lower rates, left schools with inferior skills, were far less likely to find a job, and, in general, were unprepared to live in their communities as adults (National Council on Disability, 1994; Wagner, Blackorby, Cameto, & Newman, 1993; Wagner et al., 1991). The National Association of State Boards of Education (NASBE, 1992) charged that special education had become a separate education system serving students with disabilities, isolated from the general education system. The NASBE report states, "Rather than special education supporting the general education system, the two commonly function in separate orbits that may or may not be connected with actual student learning or the needs of the child as a whole" (p. 8). Indeed, a commonly heard, if pessimistic, rallying cry in the late 1980s was "Special education isn't special and isn't education" (Merrow, 1996). Thus, as the following section will show, efforts to implement inclusive education were based on both social values and the perceived need for reform of special education.

INCLUSIVE EDUCATION DEFINED

In part because the terms *inclusion* or *inclusive education* do not appear in the law, and because inclusion grew out of a grassroots movement, there has been confusion over the exact meaning of the terms. Another source of confusion is that inclusion had its origins in a philosophy or set of values about the rights of children with disabilities. However, inclusive education (i.e., educating children in general education classrooms) is supported by proponents not only for its "correctness," but for its educational utility—that is, because it produces better educational and social outcomes for children. (This situation of multiple interpretations and origins has led not only to confusion about definitions, but to lack of clarity and focus in the debate between pro- and anti-inclusionists.)

This book adopts the following definition of *inclusive education*: "The practice of providing a child with disabilities with his or her education within the general education classroom, with the supports and accommodation needed by that student. This inclusion typically takes place at the student's neighborhood school" (National Information Center for Children and Youth with Disabilities, 1995, p. 3). Inclusive education suggests a number of practices and poli-

cies, not only in the classroom, but within the school and school district. Exhibit 1–1 describes eight such practices. Because inclusive education has not always been implemented carefully or correctly, a number of practices have emerged that can be considered *noninclusive* practices. They are delineated in Exhibit 1–1.

The practice of inclusive education is based on a philosophy that assumes general and special (and vocational) education can work together in a unified system that embraces all students and accommodates their diverse talents and needs. There is ample evidence from schools across the country that educators who attempt inclusive education without first explicitly articulating clear values to guide their practice typically fail. Beginning with the unconditional acceptance of all children and commitment to provide as much support as the child needs to be successful, inclusive education focuses on what the child *can* do, rather than on what he or she cannot do.

THE SUCCESS OF INCLUSIVE EDUCATION

There is no question that inclusive education, when planned and implemented thoughtfully, has been successful. This success has been documented through both anecdotal accounts and a growing body of research data. At a systems level, inclusive education eliminates the dual curriculum in place in many school districts—separate general and special education curricula by grade level and content area, often with little coordination between programs. Such a system jeopardizes the opportunity for students with disabilities to complete the coursework necessary for graduation or to acquire the knowledge and skills required for postsecondary instruction or work. Inclusive education identifies that students with disabilities should have the opportunity to be included in school assessment measures, especially those that serve as barrier tests (e.g., a requirement for graduation).

In summarizing the outcomes of inclusive education, this section is organized around four groups of individuals who are affected by inclusive educational practices: learners with disabilities, classmates without disabilities, family members, and teachers and other school personnel.

Learners with Disabilities

The evidence of success of inclusive education for learners with disabilities has been based, until recently, on case histories and anecdotal reports from general and special education teachers, parents, and classmates (e.g., Farlow, 1996; Hoover, 1993; Martin, 1994; Smith, 1994). Viewed collectively, however, these reports represent impressive support for inclusive education, from elementary through secondary schools, from California to Maine. Parents have shared stories about their children learning new skills more

Exhibit 1–1 Inclusive and Noninclusive Practices

Inclusive Practices

1. School has a philosophy that respects all students as learners and contributing members of the classroom and school community and holds the highest aspirations for all students.
2. Students attend the school and class they would attend if they did not have disabilities, following same schedule as other students and receiving support services in or out of the classroom.
3. Students attend general education classes with their age peers.
4. General education classes have a natural proportion of students with and without disabilities in the class (approximately 10–15 percent of students in the class).
5. Students with disabilities receive the supports they need to be successful in the classroom (e.g., curriculum adaptation and modification, assistive technology, adult and peer assistance).
6. Teachers who have students with disabilities in their classrooms receive the supports necessary for them to teach all students in their class successfully (e.g., planning time, consultation and collaboration with specialists, classroom support, training).
7. Parents of students with disabilities are given every opportunity to be full participants in their child's education.
8. As a new educational practice, planning and training precede implementation.

Noninclusive Practices

1. Placing children with disabilities into regular classes without prior planning or the necessary supports and services ("dumping")
2. Reducing or eliminating special education services needed by the child with disabilities or the other children in the classroom
3. Educating all children the same—learning the same thing, at the same time, in the same way; ignoring each child's unique needs
4. Asking teachers without prior training or without concurrent support to teach children who have disabilities
5. Sacrificing the education of all children so that children with disabilities can be integrated
6. Working toward a goal of placing students with disabilities in the general classroom rather than a goal of meeting the education needs of each student, resulting in an overall reduction in the quality of education

Courtesy of PEAK Parent Center, Inc., Colorado Springs, Colorado, and University of New Hampshire Institute on Disability, Durham, New Hampshire.

quickly by watching classmates and feeling like they belonged, teachers have reported how formerly difficult behaviors were handled efficiently and positively by classmates, and classmates have spoken of making new friends (Tashie et al., 1993b).

With the practice of inclusive education on the rise, researchers and educators have been able to document more rigorously the outcomes for children with disabilities. In one of the first such studies, Kozleski and Jackson (1993) examined the experiences of educators and children as they participated in the "full inclusion" of Taylor, a girl with severe disabilities, over a three-year period—from third through fifth grades. All of the respondents indicated that Taylor's opportunities for social participation and friendship improved over the three years. Over time, for example, classmates began to initiate phone calls and to include Taylor in parties and after-school play. Moreover, the staff and parents reported numerous positive changes in Taylor's adaptive skills attributable to being in an inclusive setting.

More recently, a group of general educators reported on their experiences with children included in their fourth- and fifth-grade classrooms:

According to individualized education plans [sic] (IEPs) and other student performance measures, all students with disabilities in our inclusive classrooms are doing as well as or better than they did in previous years in self-contained classrooms. Their on-task behavior is equal to or greater than similar students in self-contained classes. (Rankin et al., 1994, p. 235)

In general, students with disabilities in inclusive settings have shown improvement in standardized tests, acquired social and communication skills previously undeveloped, shown increased interaction with peers, achieved more and higher-quality IEP goals, and are better prepared for postschool experiences (Hardin & McNelis, 1996; Hunt, Farron-Davis, Beckstead, Curtis, & Goetz, 1994; Laski & Henderson, 1996). This does not mean, of course, that every student will automatically perform better academically in an inclusive classroom. Indeed, some researchers in the field of learning disabilities and emotional disturbances (e.g., Kauffman, Lloyd, Baker, & Riedel, 1995; Zigmond, Jenkins, Fuchs, Deno, & Fuchs, 1995) suggest that the answer to that question is, at best, equivocal at this point in our knowledge.

We also do not know what the long-term effects of inclusive education will be. Many proponents have advanced their cause on the belief that all children belong. It is possible that inclusive education need not be proven superior to other models academically or behaviorally, but that it is sufficient to obtain equivalent results while affording students the opportunity to be educated in a nonsegregated environment. The benefits may be the *feeling* of belonging, the increase in self-esteem, and a greater receptivity to learning. There is also evidence that inclusive settings can expand a student's personal interests and knowledge of the world, which is excellent preparation for adulthood (Tashie et al., 1993b). For now, however, it is safe to say that many learners have matured and prospered in general education classrooms with appropriate supports and services.

Classmates

The positive effects of inclusive education on classmates without disabilities have been well documented. Both research and anecdotal data have shown that typical learners have demonstrated a greater acceptance and valuing of individual differences, enhanced self-esteem, a genuine capacity for friendship, and the acquisition of new skills (Janney, Snell, Beers, & Raynes, 1995; Tashie et al., 1993b; York, Vandercook, Macdonald, Heise-Neff, & Caughey, 1992; Zeph, Gilmer, Brewer-Allen, & Moulton, 1992). Hardin and McNelis (1996) reported improvements in course grades and standardized tests for general education students. They noted that low-achieving students benefited from the review, practice, clarity, and feedback provided to students with disabilities.

In their study of Taylor's inclusion into general education, Kozleski and Jackson (1993) reported that the majority of students in Taylor's fifth-grade class believed that they got along better with one another than students in other (i.e., noninclusive) classes. Rankin et al., who are general educators, provided specific examples of the participation of classmates in inclusive classrooms they visited:

> I saw students . . . actively involved in solving real problems of including the student with severe disabilities and that student being functionally involved in his actual community of ten-year-old peers. I saw students in general education becoming intensely interested in how their peers with disabilities learned. I saw [them] beginning to be intensely interested in their own learning. (1994, p. 236)

When inclusive education is implemented appropriately, such reports from school personnel are the rule, rather than the exception.

Even more affecting and telling, however, are the comments from the children themselves. Many of the children remark about the opportunity both to learn from and to teach others. Nine-year-old April wrote:

> I learned alot from Mike. I learned that he can't talk with his mouth, but, he can talk with his eyes and his movements. At first I didn't like him because I thought he was different, but as the year passed I learned that he is not much different than I am. He is very special. I am glad he is in my class. Every body in my class gets a chance to be his helper. I am glad when it is my turn. (Zeph et al., 1992, p. 16)

Many of the children, however, speak in even simpler terms, such as Jessica, a first grader: "I feel good, and glad that we have him here. And he's my friend" (Zeph et al., 1992, p. 13).

Family Members

To the degree that inclusive education enhances the academic and social outcomes of children with disabilities, families clearly benefit, as well. Some of the benefits are direct. For example, in the Kozleski and Jackson (1993) study, Taylor's mother noted increases in Taylor's independent living skills, such as food preparation, hygiene, and shopping. The efficiency of inclusion in achieving certain goals is summed up in the words of a mother of a 13-year-old girl: "For years my daughter had objectives on her IEP to teach her how to become more social. Now that she is in 8th grade classes all day, her friends have taught her how to be a regular teenager" (Tashie et al., 1993b, p. 6).

Other benefits are indirect. Because inclusive education typically is provided in the neighborhood school, the parents of children moved to an inclusive class in a new school may suddenly discover less-complicated logistics, especially if they have more than one school-age child. The family also gains the benefit of heightened connection to other families in the community. One father wrote:

> We had been living on Maple Street for many years when our daughter Erika began attending our neighborhood school. When a classmate called to invite Erika to a party, I was shocked to find out that the girl lived right down the street from us. We had lived here all of these years and the girls had never met before. (Tashie et al., 1993b, p. 6)

But perhaps the biggest benefit to inclusive education for parents is that general education often is the vehicle to realizing the family's dreams for their child. These dreams typically include acceptance and belonging. (See Chapter 7 for more information on dreams and families.) They may also include greater independence as an adolescent and adult. One family shared the following story about their son, Shawn, who was born with Down syndrome. Shawn is now a young adult working at a local bank.

> At age 15, [Shawn] told us that he would someday like to live on his own and have a job. We realized then that we had to create more opportunities for Shawn to develop his independence and help him become more involved in his community high school. . . . [H]e started a part-time job. He began to take high school classes that would help him in the business world. (Dillon et al., 1994, unpaginated)

Finally, parents of students without disabilities come to appreciate the more cooperative social milieu that inclusive classrooms bring. They are also grateful for the positive changes they see in their own children, such as increased sensitivity to others (Laski & Henderson, 1996).

Teachers and Other School Personnel

Because organizing and conducting an inclusive education program takes a great deal of time and work, and because the teaching and administrative staff are so critical to its success, it is important to accrue benefits to school personnel. The research shows that teachers in inclusive settings collaborate more and spend more time planning, learn new techniques from one another, participate in more professional development activities, show a greater willingness to change, and use a wider range of creative strategies to meet students' needs (Laski & Henderson, 1996).

Teachers and other staff have spoken movingly, not only of the successes of their students, but also of what working in inclusive classrooms and schools has meant to them professionally and personally. In one of the earliest studies of the impact of inclusion on teachers (Giangreco, Dennis, Cloninger, Edelman, & Schattman, 1993), general education teachers who experienced increased ownership and involvement with their newly included students discussed how their experiences changed them. Several teachers reported being more reflective, and others talked about the importance of their serving as a positive model for the class. Still other teachers felt proud at their openness to change and more confident in their ability to approach teaching flexibly. Finally, the teachers' experiences with inclusion had an impact on how they taught *all* of their children:

> I've used a lot of the ideas that I started out using last year because I spent a lot of time thinking about them to incorporate Katie. I've used them again this year even though I don't have a special needs kid and because I found them successful with the regular ed [sic] kids. But my purpose in

developing them was thinking about Katie. (Giangreco et al., 1993, p. 370)

The use of case study and qualitative methods of measuring the impact of inclusive education is appropriate. After all, one of the hallmarks of special education has always been the design of supports and services for the individual learner. To borrow from the television commercial of a well-known investment firm, "We measure success one [student] at a time." What proponents of successful inclusive education have discovered is that the model is very effective for many learners. One of the secrets of that success lies in the attitudes and beliefs of the personnel. This and other elements underlying successful inclusive education are now fairly well known and are described in the following section.

ELEMENTS OF SUCCESSFUL INCLUSION

Establishing successful inclusive education takes a mixture of vision, leadership, commitment, collaborative planning, knowledge, and time. Inclusive education involves looking at the big picture and attending to the details. And inclusive education requires tremendous commitment to change. This section outlines these and other elements that educational personnel and parents have described as important contributors to successful inclusive education programs. (Subsequent chapters treat these elements and processes in greater detail.) For clarity, this section is primarily organized around three broad levels of planning and implementation: state-level activities, school district activities, and school and classroom activities. Success at any level requires both an initial spark and the ongoing commitment from individuals who care about the education of children and who have the power and determination to make change happen.

State-Level Activities

Although it is often not necessary for states to do anything for inclusive education to be successful in individual schools or school districts, state support makes it more likely for local administrators to undertake a difficult job. Moreover, state governments and education agencies are in a valuable position to help the schools implement inclusive education more effectively and efficiently.

Some of the actions states can take to support local schools include the following (National Association of State Boards of Education, 1992; National Council on Disability, 1994):

- Remove school finance policies that encourage segregated or categorical placements.
- Modify teacher training and certification regulations to prepare teachers better to work with a broad range of learners.

- Create incentives to place students in a neighborhood school (e.g., have the money that would otherwise have been spent in a segregated placement follow the child to the inclusive placement).
- Require the involvement of parents and persons with disabilities in local decision making.
- Require that special education be included in education reform efforts, including reform of state assessment programs.
- Provide grant programs to develop effective models.
- Work across state agencies to integrate funding for school-linked services.
- Establish statewide technical assistance and ongoing professional development for school personnel on planning for and implementing inclusive education.

While several states have supported inclusive education, Vermont's efforts and achievements are instructive. Of children with disabilities in Vermont, 83 percent are served in general education classrooms (Thousand & Villa, 1995). Some of the actions the state took to get to this point are described below.

- In the late 1960s, rather than establishing categorical and separate programs for students with learning and other mild disabilities, Vermont focused on staff development and supports for local schools. These supports were expanded in the mid-1970s for learners with severe disabilities through the creation of statewide interdisciplinary support teams (I-teams). During the 1980s, Vermont, in conjunction with the state universities, and through the continuing provision of technical assistance, "brought home" hundreds of students from regional programs to general education classrooms in local schools.
- In 1987, the state board of education, state legislators, the state department of education, and education advocacy groups developed a document (*Vermont Education Goals*) that articulated the restructuring of schools "to support the high performance of every student and a vision of 'no special education as we used to know it'" (Thousand & Villa, 1995, p. 290). In response, the state legislature "created a funding formula that allowed funding of special services for a student regardless of the *place* in which the services were delivered" (Thousand & Villa, 1995, p. 290). A subsequent modification of the funding formula in 1990 further removed monetary incentives for labeling students "by distributing a large block grant portion of the formula to school districts based on each district's *total school enrollment* rather than on the *number of students identified* as eligible for special education" (Thousand & Villa, 1995, p. 290).

- This same state statute required that "each local school district design and implement, in consultation with parents, a comprehensive system of education services that will result . . . in all students succeeding in the regular classroom" (quoted in Thousand & Villa, 1995, p. 290). The statute further specified that (1) 1 percent of the total state special education budget be dedicated to the training of teachers and administrators toward this end, and (2) each school establish an instructional support team to help teachers avoid special education referrals of children who might be better served by additional classroom support.

Vermont is but one state, and its small size and relative homogeneity simplify the delivery of services. Nevertheless, Vermont's broad-scale achievements offer lessons for other states. Success can be largely attributed to strong state leadership and coalition building; innovative policies on funding, placement, and personnel; and ongoing technical assistance and support to localities. Above all, changes in educational practices for students with disabilities were driven by policies and desire for reform for *all students*.

School District Activities

Local school districts decide to adopt inclusive education for a variety of reasons. As Roach (1995) observes, the move to inclusive services represents a logical and desirable step for some districts. Other districts undertake inclusion in response to external forces, such as litigation or the necessity of closing a regional facility. Similarly, the planning and implementation phases are driven by various practical and ideological factors. Some districts use an evolutionary process, accommodating the requests of individual parents to include their children or initiating inclusion through pilot projects, often funded externally. There are problems with both of these approaches; the episodic and narrow focus often results in failure after the external stimulus is gone. The system does not change, because it has not been forced to consider how it needs to restructure to accommodate all of its students (Roach, 1995). Successful districtwide inclusive education efforts, like successful statewide efforts, grow out of a genuine desire by the school's leadership to embrace and more effectively educate *all* learners, including those with disabilities.

One of the advantages of a district's gradually phasing in inclusion (i.e., by grade level or school) is that support is built in as implementation progresses. This approach helps to sustain inclusive education, and it is not dependent on a particular superintendent or school board member (Roach, 1995). Some smaller or more rural districts, however, have been successful in converting all their schools to an inclusive model in a short (one- to two-year) period.

Most local school districts take steps to ensure that funds previously used to support students with disabilities in separate placements are carried with those students into the general education classroom. Some districts have used the cost savings of closing separate facilities to hire additional classroom assistants to support inclusive education. As Roach (1995) cautions, however, "undertaking inclusion as a cost-saving measure dooms it to resistance, suspicion, and, ultimately, failure" (p. 297). (See Chapter 5 for more information on financing inclusive education.)

Apart from making broad decisions about funding and the scope of the inclusion effort, district administrators can take specific actions to promote inclusive education in their schools. Janney et al. (1995) conducted interviews with general and special education teachers and administrators in five school districts where students with disabilities had recently been integrated into general education schools and classrooms. In school districts that experienced success, district administrators not only "gave a green light" to change, but secured technical assistance and engaged in several months of planning and preparation. Each of the district administrators Janney et al. interviewed "spoke of the challenge of providing direction and assistance while at the same time ensuring participatory planning, site-based decision making, and teacher autonomy" (p. 436).

School and Classroom Activities

Not surprisingly, the greatest attention has been paid to successful elements of inclusive education at the level of the school and classroom. It is at this front-line level where decisions are made daily—sometimes minute-to-minute—and where real change in school culture can be seen. Moreover, there is a great deal going on within schools—from curriculum decisions, to the school culture, to team meetings, to home-school relationships. All of this activity involves a tremendous number of people: general and special education teachers, teaching assistants, related services personnel (therapists, librarians, art teachers, and others), principals and other building administrators, school support staff (secretaries, food services and maintenance workers, bus drivers, and others), and—of course—the *students*. Following is a list of activities that school personnel view as important indicators of successful inclusion (Janney et al., 1995; National Information Center for Children and Youth with Disabilities, 1995; Rankin et al., 1994; Roach, 1995; Tashie et al., 1993b):

- *Begin with a philosophy that supports appropriate inclusive practices.* A clear philosophy about the value of *all* students, developed by all staff and families, can serve as an important bridge builder across different groups of people, as well as an anchor during difficult periods of implementation. A philosophy statement also offers decision makers the authority to commit resources to support the decisions that are made (National Information Center for Children and Youth with Disabilities, 1995). Ideally, a philosophy will be developed not only at the school level, but at the state and district levels, too.

- *Plan carefully and thoroughly.* It is clear that inclusive education does not occur by happenstance. School personnel who have implemented inclusive education identify the planning stage as critical to success. The planning process should include everyone. Many schools develop core planning groups or teams, who maintain contact with other school staff and families. Early planning sessions should enable teachers and others to ask questions freely in a nonthreatening environment and should deal with anticipated fears about inclusion. Successful planning also involves discussion of how staff will work together. More specific issues will also arise, such as how grades will be determined and how teachers will be held accountable for progress of students with disabilities. "Successfully involving teachers in planning is based on empowering teachers to take control of and responsibility for the change to inclusion" (Roach, 1995, p. 298).

- *Involve the principal as a change agent.* School principals set the tone for success of any education initiative, inclusive education being no exception. Teaching staff reported that the principal was important in establishing a positive tone, in demonstrating respect for teachers as professionals, in maintaining communication, in bringing in new information, and in dealing with logistical issues (Janney et al., 1995).

- *Involve parents.* Families need to be involved from the beginning stages of planning. Apart from their obvious stake in the outcomes, parents bring valuable perspective and information to the table that cannot be matched. School personnel can enhance successful inclusion by communicating openly and honestly, by respecting families' cultural patterns and beliefs, and by listening carefully to their suggestions and concerns (Tomey, 1994).

- *Provide necessary training and supports to staff.* This is one of the single most important elements of successful inclusive education. In a survey of general and special education teachers involved in inclusion in Pennsylvania (Wolery, Werts, Caldwell, Snyder, & Lisowski, 1995), all respondents indicated a high need for personal support and training. More interesting, "the teachers who rated themselves as successful and those who rated themselves as unsuccessful were in some cases from the same district, but they reported different levels of access to training resources and supports" (pp. 23–24). Helpful training for inclusion includes (1) site visits to inclusive classrooms and to current placements from which students will come, (2) situation-specific problem-solving sessions, especially after the teachers have had some experience in their inclusive settings, (3) sessions on instructional strategies and curricular adaptations, and (4) inservice sessions on the change process itself (Roach, 1995).

- *Provide structure and support for ongoing collaboration.* Since inclusive education is based on a unified general and special education system, success depends on the ability of various educators to work together. One group of general educators (Rankin et al., 1994) stated bluntly, "We have come to the realization that providing time for teachers to reflect and plan together *is* the most effective staff development available" (p. 237). The principal plays an important role in making this time available in staff schedules.

Clearly, there are many other specific tasks that classroom staff and teams within schools need to perform to make inclusive education successful. These include, for example, reviewing and rewriting IEPs; modifying tasks, materials, and instruction; and developing strategies for evaluating student performance. These and other tasks are described in subsequent chapters.

Finally, in implementing inclusive education, team members must be able to confront resistance successfully. Some level of resistance is an inevitable response to impending change that affects people personally or represents a fear of the unknown (Janney et al., 1995). Typically, most of the opposition dissipates with planning, preparation, and implementation (Roach, 1995). Resistance fades as legitimate concerns are attended to, with open lines of communication for sharing information.

REACTIONS TO INCLUSION INITIATIVES

Resistance to change within a school where inclusive education is being actively implemented accounts for only one source of opposition—and one that is understandable and typically manageable. Like any initiative, inclusion does not enjoy universal favor. This section examines the reaction to inclusion within the education community and by the public, including the popular media.

Education Community

The reaction of the education community to efforts to implement inclusive education is varied. Appendix A includes the policy and position statements of 15 education associations. The reactions of these groups range from wholehearted support, to expressions of concern, to negativ-

ity. Exhibit 1–2 depicts how each association defines *inclusion*, either explicitly or by usage. A handful of organizations (e.g., The National Association of State Boards of Education, The Association for Persons with Severe Handicaps) address inclusion as a philosophy of education. Others provide a factual accounting of the nature of inclusion—what inclusion looks like in a school building (e.g., The Council for Exceptional Children, National Association of Elementary School Principals). A third approach can be detected in the statements that stress the limitations experienced by members of the association (e.g., the American Federation of Teachers [AFT], Learning Disability Association of America). The differences in perspective are instructive because they help educators identify the features that enable success (e.g., a philosophy that embraces all children) as well as features that create barriers (e.g., perceptions that placements are made without regard to individual needs of students).

Despite these clear successes associated with including students with disabilities, general and special educators, administrators, and parents have also endured poorly planned and executed attempts to include students. These experiences have generated barriers to further inclusion. The strong position taken by the AFT, which calls for a moratorium on the placement of children with disabilities in general education classrooms (Shanker, 1994/1995), is illustrative of the barriers created by the failed efforts. The AFT's survey of its members revealed that three-quarters would object to the adoption of a full-inclusion policy for their school (Richardson, 1994). A review of these teachers' experiences explains their strong reaction. Many teachers received minimal support from special education staff and their administration. Teachers also reported high numbers of students with disabilities compared to the number of students without disabilities.

The costs of special education, frequently termed "staggering" (Elam & Rose, 1995), has also caused some to view inclusive education negatively. For instance, Douglass Otto, superintendent of the Anoka-Hennepin Independent School District #11 in Minnesota, calls the special education programs "untouchable" (Schnaiberg, 1995). Special education programs are consuming proportionately greater percentages of school district budgets. Reactions run high when special education is untouched by budget-cutting measures, while other education programs are significantly curtailed. Superintendent Otto is concerned about this imbalance: "I have to protect the rights of special-education children at the expense of the rest of the student population" (Schnaiberg, 1995, p. 28). There is great concern that the federal government has mandated the provision of costly special education services, yet has failed to provide adequate funding (Elam & Rose, 1995).

Efforts to promote inclusive education often run up against these perceived budget inequities (McCormick &

Exhibit 1–2 Definitions of Inclusion Used by Education Associations

Association	Definition
American Federation of Teachers, *AFT Resolution on Inclusion of Students with Disabilities*	"Inclusion [is] the placement of all students with disabilities in general education classrooms without regard to the nature or severity of the students' disabilities, their ability to behave and function appropriately in the classroom, or the educational benefits they can derive."
American Speech-Language-Hearing Association, *Inclusive Practices for Children and Youths with Communication Disorders*	"Inclusive-practices philosophy emphasizes serving children and youths in the least restrictive environment that meets their needs optimally."
Children and Adults with Attention Deficit Disorders, *CHADD Position on Inclusion*	"The concept of inclusion should reflect society's commitment that every child be educated in the environment that is most appropriate to that child's identified needs."
Council for Exceptional Children, *CEC Policy Regarding Inclusive Schools and Community Settings*	"In inclusive schools, the building administrator and staff, with the assistance from the special education administration, should be primarily responsible for the education of children, youth and young adults with disabilities."
Division for Early Childhood, Council for Exceptional Children, *DEC Position on Inclusion*	"Inclusion, as a value, supports the right of all children, regardless of their diverse abilities, to participate actively in natural settings within their communities. A natural setting is one in which the child would spend time had he or she not had a disability."
Division for Learning Disabilities, Council for Exceptional Children, *Inclusion: What Does It Mean for Students with Learning Disabilities?*	"A 'full inclusion' program, as defined by its advocates, provides placements only in general education classes for students with learning disabilities."
Learning Disabilities Association of America, *Position Paper on Full Inclusion of All Students with Learning Disabilities in the Regular Education Classroom*	"'Full inclusion,' 'full integration,' 'unified system,' 'inclusive education' are terms used to describe a popular policy/practice in which all students with disabilities, regardless of the nature or the severity of the disability and need for related services, receive their total education within the regular education classroom in their home school."
National Association of Elementary School Principals, *Position Statement on Inclusion*	"... inclusion of special education students, as appropriate, in regular classrooms with their peers in their neighborhood schools."
National Association of School Psychologists, *Position Statement: Inclusive Programs for Students with Disabilities*	"Inclusive programs are those in which students, regardless of the severity of their disability, receive appropriate specialized instruction and related services within an age-appropriate general education classroom in the school that they would attend if they did not have a disability."
National Association of State Boards of Education, *Resolution on Students with Special Needs*	"Inclusion is not a place or a method of delivering instruction; it is a philosophy of supporting children in their learning that undergirds the entire system." "The inclusive philosophy of supported education espoused is truly grounded in the belief that *all* children can learn and *achieve*."

continues

Exhibit 1–2 continued

Association	Definition
National Center for Learning Disabilities, *An NCLD Statement on Inclusion*	"The concept of inclusion refers to an administrative arrangement within schools and classrooms whereby all children, regardless of handicap, receive education services within a 'regular' classroom environment. Inclusion, therefore, refers to an educational concept where children receive even specialized services within the context of the general classroom."
National Education Association, *Policy Statement on Appropriate Inclusion*	"Appropriate inclusion is characterized by practices and programs which provide for the following on a sustained basis: . . . full continuum of placement options and services within each option."
National Joint Committee on Learning Disabilities, *A Reaction to Full Inclusion: A Reaffirmation of the Right of Students with Learning Disabilities to a Continuum of Services*	"The idea that all students with learning disabilities must be served only in regular education classrooms, frequently referred to as full inclusion." "Full inclusion violates the rights of parents and students with disabilities."
The Association for Persons with Severe Handicaps, *Resolution on Inclusive Education*	"A definition of inclusion . . . begins with the educational and moral imperatives that students with disabilities belong in general education classrooms and that they receive the supports and services necessary to benefit from their education in the general education setting."
The Orton Dyslexia Society, *The Orton Dyslexia Society Position Statement on Inclusion*	"Inclusion is the opportunity for all students with disabilities to have access to and participate in all activities of the school environment in neighborhood schools. Inclusion allows some or all of a student's special education and related services to be provided in regular education classes."

First, 1994). When examining a budget in which the cost of educating a student in special education is more than twice the cost of educating a student in general education, policymakers are often hesitant to embrace a new approach to special education. (This is one important reason, as suggested earlier, for framing inclusive education as an *educational*, not a *special* educational, concern.) Although federal law requires decisions to be made apart from financial concerns, these financial concerns are ever present in the minds of superintendents, school board members, and local government officials. The cost savings associated with returning students from private day or residential special education placements are often overlooked. In addition, local districts are often limited in their ability to introduce a program or service that has the potential for future cost-savings, but that has present costs associated with the completion of physical space adaptations, equipment purchases, and staff development. (See Chapter 5 for data on specific costs of implementing inclusive education.)

Other arguments come from educators, parents, and advocates who value separate programs (e.g., Fuchs & Fuchs, 1994/1995; Webb, 1994). Some parents are protective of their children and do not want them exposed to the general education population (and vice versa). Advocates

for students with learning disabilities argue that the unique educational needs associated with dyslexia and other conditions cannot be met in general education classrooms (e.g., Maloney, 1994/1995; Zigmond et al., 1995). The Deaf community is strongly committed to the maintenance of residential schools for the deaf, places where the student's identity within that community is nurtured. Some believe that students with emotional and behavioral disabilities require highly structured environments with large numbers of staff (Kauffman et al., 1995). These parents and professionals argue that separate programs can be equal, if not superior.

Public and Popular Media

Beyond the concerns expressed by parents and professionals, the public at-large has expressed its views. The 1995 results of the annual Phi Delta Kappa/Gallup education poll are revealing (Elam & Rose, 1995). Two-thirds of the respondents believed that children with learning problems should be placed in special classrooms. More than a third of the respondents believed that the inclusion of students with learning problems in general education classrooms would have a negative effect on other students and on the students with disabilities, whereas another third believed it would have neither a positive nor negative impact.

Because the vast majority of the public have little or no direct contact with inclusive education, it is reasonable to assume that their attitudes are shaped to some extent by what they read in newspapers and magazines and what they see on television. Like the reactions within the education community, the reports in the media have been mixed. Local stories are covered by local or regional newspapers and typically have human interest value or are written in response to a newsworthy event, such as a highly visible due process hearing or court case. Such articles can trigger either local support for or opposition to inclusion. An editorial in the *Roanoke (Virginia) Times and World-News*, which concerned the case of a family that moved to Montgomery County, Virginia, because of the district's renown for inclusive education, raised timely and provocative issues:

> For parents . . . who think their disabled children should be in regular classrooms . . . is mainstream-minded Montgomery becoming a magnet? If so, should Montgomery taxpayers subsidize the education of youngsters who in other jurisdictions have been deemed too disruptive to be taught in regular classrooms? Should schools in one district be forced to take in children whose parents . . . don't like the schools in another district where they've been living and paying taxes? ("Main-streaming in Montgomery," 1995, p. A6)

Sometimes, local issues are picked up by the national media, and then the story becomes expanded through quotes by state and national authorities. The story about the nine-year-old boy and his family, editorialized in the Roanoke, Virginia, paper is a case in point. The *Washington Post* and *People* magazine wrote articles examining both sides of the inclusion debate.

National exposure of inclusive education issues is also provided through first-person stories. The *New York Times*, for example, ran op-ed pieces by a sign language interpreter for a deaf student and a man with an autistic nephew in an inclusive school (Cohen, 1994; Martin, 1994). The two columns were opposed to and supportive of inclusion, respectively. The *New York Times* also carries a regular Sunday column on education issues written by Albert Shanker, president of the AFT. Although Shanker's column is a paid advertisement, its prominence and regularity undoubtedly cause it to be read by thousands of people. One of Shanker's regular targets is inclusive education; unfortunately, he sheds little light on the issue. For example, Shanker turned over one of his columns to a woman who reared a son with Down syndrome (Wyllie, 1996). What makes this interesting is that her son is 37 years old—which means he *completed* his public school education around the time the Education for All Handicapped Children's Act was signed into law. Yet the mother asserts that had her son been included "in a regular elementary classroom with his own age group, he would have foundered as he struggled to learn. Failure would have destroyed his self-esteem" (p. 7).

Treatment of inclusive education in the electronic media is less prevalent. Although occasional stories have been broadcast on network news shows, such as *Today*, there has not been the same attempt to depict the complexity of the issues. One notable exception was a May 10, 1996 broadcast on public television, *The Merrow Report*. Merrow interviewed parents, teachers, and administrators both for and against inclusion; individuals with disabilities; and key federal officials in the U.S. Department of Education. Previously uninformed viewers likely came away with a sense of the depth of feeling on both sides of the inclusion debate and could form their own opinions.

THE FUTURE OF INCLUSIVE EDUCATION

Where is inclusive education heading? Without purporting to be fortune tellers, the authors advance several ideas in this final section of the chapter.

First, the trend toward inclusive education will increase steadily. This conclusion is based on several factors: (1) the data are convincing school districts already engaging in inclusive education to continue the practice and for new school districts to get on board; (2) parents whose children have been successfully included do not want to return to segregated alternatives; and (3) the trend in court decisions has been to support the education of learners with disabilities in general education classrooms, with supplemental supports and services, before attempting more restrictive alternatives. A survey of educators regarding future directions in education of students with disabilities (Putnam, Spiegel, & Bruininks, 1995) supports this contention. For the decade of the 1990s and after the year 2000, respondents predicted an increasing movement toward inclusion and predicted that the belief will prevail that people with disabilities have a right to participate in inclusive environments.

Second, with increasing numbers of schools changing the question from *whether to* include children to *how to* include them, specialized training will become highly sought. This need eventually will change university personnel preparation programs to become less categorical in nature and, in the meantime, to offer more information on learners with disabilities to general education majors. In addition, the need for ongoing technical assistance and supports within schools will require administrative staff to acquire more information and to locate knowledgeable resources for themselves and the teaching staff. Another outcome will be an enhanced dialogue within schools and school districts about the purpose of education and about school restructuring.

Third, states and school districts will develop more sophisticated strategies for financing education and for staffing inclusive classrooms. They will convert cost savings associated with eliminated segregated placements to financial support for inclusive efforts.

Fourth, schools will need to develop solutions to newly emerging issues. For instance, some disability-rights advocates believe that if people with disabilities are to have a well-developed sense of identity as adults, they need to have opportunities in their school years to associate with others with similar characteristics and interests (e.g., Ferguson & Asch, 1989). Stainback, Stainback, East, and Sapon-Shevin (1994) propose the development of support groups that would allow students to share information, support, and strategies. It is easy to imagine that a school environment where inclusive education is the norm will give rise to other social and philosophical issues that will need to be addressed.

CONCLUSION

Given some of the problems associated with implementing successful inclusion programs, why do many educators and parents continue to advocate for inclusive placements? A fundamental reason is that it is the right thing to do. To deny a student with disabilities the opportunity to receive an education in the general education environment, when it is the appropriate placement, is, quite simply, discrimination. The promotion of segregated placement for a class of students maintains the idea that society needs to be "charitable" to persons with disabilities. This charity falls short, however, when students with disabilities enter the adult world. Our culture cannot afford to be this charitable! Enabling students with disabilities to become independent adults is possible only by giving students the skills and experiences necessary to interact in an inclusive society.

REFERENCES

American Federation of Teachers. (1994). AFT resolution on inclusion of students with disabilities. In *Special education source book.* Washington, DC: Author.

American Speech-Language-Hearing Association. (1996, Spring). Inclusive practices for children and youths with communication disorders: Position statement and technical report. *Asha, 38* (Suppl. 16).

Appalachian Educational Laboratory, Inc. (1995, Spring-Summer). *The Link, Special Issue, 14*(1).

Association for Persons with Severe Handicaps, The. (1993). *Resolution on inclusive education.* Baltimore: Author.

Brown v. Board of Education of Topeka, 347 U.S. 483 (1954).

Children and Adults with Attention Deficit Disorders. (1993). *CH.A.D.D. position on inclusion.* Plantation, FL: Author.

Cohen, L.H. (1994, February 22). An interpreter isn't enough. *The New York Times.*

Council for Exceptional Children. (1995). CEC policy regarding inclusive school and community settings. *CEC policy manual.* Reston, VA: Author.

Dillon, A.D., Tashie, C., Shapiro-Bernard, S., Nisbet, J., Schuh, M., Dixon, B., & Zoellick, L. (1994). *Daring to dream.* Concord, NH: University of New Hampshire, Institute on Disability.

Division for Early Childhood, A Division of the Council for Exceptional Children. (1993). *DEC position on inclusion.* Pittsburgh, PA: Author.

Division for Learning Disabilities of the Council for Exceptional Children. (1995). *Inclusion: What does it mean for students with learning disabilities?* Reston, VA: Author.

Elam, S.M., & Rose, L.C. (1995). The 27th annual Phi Delta Kappa/Gallup Poll of the public's attitudes toward the public schools. *Phi Delta Kappan, 76,* 41–56.

Farlow, L. (1996, February). A quartet of success stories: How to make inclusion work. *Educational Leadership, 53,* 51–55.

Ferguson, P., & Asch, A. (1989). Lessons from life: Personal and parental perspectives on school, children, and disability. In D. Biklen, D. Ferguson, & A. Ford (Eds.), *Schooling and disability* (pp. 108–140). Chicago: National Society for the Study of Education.

Fuchs, D., & Fuchs, L.S. (1994). Inclusive schools movement and the radicalization of special education reform. *Exceptional Children, 60,* 294–309.

Fuchs, D., & Fuchs, L.S. (1994/1995, December/January). Sometimes separate is better. *Educational Leadership, 52,* 22–26.

Gartner, A., & Lipsky, D.K. (1987). Beyond special education: Toward a quality system for all students. *Harvard Educational Review, 57,* 367–395.

Giangreco, M.F., Dennis, R., Cloninger, C., Edelman, S., & Schattman, R. (1993). "I've counted Jon": Transformational experiences of teachers educating students with disabilities. *Exceptional Children, 59,* 359–372.

Hardin, D.E., & McNelis, S.J. (1996, February). The resource center: Hub of inclusive activities. *Educational Leadership, 53,* 41–47.

Hoover, M.J. (1993, June). "Inclusion" of disabled students works. *Virginia Journal of Education, 86,* 3.

Hunt, P., Farron-Davis, F., Beckstead, S., Curtis, D., & Goetz, L. (1994). Evaluating the effects of placement of students with severe disabilities in general education versus special classes. *Journal of the Association for Persons with Severe Handicaps, 19,* 200–214.

Individuals with Disabilities Education Act, 20 U.S.C., § 1400–1485. (1975).

Janney, R.E., Snell, M.E., Beers, M.K., & Raynes, M. (1995). Integrating students with moderate and severe disabilities into general education classes. *Exceptional Children, 61,* 425–439.

Kauffman, J.M., Lloyd, J.W., Baker, J., & Riedel, T.M. (1995). Inclusion of all students with emotional or behavioral disorders? Let's think again. *Phi Delta Kappan, 76,* 542–546.

Kozleski, E.B., & Jackson, L. (1993). Taylor's story: Full inclusion in her neighborhood elementary school. *Exceptionality, 4,* 153–175.

Laski, F., & Henderson, B. (1996, February/March). Upfront. *TASH Newsletter,* 3.

Learning Disabilities Association of America. (1993). *Position paper on full inclusion of all students with learning disabilities in the regular education classroom.* Pittsburgh, PA: Author.

Lipsky, D.K., & Gartner, A. (1989). *Beyond separate education: Quality education for all.* Baltimore: Paul H. Brookes.

Mainstreaming in Montgomery. (1995, March 7). *Roanoke Times and World-News*, p. A6.

Maloney, J. (1994/1995, December/January). A call for placement options. *Educational Leadership, 52,* 25.

Martin, R. (1994, February 22). Stepping into the world. *The New York Times.*

McCormick, C., & First, P.F. (1994). The cost of inclusion: Educating students with special needs. *School Business Affairs, 60,* 30–36.

Merrow, J. (1996, May 10). What's so special about special education? *The Merrow Report.* New York and Washington, DC: Public Broadcasting Service.

National Association of Elementary School Principals. (1994). *Position statement on inclusion.* Alexandria, VA: Author.

National Association of School Psychologists. (1993). *Position statement: Inclusive programs for students with disabilities.* Bethesda, MD: Author.

National Association of State Boards of Education. (1992). *Winners all: A call for inclusive schools.* Alexandria, VA: Author.

National Association of State Boards of Education. (1995). Resolution on students with special needs. *System-wide educational reform for ALL students, NASBE issues in brief, 15*(2).

National Center for Learning Disabilities, Inc. (1994). *An NCLD statement on inclusion.* New York: Author.

National Council on Disability. (1994, December 30). *Inclusionary education for students with disabilities: Keeping the promise.* Washington, DC: Author.

National Education Association. (1993). *Policy statement on appropriate inclusion.* Washington, DC: Author.

National Information Center for Children and Youth with Disabilities. (1995, July). Planning for inclusion. *News Digest, 5.*

National Joint Committee on Learning Disabilities. (1994). A reaction to *Full Inclusion:* A reaffirmation of the right of students with learning disabilities to a continuum of services. In *Collective perspectives on issues affecting learning disabilities: Position papers and statements* (pp. 95–96). Austin, TX: Pro-Ed.

Orton Dyslexia Society. (1994). The Orton Dyslexia Society position statement on inclusion. *Perspectives on Inclusion, 20*(4), 2–3.

Osborne, A.G., Jr., & Dimattia, P. (1994). The IDEA's least restrictive environment mandate: Legal implications. *Exceptional Children, 61,* 6–14.

Putnam, J.W., Spiegel, A.N., & Bruininks, R.H. (1995). Future directions in education and inclusion of students with disabilities: A Delphi investigation. *Exceptional Children, 61,* 553–576.

Rankin, D., Hallick, A., Ban, S., Hartley, P., Bost, C., & Uggla, N. (1994). Who's dreaming? A general education perspective on inclusion. *Journal of the Association for Persons with Severe Handicaps, 19,* 235–237.

Regular classroom placement gaining support in nation's courts (1993, November 16). *The Special Educator, 9*(7), 99–101.

Richardson, J. (1994, August 3). AFT says poll shows many oppose "inclusion." *Education Week, 30*(40), 14.

Roach, V. (1995). Supporting inclusion: Beyond the rhetoric. *Phi Delta Kappan, 77,* 295–299.

Rogers, J. (1993, May). The inclusion revolution. *Research Bulletin, 11,* 1–6.

Schaffner, B., Buswell, B., Summerfield, A., & Kovar, G. (1988). *Discover the possibilities.* Colorado Springs, CO: PEAK Parent Center.

Schnaiberg, L. (1995, May 31). No easy answers. *Education Week, 14*(36), 27–32.

Separate and unequal (1993, December 13). *U.S. News and World Report,* 46–60.

Shanker, A. (1994/1995, December/January). Full inclusion is neither free nor appropriate. *Educational Leadership, 52,* 18–21.

Slavin, R.E., & Stevens, R.J. (1991). Cooperative learning and mainstreaming. In J.W. Lloyd, A.C. Repp, & N.N. Singh (Eds.), *The Regular Education Initiative: Alternative perspectives on concepts, issues, and models* (pp. 177–191). Sycamore, IL: Sycamore.

Smith, A.W. (1994). *Deaf-blind success stories.* Monmouth, OR: TRACES Project.

Stainback, W., Stainback, S., & Bunch, G. (1989). Introduction and historical background. In S. Stainback, W. Stainback, & M. Forest (Eds.), *Educating all students in the mainstream of regular education* (pp. 3–14). Baltimore: Paul H. Brookes.

Stainback, S., Stainback, W., East, K., & Sapon-Shevin, M. (1994). A commentary on inclusion and the development of a positive self-identity by people with disabilities. *Exceptional Children, 60,* 486–490.

Tashie, C., Shapiro-Bernard, S., Dillon, A.D., Schuh, M., Jorgensen, C., & Nisbet, J. (1993a). *Changes in latitudes, changes in attitudes.* Concord, NH: Institute on Disability, University of New Hampshire.

Tashie, C., Shapiro-Bernard, S., Schuh, M., Jorgensen, C., Dillon, A.D., Dixon, B., & Nisbet, J. (1993b). *From special to regular, from ordinary to extraordinary.* Concord, NH: University of New Hampshire, Institute on Disability.

Thousand, J.S., & Villa, R.A. (1995). Inclusion: Alive and well in the Green Mountain State. *Phi Delta Kappan, 77,* 288–291.

Tomey, H.A. (1994, Fall). Inclusion: A responsible approach. *Perspectives, Special Issues, 20*(4), 15–16.

Wagner, M., Blackorby, J., Cameto, R., & Newman, L. (1993). *What makes a difference? Influences on postschool outcomes of youth with disabilities.* Menlo Park, CA: SRI International.

Wagner, M., Newman, L., D'Amico, R., Jay, E., Butler-Nalin, P., Marder, C., & Cox, R. (1991). *Youth with disabilities: How are they doing?.* Washington, DC: U.S. Department of Education.

Webb, N. (1994). With new court decisions backing them, advocates see inclusion as a question of values. *The Harvard Education Letter, 10*(4), 1–3.

Will, M. (1986). *Educating students with learning problems—A shared responsibility.* Washington, DC: U.S. Department of Education, Office of Special Education and Rehabilitation Services.

Wolery, M., Werts, M.G., Caldwell, N.K., Snyder, E.D., & Lisowski, L. (1995). Experienced teachers' perceptions of resources and supports for inclusion. *Education and Training in Mental Retardation and Developmental Disabilities, 30,* 15–26.

Wolfensberger, W. (1972). *The principle of normalization in human services.* Toronto, ONT: National Institute on Mental Retardation.

Wyllie, R. (1996, April 21). Inclusion can hurt everyone. *The New York Times,* p. 7.

York, J., Vandercook, T., Macdonald, C., Heise-Neff, C., & Caughey, E. (1992). Feedback about integrating middle-school students with severe disabilities in general education classes. *Exceptional Children, 58,* 244–258.

Zeph, L., Gilmer, D., Brewer-Allen, D., & Moulton, J. (Eds.). (1992). *Creating inclusive educational communities. Number 3: Kids talk about inclusive classrooms.* Orono, ME: University of Maine, The Center for Community Inclusion.

Zigmond, N., Jenkins, J., Fuchs, D., Deno, S., & Fuchs, L.S. (1995). When students fail to achieve satisfactorily: A reply to McLeskey and Waldron. *Phi Delta Kappan, 77,* 303–306.

CHAPTER 2

Inclusion and School Restructuring: Meeting the Needs of All Children

Joyce L. Videlock, Melody A. Nay Schaff, and Gail McGregor

INTRODUCTION: INCLUSION AND SCHOOL RESTRUCTURING

The demand for educational change and reform in our nation is long-standing (National Commission on Excellence in Education, 1983). Over the past decade and a half, schools have been increasingly pressured to show that students are being adequately prepared to succeed in the 21st century. Today schools are challenged to identify and teach critical skills required in a fast-paced, high-technology work environment. Concurrently, there is a growing belief that schools must be more effective in preparing students to become responsible and caring citizens. The increasingly diverse population in schools and in the workplace demands that people interact and work well together (Villa & Thousand, 1995). Indeed, it has been argued that a key responsibility of schools is to model the values of caring and interdependence in the classroom and within the larger community (Villa & Thousand, 1992b).

It is the thesis of this chapter that the movement toward inclusive schools and the instructional practices that characterize them represent not only a vehicle, but a catalyst, toward school restructuring that meets the needs of all students. Inclusive schools represent best practices for all students. A chronology of events is traced to contrast narrow school reform movements with broader, future-focused efforts at restructuring. Effective instructional practices from general and special education pedagogy are reviewed to show how each contributes to the goals of an inclusive school. Critical features and supports required to facilitate change are briefly highlighted to foreshadow in-depth discussion in subsequent chapters. Finally, key components that create a school climate where diversity is valued are examined.

A FOCUS ON REFORM AND RESTRUCTURING

Demographic information about the student population of this country's schools indicates that by the year 2020, the majority of students will be living in circumstances that place them at considerable risk for educational failure (Natriello, McDill, & Pallas, 1990). Currently, about one in seven of this country's children between the ages of 5 and 17 speaks a language other than English in the home, and the number of such children is growing (General Accounting Office, 1994). Increasing numbers of single-parent households and homes in which both parents are working are other notable and visible changes in the social fabric in which the public schools are embedded.

Although these circumstances may seem to be relatively new challenges to the educational system, concern about conditions associated with educational "risk" are as old as the public schools themselves (see Cuban, 1989, for a historical review). It is hoped that what *is* beginning to change is the framing of the educational challenges associated with students who are considered "at risk" and students with identified disabilities. The most common explanations for poor student performance have placed responsibility for low achievement on the children themselves and/or their families. Cuban explains that when child deficits are viewed as the root of a learning problem, the solutions offered by schools have been "more intense doses of what the children were already getting or should have been getting" (p. 781). When poor student performance is attributed to family issues, solutions have focused on teaching adults better child-rearing practices.

Retention and dropout rates, and unacceptably high rates of unemployment among this segment of the student population, suggest that these remedies have not been successful

(Blackorby & Wagner, 1996). Cuban (1989) provides an alternative, but less popular, framing of this issue. In his view, responsibility for school failure rests with the schools themselves. "The structure of the school is not flexible enough to accommodate the diverse abilities and interests of a heterogeneous student body. Programs are seldom adapted to children's individual differences. Instead, schools seek uniformity, and departures from the norm in achievement and behavior are defined as problems" (Cuban, 1989, p. 781).

Educational Reform

The roots of educational reform extend beyond the needs of the growing population of at-risk students that have motivated urban school reform efforts since the 1960s. It has been more than 10 years since the publication of *A Nation at Risk: The Imperative for Educational Reform* (National Commission on Excellence in Education, 1983). In this report, America's loss of standing in commerce, science, and technological innovation was directly linked to prevailing educational practices. Schools were described as "ineffective" in preparing this country's students to compete in the global marketplace. The report concluded that a complete overhaul of the public school system would be necessary to change this situation. This set into motion more than a decade of political and educational initiatives falling under the general descriptor "educational reform."

The educational reform movement has gone through three distinct waves of activity (McDonnell & Kiefer-O'Donnell, 1992). The first two waves of reform, based largely on the effective schools research literature (e.g., Coleman et al., 1966; Edmonds, 1982; Purkey & Smith, 1985; Weber, 1971) focused on improving specific components of school operation such as policy, teacher preparation practices, and structural characteristics of schools. The limited results of these initiatives suggest that their scope was insufficient to produce significant and enduring outcomes for many students (Kirst, 1990; Murphy, 1990).

The third wave of educational reform has a broader focus, emphasizing the need for a more complete change in the ways schools operate (Hawley, 1988; Metz, 1990). As described by McDonnell and Kiefer-O'Donnell (1992), current efforts at reform are grounded in the belief that improvements cannot be achieved until: "(a) the public school system is structured to empower students and parents in the design and implementation of the educational program, and (b) educational agencies work collaboratively with other community agencies to develop a comprehensive system of services that can address the complex needs of children in today's society" (p. 54).

Concurrent Trends in Special Education Service Delivery

Services to students with disabilities were not considered in the discussion and implementation of the first and second waves of reform activity. However, concurrent events within special education echo the sentiment of general education reformers that the status quo is in need of major change. Impetus for change in special education practices can be seen in the following trends:

- The growing number of students identified as having mild disabilities (Lipsky & Gartner, 1989) is generating considerable concern about the validity and instructional value of the current approach to identification and classification of disability. Categorization continues, however, and is on the rise as a result of the advocacy efforts of parents of students identified as having learning disabilities and attention deficit disorders/attention deficit hyperactivity disorders (McLaughlin & Warren, 1994).

- The discouraging data generated by special education follow-up studies have stimulated greater interest in program accountability for special education than is compatible with the movement toward outcome-based education in general education (McDonnell & Hardman, 1986; Rusch, DeStefano, Chadsey-Rusch, Phelps, & Szmanski, 1992; Wehman, 1992).

- Several years ago, Danielson and Bellamy (1989) published a comparison of placement practices across all 50 states, revealing great variability in the extent to which states relied upon separate and residential placements for students with disabilities. More recently, a series of federal court decisions has found that special education placement procedures frequently violate the intent of the "least restrictive environment" clause of federal law. In many districts, students are placed in segregated programs based on their classification without first considering the feasibility of general education placement with the use of supplemental services and supports (*Board of Education v. Holland* [1992]; *Oberti v. Clementon* [1992, 1993]). See Chapter 4 for further discussion.

For these and many other reasons, the system of special education that has emerged since the passage of the Education for All Handicapped Children Act of 1975 is now a target for reform and restructuring. Even among those who are vocal in their criticism of the current trend toward inclusion:

Recognition grows that a meaningful connection with general education is necessary; that a "Lone Ranger" strategy for special education is self-defeating. More and more special educators are resonating to a view first expressed by Dunn (1968) more than 25 years ago. To wit: Special education is not a Nantucket or Martha's Vineyard, but a town on the mainland, and its students and teachers are served better when its business is coordinated closely with mainland business. (Fuchs & Fuchs, 1994, p. 295)

School Restructuring Rather Than Reform

There is a growing consensus that school restructuring is the only viable means of implementing the fundamental changes necessary to respond to the needs of this country's diverse student population. Recent comments of Seymour Sarason, a highly influential voice in the field of education, underscore the importance of rethinking current approaches to school improvement: "The 'system'— by virtue of history, tradition, and overlearned attitudes—is allergic to change. The preventive orientation is virtually nonexistent, and what passes for education reform is almost always working in the repair mode" (Sarason, 1995, p. 84).

Unlike early reform initiatives that tended to involve new methods to recreate or maintain practices of the past, restructuring is future-focused (Whitaker & Moses, 1994). Restructuring does not merely encompass a change in organizational structure or curriculum. Rather, it involves "the total alignment of all aspects of the organization to achieve the purposes for which the organization was originally created" (Reavis & Griffith, 1992, p. 73). In education, this means that instructional, curricular, assessment, and disciplinary practices are supportive of one another, reflecting an articulated vision and mission for a school developed with the involvement of diverse constituencies within the school community.

CURRICULAR AND ORGANIZATIONAL STRATEGIES THAT ARE RESPONSIVE TO STUDENT DIVERSITY

A common theme of school restructuring efforts is the adoption of instructional practices that are responsive to student diversity and foster motivation through active learning, relevant themes, and increased student interaction. In these dynamic classrooms and schools, the teacher becomes a facilitator and guide who adjusts activities to meet the needs of students. This flexibility is highly valued by teachers, who report that they can observe, assess, and assist students in ways that were not possible in traditionally structured classrooms. As general and special educators join in teams to plan and implement inclusive classroom practices, they are identifying mutual concerns and benefits. They are sharing strategies and discovering that, collectively, they hold a broad base of knowledge and skills to meet the needs of all learners (York, Doyle, & Kronberg, 1992).

Practices Drawn from General Education

With few notable exceptions, future general and special educators are professionally prepared in separate programs at the preservice and graduate levels. As a result, general and special education teachers are trained with seemingly different disciplines, vocabularies, expectations, and philosophies. However, if one looks underneath the vocabulary to the pedagogical principles that underlie innovative practices across disciplines, it is evident that there are common and complementary practices that, in combination, create educational environments that are responsive to student diversity.

Heterogeneous Grouping Structures

Research over the past 20 years has shown that ability grouping has a negative effect on student achievement and self-esteem, particularly for students perceived as low achievers or slow learners in language arts and mathematics. For these students, long-term assignment to the same group based on achievement and/or label can mean low expectations and lack of exposure to challenging instructional materials and varied classroom practices (Oakes, 1985). A recent review of research on ability grouping (Gamoran, 1992) concluded that the most rigid forms of ability grouping, such as tracking in high school or assigning a student to an entire elementary school career in the low-achieving reading group, perpetuates low achievement and contributes to a widening gap between high- and low-achieving groups, with no real gains in overall achievement. Advocates of programs for gifted and talented youth argue that homogeneous grouping for this population leads to significant academic gains that could be jeopardized by inclusive practices. Some fear that heterogeneous grouping will lead to a "watered down" curriculum that fails to challenge high-achieving students. While it is true that children who participate in programs for the gifted show strong academic achievement, there is no evidence to suggest that these achievements are dampened by participation in an inclusive school environment. Furthermore, evidence suggests that typical students develop increased positive interpersonal behaviors and attitudes in inclusive settings (Lipsky & Gartner, 1995). Finally, it is important to recognize that inclusive practices do not preclude homogeneous groupings. The key here is that groupings are varied and flexible, and that all students have the opportunity to benefit from interactions with a diverse peer group. Consequently, restructured schools are shifting away from a preponderance of ability grouping to a variety of heterogeneous grouping structures. Flexible grouping and cooperative learning are two instructional practices that promote heterogeneous grouping.

Flexible Grouping. Flexible groupings range in size from large groups of students to small groups, triads, or dyads. Groups may form and re-form based on varying criteria such as student need, interest, task, learning strategies, student choice, or random selection. Cooper (1995) has developed a design for literature-based reading instruction in a heterogeneously grouped classroom. In this structure, children begin in the large group, where the teacher introduces the book and relates it to experiences and knowledge within the group. From there, students move into one of at least three choices that can include teacher-supported reading (read aloud, shared reading, or guided reading), cooperative reading (partners), or independent reading. Whole class, literature circle, extension, or supportive activities can follow.

Implementation of flexible grouping requires teachers to make decisions around three important variables: the basis for grouping, the format of each group, and the materials to be used. For example, one teacher may determine that small, student-led groups based on interest are most appropriate to research topics within a science unit on space exploration. Ongoing student assessment can guide teachers' decisions around these dimensions of flexible grouping (see Flood, Lapp, Flood, & Nagel, 1992, for an in-depth discussion of forming flexible groups).

Given a variety of group activities and materials, flexible grouping can be an effective strategy in an inclusive classroom. Children have opportunities to interact with all classmates because a broad range of student learning and social needs can be accommodated through group membership and material selection. For example, a student may participate in one group for verbal and social interaction, shift to another skill-based group for direct instruction, or to yet another group based on interest. In this way, over time, students are more likely to interact with and learn from a variety of their classmates. Individual students do not become associated with a particular group or set of learning materials, and each student has the opportunity to participate in a variety of learning experiences.

Cooperative Learning. In the broadest sense, cooperative learning refers to a set of instructional methods and experiences in which students work in groups toward interdependent goals (Johnson & Johnson, 1984; Sharan & Sharan, 1976; Slavin, Stevens, & Madden, 1988). Four key elements distinguish cooperative learning groups from other small learning groups: (1) positive interdependence (achievement of goals for the individual is dependent on that of other group members; students become responsible for one another's learning); (2) individual accountability (each student is assessed on his or her mastery of the content); (3) collaborative skills (leadership, decision making, trust building, communication, and conflict management are taught, practiced, and monitored); and (4) group processing (group members learn procedures for examining how well they are working together) (Johnson & Johnson, 1986).

Research on the effects of cooperative learning with typical students has shown positive effects on academic achievement, intergroup relations, and student self-esteem (Sharan & Shacar, 1988; Slavin, 1990, 1991). There is a growing body of evidence to show the positive effects of cooperative learning on academic achievement, most notably in reading comprehension and math computation, for children with disabilities who are integrated into the regular classroom setting (Slavin et al., 1988; Stevens, Madden, Slavin, & Farnish, 1987). Furthermore, there are documented benefits in social skills for all students involved (Johnson, Johnson, Waring, & Maruyama, 1986; Madden & Slavin, 1983).

The fundamental principle of cooperative learning is the formation of supportive, heterogeneous groups. Thus, it is not surprising that this instructional design is frequently used in inclusive classrooms. According to Sapon-Shevin, Ayres, and Duncan (1994):

> Including a child with a significant disability in an activity and structuring that activity cooperatively gives us an opportunity (and sometimes forces us) to examine the curriculum critically and unleash our creative pedagogical and curricular inventiveness. . . . Combining a commitment to inclusion with an orientation toward cooperative learning can be a catalyst for thinking carefully about the following questions: What is really important for students to learn? How can I make learning meaningful and functional for all students? (p. 51)

Developmentally Appropriate Practices

Developmentally appropriate practices (DAPs) are instructional approaches that are based on what we know about how children develop and learn (Bredekamp, 1987). Interest in DAPs has grown in response to the trend over the last 20 years to introduce primary grade academics during the preschool and kindergarten years. This "push-down" curriculum is often used with young children in the same manner in which it is used in the primary grades. Preschool, kindergarten, and first-grade children may be expected to master paper-and-pencil skills, to attend during extended periods of teacher-directed whole group instruction, and to learn through drill and practice with a de-emphasis on play and social interaction. These practices are viewed by child development specialists and educators as both detrimental and inefficient (Katz, 1988). Young children can gradually lose interest, enthusiasm, and self-confidence in classrooms when they are required to perform tasks and to retain information in ways that make no sense to them.

In 1990, the National Association for the Education of Young Children (NAEYC), in collaboration with the National Association of Early Childhood Specialists in State Departments of Education (NAECS/SDE), issued guidelines to assist educators in making decisions about appropriate curriculum and assessment for young children from ages three through eight (NAEYC, 1990). These guidelines are theoretically based and reflect the belief that learning is an interactive process (i.e., children construct knowledge and gain meaning from their experiences). The way in which adults choose to structure and provide these experiences can affect not only what children learn, but how they feel about learning. While each of the 20 guiding principles is consistent with and supportive of inclusive philosophy, seven of them are virtually indistinguishable with principles of inclusive practices. They are as follows:

1. Curriculum content is designed to achieve long-range goals for children in all domains—social, emotional, cognitive, and physical—and to prepare children to function as fully contributing members of a democratic society.
2. Curriculum addresses a broad range of content that is relevant, engaging, and meaningful to children.
3. Curriculum content reflects and is generated by the needs and interests of children within the groups. Curriculum incorporates a variety of learning experiences, materials and equipment, and instructional strategies to accommodate a broad range of children's individual differences in prior experience, maturational rates, styles of learning, needs, and interests.
4. Curriculum respects and supports individual, cultural, and linguistic diversity. Curriculum supports and encourages positive relationships with children's families.
5. Curriculum emphasizes the value of social interaction to learning in all domains and provides opportunities to learn from peers.
6. Curriculum builds upon what children already know and are able to do (activating prior knowledge) to consolidate their learning and to foster their acquisition of new concepts and skills.
7. Curriculum is flexible so that teachers can adapt to individual children or groups.

As these guidelines depict, the classroom with DAPs incorporates critical features such as heterogeneous groupings, social interaction, and long-range goals that support inclusive practices. The classroom environment is structured to capitalize on children's natural curiosity through active learning, thematic instruction, and learning centers. Teachers operating from these principles provide a variety of experiences and materials in a range of activities. In this type of environment, tasks can be more easily adapted to meet the needs of individual children, in contrast to the more traditionally structured classrooms where children are expected to do the same tasks in the same way in the same amount of time.

Multiple Intelligences

The theory of multiple intelligences (MI) was introduced by Howard Gardner (1983, 1993) in an attempt to explain observations and research findings that suggested a range of human intelligence extending beyond the prevailing construct of verbal and performance abilities. Gardner has identified seven intelligences: logical-mathematical, linguistic, musical, spatial, bodily-kinesthetic, interpersonal, and intrapersonal. MI theory holds that these intelligences exist in all humans, but each of us has a different pattern of relative strengths. Gardner posits that these intelligences operate independently, relying on different ways of processing information. Furthermore, MI theory yields a philosophy of intelligence assessment based on fair, culturally appropriate, and naturalistic contexts, diverging from traditional approaches to assessment (Gardner & Hatch, 1989).

Although Gardner's initial audience was the psychological community, educators have gained his support for their enthusiastic efforts to apply his theory to educational design and delivery (Armstrong, 1994a, 1994b; Campbell, 1991; Gardner & Hatch, 1989). For example, in one third-grade classroom, children rotate through learning centers designed to teach specific curriculum content through each of the seven intelligences (Campbell, 1991). In another elementary school, each child sets individual annual goals around each of the seven areas (Ellison, 1992); this occurs in the context of a parent-student-teacher conference that focuses on child strengths. Faculty study and experimentation over time have resulted in pervasive influences of MI theory on student assessment and reporting in the New City School in St. Louis, Missouri (Hoer, 1994). Portfolios, student MI profiles, individualized progress reports, and performances are used to track progress, design instruction, and communication with parents.

MI theory is based on a "growth paradigm" (Armstrong, 1994a), consistent with inclusive practices. The focus is on strengths and capabilities instead of deficits. Assessment seeks to identify the ways in which the child can learn, rather than to identify the disability category. Although MI "acknowledges difficulties or disabilities, [it] does so within the context of regarding special-needs students as basically healthy individuals" (Armstrong, 1994a, p. 136). The instructional environment, then, is designed to provide opportunities for students to learn in a way that capitalizes on each area of intelligence. This is beneficial for all students, not just those with identified learning difficulties.

Alternative Approaches to Assessment

Broad-based changes in instructional practices cannot occur without corresponding changes in assessment practices. The development of alternative forms of assessment has been a top priority for many educators dissatisfied with the limited scope of standardized testing and the perceived failure of traditional assessment to capture student growth in the learning process (Baker, 1989). While standardized achievement testing addresses annual progress and permits comparisons of the individual to a larger population, this global approach cannot capture the multidimensional nature of student learning and performance. For example, active, student-centered, project-driven learning requires an assessment approach that takes into account both the process and the product. A variety of terms (direct, performance, and authentic) have been used to describe new approaches. However, "all are viewed as *alternatives* to traditional multiple-choice, standardized achievement tests, . . . [and] all refer to direct examination of student performance on significant tasks that are relevant to life outside of school" (Worthen, 1993, p. 445).

Performance-Based Assessment. One currently popular alternative is performance-based assessment that focuses on direct observation of students performing specified tasks. Student performance may vary in terms of time frame and content. For example, oral presentations of research results, written work rated according to a predetermined rubric, project development, or demonstration of creative work are all examples of potential performance-based assessments. Alternative forms of student expression and demonstration such as artistic or musical performances are characteristic of this approach. In many schools, demonstrations of a student's performance are collected and organized in a portfolio. Portfolio assessment refers to the process by which these student products are selected and examined.

Herman, Aschbacher, and Winters (1992) caution that the development of alternative assessment protocols should be based on the same principles as those used for traditional test development. These include the following:

1. Specify the nature of the skills and accomplishments students are to develop.
2. Specify illustrative tasks that would require students to demonstrate these skills and accomplishments.
3. Specify the criteria and standards for judging student performance on the task.
4. Develop a reliable rating process.
5. Gather evidence of validity to show what kinds of inferences can be made from the assessment.
6. Use test results to refine assessment and improve curriculum and instruction; provide feedback to students, parents, and the community. (p. 8)

Advantages of alternative assessment approaches stem from their inherent link to both curriculum and instruction. Students know what the expected outcomes are, and criteria for assessment are clearly defined. While performance-based assessment may be labor-intensive for teachers and administrators, this approach lends itself well to the needs of a diverse student population. Performance outcomes may be consistent for all students, but the way in which those outcomes are demonstrated may vary according to student need. In general, these approaches "provide a more equitable and sensitive portrait of what students know and are able to do" (Herman & Winters, 1994, p. 48). Proponents argue that performance-based approaches have effected profound changes in curriculum and instruction. While there is a clear need for continued research showing the technical quality of these approaches (Herman & Winters, 1994; Worthen, 1993), alternative assessment is a promising practice for educators seeking ways to address the diverse needs and talents of their students.

Curriculum-Based Assessment. Standardized, norm-referenced approaches to testing, especially for high-stakes purposes like program evaluation or eligibility determinations, have been the mainstay of general and special education. For the classroom teacher, however, these approaches provide little instructional guidance. In contrast, curriculum-based assessment (CBA) approaches provide frequent student progress data for the purpose of improving instruction. Although these approaches differ in the type of data collected and the focus of intervention, the purpose of CBA is to identify effective instructional strategies. (See Shinn, Rosenfield, & Knutson, 1989, for a thorough review of four CBA models.)

CBA for instructional design (Gickling & Havertape, 1981) is of interest here because of its focus on the identification of instructional and curricular factors that, when adjusted, improve student performance. The basic premise of Gickling's approach is that academic failure is, to a large extent, rooted in the mismatch between the demands of the curriculum and the skills students bring to the task. "Problems occur . . . because adjustments have not been made in the curriculum to fit . . . individual needs" (Gickling & Thompson, 1985, p. 209). CBA aims to eliminate the mismatch and accompanying student frustration by controlling task characteristics (e.g., the amount of new information presented at one time [unknown], the number of items presented, the number and type of demonstrations provided, and the time allocated for review and practice). By continually assessing student performance in relation to task characteristics, the teacher can identify and maintain the optimal learning conditions, the "instructional level," for students. The result is increased task completion and comprehension.

Because CBA identifies the optimal learning conditions for any student, an outcome of this process is a precise description of the adaptations and accommodations required for students to be successful. Thus, it has great utility for programs that seek to maintain students with disabilities, to the maximum degree possible, in the general education program. In Pennsylvania, CBA is being used by instructional support teams to create and maintain successful learning environments for students, with and without individualized education programs (IEPs) (Kovaleski, Lowery, & Gickling, 1995; Kovaleski, Tucker, & Duffy, 1995). An important aspect of this process is the use of CBA to measure the student's response to instruction (i.e., precisely how much was learned and retained). This type of formative assessment is viewed as a valuable tool to determine what instructional strategies and supports are needed to maintain student success. In the words of one Pennsylvania school psychologist:

> Through my use of CBA, the focus of the evaluation transferred from the learning problems of the student to the student's level of success within the context of the classroom. The curriculum and its instructional presentation within the learning environment of the classroom gave me a wealth of information which I had not previously considered. I began to ask such questions as: (1) Does the curriculum and instruction in the classroom match the needs of the student? (2) Are the curriculum and instruction assets or detriments to the student's learning? (3) Is the curriculum presented at the student's instructional level? and (4) Does the teacher modify curriculum and is instruction based on individual student's needs? (Chick, 1995, p. 16)

Practices Drawn from Special Education

Several premises fundamental to the field of special education, like the practices above, focus instructional effort on meeting the individual student's needs. The inherent nature of special education is to focus on the individual through individualized assessment approaches and curricular adaptations. These features facilitate inclusive practices by providing the framework for examining a student's special needs in the context of the overall educational program.

Focus on the Individual

A defining principle of special education is that schools are obligated to meet the unique needs of children who are found eligible for specialized instruction. The Individuals with Disabilities Education Act of 1990 (IDEA) provides the general framework by which state education agencies and local school districts deliver services and protect the rights of these students. IDEA is an outgrowth of earlier legislation designed to ensure that individuals with disabilities receive the same protections (due process) and access to educational services that are available for individuals without disabilities.

Individualized Assessment Approaches

The IEP is the outcome of a comprehensive evaluation process to identify the individual student's learning strengths and needs, as well as a description of the optimal learning conditions for the student. This is accomplished though assessment approaches that focus on the individual student's learning characteristics and factors in the instructional environment. Special education has spawned a variety of individualized assessment practices that include, among others, interviewing, direct systematic observation, and task analysis methods. Rosenfield (1987) provides a comprehensive discussion of these techniques as they pertain to instructional consultation.

These activities are usually performed by educational specialists such as school psychologists, special educators, and related services personnel. However, as partnerships between general and special educators emerge, it is anticipated that classroom teachers with support staff will employ these methods to design effective learning environments and to monitor student progress on an ongoing basis. Specialists need to share their skills through modeling and demonstration for classroom teachers so that all members of student planning teams can use these techniques and procedures in the classroom.

This trend is emerging through inclusive practices that require teachers to shift from a "deliverer of instruction" to a "guide/facilitator." This new role involves ongoing assessment and, consequently, teachers are developing these skills. For example, structured observation—"kid watching"—is a central feature of developmentally appropriate practices. As a framework for observation, the teacher may be guided by questions like: "What can the child do?" "What areas of growth are observed?" "What patterns are emerging?" (Griffin, 1993). Here the emphasis is on discovering how the child responds under different learning conditions—particularly, which conditions are most beneficial. Likewise, the student interview and task analysis are key components of assessment to decide the optimal learning conditions and effective strategies for students with diverse learning needs.

Curricular and Instructional Adaptation

Specially designed instruction is, by definition, adaptation of curriculum and instruction to meet student needs. In the inclusive school, the goal of the adaptation process is to design student activities and experiences that address individualized program goals while enabling students to participate with age peers to the maximum degree possible. Special educators have developed a variety of approaches to creating curricular and instructional adaptations.

Giangreco and Putnam (1991) describe ways to address a wide range of outcomes within a group structure. Schumm, Vaughn, and Leavell (1994) present a comprehensive planning approach to assist teachers in designing learning outcomes across broad curricular areas. A systematic decision-making model proposed by Udvari-Solner (1994) provides a series of questions to guide teachers through a hierarchy of instructional strategies. Changes in task structure, task demands, the learning environment, the way the task is done, and the support provided are considered. (See Chapter 6 for an in-depth discussion of curricular adaptations.)

DEVELOPING SCHOOLS AS INCLUSIVE LEARNING COMMUNITIES

Much has been written about the phenomenon of change as it relates to innovation in education (see the September 1993 issue of *Educational Leadership* for a series of articles about systems change). This body of literature offers the reader insight into and an appreciation of the complexity of dealing with human behavior in the context of well-established bureaucracies. At a systems level, it is useful for administrators to recognize key stages that characterize the process of change within the organization (Anderson, 1993). Likewise, it is critical for the organization to recognize that change is accomplished by individuals who must feel invested in the process (Evans, 1993).

Supports To Facilitate Adoption of Inclusive Practices

Regardless of the specific framework used to help understand the phenomenon, several common themes emerge as critical supports to facilitate the change process. These include articulating a *vision* for the organization about the educational innovation, providing strong *leadership* around the innovation, making available *training and technical assistance* to all stakeholders in the process, and using *teaming and collaborative structures* to plan and prepare for the change. All these elements are critical to transform a segregated special education system to a child-centered service delivery system that supports all the needs of its learners. These concepts are addressed, with practical suggestions, throughout this book.

Restructuring To Support Diversity

As schools develop action plans motivated by an interest in meeting the needs of its entire student population, the following principles should be considered.

Children Attend Their Neighborhood School in a Natural Proportion

The principle of natural proportion is critical to the development of an inclusive learning community (Brown et al., 1989). This principle says that students with disabilities should attend the school they would attend if they did not have a disability. If this principle guides placement patterns, the number of students requiring specially designed instruction and support services will be relatively uniform across all the schools in a district. In addition, the ratio of students with disabilities will reflect the proportion of individuals with disabilities in our society. Conversely, if the school has an "unnatural" proportion of students with disabilities due to cross-district or categorical programs, it will quickly deplete its resources and its ability to provide specially designed support services to these students in general education classrooms. Furthermore, when there is a high density of students with disabilities within a school, it is more likely that these students will be treated as a group rather than as individuals (Roach, 1994; Stainback & Stainback, 1990).

It must be acknowledged, however, that the idea of natural proportion within the neighborhood school may not apply for deaf or hearing-impaired individuals who seek the unique characteristics and support of the deaf community. Villa and Thousand (1995) point out the difficulties that exist with current educational systems for this population. Pull-out instruction, interpreters within the general education environment, and sign language instruction for hearing students are solutions frequently implemented by school districts to meet the needs of hearing-impaired students. Regional or magnet schools may offer valuable resources, yet children are segregated from family and community. Chapter 17 discusses issues associated with inclusive education programs for students who are deaf and hard of hearing.

Student Experiences and Environments Are Varied

Inclusive learning communities embrace diversity and are designed to support all children. To meet the diverse learning needs in heterogeneous classrooms, educators must use a wide array of grouping structures, instructional strategies, and classroom management tools. Such grouping structures include but are not limited to multiage and flexible grouping. Kasten and Clarke (1993) define multiage as "any deliberate grouping of children that includes more than one traditional grade level in a single classroom community" (p. 3). *Nongraded* and *vertical grouping* are alternative terms for the multiage classroom. The goal of this structure is to create a "balanced collection of students from the school population with consideration for heterogeneity in gender, ability, ethnicity, interest and age levels" (Villa & Thousand, 1995, p. 96). Furthermore, when the individual needs of students cannot be met within the classroom setting, instruction in other school and community settings is also made a part of a student's instructional program.

Support Structures Are Classroom-Based and Generic

When students with disabilities are members of general education classrooms, support services are provided within this context unless the team decides that another arrangement makes better instructional sense. The first step in developing an inclusive learning community is to identify who and how many individuals within a school community are available to provide services and support to students. Special education teachers, enrichment teachers, instructional assistants, Title I teachers and aides, therapists (occupational, physical, speech, recreation/leisure), mobility specialists, guidance counselors, cross-age and peer tutors, parent and grandparent volunteers, and community business partners are all potential sources of support. Building-based planning is necessary to develop schedules that match the support needs within individual classrooms with the expertise and schedules of support personnel.

Diversity Is Valued and Embedded within the Curriculum

Traditional educational approaches such as tracking and categorical special education practices are based on the assumption that the more homogeneous the classroom, the better a teacher can meet students' needs. Diversity among students is viewed as a threat to instructional integrity. In contrast, diversity is viewed as a strength in inclusive schools and classrooms. Recognizing that a truly homogeneous group of students does not exist, teachers in inclusive schools plan for the natural diversity they know exists among students. Thus, they use teaching methods, materials, and response modalities that are based on the recognition that we all learn and show what we know in different ways. Furthermore, this diversity is acknowledged, celebrated, and elevated to an issue that merits study as part of the curriculum.

Organizational Targets for Change in Inclusive Schools

Restructuring toward inclusive practices requires schools to modify or even eliminate organizational structures that are inconsistent with an inclusive philosophy. Categorical service delivery and separate special and general education administrative structures often become strategic targets for change in the emerging inclusive school.

Categorical Service Delivery

Over the past two decades, there has been a proliferation of categorical programs that separate children according to

labels such as mildly mentally retarded, learning disabled, or low achieving. While categorization and separation might be justified if the labels were associated with specific, mutually exclusive learning strategies and instructional approaches, this is not the case. In fact, the learning profiles of these children are often indistinguishable (Algozzine & Ysseldyke, 1983; Wang, Reynolds, & Walberg, 1994). Furthermore, the need to account for categorical funding streams has had a chilling effect on integrated service delivery. Tracking the use of funds, materials, and personnel is easier when the service delivery is separate and autonomous. As a result, categorical approaches have become synonymous with "pull-out" forms of service delivery, resulting in fragmented instruction and focusing on deficits within the student rather than conditions in the instructional environment. Fortunately, the new Title I law (Elementary and Secondary Education Act of 1965 [ESEA], Title I Amendment) permits greater flexibility in the use of funds to raise academic achievement for all children within a school. Under the new guidelines, funds from most federal programs can be combined with Title I dollars to address the needs of the entire school population, removing at least one barrier to categorical service delivery. This does not apply, however, to IDEA funds. Nevertheless, Title I funds could be used to support instruction in heterogeneously grouped classrooms.

Separate Special and General Education Administrative Structures

Administrative policies and structures are also targets of change for the emerging inclusive school community. Lipp (1992) identifies a shift from centralized control to building-based program design and implementation for special education. As a result, roles and responsibilities of special education leadership change from supervision of direct service to provision of technical assistance and support. For example, in one Vermont school district, the separate special and regular education programs have been merged (Villa & Thousand, 1992a). Labels for students and for teachers have been eliminated, and the special education and pupil personnel services departments have been replaced by a director of instructional services, whose responsibilities include support service management and staff development for all teachers.

Creating a Climate in Which Diversity Is Valued

The research literature about effective schools reinforces the notions held by many educators and families about what makes a good school and classroom. *Community* emerges in both the professional literature and in conversation as a defining element. Successful schools and classrooms create

Exhibit 2–1 Examples of Educational Practices That Build upon Student Diversity

Educational Strategy	Practices That Relate to Student Diversity
Curricular infusion (Hamre-Nietupski, Ayres, Nietupski, Savage, Mitchell, & Bramman, 1989)	The practice of introducing information about diversity at naturally occurring opportunities in the general education curriculum. The purpose of curricular infusion is to promote understanding and acceptance of diversity, including differences associated with disability.
Multiple ability treatments (Cohen, 1994)	A strategy used to design and orchestrate cooperative learning groups that is built upon the expressed assumption that different skills are necessary to complete the task, and that no one person can perform each aspect of the task well. The process makes explicit the notion of positive interdependence that is characteristic of cooperative learning tasks.
Multiple intelligences (Campbell, 1991; Gardner, 1983)	Instructional strategies based on the premise that human intelligence consists of seven distinct ability areas, suggesting different areas of strength for each individual. Teaching strategies developed based on this framework incorporate learning strategies and activities that take into account the many ways of learning and demonstrating knowledge.
Collaborative problem solving (Giangreco, Cloninger, Dennis, & Edelman, 1994)	A process by which children and adults work together to resolve conflicts and problems. It is a useful strategy to help resolve barriers associated with inclusion.
Flexible groupings (Flood, Lapp, Flood, & Nagel, 1992)	Use of multiple strategies to group students, different formats for group instruction, and varying strategies about the materials provided to group members. This provides many alternatives to grouping that do not reflect the variable of *ability*.
Peer-mediated instruction (Harper, Maheady, & Mallette, 1994)	Teaching arrangements in which students serve as instructional agents for their classmates and/or other students.
Democratic schools (Apple & Beane, 1995)	Democratic schools rely upon widespread participation in issues of governance and policy making by staff, students, parents, and community members. Equity is a critical underlying belief of a democratic school.

a climate that can be described as an extended family, where concern for achievement is conveyed in the context of caring and belonging. Differences are not only tolerated; they are viewed as an asset.

Several specific strategies that reinforce a sense of community in the classroom are highlighted in Exhibit 2–1. This is not an exhaustive list or a "recipe." Rather, these practices are provided as examples of strategies that are congruent with a climate in which diversity is celebrated and viewed as an educational asset.

CONCLUSION

The creation of inclusive schools must be viewed within the context of the overall school restructuring effort. For school districts moving in this direction, inclusion cannot be considered a separate initiative, removed from the planning and development of the general education system. Rather, school leadership must recognize that, with few exceptions, effective general instructional practices work for everyone. The dynamic, interactive classroom of the 21st century is an environment that facilitates learning *and* inclusion.

REFERENCES

Algozzine, B., & Ysseldyke, J.E. (1983). Learning disabilities as a subset of school failure: The over sophistication of a concept. *Exceptional Children, 50*, 242–246.

Anderson, B. (1993). The stages of systemic change. *Educational Leadership, 51*(1), 14–17.

Apple, M.W., & Beane, J.A. (1995). *Democratic schools*. Alexandria, VA: Association for Supervision and Curriculum Development.

Armstrong, T. (1994a). *Multiple intelligences in the classroom*. Alexandria, VA: Association for Supervision and Curriculum Development.

Armstrong, T. (1994b). Multiple intelligences: Seven ways to approach curriculum. *Educational Leadership, 52*(3), 26–28.

Baker, E. (1989). Mandated tests: Educational reform or quality indicator? In B.R. Gifford (Ed.), *Test policy and test performance: Education, language, and culture* (pp. 3–23). Norwell, MA: Kluwer Academic.

Blackorby, J., & Wagner, M. (1996). Longitudinal postschool outcomes of youth with disabilities: Findings from the National Longitudinal Transition Study. *Exceptional Children, 62,* 399–413.

Board of Education, Sacramento City Unified School District v. Holland, 786 F. Supp 874 (E.D. Cal. 1992).

Bredekamp, S. (Ed.). (1987). *Developmentally appropriate practice in early childhood programs serving children from birth through age 8* (expanded ed.). Washington, DC: National Association for the Education of Young Children.

Brown, L., Udvari-Solner, A., Davis, L., VanDeventer, P., Ahlgren, C., Johnson, F., Gruenewald, L., & Jorgenson, J. (1989). The home school. *Journal of the Association for Persons with Severe Handicaps, 14,* 1–7.

Campbell, B. (1991, Winter). Multiple intelligences in the classroom. *Context Quarterly,* 95–98.

Chick, K. (1995). Evaluating student needs within the context of the classroom. *Communique, 24*(2), 16.

Cohen, E.G. (1994). *Designing groupwork. Strategies for the heterogeneous classroom* (2nd ed.). New York: Teachers College.

Coleman, J.S., Campbell, E.Q., Hobson, C.J., McPartland, J., Mood, A.M., Weinfeld, F.D., & York, R.L. (1966). *Equality of educational opportunity.* Washington, DC: U.S. Government Printing Office.

Cooper, J.D. (1995, August). *Meeting individual needs in a literature-centered classroom.* Workshop presentation at Montgomery County Intermediate Unit 23, Norristown, PA.

Cuban, L. (1989). The "at-risk" label and the problem of urban school reform. *Phi Delta Kappan, 70,* 780–784, 799–801.

Danielson, L., & Bellamy, G.T. (1989). State variation in placement of children with handicaps in segregated environments. *Exceptional Children, 55,* 448–455.

Dunn, L.M. (1968). Special education for the mildly retarded: Is much of it justifiable? *Exceptional Children, 34,* 5–22.

Edmonds, R. (1982). Programs of school improvement: An overview. *Educational Leadership, 40*(3), 4–11.

Ellison, L. (1992). Using multiple intelligences to set goals. *Educational Leadership, 50*(2), 69–72.

Evans, R. (1993). The human face of reform. *Educational Leadership, 51*(1), 19–23.

Flood, J., Lapp, D., Flood, S., & Nagel, G. (1992). Am I allowed to group? Using flexible patterns for effective instruction. The *Reaching Teacher, 45,* 608–616.

Fuchs, D., & Fuchs, L. (1994). Inclusive schools movement and the radicalization of special education reform. *Exceptional Children, 60,* 294–309.

Gamoran, A. (1992). Synthesis of research: Is ability grouping equitable? *Educational Leadership, 50*(2), 11–17.

Gardner, H. (1983). *Frames of mind: The theory of multiple intelligences.* New York: Basic.

Gardner, H. (1993). *Multiple intelligences: The theory in practice.* New York: Basic.

Gardner, H., & Hatch, T. (1989). Multiple intelligences go to school: Educational implications of the theory of multiple intelligences. *Educational Researcher, 18*(8), 104–110.

General Accounting Office. (1994, January). *Limited English proficiency: A growing and costly educational challenge facing many school districts.* Report to the Chairman, Committee on Labor and Human Resources, U.S. Senate, Washington, DC.

Giangreco, M.F., Cloninger, C.J., Dennis, R.E., & Edelman, S.W. (1994). Problem-solving methods to facilitate inclusive education. In J.S. Thousand, R.A. Villa, & A.I. Nevin (Eds.), *Creativity and collaborative learning* (pp. 321–346). Baltimore: Paul H. Brookes.

Giangreco, M.F., & Putnam, J. (1991). Supporting the education of students with severe disabilities in regular education environments. In L. Meyer, C. Peck, & L. Brown (Eds.), *Critical issues in lives of people with severe disabilities* (pp. 245–270). Baltimore: Paul H. Brookes.

Gickling, E., & Havertape, J.F. (1981). Curriculum based assessment. In J.A. Tucker (Ed.), *Non-test based assessment.* Minneapolis: University of Minnesota, The National School Psychology Inservice Network.

Gickling, E., & Thompson, V. (1985). A personal view of curriculum-based assessment. *Exceptional Children, 52*(3), 205–218.

Griffin, E.M. (1993, August). *Structured child observation: Kid watching.* A Griffin Center Professional Development Workshop. Seven Springs, Pennsylvania.

Hamre-Nietupski, S., Ayers, B., Nietupski, J., Savage, M., Mitchell, B., & Bramman, H. (1989). Enhancing integration of students with severe disabilities through curricular infusion: A general/special educator partnership. *Education and Training in Mental Retardation, 24,* 78–88.

Harper, G.F., Maheady, L., & Mallette, B. (1994). The power of peer-mediated instruction: How and why it promotes academic success for all students. In J.S. Thousand, R.A. Villa, & A.I. Nevin (Eds.), *Creativity and collaborative learning* (pp. 229–241). Baltimore: Paul H. Brookes.

Hawley, W.D. (1988). Missing pieces of the educational reform agenda: Or why the first and second waves may miss the boat. *Educational Administration Quarterly, 24,* 416–437.

Herman, J., Aschbacher, P., & Winters, L. (1992). *A practical guide to alternative assessment.* Alexandria, VA: Association for Supervision and Curriculum Development.

Herman, J., & Winters, L. (1994). Portfolio research: A slim collection. *Educational Leadership, 52*(2), 48–55.

Hoer, T.R. (1994). How the New City school applies multiple intelligences. *Educational Leadership, 52*(3), 29–34.

Johnson, D.W., & Johnson, R. (1984). *Cooperation in the classroom.* New Brighton, MN: Interaction.

Johnson, D.W., & Johnson, R. (1986). Mainstreaming and cooperative learning strategies. *Exceptional Children, 52*(6), 553–561.

Johnson, D.W., Johnson, R., Waring, D., & Maruyama, G. (1986). Different cooperative learning procedures and cross-handicap relationships. *Exceptional Children, 53*(3), 247–252.

Kasten, W., & Clarke, B. (1993). *The multi-age classroom: A family of learners.* New York: Richard C. Owen.

Katz, L. (1988, May). The disposition to learn. *Principal, 67*(5), 14–17.

Kirst, M.W. (1990). Recent state education reform in the United States: Looking backward and forward. In S.B. Bacharach (Ed.), *Educational reform: Making sense of it all* (pp. 20–29). Boston: Allyn & Bacon.

Kovaleski, J.F., Lowery, P., & Gickling, E. (1995). School reform through instructional support: Instructional evaluation (Part II). *Communique, 24*(2), 14–17.

Kovaleski, J.F., Tucker, J.A., & Duffy, D.J. (1995). School reform through instructional support: The Pennsylvania Initiative (Part I). *Communique, 23*(8), insert.

Lipp, M. (1992). An emerging perspective on special education: A development agenda for the 1990's. *The Special Education Leadership Review, 1*(1), 10–39.

Lipsky, D.K., & Gartner, A. (1989). The current situation. In D.K. Lipsky & A. Gartner (Eds.), *Beyond separate education. Quality education for all* (pp. 3–24). Baltimore: Paul H. Brookes.

Lipsky, D.K., & Gartner, A. (1995). Common questions about inclusion: What does the research say? *Exceptional Parent, 25,* 36–39.

Madden, N.A., & Slavin, R.E. (1983). Cooperative learning and social acceptance of mainstreamed academically handicapped students. *Journal of Special Education, 17*, 171–182.

McDonnell, J., & Hardman, M.L. (1986). Planning the transition of young adults with severe handicaps from school to community services: A framework for high school programs. *Education and Training in Mental Retardation, 21*, 275–286.

McDonnell, J., & Kiefer-O'Donnell, R. (1992). Educational reform and students with severe disabilities. *Journal of Disability Policy Studies, 3*, 53–74.

McLaughlin, M.J., & Warren, S.H. (1994). Restructuring special education programs in local school districts: The tensions and the challenges. *The Special Education Leadership Review, 2*, 2–21.

Metz, M.H. (1990). Some missing elements in the educational reform movement. In S.B. Bacharach (Ed.), *Educational reform: Making sense of it all* (pp. 141–154). Boston: Allyn & Bacon.

Murphy, J. (1990). The educational reform movement of the 1980's: A comprehensive analysis. In J. Murphy (Ed.), *The educational reform movement of the 1980's: Perspectives and cases* (pp. 3–55). Berkeley, CA: McCutenhan.

National Association for the Education of Young Children. (1990). *Reaching potentials: Appropriate curriculum content and assessment for young children.* Washington, DC: author.

National Commission on Excellence in Education. (1983). *A nation at risk: The imperative for educational reform.* Washington, DC: U.S. Government Printing Office.

Natriello, G., McDill, E.L., & Pallas, A.M. (1990). *Schooling disadvantaged children: Facing against catastrophe.* New York: Teachers College.

Oakes, J. (1985). *Keeping track: How schools structure inequality.* New Haven, CT: Yale University.

Oberti v. Board of Education of the Borough of Clementon School District, 789 F. Supp. 1322, 75 Ed.Law Rep. 258 (D.N.J. 1992); 801 Supp. 1393 (D.N.J. 1992); *aff'd* 995 F.2d 1204, 83 Ed.Law Rep. 1009 (3d Cir. 1993).

Purkey, S., & Smith, M. (1985). School reform: The district policy implications of the effective schools literature. *Elementary School Journal, 85*(4), 427–452.

Reavis, C., & Griffith, H. (1992). *Restructuring schools. Theory and practice.* Lancaster, PA: Technomic.

Roach, V. (1994, November). The superintendent's role in creating inclusive schools. *The School Administrator,* 20–27.

Rosenfield, S. (1987). *Instructional consultation.* Hillsdale, NJ: Lawrence Erlbaum.

Rusch, F.R., DeStefano, L., Chadsey-Rusch, J., Phelps, L.A., & Szmanski, E. (1992). *Transition from school to adult life: Models, linkages, and policy.* Sycamore, IL: Sycamore.

Sapon-Shevin, M., Ayres, B., & Duncan, J. (1994). Cooperative learning and inclusion. In J. Thousand, R. Villa, & A. Nevin (Eds.), *Creativity and collaborative learning* (pp. 45–58). Baltimore: Paul H. Brookes.

Sarason, S.B. (1995). Some reactions to what we have learned. *Phi Delta Kappan, 77*, 84–85.

Schumm, J.S., Vaughn, S., & Leavell, A.G. (1994). Planning pyramid: A framework for planning for diverse student needs during content area instruction. *The Reading Teacher, 47*(8), 608–615.

Sharan, S., & Shacar, C. (1988). *Language and learning in the cooperative classroom.* New York: Springer.

Sharan, S., & Sharan, Y. (1976). *Small group teaching.* Englewood Cliffs, NJ: Educational Technology.

Shinn, M., Rosenfield, S., & Knutson, N. (1989). Curriculum-based assessment: A comparison of models. *School Psychology Review, 18*(3), 299–316.

Slavin, R.E. (1990). *Cooperative learning: Theory, research and practice.* Englewood Cliffs, NJ: Prentice-Hall.

Slavin, R.E. (1991). Synthesis of research on cooperative learning. *Educational Leadership, 48*(5), 71–82.

Slavin, R.E., Stevens, R.J., & Madden, N.A. (1988). Accommodating student diversity in reading and writing instruction: A cooperative learning approach. *Remedial and Special Education, 9*(1), 60–66.

Stainback, W., & Stainback, S. (1990). *Support networks for inclusive schooling: Interdependent integrated education.* Baltimore: Paul H. Brookes.

Stevens, R.J., Madden, N.A., Slavin, R.E., & Farnish, A.M. (1987). Cooperative integrated reading and composition: Two field experiments. *Reading Research Quarterly, 22*, 433–454.

Udvari-Solner, A. (1994). A decision-making model for curricular adaptations in cooperative groups. In J. Thousand, R. Villa, & A.I. Nevin (Eds.), *Creativity and collaborative learning* (pp. 59–77). Baltimore: Paul H. Brookes.

Villa, R., & Thousand, J. (1992a). How one district integrated special and general education. *Educational Leadership, 50*(2), 39–41.

Villa, R., & Thousand, J. (1992b) *Restructuring for caring and effective education: An administrative guide to creating heterogeneous schools.* Baltimore: Paul H. Brookes.

Villa, R., & Thousand, J. (1995). *Creating an inclusive school.* Alexandria, VA: Association for Supervision and Curriculum Development.

Wang, M.C., Reynolds, M., & Walberg, H. (1994). Serving students at the margin. *Educational Leadership, 52*(4), 12–17.

Weber, G. (1971). *Inner city children can be taught to read: Four successful schools* (Occasional Paper No. 18). Washington, DC: Council for Basic Education.

Wehman, P. (1992). *Life beyond the classroom: Transition strategies for young people with disabilities.* Baltimore: Paul H. Brookes.

Whitaker, K.S., & Moses, M.C. (1994). *The restructuring handbook. A guide to school revitalization.* Needham Heights, MA: Allyn & Bacon.

Worthen, B.R. (1993, February). Critical issues that will determine the future of alternative assessment. *Phi Delta Kappan, 74*, 444–456.

York, J., Doyle, M.B., & Kronberg, R. (1992). A curriculum development process for inclusive classrooms. *Focus on Exceptional Children, 25*(4), 1–16.

CHAPTER 3

Planning, Implementing, and Evaluating Inclusive Education within the School

Ray E. Van Dyke, Cynthia R. Pitonyak, and Christina Thomasson Gilley

INTRODUCTION

Inclusive education begins with a belief and a vision. Realizing the fulfillment of that vision occurs because of the hard work of school teachers, administrators, and staff, working cooperatively with families. This chapter describes the experiences of the authors in implementing an inclusive education program in elementary schools in Montgomery County, Virginia (VanDyke, Stallings, & Colley, 1995). The experiences shared here are designed to stimulate educators in other schools; they are not meant to be the only or best way to approach inclusion.

The chapter is organized around three broad stages—planning, implementation, and evaluation—and discusses the importance of each stage as a school begins the process of inclusion.

PLANNING

Overview

Simply placing students with disabilities into general education classrooms is *not* inclusion. Inclusive education involves thoughtfulness and commitment on the part of everyone within the school to establish a system of education and supports that will be effective for each individual learner. Inclusion involves considering the interests, knowledge, and preparation of the instructional personnel and the resources of the school. And inclusion requires working cooperatively with and being considerate of the interests of families. In short, successful inclusion demands careful, coordinated, and long-term planning. The remainder of this section describes the steps of the planning process, most of

which must occur *before* the student with the disability joins the general education classroom.

Articulate Values and Develop the Vision

A plan for inclusive education begins by an open discussion of the values of the individuals and the system (i.e., district and school). These values form the basis for articulating a clear vision for serving students. Ideally, a school's vision for inclusive education is directly tied to existing philosophy statements for the school district. Philosophy statements included in existing goals or plans typically specify the school's desire for all students to succeed; a shared commitment to education by staff, teachers, parents, and community; and a belief that each student's education is important.

Because the shift from the traditional organization of special education to inclusive education for students with disabilities often spurs fear and disagreement, it is imperative that the vision for inclusion be developed by a group of persons representing all stakeholder groups. This group, an inclusion committee, should be established at the school level and led by the principal. (This committee should be different from any districtwide inclusion committee, although some persons may be members of both committees.) Committee members should have a special interest in and enthusiasm for the change to inclusive education. Especially in the beginning, the members of this site-based inclusion committee should be stakeholders who actively support inclusive instruction and who will take a proactive, problem-solving approach rather than a hand-wringing approach to difficult issues. The principal's leadership is critical in getting the committee organized, moving, and highly visible in the school (see Exhibit 3–1).

The inclusion committee should look at existing plans within the school and district to articulate the actual planning

The authors thank Brian Cullen and George Flynn of Ontario, Canada, for their inspiration.

Exhibit 3–1 Inclusion Committee

MEMBERSHIP

Characteristics:
- voluntary participation
- people committed to inclusive programming

Suggested members:
- teachers (general and special education, grade level or grade clusters, support personnel)
- related services personnel
- parents
- students, as appropriate
- principal as chairperson

MEETING FORMAT AND CONSIDERATIONS

- scheduled monthly meetings for one hour
- mechanism for calling a crisis meeting
- system for efficient use of time
- system for taking minutes
- system for informing members who are not present of essential deliberations

RESPONSIBILITIES

- Develop a philosophy statement or vision.
- Provide information:
  - Identify inservice/training.
  - Secure resources for staff and parents.
  - Actively seek best-practice information.
- Provide opportunities for teacher involvement:
  - site-based, collaborative planning
  - site-based management of resources
- Provide systematic support for staff:
  - Use a creative, team approach to problem solving.
  - Celebrate successes together!

---

steps to achieve inclusive education. Many schools work from biennial plan documents, staff development plans, five-year instructional plans, and individual teacher or principal work plans, all of which lend themselves to a framework for planning and implementing inclusive education.

Montgomery County Schools tied its five-year instructional plan goal for special education to the school board's one-line philosophy statement: "Montgomery County Public Schools accepts the responsibility for the success of every student" (Montgomery County, Virginia, Public Schools). A committee comprised of volunteer members representing general education teachers and parents, special education teachers and parents, administrators, community members, the local special education advisory committee, and a representative from the Montgomery County Public Schools' Parent Resource Center,* developed a visionary goal statement tied directly to the "success of every student" goal. The vision called for ". . . provision of integrated home-school placements for special education students whenever possible in order to educate all students in the least restrictive environment and to expand the quality and opportunities of instruction to all students in Montgomery County Public Schools." This vision guided the planning and implementation process for inclusion and served as the "litmus test" for each step of the process.

Maintaining commitment to the values articulated by the vision means keeping the vision statement in front of the group at all times, both literally and figuratively. This can keep the group focused and help members clarify their own values as they work through the process.

Listen to the People Affected by the Change

Because inclusive programming represents a total community change, it is critical from the very beginning to create formal and informal opportunities to share information and to listen to the people who will be affected by the change.

Teachers are the primary group directly affected by a move to inclusive education. When the building principal and the teaching staff together examine the options available to bring about this change, teachers feel a greater sense of choice and control in the process. One way to assist teachers in expressing and addressing concerns is to remind them that there is no single right or wrong way to go about making this change. Discussing multiple options can help teachers feel ownership of the process.

The principal should ask general and special education teachers what they need to provide a successful inclusive education. It can be especially useful in the beginning to remind teachers that delivering special education services is still the primary responsibility of the special education staff. The job of the general education teacher at this point is to maintain a classroom community that welcomes and includes identified special education students as integral members, and to develop a smooth, cooperative working relationship with special education staff. It is completely natural for teachers to be unsure about exactly what they will need to be successful until they have had the opportunity to experience the situation. Questions expressed at this point in

---

* This Parent Resource Center, staffed by a parent and an educator, provides training for parents. The focus is on parents of children with disabilities.

the process may be related to: access to help and support when problems arise, when and where special education support will be available, clearly defined individual responsibilities, and assurances that all students receive quality instruction.

Because teachers may not be able to envision clearly what supports they will need for success, it is particularly important for administrators in this listening part of the planning process to hear the underlying need for safety nets if things go wrong. The planning process should include clear descriptions of supports to which teachers can gain access in the building for help with planning and problem solving. The building principal, the site-based inclusion committee, and colleagues in the building who are dealing with similar issues should be especially accessible for support throughout the planning and implementation stages. Principals can do much to create a feeling of comfort for teachers by emphasizing the initial effort as a *learning process*. Mistakes are not only permissible, but expected. The commitment is to the vision, not to the structure or to the procedures that are developed to make the vision a reality. Aspects of the program that do not work will be revised, and open and honest communication is valued above everything else.

Parents are another primary group affected by the move to inclusive education. The building principal, with the support of the inclusion committee, should establish forums for sharing information on inclusive education with parents and allow for open discussion of their concerns. Parents of students in special education who may be moving to new schools must be consulted and their agreement secured prior to any placement change. Parents, like teachers, are concerned about the availability of adequate supports for their children in general education classes. At this point, however, a specific plan should be developed for sharing information with parents of special education students who live in the school attendance area. (The following section on implementation presents some specific strategies for enlisting parent support and guidance in the transition process for individual students.)

Parents of all students who attend the school should be informed of the upcoming changes and given an opportunity to ask questions and express concerns. It is important that the information be presented in a consistent, clear, and concise format, and it should focus on benefits to the total school community. The vision statement should be a prominent feature of this communication, and benefits and desired outcomes for all students should be emphasized. These communications provide practical information about what the changes will mean for a particular school. It is not necessary (and it breaks confidentiality requirements) to give parents details about specific students; instead this meeting should focus on concrete ways that special education resources can be merged with general education resources to create a more

individualized learning environment for all students. In most schools, Parent Teacher Association (PTA) meetings offer a logical forum for this type of presentation and discussion. Information should also be shared in written form through parent newsletters and PTA publications.

In the initial planning stages, information provided to parents, teachers, and others should be concise, consistent, and relatively low key. The listening step of the change process should be an ongoing effort, as changes are implemented and outcomes evaluated. In the beginning, the goal should simply be to keep people informed and to create a pattern of open dialogue and discussion.

The inclusion committee should involve certain key community agencies (e.g., the local parks and recreations department, local agencies that exclusively serve students with disabilities). These groups could participate in the initial forums, or they may be invited to a separate presentation. In Montgomery County, community groups became more interested in discussing inclusive services during the implementation stage when they began to see the signs of being directly affected by the changes taking place in the school. For example, parents whose children spend the school day with peers without disabilities begin to expect that community recreational programs available to children without disabilities, such as Little League baseball, will be available to their children as well. Parents may begin to question whether it is a good idea to send their children to summer camp that children without disabilities do not also attend. Local community children's programs are often very interested in including students with disabilities when they begin to receive direct requests from parents to do so. In Montgomery County, Virginia, agencies that initially served students with disabilities exclusively have had major gains in combining services with other community programs to provide more inclusive community opportunities for their customers. (Chapter 8 provides more information on working with community agencies.)

The building administrator must find the time for members of the inclusion committee to do the listening during the first year, including gathering needed information and organizing the forums for discussion outlined in this section. In addition, the committee members should meet to plan the next steps and should be available for planning and problem solving throughout the first year. Staff serving on this committee must be relieved of other nonessential, nonteaching responsibilities to allow time for leadership and support. More time is needed in the first few years of implementation than after inclusive services are well established. Serving on the inclusion committee is not a task to be taken on in a teacher's limited spare time. Principals sometimes can fund substitute teachers to allow release time through grants or inservice funds, or conference leave. Strategies developed for collaborative teaching, planning, and problem solving during the first year can be shared with other teachers through inservice sessions in subsequent years.

Provide Transformative Experiences

Individuals who change from traditional special education to inclusive education often undergo transformative experiences in which they are able to see a new or different paradigm. Such experiences help people to change their context for thinking, to redefine their skills, and to provide a strong value system upon which they can base their future actions. Transformative experiences may include classroom or school visitations, inservice workshops, training programs, or "celebrations" that provide individuals with visual examples and personal experiences that are proof that inclusive education can work.

Visiting classrooms and schools that reflect good quality inclusive education programming is essential in the development of inclusive education. Appropriate sites can be identified through state departments of education, local universities with special education programs, and state parent information and advocacy centers. Visits should be made to the sites that are recognized for their belief in inclusive education as well as their dedication to quality educational services. A school team comprised of general education teachers, special education teachers, and the principal should visit inclusive schools as part of their responsibility as members of the site-based inclusion committee. Members of this team should be provided release time with substitutes and travel expenses. The school team should have a clearly defined goal and a specific list of questions. To allow staff to transfer knowledge and solve problems relevant to school planning after the visit, discussion and planning opportunities should be arranged with resource people from the model district, local universities, or other sites.

Classroom visitations are especially beneficial for teachers who will be including students with disabilities within their classrooms for the first time. Once the needs of the student and the teacher(s) are identified, an observation of an inclusive classroom with a similar student helps the teacher establish specific instructional strategies, technologies, and collaboration techniques that can be implemented. These visits should allow teachers time to talk with one another about fears, questions, and concerns.

Staff development, reflecting the visions and beliefs of inclusive education, can assist with the transformative process. A staff development plan is critical to the systematic acquisition of necessary skills and to the continued realization of the values and beliefs necessary to sustain the process of changing to an inclusive education. Staff at every level within the school should be involved in an information network that includes conferences, workshops, and newsletters. A packet of facts and information should be provided to all staff and parents that describes the following: what inclusion is and is not; the benefits of inclusion for all children; basic strategies to support students in general education classes; and the value, best practice, and legal basis for inclusion. Videos that depict inclusive education programs or experiences and that present some of the struggles and successes may be useful. Visible support and participation from administrators, general and special education teachers, support staff, and parents are important. Staff development programs should also identify resource people who could assist with planning and implementation.

Local successes should be highlighted throughout the school or division with opportunities for colleagues to observe within classrooms and to have access to peers for support and technical assistance. The process of change takes time, and the move toward inclusive programming within a school, classroom, or division is no exception. Providing transformative experiences for staff, students, and parents is one of the strongest change agents available. Personal positive experiences empower individuals to take the next step with more confidence. Peer validation, confirmation, and support provide a safety net, while resources outside the school or division offer guidance necessary to the planning and implementation of inclusive education for students with disabilities.

Plan for Bringing Students to Their Neighborhood Schools

One primary element in inclusive programming is the concept of the neighborhood school. Moving from a center-based system, in which students are bused to certain schools to receive special education services, to a neighborhood school system, in which students attend schools they would attend if they did not have a disability, can represent a major student population shift for some schools. Principals can take advantage of the opportunity to analyze the impact of such a shift and thus involve teachers in planning and organizing from the very beginning.

Principals can initiate this process by gathering information about the student population in the school's attendance zone. The principal and teachers discuss the options for facilitating this population shift:

- Should all students who now attend other schools be brought back "home"? Are there other students who are bused to the school for special education services? Are the student's neighborhood schools prepared to bring them "home" as well? Should students who have only one more year before moving to another level (e.g., elementary to middle school) be moved at this time?
- Should only some of the students who now attend other schools be brought back? Should the process

begin with certain grade levels? What about students whose parents express an interest in such a move?

- Should the process begin with students who are newly identified as eligible for special education services? Could the program be adjusted along the way to continue serving those students in the school rather than busing them to programs in other schools?
- Should the process begin with students at entry level in the school, maintaining inclusive services for those students as they move through the grade levels? (For example, an elementary school would set up inclusive services for all entering kindergarten students during the first year, and move the next year to maintaining services for those students in first grade while continuing kindergarten services. This way, the school would add inclusive programming one grade level at time. By the time the entering kindergartners exited fifth grade, all special education services in the school would be inclusive.)
- Should only those students who already attend the school, receiving special education services in special education classes, be first included? A note of caution here: If the school is a center for special education classes and serves many students who are bused in from other attendance areas, general education classrooms can quickly become overwhelmed by trying to include unnaturally high numbers of students with disabilities. This option might be appropriate for a school with small numbers of special education classes (e.g., a school with one resource room or one self-contained special education class serving students from several grade levels).

These options represent only a few of the many possibilities for shifting to a natural neighborhood-school population of students receiving special education. In all cases, decisions must be made on an individual basis for each student, as part of the individualized educational program (IEP) process. In Montgomery County, different schools selected different options as a means of getting started. As teachers and administrators in a school work together to identify options for inclusive education, two things should be constantly emphasized: (1) commitment to the values articulated by the vision, and (2) development of realistic options for a particular school and the children it serves.

After identifying students who may be candidates for returning to their neighborhood schools, the inclusion committee should learn more about these students. A first step is to visit the students in their current schools to get a sense of their strengths and needs. This step is important because all team members must be given as much information as possible to ensure a smooth transition to new schools. It is also important that all persons who work with a particular student be involved in the transition. The principals of the two schools should work closely to coordinate visits, share ideas, and provide support for the transition process.

Meet with Parents and Prepare IEPs

After appropriate contacts have been made, the principal should invite to school the parents of students who may be included to discuss their opinions of whether students should be placed in a general education class in their neighborhood school instead of a self-contained classroom in another school. Schools can find success in having the parents, principal, special education teacher, central office special education representative, and classroom teacher meet to discuss the advantages and disadvantages of having the students move to the neighborhood school. It is vitally important that the people in this meeting be open about their concerns and perceived needs. The parents, in particular, must be given a chance to express their fears and hopes about having their child in an inclusive setting. Many parents say they leave this meeting with very mixed feelings. They are fearful for their child to be in a real-life setting for the first time after the relatively safe environment of a self-contained classroom. This fear is often twofold: parents fear that their child may suffer physically or emotionally from encounters with students in the general education population, and they sometimes fear that their child may cause injury to the general education students.

This meeting should focus on the supports needed for the student to be included. The first question is: "What are the supports needed for this student to be successful in our school?" The answer to this question must come from all stakeholders—from parents, to principal, to classroom teacher. Once the answer is determined, the next question is: "Can we provide those supports in our school?" If a support is missing, then the meeting participants must identify the options for finding and providing the support. If it is determined that the supports are available, then the group must discuss the benefits and drawbacks for a student's remaining in the self-contained setting and for moving to the neighborhood school. The experience of the authors has consistently been that the benefits of attending the neighborhood school have led the team to choose inclusion. However, it is important that this be a team decision, made individually for each student.

In Montgomery County, Virginia, a useful strategy for increasing teacher and parent understanding of special education service delivery options has been to identify and describe specific types of services that are available to students. Rather than defining services in terms of *where* they will be delivered (e.g., resource room versus self-contained classroom), Montgomery County IEP committees now identify *which type* of special education service is appropriate for each student in each area where disability is a factor:

- *Instruction* is used on IEPs to identify times and subjects where specialized instruction from a special education teacher is needed.
- *Support* is used to identify times and subjects that may be taught within the context of general instruction with support and accommodations provided by an instructional assistant under the supervision of a special education teacher.
- *Consult* refers to those times and subjects that may be taught within the context of general instruction with only periodic consultations from a special education teacher.

Using this approach, services delivered to students may be highly individualized and are developed with consideration given to resources already available within the general education classroom. It is not unusual for one student to receive all three kinds of services at different times during the day or week in different academic areas. IEP committees can specifically determine which types of services work best for certain students in certain subject areas; this information is valuable for future planning and program development. Parents appreciate having services described in these terms; they can advocate more effectively as their children move through grade levels when they know specifically what kinds of services are most beneficial.

The next step is to finalize the IEP. The IEP will specify the placement, services, and supports necessary for the student.

Consider Staffing and Physical Resources

After IEPs are completed, the inclusion committee will identify immediate needs for reorganization of staff, resources, and physical space. Staff responsibilities may need to change to meet the needs of the students. For example, an instructional assistant who worked primarily with a self-contained class in the past may now need to become an assistant in several general education classrooms. The most obvious staff changes to be planned are the roles of the general education teacher and the special education teacher (discussed in the implementation section of this chapter). It is possible that the needs of some students may require additional staff, which should be planned for immediately (Snell & Raynes, 1995). This need for extra staff can be a problem if the budget has been finalized and no more positions are available. Coordination with the central office administrators may identify available resources.

The inclusion committee should plan for resources such as instructional supplies. These supplies may have been purchased through separate funds and labeled as general education and special education in the past. If students will spend most of their time in the general education classroom, then the general education supplies should be increased and special education funds may not be necessary. Ideally, instructional supply needs can be accommodated without earmarking them as general or special education, thus allowing funds to merge. This decision may be made at the central office or at the site, depending on the funding structure of the school district. (See Chapter 5 for further discussion of fiscal issues.)

In addition to supplies, physical space may become an issue. Classrooms that once were used for self-contained classes may become offices, storage space, or resource rooms for small-group work. Some students may have difficulty at first with the transition from special education to general education classrooms and may benefit from having a "break." A quiet, private place is needed for the occasional times when the overstimulation of the general classroom becomes overwhelming for some students. These spaces should be available to all students, not just students with disabilities.

Some schools may be faced with using a facility that is outdated or in poor condition. This is a concern for students who use wheelchairs or walkers. Fortunately, many schools have already made alterations to ensure access for all people to comply with the Americans with Disabilities Act. Flexibility is the key to resolving problems with physical access. Although at times it may be necessary to construct a ramp, it is also possible for a particular class to move for one period to another room that meets the needs for access. (See Exhibit 3–2 for a list of issues related to space.)

Exhibit 3–2 Questions Related to Space

- What do we need space for (e.g., small-group instruction, place for "breaks" when a student needs it, equipment storage)?
- How often will the space be needed (e.g., daily at the same time, once a week)?
- What are all the possible spaces that are available? (Be creative!)
- Which supplies and equipment are used on a daily basis as compared to those used weekly or monthly? What are the implications for space?
- What activities need more privacy (e.g., toileting, some medical procedures)?
- How can the use of existing space be modified? (Consider even short periods of space availability.)

Resolve Transportation Needs

Transportation can be a critical aspect of success. The director of transportation of the school system should be included in discussions of inclusion early in the planning process. Because the director is instrumental in working out the logistics of bus routes for students with special needs, he or she should agree to the vision of inclusive education and support the vision by alleviating bus problems as they arise.

In most cases, an inclusive education program reduces transportation needs, and no additional funds are necessary. The focus should be on planning for the students' needs within the existing transportation system. Assistance on the "regular" bus may be necessary; this assistance may come from older students or an adult assistant. Training must be provided so bus drivers know the needs of the students. In some situations, a specialized bus may still be needed because of a student's physical disability.

One common issue is the length of the school day for students with disabilities. The day should not be shortened to accommodate transportation.

Another concern is the need for specialized buses for field trips to accommodate students with physical disabilities. These buses obviously add expense to the field trip, but often students in general education may ride with students on the specialized bus.

Teach Skills Needed for the Change Process

Once people begin to envision what successful inclusive special education might look like, they have many questions about how to realize that vision. At first, most of the questions have to do with *implementation*: "What if I am teaching a unit on the Civil War and a student with a severe intellectual disability is in my class? What will she do during our discussions?" "What if I am conducting a chemistry lab and a student in my class has physical disabilities and is blind? Won't that be dangerous?"

There are numerous "how to" questions, and teachers usually want answers before they begin. The most common scenario is one in which the teacher is standing in front of the classroom, confronted all at once with the demands of everyday teaching (which are quite significant) and with a student who does not understand the lesson in any way and for whom the teacher is, nevertheless, responsible. This teacher may be wondering how to teach simple addition and calculus at the same time. Meeting the needs of diverse groups of learners has always been a formidable challenge to educators. "Upping the ante" with a student with special needs pushes that challenge to extremes in the minds of some teachers.

What is missing in the scenarios described here is the presence of special education support. Take the same pictures and add the special education teacher. The teacher can assist with adapting the curriculum and instruction (see Chapter 6) and demonstrating specific teaching strategies. This teacher is very familiar with the lesson plan and the student's IEP and objectives. For example, with a child with severe disabilities, there are opportunities for social skill development (answering roll call, socializing during transitions between activities), movement training (distributing and collecting papers), and functional math (counting out and assembling materials students will need for the upcoming lab activity). This special education support may be available all day or for part of the day, depending upon the specific situation.

Especially in the beginning, planning relevant instruction for the student with an IEP is not the general education teacher's primary concern. The special education teacher already knows how to plan relevant instruction for students with disabilities. In addition, becoming an expert in the general education curriculum is not the primary concern of the special education teacher. The general classroom teacher already has that expertise. The skill that is most important for successful implementation is both teachers' ability to *communicate* and *collaborate* to create lessons and to provide classroom experiences that will work for all of the students. Learning to function as a team, communicate effectively, and deal with change are the most important skills teachers can acquire.

The inclusion committee should be prepared to come together quickly in crisis situations—when events arise that challenge the stability of instruction in a classroom (e.g., escalation of behavioral problems for a student, a serious disagreement between the general and special education teachers working together as a team). This group needs to stay enthusiastic and energized; the more they learn to communicate and collaborate, the less they will need the direct leadership of the principal.

Schools in Montgomery County, Virginia, have found issue/action planning to be a simple, effective way for structuring meetings. This format provides an action-oriented focus, which is invaluable given the time constraints that most teachers experience. Anyone voicing a concern leaves the meeting with suggestions for dealing with the concern and with the knowledge that someone is responsible for following up on the solution. Short but highly productive meetings need to become "normal operating procedure" in a school moving toward inclusion. (See Exhibit 3–3 for issue/action planning strategy.)

Members of the inclusion committee should become familiar with the change process itself in order to understand the events that occur as they begin planning for implementation. Knowing that change is difficult and that groups and individuals go through certain developmental stages as they experience change can be invaluable.

Exhibit 3–3 Issue/Action Planning Strategy

Issue/action planning works as follows:

1. The group agrees on a set period of time within which to conduct the meeting.
2. The chairperson checks with each member of the group regarding issues that he or she may wish to bring forward. The group looks at the agreed-upon time period and determines roughly how much time will be spent on each issue.
3. The group addresses one issue at a time, with the chairperson or someone else taking notes. For each issue brought forward, actions are discussed and noted, along with the names of persons responsible for making sure each action is carried out.
4. The date and members attending the meeting are recorded at the top of the planning form. Members who are absent are also recorded. Everyone in the group gets a copy of the minutes.

For example, it may be useful to realize that one of the first responses of a group moving into a real community change is to go through a period of "faking it." Members of the group may attempt to avoid disagreement at all costs. It is critical to move past this stage, because a school community that practices inclusive education must learn to *resolve* rather than *avoid* conflict. As daily inclusive instruction begins and problems arise, staff may feel themselves moving into a period of "chaos" as conflicts come to the surface and teams struggle to learn to work together. If the group understands that this chaos is a normal part of change, they may not waste so much time trying to avoid conflict. Working through the chaos stage means dropping preconceptions, expectations, and prejudices and avoiding the need to control situations. As the groups work through the change process together, they will learn to face and resolve conflicts and work together to develop creative solutions. Inservice training about what to expect during the process of change is an excellent investment.

IMPLEMENTATION

Following the planning year, it is time to move into implementation. In reality, these stages are not so clearly defined. Planning must be continuous throughout the entire process, and small efforts toward implementation should begin during the planning stage.

Develop the Master Schedule

One of the principal's first tasks is to develop the master schedule. An often-repeated concern is the belief that the schedule of the students who receive special services drives the entire master schedule. However, this is not necessary. One of the most effective ways to develop the master schedule is to have a committee of special and general education teachers work with the principal. These teachers then begin to see the limitations placed on each group as they attempt to meet student needs. Often, if a staff can get beyond traditional beliefs (e.g., language arts must be taught in the morning when students are still "fresh"), teachers may find that the new master schedule would also have been the most efficient one under the traditional model of special education.

In the early stages of inclusion, it is advisable to give teachers a choice about having students with special needs included in their classrooms. This choice may be easier to implement in schools with multiple sections per grade level. In smaller schools, it may be necessary for principals to offer teachers the choice to move from one grade level to another if they are uncomfortable with inclusion at first. If no opening exists at a grade level the teacher prefers, then it may be necessary for the principal to move a teacher to another grade level. Some schools have used various forms of cluster grouping of students in classrooms to make the best use of the instructional assistants. However, schools should always strive not to exceed natural proportions when placing students with disabilities in classrooms.

The principal may consider keeping the class size smaller than other classes on the same grade level by "weighting" the students with disabilities. This process involves assigning extra "weight" to a student with disabilities when counting the number of students in the room. For example, a student with severe disabilities may "count" as two students. The "weight" can depend on several factors (e.g., specialized equipment in the room, emotional or physical needs that may require more of the teacher's time, or the use of resource people—speech-language pathologist, physical therapist—in the classroom).

Use Consultant Teachers and Inclusion Specialists

One strategy that was particularly effective in Montgomery County, Virginia, was the creation of a consulting teacher position in each school. The consulting teacher serves as a leader for special education in the building. He or she is responsible for ensuring that services are delivered in compliance with the state and federal regulations. The consulting teacher chairs eligibility meetings and monitors the special education process for each student, from referral through IEP development. The consulting teacher also provides on-site technical assistance to teachers, administrators, students, and parents. This assistance can take the form of support for crisis intervention, model teaching, facilitation of collaboration among members of instructional teams, and ongoing staff development activities within the building. Many consulting teachers within Montgomery County Schools also help conduct educational evaluations for eligibility and are responsible for a small caseload of students with particularly challenging educational disabilities. The consulting teacher model can be an effective way to provide individualized support and assistance to teachers in gaining skills needed to teach in inclusive classrooms. (See Exhibit 3–4 for a description of the responsibilities of the consulting teacher.)

A strategy for increasing skills in individualizing instruction for students with the most severe disabilities has been the development of an itinerant inclusion specialist. Inclusion specialists are teachers with training and expertise in teaching students with severe or multiple disabilities. Because of the relatively small number of these students in any school district, it is often not feasible to begin implementation with a properly endorsed staff person in each building. The inclusion specialists travel between schools, providing training and support to general education teachers

Exhibit 3–4 Consulting Teacher Job Description

ADMINISTRATIVE/SUPERVISORY DUTIES

- Develops student groups and special education staff assignments for master schedule.
- Maintains knowledge of current regulations and provides information to staff in building.
- Monitors maintenance of special education confidential files as required.
- Develops contacts with people in the school system and the community to aid in special education cases.
- Keeps abreast of current research in area.
- Coordinates transition of students to or from schools.
- Ensures that all legal regulations and requirements for special education are met.
- Observes classroom activities as part of the evaluation process (aides/students).
- Monitors all cases that require special attention.
- Meets with parents of incoming students to explain the program.
- Provides required/requested information to special education office regarding caseloads, schedules, etc.
- Completes observations of students for evaluations, as requested.
- Reviews all IEPs for quality and compliance.
- Monitors related service delivery within the building.
- Chairs eligibility meetings and ensures compliance with regulations.
- Conducts or attends out-of-school suspension meetings for special education students.
- Assists in evaluation of instructional aides, as required.
- Monitors procedures for the following for identified special education students:
  - screenings
  - temporary placements
  - referrals for special education evaluation
  - suspensions
  - grades
  - attendance
- Responds to correspondence.
- Maintains materials and equipment inventories.
- Purchases supplies as needed.

WORK ACTIVITIES

Teaching Duties

- Provides direct instruction and support for crisis intervention, as needed.
- Reviews/consults on lesson plans, as needed.
- Teaches learning units as invited (with the assistance of an instructional aide, where applicable).
- Provides appropriate individualized programs for assigned students through the development, implementation, and evaluation of the student's IEP.
- Assists with instruction in other classrooms as required.
- Completes diagnostic testing of new referrals as required.
- Collaborates with teams and individual teachers and instructional aides, as needed.

Meeting Duties

- Attends faculty meetings, as required.
- Attends PTA meetings, as necessary.
- Participates in child study meetings, as requested.
- Chairs special education eligibility committee meetings in schools.
- Meets with other interdisciplinary teams to discuss special cases.
- Plans special education inservice meetings for personnel within building.
- Meets with special education teachers and counselors to determine a student's individual needs or to discuss specific problems.
- Chairs special education staff meeting within building.
- Plans agenda for special education staff meetings within building, as requested.
- Attends planning meetings for IEPs, as requested.
- Attends and/or presents information in local, state, or national conferences.
- Attends meetings as required by special education and central office.
- Attends inclusion support committees at school site.

and instructional assistants working with students with severe disabilities. They collect lesson plans or a description of class activities from general education teachers on a weekly basis and plan adapted lessons according to student IEPs. These adapted lessons are carried out by the instructional assistant. Inclusion specialists are responsible for facilitating positive peer relationships between students with disabilities and their classmates. They also work directly with students for a few hours each week, which gives them an opportunity to model appropriate instructional techniques, to check progress, and to provide on-the-spot problem solving as needed. Inclusion specialists coordinate related services for students with severe disabilities. They also assist the classroom teacher in facilitating parent involvement and participation in the instructional program.

Develop Instructional Teams

Moving toward inclusive programming for all students means significant changes in the way daily classroom instruction is conducted. Instructional teams become the norm in inclusive classrooms, with the goal that each team member carries part of the load for meeting the diverse needs of all the students in the classroom. No longer does the classroom teacher assume this responsibility. Similarly, rather than serving students by disability labels, special education teachers may begin serving students by grade level.

Special and general education teachers who are new to inclusive situations tend to move through three phases as they learn to work together. At first, teachers have a tendency to instruct in a *parallel* fashion, where the class is divided so that some students meet with the special education teacher and some meet with the general education teacher. Next, teachers tend to work in a *cooperative* fashion, taking turns in presenting portions of each lesson or unit to the entire class or to small groups. As time passes and teachers develop a good working relationship, develop respect for each others' skills and style, and learn to plan efficiently, they move at last into a *collaborative* teaching relationship. They develop instructional units together, and teachers' roles vary according to the type of lesson, the students' needs, and the teachers' personal preferences and styles.

The teaching assistant is a key player in the instructional role. The role of the teaching assistants includes:

- providing ongoing assistance and support to individual students as described on IEPs and as directed by the teachers
- implementing adapted lesson plans with individuals or small groups
- monitoring student performance in daily activities and reporting progress to teachers
- assisting the classroom teacher
- making materials as needed

The instructional team meets regularly to plan and to evaluate the team's success in meeting the needs of all the students. The roles of team members may change according to the specific needs of the class, including students with general needs and those with special needs. Information obtained from inclusion committee meetings may also require that the team examine its format and make changes. Flexibility becomes a vitally important trait for the staff members on the team.

Adjust Policies and Procedures

As the roles and responsibilities of team members change, it may be necessary at times to request assistance from the division special education office or even the state department of education to deal with regulations and policies that may be disincentives or barriers to inclusive educational programming. For example, when team members brainstorm about ways of dealing with a problem, a seemingly easy solution may involve dealing with prohibitive regulations. These regulations can often be changed if one goes through appropriate channels. Similarly, what is presumed to be impossible due to regulations can sometimes be accomplished. Staff members find that they can sometimes request waivers of regulations to obtain the needed flexibility. In approaching these barriers, it is necessary for staff members to find out if the barrier exists because of district policy, state regulations, or federal regulations. It is important to read these policies carefully to ensure that assumed barriers are actually there.

Schools must make ongoing adjustments as they implement inclusive programming. Staff quickly realize that they never reach the level at which they have solved all problems and mastered all techniques. Each time a new student enters the school, a new staff member may be hired; even when a student moves from one grade level to another, the program must be adjusted.

Develop a Solution-Oriented Approach to Problems

A teacher who is widely regarded in Montgomery County Schools as very successful with inclusive instruction reported that the most helpful question she asks herself when she gets discouraged is not, "Do you believe inclusion works?" but rather, "Do you believe inclusion *can* work?" According to this teacher, nothing works every day; on the days when everything seems to go wrong, what she needs to do is to remember the experiences she has had and the examples she has seen of "inclusion at its best." Telling herself that inclusion should work all the time only makes her feel like a failure on those tough days. Keeping the most positive experiences clearly in mind and collecting new ones can encourage and motivate teachers and support staff through the bumpy times that are sure to arise as the implementation stage begins.

As the inclusion committee meets with staff and works to resolve issues that arise on a daily basis, it is a good idea to keep a record of the various problems that seem most prevalent in the building. If the committee uses the issue/action planning strategy discussed previously, an ongoing record of issues is automatically maintained. The principal should then seek out programs in other areas that are working through similar issues. Whereas in the planning stage, the principal hopes to provide staff with a positive "big picture" of inclusive programming, during the implementation stage the focus should be on looking for creative solutions to specific problems. The principal or the committee should approach other school districts about their solutions to typical problems, such as creating planning time for teachers, providing inclusive instruction in whole-language classrooms, and scheduling support staff. Some schools may have discovered effective ways to work with students with special challenges, such as behavioral or emotional disabilities. Opportunities to observe similar programs provide teachers with a valuable source of transformative experiences during the implementation stage.

When staff have the opportunity to observe colleagues in other settings, it becomes clear that there is no one "right way" to practice inclusive educational programming. Team members will see ideas for addressing problems that will be helpful to them. They will also see aspects of the programs they observe that do not seem to work as well as their own strategies. This in itself can be a powerful transformative experience. Inclusive programming represents an ongoing and continuous process for collaborating to meet individual students' needs and to capitalize on the strengths of students and staff in the learning process. Freeing themselves of the notion that they must figure out the right way to conduct their classes allows teachers to address problems creatively.

Often, the "model schools" that teachers and staff visit are interested in exchanging information, perhaps even making a reciprocal visit to the visitors' school. Encouraging observers and giving teams opportunities to speak publicly about their ideas and successes bolster confidence and provide some well-deserved recognition.

Sources of transformative experiences are also available right within the school building. During the implementation stage, the inclusion committee should create regular opportunities to highlight "success stories" within the building. One activity that worked well during the initial years of implementation in Montgomery County was an "inclusion get-together." This voluntary, after-school opportunity let teachers share experiences. At the first get-together, the group formed a list of topics that everyone was interested in discussing. Teachers and support staff shared aspects of inclusive instruction that they believed were working well for them.

Future get-togethers were scheduled on a topical basis, working through the list generated by teachers at the first meeting. Teachers who had positive experiences or special expertise were asked to present to the group, and plenty of time was allowed for questions or discussion. Snacks were provided, and the atmosphere was relaxed, social, and positive.

Another opportunity for highlighting successes in the building occurs on a regular basis at inclusion committee meetings. Regardless of the meeting format, every meeting can be structured to begin or end (or both) with recounting of funny stories or success experiences. This strategy brings a positive note to even the most potentially stressful meeting, and helps teachers keep the change process in perspective as an experience rich with stories and creative struggle. Especially in the beginning, it will be up to the principal to deliberately structure opportunities for telling positive or funny stories lest most of the discussions become overwhelmingly problem-oriented. Transformative experiences in the implementation stage include deliberately highlighting and celebrating successes, and specifically visualizing ways to address problems through observations and consultations.

Teach Skills Needed for Inclusive Instruction

Another step of the implementation stage is teaching skills necessary for success in inclusive classrooms. At this point, instructional teams need staff development in the basics of daily classroom operations.

Teachers must be very clear about the strategies they will use to individualize instruction of special education students within daily lessons. The most common ways of individualizing within regular class instruction are adapting instruction and providing instructional accommodations. The special and general education teachers should adapt instruction when the entire range of mastery objectives being used to measure student success is inappropriate for some special education students. For example, in a fifth-grade unit on the Civil War, the mastery objectives may include independently researching information on the Civil War, reading works of fiction from this period, writing an essay outlining the major themes of the war, identifying key historical figures, and relating how people's lives today are affected by the war's outcome. These objectives may not be appropriate for a student in the class who has significant difficulty understanding abstract concepts, so the mastery objectives and daily lessons for this unit of instruction would be adapted. Rather, this student's learning objectives may deal with very basic information about the Civil War: the basic conflict between North and South, the time frame, several of the major issues, and perhaps identifying pictures of General Grant and General Lee as major figures. Along with this information, the student may use these lessons as opportunities to work on socialization and fine motor skills as he or she participates in cooperative groups working on class projects. An adapted lesson generally requires an alteration of the learning objectives, and alternative materials or alternative uses of materials used in instruction with the rest of the class. (See Chapter 6 for further information on adapting curriculum.)

Another common method for individualizing instruction is providing accommodations to give students with disabilities equal access to the instruction. Accommodations are modifications or extra supports that can be made within the context of the instruction available to the entire class, without changing the content of the instruction. Students who would benefit from accommodated lessons are those for whom the learning objectives are appropriate. These students will be able to master the concepts presented, but their disabilities may prevent them from using some instructional materials, producing some required products, or completing assignments within the same time frame. Using the example of the Civil War unit, such students may need access to accommodations to participate in daily lessons. A student with a reading disability, for example, may need written material to be read aloud or to have cue words to find reference materials. It may be necessary for a student with a reading disability to dictate the essay and then copy it, rather than generate the writing independently. Students who have difficulties with organization or who need more repetitions to remember material may need access to a study guide or extra practice sessions. Students with attention difficulties may need help in structuring long-term projects to ensure completion. (See Chapter 18 for additional examples of accommodations for students with reading disabilities.)

Celebrate Accomplishments

There should be open and public opportunities for celebration of accomplishments and benefits. Staff and community need to share in the public recognition of a job well done that is recognized and attended by all interest groups within the school or district, including school board members, the superintendent and central office staff, building administrators, teachers, PTA leaders, special education advisory members, students, and parents. All levels of the organization should be present, as well as a mixture of general and special education staff members. Celebrations of accomplishments are positive experiences within which we can solidify or begin relationships with community agencies, universities, advisory committees, school boards, and parent groups. Parent testimonials provide moving, positive, personal accounts of the results of inclusive education that can help to balance the best-practice foundation by emphasizing the important value basis for inclusion. Celebrations may be the transformative experience for some, leading to a change in vision toward inclusive service.

EVALUATION

Create Process To Evaluate Outcomes

Inclusive educational programming for students with disabilities should focus on high-quality educational services and benefits for all students, measured by student outcomes. The outcomes should be identified in the planning and IEP process. It is imperative that general education and special education staff openly share the responsibility for implementing the evaluation process. This cooperative effort provides evidence of the shared commitment to inclusive programming as well as further evidence of the actual merger of general and special education.

The inclusion committee of educators and administrators should develop the instruments, timeline, and methods of evaluation under the direction of a professional educational evaluator. A committee approach is critical to obtain input from all interested parties and to provide opportunities for in-house staff to become familiar with the evaluation procedures. The trained evaluator establishes educational validity of the test instruments and methods selected or developed.

Formal evaluation methods should be developed that provide opportunities for individuals to share feedback on every level: systemwide evaluation among administrators, teaching staff, and community; and building-level evaluation among administrators, teachers, students, and parents. Rating scales, guided interview formats, and other data collection strategies should be designed specifically to address the outcomes that have been identified and to elicit informal feedback or input from individuals or groups. All strategies must be designed with consideration given to the resources available for distribution of the instruments and for collection and analysis of the data. Release time for staff must be provided so that personnel are required to complete evaluation tasks in addition to their other responsibilities. The process of implementing inclusion is very time consuming and emotionally draining. It is often difficult to have the time to evaluate what you are doing while you are doing it.

Informal evaluation procedures provide necessary information to correct or alleviate problems that arise, and they provide information critical to continued program and service development. Issue/action planning formats (Exhibit 3–3) are useful in articulating the specific issues being addresses and in determining strategies, actions, and individuals to address the issues. This format may be used by a single person, team, or group for evaluation of student or process outcomes. Another informal procedure would allow key groups or individuals to list their concerns related to inclusive programming and the benefits derived from inclusive programming. Although this process has a positive end, listing all of the concerns can be discouraging. Listing benefits, as well as concerns, helps staff to see the good things that are occurring and takes the negative slant off of the process. The benefits noted should be openly celebrated and acknowledged in order to validate the efforts of individuals who are working hard for quality inclusive education; the concerns listed should be openly and systematically addressed by the site-based inclusion committee.

Another powerful tool involves a process of assessing needs, barriers, and strategies. The process involves providing the group with unlimited time to develop an exhaustive list of concerns or needs. Individuals should feel that they have been heard and that all of their needs or concerns have been included in the list. The facilitator clarifies what the individual means so that the list is truly representative of the group's ideas rather than an interpretation of their needs. The facilitator then assists the group to identify the barriers that may interfere or prevent their needs from being met. This is an important part of the process because it clarifies the actual obstacles that must be overcome to reach the goal of inclusive services. The final step of the process is to develop strategies to remove the identified barriers. This technique can be used to evaluate student and process outcomes and to plan for future program development.

Is the Vision Growing As the Team Grows?

Once evaluation procedures have been completed, it is important to establish a system to use the data in a meaningful and proactive way. It is imperative that collected data be incorporated into an annual planning process to further the inclusion efforts in the school or system. The evolutionary process of inclusion is best represented visually as a circle that begins with planning, moves to implementation, then moves to evaluation, and finally returns to the first step of planning. Evaluation results should be the cornerstone of the systematic planning process and should clearly delineate what should be altered or addressed and what should be left alone.

As schools continue to move through the change process, it is necessary for the inclusion committee to revisit the original vision and to continue to listen actively to stakeholders. The committee should review policies and procedures regularly to ensure that they are working to bring about desired outcomes. At the end of each year of implementation, it is a good idea to take a thorough, honest look at special education services delivered in the building, grade level by grade level.

The inclusion committee should carefully review students' IEPs at this point in the process and list the types of services offered. Comparing this list with the continuum of services can provide information needed to assess whether students have access to the entire range of services. This is an important step; with the move into inclusive education, special education staff are serving a much broader range of students, and services should reflect this range. Especially after the first year or two of implementation, special education staff must be sure that they are not continuing to provide the same old services to a broader range of students. Services must meet the instructional needs of the students who are served. Are affective skills being taught? Should changes be made to the environment to create opportunities for success? Is further inservice training needed?

Are Policies and Procedures Working To Move the Vision to Reality?

Periodically, the special structures that have been put into place to get an inclusive program off the ground should be evaluated. Are those structures still needed? Should their functions change? It is helpful to begin by evaluating the inclusion committee. Although this group may be needed for several years, or even indefinitely, its function will change over time. Is the meeting schedule still appropriate? Is the group still functioning in a crisis-management capacity? How much time are members putting in? Is duty relief still important? Should the focus of the inclusion committee still be students with disabilities? Is it time for the committee to evolve into a planning/problem-solving group available to teachers for all issues? If so, how will this committee differ from the child study committee? In Montgomery County, Virginia, special education has, over time, become a very minor issue in the day-to-day operation of most classrooms. Special and general education teachers functioning as collaborative teams are concerned with the needs of all of the students in their classrooms. Singling out the students who have IEPs as a special topic for discussion eventually becomes irrelevant. The need for special events like the inclusion get-togethers described earlier is greatly reduced after the first year or two of implementation, although the need to base staff development activities on concerns articulated by the staff is ongoing.

Another procedural target for review and evaluation should be any special positions created during the implementation stage, especially those designed to serve specific student populations. In Montgomery County, the inclusion specialist position was created originally to serve the relatively small population of students with severe disabilities. As implementation has continued, it has not made sense to continue putting resources into spreading itinerant teachers throughout the division to plan for these students. There are students with severe disabilities in nearly every school. Montgomery County is working now to establish the expertise needed to plan for these students within every school. The inclusion specialists have provided intensive staff development for special education teachers on best practices in instruction of students with severe disabilities. Each inclusion specialist works extensively in only one or two schools and serves students with a range of disabilities. During this transition period, time is allotted for teachers who are new to this type of instruction to consult regularly with the inclusion specialist. Teachers working with students with severe disabilities have an opportunity to meet regularly to share ideas and problem solve around specific issues or students. The identity of an established inclusion specialist is beginning to fade as staff in every building gain expertise in teaching these students.

When Montgomery County schools first began to move into inclusive programming, they made a commitment to expand the options available for students rather than dismantling existing programs. The staff believed that existing programs that were no longer needed would "die a natural death" as inclusive options became widely available. This same philosophy can apply to structures created to establish inclusion in the building, as long as the educational program in the building is continuing to grow and improve. If one's vision is to merge special and general education programs in order to improve the quality of education for all students, then one must not "get stuck" along the way. Policies and procedures should be vehicles for achieving the vision. They must be evaluated regularly and changed as needed.

Which Skills Do We Need To Continue To Teach?

Evaluation results should be used to help plan future staff development sessions for current and new staff members for the upcoming school year. Areas of continued need or concern that are identified through the evaluation procedures should be included as training sessions or workshops in the upcoming inservice plan. Identified needs will drive inservice planning for existing staff and will indicate areas in which new staff may need additional assistance or training. Areas that are noted as currently effective should be required for new staff only. Evaluation data should also help identify the degree to which staff development provided during the planning and implementation process has been effective. Finally, evaluation offers information about areas that were missed in the inservice training provided to existing staff. The individuals who provide inclusive educational services on a daily basis are the best source of information when determining what skills are needed to begin this effort or to continue moving forward in the effort; therefore, the information these individuals provide through their evaluation is critical to inservice planning.

Evaluation results in Montgomery County schools made it clear that the two areas overlooked in the initial training for inclusion were team building and handling change. The initial training sessions had focused heavily on answering the questions "What?" "Why?" and "How?" Change and team building should be addressed through inservice training prior to specific workshops on inclusion.

Are Our Outcomes Still Relevant?

Within the evaluation process, it is important to evaluate the evaluation. Individuals and groups must continually look at the outcomes and compare them to the actual vision and plan that were developed at the inception of the change process toward inclusive education. It may be necessary to replace original outcomes that have been attained. Often, inclusive efforts begin with a focus on physical placement of students with disabilities within general education classrooms. Once this goal is realized, it is necessary to move to inclusive services within the entire school community that go beyond setting and that embrace coteaching and collaboration for staff and equal opportunity for students. It may also be necessary to redefine original outcomes as they become outdated or are no longer relative to the plan and goals.

Once formal and informal evaluation data are interpreted, members of the inclusion committee or key representatives of the vision should determine if the evaluation format continues to address the needs of the school or district. The evaluation should be modified to incorporate all of the criticisms or shortcomings that have been voiced within the evaluation process itself or as a result of comments from the public. The criticisms of skeptics should be heard and considered in the redefinition of the evaluation process.

CONCLUSION

Inclusion has become an increasingly accepted practice in Montgomery County, Virginia, schools. The school district continues to listen to the concerns of the stakeholders. The schools have begun to view the term "inclusion" to mean more than just the inclusion of students with special education needs. The schools now listen to the local community speak of the idea of inclusion as the acceptance of diversity and uniqueness brought to school by each student. The school district believes that all students—regardless of academic ability, ethnic background, or any other characteristic—should be embraced by the school system and included as a valuable part of society.

In many ways, Montgomery County schools have moved from questioning the value of inclusion to regarding it as an accepted community practice. They no longer spend time explaining to stakeholders *why* students should be included. Educators now talk about *how* they should include students. Although they continue to deal with questions and concerns about inclusion, they are beginning to see it as an accepted practice in the school community. The school system still listens to teachers who have fears and are unsure of how to respond to a particular student. It continues to encourage these teachers to observe inclusive classrooms, and it provides staff-development opportunities as needed. Most often, the schools no longer ask teachers to volunteer to have students with disabilities included in their classrooms. Teachers and community members have grown to accept students with disabilities as simply students with unique needs, just as all children have unique needs.

REFERENCES

Snell, M., & Raynes, M. (1995). Changing roles in inclusive schools: Staff perspectives at Gilbert Linkous Elementary. *Kappa Delta Pi Record, 31,* 104–109.

Van Dyke, R., Stallings, M.A., & Colley, K. (1995). How to build an inclusive school community: A success story. *Phi Delta Kappan, 76,* 475–479.

CHAPTER 4

Legal Concerns

Kathe Klare

INTRODUCTION

This chapter introduces the educator and other professionals to the laws that affect the education of children with disabilities.[1] More specifically, it focuses on the concepts of least restrictive environment, mainstreaming, and inclusion as defined by the legal system. The discussion is limited to least restrictive environment, mainstreaming, and inclusion as they are interpreted by the federal statutes, appellate case law, and the U.S. Department of Education.

THE SOURCES OF LAW

The Individuals with Disabilities Education Act (IDEA) was signed into law in 1975.[2] Formerly called the Education for All Handicapped Children's Act (EAHCA), the act was commonly referred to as the EHA, or Public Law 94-142. IDEA is a federal statute or law that was developed and passed by Congress. IDEA also has implementing regulations developed by the U.S. Department of Education that are more specific than the broader language contained in the statute. One example is the term *least restrictive environment*. The law contains language that identifies the state's responsibility for placing a student in the least restrictive environment if the state wants to receive funds under IDEA. The statutory language requires the state to have procedures in effect that

> ensure that to the maximum extent appropriate, children with disabilities, including children in public or private institutions or other care facilities, are educated with children who are not disabled, and that special classes, separate schooling, or other removal of children with disabilities from the regular educational environment occurs only

when the nature or severity of the disability is such that education in regular classes with the use of supplementary aids and services cannot be achieved satisfactorily.[3]

Although this language is repeated in the regulations, the regulations also contain more specific language to assist the states in implementing least restrictive environment. This language establishes the legal criteria for interpreting the least restrictive environment requirement. For example, one criterion contained in the regulations relating to the selection of the least restrictive environment is whether consideration should be given to any potential harmful effect a specific placement may have on the child, or on the quality of services that he or she needs.[4]

In addition to the federal statute and supporting regulations, state legislative bodies also pass laws related to special education. These state statutes may have state implementing regulations as well. Generally, state agencies are also given the authority to develop the state regulations. A state education department often serves this function. While state statutes and regulations are often identical to the federal statutes and regulations, this is not always true. For example, federal statutes and regulations are silent on some points, such as the procedures used for invoking discipline for students with disabilities, and Congress has permitted states to develop independent standards in a particular area, if they so choose. A state may provide for additional rights not provided under the federal law. The state laws, however, cannot deny the protections, rights, or services guaranteed under the federal law. For example, a state may pass a law that requires maximization of potential. That is, the state requires delivery of the best education for individuals with disabilities that differs from the federal requirement, which provides for delivery of an appropriate education.

This state-mandated right would be in addition to the rights afforded under the federal law and, thus, would impose different and higher standards than the federal law alone.

DISPUTE RESOLUTION SYSTEMS

Administrative and Court Hearings

Disputes regarding educational issues often arise between the parents and the agencies delivering the services. These differences may ultimately end up in court, the outcome depending on an interpretation of the statutes and regulations. This resolution of disputes can occur in several forums. An administrative hearing is usually the first step in the legal proceedings under IDEA.[5] Generally, cases brought under IDEA require exhaustion of these administrative remedies. The losing party may then appeal to either state or federal court.[6] The typical state court system requires the final decision of the administrative hearing officer or agency to be appealed to a trial court. Further appeal can be made to an intermediate appellate court, and finally to the state supreme court.[7] The losing party may also appeal a final administrative decision through the federal system. The case would first be brought in the federal district court, then to the federal court of appeals in a particular circuit. The final appeal would be to the U.S. Supreme Court. Figure 4–1 contrasts the typical state court system with the federal court system.

Generally, state supreme courts are regarded as establishing precedent for the state in which the court is located. Precedent is a legal principle requiring that the legal conclusion be followed the next time the court hears a similar case involving the same legal issue. Federal appellate courts cover a specific area called a circuit (see Exhibit 4–1 for the states included in each circuit court). The federal appellate court (called a Circuit Court of Appeals) also establishes precedents, and its decisions are binding on the lower courts in that circuit. Although the state and federal courts function independently of one another, the judges often consider decisions from other jurisdictions and courts, not as binding precedent, but as persuasive authority. Decisions rendered by the U.S. Supreme Court must be followed by all states. Because appeals can be taken to either state or federal court, and because both state and federal law apply, both state and federal law should always be checked.

Mediation

Administrative hearings and court proceedings are not the only means for resolving disputes. Mediation is also an available method.[8] Although not required by law, mediation is often used as an intervening step prior to conducting a formal due process hearing. Mediation is a nonadversarial procedure unlike due process hearings and court proceedings. The focus of mediation is on developing a mutually acceptable agreement to meet the unique needs of the child.

An impartial neutral mediator meets with the parties involved—generally the parents, educators, and related agencies—to assist in reaching mutually agreeable goals for a child. Each person has an opportunity to explain the issues from his or her viewpoint. The mediator works to clarify the issues, needs, and interests of everyone and facilitates the process as each person discusses ideas for resolution. The mediator does not determine who is right or wrong. Mediation does not affect the right either party has to

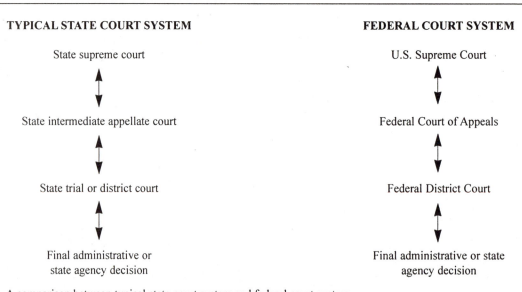

TYPICAL STATE COURT SYSTEM

State supreme court

↕

State intermediate appellate court

↕

State trial or district court

↕

Final administrative or
state agency decision

FEDERAL COURT SYSTEM

U.S. Supreme Court

↕

Federal Court of Appeals

↕

Federal District Court

↕

Final administrative or state
agency decision

Figure 4–1 A comparison between typical state court system and federal court system

Exhibit 4–1 Federal Circuit Courts

First Circuit	Puerto Rico, Maine, New Hampshire, Massachusetts, Rhode Island
Second Circuit	New York, Vermont, Connecticut
Third Circuit	Pennsylvania, New Jersey, Delaware, Virgin Islands
Fourth Circuit	West Virginia, Maryland, Virginia, North Carolina, South Carolina
Fifth Circuit	Texas, Louisiana, Mississippi
Sixth Circuit	Ohio, Kentucky, Tennessee, Michigan
Seventh Circuit	Wisconsin, Indiana, Illinois
Eighth Circuit	North Dakota, South Dakota, Nebraska, Arkansas, Missouri, Iowa, Minnesota
Ninth Circuit	Alaska, Washington, Oregon, California, Hawaii, Arizona, Nevada, Idaho, Montana, Northern Mariana Islands, Guam
Tenth Circuit	Wyoming, Utah, Colorado, Kansas, Oklahoma, New Mexico
Eleventh Circuit	Alabama, Georgia, Florida
District of Columbia Circuit	Hears cases from the U.S. District Court for the District of Columbia
Federal Circuit	Sitting in Washington, D.C., the U.S. Court of Appeals, Federal Circuit hears patent and trade appeals and certain appeals on claims brought against the federal government and its agencies.

request a due process hearing if the results are unsatisfactory. In fact, the hearing can be requested while mediation is ongoing, as this process can provide an effective environment for positive and effective communication. Negotiation is different from mediation in that it involves the parties themselves, without impartial third-party involvement. It can also foster positive results if a cooperative, problem-solving approach is used. This can be successful because it promotes collaboration in looking for means to identify, discuss, and provide possible solutions to the problems.

STATUTORY OVERVIEW

The two primary federal statutes relating to special education are IDEA and Section 504 of the Rehabilitation Act; they have significant interplay. (Relevant sections of both statutes can be found in Appendix B.) The Infants and Toddlers with Disabilities Act (ITDA), a subchapter of IDEA, relates to providing coordinated services to infants and toddlers with disabilities and their families. Another federal statute under which special education actions may be brought is the Americans with Disabilities Act (ADA).

Individuals with Disabilities Education Act (IDEA)

IDEA is a funding law that provides both a substantive right to a free and appropriate education (FAPE) for students with disabilities and procedural protections to ensure the provision of the substantive right (see Appendix B–1).

In order to receive federal special education funds, each state must submit a periodic state plan to the U.S. Secretary of Education ensuring that the state educational agency (SEA) assumes "responsibility for effecting a policy that assures a free and appropriate public education (FAPE) is being provided by local agencies to all children with disabilities."[9] Since all states presently receive this federal funding, all states are required to develop and implement a program to monitor each public school's provision of special education and related services.

The overriding states' responsibility under the IDEA is the requirement to provide a FAPE to students with disabilities. A *free and appropriate public education* is defined as providing special education and related services, in conformity with the requirements of IDEA. These requirements are that special education and related services (a) be provided at public expense, under public supervision and direction, and without charge; (b) meet the standards of the SEA, including the requirements of this part; (c) include preschool, elementary school, and secondary school education; and (d) be provided in conformity with an individualized education program (IEP).[10] The local educational agency (LEA), typically a school district, is required to develop this IEP and to revise or update it at least annually. The IEP must include the child's present educational functioning and describe specific long- and short-term educational goals and objectives.[11] In addition, the law requires that the education program developed through the IEP process provides for placement in the least restrictive environment.[12]

Children and families are also given certain procedural protections under IDEA.[13] They include identification of the child,[14] evaluation conducted by a multidisciplinary team,[15] determination for eligibility,[16] development of an IEP with parental participation,[17] placement based on the goals and objectives in the IEP,[18] multidisciplinary and nondiscriminatory testing,[19] reevaluation every three years,[20] and an opportunity for a multidisciplinary, independent educational evaluation.[21] As stated before, if a disagreement occurs between the parents and the school district, a due process hearing may be requested.[22] After this administrative hearing, the state may be asked to conduct a state-level review.[23] After completing this administrative process, the suit may be filed in either state or federal court.[24]

Infants and Toddlers with Disabilities Act

Enacted in 1986, ITDA is a subchapter of IDEA.[25] This legislation, often referred to as Part H, or Public Law 99-457, was enacted to satisfy a need to identify and provide coordinated services to infants and toddlers with disabilities as well as their families through a multidisciplinary and multiagency approach.[26] The eligible children served under Part H are those children age birth to two who need early intervention services because they have developmental delays or have been diagnosed with physical or mental conditions that have a high probability of resulting in developmental delay. The state may, at its discretion, include those children who would be at risk of substantial developmental delay were the early intervention services not provided.[27]

Like IDEA, ITDA is a funding statute.[28] The states must agree to certain conditions in order to receive funds. Early intervention services under ITDA are defined as developmental services provided under public supervision, at no cost to the families unless state or federal law requires payment, which meet the developmental needs of the infants or toddlers with disabilities.[29] The delays can occur in any of the following areas of development: physical, cognitive, communication, social, emotional, or adaptive.[30] Early intervention services must also meet state standards that require inclusion of services such as family training and counseling, occupational and physical therapy, case management, and transportation, to name a few.[31] These services, which must be provided by qualified personnel, are provided in "natural environments including the home, and community settings where children who do not have disabilities also participate."[32] Each child and family served must have an individualized family service plan (IFSP), a written plan that includes case management services. The services provided to the children are evaluated annually, but the family must be provided a review of the plan every six months.[33] The IFSP has eight components. One component is "a statement of the early intervention services necessary to meet the unique needs of the child and family."[34] The frequency, intensity, method of delivery, and location of the delivery of the services and method of payment if required must be included."[35] This delivery of services obviously incorporates the inclusion model. Specifically, the statute requires that the services must be provided in environments where children without disabilities normally participate.[36] Parents are also entitled to procedural protections under ITDA.[37]

Section 504 of the Rehabilitation Act

Section 504 of the Rehabilitation Act of 1973, revised as of July 1, 1995, is an antidiscrimination law that also affects mainstreaming and inclusion (see Appendix B). Section 504 was enacted to prohibit discrimination on the basis of disability in programs or activities receiving federal financial assistance.[38] Specifically, Section 504 requires education of an individual with a disability with individuals without a disability to the maximum extent appropriate to the needs of the individual with a disability. This requirement applies to both academic and nonacademic extracurricular activities and services.[39] The statute also specifically provides that in order to protect the procedural rights of the parents and children, the schools can use the same system developed for use under IDEA. For example, there must be an opportunity to challenge decisions with which the parents do not agree. It can be the identical impartial due process system developed under IDEA, which includes an impartial hearing that allows participation by the parents with the right to be represented by counsel and a review procedure.[40] The system must also have procedures for identifying, evaluating, and placing students with disabilities, and protecting student and parental rights regarding notice and inspection of records. Unlike IDEA, however, the state and public schools do not receive funds for compliance under Section 504. The public schools are obligated to comply with the statute and its implementing regulations.[41] Like IDEA, the regulations also require that the child be placed in the least restrictive environment to the maximum extent appropriate. This includes placement in the regular education environment with the use of supplementary aids and services.[42] Another similarity between IDEA and Section 504 is the concern for children who may disrupt the educational environment. Both laws indicate that a regular education placement may not be appropriate to the needs of the child with a disability if the disruptive behavior significantly impairs the rights of the children without disabilities.[43]

Americans with Disabilities Act

In 1990, the Americans with Disabilities Act (ADA) was enacted, providing a national mandate to eliminate and address discrimination in more than just education. These areas include employment, transportation, public accommodations, and telecommunications. Generally, however, a school district's obligations under ADA and Section 504 are the same. For example, Section 504 regulations require a district to provide a FAPE to students with disabilities and due process to their parents. ADA regulations do not specifically address FAPE and due process, but these provisions are incorporated in Title II of the act by reference to Section 504. Thus, a district must provide FAPE and due process in order to comply with ADA. ADA is similar to Section 504, and the courts look to case law under Section 504 for interpreting ADA.

The significant difference between Section 504 and Title II of the ADA is the type of programs covered. Section 504 was enacted to prohibit discrimination on the basis of disability in programs or activities receiving federal financial assistance.[44] Title II simply extends certain rights, procedures, and remedies enunciated in Section 504 to all programs and services provided by state and local governments. Thus, Title II prohibits discrimination of qualified individuals with disabilities from being excluded from participating in or being denied the benefits of the services, programs, or activities of public entities.[45] Within ADA, Title II then potentially affects special education service delivery.

An ADA claim may also be brought under Title III, which applies to public accommodations. For example, in *Orr, Huffstutler v. Kindercare Learning Centers, Inc.*,[46] although not decided on the merits, the court discussed the issue of whether Kindercare, a day care program, violated the general and specific prohibitions against discrimination when it refused to let Jeremy attend Kindercare based on the severity of his disability.[47] This requirement is similar to Section 504, which prohibits discrimination on the basis of a person's disability or the denial to an individual of the benefits of services, facilities, or accommodations of an entity.[48] Under ADA, discrimination includes

> failure to make reasonable accommodations in policies, practices, or procedures when such modifications are necessary to afford such . . . services . . . to individuals with disabilities, unless the entity can demonstrate that making the modifications would fundamentally alter the nature of such . . . services.[49]

In this case, the parents believed that Kindercare's refusal to allow an aide to attend with Jeremy violated his rights regarding reasonable accommodations.

The Carl D. Perkins Vocational Applied Technology Education Act

The Carl D. Perkins Vocational Applied Technology Education Act falls under the regulations of the Vocational and Applied Technology Education Programs, the purpose of which is to develop the academic and occupational skills of all segments of the population by concentrating resources on improving educational programs leading to academic and occupational skill competencies needed to work in a technologically advanced society.[50] This includes funding for programs for individuals with disabilities. Vocational education is specifically contained in the definition of special education as meaning organized educational programs that relate directly to the preparation of individuals for paid or unpaid employment or for additional preparation for a career requiring other than a baccalaureate or advanced degree.[51] IDEA provides for the coordination of educational programs with vocational programs. The Carl Perkins Act permits agreements with the Secretary of Education to develop projects and improve the delivery of services in integrated settings.[52] Inclusive vocational education will assist in preparing students for productive lives and full membership in their communities. (See Chapter 13 for further discussion of vocational education.)

LEAST RESTRICTIVE ENVIRONMENT, MAINSTREAMING, INCLUSION—LEGAL DEFINITIONS[53]

As the above discussion suggests, IDEA and Section 504 provide the primary bases for measuring educational requirements. Neither law, however, uses the term *inclusion* or *mainstreaming* in addressing placement options. Under IDEA and Section 504, both the statute and the implementing regulations define the placement where a child is to receive educational services as the "least restrictive environment." The least restrictive environment obligation requires that each public agency ensure that (1) to the maximum extent appropriate, children with disabilities, including children in public or private institutions or other care facilities, are educated with children without disabilities; and (2) special classes, separate schooling, or other removal of children with disabilities from the regular educational environment occurs only when the nature or severity of the disability is such that education in regular classes with supplementary aides and services cannot be achieved satisfactorily.[54]

There is some confusion over what the requirement "to the maximum extent appropriate" means.[55] Quite often, among both courts and commentators, this requirement is referred to as either a least restrictive environment requirement, a mainstreaming requirement, an integration requirement, or an inclusion requirement. IDEA's requirement is a least restrictive environment requirement. The child is to be educated in an environment that, given the child's individual educational needs, provides the fewest restrictions not encountered by the child without a disability. One aspect of this least restrictive environment requirement is a presumption that this placement be with children without disabilities in regular classrooms. The requirement is for the least restrictive environment in which educational progress can be made.[56]

Mainstreaming (inclusion) is a presumptive requirement under IDEA, and the agency has the burden of establishing that any mainstreamed (inclusive) placement will not provide a FAPE.[57] In selecting the least restrictive environment, consideration must be given to any potential harmful effect on the child or on the quality of services he or she needs. It is clear, therefore, that placement in the least restrictive environment is not an absolute right. Merely because the placement is private, or even residential, does not mean it fails to meet the least restrictive environment requirements of IDEA. The least restrictive environment requirement must be viewed in light of the individual needs of the child. The individual nature of these decisions cannot be overemphasized. Indeed, children with very similar situations often receive very different determinations.[58]

IDEA, Placement, and Least Restrictive Environment

As mentioned previously, the obligation to provide a FAPE requires the provision of special education and related services. Special education is defined as specially designed instruction, at no cost to the parents or guardians, provided to meet the unique needs of a child with a disability. This definition includes classroom instruction; instruction in physical education; home instruction; and instruction in hospitals, institutions, and other settings. Special education can also include vocational educational and related services if the related services are considered special education under the state definition. An example of a related service that would be classified as special education would be speech and language services.[59]

In general, all placement decisions must be based on a variety of information made by a group of persons who are knowledgeable about the child.[60] The information for making the placement decisions should include aptitude and achievement tests, teacher recommendations, physical conditions, social or cultural background, and adaptive behavior.[61]

Public agencies must have available alternative placements along a continuum where children with disabilities can be placed. The continuum has to include the placements listed under the definition of special education (see above). The placement decision must then be based on the IEP, which must comply with the least restrictive environment requirements.[62] In addition, the continuum of placements requirement includes the important provision that supplementary services should be provided in conjunction with the regular education placement.[63] Included in this obligation to provide a FAPE is the requirement to provide the special education in the "least restrictive environment."

The main factors to consider in making a placement in the least restrictive environment include making the decision annually based on the child's IEP, and making the placement as close to the child's home as possible in the school the child normally would attend. If the placement is to occur in a school other than the school the child normally would attend, the placement must be included on the IEP. Another factor to consider for placement in the least restrictive environment is whether it is potentially harmful to the child or to the quality of services that he or she will need.[64]

Preschool-age children covered under the ITDA are also entitled to the same considerations for placement in the least restrictive environment as older children who are covered under Part B of IDEA. The programs can be provided in the public elementary school or in other agencies such as Head Start. In addition, services can be provided in private early childhood education or elementary school programs where children with and without disabilities are educated together.[65] (See Chapter 9 for further discussion.)

In addition to academic services, the law also requires that nonacademic services be provided in the least restrictive environment. Nonacademic and extracurricular services and activities may include recess, meals, athletics, recreational activities, special interest groups, and clubs, to name a few. Thus, these services must be provided with peers without disabilities to the maximum extent appropriate to the needs of the child with a disability.[66] The least restrictive environment requirement does not apply only to children being educated in public schools. If a child is placed in a public or private institutional setting for reasons other than receiving educational benefit and is able to receive educational benefit in a public school setting, the child may not be denied this type of education because he or she has a disability.[67]

The law addresses obligations for teachers and administrators to ensure that the least restrictive environment component is implemented. Therefore, teachers and others working in special education should be well informed about the least restrictive environment requirements. The SEA, for example, has a responsibility to inform teachers and administrators to provide technical assistance and training necessary to carry out placement in the least restrictive environment.[68] The SEA has ultimate authority for monitoring the correct and full implementation of the least restrictive environment requirement.[69]

Section 504 and Least Restrictive Environment

Section 504 language is similar to the language under IDEA regarding the term *least restrictive environment*. For example, Section 504 requires that an individual with a disability be educated with nondisabled persons to the maximum extent appropriate to that individual's needs.[70] Section

504 regulations require that the person with a disability be placed in the regular education environment unless the education in the regular environment cannot be achieved satisfactorily with the use of supplementary aids and services.[71] Similar to IDEA, which requires that placements occur as close to home as possible, Section 504 requires that when an individual with a disability is placed in an alternative setting, the proximity to his or her home must also be considered in the final placement decision.[72]

JUDICIAL INTERPRETATION OF LEAST RESTRICTIVE ENVIRONMENT

Although least restrictive environment requirements have existed since the implementation of both IDEA and Section 504, questions continue to arise about their meaning and, more specifically, in reference to the least restrictive environment requirement and inclusion. A line of cases, often referred to in discussions of least restrictive environment, provide the legal parameters for determining the degree and appropriateness of mainstreaming or inclusion. (Appendix B–4 provides further information on these cases.) As a result of the decisions, different circuits have developed different standards for determining the least restrictive environment requirement.

Rowley Standard

In order to understand whether school systems are meeting their statutory obligation under IDEA to place children in the least restrictive environment, it is necessary to look to the U.S. Supreme Court's first case that interpreted IDEA. In *Hendrick Hudson District Board of Education v. Rowley,*[73] the U.S. Supreme Court addressed for the first time in 1981 the meaning of a FAPE. The Court held that a FAPE "consists of educational instruction specifically designed to meet the unique needs of the handicapped child, supported by such services as are necessary to permit the child to 'benefit' from that instruction."[74] Thus, FAPE consists of individualized and unique instruction that qualifies and limits Congress's preference for educating children in regular education classes.

The Court also enunciated a two-prong test for determining whether a FAPE was being provided.[75] In the first prong, the Court asked whether the state complied with the procedures set forth in the act (IDEA). Second, the Court asked if the IEP developed through the act's procedures was reasonably calculated to enable the child to receive educational benefits.[76] Thus, a FAPE was viewed as both a procedural and substantive right. The failure to provide either right results in a violation of IDEA.

In addition, the *Rowley* decision noted that states are not required to offer the same educational experience to all children; instead, states must address the unique needs of the child, recognizing that the child who receives special education may benefit differently from being served in the regular education class than the other students who do not receive special education. The fact that the child will learn differently, however, does not justify exclusion.[77] Thus, the tension that exists between mainstreaming and tailoring a program to the individual needs is qualified and limited by the Court's interpretation of a FAPE.

Least Restrictive Environment Standards

A number of federal circuit courts have consistently noted that the two-prong test of Rowley is inadequate to determine compliance with the least restrictive environment requirement of the law. The courts, therefore, have employed their own tests as to whether this standard is being met. Although these courts, along with the *Rowley* Court, recognized the congressional preference for mainstreaming, they acknowledged that the least restrictive environment requirement does not provide an absolute right to an education in a mainstream environment.

Best versus Appropriate Standard

The issue of least restrictive environment was addressed as integration in *Mark A. v. Grant Wood,* an Eighth Circuit case where the child had been educated in an integrated, private preschool program because the state at the time did not provide integrated, public preschool programs. When it came time for placement in the public school, the district recommended placing the student in a public preschool developmental program. The issue confronting the court was whether the decision to place the student in a public program for children with disabilities only, rather than in a private placement where the children were integrated, was a violation of the least restrictive environment requirement. The court noted that educating children with disabilities in a school with only other children with disabilities did not necessarily violate the least restrictive environment requirement. The court went on to state that no requirement exists to provide for the "best" educational environment but rather only to provide an appropriate one.[78] Thus, the tension between FAPE and least restrictive environment was decided on the appropriateness versus the best standard.

Superior Services in Segregated Setting versus Services in Nonsegregated Setting Standard

The Sixth Circuit Court of Appeals in *Roncker v. Walter*[79] developed criteria to determine the appropriate level of mainstreaming. In *Roncker,* the parents of a nine-year-old boy with severe mental retardation wanted him placed in a nonsegregated setting where he could interact with his peers without disabilities.[80]

This case established the standard that must be applied when issues of mainstreaming are decided in the Sixth Circuit. The standard applied was that, where a decision has been made to place a child in a segregated facility that is considered superior, the court needs to make a determination as to whether the services that make that placement superior could feasibly be provided in a nonsegregated setting. If those services could feasibly be provided in the nonsegregated setting, then the placement in the segregated school would be inappropriate under IDEA.[81] Under the *Roncker* test, if the child must be placed in the segregated setting, no further analysis is required. There is no further determination by the court to see if the child is included with peers without disabilities to the maximum extent appropriate while in the alternative setting.

Supplemental Aids and Services Standard and Mainstreamed to Maximum Extent Appropriate Standard

Another standard for determining mainstreaming developed subsequent to the *Roncker* decision is the two-part test established in *Daniel R.R. v. State Board of Education*,[82] a Fifth Circuit case. This court declined to follow the test developed in *Roncker*, because it believed that the decision of whether services could be offered in the regular education environment belonged to the school administration. This court also believed that the *Roncker* court did not analyze the mainstreaming requirement in reference to the statutory language of IDEA.[83] Thus, the Fifth Circuit disagreed with the *Roncker* view that as a prerequisite to the mainstreaming requirement, the court would require the child with a disability to learn at the same level as his or her classmates without disabilities.

In addition, the Fifth Circuit observed that the *Roncker* court placed too much emphasis on the ability of the child with a disability to achieve educational benefits, and this analysis does not account for educational differences. The Fifth Circuit rejected this premise because the lower court failed to take into account the principles in *Rowley*. The U.S. Supreme Court in *Rowley* explained:

> States must tolerate educational differences; they need not perform the impossible; erase those differences by taking steps to equalize educational opportunities. As a result, the Act accepts the notion that handicapped students will participate in regular education but that some of them will not benefit as much as nonhandicapped students will. The Act requires states to tolerate a wide range of educational abilities in their schools and, specifi-

cally, in regular education—the EHA's preferred educational environment. Given the tolerance embodied in the EHA, we cannot predicate access to regular education on a child's ability to perform on par with nonhandicapped children. We recognize that some handicapped children may not be able to master as much of the regular education curriculum as their nonhandicapped classmates. This does not mean, however, that those handicapped children are not receiving any benefit from regular education. Nor does it mean that they are not receiving all of the benefit that their handicapping conditions will permit. If the child's individualized needs make mainstreaming appropriate, we cannot deny the child access to regular education simply because his educational achievement lags behind that of his classmates."[84]

It is evident that the child with a disability can also benefit from the mainstreaming experience from a nonacademic perspective.

In determining the appropriate level of mainstreaming, the court in *Daniel R.R.* adopted a two-part test that requires the courts to ask: (1) whether education in the regular classes with the use of supplemental aids and services can be achieved satisfactorily for a given child; and (2) if it cannot, and the school intends to provide special education or remove the child from regular education, whether the school has mainstreamed the child to the maximum extent appropriate. The court then provided a list of factors that it deemed relevant to the mainstreaming issue.

1. The court determined whether steps were taken to accommodate the child in the regular education class and, if so, whether those steps were sufficient. The accommodations did not need to include every conceivable accommodation, nor did they need to include devoting all or most of the teacher's time to one child. The modifications to the curriculum did not include modifying the curriculum beyond recognition.
2. The court asked whether the child received educational benefit from the regular education class. The focus of this inquiry is on the ability of the child with a disability to grasp the essential elements of the regular education program. Next, the court examined the overall educational experience in the mainstreamed environment, balancing the benefits of regular and special education to each individual child. This analysis included not only measuring the amount the child is able to absorb of the regular education curriculum, but also analyzing the benefits the child absorbs as a result of imitating appropriate language or behaviors.[85]

3. The court asked about the effect of the presence of the child with a disability on the regular education environment and education of other students.

The second part of the *Daniel R.R.* test is where the regular education environment is found to be an inappropriate placement. The question that follows then must be whether the child has been mainstreamed to the maximum extent appropriate to meet his or her needs. After applying the facts of this case to this analysis, the court found that Daniel should be educated in the placement recommended by the school district. Thus, for him, mainstreaming did not include inclusion in the regular education environment for any academic subjects.[86]

Supplemental Aids and Services Standard

The Third Circuit Court of Appeals in *Oberti v. Board of Education of the Borough of Clementon School District* [87] articulated another test for determining whether the mainstreaming requirement is met. This court held that the school district improperly reached its placement decision before considering the complete range of supplemental aids and services that might have facilitated the child's placement. The court also noted that a special education placement cannot be justified on the basis that a child might make greater academic progress outside of the regular education environment. In addition, the court noted in its holding that several factors must be considered to decide whether the child can be educated satisfactorily with the use of supplementary aids and services.

The factors considered under this test include: (1) whether the district has made reasonable efforts to accommodate the child in the regular classroom; (2) the educational benefits available to the child in the regular classroom with the use of appropriate supplementary aids and services; and (3) the possible negative effects of the child's inclusion on the other students in the class.

The Oberti appeal arose from the federal district court's finding that the school had not proved that Rafael, an eight-year-old child with Down syndrome, should be educated in a segregated setting. The *Oberti* decision was one of the first cases where the word *inclusion* was used. The court recognized that in recent years the use of the word *mainstreaming* had not been favored by some educators, because the term suggests shuttling children with disabilities in and out of a regular class without altering the class to accommodate the child. These authorities, according to the Obertis, prefer the term *inclusion* because of its greater emphasis on the use of supplementary aids and services.[88]

The court specifically ordered the school to "develop a more inclusive program"[89] for Rafael in compliance with IDEA. The district court noted that supported inclusive education (or inclusion) is when a child with a disability is placed as a full member of a regular class with the provision of supplementary aids and services. The middle of the continuum contains mixed placements, in which a child might be a member of a regular class but obtain supplementary services in a separate "resource room," or where the child might be a member of a self-contained special education class, but spend a portion of his or her time "mainstreamed" in regular classes along with nondisabled students in other activities such as recreation or lunch.[90]

Daniel R.R. Test

In 1991, the Eleventh Circuit in *Greer v. Rome City School District* [91] addressed the issue of mainstreaming. The issue in this case was whether Christy Greer's IEP violated the least restrictive environment requirement of IDEA. The school recommended that Christy be placed in a self-contained class at a school other than the neighborhood school. The parents wanted placement in regular education at the neighborhood school. Christy, a 10-year-old child with Down syndrome, who had speech and learning disabilities, was placed in a regular kindergarten class while the case was undergoing administrative proceedings. The court applied the *Daniel R.R.* test in making its fact-specific inquiry. The court noted several factors that the school district might need to consider in determining whether the education in the regular environment may be achieved satisfactorily. The first factor the court reviewed is comparing the educational benefits of being educated in a regular class, with the aids and services, against the benefits of the self-contained class.[92] This balancing requires more than academic achievement, and must consider other achievements such as language development and role modeling.[93] Second, the school district must consider the effect the presence of the child with a disability has on the other children. The court noted that the child who merely requires more teacher attention than most other children is not likely to be so disruptive as to significantly impair the education of other children.[94] Third, the school may consider cost of the supplemental aids and services. If the cost is incrementally more expensive, the school may not decline to provide the services; but, if the services require a full-time aide or teacher, these services must be balanced against the impact they have on the other children in the district.[95]

In reviewing the facts of this particular case, the court decided that it needed only to inquire about the first part of the test, because the evidence indicated that the school district did not make efforts to provide supplemental aids and services. Rather, because of Christy's "severe impairment" the school justified her placement in a self-contained class.[96] The school district also did not attempt to modify the curriculum, but only spent extra time with Christy. Finally, although the school requested that the parents comment on their proposed placement, the school did not inform the parents of the range of supplemental aids and services available.[97] The court also noted that the decision regarding mainstreaming must be made during the development of the IEP and not afterward. Thus, the court did not have to reach the second prong of this test.

The court's holding was that the school district failed to comply with the first part of the two-part test applicable to mainstreaming by not taking steps to accommodate Christy in the regular class and determining whether her education could be achieved satisfactorily with the aids or services. This, the court noted, was not an invasion of the school's administrative obligations in selecting education methodologies, because this deference is due only to the school "once a court determines that the requirement of the Act has been met."[98] Thus, since alternative methods of education for Christy were not tried, the school had not complied with the act.[99]

Daniel R.R. and *Roncker* Standard

In *Sacramento City Unified School District, Board of Education v. Holland,*[100] the Ninth Circuit developed, approved, and adopted the district's court test in its review, which considered factors from both *Daniel R.R.* and *Roncker.* In this case, the court held that the appropriate placement for Rachel, an 11-year-old girl with moderate mental retardation, was a full-time, regular second-grade class with some supplemental services. The district court examined the following four factors: the benefits of placing the child in a full-time, regular education program; the nonacademic benefits of such a placement; the effect that the child had on the teacher and other students in the regular class; and the costs associated with the placement. The school district contended that the appropriate placement for Rachel was spending half her time in a special education class and half her time in a regular education class for her nonacademic subjects. This placement would have required Rachel to make six moves per day between classes.[101] The court specifically found that the educational benefits of regular education weighed heavily in Rachel's favor. The court noted that the school district's evidence focused on Rachel's limitations, but the school did not establish that the educational opportunities available through special education were better than or equal to those available in a regular classroom.[102]

Because Rachel had been placed by her parents in a private, regular class, the court gave greater weight to the testimony of the parents' experts, since "they had more background in evaluating children with disabilities placed in regular classrooms and . . . they had a greater opportunity to observe Rachel over an extended period of time in normal circumstances."[103] Thus, the district court found that all of her IEP goals could be implemented in a regular class with some modification to the curriculum and with the assistance of a part-time aide.[104] As to the nonacademic benefits, the district court found that the benefit to Rachel weighed in favor of placing her in a regular class. Rachel developed social and communication skills and increased her self-confidence. Again, the evidence from the school and the parents was contradictory. The court chose to give greater weight to the parents' testimony.[105]

The district court addressed the issue of Rachel's effect on the teacher and the other children in the class from two aspects. The first issue was whether Rachel was too disruptive, distracting, or unruly, resulting in a detrimental impact on the class. Second, the court looked at whether Rachel took up too much time or deprived the other students of the teacher's attention.[106] The evidence indicated that Rachel followed directions, was well behaved, and was not a distraction in class. She would need only a part-time aide in a regular classroom.[107]

The last factor the court reviewed was the cost to the school division. The school district contended that it would cost $109,000 to educate Rachel. This included the cost of hiring a full-time aide, plus the cost of providing schoolwide sensitivity training at the cost of approximately $80,000. The court found the school district unpersuasive on this issue, since the state could have provided the sensitivity training for free and Rachel did not require a full-time aide. Moreover, because the cost for the training would benefit other children with disabilities, the cost should not have been assigned totally to Rachel.[108] The court found that the comparison of costs should have been between placement in a special education class with a full-time special education teacher and two full-time aides with 11 other children, versus placement in a regular education class with a part-time aide.[109]

The district court also was not persuaded by the school's argument that it would lose significant funding if Rachel did not spend 51% of her time in a special education class, since the school district could have applied for a waiver from the state department of education.[110] Thus, cost did not weigh against mainstreaming Rachel. During the presentation of evidence in the district court, disagreement arose as to the meaning of the terms *mainstreaming* and *full inclusion.* The court accepted the following definition of *full inclusion*:

> [The child with disabilities] is a full member of a regular education class . . . the child need not be in the classroom 100% of the time . . . the child may be removed from that class to receive supplementary services such as physical or speech therapy when these services cannot be provided in the

classroom. Under full-inclusion, the child's primary placement is in the regular education class, and the child has no additional assignment to any special class for handicapped children.[111]

In affirming the district court, the appeals court also stated that they did not agree or reach a decision on the school's position that there was a requirement for the child to receive her academic and functional curriculum in the special education class from a teacher certified in Rachel's particular area of disability, as required by state law. The district court found that this proposition that Rachel must be taught by a special education teacher conflicted with the federal law and its preference that children with disabilities be educated in regular classes with children who are not disabled.[112]

Appropriateness and Cost Standards

The Eighth Circuit Court of Appeals, in *A.W. v. Northwest R-1 School District*,[113] first adopted the cost factor for consideration in mainstreaming cases. In this case, the parents wanted their son with Down syndrome placed in a public elementary school. The school district recommended a private institution designed for and attended only by children with disabilities. The least restrictive environment was found to be a segregated setting. In this finding, the court noted that the preference for mainstreaming was not absolute, because the regular classroom is not suitable for many children with disabilities.[114] The marginal benefits that would be received by mainstreaming the child were outweighed by the deprivation of the benefits to other disabled children.[115] This deprivation of benefits was financial because, if placed in a regular class, the student would require an additional special education teacher. Hiring an additional teacher would result in decreased funds available to other students. Thus, mainstreaming was not required.

The Neighborhood Test

Courts have considered additional factors in determining the least restrictive environment. One such factor is the location of the program. In *Barnett v. Fairfax County School Board*,[116] the court addressed the issue of placement and its relationship to FAPE by interpreting the regulations regarding least restrictive environment. In this case, a 16-year-old student with profound deafness was receiving special education services in the regular class with the assistance of a cued speech interpreter.

Although cued speech was appropriate, the student was not receiving his education in his home-based school, but in a school approximately five miles away. The regulations regarding placement state that the public agency shall ensure that the placement "is as close as possible to the child's

home." This is only one of the factors to be considered, and parents who disagree have a right to challenge the placement.[117] The court held that IDEA did not require the board to duplicate the highly specialized services at the student's base school.[118] The district was therefore able to provide services in a central location. Thus, IDEA did not create an absolute right to have a FAPE in the neighborhood school.

A more recent case, which also focused on least restrictive environment and the issue of placement at the neighborhood school, is *Tarah P. v. Board of Education of Fremont School District 79*.[119] The issue in this case was whether the school district had an obligation to place Tarah, a seven-year-old with physical and visual impairments, in her neighborhood school. The disagreement centered not on the concept of mainstreaming per se, but on the interpretation of least restrictive environment and placement in the neighborhood school.[120] The only difference in these two programs was the access to a full-time special education teacher. In either program, Tarah would be in the regular education class. The court noted the desire to place the child as close to home as possible and that the obligation to provide quality services would create inevitable tensions. Thus, the case turned on methodology. As the court noted in *Lachman*, "Rowley and its progeny leave no doubt that parents, no matter how well-motivated, do not have a right to compel a school district to provide a specific program or employ a specific methodology in providing for the education of their handicapped child."[121] Thus, mainstreaming is not equal to placement in the neighborhood school.

In *Murray v. Montross County School District*, the court held that there is no presumption that the neighborhood school is part of the child's least restrictive environment.[122] The Murrays, relying on the statute, regulations, and legislative history, argued that the meaning of "regular educational environment" implicitly included neighborhood schools, that "special classes" means nonregular classes, and that "separate schooling" means non-neighborhood schools. Their argument continued that Congress has declared that "the neighborhood is the appropriate basis for determining public school assignments"; thus, the reference to "removal" in IDEA must mean removal from the neighborhood school.[123] The parents then argued that "supplementary aids and services must be fully explored before a child can be removed from both the neighborhood school and the regular classroom with nondisabled children."[124]

The court noted that this interpretation strained the meaning of the statute. The court stated that the statute says nothing, expressly or by implication, about removal of children with disabilities from neighborhood schools. The statute, although requiring mainstreaming as much as possible, says nothing about where within a school district that inclusion shall take place.[125] The Murrays argued that two of the implementing regulations, in conjunction with the statute, create a presumption for placement in a neighborhood school. One of the regulations requires that the placement be as close to home as possible.[126] The other regulation requires the child to attend the school he or she would normally attend if not disabled, unless of course, the IEP indicates some other arrangement.[127]

This decision in the Third Circuit disagreed with the *Oberti* decision, in that *Oberti* notes that IDEA encompasses a presumption of placement in the neighborhood school, whereas the Third Circuit believes it is only a preference.[128] Thus, a school district is not obligated to explore aids and services fully before removing a child from a neighborhood school, although it is required to explore them before removing a child from a regular classroom.

Summary of Judicial Interpretation

The courts, generally, are interpreting IDEA as favoring inclusion. Courts, however, review each case on an individualized basis, viewing the specific facts that are presented. Therefore, no single standard may be appropriate, and the placement options along the continuum must continue to exist. The school district, however, should take the appropriate steps to educate a child with disabilities in the regular class. A number of factors should be considered on an individualized basis each time a student's placement is considered:

- Whether supplementary aids and services have been provided to accommodate the students in the regular class. These include visual aids, tape recorders, note-taking assistance, oral tests, and frequent breaks. The fact that accommodations must be considered does not mean that every conceivable accommodation should be tried but that the accommodation must be more than a token gesture.
- The amount of time that would be required for the teacher to assist the student. This does not include devoting most of a teacher's time to one student.
- The degree of modification of the curriculum and the student's ability to grasp the curriculum are to be considered. Yet the child is not expected to achieve at the same level as the child without disabilities. The curriculum does not have to be modified beyond recognition. The kind and amount of benefit the student will receive in the inclusive setting, considering the nature and severity of the disability and the goals of the curriculum, is also a factor to consider.
- Both the academic and nonacademic benefits to students with disabilities must be evaluated. The nonacademic benefits would include social interactions, behavioral models, and language models. If the inclusive placement would be detrimental to the child, then it may not be appropriate.

- Another factor to consider is the child's presence and negative effect on the other students.
- The last factor for consideration is the cost.

In developing IEPs, schools must consider the regular education class as the first option under the least restrictive environment requirement. Courts seem less willing to place children in segregated placements.

FEDERAL AGENCY INTERPRETATION OF LEAST RESTRICTIVE ENVIRONMENT

The courts are not the only bodies that interpret the statutes and the regulations. Offices designated within the U.S. Department of Education also have this authority. These offices interpret the law by issuing policy letters and by monitoring the states' compliance with each agency's respective laws. These policy letters are disseminated to chief state school officers and help provide guidance for proper implementation of the laws.

One of these offices is the Office of Special Education Programs (OSEP), located within the Office of Special Education and Rehabilitative Services (OSERS). OSEP is authorized through Section 1402 of IDEA to be the "principal agency in the Department for administering and carrying out [IDEA]."[129] The other office that interprets the law is the Office of Civil Rights (OCR), which has responsibility for monitoring state compliance with the provision of Section 504. In furtherance of this requirement, OCR publishes a number of documents useful to educators, lawyers, other professionals, and parents. OCR publishes both formal and informal policy interpretations, which are written in response to specific inquiries regarding OCR's interpretation of Section 504. Neither OSEP, OSERS, or OCR policy interpretations have the force of law. The policy interpretations are viewed as having persuasive authority, which means that courts will give deference to the agencies' interpretation of the regulations. Several of these policy memos address the issues of least restrictive environment, mainstreaming, and inclusion.

Least Restrictive Environment

In 1994, OSEP issued a policy memorandum that included a comprehensive set of questions and answers that summarizes the position of the U.S. Department of Education on several aspects of IDEA's least restrictive environment requirements. The first issue discussed is the least restrictive environment requirements of Part B and the assurances a state must make in order to receive federal funding for special education purposes. For states to be eligible, they must give certain assurances to OSEP. These assurances include availability of a FAPE and development of an IEP under proper procedures, including meaningful parental input. The IEP must also include all components necessary to meet the child's unique needs. This properly constructed IEP then serves as the basis for entitlement to an individualized and appropriate education.

In addition, states must also have procedures to ensure that children with disabilities are educated to the maximum extent appropriate with their peers without disabilities. Thus, removal from the regular education environment can occur only when the nature or severity of the disability prevents satisfactory achievement in the regular education class when supplementary aids and services are used.[130]

OCR also issues letters of findings on the issue of least restrictive environment. A 1993 letter addressed a complaint that alleged that the method of providing special education to disabled children was changed from a pull-out model (i.e., providing resource room services) to an inclusive model (i.e., providing services in a regular class). The district was found to be out of compliance because student placements were changed contrary to the regulations, which required an evaluation to be conducted prior to implementing a significant change in placement, and because the district failed to provide proper notice to the parents.[131] Thus, the move to an inclusive educational environment must be completed following proper procedures and must meet the unique needs of a child.

Definition of Inclusion

Returning to the 1994 OSEP policy memorandum, the second issue relates to the definition of the term *inclusion*. OSEP stated that neither IDEA nor the U.S. Department of Education defines inclusion. IDEA does require school districts to place children with disabilities in the least restrictive environment in the school the children would normally attend. This requirement can be altered if the IEP dictates a different placement.[132]

Supplemental Aids and Services

The third issue is implementation of IDEA's requirement that proper consideration is given to whether a student with a disability can be educated in the regular educational environment with the use of supplementary aids and services before the school district considers and places a student outside of the regular classroom setting. The IEP functions as the centerpiece of IDEA and defines the least restrictive environment for that individual. The IEP is developed through a joint process with the parents and the appropriate school personnel and consists of the development of the student's goals and objectives. Once these are properly developed, then—and only then—can the appropriate placement

be decided. Thus, the finalized IEP is the determining factor for the ultimate placement for each student.

Several components must be included in the IEP. One of these specific components includes a "statement of the specific special education and related services to be provided to the child and the extent that the child will be able to participate in regular educational programs."[133] The IEP meeting is where the supplementary aids and services that facilitate placement in the regular educational environment are considered. As mentioned previously, the courts have put some limitations on the range of services that would need to be implemented based on the cost of those services. Cost, however, is only one of the factors considered, as each case is decided on its own facts.

Supplementary aids and services must also be included in the IEP. OSEP stated that "if modifications and supplementary aids and services to the regular education program are necessary to ensure the child's participation in that program, those modifications must be described in the child's IEP (e.g., for a child with a hearing impairment, special seating arrangements or the provision of assignments in writing)."[134] This applies to any regular education program in which the student may participate, including physical education, art, music, and vocational education.[135]

The IEP team must be prepared to ask whether the student's IEP can be implemented satisfactorily in the regular educational environment with the provision of appropriate supplementary aids and services. Although IDEA does not define the term *supplementary aids and services*, decisions as to what services and aids may be used have included: modifications to the regular class curriculum, assistance of an itinerant teacher with special education training, special education for the regular education teacher, use of computer-assisted devices, provision of note takers, and use of a resource room.[136]

Review of Placements

The OSEP memo also discussed the requirements for the time periods when a placement should be reviewed. This review must occur at least annually. The student's placement, as mentioned previously, is based on the IEP, and the student should be placed in the school as close to his or her home as possible. The placement decision must be made by a group of persons who know the student and who know the meaning of the evaluation data of the student. It is extremely important, as well as required, that this group of persons also know about the various placement options. Although the placement can be changed prior to an annual review, it cannot be done without reconvening an IEP meeting. This can be requested by the school district or the parents. Any time an IEP is reviewed, the placement should also be reviewed.[137]

Teacher Training

Teacher training is another issue discussed in this OSEP memo. If the IEP placement of a student with a disability should be in a regular class, school administration cannot lawfully prevent this placement by their lack of adequate personnel or resources. The school would still have an obligation to place the child in the least restrictive environment. The language in Section 504 of the Rehabilitation Act specifically prohibits exclusion of a student with a disability from an appropriate placement if that exclusion is based solely on the student's disability. Under both IDEA and Section 504, however, placement in a regular class is permitted based on the qualifications of a specific teacher. The school also has an affirmative obligation to ensure that a sufficient number of qualified teachers are available to provide services. The U.S. Department of Education recommends that several factors be examined when considering available resources for the education of students with disabilities. These include cooperative learning, teaching styles, physical arrangements of the classroom, curriculum modifications, peer-mediated supports, and equipment.[138]

Placement

If the child cannot be educated satisfactorily in the regular educational environment, the placement must be based on the individual needs of the child. Basing placement on the individual needs of the child is also a component of placing a child in a regular class. Thus, a continuum of placement options must be offered by the schools. These include instruction in regular education, special classes, special schools, home instruction, and instruction in hospitals and institutions.[139] If the child's IEP requires education in other than the regular class, then the child must be educated in an environment that maximizes the opportunity for the student to interact with students without disabilities.

IDEA requires written notice to the parents of a child with a disability before an agency implements a proposal or refuses to initiate or change the identification, evaluation, or educational placement of the child or provision of a FAPE. This notice requirement must include the availability of the continuum of placements, as well as the placement options considered and the reasons the options were rejected.[140]

Appropriate factors to consider when determining the individualized placement for a child include: the educational benefits available to the student in a regular class when supplemented with appropriate aids and services (this must be compared to the educational benefits the student can receive from a special education classroom); the nonacademic benefits the student with a disability can receive from interacting with students without disabilities; and the degree of disruption that occurs in the education of the other students, which would result in the inability to meet the unique needs of the student with the disability. OSEP's position is that school districts may not make placement decisions solely on the basis of the category or severity of the disability, the model of the delivery system in the school division, the availability of the educational or related services, space, or convenience to the administration of the school district.[141]

IDEA does permit school districts in placement decisions to consider any potential harmful effects the placement may have on the student, as well as on the quality of the services the student receives. If the behavior of the student is too disruptive, even with the needed aids and services, or if the behavior significantly impairs the education of other students, then placement in the regular class may be inappropriate.

In making placement decisions, IDEA also permits consideration of the effect of the child's presence on the children without disabilities. Some federally funded research projects have made significant findings regarding the impact of students with disabilities on typical learners when educated in the same class. The studies found that the performance of students without disabilities on achievement tests was equal to or better than the performance of a group of children who were not integrated; that the students without disabilities developed more positive attitudes toward peers with disabilities; and that self-concept, social skills, and problem-solving skills improved for all students in inclusive settings.[142]

Another letter of inquiry to OSEP in 1994 concerned the issue of the implementation of inclusion by order of the Civil Rights Commission, which was often contrary to parents' desires for placement.[143] The letter also stated that schools where children have the opportunity to be mainstreamed, included, and not segregated are stymied by classroom teachers who are not trained or equipped to deal with the complexities of integrating "special needs" approaches appropriately. The letter went on to state that the "result of forcing this on our parents and schools could be frustration, resentment, and a seriously diminished level of educational service to those most desperately in need."[144] In response, OSEP reiterated its position regarding the necessity of having a continuum of placements, that the first placement option considered should be the regular education class in the neighborhood school, and that FAPE must be made on an individual basis.[145]

Preschool Services

In 1993, OSEP responded to an inquiry about the type of services provided to a preschool child with a disability and the responsibility for payment of these services. Public agencies do not generally operate programs for children without disabilities and thus may consider alternative methods for meeting the child's unique needs in the least restrictive environment. These methods include providing opportunities for participation with children without disabilities in other preschool programs operated by public agencies or by private school programs for preschool children without disabilities or by private preschool programs that integrate students with and without disabilities, or providing classes for preschool children with disabilities in regular elementary schools.[146]

When the public agency places a child in a private preschool program for the purpose of receiving a FAPE, the entire early childhood educational program, including tuition, is at no cost to the parents and may be the responsibility of the public agency. This same inquiry also addressed the issue of least restrictive environment and its relationship to "stand-alone services."[147] Although OSEP does not refer to stand-alone services, OSEP recognizes that a placement team may determine that a specific service required by a preschool child may not require interaction with other children. These services, such as physical therapy, may be provided in a variety of settings such as the child's home, the provider's office, or a day care center. If, however, the placement team determines that the least restrictive environment can be met only in a full-day or part-time preschool program so that the child with disabilities is integrated with children without disabilities, then the public agency is responsible for all costs associated with that placement, regardless of whether single or multiple services are provided.[148]

DISCIPLINE

Discipline of students should not be a concern in the inclusive environment because, if the student is disruptive, the placement may not be appropriate. Regarding the issue of discipline, however, as long as the child's educational placement does not change, the disciplinary measures available to the school are the same for students with disabilities as for other students.[149] In addition, there is often a close relationship between discipline and the educational needs of a particular student, and the IEP may state particular modes of discipline.[150] A significant limitation on the agency's ability to discipline the student exists if such discipline constitutes a change in placement. (See Chapter 15 for further discussion.)

The U.S. Supreme Court, in *Honig v. Doe*,[151] relying on the stay-put provision[152] of IDEA, held that suspension from school for longer than 10 days constitutes a change in placement and, absent agreement of the parties, this change in placement is subject to all the other protections associated with other placement changes. The Court found Section 1415(e)(3) of IDEA to be unequivocal: during pendency of proceedings initiated under IDEA, "the child *shall* remain in the current educational placement." Congress intended to strip schools of unilateral authority to exclude children with disabilities from school. No "dangerousness exception" is to

be added to IDEA. A school, however, may use normal procedures for dealing with children who endanger themselves and others. The Court listed the following alternative factors: study carrels, time outs, detention, restriction of privileges, and suspension up to 10 days. In exceptional cases, the school system's hands are not completely tied. In cases where the parents of a truly dangerous child adamantly refuse to permit any change in placement, the schools can use the 10-day respite to go to court to seek a preliminary injunction. If successful, the injunction prohibits the child from returning to school for a temporary period of time. The exclusion will last until there has been an administrative determination of the questions regarding the change in placement.[153]

Prior to implementing disciplinary measures, the school districts have certain obligations. OSEP has issued guidance to clarify the requirements for disciplining students with disabilities.[154] This OSEP memo addresses the common questions that arise concerning discipline issues. Some of these include the proper procedure for deciding whether a student may be expelled or suspended for more than 10 days from school, the continuing obligation of the school once a student is suspended or expelled, and the proper procedure for removal of a student from school when the child has brought a firearm to school. The proper procedure required for schools to follow when considering a suspension of more than 10 days or an expulsion is for the school district to make a determination whether the student's misconduct was a manifestation of the student's disability. This decision must be made by a group of persons knowledgeable about the student.[155] If the student's misconduct is found to be a manifestation of the disability, then the student may not be suspended for more than 10 days or expelled. Other procedures, however, may be used to address the misconduct if there is a finding of no manifestation. Figure 4–2 displays a flowchart related to the discipline of students with disabilities. Exhibit 4–2 presents steps to take during disciplinary actions.

Under IDEA, school districts have a continuing obligation to provide appropriate educational services designed to meet the student's unique educational needs during the period of disciplinary exclusion. These services do not have to be provided in the school but can be provided in the student's home, an alternative school, or other settings. If, a student is being provided educational services under Section 504 and there is a finding that the misconduct is not a manifestation of the disability, then the student can be treated in the same manner as a student without disabilities. This means that the student can be suspended for more than 10 days or expelled, and the school district has no obligation to continue to provide educational services.

If a student brings a firearm to school, the procedures are different. Before the school district makes a determination as to whether the misconduct was a manifestation of the dis-

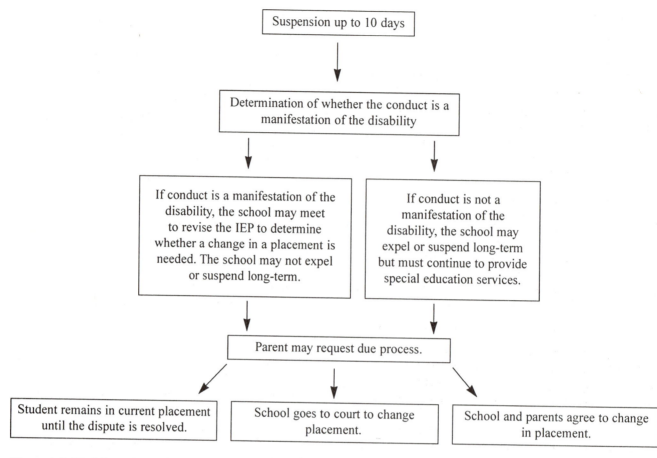

Figure 4–2 Disciplinary procedures for students with disabilities (not including firearms)

ability, the school may place the student in an interim alternative educational placement for up to 45 days. This placement must occur according to the respective laws of each state, as well as according to appropriate procedures. If, however, the parents initiate a due process proceeding, the student's placement will be the interim placement unless the parents and the school agree to a different placement. This interim placement can last for more than 45 days. This situation is different from suspending a student for more than 10 days or expelling a student whose misconduct did not involve bringing a firearm to school. In this situation, if the parents initiate a due process proceeding, the student would remain in the last agreed-upon placement, which is the program the school is trying to remove the student from, unless the parents and the school district agree to another placement.

LIABILITY ISSUES

In Loco Parentis

As the movement heightens toward including students with disabilities with their nondisabled peers in regular classes, teachers and administrators may be increasingly concerned regarding their liability. Specifically, staff may become concerned if a student with disabilities gets injured or injures another student.[156] Courts have consistently recognized that school administration and personnel must have authority to maintain a safe and orderly educational environment where learning can occur. The legal principle of *in loco parentis*, derived from common law,[157] views the teachers and administrators as standing in the place of the parents when it becomes necessary to exert control in order to maintain a conducive learning environment.

In loco parentis is invoked when a child is placed in the school system. It exists unless removed by state law or school board policy. *In loco parentis* then provides the teacher and/or administrator with the authority to guide, correct, and discipline student behavior when it is done in order to accomplish educational objectives. The general principle underlying this intervention is that the guidance, correction, or discipline must be reasonable in light of the circumstances surrounding the action.

If claims arise as a result of school personnel intervention, there are several defenses school divisions can invoke.

Exhibit 4–2 Steps To Take in Disciplinary Actions with Students with Disabilities

Based upon Section 504 of the Rehabilitation Act and IDEA requirements together, the following steps must be followed before disciplinary action that results in a change of placement:

1. Individuals familiar with the child and knowledgeable about special education (placement or IEP) determine whether behavior has a causal connection with the disability.
2. If there is no causal connection, normal disciplinary actions may be taken. Under IDEA, however, alternate educational programming must be provided.
3. If there is a causal connection, suspension may not exceed 10 days without implementing a change in placement. If school seeks to suspend for longer than 10 days, and the parents have not agreed to the change, procedures for a change in placement must be followed *before the suspension for longer than 10 days can begin.*
4. If the child is "truly dangerous," agency may seek preliminary injunction excluding child from school pending administrative determination of necessity to change placement.
5. Under Section 504, there must be a reevaluation of the child. Notice of this evaluation must be provided to the parents.
6. An IEP meeting must be convened, notice of which must have been provided to the parents.
7. If parents and school agree, IEP is revised.
8. If IEP is revised, notice must be provided to parents of intent to change placement.
9. Placement may then be changed.
10. Under IDEA, alternate educational programming must be provided.
11. If at any point in the process a disagreement occurs between the parents and the agency, a due process hearing may be initiated.

One is governmental or sovereign immunity, a common defense that protects a state agency against liability for its torts. It developed long ago from the belief that "the King can do no wrong" and continues today unless the courts or legislature abrogate this immunity. Governmental immunity for school divisions is followed by about half the states. A state may be liable if it can be said to have acted affirmatively to create or exacerbate a danger to victims.[158] Although there are several possible defenses that a teacher or administrator may invoke for an alleged negligent act, they may be liable for their own tortious conduct. (Tortious conduct is wrongful conduct whether by act or omission.)

Actions may also be brought under a constitutional law theory under the Civil Rights Act of 1871.[159] Under this doctrine, public officials who violate the statutory or constitutional rights of a student may be personally liable. This includes local government or institutions. The local government, institutions, and public officials may, however, have qualified or conditional immunity, which means they may not be liable as long as they are acting within the scope of their authority.

When intervention with students is necessary, one must consider the nature of the act committed by a student; the ability, attitude, and behavior of the student; the nature and severity of the intervention; and whether another, less intrusive intervention can occur. It's important to know state law and school policies. This chapter is not intended to substitute for legal advice. Readers who have questions are encouraged to consult legal counsel.

NOTES

1. *Children with disabilities* refers to preschool and school-age children and is used interchangeably throughout with the term *students with disabilities.*
2. Individuals with Disabilities Education Act, 20 U.S.C. § 1400–1485. (1975).
3. 20 U.S.C. § 1412 (5)(B).
4. Section 504 of the Rehabilitation Act of 1973, 34 C.F.R. § 300.552 (d) (1973, rev. 1995).
5. 20 U.S.C. § 1415 (b)(2); 34 C.F.R. § 300.504(a)(1) and (2); § 300.506.
6. 20 U.S.C. § 1415; 34 C.F.R. § 300.511.
7. The court system including the titles of the courts can vary from state to state.
8. *See* 34 C.F.R. § 300.506. Mediation may not be used to deny or delay a parent's rights under present law. There is a possibility with the reauthorization of the law that mediation could be required.
9. 20 U.S.C. § 1412(1).
10. 20 U.S.C. § 1401(a)(18); 34 C.F.R. § 300.8. See Appendix B–1.
11. 20 U.S.C. § 1401(19); § 1412(4); § 1414(a)(5); 34 C.F.R. § 300.343(d); and § 300.346.
12. 20 U.S.C. § 1412(5)(B); § 1414(a)(1)(c)(iv); 34 C.F.R. § 300.550–554.
13. For a more thorough discussion of both substantive and procedural protections under IDEA, *see* Guernsey, T.F., and Klare, K. (1993), *Special Education Law*, Durham, NC: Carolina Academic Press; and the regulations contained in 34 C.F.R.
14. 20 U.S.C. § 1414(a)(1)(a); 34 C.F.R. § 300.220.
15. 20 U.S.C. § 1412(5)(C); 34 C.F.R. § 300.531.
16. 34 C.F.R. § 300.343–345.
17. 20 U.S.C. § 1401(20); 34 C.F.R. § 300.345.
18. 34 C.F.R. § 300.542; .342(b)(1); Pt. 300, App. C, Question 42, which states that objectives must be written before placement and once a child is placed more detailed lesson plans or objectives may be written.

19. 20 U.S.C. § 1412(5)(C); 34 C.F.R. § 300.532.

20. 34 C.F.R. § 300.534.

21. 20 U.S.C. § 1415(b)(1)(a); 34 C.F.R. § 300.503.

22. 20 U.S.C. § 1415(b)(1)(a); 34 C.F.R. § 300.503.

23. 20 U.S.C. § 1415 (b)(1)(a).

24. 20 U.S.C. § 1415(c).

25. 20 U.S.C. § 1471.

26. OSEP Policy Memorandum 90-14 (March 20,1990) provides a discussion of Part H regarding entitlement and eligibility, fiscal responsibility, monitoring requirements, and timelines.

27. 34 C.F.R. § 300.16; 34 C.F.R. § 300.300.

28. A state application for funds requests both general and specific information in addition to specifically identified assurances. 20 U.S.C. § 1478; 34 C.F.R. § 303.140–146; § 303.120–127.

29. 20 U.S.C.§ 1401–1418; § 1420; § 1483; 34 C.F.R. § 303.4(b)(1)(2).

30. 20 U.S.C. § 1472(2)(C).

31. 20 U.S.C. § 1472(2)(E).

32. 20 U.S.C. § 1472(2)(F)(G).

33. 20 U.S.C. § 1477; 34 C.F.R. § 303.342.

34. 20 U.S.C. § 1477(3)(d)(4); 34 C.F.R. § 303.344.

35. 20 U.S.C. § 1477(d); 34 C.F.R. § 303.344.

36. 20 U.S.C. § 1472(2)(G).

37. 20 U.S.C. § 1480(1)–(8); 34 C.F.R. § 303.420–423, 460(a).

38. 29 U.S.C. § 794.

39. 34 C.F.R. § 104.34(a); and (b). See Appendix B–2.

40. 34 C.F.R. § 104.36.

41. 29 U.S.C. § 794; 34 C.F.R. § 104.31 *et seq*. Section 504 provides: "No otherwise qualified handicapped individual . . . shall solely by reason of his handicap, be excluded from participation in, be denied the benefits of, or be subjected to discrimination under any program or activity receiving federal financial assistance." Rehabilitation Act of 1973, revised July 1, 1995, Section 504.

42. 34 C.F.R. § 104.34(a).

43. 34 C.F.R. § 104.34(a); 104.37; Pt. 104, App. A, Question 24, which states that where a handicapped child is so disruptive that the education of other students is significantly impaired the needs of the handicapped child cannot be met in that placement.

44. 29 U.S.C. § 794.

45. 42 U.S.C. § 12132.

46. 23 IDELR 181 (June 9, 1995). This case involves an action by the parents alleging discrimination on the basis of denying the plaintiffs the opportunity to participate in or benefit from the services offered by Kindercare by failing to make reasonable modifications to its policies, practices, and procedures in violation of the ADA. The court ordered the center to retain the child until a hearing on the merits occurred.

47. 42 U.S.C. § 12182.

48. 42 U.S.C. § 12182(b)(1)(a)(I).

49. 42 U.S.C.§ 12182(b)(1)(a)(ii).

50. 20 U.S.C. § 2301; 34 C.F.R. § 400.1.

51. 34 C.F.R. § 300.17; 20 U.S.C. § 14019(16).

52. 20 U.S.C. § 1424.

53. These terms will be used as they are in the law and the cases.

54. 20 U.S.C. 1412(5)(B); 1414(a)(C)(iv); 34 C.F.R. § 300.550.

55. The text that follows in this paragraph is reprinted with permission from Guernsey, T.F., & Klare, K. (1993). *Special Education Law* (pp. 103–107). Durham, NC: Carolina Academic Press.

56. Board of Education v. Diamond, 808 F.2d 987 (3rd Cir. 1986).

57. Thornock v. Boise Idaho Independent School District, 556 Educ. Handicapped L. Rep. (CRR) 477, 482–483 (Dist. Ct. Idaho 1985) *aff'd*, 115 Idaho 466, 767 P.2d 1241 (1988), *cert denied*, 490 U.S. 1068 (1989).

58. Compare Bondonna v. Cooperman, 619 F. Supp. 401 (D.N.J. 1985) (ruled that hearing-impaired student should be mainstreamed where she was capable of functioning at above average intellectual level, adjusted to regular classroom, and was learning. LEA could transport to resource program for supplemental instruction) with Vesaco v. School District, 684 F.Supp. 1310 (W.D. Pa. 1988) (ruled that private school for hearing impaired was least restrictive because move to public school would interrupt acquiring needed language skills).

59. 20 U.S.C. § 1401(16); 34 C.F.R. § 300.17(a)(1–3).

60. 34 C.F.R § 300.553.

61. 34 C.F.R. § 300.553(a)(1).

62. 34 C.F.R. § 500; 34 C.F.R. § 533(a)(4) and (b).

63. 20 U.S.C. § 1412(5)(B); 34 C.F.R. § 300.551. The term *regular education* is used throughout this chapter and means the same as general education.

64. 20 U.S.C. § 1412(5)(B); 34 C.F.R. § 300.552.

65. 34 C.F.R. § 300.552. See Note to this section.

66. 34 C.F.R. § 300.306; 34 C.F.R. § 552.

67. 34 C.F.R § 300.554.

68. 20 U.S.C. § 1412(5)(B); 34 C.F.R. § 300.555.

69. 34 C.F.R. § 300.556.

70. 34 C.F.R. § 104.34.

71. *Id*.

72. *Id*.

73. Hendrick Hudson District Board of Education v. Rowley, 458 U.S. 176 (1981).

74. *Id*. at 188–89.

75. *Id*. at 206–7.

76. *Id*. at 202.

77. *Id*.

78. Mark A. v. Grant Wood Area Education Agency, 795 F.2d 52 (8th Cir. 1986).

79. Roncker v. Walter, 700 F.2d 1058 (6th Cir.).

80. The Eighth and Fourth Circuits have also adopted this test.

81. 874 F.2d 1036, 1050 (5th Cir. 1989). This test has been adopted by the Third, Fifth, and Eleventh Circuits.

82. Daniel R.R. v. State Board of Education, 874 F. 2d 1036, 1045 (6th Cir. 1983).

83. *Id*. at 1046.

84. Board of Education v. Rowley, 458 U.S. 179, 181 (1981).

85. Daniel R.R. v. State Board of Education, 874 F.2d 1036, 1049 (1989).

86. *See* Mavis v. Sobol, 839 F.Supp. 968 (1994), where the court held for the parents since the school district failed the first part of the two-part test established in Daniel R.R.

87. Oberti v. Board of Education of the Borough of Clementon School District, 995 F.2d 1204 (3rd Cir. 1993).

88. *Id*. at 1207, n. 1.

89. *Id*. at 1224.

90. Daniel R.R. v. State Board of Education, 874 F.2d 1036, 1050 (5th Cir. 1989).

91. Greer v. Rome City School District, 950 F.2d 688 (11th Cir. 1991).

92. *Id.* at 691.

93. *Id.*

94. *Id.* at 697.

95. *Id.*

96. *See* OCR opinion Chicago (Ill.) Pub. Sch. Dist. no. 299, where virtually all students with severe cognitive disabilities were placed in private day schools. 20 IDELR 699 (Dec. 3, 1993).

97. Greer v. Rome City School District, 950 F.2d 688, 698 (1991).

98. *Id.* at 699 citing Board of the Hendrick Hudson Central School District v. Rowley, 458 U.S. 176, 208 (1992).

99. The severity of the disability in Christy's case was not sufficient justification for placement, but in De Vries v. Fairfax County School Board, 882 F.2d 876 (9th Cir. 1989), the student's disabilities were the reason for not placing the child in a regular education class. In DeVries, the cognitive differences between the student with disabilities and the students without disabilities were so great that the high school student with disabilities would be simply "monitoring" the regular classes. *Id.* at 879.

100. 786 F.Supp. 874 (E.D. Cal. 1992); 14 F.3d 1398 (9th Cir. 1994). *But see* Clyde K. v. Pallyup School District, 35 F.3d 1396 (9th Cir. 1994) where the court found that a self-contained placement was appropriate because the nonacademic benefits were minimal. The court stated that "while school officials have a statutory duty to ensure that disabled students receive an appropriate education, they are not required to sit on their hands when a disabled student's behavioral problems prevent him and those around him from learning." *Id.* at 1402.

101. Sacramento City Unified School District Board of Education v. Holland, 786 F.Supp. at 876.

102. *Id.* at 881–82.

103. *Id.* at 881. The court found that the differing evaluations as to nonacademic benefits in large part reflected the predisposition of the evaluators.

104. *Id.* at 882.

105. *Id.*

106. *Id.* at 883.

107. *Id.* at 884.

108. *Id.* at 883.

109. *Id.* at 883–84.

110. *Id.* at 884.

111. Sacramento City School District v. Holland, 786 F.Supp. 874, 878, n. 6 (E.D. Cal. 1992).

112. Sacramento City School District v. Holland, 14 F.3d 1398, 1404, 1405 (9th Cir. 1994), which held that the school's proposition conflicted with 20 U.S.C. § 1412(5)(B).

113. A.W. v. Northwest R-1 School District, 813 F.2d 158 (8th Cir. 1987).

114. *Id.* at 163.

115. *Id.* at 164.

116. Barnett v. Fairfax County School Board, 721 F.Supp. 757 (E.D. Va. 1989).

117. 34 C.F.R. § 300.552.

118. Barnett v. Fairfax County School Board, 721 F. Supp. 757, 758 (E.D. Va. 1989).

119. Tarah P. v. Board of Education of Fremont School District, 1995 W.L. 66283 (N.D. Ill. 1995).

120. *See* C.F.R. § 300.552.

121. Lachman v. Illinois State Board of Education, 852 F.2d 290, 297 (7th Cir. 1988). This case involved placement in a school outside the neighborhood school where the school provided a particular method of teaching hearing-impaired students; the parents objected, believing that the method could have been used successfully in the neighborhood school.

122. Murray v. Montross County School District, 51 F.3d 921 (10th Cir. 1995).

123. *Id.* at 928; 20 U.S.C. § 1701(a)(2); 20 U.S.C. § 1412(5)(B).

124. *Id.* at 929.

125. *Id.* at 928–9.

126. 34 C.F.R. § 300.552(a)(3).

127. 34 C.F.R. § 300.552(c).

128. Oberti v. Board of Education of the Borough of Clementon School District, 995 F.2d 1204, 1224, n. 31.

129. 20 U.S.C. § 1402(a).

130. OSEP Memo 95-9, Judith E. Heumann, Assistant, Thomas Hehir, Director, 21 IDELR 1152 (November 1994).

131. Kelso (WA) Sch. Dist. No. 4, 20 IDELR 1006 (August 13, 1993).

132. *Id.* at 1153–54.

133. 34 C.F.R. § 300.346(a)(3).

134. OSEP Memo 95-9, 21 IDELR 1152, 1154 (November 1994).

135. 34 C.F.R. Pt. 300, App. C 48.

136. OSEP Memo 95-9, 21 IDELR 1152, 1154 (November 1994).

137. *Id.* Question 5 at 1154.

138. *Id.* Question 6 at 1154–5.

139. *Id.* Question 7 at 1155; 34 C.F.R. § 300.17; § 300.551(b)(1).

140. *Id.* at 1155; 34 C.F.R. § 300.504.

141. *Id.* Question 8 at 1155.

142. *Id.* Question 9 at 1156.

143. OSEP Memo to Honourable John M. Spratt, Jr., 20 IDELR 1457 (January 12, 1994).

144. *Id.*

145. *Id.* at 1458. *See also* Letter to Johns, 21 IDELR 571 (April 8, 1994) and Letter to Goodling (18 IDELR 213) where the inquiry was regarding OSERS position on placing all disabled students in regular education classes and the response was that some children may require placement in settings other than regular education in order to be provided with education designed to meet their unique needs.

146. Letter to Thomas B. Neveldine, 20 IDELR 181, 182 (January 29, 1993).

147. *Id.* at 181.

148. *Id.* at 181.

149. *See* Comment, 34 C.F.R. § 300.513 (cited with approval in Honig v. Doe, 484 U.S. 305, 325 (1988)); *see also* 20 U.S.C. § 1415(e)(3).

150. *E.g.*, Hayes v. Unified School District No. 377, 877 F. 2d. 809 (10th Cir. 1989).

151. Honig v. Doe, 484 U.S. 305 (1988).

152. 20 U.S.C. § 1415(e)(3).

153. The text from note 149 to note 153 has been reprinted with permission from Guernsey, T.F., & Klare, K. (1993). *Special Education Law.* (pp. 137–138) Durham, NC: Carolina Academic Press.

154. OSEP Memo 95-16, 22 IDELR 531 (April 1995).

155. 34 C.F.R. § 300.553(a)(3) and 34 C.F.R. § 300.344(a)(1)–(5).

156. State laws vary significantly on liability issues. Check with legal counsel for any questions.

157. *Common law* refers to law that develops from usages, customs, and cases. It excludes law derived from the legislature.

158. D.R. v. Middle Bucks Area Voc. Tech. School, 972 F.2d 1364, 1374 (3d Cir. 1992).

159. Civil Rights Act of 1871, 42 U.S.C. § 1983.

CHAPTER 5

Financing Inclusive Education Programs

Leslie W. Jones and Lissa A. Power-deFur

INTRODUCTION

Any discussion of inclusion must consider financing its implementation. What are the costs associated with inclusion? Does inclusive education cost more? Does it cost less? Some suggest that inclusion creates an opportunity to save money at the expense of students in special education (Shanker, 1994/1995). Others, such as local school district superintendents and school board members, fear that inclusion costs are prohibitive and will reduce services for other students (Beales, 1993). However, recent studies have identified minimal cost increases associated with an inclusion delivery model, compared with the traditional service delivery model (Inclusive Education Programs, 1994; McLaughlin & Warren, 1994b).

This chapter outlines the issues involved with financing an inclusive education program. It discusses the major sources of funding, including the relationship between federal, state, and local funding. It talks about how various funding methodologies can encourage or discourage certain types of placements and services—and, thus, how they can support or hinder efforts to place students in inclusive settings. In addition, the high cost of education—and of special education, in particular—is reviewed, with a focus on how this cost affects the perceptions of policy makers. The resource implications of inclusive practices on personnel, transportation, facilities, materials and equipment, and professional development are discussed, with examples drawn from local school districts. The chapter closes by returning to the above-mentioned questions: "Does inclusion cost more?" "Does it cost less?" The conclusion is that inclusive education programs do not necessarily cost more or less than traditional special education programs. The costs are simply different from those for carrying out traditional special education programs.

THE INFLUENCE OF FINANCIAL POLICY ON SPECIAL EDUCATION PLACEMENTS

In the United States, the responsibility for funding public education falls to state and local government. The federal government provides funding to support certain initiatives of national importance or to rectify issues related to civil rights. In 1975, funding associated with the Education for All Handicapped Children Act (EHA), now the Individuals with Disabilities Education Act (IDEA), was directed toward supporting state and local governments in establishing special education and related services for students with disabilities who had previously been excluded from public education. Federal funding accounts for a small portion of special education funding—less than 10% nationwide—with wide variability across the states. The cost of public education has grown over the last few decades, and special education costs are significant in every education budget (Parrish & Verstegen, 1994).

All education policy is influenced by economic factors, and special education is no exception. The practice of categorical labeling and specialized placement for students with disabilities (Dempsey & Fuchs, 1993) has resulted in differentiated funding—funding that provides more financial support for certain categorical labels or certain placements. For example, many states provide additional financial support to localities when a student's individualized educational program (IEP) calls for a high-cost placement such as a residential setting. As a result, a fiscal incentive exists to place challenging students in restrictive placements, especially if the provision of services locally would result in costs to the locality for which there is no state reimbursement. Conversely there are few financial incentives to encourage school districts to place students in an inclusive, less restrictive environment. Thus, finance policies have played a significant role in influencing special education placements and implementing the least restrictive environment requirements (Hasazi, Liggett, & Schattman, 1994; Parrish, 1993a; Parrish & Verstegen, 1994).

The cost of special education services is higher than the cost of general education. At the inception of EHA in 1975, the added cost to educate a student with a disability was approximately twice the average per pupil expenditure (Chaikind, Danielson, & Braven, 1993). The additional cost associated with educating a student eligible for special education and related services (excess costs), when added to the cost of educating any student in a school system (average per pupil expenditure) created a total cost that was twice the cost of educating a child without a disability. Today, this cost has grown to 2.3 times the average per pupil expenditure (Chaikind et al., 1993). In addition, the number of students eligible for special education has increased by 40% since 1977, from 8.2% to 11% of school-aged enrollments (U.S. Department of Education, 1994). The rate of growth of children in special education exceeds the rate of growth of all children enrolled in public education (U.S. Department of Education, 1995). In addition to the per child costs of special education, there are costs associated with evaluation of students who are not found eligible for special education and the special expense of transporting students with disabilities (Moore, Strang, Schwartz, & Braddock, 1988; Parrish, 1993a).

One unfortunate by-product of this high cost of special education is the perception that special education is too costly and is taking funds away from other necessary educational programs and services. Perceptions such as these can have an impact on policy makers and dampen efforts to start new programs and services. For example, school board members may not support a proposal for additional funding for staff development and additional instructional assistants to start an inclusive education program in an elementary school if their constituents perceive that special education has already gotten "its share," and that other education programs must be supported. The beliefs and opinions of local governing bodies; local school boards; parent associations; special education interest groups; superintendents; principals; general, vocational, and special education teachers; related service staff; and students will influence efforts to create new programs.

SOURCES OF FUNDING FOR SPECIAL EDUCATION

Three sources support the funding of special education and related services: federal, state, and local government. Support across these three areas naturally varies by state and locality. In their analysis of funding for special education in 1988, Parrish and Verstegen (1994) found that when averaged across states, federal funds accounted for 8% of the cost of special education, state sources supported 56% of costs, and local government supported 36% of costs. In recent years, many states have changed their special education funding formulas, so the relationship between the amount of federal, state, and local dollars has changed.

Federal Sources

IDEA

IDEA is the most influential source of funding, since funding is tied to one of the primary assurances of special education, the free and appropriate public education (FAPE) requirement. The data collection required to support reporting under IDEA created a system that tends to categorize and place students according to their disability label. In addition, the reporting of level of service (e.g., regular education, self-contained special education, separate school) created distinctions in placement rather than services. This data collection system, although not the basis for federal funding, has created the impression in the minds of many that funding is specifically associated with a categorical label and the student placement.

In addition, Part D of IDEA supports personnel development and, over the years, has offered significant support in higher education. The categorical nature of the data collection for the annual reporting requirements influenced the creation of categorical teacher-training programs at colleges and universities. The categorical training programs have limited cross-disciplinary training both within special education and between special education and general education. Because of this separate training, teachers often develop a limited conception of their capabilities and competencies: special education teachers are uncomfortable teaching general curriculum, and general education teachers believe they are incapable of working with students who have disabilities. This perception influences teachers and administrators, creating the impression that the general and special education programs must be separate and, perhaps, segregated.

Federal funding flows through states to localities based on data from the previous year. (This is generally the case for state funding as well.) As a result, localities have to pay in advance the cost of serving new students, as the funding from state and federal levels will not "catch up" for at least a year.

Part B. Passed in 1975, EHA reauthorized as IDEA created a federal funding formula to help states set up special education and related services. Funding is based upon compliance with federal regulations. (This is in contrast with Section 504 of the Rehabilitation Act of 1973, which includes many of the same provisions as IDEA, but is a civil rights statute and carries no funding for implementation. See Chapter 4 for further information.) Originally, the intent of the federal legislation under EHA was to fund 40% of the excess costs of educating students with disabilities. The $251.7 million appropriation in 1977 reflected a $71 per child allocation. Although the appropriation has grown nearly tenfold (to $2.1 billion in fiscal year 1994), the per child allocation remains low ($413 in fiscal year 1994) (U.S. Department of Education, 1995). The current funding, however, is less than one-tenth of the estimated excess costs. This creates a belief that IDEA is an "unfunded mandate."

It is important to remember that students with disabilities have the right to be educated with peers without disabilities, to the maximum extent appropriate. Although IDEA has major funding provisions, it is a law establishing the civil rights of students with disabilities. As such, the role of the federal government in financing special education is to assist, not to provide full funding (Verstegen, 1995). The mandate for special education is "sum sufficient"; that is, the services must be provided. It is not acceptable to deny services based on insufficient funds. Case law interprets federal statutes and regulations, and, in recent years, fiscal matters have been addressed by the courts. Chapter 4 provides a discussion of these court cases.

Part B distributes funds to states according to the total number of students with disabilities aged 3 through 21 reported as receiving special education and related services in the previous year. Localities report this information in the December 1 child count. The federal allocation is equal for all children, regardless of the nature of their disability or the level of service they receive. States retain no more than 25% for administration and projects (e.g., staff development, technical assistance, or research). The remainder is distributed to localities, based on a state-approved local application for special education. Central to this and many federal programs is the matter of *supplanting*—using federal funds to replace state and/or local funds (e.g., funding a special education teacher position previously supported by state and local dollars). This practice is not allowed under IDEA; rather, the intent of Part B funds is to pay for *additional* (increased) services.

Section 619—The Preschool Grants Program. This program provides funds to states for each preschool-age child, ages three through five. To be eligible for a preschool grant, states must make FAPE available to all children ages three through five. States are awarded funds based on the number of children ages three through five who received special education and related services on December 1 of the previous year. State departments of education must pass at least 75% of the funds on to localities. Of these funds, 5% may be used for administrative purposes by the state, and 20% may be managed at the state level to support such programs as technical assistance to teachers, training costs, or special-

ized evaluations. The process of data collection and disbursement of funds is similar to the Part B program, to include matters of supplanting.

Part H. As part of P.L. 99-457 (1986), Congress established incentives for early intervention services for children with significant developmental delays, from birth to age three, and for their families. States are not required to participate in Part H. Participating states identify the agency with responsibility to manage the Part H program (e.g., education, social services, mental health and mental retardation). Grants support a statewide, comprehensive, multidisciplinary, interagency coordination program of early intervention for infants and toddlers who meet the state's eligibility criteria. In fiscal year 1993, more than $213 million was allocated to states (U.S. Department of Education, 1995).

Funds to support services for children served by Part H may come from many sources, including: Part H grants, Medicaid, Maternal and Child Health block grants, state funds, local funds, private insurance, nonprofit sources, parental payment. Eligibility criteria for each funding source must be met (U.S. Department of Education, 1995).

Carl D. Perkins Vocational and Applied Technology Education Act (1994)

Uses of funds under this act include vocational education sites and programs that serve the highest concentrations of individuals who are members of special populations—that is, programs that provide equitable participation in vocational programs for students with disabilities. The federal regulations governing this program are not specific regarding numbers of students with disabilities who must participate. It simply requires equitable participation. Outcomes for use of these funds must consider the integration of academics and vocational education so that students achieve both academic and occupational competencies. Economic development influences program efforts in the state and the locality.

Head Start Program

This federal grant program provides preschool services for children whose families fall below the poverty level. Programs are generally offered by local, nonprofit organizations. Federal funds flow directly to local grantees. Not less than 10% of program enrollment must be available to children with disabilities. Income eligibility does not apply to this 10%, yet many programs prefer to honor the low-income requirement. Fiscal coordination of this program with special education programs is important. Local budgeting should include an increase in certain related services such as speech-language services, occupational and physical therapy, and parent counseling.

Chapter I Program for Children with Disabilities

Chapter I of the Elementary and Secondary Education Act (ESEA) helped with the education of children with disabilities in state-operated programs beginning in 1965. The program was phased out, with the reauthorization of ESEA as the Improving America's Schools Act (IASA). Funds for services to eligible children are now provided under Part B of IDEA. This policy decision eliminated any potential financial benefit associated with placing a child in a state-operated program as opposed to educating the child within the local education agency.

Improving America's Schools Act, Title I

This program, formerly Chapter I of ESEA, is designed to improve educational opportunities for children from low-income families who perform below grade level. Funding is based on the number of children in poverty. Children with disabilities who live in Title I attendance areas and meet school districts' "greatest-need" standard are eligible.

Medicaid

Changes in the Medicaid requirements in the late 1980s permitted states to use Medicaid funds to support certain special education and related services. A variety of services—including occupational and physical therapy, speech-language services, and psychological services—may be billed if the child is eligible. Certain components of student assessment used for determining eligibility may also be billed (e.g., medical, psychological, audiological). The Medicaid compliance requirements are substantial, which may deter school systems from using this source. In some localities, private vendors can provide the service and bill Medicaid for the school district. Many local school districts have found that the funding received from Medicaid is significant and worth the administrative burden. Readers should contact their state's department of education and Medicaid offices to determine if their state's Medicaid plan permits use of Medicaid funding in the schools and to discover the procedures for obtaining Medicaid reimbursement for services.

State Sources

State support for special education and related services varies considerably from state to state. According to the U.S. Department of Education's Fourteenth Annual Report to Congress, in 1993 state support ranged from more than 90% of total special education costs to 17% (Parrish & Verstegen, 1994). However, state funding formulas vary widely, and readers are urged to contact their state department of education to understand how state funds are designated for special education in their state. In addition, readers may wish to contact The Center for Special Education Finance, the National Association of State Directors of Special Education, or the U.S. Department of Education.

The 1992 report from the National Association of State Boards of Education, *Winners All: A Call for Inclusive Schools*, speaks to the influence of different state funding formulas on special education placements. The report notes that most states use one of five basic special education funding formulas:

1. *Flat grants per teacher or classroom unit.* The state provides a fixed amount of money for each special education classroom needed.
2. *Percentage of excess cost.* The state reimburses districts for a percentage of the excess cost of educating students with disabilities.
3. *Percentage of teacher salaries.* The state provides a percentage of salaries of special education teachers and other special education personnel.
4. *Weighted pupil.* The state pays districts a multiple of the average per pupil costs (or other base rate). The multiple depends on the pupil's disability label or special education program. Weighted formulas may include funding general education programs or other categorical, non–special education programs.
5. *Weighted teacher/classroom.* The state pays districts an amount based on a multiple of allowable teachers or classrooms. Weights may vary by disability category or program.

State fiscal policies create incentives and disincentives that influence programs and services (Farrow & Tom, 1992; Parrish & Verstegen, 1994). Funding policies that rely on labeling and special placements, although originally designed to ensure that all eligible students receive services, may encourage identification and placement to receive funding (National Association of State Boards of Education, 1992). These policies contribute to the separation and segregation of students. Other policies result in financial incentives for placing students in highly restrictive placements; these provide additional assistance for students in special and regional facilities rather than students served in home districts. In addition, some policies pay in advance for expensive, restrictive, out-of-district placements, rather than reimburse districts at the end of the academic year. Such funding policies penalize efforts to meet the needs of students in less restrictive settings.

In recent years, efforts have been under way in some states to alter the relationship between funding and placements. Vermont's efforts to develop inclusion opportunities statewide are illustrative: "[O]ne monumental barrier to widespread implementation of inclusion in Vermont remained—a barrier that could not be moved by all the training, model demonstrations, guidelines for best practice, and technical assistance that the Green Mountain State could offer. This barrier was a 20-year-old state funding formula for special education that favored restrictive placement" (Thousand & Villa, 1995, p. 289). The first step for Vermont was to change the funding formula to one that funded the locality for each student with a disability despite the placement or extent of services. In other words, there was a need for a placement-neutral funding formula. Vermont went one step further to create incentives. The funding formula changed to a block grant based on the total school enrollment for the school system. The block grant approach gave school districts in Vermont the flexibility to spend these state funds on remedial and compensatory services. In addition, Vermont policy makers created an incentive in their realignment of state funds. Legislation specified that 1% of the special education budget had to be spent on training of teachers and administrators (Thousand & Villa, 1995).

Other states (e.g., Pennsylvania, Massachusetts, Idaho, and Montana) have also revised their funding allocation methodologies. Funding in these states is based on the total school-age enrollment for the school system. School systems receive the same funding regardless of the number of students with disabilities served. The fiscal incentive to identify and label students for special education is removed (Parrish & Verstegen, 1994).

In some states, special funding may support transportation costs for students with disabilities. These policies may have been originally created with good intention—to support local efforts to purchase and operate specially equipped buses for certain students with disabilities. Special funding streams, however, often discourage or prohibit transporting students without disabilities on buses for students with disabilities. Although established in good faith, such fiscal policy leads to separate and segregated transportation systems. Readers should contact pupil transportation specialists in the state department of education for information on the funding mechanism in their state.

Local Sources

Parrish and Verstegen (1994) reported that the local contribution across states ranged from 3% to more than 70% of total special education expenditures. Exhibit 5–1 presents the relationship between the various funding sources for Virginia in the 1994–1995 school year (Virginia Department of Education, 1996). The relationship between the three funding sources varies from state to state. Generally, the lion's share of the excess costs for educating students with disabilities is borne by local government. The locality bears most of the cost of special education, neutralizing any incentive to over-identify created by state and federal funding formulas.

A source that can be tapped at the local level is inter-agency support and funding for certain youth (Farrow &

Tom, 1992). Many states have created interagency initiatives to contain the costs and increase the flexibility in use of funds for students with emotional and behavioral disorders (Hill, 1996). These initiatives involve education, social services, mental health, and the juvenile court; some also include health, rehabilitation, employment, and law enforcement. Many of these initiatives pool resources from multiple sources (e.g., special education, social services, and health) to support the costs of services for children and their families. (See Chapter 8 for more information on community-based support for inclusive education programs. See Appendix 5–A for sources of information regarding funding of special education programs.)

FUTURE TRENDS IN FEDERAL AND STATE FUNDING

In recent years, considerable discussion has been focused on the value of changing the way in which federal and state funding supports special education. The National Association of State Boards of Education recommended severing the link between funding, placement, and disability label (1992). It suggested that changing to a flat reimbursement formula would be an improvement. This approach would assign a single weight, reflecting a percentage of the general education formula to be reimbursed, based on the national percentage of students with disabilities. This method would eliminate benefits for over- and underidentification or for level of service. It also allows for increased flexibility, allowing special education funds to be

---

Exhibit 5–1 Relationship between Federal, State, and Local Funding of Special Education for the State of Virginia, 1994–1995

Percent of per child special education expenses	
from federal funds	8.8%
from state funds	24.2%
from local funds	67.0%
Average total of expenditures for special education	$9,807.00
Average contribution from federal funds	$ 863.00
Average contribution from state funds	$2,373.00
Average contribution from local funds	$6,571.00

Note: Data based on expenditures reported by local school divisions for special education in 1994–1995.

Source: Adapted from *Statewide Cost of Special Education in Virginia's Schools,* March 29, 1996, Virginia Department of Education.

used to support general education programs that include students in special education.

The Center for Special Education Finance also discussed the importance of changing funding mechanisms (Parrish, 1993b; Parrish & Verstegen, 1994). The center made the following arguments supporting the need to change federal funding policy: (1) serving students outside special education is more cost-effective, and certain students are better served outside special education; and (2) overidentification is a major issue facing states and localities. The center pointed out a number of disadvantages to funding based on total enrollment: (1) it would not be fair to states and school systems with high numbers of students identified; (2) it could usher in a retreat of the traditional role of the federal government in promoting special education; and (3) current federal funding could be jeopardized, as could accountability for spending special education funds on students in special education. The arguments for and against this funding approach are compelling. Concerns about losing federal support and leadership are real. Parrish and Verstegen (1994) argue that, despite these concerns, the current system of funding stands in the way of efficiency of services.

The Vermont finance reform included a block funding approach. At the federal level, this approach means consolidating major elementary and secondary federal assistance programs for children with special learning needs. These programs target certain categories of children such as economically disadvantaged children (ESEA, Title I), children with limited English proficiency (ESEA, Title VII), or students with disabilities (IDEA, Part B). These federal programs have strict conditions for funding, with minimal local flexibility. However, localities desire more flexibility for efficiency of service delivery and for better program coordination (Parrish, 1995; Verstegen, 1995).

RESOURCES AFFECTED BY INCLUSIVE EDUCATION PROGRAMS

Refining school finance accounting to the level needed to track exact costs associated with financing special education and related services is difficult, if not impossible. Local budget and accounting practices are established to conform to local and state budgetary categories and reporting needs. These categories do not always allow for the specificity needed to distinguish between costs for special education and those for general education, transportation, or staff development (McCormick & First, 1994). Some distinctions can be made, such as the costs for personnel (e.g., special education teachers and instructional aides). Other areas, such as costs for assessment services or school facilities, present a significant challenge. The challenge is deciding what percentage should be designated for students with disabilities and what percentage should be designated in other

categories. Constructing budget categories and line-item budget practices at the level of detail often requested by policy makers is often not cost-effective.

As stated in the beginning of the chapter, there are varying perceptions about the cost of implementing inclusive education programs. One primary source of the different perceptions about cost is the time frame used for gathering data and drawing conclusions. For example, there may be an increase in costs in the first year to provide physical plant accommodations and staff development, yet these costs would not be present in later years. To date, no longitudinal study of the costs associated with inclusion has been completed. Assessing the impact on a case-by-case basis may also result in a skewed analysis of the costs. For example, the cost of a one-on-one instructional aide for a child with moderate mental retardation in a general education kindergarten class would be $10,000 for one school year. If 20 children with moderate mental retardation required the same type of instructional aide, the costs of an inclusive education program could be determined to be $200,000. In a school system of 15,000 students, this is a significant increase in costs and would result in a cost overrun for the system. However, this approach assumes a one-size-fits-all mentality for children with disabilities. Whereas the use of an instructional aide may be the most effective support for one child, other children may need different supports and services. Decisions must be made on an individual basis, and generalizing a decision for one child to all children with disabilities will result in incorrect assumptions regarding costs.

A few case studies of the cost of carrying out inclusive education programs have been conducted. A southern Indiana cooperative found no difference in the cost per pupil between an inclusive service delivery program and a traditional service delivery program (Inclusive Education Programs, 1994). The costs remained relatively constant. The cooperative reported that these same resources were previously used in different ways before being shifted to accomplish inclusion outcomes. McLaughlin and Warren have conducted a thorough study of the costs associated with inclusion (1994a, 1994b). In an analysis of 14 school districts that have implemented inclusive education programs, they concluded that inclusive schools cost less per pupil ($4,096 per student) than traditional schools ($4,267). These authors reported an increase in expenditures for adaptive materials and building renovations, but indicated a reduction in transportation costs. However, readers were cautioned that it was difficult to arrive at exact costs in their study.

Personnel

Implementation of inclusive education programs creates a significant change in the assignment of special education personnel. Special education teachers may move from self-contained settings to general education classrooms. Paraprofessionals may be assigned to a general education classroom or to a student on a full-time basis. McLaughlin and Warren (1994b) found that only 1 of the 14 sites experienced a reduction in staff. In this district, a full-time professional position was converted to 2.5 instructional assistant positions. Several sites experienced an increase in staff, most notably in the number of paraprofessionals providing direct instructional support. See the case study presented in Exhibit 5–2.

The specific cost differences associated with inclusive education programs depend upon the staffing patterns required in the school. Districts must plan for the costs associated with increasing the number of instructional assistants or other paraprofessional staff. However, as demonstrated in Exhibit 5–2, many school districts find this to be a temporary cost. McLaughlin and Warren reported that, as instructional staff gained in their skills and confidence, the need for an additional instructional assistant was reduced (1994b). They found that many school districts identified a significant change in the role of the instructional staff. Teachers who had previously served as teachers in self-contained special education classrooms assumed the role of consultant-teacher. With planning and preparation, such a change in roles can be accomplished without additional staff.

Transportation

Transportation is one of the largest line items in most school district budgets. Districts that transport many students with disabilities outside their neighborhood (and outside the district) may experience significant cost savings by creating inclusive education programs at students' home schools.

Casey and Dozier identified significant savings in the district's transportation budget when the district discontinued the practice of placing many students with disabilities out of district and organized its own classes for students (1994). Some districts experience an initial increase in transportation costs if they have to increase the number of buses that can transport students with disabilities. These are one-time costs associated with purchasing new buses or retrofitting existing ones. Because the fiscal impact on transportation will reflect capital costs (purchasing/retrofitting buses) and day-to-day costs (number of bus runs, length of bus ride), accurate analysis of the effect on transportation costs must be done on a systemwide basis, over a period of time. McLaughlin and Warren (1994b) reported that one school district reduced the number of students who needed specialized transportation from 300 to 125 within three years. Exhibit 5–3 illustrates the costs associated with including students with physical disabilities in their home school. Unfortunately, as McLaughlin and Warren point out, savings in transportation costs are realized in a separate budget and seldom attributed to changes in special education programs. Further, cost savings are seldom transferred to the source to offset any increase in costs associated with carrying out an inclusive school program.

Facilities

A fundamental feature of an inclusive school is the accessibility of the school to all students. Including students with physical disabilities may require physical plant modifications. Again, McLaughlin and Warren (1994a, 1994b) found wide variability in facilities cost, which related directly to prior accessibility and renovation costs. The most frequent renovation costs were associated with increasing

Exhibit 5–2 One-on-One Instructional Assistant at the Elementary Level: A Case Study

Over a period of three years, several parents requested that their child with a disability be fully included in a general classroom at the elementary level. In each case, it was the expectation of the parents and the desire of the general classroom teacher that a full-time instructional assistant be assigned one-on-one with the student. The parents and the general classroom teacher believed that this instructional assistant was necessary to ensure the success of the student in the fully included environment. Each student's individualized educational program (IEP) was carried out to emphasize the development of academic, social, and communication skills. The instructional assistant provided instructional accommodations to the curriculum to support the development of academic skills, under the guidance of both the special education and the general education teachers.

After a few months, it became apparent in each case that the one-on-one instructional assistant was no longer needed on a full-time basis for the child. The IEP committee, including the parents, discerned that as the general classroom teacher increased her understanding of the educational needs of her new student, the reliance on the instructional assistant decreased. The teacher and classmates became comfortable with the student in the classroom. This experience showed that an instructional assistant is not always the key to success. Rather, the presence of the aide provided support while the teacher was learning new skills and adjusting to the new teaching environment.

The school district now assigns an additional instructional assistant to a school when a new student is identified who requires intensive support during his or her initial placement in an inclusive education program. Assigning the assistant to the building allows the principal, with the IEP team's concurrence, to shift the assistant's responsibility to other areas when the intensity of required involvement with the student is reduced.

Exhibit 5–3 Changing Transportation Needs Associated with Implementation of Inclusive Education at an Elementary School: A Case Study

An inclusive education program was started in an elementary school. All students with disabilities in the school's attendance zone attended their neighborhood school. A full year of planning and preparation preceded implementation, involving the principal, the school's instructional staff, parents, and the transportation director.

As a part of the planning team, the transportation director identified the transportation routes and vehicles that would accommodate the students with disabilities in an inclusive manner. The director determined that there was no need to purchase a new bus (or retrofit an existing bus) to transport the students to their neighborhood school, as sufficient buses were available. Previously, these students had been "chauffeured" with one to two students per bus, to their separate special education school. Many of these schools were long distances from the students' homes. The transportation director predicted an immediate reduction in transportation costs because the students with disabilities could be transported with other children from their neighborhood. If a student required a specially equipped bus, students without disabilities joined the student who required the special accommodation, so that the bus was full.

the size of bathrooms, creating "curb cuts," and installing ramps. Creativity by school personnel often solved some high-cost accessibility issues (e.g., moving a class to the ground level). It should be noted, however, that school districts are required to assume the costs of making the facilities accessible to comply with the Americans with Disabilities Act (Mawdsley, 1995).

In some circumstances, there may be a cost savings associated with facilities. For example, the use of a team-teaching model may eliminate the cost of additional special education classrooms or reduce the need to purchase trailers in a building that is at capacity. In other buildings, team teaching may make a classroom available for other purposes. Many districts identify the need for additional space for teachers and specialists to come together for planning, consultation, and problem solving; a "freed-up" classroom could be used for such a meeting room. This scenario will be more important in school districts with a growing student population where classroom space is at a premium.

Materials and Equipment

The categorical nature of education programs has frequently resulted in the purchase of materials and equipment by a specific funding source (e.g., special education, Title I, Title II). The belief that use of these materials and equipment by persons outside the categorical area violates a sup-

planting requirement has resulted in many duplicate purchases, or instances when valuable materials have been left unused. Through inclusion, many educators have recognized that their materials and equipment can be used in multiple settings. Further, a cost savings can be realized by elimination of duplicate purchasing. McLaughlin and Warren (1994b) identified an additional area of savings—purchasing materials for students in special education from general education catalogs. Through collaboration, special education teachers identified many general education materials that are similar to those available, generally at a higher price, from specialty catalogs.

In some cases, there has been an increase in the costs associated with materials and equipment during the initial stages of implementation of inclusive education. For example, the district may need to purchase additional adaptive equipment to ensure its availability at students' home schools (e.g., positioning boards or specialized chairs) (McLaughlin & Warren, 1994b).

Professional Development

The cost associated with professional development is, perhaps, the one cost that is found in all districts successfully using inclusive education practices. Teachers, related service staff, support staff, and administrators cannot be expected to carry out any school reform initiative, including inclusive education, without widespread professional development. Because teacher education programs generally do not provide cross-disciplinary course work or experience for general and special educators, most school districts find they need to prepare all staff. Preparation ranges from developing specific skills to modifying attitudes. It also includes opportunities for instructional staff to visit other schools. Professional development is incomplete if offered only once, and districts need to provide regular opportunities for learning. Giving teachers time to plan, problem solve, and share techniques and strategies is another important component of professional development. Most school districts that operate successful inclusive education programs also identify the need to provide specialized professional development for their instructional assistants.

The costs associated with professional development may include guest speakers, handouts and materials accompanying inservice presentations, and travel costs to permit teachers to visit other programs. Exhibit 5–4 provides an example of how professional development supported successful team teaching at the middle school level.

Special Situation: Private Residential Placements

Placement of students in residential settings can be costly to a school system. Many students can be returned from such restrictive, costly placements to their communities through the supports and services made available through inclusive education. Casey and Dozier (1994) found that the costs saved by returning students from expensive, out-of-district placements provided the district with fiscal resources for creation of new programs in local schools.

For a student who has been placed in a residential placement, the prospect of returning to a general education environment can be frightening. The transition back to the community and the school setting must be carefully planned. Schools may find that services of an instructional aide or a behavior management specialist, along with a teacher who specializes in behavior management and counseling, may be an important element in making the new placement work. All staff must be prepared to help reduce anxiety and stress for the student. Sometimes, a student cannot move from a residential placement directly to a neighborhood school placement. The student may need to make the transition through a combination of a private day program and the public school, and then to a full-time placement in the public school. In addition, many students and families will benefit from other support services.

The student's family is critical to the student's success. Community in-home services may be necessary to help establish and maintain a stable home environment. The collaborative efforts of a treatment team may be needed to maintain the support system and training for the family until they can become independent. (Chapter 8 provides further information on how community-based services can support schools in their efforts to include students with disabilities.)

What are the costs? Cost savings are associated with eliminating the expensive residential setting and the associated transportation costs. The use of additional, specialized staff is costly, yet less expensive than the residential placement. Inclusion of a transition period increases the short-term costs. However, some students cannot be placed in a community setting without such a transition, so the costs associated with the transition placement may be needed to prevent a return to the more restrictive residential placement. Though the costs for the in-home services may be borne by other agencies (e.g., social services or mental health) or an interagency pool of funds, these are costs that the community must bear. In time, additional services may be phased out or reduced to allow the student as much independence as possible.

INCLUSIVE EDUCATION COSTS ARE "DIFFERENT"

The statement that inclusive education programs cost the community more money is not true. Nor is it accurate to suggest that inclusion will cost less. Very few local school districts have implemented an inclusive education program and concurrently gathered information regarding costs for a sufficient period to draw conclusions regarding costs. It is difficult to determine if inclusive education costs resources

Exhibit 5–4 Professional Development To Implement Team Teaching Successfully at the Middle School: A Case Study

A middle school team-teaching approach was modified by adding a special education teacher to the seventh-grade team of three teachers. The special educator is available for one-on-one instruction within the classroom, with groups of students with disabilities or without disabilities, or for consultation with the general education teacher. Before setting up this new variation of team teaching, special and general education teachers received staff training. Activities focused on working as a team, adapting instruction, and improving everyone's understanding of the special needs of adolescents with disabilities

This team teaching benefited many more students than those found eligible for special education. Students with attention deficit disorder, at-risk students, students who spoke English as a second language, and the general education students all benefited from the joint expertise of the four teachers.

Staff development activities cost money. However, the principal recognized that the staff development activities could fit into the school's six-year plan of instruction, and, as a result, identified funding in existing staff development resources.

or saves resources for a school district. Determination of the fiscal impact of inclusion must be done on a school-by-school or district-by-district basis. Further, analysis must be conducted over a number of years—perhaps as long as five years—to ensure that start-up costs (e.g., staff development, equipment, or facility renovation) do not skew the data. Comparison of the cost of inclusion with the traditional special education system will be difficult, because identifying the costs associated with the traditional program are also challenging.

Inclusive education programs will require resources in personnel, staff development, facilities, equipment, materials, and transportation. Each of these categories must be examined with respect to where a system is in its movement toward inclusion. Initially, every category may generate a significant increase in costs. Over time, however, the school system may see a leveling of costs in each area. Eventually, the positive outcomes, as measured in benefits to students and school personnel, outweigh the added initial costs. Districts considering inclusive education programs should decide placement based on individual needs. After placement decisions are made, creative administrators can identify cost savings in areas such as transportation, private tuition, and out-of-district placements, to help support costs associated with implementation (e.g., personnel, equipment, and professional development). In the end, inclusion must be started because it is the "right thing to do," not because it will the save the district money.

REFERENCES

Beales, J.R. (1993). *Special education: Expenditures and obligations.* Los Angeles, CA: Reason Foundation.

Carl D. Perkins Vocational and Applied Technology Education Act, 20 U.S.C. § 2301 (1994).

Casey, C.M., & Dozier, P.W. (1994, October). Cutting costs in special education. *The American School Board Journal,* 27–30.

Chaikind, S., Danielson, L.C., & Braven, M.L. (1993). What do we know about the costs of special education? A selected review. *Journal of Special Education, 26*(4), 344–370.

Dempsey, S., & Fuchs, D. (1993). "Flat" versus weighted "reimbursement" formulas: A longitudinal analysis of statewide special education funding practices. *Exceptional Children, 59*(5), 433–443. (From Policy Paper No. 2. Palo Alto, CA: Center for Special Education Finance, American Institutes for Research.)

Farrow, F., & Tom, J. (1992). Financing school-linked integration services. *The Future of Children, 2*(1), 56–67.

Hasazi, S.B., Liggett, A.M., & Schattman, R.A. (1994). A qualitative policy study of the least restrictive environment provision of the Individuals with Disabilities Education Act. *Exceptional Children, 60*(6), 491–507.

Hill, E.B. (1996). *Comprehensive services for students with serious emotional disturbance: An analysis of state legislation and policy.* Unpublished doctoral dissertation, The College of William and Mary, Williamsburg, Virginia.

Inclusive Education Programs. (1994). *Funding issues: Does inclusion cost more? 1*(4–5).

Individuals with Disabilities Education Act, 20 U.S.C. § 1400–1485 (1990).

Mawdsley, R.D. (1995). Does inclusion cost more? The cost of special education. *School Business Affairs, 61,* 27–31.

McCormick, C., & First, P. (1994). The cost of inclusion: Educating students with special needs. *School Business Affairs, 60,* 30–36.

McLaughlin, M., & Warren, S. (1994a). *Resource implications of inclusion: Impressions of special education administrators at selected sites* (Policy Paper No. 1). Palo Alto, CA: Center for Special Education Finance, American Institutes for Research.

McLaughlin M., & Warren, S. (1994b, November). The costs of inclusion. *The School Administrator, 51,* 8–19.

Moore, M.T., Strang, E.W., Schwartz, M., & Braddock, M. (1988). *Patterns in special education service delivery and cost.* Washington, DC: Decision Resources.

National Association of State Boards of Education. (1992). *Winners all: A call for inclusive schools.* Alexandria, VA: Author.

Parrish, T.B. (1993a, Fall). *Federal policy options for funding special education.* (Brief No. 1). Palo Alto, CA: Center for Special Education Finance.

Parrish, T.B. (1993b, Fall). *State funding provisions and least restrictive environment: Implications for federal policy* (Brief No. 2). Palo Alto, CA: Center for Special Education Finance.

Parrish, T.B. (1995, August). What is fair? Special education and finance equity. *School Business Affairs,* 26–31.

Parrish, T.B., & Verstegen, D. (1994). *Fiscal provisions of the Individuals with Disabilities Education Act: Policy issues and alternatives* (Policy Paper No. 3). Palo Alto, CA: Center for Special Education Finance, American Institutes for Research.

Rehabilitation Act of 1973, 29 U.S.C. § 794.

Shanker, A. (1994/1995). Full inclusion is neither free nor appropriate. *Educational Leadership, 52,* 18–21.

Thousand, J., & Villa, R. (1995). Inclusion: Alive and well in the Green Mountain State. *Phi Delta Kappan, 77,* 288–291.

U.S. Department of Education. (1994). *Sixteenth annual report to Congress on the implementation of The Individuals with Disabilities Education Act.* Washington, DC: Author.

U.S. Department of Education. (1995). *To assure the free appropriate public education of all children with disabilities: Seventeenth annual report to Congress on the implementation of The Individuals with Disabilities Education Act.* Washington, DC: Author.

Verstegen, D. (1995). *Consolidated special education funding and services: A federal perspective* (Policy Paper No. 6). Palo Alto, CA: Center for Special Education Finance.

Virginia Department of Education. (1996, March 29). *Statewide cost of special education in Virginia's schools.* Richmond, VA: Author.

Sources of Information Regarding Funding of Special Education

Center for Special Education Finance (CSEF)

The Center for Special Education Finance is supported through a cooperative agreement with the U.S. Department of Education, Office of Special Education Programs. Information can be obtained from:

Center for Special Education Finance
American Institutes for Research
1791 Arastradero Road
P.O. Box 1113
Palo Alto, CA 94302

Materials and publications from this center can be obtained through:

CASE Research Committee
Smith Research Center, Room 103
2805 East 10th Street
Bloomington, IN 47405

National Association of State Directors of Special Education (NASDSE)

NASDE
2021 K Street, NW
Washington, DC 20006
(202) 296-1800

U.S. Department of Education

U.S. Department of Education
Office of Special Education Programs
600 Independence Ave., SW
Washington, DC 20202-2524

CHAPTER 6

Adapting Curriculum and Instruction in Inclusive Classrooms

Alice Udvari-Solner

INTRODUCTION: THE CHALLENGE OF EDUCATING DIVERSE LEARNERS IN INCLUSIVE CLASSROOMS

An inclusive classroom is characterized by a heterogeneous group of students learning together while individual differences in culture, communication, learning styles, and preferences are acknowledged and accommodated. Students who had been previously labeled, excluded, or educated in separate settings are accepted into the membership of a general education class without conditional performance expectations or arbitrary prerequisite skills (Falvey, Givern, & Kimm, 1995; Stainback & Stainback, 1992). Specialized services and instruction are delivered and integrated within the context of general education.

The diversity inherent in such classrooms has been the impetus for significant change with regard to instructional practice and the roles and responsibilities of educators. The practices of general and special education teachers, formerly instructed and implemented in separate worlds, are now becoming blended and integrated into one body of professional knowledge. General and special educators are required to collaborate in the planning and development of curriculum and consequently carry out instruction in ways that are coordinated and complementary. Together, as educators for all children, general and special educators must critically examine their existing approaches to instruction and create learning experiences that are meaningful and appropriate for a wide range of learners. In inclusive class-

rooms, both groups of professionals must have in their repertoire the skills to link the design of curriculum and instruction with effective forms of accommodation.

This chapter provides an overview of educational practices and adaptive strategies that are effective in educating students with diverse learning needs. First, a number of best educational practices in general education are presented, which by design are inherently accommodating. Second, adaptations within curriculum and instruction are defined. Third, three approaches to the development and implementation of adaptive practices are offered. Practical considerations for evaluating the impact and effectiveness of adaptations conclude the chapter.

RESPONDING TO STUDENT DIVERSITY: BEST PRACTICES AND ADAPTIVE STRATEGIES

Best Practices in General Education That Hold Promise for Accommodating Diverse Learners

The school restructuring and reform movements of the past decade have sought to establish organizational, curricular, and instructional practices that promote democracy (Apple & Beane, 1995; Goodlad, Soder, & Sirotnik, 1990), multicultural understanding (Banks & McGee Banks, 1989; Sleeter & Grant, 1994), student-centered and process-oriented learning (Gardner, 1983; Greene, 1995; Lipsky & Gartner, 1992), and authentic views of student performance (Perrone, 1991; Wiggins, 1995). From these reforms, a number of best or promising practices have emerged that hold great promise in responding to student diversity. Several of these practices, already mentioned in Chapter 2, include heterogeneous grouping structures, cooperative learning, developmentally appropriate practice, multiple intelligences theory, and alternative assessment. The reader

The author would like to thank Maureen Keyes, Debra Enburg, and Catherine Witty for their research and summaries of information during the drafting of this chapter. Fond appreciation is expressed to Julie Frentz for her support, proofreading, and contribution of ideas.

also is referred to Udvari-Solner and Thousand (1995) for further discussion of supportive practices in general education. In addition to these approaches, a coherent/interdisciplinary curriculum, constructivist learning, and activity-based and experiential learning should be mentioned specifically, as the principal features of each practice appear to be inherently accommodating. Furthermore, the tenets underlying these practices are congruent with the philosophy of inclusive education. Consequently, where these practices are employed, all students with unique learning needs, including those with disabilities, often are able to be integrated with fewer formal or prescribed adaptations.

A Coherent/Interdisciplinary Curriculum

Teachers have long taught discipline-based information to students in isolated chunks (e.g., 50 minutes for history, followed by 50 minutes of science, followed by 50 minutes of math). Beane (1995) uses the jigsaw metaphor to describe students' typical learning experiences. Essentially, students are given a pile of jigsaw pieces—disconnected and fragmented segments of information or skills—without ever being privy to the picture the pieces were intended to construct. Educators have assumed that by teaching subject matter side-by-side or successively within a day, students will "see" the connections between these areas of content and integrate them into their thinking, thereby creating the picture in the metaphor. Palmer (1995) reports that this simply isn't happening for the majority of students and believes "they need to be consciously guided to see, discuss, internalize, and then discover the nature of the connections in what they are studying" (p. 56). The teaching and learning process described by Palmer has been referred to as an interdisciplinary, integrated, connected, or coherent curriculum.

An interdisciplinary approach is a curricular orientation involving both process and product that employs methodology and language from multiple disciplines to examine central themes, issues, problems, topics, or experiences (Jacobs, 1989; Palmer, 1995). The curriculum becomes coherent when its parts are effectively unified and connected by a sense of the whole. When a problem or issue arises in our daily lives, we bring to its solution a constellation of skills that intersect many disciplines. Interdisciplinary approaches are premised on the idea that knowledge and skills are integrated and used in real-life experiences. Thus, teachers and students must come together in a learning partnership to examine selected areas of concern in depth from complex and multiple perspectives.

Interdisciplinary orientations can promote inclusive efforts. For students with disabilities, the learning environment created by an interdisciplinary approach helps to clarify how categories of information are connected. Interdisciplinary experiences reduce the need for the student to create bridges between seemingly unrelated splinters of information. Therefore, generalization of information and the transfer of skills from one setting to another, difficult tasks for many students with unique learning needs, are addressed in the design of the curriculum. Students not only are encouraged to see the connections but are provided a context to blend the use of several different skills to approach an obstacle. Thus, opportunities are created for integrated problem solving that more closely resemble those encountered in postschool life. Students with unique learning needs have consistently been challenged in general education classrooms to keep up with an endless barrage of content-oriented facts, details, and particulars. For many, selecting and using the most meaningful information is an insurmountable challenge. A commitment to an interdisciplinary approach almost always requires teachers to rethink the way areas of study are selected, deciding not only what should be taught, but what should be eliminated. The extent of discipline-based content that can be addressed must be streamlined, thereby emphasizing quality and relevance over quantity (Ackerman & Perkins, 1989).

Constructivist Learning

Constructivism is a theory about learning and knowledge. Learning, within the paradigm of constructivism, is defined as a "process by which new meanings are created (constructed) by the learner within the context of . . . current knowledge" (Poplin & Stone, 1992, p. 161). Questioning, observing, and developing skills and new knowledge are prompted when students seek to resolve incongruities between old patterns and new experiences (Sergiovanni, 1994). Thus, in constructivist classrooms teachers act as facilitators to bring together a balance of novel and unfamiliar activities. Instructional activities are designed for students to gain information by experiencing concepts so that new information can be connected meaningfully to what is already known. The relationship and dialogue between teacher and student and among students are an essential vehicle for refining ideas and cementing new learning (Grennon-Brooks & Brooks, 1993; Poplin & Stone, 1992).

Constructivist teaching and learning processes can support the inclusion of a student with disabilities in the following ways. The perception of the learner by teachers who use constructivist theory is that each person—regardless of his or her academic history, diagnosed disability, or educational characteristics—is capable of constructing knowledge. Teachers expect that *all* students will learn, acknowledging that learning will most likely take place in different ways and at different rates. Learning is viewed as an intrinsic ability that requires the teacher to use multiple methods to assist students to demonstrate their knowledge. Consequently, adaptation and individualization are commonplace and available to all children (Udvari-Solner, 1996b).

Constructivist teachers present concepts to students holistically as opposed to fragmenting a concept into sequential steps or skills (Poplin & Stone, 1992). Thus, students are exposed to and involved with more complete and complex concepts without having to demonstrate an arbitrary or unrelated set of prerequisite academic skills. After "seeing" a concept in its entirety, learning essential skills or parts of the whole can be more meaningful.

Lessons are designed to be open-ended and have built-in flexibility to allow for individual accommodation. The aim is to create a context for learning; each student, however, enters the setting with a different level of understanding and with different personal strategies for negotiating the learning experience. Students' suppositions and viewpoints shape the sequence of curriculum. Consequently, teachers in these settings foster a dynamic and changeable atmosphere. Rigid adherence to a standard sequence of study is antithetical to the learning processes that are to be fostered.

A critical tenet of constructivism is that knowledge is socially and culturally mediated. Therefore, joint inquiry among students and collaborative discourse are encouraged. These interactive experiences establish the opportunity for learners with disabilities to observe the thinking and problem-solving processes of peers, thus advancing their own personal strategies.

Activity-Based and Experiential Learning

When teachers use interdisciplinary or constructivist orientations, the nature or form of the learning experience becomes activity-based or experiential. Activity-based or experiential learning is characterized by students engaged in discovery; movement; interaction with the environment; manipulation of materials or variables; and using reading, writing, and communication skills with a clear purpose (Stover, Neubert, & Lawlor, 1993; Udvari-Solner, 1994). This orientation promotes planning, self-management, group processing skills, and critical thinking. Children are naturally curious and have an inherent need to explore and manipulate. Sergiovanni (1994) indicates that this need should be fulfilled by engaging in multisensory experiences with real things—that is, objects, events, processes, and relationships. When students are physically active in carrying out processes and procedures that are concrete and real, information is retained in a manner that facilitates recall and retention. These learning conditions facilitate integration and application of skills, and promote the conceptualization of new information.

Students with diverse learning needs often are unable to learn, retain, and apply knowledge when skills are presented in isolation or in a passive mode—common in classrooms where lecture and independent seat work are primary forms of instruction. Students with disabilities often benefit from the opportunity to experience learning in actual and realis-

tic contexts. The act of engaging in meaningful activity may allow students to demonstrate their knowledge or skills in ways that may not be evident or elicited during conventional learning situations. Because experiential lessons use real-life activities and real-life materials, the need to generalize or transfer skills from one setting to another is decreased (Udvari-Solner, 1994). Through the means of activity, significant factors are remembered and applied. The process of remembering and visualizing the activity at a later date can assist students with disabilities in grasping and retaining the concept.

Activity-based and experiential learning provide an opportunity to use a variety of environments where learning can take place. Beyond the use of school environments, instruction can take place in the community where skills necessary to lifelong functioning can be taught and applied (Ford & Davern, 1989; Udvari-Solner & Thousand, 1996). Students with and without disabilities are enabled to connect with the larger community and learn skills in settings that are personally meaningful and prepare them for postschool functioning.

Creating Individualized Adaptations in the Context of General Education

An *educational adaptation* can be defined as any adjustment or modification in (1) learning expectations, (2) curriculum content, (3) the physical and sociocultural environment, (4) organization of the lesson or delivery of instruction, (5) the materials or media used for learning, (6) ancillary support, (7) classroom management, and (8) evaluation strategies that enhance a person's performance or allow at least partial participation in an activity (Cohen & Lynch, 1991; Udvari-Solner, 1995). Implicit in this definition is that adaptation must occur on two levels: *what* to teach and *how* to teach. The question regarding what concepts and content to teach is a curriculum decision. After curriculum development is completed, the curriculum can be used for instructional design or the details of how to teach.

Curriculum can be conceptualized as the selection of content and the planned learning experiences that have intended educational outcomes (Armstrong, 1990; Hoover, 1988). Adaptation to or differentiation in curriculum are variations in the scope, depth, breadth, and complexity of what is taught. Traditionally, our schools have offered a narrow band of issues and content to students. Much curriculum content is based upon preestablished genres and categories and predefined bodies of knowledge (Grennon-Brooks & Brooks, 1993; Stainback, Stainback, & Moravec, 1992). Sergiovanni (1994) indicates that content or curriculum must be viewed as more than subject matter. Content that is embedded in an environment of people, things, and symbols is the vehicle through which the child acquires the values, concepts, information, opinions, techniques, learning strategies, and skills. Therefore, the teacher and student should be involved in choosing content. To effectively teach students with diverse learning needs in general education classrooms, such a student-centered approach must be adopted. When curriculum is predefined and inflexible, educators start with the curriculum instead of the student. Instead, learner outcomes that consider what the student already knows and what he or she needs to know should direct curriculum development. The heterogeneous nature of inclusive classrooms presumes that students will have multilevel curricular goals and, therefore, the curriculum must be multilevel as well.

Flexible, multilevel, or student-specific learning outcomes allow educators and parents to define individualized curricular goals that are based upon the learner's unique needs, skills, interests, and abilities. These student-specific learning outcomes, in turn, affect the scope and orientation of the curriculum. Student-specific learning outcomes may be designed to (1) relate to the same curricular content with the focus being more or less complex; (2) address the same content but require the student to use different response modes to demonstrate his or her knowledge (e.g., to speak rather than write, to point rather than speak) (Nevin, 1993); (3) increase or decrease the rate of completion or pacing of the content; (4) change the expectations in the level of mastery, degree of quality, or quantity of the curricular requirements; and (5) focus on similar content but with functional applications.

Figure 6–1 illustrates curriculum in a fifth-grade unit of study that has been differentiated based upon the needs of a range of learners. The focus of study was the broad topic of inventions and discoveries. In the past, the teacher had centered the curriculum on famous inventors and their inventions throughout history. Students engaged in individual research/book reports regarding an inventor of their choice. The basic learning outcomes that guided the selection of curriculum included the following:

- Identify well-known inventions and associate them with their originators.
- Use research skills to prepare a 5- to 10-minute report about a specific inventor and his or her inventions.
- Situate inventions and inventors in a historical time-line.

Within this class were a number of students with a proclivity toward math and science, as well as a student with severe multiple disabilities. More appropriate learning outcomes for those students who required a more complex orientation were:

- Trace the development of knowledge of a specific invention.

- Compare and contrast past and modern inventions that have evolved or been transformed by new technology (e.g., the introduction of the microchip to telecommunications, the evolution of the record to compact disk technology).
- Predict, speculate, or theorize a future invention/discovery. State the rationale for your prediction.

For the student with disabilities to participate effectively, his learning outcomes required an applied, practical approach to the subject:

- Participate in the design, construction, and marketing of an invention that can be used in your personal life.
- Use planning, budgeting, and purchasing skills to construct the invention.
- Employ communication and cooperation skills to work with a small group in the development of an invention.

Attention to these multilevel outcomes allowed the curriculum to include investigations into contemporary and local inventions and an experiential approach to the design and development of inventions. The shaded branch of the figure indicates the area of primary study for the student with the most significant disabilities. However, the three strands of study represented here improve and enrich the overall curriculum.

As exemplified in Figure 6–1, the inclusion of students with unique learning needs can be a needed catalyst to reexamine the existing curriculum and expand the learning options for all students.

Instructional Modifications To Achieve Student-Specific Curricular Goals

Instructional adaptations in the areas of classroom environment, organization of the lesson or delivery of instruction, the materials or media used for learning, ancillary support, management techniques, and evaluation strategies are far too extensive for a comprehensive listing here. Appropriate selection of instructional approaches is logical only when presented in concert with the needs of a specific learner. Wang (1991) stated that teachers who are effective in creating appropriate adaptations

> know the subject matter and their students. They know what individual students can do, their unique learning styles, and their characteristic behaviors in a variety of instructional-learning situations. They incorporate information about their students when adapting their instruction and prescribing learning activities that enhance students' ability to profit from instruction. (p. 146)

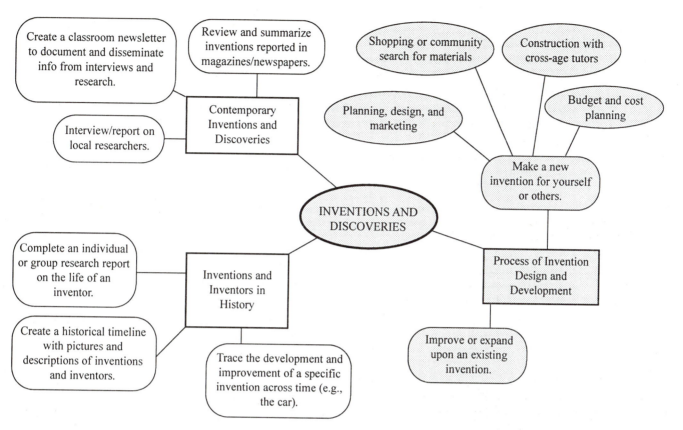

Figure 6–1 Curriculum options for a fifth-grade unit in the study of inventions and discoveries. The shaded branch indicates the area of primary study for the student with the most significant disabilities.

Students will vary in their need for adaptation. The changes for some students will be complex and comprehensive; for others, cursory or superficial variations will suffice. To address these extensive and individualized decisions, a range of instructional accommodations is illustrated within the sections that follow.

THREE APPROACHES TO ADAPTING CURRICULUM AND INSTRUCTION

As the professional lives of general and special educators overlap within inclusive classrooms, tools for communication, decision making, and classroom organization become critical. In this section, three approaches or models to planning, adapting, and implementing instructional practices are described. The first approach, advanced by Giangreco, Cloninger, Dennis, and Edelman (1994) uses the Osborn-Parnes creative problem-solving (CPS) model as a general strategy for defining critical issues and generating potential solutions in inclusive settings. The second approach is a more specific decision-making process developed by Udvari-Solner (1995; in press) that uses a series of distinct reflective questions to guide the dialogue of educators as

they collaboratively design curriculum and instruction. Third, the adaptive learning environments model (ALEM), developed by Wang (1980), provides a method of classroom operation and organization that embeds strategies of accommodation into daily practice.

The Osborn-Parnes Creative Problem-Solving Model

Originally developed by Alex Osborn (1953) and elaborated over time by Sidney Parnes, the Osborn-Parnes CPS model (Parnes, 1992) has been applied in both business and educational settings. Giangreco et al. (1994) have suggested that teachers who work in inclusive settings can benefit from the use of this model "to address—individually or in groups—a range of academic, social, or personal challenges" (p. 330). The process involved in the model can assist teachers to engage in inventive thought, organize their thinking, and generate multiple solutions for involving students with disabilities in the general education classroom. CPS includes the components of visioning or objective finding, fact finding, problem finding, idea finding, solution finding, and acceptance finding. Following is an overview of these components and the advantages of establishing this process as an integral part of collaborative planning.

Visioning or Objective Finding

During the first stage of CPS, educational personnel are in a position to decide among a number of objectives that are most critical in fulfilling the student's educational needs. It is important that the chosen objective be small enough to be accomplished during a designated period of time. The old cliché "pick your battles carefully" is apropos. In doing so, there is greater likelihood that the objective will be achieved. Furthermore, working to solve smaller, yet still high-priority components can seem more manageable or achievable by a team. When success is experienced in one area, team members often become more willing and motivated to work on more difficult challenges. Objective finding requires parents, teachers, and resource personnel to perform as a team to (1) identify the potential areas that require problem solving, (2) determine which of those areas is the first to be addressed, and (3) commit to developing creative solutions to improve educational programming. Participants in the CPS process are encouraged to move from divergent to convergent thinking by first generating a range of potential problems that need resolution, then narrowing the focus by selecting a primary issue for deliberation.

To illustrate each step of the CPS process, a student case example is offered. Abby is a sixth-grade student with learning disabilities that affect her reading, writing, expression, and organizational skills. She is a shy young woman, often choosing to be on the periphery of social and interactive activities. To those who know her learning style, she is a serious and conscientious student. However, due to difficulties in spelling, writing, and expressive skills, it is laborious for her to transfer her thoughts to paper. When given sufficient time and support to organize her ideas, she can be extremely thoughtful and perceptive. When faced with a challenging academic task, she will attempt it only with ongoing and intensive assistance from a teacher or other adult. If adult assistance is not available, she would rather not complete the activity than complete it incorrectly. To teachers unfamiliar with Abby, this coping strategy is often misinterpreted as laziness or unwillingness to try. Abby tends to seek out the company of younger children rather than children her age. In the presence of younger children, she is a natural storyteller and enjoys embellishing traditional stories and folktales.

During the visioning or objective-finding phase, Abby's team identified the following challenging time periods or activities during which Abby depends upon adult assistance or struggles to participate: test taking across subject areas, presenting orally, having an active role in the sixth-grade play, initiating conversations with peers during lunch or unstructured study halls, and engaging in journal writing. Journal writing was selected as a high-priority area because it is a daily activity, and solutions for participation would affect her performance throughout the week. The writing, reading, and language skills required in this activity are current learning objectives in Abby's individual educational program. Additionally, the adaptations generated for this activity would likely apply to similar language and writing-based activities expected at the secondary level.

Fact Finding

During this particular stage, the team generates descriptive facts related to the objective of primary importance. Careful anecdotal records should be maintained pertaining to each team member's ideas. At this point, it is more important that the team list as many ideas as possible and not be concerned about explanations or justifications. Only five to eight minutes should be allocated for fact finding. Fact finding helps the team to clarify realities and define the problem, thereby creating a context from which to generate solutions. A selected listing of facts about journal writing generated by Abby's team is presented in Exhibit 6–1.

Giangreco et al. (1994) offer the following tips to increase the likelihood that a larger pool of ideas will be generated:

- Rely upon all perceptions including feelings and emotional responses to describe what is known about the challenge.
- Use "who, what, why, where, when, and how" questions to clarify the details and circumstances around the issue.
- Accept a divergent list of ideas without focusing concern upon the appropriateness of those particular thoughts. At this point accept them as matter of fact to perpetuate the accumulation of ideas from each of the team participants. Allow members to speak of aspects beyond the obvious or concrete.
- Formulate a subset of facts to assist problem solving during the subsequent stage of CPS.
- Carefully record all of the ideas shared during the process of fact finding to enable the team to reflect upon them during later stages of CPS.

Problem Finding

The purpose of problem finding is to delineate the target problem more clearly. To facilitate problem definition, the team identifies alternative ways of viewing the issue. This process can be prompted by adopting the positive starter phrase, "In what ways might we . . . ?" In Abby's case, the starter phrase yielded this question: "In what ways might we assist Abby to generate ideas for her daily journal and to express her thoughts in a manner that does not require extensive writing?" The problem was framed in yet another way by this question: "In what ways might we reduce the emphasis on independent seat work and individual writing

Exhibit 6–1 Fact Finding, Problem Finding, Idea Finding, and Solution Finding for Participation in Journal Writing

Note: Shading indicates viable solutions identified by the team based upon the evaluation criteria represented in column IV (see text for full discussion).

I Fact Finding	II Problem Finding	III Idea Finding	IV Solution Finding — Addresses Student's Learning Objectives	Facilitates Interactions/ Relationships	Enhances Status and Is Acceptable to the Student	Is Feasible To Implement by Education
1. Students reflect on an activity or event in their day.		Use voice-activated word-processing program to "write" journal entry.	–	–		–
2. Students write a one-page description in their journals.	"In what ways might we assist Abby to generate ideas for her journal and to express her thoughts in a manner that does not require extensive writing?"	Allow "talk" time between pairs of students to share events/ feelings. Sample questions to guide dialogue are given to entire class.	+	+	+	+
3. Students refer to a previous day's work to edit, elaborate, or write a response.		Abby dictates her ideas to a peer.	+	+	+	+
4. Teacher circulates among students to review selected passages and provide feedback on grammar/style.		Generate writing ideas by passing a paper among students in a round robin fashion. Ideas are used as starters for all students.	+	+	+	+
5. Students work alone.		Abby audiotapes her ideas and transcribes them during study hall.	+	–	+	–
6. The room is silent.		Students work in writing pairs to provide feedback, ask questions, and prompt elaboration.	+	+	+	+
7. Some students seem to want time to talk about important or stressful events.		Students are given option of compiling a video journal.	–	+	+	–
8. Abby is able to write three or four sentences in the time other students write one page.		Abby carries handheld tape recorder to capture thoughts/events during nonschool hours.	+	–	–	+
9. Abby's entries are usually simple, without much detail.		Allow Abby to draft short stories that are read to younger students in a cross-age peer tutor relationship.	+	+	+	+
10. When Abby is asked to describe what she wants to write about, she typically says "Don't know."						
11. After asking Abby a number of leading questions (e.g., did you see anyone this weekend?), she will begin to talk about the event in expanded and rich detail.						

while encouraging interaction, collaboration, and sharing of reflective thought between Abby and her classmates?" One can see how the problem is more clearly identified in these statements than at the beginning of the process. Further, one question focuses on how the task might be changed for Abby, while the second question addresses the structure of the existing activity and the participation of all students. This step should be repeated until the team identifies a statement that best represents the issues that they feel should be addressed (Giangreco, 1993). The team should also be careful to ensure that consensus has been reached among all of its members. It is only after this phase of CPS that ideas and solutions to the problem may be explored.

Idea Finding

During this phase of CPS, it is useful for team members to implement a brainstorming approach to proliferate a number of ideas that may later become solutions to the challenge statement. This phase, too, should be limited to 5 to 10 minutes, with ideas being presented in single words or short phrases, as opposed to full sentences. The goal here is to accumulate as many ideas as possible from each of the team participants. Once a list of ideas has been generated, it is then possible for some of the ideas to be combined and communicated as potential solutions. A partial listing of solutions for Abby is provided in column III of Exhibit 6–1.

Solution Finding

The stage of solution finding requires that participants analyze carefully each of the ideas generated during the preceding stage. It is during this stage that the team members will determine the importance and feasibility of incorporating various accommodations. According to Giangreco (1993), this procedure can best be facilitated by the use of a matrix. In such a matrix, the "ideas" are listed down one side and the "criteria for selection" appear across the top. Options for rating systems include a plus or minus notation or a weighted score for each criterion. The resulting visual representation allows participants to consider the virtues of each potential solution. A standard set of criteria by which all ideas are compared does not exist. Instead, teams are encouraged to determine the most appropriate criteria for the child, the issue, and the setting. Critical criteria for the evaluation of the ideas developed by Abby's team are represented in column IV of Exhibit 6–1. As a result of the evaluation, five ideas emerged as viable; these are highlighted in column III of Exhibit 6–1. These solutions could be implemented separately or combined into a more complex plan of accommodation.

Acceptance Finding

The last stage of CPS is characterized by the development of an agreed-upon plan of action. Minimally, the plan should articulate the following: what needs to be done, the person(s) responsible, and a timeline for completion or implementation. Additionally, it is necessary for the team to continually evaluate the effectiveness of the prescribed plan and provide follow-up information that may indicate the need for further changes or improvements.

The basic elements of the CPS process have been described here. There are many nuances and useful variations to this process that aid in idea generation. For more detailed treatment of this approach, the reader is referred to the original sources by Osborn and Parnes. Giangreco and his colleagues (1994) have enriched and expanded upon the generic problem-solving model by capitalizing on the involvement and creative power of nondisabled peers. In variations of the CPS approach, the teacher serves as facilitator and students fill roles as problem solvers. The variations are designed expressly for classes where students display a diversity of ability levels and characteristics.

The Osborn-Parnes CPS model is one tool that teams can use to implement effective solutions to curricular and educational issues that can arise in inclusive settings. The general problem-solving structure lends itself to a variety of situations and could be infused easily into weekly or biweekly planning sessions among educators. The process is simple, requiring no expert knowledge to be a meaningful contributor. Thus, it is conducive to and improved by the involvement of parents and peers. This method requires participants to analyze problem issues collectively and proactively and to engage in the process of evaluation after programmatic changes have occurred.

A Reflective Decision-Making Process for Designing Curricular Adaptations

The Decision-Making Process As a Reflective Protocol

Teachers, both general and special, are beginning to define their professional teaching behaviors by using the term *reflective practice* (Liston & Zeichner, 1986; Prawat, 1991). Examples and references of reflective teaching practices are found in the literature, dating back to the early 1900s (Brubacher, Case, & Reagan, 1994). A definition for reflective practice found within current literature states: "It is an integrated way of thinking and acting focused on learning and behavioral change; it is individuals working to improve organizations through improving themselves" (Osterman & Kottkamp, 1993, p. 1). For Dewey (as cited in Brubacher et al., 1994), "true reflective practice takes place only when the individual is faced with a real problem that he or she needs to resolve and seeks to resolve that problem in a rational manner" (p. 19). Successful inclusion rests upon practices and methods that engage and challenge all learners—a pressing problem needing rational solutions.

The reflective decision-making process articulated by Udvari-Solner (1995; in press) provides an effective tool for general and special educators to frame pedagogical discussions and begin to generate solutions for the very real day-to-day challenges of accommodation. This reflective decision-making process resulted from a research study designed to document and promote innovative strategies for including students with disabilities in general education classrooms (Udvari-Solner, 1996a; in press). During the first phase of the study, an attempt was made to reconstruct the thinking and planning process in which teachers engage, either alone or in teams, to design effective curricular adaptations. Teachers who were particularly successful instructing students with significant learning differences were constantly questioning, assessing, and retooling their practice; essentially, they engaged in reflective thinking. Specifically, educators reflected upon the content and structure of their teaching in relationship to nontraditional learners. Teachers who were most effective made modifications in the way the overall lesson was designed, which included devising student-specific outcomes, instructional groupings and instructional sequences that promoted active participation, and individually appropriate teaching strategies. When these forms of modifications were "front-loaded" (determined at the onset of lesson planning), the learner's needs were accommodated in an unobtrusive manner. The need for intensive, specialized support, modified materials, or changes in the environment appeared to lessen when well-conceived and interactive lessons were in place. The decision-making process is designed to be used by teams of educators during weekly curriculum planning meetings. The protocol is student-specific so the involvement of parents in the design process is desired and valued. As teams become adept at using the process, they can move from the discussion of one student to the needs of any learner who poses unique challenges in the classroom.

To depict and promote critical reflection, a protocol was developed mirroring teacher thinking, talk, or dialogue that shaped the development and infusion of curricular adaptations in lesson design. A series of questions, presented below, is used to represent key decisions in the planning process. In practice, these questions have served to structure the interaction among team members so that each form of adaptation is considered and the least obtrusive means of modification are appraised first.

1. *Can the student actively participate in the lesson without modifications and achieve the same essential outcomes as peers without disabilities?* This is an important starting point. If the answer to this question is "no," the team must select or design appropriate adaptations represented in subsequent questions of the decision-making process.

2. *Is it necessary to identify student-specific learning outcomes?* If a learner cannot achieve the same outcome as classmates, then teachers must be explicit about the student-specific goals that are necessary for the individual to benefit from the lesson. As mentioned earlier, when student-specific goals are articulated, they may be a catalyst for reexamining the appropriateness of the curriculum for all students and therefore prompt the process of differentiation. Evaluation (e.g., assessment or grading) and management strategies are also defined when student-specific outcomes are developed.

3. *Can the student's participation be increased by changing the instructional arrangement?* Instructional arrangements are the configurations teachers use to group students for teaching. Instructional arrangements dictate whether a student will be working alone, functioning as part of a large group, or operating in coordination with a small number of classmates. Changes in instructional arrangement from traditional whole group and independent seat work to small groups, cooperative groups, peer partnerships, or peer-tutoring systems offer many more opportunities for students with disabilities to be actively engaged, act as initiators, interact with others (both with teachers and classmates), and receive spontaneous support from their peers and the general educator.

4. *Can the student's participation be increased by changing the lesson format?* The use of activity-based, experiential, and community-referenced lesson formats is considered at this juncture. Teachers should consider process-oriented and interactive formats such as games, role-plays, simulations, and exhibitions of learning in lieu of lessons based upon the traditional lecture-demonstration-practice format.

5. *Can the student's participation and understanding be increased by changing the delivery of instruction or general educator's teaching style?* All elements of teaching style should be considered: language, vocabulary, speech, cues, prompts, pacing, physical proximity, frequency of interaction and feedback, and the manner in which criticism or encouragement is given. When educators consciously and selectively engineer their teaching style relative to particular learners, appropriate student-specific teaching strategies are designed.

6. *Can changes be made in the physical or social classroom environment that will facilitate participation?* Changes in lighting, positioning of materials, the removal or addition of specific equipment, and the student's location in the classroom are potential physical modifications to the setting. Teachers should observe for any intermittent auditory and visual dis-

tractions (e.g., chair movement, pencil sharpeners, hall movement, audiovisual equipment noise). Educators may also need to attend to the implicit and explicit rules and symbols that establish a social climate and classroom culture.

7. *Will different instructional materials be needed to ensure participation?* Adaptive materials may be needed for students who do not acquire information or express their knowledge in conventional ways (e.g., through reading, writing, speech). Materials should be designed to allow several modes of input to and provide multiple modes of output by the student. To design modified materials for any subject area, it is helpful to identify the conceptual, academic, and communication skills needed to participate in upcoming learning activities. The materials that are developed should compensate for, replace, or help to strengthen skills within weak performance areas. For example, the team determines that the skills needed to conduct a science experiment and record the results on a graph are: writing, reading, note taking, measuring, and plotting a graph. Materials specific to each performance area can then be developed to promote the student's active participation and learning (e.g., directions may be audiotaped, a three-dimensional graph may be constructed with manipulable objects, and measuring cups may be marked with raised and colored lines). These material changes then can be employed any time similar skills are required across activities and subject areas.

8. *Will personal assistance be needed in the form of natural support and supervision to ensure participation?* The nature of the activity defines the method and frequency of support; thus, accurate supervision and support plans are best devised after all the previous forms of adaptations have been established. Spontaneous and planned assistance from peers and general educators are highly preferred methods of support and should be considered first before employing specialized personnel.

9. *Is it necessary to design an alternative activity for the student and a small group of peers?* An alternative activity is defined as a learning experience that is most often activity-based, experiential, or community-referenced, which includes the student with disabilities and a small group of peers without disabilities. The activity relates to the curricular content of the class and must be meaningful and age-appropriate for all students involved (Udvari-Solner, 1995). An alternative activity may be designed to supplement or replace classroom experiences when the previous forms of adaptation have been inadequate in addressing the student's learning priorities.

The essential elements of the decision-making process are illustrated in a planning form shown in Exhibit 6–2. The form was developed in coordination with educational planning teams to prompt team members to employ the process in an efficient and coordinated manner.

Case Study: Designing Curricular Adaptations Using the Reflective Decision-Making Process

The reflective decision-making process is exemplified below in a case drawn from a high school sophomore ceramics class that has as one of its members a student with significant multiple disabilities, named Travis. Although several students with unique educational needs are present in the class, the adaptations developed for Travis are the focus of this illustration. Travis has a visual impairment, moderate intellectual disabilities, and cerebral palsy that causes low muscle tone affecting his fine motor skills. He is somewhat unstable when standing and uses a walker to guide his gait. Travis uses a limited range of single words for expression but understands conversational language. Note that the descriptions associated with each form of adaptation are presented in a slightly different order from the sequence of questions in the decision-making process. This variation was made to better communicate the case example to the reader.

The current unit of study within the ceramics course is the sculpting of human forms. The art instructor originally intended each student to fashion a human figure in the style of an abstract or realist sculptor. The instructor required individual research reports about the sculptor and oral presentations illustrating how the artist's techniques were incorporated into student representations. Given the individual and academic nature of this project, Travis would be unable to participate without intensive assistance from an adult. Using the decision-making process, the lesson was transformed in the following ways.

Instructional Arrangement and Lesson Format. The individual art project was changed to a cooperative group arrangement. Teams of three students were assigned to work together to develop a "progressive" sculpture. Each team selected an artist to emulate.

Realism includes the work of such masters as Degas, Rodin, and Michelangelo. Nonobjective or abstract artists include Picasso, Henry Moore, and Archipenko. Travis was assigned to a group working with abstract techniques. The less restrictive methods used to craft the final product in an abstract style were a good match with Travis's motor abilities. The sculpture was developed sequentially and progressively among the team members. Starting with a lump of clay, one member added an element, then passed the piece in a round-robin fashion to the next member, who added another element or refined the previous feature. In this manner, Travis could contribute elements to the sculpture with-

Exhibit 6–2 A Planning Form To Prompt the Use of Reflective Decision-Making Process To Design Curricular Adaptations

CURRENT INSTRUCTIONAL PLAN Date:	DO CHANGES NEED TO BE MADE IN:	
Content area/subject or theme: Instructor(s): Estimated time: Activity: Materials:	**Instructional Arrangement** ___ Cooperative groups ___ Cooperative structures (e.g., jigsaw, think-pair-share, say and switch) ___ Peer partnerships ___ Small group _____ Student-directed _____ Teacher-directed ___ Peer or cross-age tutor ___ Other **Curricular Goals/Learning Outcomes** ___ Adjust performance standards ___ Adjust pacing ___ Reduce complexity ___ Adjust functional/direct applications ___ Adjust the grading/evaluation system ___ Adjust behavior management system ___ Other **Natural Support/Personal Assistance** ___ General educator ___ Peers ___ Special educator ___ Therapist ___ Paraprofessional ___ Volunteer ___ Other What does the support look like and how frequently will it be provided?	**Lesson Format** ___ Interdisciplinary/thematic ___ Self-directed study ___ Language experience approach ___ Group investigation ___ Discovery learning ___ Learning centers ___ Demonstrations ___ Activity-based ___ Games ___ Role-plays/simulations ___ Multimedia ___ Experiential **Social/Physical Environmental Conditions or Lesson Location** ___ With selected others ___ In specified classrooms ___ In another part of school building ___ In the community ___ Altered environmental factors (light, sound, physical access) ___ Change or develop social rules ___ Other **Alternative Activity or Additional Adaptations** The alternative activity should: ___ include the student with disabilities and a partner or small group of peers without disabilities ___ be similar or related to the curricular content of the class ___ be meaningful and age-appropriate for all students involved Potential location for the alternative activity: ___ within the classroom ___ within other general education settings in the school (e.g., computer lab) ___ in the community	**Student-Specific Teaching Strategies** ___ Adjust sequence of instruction ___ Repeat key points/directions ___ Periodically check performance ___ Provide physical guidance/prompts ___ Back up verbal instruction with other modes of input ___ Foreshadow events, concepts ___ Use clear, concise language, reduce unnecessary information ___ Provide demonstrations, role-plays while using concrete materials and props ___ Other **Modified Materials** What skills will be used within the lesson? ___ Note taking ___ Reading ___ Writing ___ Test taking ___ Computer skills ___ Math skills ___ Oral presentation skills ___ Musical, art, or physical performance skills Will the materials associated with these skill areas need to be changed to ensure that the student can access information and express his/her knowledge?

out the expectation of completing a figure single-handedly. He could easily add essential features (e.g., the head, arms, legs) while other team members stylized the attribute.

The academic component was also transformed from an individual to a group research assignment. Each week, student groups devoted two class periods to the development of their sculpture and two class periods to research. Travis's participation in this aspect of the lesson is addressed within the section outlining alternative activities.

Student-Specific Learning Outcomes. The general goals for the class were to research the work of a master sculptor and incorporate elements of his or her style and techniques into the development of a personal sculpture. Travis's desired learning outcomes reflected his need to develop better communication and fine motor skills. These goals included: engaging in reciprocal interactions with peers; requesting assistance from others; speaking in two-word combinations; communicating key concepts using speech, gestures, and picture representations; and improving dexterity and hand strength through the preparation and manipulation of the clay. The cooperative and progressive nature of the art project allowed Travis to have multiple opportunities to interact for the purpose of building communication while engaging in an artistic venture.

Teaching Style and Delivery of Instruction. To explain the procedures of constructing a progressive sculpture, the art instructor enlisted Travis's group to demonstrate the process for the entire class. Acting as a member of this demonstration/role-play, the instructor was able to illustrate how the sculpture should be passed to each member and also modeled positive communication skills in the provision of feedback and criticism. Using Travis's group as part of the demonstration enabled the instructor to nonchalantly prompt interactions and facilitate contributions by Travis. As students began working in teams, the art instructor dropped into a group as a member to demonstrate, guide, or advance their techniques. The instructor provided physical guidance and positive encouragement to Travis each time he sat in as a member of his group.

Environmental Considerations. The tall workstations in the art room required class members to stand or sit on high stools. Given Travis's physical need for stability, his group used a round table with conventional chairs as their work space. The smaller table also created a more relaxed and supportive social climate for the group, thus enhancing face-to-face interactions.

Instructional Materials. To select an artist for the project, Travis's group used a series of pictures representing the most famous and recognizable works. This activity allowed Travis to make an informed choice in the selection of a sculptor. The nature of the activity and the use of abstract techniques eliminated the need for more complex material changes.

Support and Supervision. Natural support for Travis was intrinsic to this cooperative project. Peers within the group provided spontaneous and ongoing prompts, cues, and guidance as the sculpture moved from person to person. The art teacher had consciously engineered this support by visiting each group every 10 to 15 minutes. Consequently, he was able to catch any potential breakdowns in communication or cooperation that occurred with Travis. Specialists were present in the classroom on alternate days. The special educator was present during one project and one research day; during this time, she acted in a team-teaching capacity with the art instructor. The speech-language pathologist and occupational therapist also offered support by periodically joining Travis's group to model instructive techniques.

Alternative Activities. An alternative activity was designed for Travis and his group members to carry out the academic research component of the project. As originally designed, the group research report offered few avenues for Travis's meaningful participation. An alternative activity was designed by the general and special educators that would be enriching for all of the group members by connecting them with the local art community. Travis's group was assigned to interview a local sculptor about his artistic influences, videotape the interview, and take slides of his work to share with the class. This alternative activity took the group into the community and ultimately brought the community back to the classroom. The research team had to generate appropriate questions for the artist, summarize and present the information, and use video and slides to supplement their presentation. Using a series of pictures representing the work of key artists, Travis participated in the interview by asking the sculptor about his influences. To clarify his speech in the interview, Travis was equipped with a communication card stating: "Which artist(s) have influenced your style as a sculptor? Please point to the picture(s)." Travis also had a role in taking slides of the artist and his studio. During the presentation, Travis shared the response to his interview question by showing the pictures selected by the artist. He was also in charge of operating the slide projector and offering one- to two-word statements about each image. Further explanations were provided by group members to clarify or expand upon Travis's contribution.

The process of decision making presented here serves teams as a recall protocol to prompt dialogue and ensure that learners' needs are being considered. For those using this process, the sequence of questions and categories of adaptations provide team members with a shared or common language with which to structure discussion, thus improving efficiency and understanding in communication. The decision-making process can provide a workable template on which to base joint teaching decisions for educational support teams implementing inclusive educational practices.

Adaptive Learning Environments Model

The adaptive learning environments model (ALEM), developed and extensively field-tested by Wang (1980), establishes a classroom instructional model aimed at accommodating heterogeneous learners. Originally developed for preschool and early elementary grades, ALEM has since been extended and applied in secondary settings (Wang & Birch, 1984; Wang & Zollers, 1990). A basic tenet of ALEM is that the diverse academic and social needs of all students, including students with exceptional talents or special needs, can be met in a regular classroom setting. Individual differences are accommodated through the use of a variety of instructional methods, alternative learning sequences, and options. Special services are delivered based on individual needs. This approach differs significantly from traditional approaches of grouping students by ability or diagnostic labels.

Many of the elements in ALEM are not new or radical in and of themselves. What is unique about this approach is that it systematically integrates the components of adaptive instruction with classroom management and resource supports to make a comprehensive program. Five major components of ALEM outlined by Epps and Tindal (1987) are: (1) a basic skills curriculum of highly structured learning activities and more open-ended exploratory learning activities that are derived from diagnostic-prescriptive information about the student; (2) an instructional/learning management system designed to maximize the use of classroom and school resources such as curricular materials and time; (3) planned and coordinated family involvement to interface school and home learning experiences; (4) a team system, bringing together general educators, specialists, and other resource personnel in flexible instructional arrangements; and (5) a data-based staff development program for training personnel in the philosophy and implementation of ALEM.

An expected outcome of ALEM is that "students will become more competent and confident in their abilities to successfully acquire skills in academic learning and in the management of the classroom environment" (Wang, 1992, p. 101). When ALEM is implemented effectively, findings have shown it to decrease student-teacher interactions for management purposes and increase student self-responsibility for managing behavior. Also noted were higher levels of student-initiated interactions with teacher(s) for instructional purposes, increased time on task, and increased time spent in cooperative learning. Overall, students in a classroom using ALEM tend to demonstrate greater perceptions of self-competence and academic gains.

ALEM is a multicomponent approach that influences classroom structure, instructional design, and service delivery. The primary design features that promote adaptation for students with unique learning needs are delineated and described below. (ALEM also has design features to provide district-wide and schoolwide support for implementation [i.e., the data-based staff development program], but they are not addressed here.)

The Diagnostic-Prescriptive Process

A key element of success in an educational setting is the accurate identification of student learning needs. Entry-level learning behavior and performance of each student with and without disabilities are assessed in the basic subject matter areas using criterion-referenced and curriculum-based diagnostic techniques. Individual learning plans are developed, and appropriate educational tasks for each student are determined based on results from these formal and informal assessments. Frequent and ongoing monitoring, as well as systematic reassessments of learning progress, leads to modification of instructional prescriptions as they are needed. Appropriate amounts of time and instructional supports are provided to students in the form of curricular options and various grouping arrangements based on student interests and abilities, while allowing for individual differences. Support may be offered in the form of extra tutoring with a general or special educator, paraprofessional, or peer. Remedial or supplementary activities, such as additional worksheets, games, or exploratory projects, are used when appropriate or when needed to reinforce concepts. In the diagnostic-prescriptive process, teachers are considered "field researchers," as they continually gather information about student performance and modify teaching strategies in an effort to enhance student learning. Changes in instructional strategies also are made, based on the information gathered.

Individualized Progress Plans

Individual progress plans are developed to address each student's learning needs and characteristics by using information gathered from diagnostic tests, records indicating student progress rates, and teacher observations. A basic premise of adaptive instruction is that learning experiences should be built on initial competence and continued responsiveness to individual learning needs. Typically, progress plans are divided into two learning or curriculum components. A highly structured and prescriptive component is designed to address mastery of basic skills in academic content areas. The other component is designed to promote exploratory learning, processes of inquiry, social cooperation, and self-responsibility. These two curriculum components combine elements of direct instruction with features of informal or open education for all students in the classroom. Because instruction is individually planned, it is expected that students will progress through the curriculum at different rates. Learning tasks are broken down into small steps, allowing frequent opportunities for evaluation. Consequently, when issues in learning arise, the difficulty can be pinpointed and addressed before more serious learning problems develop.

The Self-Schedule System: An Instructional Management Tool

Increasing students' ability to manage their own learning is a primary goal of adaptive education. Just as instruction is adapted for the teaching of math or reading, the teaching of self-management skills must also be adapted to address individual differences. The self-schedule system (Wang, Gennari, & Waxman, 1985) was designed to help students play a more active role in their own education. A self-schedule sheet, designed by the teacher and based on individual learning needs, serves as a daily and weekly planning guide for the student. The self-schedule prompts the student to manage work time, set priorities for assignments, and plan the coordination of multiple tasks.

The self-schedule system is premised on the following assumptions (Wang, 1992):

- Self-management abilities are not acquired automatically as the student grows older. Instead, these abilities are based upon a distinct set of skills that must be learned.
- Assuming responsibility for school learning requires a variety of abilities in decision making, self-assessment, and time management.
- The development of self-management skills should be taught in a progressive and guided manner by beginning with few demands of responsibility and working up to more intensive levels.

Based on these assumptions, objectives for the development of self-management skills are arranged in order of complexity. The system is hierarchical in design, beginning with relatively simple skills, such as deciding the order in which to complete two or more tasks. Learning tasks are both teacher-prescribed and self-selected. Although students progress through the curriculum at their own pace, time limits are set jointly with the teacher. As changes are made in the classroom environment, the content and format of the management sheets are also changed or modified.

A documented, positive outcome from the use of this system is that students develop the ability to manage their time and the tasks they are expected to complete (Wang, 1991). As students become more confident and self-sufficient, teachers typically become more available to provide instruction in one-to-one, small group, and large group settings.

Adaptive Program Delivery System

To provide opportunities and instruction for all students in the general classroom setting, emphasis has been placed on instructional teaming. An instructional team is formed, whose membership may include two or more general education teachers, specialists (e.g., special education teachers, school psychologists, speech-language pathologists, Title I reading teachers), and support staff (e.g., paraprofessionals and classroom volunteers). Teaming allows for supportive intervention to be provided in the general education classroom. Collaborative team principles guide the functioning of the instructional team in order to meet the diverse student needs. A variety of options are used for instruction and program delivery that include the following:

- *Small-group instruction.* Students with similar learning needs may be placed together based on student performance and diagnostic/placement tests. However, placements are considered flexible, allowing movement between groups as needed.
- *Individual assignments/work by students.* Based on continual monitoring of student progress and individual needs, teachers may determine that individual assignments are appropriate.
- *Whole-group meetings.* This grouping is used primarily for the introduction of new concepts/skills, review of material needed by all students, and social learning activities.
- *Individual tutoring.* Tutoring may be delivered by teachers or peers in response to student requests or observed need.

Flexibility is essential to address the needs of both teacher and student. A variety of learning options are presented and available to all students. Teachers and specialists circulate to provide feedback, tutoring, and instruction to small groups or instruction to the entire class. Teachers are encouraged to organize the learning environment, create schedules, and develop various grouping options rather than follow a prescribed format. The goal of classroom organization is to have a variety of simultaneous activities occurring and to facilitate movement between groups.

ALEM represents a comprehensive instructional delivery system that has promoted shared ownership by general and special educators for heterogenous groups of students. By design, curriculum and instructional techniques are individually determined. A system of support for implementation is built in through active involvement of school administrators, instructional support personnel, related services professionals, and families. ALEM has been a forerunner in models of support and service delivery for students with gifts and talents and those with mild and moderate disabilities.

CONCLUSION

Expanding the scope, complexity, and range of the curriculum is a necessary starting point to create classrooms that are responsive to the needs of nontraditional learners. A truly differentiated curriculum begins with attention to desired student-specific outcomes. When student-specific curricular goals have been well defined, appropriate instructional accommodations can be designed to achieve those outcomes. Three approaches are offered in this chapter for designing appropriate adaptations in curriculum and instruction: a general CPS model, a specific decision-making process, and a system of service delivery and classroom organization. At the heart of each of these approaches is a commitment to individualization in the development of modifications. The act of designing and selecting adaptations must be highly individualized. The reader is cautioned to question "cookbook" approaches or a standard set of strategies for specific populations, because such orientations almost always invite overgeneralization regarding the characteristics and needs of the learner.

Good adaptations must be mutable and under continual analysis to respond to improvements exhibited by the learner and the dynamic nature of the general education classroom. To complete the process of adaptation design and implementation, educational teams are encouraged to evaluate the effectiveness of adaptations in inclusive settings. Each adaptation should be evaluated on at least the following dimensions:

- adequately addresses the problem or learning issue
- maximizes opportunities for reciprocal interactions between students with and without disabilities
- increases the student's ability to be an active participant, to be an initiator, and to demonstrate his or her knowledge
- assists in making the information or learning activity relevant to the student's current and future life
- facilitates independence or partial participation
- helps match the instructor's teaching style to the student's learning needs
- is status-enhancing, age-appropriate, and deemed acceptable by students with and without disabilities

When these or similar criteria are used to assess the effectiveness of adaptations, greater reform may result in classroom structures and instructional patterns.

As the inclusion of students with disabilities in general education classrooms becomes more and more commonplace, innovative instructional strategies and classroom practices are being validated daily through demonstration and research. When teachers become cognizant of the practices available to them and use these options to renovate and improve their instruction, they most often serve all children better.

REFERENCES

Ackerman, D., & Perkins, D.N. (1989). Integrating thinking and learning skills across the curriculum. In H.H. Jacobs (Ed.), *Interdisciplinary curriculum: Design and implementation* (pp. 77–95). Alexandria, VA: Association for Supervision and Curriculum Development.

Apple, M., & Beane, J. (1995). *Democratic schools.* Alexandria, VA: Association for Supervision and Curriculum Development.

Armstrong, D.G. (1990). *Developing and documenting the curriculum.* Boston: Allyn & Bacon.

Banks, J., & McGee Banks, C. (1989). *Multicultural education: Issues and perspectives.* Boston: Allyn & Bacon.

Beane, J. (1995). *Toward a coherent curriculum: 1995 yearbook of the Association for Supervision and Curriculum Development.* Alexandria, VA: Association for Supervision and Curriculum Development.

Brubacher, J.W., Case, C.W., & Reagan, T.G. (1994). *Becoming a reflective educator.* Thousand Oaks, CA: Corwin.

Cohen, S.B., & Lynch, D.K. (1991). An instructional modification process. *Teaching Exceptional Children, 23*(4), 12–18.

Epps, S., & Tindal, G. (1987). The effectiveness of differential programming in serving students with mild handicaps: Placement options and instructional programming. In M. Wang, M. Reynolds, & H. Walberg (Eds.), *Handbook of special education: Research and practice: Vol. 1. Learner characteristics and adaptive education* (pp. 213–235). New York: Pergamon.

Falvey, M., Givern, C., & Kimm, C. (1995). What is an inclusive school? In R. Villa & J. Thousand (Eds.), *Creating an inclusive school* (pp. 1–13). Alexandria, VA: Association for Supervision and Curriculum Development.

Ford, A., & Davern, L. (1989). Moving forward with school integration: Strategies for involving students with severe handicaps in the life of the school. In R. Gaylord-Ross (Ed.), *Integration strategies for students with handicaps* (pp. 11–31). Baltimore: Paul H. Brookes.

Gardner, H. (1983). *Frames of mind: The theory of multiple intelligences.* New York: Harper Collins.

Giangreco, M. (1993). Using creative problem-solving methods to include students with severe disabilities in general education classroom activities. *Journal of Educational and Psychological Consultation, 4,* 113–135.

Giangreco, M., Cloninger, C., Dennis, R., & Edelman, S. (1994). Problem solving methods to facilitate inclusive education. In J. Thousand, R. Villa, & A. Nevin (Eds.), *Creativity and collaborative learning: A practical guide to empowering students and teachers* (pp. 321–346). Baltimore: Paul H. Brookes.

Goodlad, J., Soder, R., & Sirotnik, K. (1990). *The moral dimensions of teaching.* San Francisco: Jossey-Bass.

Greene, M. (1995). Notes on the search for coherence. In J. Beane (Ed.), *Toward a coherent curriculum* (pp. 139–145). Alexandria, VA: Association for Supervision and Curriculum Development.

Grennon-Brooks, J., & Brooks, M. (1993). *A case for a constructivist classroom.* Alexandria, VA: Association for Supervision and Curriculum Development.

Hoover, J.J. (1988). *Curriculum adaptation for students with learning and behavior problems: Principles and practices.* Lindale, TX: Hamilton.

Jacobs, H.H. (1989). The growing need for interdisciplinary curriculum content. In H.H. Jacobs (Ed.), *Interdisciplinary curriculum: Design and implementation* (pp. 1–13). Alexandria, VA: Association for Supervision and Curriculum Development.

Lipsky, D., & Gartner, A. (1992). Achieving full inclusion: Placing the student at the center of educational reform. In W. Stainback & S. Stainback (Eds.), *Controversial issues confronting special education: Divergent perspectives* (pp. 3–12). Boston: Allyn & Bacon.

Liston, D., & Zeichner, K. (1986). Reflective teaching and action research in preservice teacher education. *Journal of Education for Teaching, 16,* 213–238.

Nevin, A. (1993). Curriculum and instructional adaptations for including students with disabilities in cooperative groups. In J. Putnam (Ed.), *Cooperative learning and strategies for inclusion: Celebrating diversity in the classroom* (pp. 41–56). Baltimore: Paul H. Brookes.

Osborn, A. (1953). *Applied imagination: Principles and procedures of creative thinking.* New York: Charles Scribner's Sons.

Osterman, K.F., & Kottkamp, R.B. (1993). *Reflective practice for educators.* Newbury, CA: Corwin.

Palmer, J.M. (1995). Interdisciplinary curriculum—again. In J. Beane (Ed.), *Toward a coherent curriculum* (pp. 55–61). Alexandria, VA: Association for Supervision and Curriculum Development.

Parnes, S.J. (1992). *Source book for creative problem-solving: A fifty year digest of proven innovation processes.* Buffalo, NY: Creative Education Foundation.

Perrone, V. (1991). *Expanding student assessment.* Alexandria, VA: Association for Supervision and Curriculum Development.

Poplin, M.S., & Stone, S. (1992). Paradigm shifts in instructional strategies: From reductionism to holistic/constructivism. In W. Stainback & S. Stainback (Eds.), *Controversial issues confronting special education: Divergent perspectives* (pp. 153–180). Boston: Allyn & Bacon.

Prawat, R. (1991). Conversations with self and settings: A framework for thinking about teacher empowerment. *American Educational Research Journal, 28*(4), 737–757.

Sergiovanni, T.J. (1994). *Building community in schools.* San Francisco: Jossey-Bass.

Sleeter, C., & Grant, C. (1994). Education that is multicultural and social reconstructionist. In C. Sleeter & C. Grant (Eds.), *Making choices for multicultural education: Five approaches to race, class, and gender* (2nd ed.) (pp. 209–242). New York: Merrill.

Stainback, S., & Stainback, W. (1992). *Curriculum considerations in inclusive classrooms: Facilitating learning for all students.* Baltimore: Paul H. Brookes.

Stainback, S., Stainback, W., & Moravec, J. (1992). Using curriculum to build inclusive classrooms. In S. Stainback and W. Stainback (Eds.), *Curriculum considerations in inclusive classrooms: Facilitating learning for all students* (pp. 65–84). Baltimore: Paul H. Brookes.

Stover, L.T., Neubert, G.A., & Lawlor, J.C. (1993). *Creating interactive environments in the secondary school.* Washington, DC: National Education Association.

Udvari-Solner, A. (1994). A decision-making model for curricular adaptations in cooperative groups. In J. Thousand, R.A. Villa, & A.I. Nevin (Eds.), *Creativity and collaborative learning: A practical guide to empowering students and teachers* (pp. 59–77). Baltimore: Paul H. Brookes.

Udvari-Solner, A. (1995). A process for adapting curriculum in inclusive classrooms. In R. Villa & J. Thousand (Eds.), *Creating an inclusive school* (pp. 110–124). Alexandria, VA: Association for Supervision and Curriculum Development.

Udvari-Solner, A. (1996a). *Improving the quality of inclusive practices through the use of a reflective decision-making process to design curricular adaptations.* Manuscript submitted for publication.

Udvari-Solner, A. (1996b). Theoretical influences on the establishment of inclusive practices. *Cambridge Journal of Education, 26*(1), 101–119.

Udvari-Solner, A. (in press). Examining teacher thinking: Constructing a process to design curricular adaptations. *Remedial and Special Education.*

Udvari-Solner, A., & Thousand, J. (1995). Promising practices that foster inclusive education. In R. Villa & J. Thousand (Eds.), *Creating an inclusive school* (pp. 87–109). Alexandria, VA: Association for Supervision and Curriculum Development.

Udvari-Solner, A., & Thousand, J. (1996). Creating a responsive curriculum for inclusive schools. *Remedial and Special Education, 17*(3), 182–192.

Wang, M.C. (1980). Adaptive instruction: Building on diversity. *Theory into Practice, 19*(2), 122–127.

Wang, M.C. (1991). Adaptive instruction: An alternative approach to providing for student diversity. In M. Ainscow (Ed.), *Effective schools for all* (pp. 134–160). London: David Fulton.

Wang, M.C. (1992). *Adaptive education strategies: Building on diversity.* Baltimore: Paul H. Brookes.

Wang, M.C., & Birch, J.W. (1984). Effective special education in regular classes. *Exceptional Children, 50*(5), 391–398.

Wang, M.C., Gennari, P., & Waxman, H.C. (1985). The adaptive learning environments model: Design, implementation, and effects. In M.C. Wang & H.J. Walberg (Eds.), *Adapting instruction to individual differences* (pp. 191–235). Berkeley, CA: McCutchan.

Wang, M.C., & Zollers, N.J. (1990). Adaptive instruction: An alternative service delivery approach. *Remedial and Special Education, 11*(1), 7–21.

Wiggins, G. (1995). Curricular coherence and assessment: Making sure that the effect matches the intent. In J. Beane (Ed.), *Toward a coherent curriculum* (pp. 101–119). Alexandria, VA: Association for Supervision and Curriculum Development.

CHAPTER 7

Family Partnerships, Belonging, and Diversity

Anne Malatchi

INTRODUCTION

In his newest book, *The Very Lonely Firefly*, noted author/illustrator Eric Carle (1995) celebrates achieving the goal of completing a "very" quartet, which includes the following books:

- *The Very Busy Spider* (1984) is about *WORK* and the ability to remain on task despite many diversions. Committing ourselves to building inclusive schools is the beginning of a long journey of working together in teams that include the child, the family, and the teachers.
- *The Very Hungry Caterpillar* (1987) is about *HOPE*, progress, and metamorphosis. With the proper supports and knowledge about our learners, all of our children have a better chance to grow up, unfold their wings, and be prepared for the future.
- *The Very Quiet Cricket* (1990) is about *LOVE* and the quest to be heard. We all need a voice and someone to listen to and acknowledge us as valuable, contributing members of society.
- *The Very Lonely Firefly* (1995) is about *BELONGING* and the desire we all have to be accepted in a com-

munity. Children with disabilities often need facilitation to make friends and become members of their school community.

Children's literature often contains powerful messages for people of all ages. This chapter addresses the same issues Carle focuses on in his quartet: *hope, work, love*, and *belonging*. The chapter explores ways we can learn from and work with children and their families in all schools. What are their hopes, dreams, and visions? Why is it important to know this? How can all of us working together build a quality education and positive future for *all* learners, including those with disabilities? This chapter also discusses some of the barriers associated with the reluctance families sometimes feel about trusting and sharing information, and suggests strategies designed to overcome these barriers. For schools to be successful and inclusive, educators must believe they can learn from and value the information that children and their families have to offer, and believe that this information will lead toward more effective teaching and a higher quality of educational programming for their students.

In addition to addressing families and family partnerships, this chapter examines issues of belonging and closes with a discussion of how the quartet of books by Carle and other children's literature can be used to promote inclusive classrooms, diversity, and ability awareness.

LOOKING AT FAMILIES AND FAMILY PARTNERSHIPS

"It takes a whole village to raise a child" is an often-quoted African proverb. Similarly, proponents of successful inclusive schools might say, "It takes a whole team to teach a child," with the team including the child and family. An

The writing of this chapter was supported in part by the U.S. Department of Education, Grant No. H025A50036-95. However, the opinions expressed herein do not necessarily reflect the position or policy of the U.S. Department of Education, and no official endorsements by the department should be inferred.

The author would like to acknowledge the many families who have shared themselves and their stories with her over the past 15 years. Special thanks to Mike, Mary, Leslie, and Rachel Peterson of Virginia; Leau and Donnie Phillips of New Mexico; and Harold, Eileen, and Kit Hammar of Virginia, who allowed their personal stories to add so much to this chapter.

essential component of successful education is the involvement of families. The U.S. Secretary of Education, Richard Riley, in *Strong Families, Strong Schools* (1994), addresses all educators and all families: "Schools must become places where families feel wanted and recognized for their strengths and potential" (p. 13). Secretary Riley continues in a chapter on school-family partnerships: "For partnerships to work, there must be mutual trust and respect, an ongoing exchange of information, agreement on goals and strategies, and a sharing of rights and responsibilities" (p. 15). Moreover, he states, "teacher training needs to include general information regarding the benefits of and barriers to parental involvement, awareness of different family backgrounds and lifestyles, how to improve communication, and ways to meet families' social, educational and social service needs" (p. 17). These are powerful statements for anyone working to include learners with disabilities. The Office of Special Education Programs (OSEP), in its 17th Annual Report to Congress, also addresses the need for the active and effective involvement of families if schools are to be successful in building inclusive classrooms (U.S. Department of Education, 1995).

Some of the key words mentioned above are: *mutual trust* and *respect, strengths, wanted, partnerships, active involvement*, and *support*. How do schools become places where these words are used by families, students, and teachers to describe their partnerships? What can educators do to create situations where families want to share information, including their dreams and visions, for the futures of their children? How can we develop partnerships where all parties believe the statement: "Share the commitment; share the vision; together we will enrich each other" (Mount & Zwernik, 1988, p. 34)?

Family-School Communication

When a child enters school as a general education student, information about the child and family is typically gathered from the parent(s) during a kindergarten-screening process or from a new student questionnaire. As the school year progresses, teachers observe their students, assess and evaluate them, and share information through phone calls, notes, and parent-teacher conferences. When learners with disabilities enter elementary school, they often come with thick files from previous programs (e.g., infant intervention, early childhood special education). During the school years from ages 5 to 21, "back-and-forth books" are a common way for parents and teachers to communicate daily information about a child with a disability. Many families of children with and without disabilities feel that these avenues of communication alone are not conducive to promoting equal partnerships and encouraging families to become part of the educational team. One mother of a learner with dis-

abilities called her daughter's back-and-forth book "the bad news book" and dreaded reading about what went wrong each day in class. Back-and-forth books, one or two conferences a year, and several progress reports do not usually give a complete picture of a child with disabilities. Moreover, these forms of sharing information are all school-initiated. We must move beyond the traditional image of sharing information with families only when a child "is in trouble," when there is a meeting, or when "the school needs help with a bake sale" (Riley, 1994, p. 17).

From System-Centered to Family- and Person-Centered Practices

Changing the way we communicate with families and gather information must begin by shifting from a system-centered approach to a family/person-centered approach toward education. This involves changing our beliefs from:

- The educator is the only expert and in control of all educational decisions.
- All learners must fit into existing programs based on labels.

We must change to:

- a transdisciplinary, team approach to education
- educational plans based upon knowledge of the individual learner, including his or her dreams, strengths, and challenges

In a traditional, system-centered approach to education, learners with disabilities are placed according to labels, and curriculum decisions also are determined by label. Family input is not encouraged. "We've always done it this way for kids with autism"; "If we include him, we'll have to include others"; "Severe and profound? That classroom is in a different building" are statements reflective of a system-centered approach. In one extreme application, an individualized education program (IEP) was developed by entering the child's label into a computer program. Children with disabilities are as different from one another as children without disabilities!

A person-centered approach gathers information from the child, family, and others supporting the child, considering strengths, interests, needs, and dreams for the future. Creating person-centered teams means empowering all team members to make decisions and solve problems based upon the individual needs of the child and family, rather than on a diagnosis, label, or tradition. This shift to a person-centered approach challenges us to look at our learners and their families as allies and team members all working together for the same outcome: the best education possible. "The purpose of person-centered planning is learning through shared action. It requires collaborative action and fundamentally challenges practices that separate people and perpetuate controlling relationships" (O'Brien & Lovett, 1996, p. 11). Successful inclusive schools and classrooms have made that transition from system-centered to person-centered practices. We must be willing to rethink the role of students and families in the education process.

Forest and Pearpoint (1992) discuss three monsters that often operate as barriers when we attempt this shift: fear, control, and change. We tend to feel comfortable with the way things have always been and are fearful of the unknown. As educators, we must share power and control and encourage partnerships. Asking for information and help from team members is not a sign of weakness. We know that change is a difficult process, is very personal, and takes time (Villa & Thousand, 1992). This is especially true when change involves a shift in our attitudes and beliefs regarding power and control.

Families and educators experience these monsters of fear, control, and change. Even when educators are willing to extend a hand as an ally and partner, these monsters may still inhibit some families from sharing information and entering into partnerships. If families have been ignored, had their opinions devalued, or had their dreams shattered in the past, it is difficult for them to believe someone will value their input. Unfortunately, many education systems have been operating under an "us versus them" philosophy for many years, especially for families of children with significant challenges. Once they realize this situation, most family members and educators try to discover tools that will help them move away from this philosophy and begin the process of sharing information and collaborating as partners for the best education of their children.

In person-centered approaches to education, the team looks at dreams and visions for the future to help determine what a child with challenges needs to learn in school. Dreaming—having a vision for the future—is an important and necessary precursor to planning an educational program for a child with a disability (Orelove & Malatchi, 1996; Rainforth, York, & Macdonald, 1992). Many people are reluctant to discuss dreams and dreaming about the future, uncertain of that importance in the educational process. Yet corporate America has been focusing successfully on dreams and visions for years. In *The Fifth Discipline,* Senge calls shared visions "the force in people's hearts" and states the importance of sharing that vision so that it can be supported by many people. "Few, if any, forces in human affairs are as powerful as shared vision" (Senge, 1990, p. 206).

Shattered Dreams

Everyone has dreams and visions—for themselves and for their children. Dreaming about and planning for our children often begins when we are young, playing house, or thinking about the kind of parent we would like to become. Most of us, however, do not dream about having a child with a disability. This discovery, either before or after birth, may shatter the dreams families have for their children; once these dreams are shattered, many parents are reluctant to dream new dreams. In *Lost Dreams and Growth,* Moses (1988) talks about the impact a child with a disability has on a family and how dreams die or change. Understanding lost and shattered dreams is a beginning for the journey toward shared dreams and planning together for the future.

With the realization a child has a disability, family members go through different emotional stages, often similar to those depicted by Kubler-Ross (1969) in *On Death and Dying.* These stages include denial, anger, anxiety, fear, bargaining, guilt, depression, and acceptance. Families of children with disabilities grieve the loss of the child they had dreamed about, planned for, and expected. Additional shattered dreams involve the loss of the future the family had envisioned. One father talked about the pain he encountered when he realized, following the diagnosis at birth of his son's multiple disabilities, that he would not be able to pursue his own dream of a career in politics. He knew that a career as a politician would require too much time away from home and that he would be unable to provide the support he wanted and needed to give to his family.

The first news about a child's disability is often delivered by a doctor who is a stranger to the family. The information shared may include unfamiliar terminology, and be followed up by days, weeks, or months of tests before arriving at a diagnosis. Sometimes there is no specific diagnosis beyond "disabled" or "retarded." Families may spend years and thousands of dollars before finding a specialist who will confirm what they suspect—that their child has a disability. Still others may search for confirmation that their child does not have a disability and is "normal." Many parents, upon discovering that their child has a disability, simply stop dreaming. The following are quotes families have shared with the author: "The doctor told me he could die anytime, not to think about the future." "Dreams? Why? They've told me she can't learn anything." "I'm too busy and too scared to dream about my child's future; I just think about today."

Information about grieving and how it relates to parents of children with disabilities is not new, and it should be familiar to educators working with these families. Yet, many families believe that educators are unaware of the importance of, and their potential impact on, shattered dreams and the cyclical nature of grieving. Do educators realize, for instance, that for families of children with disabilities the feelings associated with grieving are cyclical, rather than occurring in sequential stages as might be found following the death of a loved one? Families feel that it is important for professionals to understand what situations, comments, and conversations trigger a response that takes family members back into this cyclical nature of grieving. This understanding may help educators see how fragile the family structure can become and why there may never be complete acceptance. Knowing that other families go through similar feelings is somehow comforting, as is the thought that the educators and other service providers will have an understanding of the shattered dreams circle.

What is *not* comforting is the feeling that professionals might use this knowledge as an assessment tool and wonder when families will "get over it," or "get out of the circle." Or that this knowledge might lead to feeling of pity. Families want and deserve respect and understanding, not pity. How many of us have heard a colleague talk about a mom or dad who always "appears to be angry"? How many have heard another colleague, frustrated following an IEP or other meeting, say "Can't that family accept their child's disability?" Maybe the mom and dad are, once more, experiencing some anger; maybe they are making the transition into a different stage of their child's life (such as kindergarten or middle school) and are angry because, again, they are being asked to accept something their child can't do. However, they might be angry because they have another, truer, vision of their child and his or her potential. The feelings associated with grieving and the triggers that elicit them may affect all family members (brothers, sisters, grandparents, and others, as well as the mom and dad) in different ways and at different times.

Natural triggers include developmental stages (e.g., walking and talking), milestones (e.g., riding a bicycle, getting a driver's license), and transitions (e.g., entry into kindergarten and graduation from high school). One mother of a young son related how she ended up in tears watching a group of teenagers hanging out in the mall, wondering if her child would ever have experiences like that. Often, these feelings are fleeting, while others last much longer. One father stated that he was unable to watch a football game for several years after his son was born, having lost his dreams of father-son scrimmages.

Medical expenses, which often occur throughout the life of an individual with a disability, can also elicit feelings of anger and depression. Financial issues can have a devastating effect on families and their dreams. These are, however, natural triggers that families of children with disabilities usually cannot avoid.

Imposed triggers are statements and situations that, however unintentional, throw a family member back into an emotion on the circle. Some physicians and other health care professionals offer well-meaning, but unrealistic, recommendations and predictions. Educators offer opinions about potential learning based on outdated material and traditional expectations for children with certain labels. Each assessment and evaluation can lead to the further loss of hopes and dreams, especially when a family member is

hearing more information about what their child can *not* do and how far behind other children their child might be developmentally. Parents also share stories of awkward experiences involving gatherings with relatives and others who are sharing pictures and discussing milestones. The tears that follow, while often unavoidable, sometimes make everyone uncomfortable. Evaluations still must be completed, trips to medical specialists will continue, and friends and relatives will continue to discuss their children. Having knowledge of the concept of shattered dreams can help all of us handle situations like these with respect, tolerance, concern, and understanding.

Understanding this shattered dream cycle *should* do the following:

- acknowledge to family members that grieving can be healthy and necessary for growth
- acknowledge to families that other families experience these feelings
- help educators and others learn about natural and imposed triggers
- help everyone concerned become more comfortable with the feelings associated with grieving
- establish a basis of understanding that will lead toward partnerships and collaboration among family members, educators, and other service providers

Understanding this shattered dream cycle *should not* do the following:

- provide educators and others with an assessment tool to see "where families are"
- give a mandatory, progressive, sequential "list" of feelings
- elicit feelings of pity
- mean educators can expect that all families and family members will grieve in the same way
- provide ammunition for labeling a family member (e.g.,"she's in denial")

Our society needs to accept that grieving can be healthy and necessary for growth. Identifying lost dreams enables us to begin dreaming again. "My parents always had a dream for my brothers and sisters for when they grew up, but nobody ever had a dream for me, so I never had a dream for myself. You can never have a good life if nobody ever has a dream for you unless you learn to have a dream for yourself. That's what I had to do, and now I have a dream for myself. And I believe my dreams will come true" (Martinez, 1990, p. 4).

Although current information and research on inclusion and education address the importance of dreams (Orelove & Malatchi, 1996; Rainforth et al., 1992; Romer & Romer, 1995; Thousand, Villa, & Nevin, 1994), many schools, educators, and families across the United States do not incor-

Exhibit 7–1 A Dream for Donnie

In 1985 when my new son arrived at the age of 2 1/2, everyone around me thought that what I was doing was crazy. Except my father. People around me said, "Oh, this won't last long." "What will you do when he's an adult?" "Where do people like him go?" But my father, at 78, said, "Helen Keller. That boy is going to be like Helen Keller." And I would say, "Now daddy, not really. He has this wrong and that wrong and he can't do this and that is too hard for him." But he insisted, "Helen Keller, Helen Keller." And the doctors would say, "He won't live to be 10. He isn't strong enough to grow up and you should just try to make him comfortable while you can." And my daddy would say, "He's going to teach us all, just like Helen Keller did. Think what she did for the world." He would tell visitors to his garden about his grandson that was going to be like Helen Keller.

So I started thinking maybe there was something to this future thing and I started teasing my father saying, "No, I want him to be Ray Charles, because Ray Charles makes more money than Helen Keller did." I realized that because my father had a dream for my son, I started dreaming for my son. And when I started dreaming for my son, others around him started looking at dreams for him.

And a person with a dream is viewed differently than a person with no future plans. It just takes one person to have a dream for the importance of dreaming to make a difference in the life of a family.

Courtesy of Leau Phillips.

porate this knowledge into their practices. How can we encourage families to have dreams for their children with disabilities? We need to journey together to become good listeners and encourage dreaming together. Sometimes it takes one person who believes in a dream to make a difference (see Exhibit 7–1).

Dream Catchers

Many of us in North America are familiar with the Native American legend surrounding dream catchers (see Figure 7–1). The Sioux and Ojibway Indians, along with many other tribes, consider the dream catcher the web of life, and it is hung above the bed or in the home to sift the dreams of those nearby. Good dreams are captured and stay with a person; bad dreams escape through the hole in the center of the web and are no longer a part of the person's life. Our challenge, as people who care about and support individuals with disabilities, is to become dream catchers ourselves: learning about positive dreams and helping to make them reality, and helping to avoid the nightmares for our learners with disabilities. Together we can do this! Educators and other professionals have the opportunity to join together with family members to become dream catchers in creating and realizing new dreams for children with disabilities (see Exhibit 7–2). From our dreams for the future we decide what we need to learn and do today. As Marsha Forest, a leading professional in the area of inclusion, has often stated: "We create our tomorrows by what we dream today."

In addition to the suggestions for becoming dream catchers presented in Exhibit 7–2, there are many ways educators can let all families know they want to work together to create positive, possible futures for their children. First, educators can begin by making schools "family friendly." Creating schools that are welcoming environments for everyone, especially families, should become a priority for all educators. If parents do not feel wanted in a school, they are less willing to share information, work on teams, and become partners in the education of their children. While educators would like to think that all the schools they work in are warm and welcoming, sometimes it is difficult to determine the climate in your own building. Substitute and itinerant teachers are usually excellent sources to check out the feeling of a building; because they work in so many, they can tell immediately if they are in a friendly building. Family members and PTA volunteers also have definite feelings about the friendliness of school buildings and the people who teach there. What type of climate must exist before families are willing to exchange information and feel wanted? The checklist in Exhibit 7–3 can be used to rate a school and to determine where changes are needed. Answering "yes" to all 15 items is a strong indicator that a

Figure 7-1 Dream catcher. Courtesy of A.M. Jones.

Exhibit 7–2 How To Become Dream Catchers

To become dream catchers, families, educators, and all others involved in the lives of children with disabilities should do the following:

- Dare to dream for your children and your students.
- Voice these dreams.
- Listen to and encourage the dreams of others.
- Celebrate and share stories of successes.

- Value all children.
- Believe all children can learn.
- Think "*capacity, gifts, strength,* and *ability,*" not "*deficit, weakness,* and *disability.*"
- Promote partnerships, teaming, and collaboration. Remember, "Together we can," and "Together we're better."

Exhibit 7–3 Is Our School "Family Friendly"?

	Yes	No
1. Are there signs and posters around the school welcoming families?	☐	☐
2. Do we have a family resource section in our school containing books, videos, and magazines of interest and support for families, including information for families of children with disabilities? Who selects the materials?	☐	☐
3. Are families welcome in our classrooms? If yes, what are the procedures? Are they cumbersome? Is prior authorization necessary? Is there a time limit?	☐	☐
4. Do we encourage family volunteers? How? For what tasks? (Clerical? Fund raising? Working with the kids?)	☐	☐
5. Do we have a suggestion box for families? If so, do we respond to the suggestions?	☐	☐
6. Are family members involved in all our professional committees (school improvement, curriculum, program planning, policy development, etc.)? How are they recruited? Do they represent all student populations?	☐	☐
7. Was our vision statement developed by a team that included family representatives from all populations and age levels, including those with disabilities?	☐	☐
8. Do family representatives attend our faculty meetings? Team meetings?	☐	☐
9. Do we have a family mentor program to welcome new families to our community?	☐	☐
10. Do we have an active Parent-Student-Teacher Association that addresses issues of diversity and inclusion through inservices, guest speakers, videos, and panel discussions? Does it meet at a time that encourages working parents to attend? Are parents of kids with disabilities included in PTA leadership?	☐	☐
11. Do we make it a priority to schedule family-teacher conferences and individual education program meetings at times convenient for families, including working parents?	☐	☐
12. Do we survey all our families for input on a consistent basis?	☐	☐
13. Do we have an effective, ongoing evaluation plan so we continue to be a school that welcomes families?	☐	☐
14. Are we willing to make home visits? Phone calls in the evening?	☐	☐
15. Do we believe that parents know their children best?	☐	☐

school is family friendly and has a healthy atmosphere for inclusive classrooms.

Part of becoming an inclusive school involves welcoming and belonging, and this affects parents, brothers, and sisters, as well as the child with a label. When we segregate a child, we segregate the entire family. If a child with a disability has not been welcome in a school or classroom, the family usually has not felt welcome, either. Creating family-friendly schools for all families, including those with children with disabilities, is a prerequisite for "promoting partnerships that will increase parental involvement and participation in promoting the social, emotional and academic growth of children" (Riley, 1994, inside cover).

Once a school has been made family friendly, it is time to consider the following: looking at children in terms of capacities instead of deficits (i.e., talking about things children can do); restructuring the format of IEP and other meetings to avoid beginning with a discussion of the person's deficits; and using person-first and family-friendly language and avoiding educational jargon.

Capacities, Not Deficits

All people have strengths, gifts, and talents (Snow, 1994), yet individuals who work with children with disabilities spend a great deal of time discussing what learners cannot do. Think how you would feel if you went to meeting after meeting and all you heard were lists of things your child could not do, how your child behaved inappropriately, and what he or she needed to change. Would you want to share your dreams for the future or share intimate details about your child's life? When questioned about their feelings regarding their involvement at IEP meetings, many parents indicate that it is a constant battle to be listened to and included as active, respected members of the team. Parents share their frustration at the attitude of "them versus us" that sometimes prevails, and they state that they feel isolated and defensive during an often negative, deficit-based orientation to the meetings.

IEP Meetings

IEP meetings often begin with members sharing results from assessments. The focus is placed on what the learner cannot do, punctuated by descriptors such as "performing at a six-month level" or by IQ-driven labels of "educable mentally retarded" and "severe and profound." Often there are people at an IEP meeting who have never met the child, such as a special education administrator or next year's teacher, and they develop a vision of the child's deficits. In almost every situation, parents are outnumbered by the professionals in attendance. Many teachers and administrators feel threatened when a parent arrives with a mentor, friend,

or advocate. The three monsters of fear, control, and change—discussed earlier in this chapter—are responsible for this attitude. Educators are fearful of the unexpected, fearful that what they are doing might be questioned, and fearful that they might have to relinquish or share the power and control of decision making. Even though parents have the right to bring friends to meetings, this is "not the way it's always been done." At meetings in environments that are not family friendly, the arrival of a family friend or advocate might indicate that the family is considering legal action, such as due process. Exhibit 7–4 offers some suggestions that parents and teachers have found helpful in setting a positive climate for collaboration (Malatchi, 1994b).

Often, information must be shared at meetings that can be painful to hear and discuss. If teams are sensitive to this, discuss the information with families in advance, and begin and end the meeting thinking and talking positively about learners, they will be moving much closer to achieving what everyone wants: collaboration for developing a quality education for learners. Exhibit 7–5 depicts a sample IEP meeting agenda that implements some of the aforementioned suggestions, including ways to involve families in the structure of the meeting (Malatchi, 1994b). Another example of family involvement in the IEP process can be found in a letter Mary Falvey and Richard Rosenberg sent to their son's IEP team in preparation for a meeting (Falvey, 1996). They listed their child's strengths and needs, compiled by those who knew and loved him. They requested that all information be conveyed in terms that were understandable to their son, who would be attending the meeting, and that team members address their assessment findings to their son. Finally, they identified what they hoped would be the outcomes from the meeting.

Person-First Language

Person-first language challenges us to change how we speak about people with labels, thereby increasing our respect and value of them as individuals. Instead of saying "disabled" or "handicapped person," it is preferable to use the noun first (e.g., "person with a disability"). Thus, terms like "child who uses a wheelchair" or "child with cerebral palsy" are preferred to "wheelchair kid" or "CP kid." Everyone is a person first, and the specific disability is a characteristic.

Listening and Adapting

Becoming dream catchers begins with dreaming and listening to the dreams, and proceeds with joining in the actions needed to achieve them. "The process of creating action with results involves first *listening* to a dream, then reaching agreement on the value of the dream to the listeners, finding

Exhibit 7–4 Setting a Positive Climate for Collaboration between Parents and Educators at IEP Meetings

BEFORE AN IEP MEETING

- Administrator designates a contact person (facilitator) from the school; make sure parent(s) and staff are aware of this person.
- Facilitator schedules premeetings with the parents and others on the team who are involved with the child to discuss progress, strengths, and needs, and to share ideas for goals and objectives. The number of these meetings should be decided by the team.
- Team members share assessment results with the family in family-friendly language (e.g., don't use educational jargon, demeaning labels) at a premeeting.
- Facilitator reminds the parent(s) that it is their right to bring a mentor, friend, or advocate with them.
- Facilitator asks the parent(s) to bring pictures of their child (when child is unable to attend) so that all in attendance have the opportunity to see the person who is the focus of the meeting.
- Facilitator lets everyone attending know what time the meeting will start, what time it will end, and that everyone is expected to remain for the entire meeting.
- Facilitator checks on transportation needs of parent(s) and assists if necessary.

- Facilitator sends out an agenda that includes the names of everyone who will be attending and the location of the meeting.

AT THE MEETING

- Have day care available if the parent(s) need to bring very young siblings.
- Facilitator should have copies of an agenda available for everyone (see Exhibit 7–5).
- Facilitator makes name tags for everyone, including the parent(s).
- Facilitator restates the time the meeting should end and appoints a timekeeper to let everyone know when about 15 minutes remain.
- If it is obvious that more time will be needed, decide on a future meeting time with everyone present, rather than after they have all left.
- Make sure that the language used throughout the meeting is family friendly (e.g., don't use educational jargon, acronyms).

Exhibit 7–5 Sample IEP Meeting Agenda

September 26, 1994
3:30–4:30 PM
Participants:

AGENDA

1. **Welcome:** Designated meeting facilitator welcomes participants.
2. **Introductions:** Begin with student (or pictures if he or she is not present) and family.
3. **Purpose of meeting:** State that purpose of meeting is to gather information about (child's name) in order to develop collaboratively an individualized education program.
4. **Progress and strengths:** These are presented by those who know the student; they are not limited to academic progress, but include strengths and preferences (in home, school, and community).
5. **Needs and challenges:** Consider all environments.
6. **Assessment information:** Use informal as well as formal assessment. There should be no surprises, as this information should have been shared with parents prior to the meeting.
7. **Formulating goals and objectives:** These should be based on strengths, needs, and assessment information.
8. **Student placement:** Determine location where goals and objectives will be addressed.
9. **Closure:** Develop a "wish list" by quickly going around the table and having each person share a wish for the student during the coming year. Ask parents to listen and add theirs last.

a mutually acceptable concrete expression of the dream, and, finally, planning and sharing action" (Snow, 1994, p. 44). How to engage in this action and gather information from the child and family will vary, because every school community is different and must decide what works for it. Our lead as educators must come from the families, and each family must be consulted to see what works best. Assuming that one or two families from a school are responding for all can be dangerous, especially in a diverse community with many racial and ethnic groups represented. One example of this occurred while this author was teaching a young child from Taiwan. Colleagues were concerned about the father's lack of involvement and other aspects of the child's home life. These concerns disappeared as the team developed an understanding of the cultural differences, including parental roles and attitudes toward children with disabilities. The key component in determining how to include families and gather information is to make sure to ask the families.

The Tools

Several excellent tools have been designed specifically to assist in gathering information about a learner with a disability in order to support that individual in reaching his or her dreams. Some of these tools include: choosing options and accommodations for children (COACH) (Giangreco, Cloninger, & Iverson, 1993); lifestyle planning (Romer & Romer, 1995); personal futures planning (Mount, 1992); making action plans (MAPs) (Forest & Pearpoint, 1992); and planning alternative tomorrows with hope (PATH) (Pearpoint, O'Brien, & Forest, 1995). Readers are encouraged to explore these tools and to decide, as part of a team, what works best for their situation. Each tool can be adapted for use with any individual, regardless of the person's age, disability, or racial-ethnic group. All are based on the following common values:

- The tool is person-centered instead of system-centered.
- Collaboration and partnerships are essential.
- A capacity approach is preferred to a deficit approach.
- Everyone has strengths, gifts, and talents.
- Positive futures begin with dreaming now.
- The individual the process is focusing on is the key decision maker.
- Families know their children best.

Making Action Plans

MAPs is a strategic planning and problem-solving process developed by Forest and Pearpoint (1992) to facilitate the inclusion of children with disabilities into general education classes. It is an information-gathering tool that involves individuals' meeting to answer eight questions collaboratively and create a positive portrait of an individual. MAPs, by its very design, is an excellent tool for empowering dream catchers.

There are several steps to the MAPs process. Step 1 involves selecting an individual from the school to work with a family member to coordinate the arrangements for the MAPs process.

Step 2 is determining a place and time and deciding persons who should attend. Two places that work well are school libraries and family homes. It is important to choose a location where everyone will be comfortable and that has adequate wall space. Information collected during the MAPs process will be recorded on chart paper during the meeting. Participants should be persons from home, school, or the community who know the learner well, and persons likely to work with the learner in the future. Ideally, family members and school personnel should collaborate to decide who to invite. It is important not to forget to ask the "star" of the MAPs process who he or she wants to invite. Often the child will think of someone the adults have forgotten. One young lady wanted to invite her school bus driver, who wound up contributing very significant information. Many families mail an invitation that also explains the MAPs process. At least two hours should be planned for the meeting. (Furnishing snacks for a food break is always a hit.)

Other essential participants are typical children from both school and the neighborhood. The contact person from the school can facilitate the necessary arrangements for these peers to attend. Exhibit 7–6 offers suggestions of questions to ask classmates and peers who may be unable to attend the MAPs session, but who may have valuable information to share. Although these questions are designed to elicit responses from elementary-aged students, they may be adapted for other age groups. Often a classroom teacher, assisted by a parent of the MAPs "star," gathers this information from the children. It is powerful to record the children's responses on chart paper and share them at the MAPs meeting.

In step 3, a neutral, trained facilitator leads the group through the eight questions. (If possible, the facilitator should meet with the family and other participants prior to the MAPs session so no one feels threatened and everyone understands what is involved.) Participants are asked to introduce themselves and explain their relationship to the key person. Chart paper placed on the walls helps facilitate the recording of responses. It is strongly recommended that a second facilitator be responsible for this recording. This graphic facilitator records the responses of the participants through words, pictures, and color. Many people also choose to videotape the process.

Exhibit 7–6 MAPs Questions for Classmates and Friends in Elementary School

Record the children's responses on chart paper so they can see them. Make sure someone the children know is asking the questions.

1. Ask the class: (a) do they ever tell their parents about school and, if so, (b) what do they tell their parents?
2. Explain that often teachers talk to the children's parents to let them know how their children are doing in school.
3. Today they have a chance to help (*child's name*) let (*his or her*) parents, teachers, and other people know about school, what (*child's name*) does well, how (*he or she*) needs to improve, and what they have learned from (*child's name*).
4. Ask them "What is a MAP?" (Gives us directions, tells us where motels are, tells us where to stop for the bathroom, etc.).
5. Tell them about the MAPs meeting. Explain that we need their answers to some questions because they are (*child's name*) age and very important in (*his or her*) life. Their answers will help the adults plan (*first*) grade for (*child's name*).
6. Ask them:
   - What are some things that happened with (*child's name*) this year?

- What is (*he or she*) good at?
- What does (*child's name*) do better now than at the beginning of school?
- What should (*child's name*) learn next year in (*first*) grade?
- What do you think (*his or her*) classmates next year would like to know about (*child's name*)?
- What have you learned from having (*child's name*) in your class?
- What are some things (*child's name*) friends next year should do? In the classroom? Other places around the school? After school? On weekends?
- What do you think (*child's name*) would like to be when (*he or she*) grows up?
- What else can you think of about (*child's name*) that would help others understand (*him or her*)?
- Where do you think (*he or she*) would like to live?
- What kind of a job should (*he or she*) have?
- What is your favorite thing about (*child's name*)?
- Is there anything else you think people need to know about (*child's name*) to help them understand (*him or her*)?

The following MAPs questions are addressed by the participants (Forest & Pearpoint, 1992):

1. What is a map?
2. What is the child's history?
3. What is your dream for the child?
4. What is your nightmare for the child?
5. Who is the child?
6. What are the child's strengths, gifts, and talents?
7. What are the child's needs and challenges?
8. What action plans are needed to meet these dreams and avoid the nightmares? What would an ideal day at school look like?

In question 1, after participants are asked to share their idea of a road map, the facilitator explains that this is what they will be doing—designing a MAP to help determine the direction of the child's life. Question 2 involves sharing the highlights of the student's life (i.e., the child's story). The facilitator should review this information prior to the meeting so not too much time is spent on this section. Be sure to include information regarding medical, educational, social, and communication history.

Dreams and nightmares (questions 3 and 4) for the child are the heart and soul of the MAPs process and must not be eliminated. It is up to the facilitator to make sure the family is comfortable enough to share this information. (Questions

2, 3, and 4 are usually answered first by family members, then by other participants.) Questions 5, 6, and 7 gather information about who the child is and about his or her strengths and needs. What works, what doesn't work, preferences, and needed supports should be covered in these questions. This information is crucial to developing the action plans (question 8), and deciding what needs to happen, and when and how things should happen to meet the dreams and avoid the nightmares. It is helpful if the action plans also include who will take this information (the chart papers from the MAPs meeting) and copy it for the participants. For closure, the facilitator reviews what has been recorded to make sure the words of the participants are reflected correctly and then asks for a word or two from each member of the group to express their feelings about the MAPs experience. Exhibit 7-7 provides selections from Rachel's MAPs meeting, which was held in the spring of her kindergarten year to facilitate her transition to first grade. Following the action plans section are sample responses from her classmates who were unable to attend the MAPs session. Mary, Rachel's mother, talks about the impact of the MAPs process in Exhibit 7-8.

While a MAPs process does not take the place of an IEP, families and teachers use the information gathered from MAPs to help assist with the IEP process. Some family

Exhibit 7–7 Rachel's MAPs

Selections from Rachel's MAPs session (spring 1995), held in the school's library, are presented below. Twenty-five people attended including her family, family friends, minister, neighbors, principal, current and future teachers, and therapists.

QUESTIONS

1. What is Rachel's history?

   - **Family:**
     - Rachel is six years old, diagnosed with multiple disabilities.
     - She lives with her mom, dad, and older sister, Leslie.
     - She has a large extended family.
     - Mom and Dad are very involved in the education of their children and have fought very hard for Rachel to be included successfully in school.

   - **Medical:**
     - Mary, Rachel's mother, had a normal pregnancy.
     - Developmental delays were suspected by the time Rachel was four to six months old.
     - Rachel is currently healthy, with bouts of respiratory problems and allergies.

   - **Education:**
     - Rachel was involved in early intervention programs.
     - She attended special education preschool until she was six.
     - Rachel is now in a general education kindergarten but not in the neighborhood school.

   - **Social:**
     - Rachel has a loving, supportive family and a supportive church family.
     - Rachel had very few friendships in school until this year.
     - Inclusion has increased her circle of friends.

   - **Communication:**
     - Rachel uses gestures to communicate along with a few signs and some vocalizations.
     - Rachel receives private speech therapy twice a week.

2. What are your dreams for Rachel?

   - to have friends
   - to be a friend
   - to be understood
   - to *communicate*, understand, and be understood
   - to be supported
   - to always live in a loving home
   - to be valued
   - to have a job that earns money
   - to contribute
   - to be supported to develop to full potential
   - to be accepted and included .
   - to have choices
   - to be challenged
   - for Rachel to let us know what *her* dreams are!
   - to be part of a community

continues

Exhibit 7–7 continued

3. What are your nightmares for Rachel?

- She will not be accepted by society.
- She will have no opportunities or choices.
- She will be teased and ridiculed.
- She will suffer physical and/or sexual abuse.
- She will not be valued.
- She won't have close friends.
- She will be excluded, segregated.
- People won't understand her.
- She will withdraw or shut down.
- She will be institutionalized.
- She will be rejected.
- She won't love those who love her.
- She will lose her joy for life.
- She'll be alone.

4. Who is Rachel? What does she like?

- she's a blessing
- sister, daughter, student, grandchild, friend
- happy
- independent
- stubborn
- one of the kids
- observant
- loves music, water
- delightful
- loves to play
- gentle
- fun, giggly, silly, a flirt
- a learner with lots of potential
- a member of our school
- impatient, reactive, proactive——knows what she wants
- a best friend

5. What are Rachel's strengths, gifts, and talents?

- her sister
- loving, caring, concerned, and involved family
- the staff and children at her school
- music, motor skills, curiosity, books
- tactile learner, body language, modeling
- desire for independence
- loves learning
- loves being outside
- loves kids
- she is a gift!

continues

Exhibit 7–7 continued

6. What are Rachel's needs and challenges?

- input from her friends into planning her education
- communication options
- functional, realistic goals and objectives
- for her friends to learn sign or communicate whatever way Rachel communicates
- to be included
- support in the classroom from friends as well as adults
- acceptance, patience, understanding
- recognition and appreciation of her successes
- circle of friends, extracurricular activities with friends, risk takers in her life
- health, physical, and safety needs met
- necessary supports after she's 21
- family, teachers, and others in her life to be current on "best practices"
- team at school that includes her family
- to be challenged

ACTION PLANS

- Team will be formed before end of school year (parents on it).
- Team will revise IEP before first grade begins.
- IEP will include input from MAPs.
- New IEP will contain communication and functional goals.
- Circle of friends activities will begin in her class, including sign language.
- Transition plans for moving to first grade will begin now.
- Team will develop summer options.
- Friendships will be maintained over the summer with help from family.
- School will look at alternative, appropriate assessments for Rachel (ecological).
- Matrix will be used in first grade to help with daily schedule and to address IEP goals and objectives.

SELECTED RESPONSES FROM HER CLASSMATES

1. What does Rachel do better now than at the beginning of the year?

- She's better at touching things and not putting things in her mouth.
- She knows "no" in sign language.

2. Where do you think Rachel would like to live?

- Disney World
- an apartment
- California, the beach

3. What would Rachel like to be when she grows up?

- someone who helps someone else learn to talk
- horseback riding teacher
- rock singer
- principal

4. What else can you think of about Rachel that would help others understand her?

- Other kids need to know sign language.
- She likes to be patted on the back.
- She likes to play with us.
- She loves books.
- She needs help coloring and painting.

continues

Exhibit 7–7 continued

5. What do you think Rachel's classmates next year would like to know about her?

- She isn't mean.
- Tell them her name.
- If her noises bother you, just ignore them . . . because she can't help it.

6. What should Rachel learn in first grade?

- homework
- how to talk
- how to do sign language
- how to walk better and numbers

Graphics by Paula Ropelewski.

SIGN LANGUAGE

members and educators who participate in the process ask that a statement be added to an IEP letting people know this information is available; other educators attach the information directly to the IEP. MAPs is also an extremely valuable tool at transition times (e.g., from grade to grade, school to school). The success of this process has led to adaptations for schools and teams to use MAPs creatively in solving a variety of issues. Some educators are now using the MAPs format at the beginning of the school year to gather information about all their learners, not just those with disabilities.

Exhibit 7–9 offers forms for "This Is My Life! A Snapshot of (*child's name*)" that families and teachers can use as a follow-up to a MAPs, or in lieu of a MAPs when a MAPs session is not possible. If the key participants are not available for the MAPs process, or if there has been a MAPs for the child within the last year, updating information is still important and the snapshot forms may help. This snapshot provides a positive way of sharing some of the same information about a child as in a MAPs. One mother completes these forms at the beginning of each school year as a

reminder of the information gathered at a previous MAPs session. She says this helps them all start off the year with the same information about her son. Her son's teachers now use an adapted version of this form on which they give their input before convening for an IEP meeting. An actual MAPs session is always preferable because of the interaction of the participants, with the snapshot format as a follow up.

PATH

PATH is an eight-step process used to design possible, positive futures (Pearpoint et al., 1995). While MAPs gathers information about a child, family, team, or class, PATH pushes an individual, family, or team to explore their dreams (North Star) and helps them design the journey (pathway) to get there. PATH is a very specific, powerful planning process that involves visualizing the dreams and experiencing the tension between where a person is now and where he or she wants to be in the future. The PATH process involves three roles: graphic recorder, process facil-

Exhibit 7–8 My Daughter's MAPs

With a child like Rachel, it was sometimes easy to forget that she is a whole person. She is often fragmented into bits of information such as cognitive level, gross motor, fine motor, social skills, etc. We were always addressing her need, based on what therapy or tool could help individual problems. MAPs changed all that by helping us focus on who Rachel truly is. She is a child, sister, friend, student, and—most importantly—our beloved daughter. Through the MAPs process, we came to realize that she has an enormous group of people loving and supporting her. We were able to piece together the parts, to see Rachel as a "whole" person. Even though we always knew it, MAPs reminded us that Rachel is

a little girl with many gifts and strengths and not a bunch of broken parts.

MAPs is such a powerful tool. Our hopes and visions for her future are much clearer now. We have goals that exceed far beyond just the next skill that she will master. We actually think about her future, which includes work, supportive family and friends, and fun. We want Rachel to be happy and to have a full life. We don't think that is too much to ask for anybody. MAPs was able to show us that if we start now, and don't abandon our dreams and Rachel's dreams, we can build a better life for her. It will be a lot of hard work, but it is worth the effort because she deserves a good life!

Courtesy of Mary Peterson.

Exhibit 7–9 This Is My Life! A Snapshot of (*Child's Name*)

These are the people who contributed information to this snapshot:

Attach a photo

1. Here are the basics (include family information, interests, preferences, age, where you live, highlights from your past):

2. These are my dreams:

3. These are my nightmares:

4. These are the important people in my life:

5. These are my strengths and things that work for me (including how I learn best):

continues

Exhibit 7–9 continued

6. These things are challenging (including the supports I need):

7. This is how I communicate best:

8. This is what I want to be working on this year:

9. This is what I want to learn over the next several years:

10. Here are some ways you can help me:

Source: Adapted with permission from *Inclusion News,* © 1996, Inclusion Press.

itator (or guide), and pathfinder(s). *The PATH process should not occur without these three individuals.*

All eight steps of this process are graphically recorded on a large, 10-foot by 3-foot piece of paper on which is drawn the PATH diagram (see Figure 7–2). As with the MAPs process, the PATH process takes a minimum of two hours and should not take place unless sufficient time has been allocated. The focus person, or pathfinder (the individual who the PATH is for) suggests a list of individuals who would be valuable participants at the PATH meeting. The eight steps of the PATH process are (Pearpoint et al., 1995):

1. Touching the dream (the North Star)
2. Sensing the goal: Focus for the next year
3. Grounding in the now: Where are we?
4. Identifying people to enroll on the journey
5. Recognizing ways to build strength
6. Charting actions for three or six months from now (pathfinder's choice)
7. Charting actions for the next month
8. Committing to the first step

In step 1, participants focus on the future (i.e., the North Star), and the graphic facilitator interprets this future in pictures, colors, and words. From the North Star, the pathfinder (focus person or group of people) is encouraged to step into the future and decide what positive and possible goals have been achieved in the past year that lead toward reaching the North Star (step 2). Returning to the present for step 3, participants describe what the now feels like. Much of the power of the PATH comes from feeling this tension between where we want to be and where we are now. This tension leads to the commitment to journey on this path to take the actions necessary to move into the future. In step 4, people are asked to enroll for specific responsibilities that will support the pathfinder and the actions needed over the next several months to reach the goals. Many, but not all, of these people may be present for the PATH process. It is recommended that the pathfinder enroll first by signing his or her name in the designated space, and then ask others present to stand, come forward, and write their names. It's easy to say "OK" when asked to help, but more personal when someone actually takes pen in hand and signs his or her name. Those present might also decide who will contact the other people crucial for the journey who are not there. Step 5 lists ways for enrollees to build strength for the journey and avoid burnout. Steps 6 and 7 are the action plans necessary over the next few months for achieving the desired goals. Step 8 is committing to the first steps for implementing the PATH. Dates and names are listed for specific responsibilities. Saying a meeting will occur is not adequate; specify where and when it will happen. Facilitators check in with all participants at the end of the process and ask for a word or two that reflect their feeling regarding participating in this process. These words can be written along the bottom of the PATH diagram. Then the PATH is rolled up and presented to the pathfinder (focus person). (Some print shops can make smaller, 11-by-17 inch copies for other participants.) Figure 7–2 includes an example of a completed PATH.

Some ways the PATH process has been used successfully include planning for:

- a child with a disability in an inclusive classroom
- a student's transition from school to the community
- collaboration between families and teachers
- a school staff developing their vision

While the MAPs process gathers information to help others know a child, the PATH process goes much further and sets specific goals, timelines, and action plans required to achieve the goals and journey toward the North Star. Many teams are using both the MAPs and PATH processes: MAPs for gathering information about a person and PATH for specific planning. Both MAPs and PATH allow for input in a positive way from all the participants, paint positive portraits of an individual, and strengthen the concept of inclusive schools and communities. People who are actively involved as part of a planning process find it much easier to support and participate in implementing the action plans.

BELONGING

Belonging, the need for relationships and friends, is a basic human need (Maslow, 1970). How we look at the issues of acceptance, belonging, and community is closely associated with our values. Creating schools that are welcoming for families and gathering information about the learners are important steps in the process of developing a successful climate for inclusive classroom communities. In successful inclusive schools, *all* people feel like they belong (see Figure 7–3).

To have a school where everyone feels he or she belongs, we must begin with all the adults in the building (i.e., educators, administrators, kitchen staff, paraprofessionals, as well as families) and then look at the issue of belonging for the students. In school life as well as home life, children will reflect the attitudes of the adults and peers around them. In order to develop caring school *communities*, we need to be *accepting* of differences. From this acceptance comes the feel of *belonging*. How do the adults feel about working with students with different abilities and different racial-ethnic backgrounds? Educators and administrators should take the time to survey their colleagues on these issues. Based on the results, inservice and training can be arranged to address questions, fears, and strategies. Do all

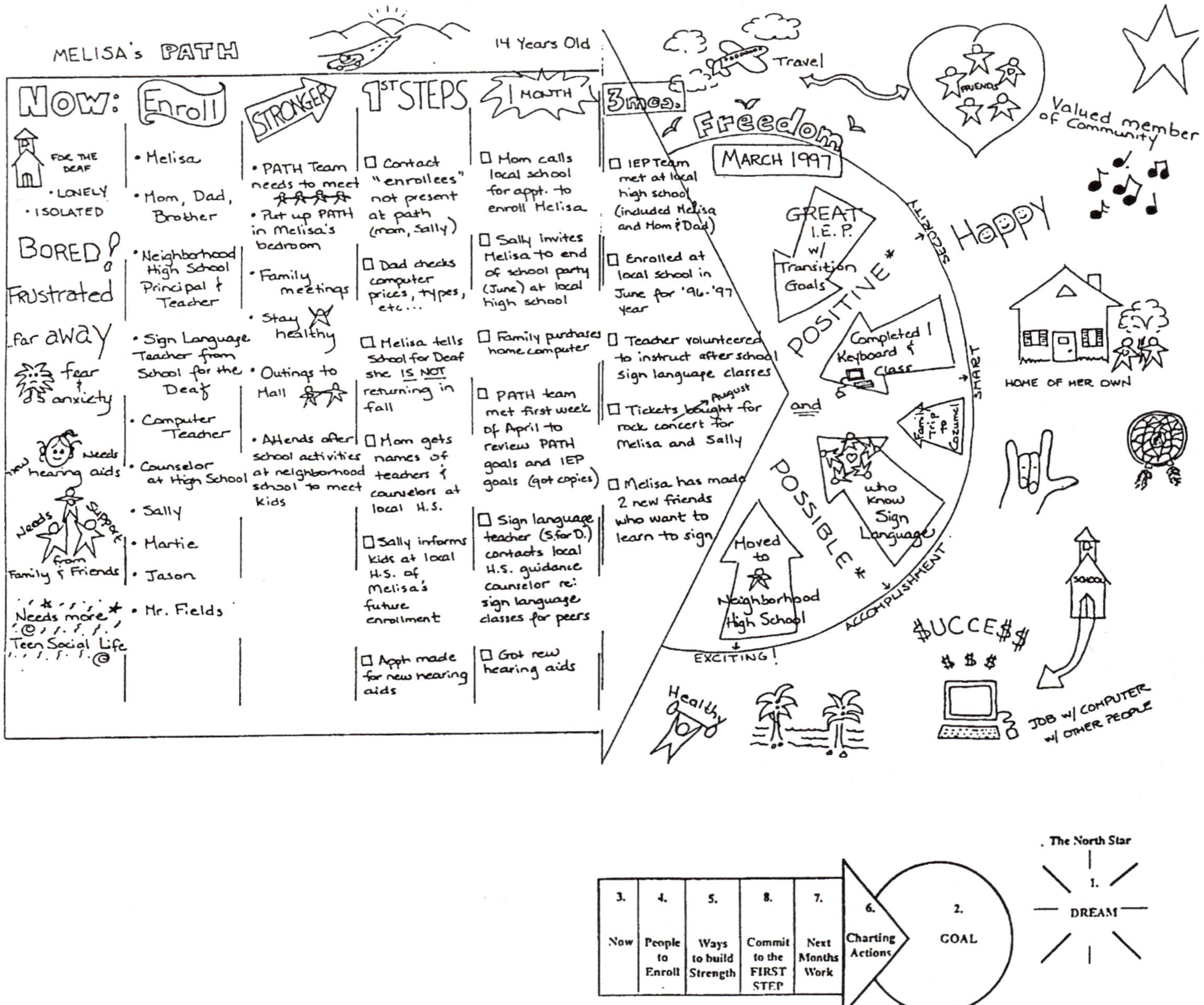

Figure 7–2 Sample PATH. *Source:* Lower portion is reprinted with permission from *Inclusion News*, © 1996, Inclusion Press. Graphics by Paula Ropelewski.

Figure 7-3 Belonging. Courtesy of Dan Wilkins, Nth Degree.

school employees have equal value? Are special education teachers as valuable as general education teachers?

Consider this example. One educator transferred from the general education field to the special education field to teach children labeled "severely and profoundly handicapped." This teacher had taught the previous 15 years in the same school system; she left in June as a general education teacher and returned in the fall as a special education teacher. Within one week, the teacher was questioning what had happened during the summer vacation. She felt left out and ignored, as if she were no longer part of the school staff. Teachers avoided her students in the hallways and seemed to have difficulty maintaining eye contact with her. She was not assigned to any grade-level team. The previous year, as a general education teacher with 15 years' teaching experience, she had a duty-free lunch time, one planning period each day, and other daily times when she had no student contact while her students were in library, physical education, art, or music. She was not assigned any before- or after-school duties, nor were any of the other general education teachers. As a special education teacher in the same school system, she found she had no scheduled lunch time away from her students, she had no planning time during school hours, she was assigned bus duty before school, and she was given a classroom as far from the center of the school as possible. Other staff members avoided her classroom. Many special education teachers across the United States share similar experiences. Why? Are special education teachers—often with advanced degrees—not as smart or as important? Are the learners they teach not as valuable as other learners?

Another example involves an educator who entered a school, asked for the classroom location of a child (who has a disability) and had an administrator respond that "the zoo classroom is over there." Adults in schools need to discover where they stand on recognizing the value of everyone, and everyone's right to feel accepted and to feel a sense of belonging.

Dan Wilkins, an advocate for inclusive communities, developed this definition of *belonging*:

> **be•long**, v. 1: to feel and be a part of . . . i.e., of a community, a workplace, a neighborhood or school 2: to enjoy a sense of contribution, value, self-worth 3: to truly believe one is a natural and equal part of the whole 4: comfortable, safe, cared for, welcome (Wilkins, 1995).

This definition of *belonging* challenges educators to look at issues of self-worth, values, equality, and welcoming. It is crucial for teams to focus on all four of these issues to make education successful for all students.

One excellent resource that explores the topic of self-worth is *Reclaiming Youth at Risk: Our Hope for the Future* (Brendtro, Brokenleg, & Van Bockern, 1990). These authors discuss a philosophy of belonging based upon the Native American circle of courage, built upon a medicine wheel symbol with the child depicted in the center surrounded by four directions. These directions portray four goals of Native American education that lead to self-worth (Brendtro et al., 1990):

- belonging—nurturing a belief in the universal need for belonging
- mastery—ensuring competency through guaranteed opportunities for success
- independence—fostering a sense of confidence and power by encouraging personal independence
- generosity—experiencing one's worth and sharing one's gifts by giving to and caring for others.

Like dream catchers, the circle of courage was designed by Native Americans. Brendtro et al. (1990) state: "We believe the philosophy embodied in this circle of courage is not only a cultural belonging of Native peoples, but a cultural birthright for all the world's children" (p. 36). To educate a child successfully, the child must have daily opportunities to experience all four parts of this educational philosophy. When one area is missing, the circle is broken. When broken, the circle cannot be fixed without first understanding where it is broken. Instead of isolating and punishing children "at risk" in our school systems, we need to "reclaim" them, bringing them into the classroom, offering guidance, and learning to support building or rebuilding self-esteem.

Certainly the efficacy of this approach has implications not just for Native American children or children at risk, but for all children. This philosophy, so fundamental to children with disabilities, is proving effective as a philosophy for alternative schools as well as for students in general and special education. While the information above refers to the education of children, the four areas of self-worth depicted by the circle of courage offer a universal philosophy beneficial to *all* individuals, regardless of age.

Belonging and Friendships

> To be alienated is to lack a sense of belonging, to feel cut off from family, friends, school or work—the four worlds of childhood.
> *Urie Bronfenbrenner* (cited in Brendtro et al., 1990, p. 6)

Students in a multicultural fifth-grade class in Virginia were asked to respond to the following questions:

- How would you feel if you didn't have any friends, and other kids avoided and ignored you? *Lonely, frustrated, angry, scared, sad, and depressed*
- What do you think you would do if you had those feelings? *Ditch school, run away, cry, hit someone, take drugs, drink booze*
- What could make someone feel that way? *Being different, looking weird, being from another country, talking another language, being a different religion than the other kids, not fitting in, not being popular*
- How many of you have ever had a day like that—a "nobody likes me, everybody hates me, think I'll go

eat worms" kind of day? *Everyone, including the teacher, acknowledged having days with those feelings*
- Can you pay attention and learn on the days when you are having those feelings? *Overwhelming no's!*

These are all pretty scary responses. The students' answers to that final question, though, are extremely powerful. This was a multicultural classroom, with learners from five countries, many religions, and various learning abilities, including one child with the label of autism. Yet, when the administration was asked to allow classroom time for ongoing discussions related to issues of diversity and belonging, the response was "it takes away from learning time." This is not an isolated incident. Schools that encourage staff development regarding inclusive classrooms and best practices are recognizing the need for including time in their schedules for issues surrounding acceptance, belonging, and diversity. Families are looking for these schools and are even willing to move to have their children attend schools that value issues of belonging, diversity, and relationships (see Exhibit 7–10).

Friends and Relationships

According to Aristotle, "Friendship is a thing most necessary to life, since without friends no one would choose to live, though possessed of all other advantages." Clearly,

Exhibit 7–10 Kit, Circles, and Belonging

It is 1990. My husband and I sit in pint-sized chairs at our local YMCA preschool program on Parents' Observation Day, watching our five-year-old son Kit. I am remembering how my palms sweat and my stomach clenched when I first called the Y to ask about enrolling our then three-year-old son in their preschool. With a forced casualness that I did not feel, I had explained that Kit had Down syndrome. I did not say that it was my most fervent wish that he be allowed to go to "regular school with regular kids." Instead, I held my breath and waited. Without missing a beat, the voice told me, "We've never had a child with Down syndrome before, or any handicap for that matter, but we would love to try with Kit. Let me check with a teacher whom I think would be perfect and then I'll be back to you." I hung up the phone still not breathing, my tears beginning to well and fall. With little ado, Kit was going to regular school.

So as we sit here now and observe, two years later, my nervousness turns to sadness. Kit's teacher is loving. She wants Kit in her class, but she has no experience in facilitating his relationships with his classmates. Kit seems happy to cruise the outskirts of the small clusters of children, playing alongside but never with any of them. His delayed language development seems a barrier to his connecting with these chattering children, but his desire to stand off and just watch is distancing him as well.

My husband and I ride home. I am fighting back tears. Kit is on the edge of things—not really a part of any circle of children, not really belonging. The isolation and separation that I have feared is before me in plain view. "Wait a while," my husband reasons with me. "Not everyone is always in the center of the circle. Sometimes we are just barely a part of the circle. Sometimes we wander on the outskirts, moving toward the circle, sometimes moving intentionally and comfortably toward the edge. But if you never get to the circle, you have no chance of ever being a part of it. We've gotten Kit to the circle. Can't we just enjoy that and take it one step at a time?" So we have the first of many celebrations of small steps.

We have spent these last six years making sure that we get Kit to the circle. For the most part, getting there has *not* been half the fun! Public school in New Jersey was not as welcoming of Kit as the Y preschool had been. Teachers and therapists struggled, often unsupported in their efforts to include Kit in regular classes. He was known as "the Down syndrome child" and I was "the inclusive parent" or, with a slip of the tongue, "the intrusive parent." There were, of course, some wonderful moments with educators whose capacity to grow and give of themselves inspired us.

Yet I still saw Kit on the edge of the circle, bravely showing up each day but not really belonging. From day one at the Y

continues

Exhibit 7–10 continued

when I asked him what he liked about school, and every time thereafter, his answer was always the same. In his staccato speech that has frustrated legions of speech therapists, he replied "Kids, mom, kids."

Then one day we moved to Virginia. We hand-picked the school that Kit would attend and bought a house in that school's jurisdiction. Administrators and teachers in this school wanted children with disabilities to be in general education classes: they *wanted* Kit! He was never referred to as my "Down syndrome child," and I was introduced as simply "Kit's mom." Special education and general education teachers were just developing a collaborative teaching model. The nucleus of a team had been formed and—oh, by the way—did I want to be part of it? We were home! My husband and I both cried.

Kit's team meets monthly. This is our third year at it. We grapple with all aspects of Kit's school life. My husband and I have shared our dreams for Kit with our fellow team members. To our great joy, we find that they have dreams for him too. While once we were Kit's only advocates, now we know when to take a back seat and listen and smile.

The team addresses social issues as well as academic concerns. Kit's teachers and therapists have brainstormed ideas with us to facilitate Kit's friendships with his classmates. Kit is seated in class next to kids with whom he is developing "rapport." Once while volunteering in Kit's class, I had to restrain myself from hugging his teacher. I overheard her warning Kit and a buddy that if they continued to talk too much during teaching time she would separate them. My Kit was talking too much—and to a friend, no less!

Early on, one of Kit's teachers noticed that he was not playing well with the other kids during recess. She observed some more and decided that Kit, and other children as well, could not

keep up with the ever-changing rules to the group games that the kids played. She picked a few games, wrote down the rules, and spent several recesses and rainy days teaching all of the children uniform sets of rules. She explained that some kids were getting confused and that it was very grown up to play by a fixed set of rules. She then facilitated for Kit and modeled for the other children how to do the same.

When some children began picking on each other, a Friday afternoon was designated "ability awareness afternoon." Activities were designed to allow the children to move in small groups through stations where they could explore ways in which they were different and the same. Talk time focused on the importance of valuing our similarities and our differences and appropriate forms of expression.

The emphasis on inclusion at Kit's school has eliminated many of the artificial barriers to belonging. Kids like Kit are no longer scary or friendless. Parents often hear volumes about Kit from their own kids long before they ever meet him. Usually they hear good things. When they do meet him, they feel much as I do; they admire him.

Kit, his dad, and I stand in the center of the circle together. We each see different things. Kit sees kids. My husband sees a place where there are choices. I see the best of all that I can give to Kit: a wealth of caring family and friends and the riches of the simple pleasures of an ordinary life.

As parents, we often feel the need to let go of our dreams for our children. It is hard to make our dreams come true without lots of help, and it is difficult to reach out and ask for that help. Yet when hands reach back and grasp not only our *hand but our child's as well, there is a great sense of relief and joy in knowing that the circle is wide enough to encompass us all.*

Courtesy of Eileen Hammar.

the need to belong and have relationships in one's life is not just a disability issue, but having friends and feeling a sense of belonging can be more difficult for someone with a disability. Some of us have an easy time developing relationships, others have a difficult time making friends and "fitting in." As we grow up, we learn about relationships, friends, belonging, and how to make choices that satisfy our needs for these things. For many reasons, children with disabilities often have a difficult time learning how to make these choices and, when they do, having opportunities to follow through. Some of the barriers are segregated classrooms, lack of mobility skills, and different communication styles. Think for a minute about the friendships in your own life. Where and how did you meet these people? What makes them so special? Were these relationships determined for you—or did you have choices? Now think about a student you know with a significant challenge.

Does this child have the same opportunities to meet and interact with other children (Schaffner & Buswell, 1992)? Educators who facilitate friendship building for children find that each experience is unique—except for one consistent, overwhelming fact: in each situation, the child with a disability is the catalyst for discovering and assisting other children, without labels, to also express their feelings and frustrations regarding making friends and feeling welcome and wanted in their schools and neighborhoods.

Circle of Friends

The circle of friends, developed by Marsha Forest, Judith Snow, and Jack Pearpoint, is a process to facilitate the building of relationships with one's peers (Forest & Pearpoint, 1992). The concept is based on looking at the relationships in different areas in the life of an individual with a disability. Using four concentric circles (see Figure 7–4), with the child in the middle, the people involved in a child's life are listed.

The innermost circle (circle of intimacy) indicates people the child loves most; the second circle (circle of friendship) depicts best friends; the third circle (circle of participation) shows individuals who participate in activities with the child, and the fourth circle (circle of exchange) indicates those paid to be in the child's life. In many instances, children with disabilities have people in the first circle (often family members), the next two circles are almost blank, and the outer circle is filled with people. Circles must be filled from the outside in. No one can pick a best friend for someone else. Relationships are formed only when there are opportunity and proximity. People paid to be in a child's life can facilitate relationship building by providing opportunities for friendships to develop and ensuring that the child is in the proximity of other children of the same age. This includes opportunities for the child with a disability to be around children with and without disabilities. Class meetings or circle-of-friends activities can be arranged to help a child have more balanced circles. These meetings empower children to discuss topics important to them and find mutual interests.

Beginning circle-of-friends activities in a classroom requires only that the adults care about and value all the students in the classroom. A classroom teacher or other adult with knowledge of circle of friends acts as facilitator (adapts activities as necessary). Someone else should be the recorder to take down each response, preferably on large chart paper for all to see. (In upper grades, the students might take turns doing this recording.) Recommended time allotment for this activity is 30 minutes, once a week. The adults model group behavior and join in the

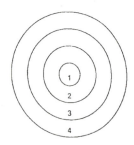

Fill circles from the outside in:
First circle: circle of intimacy
Second circle: circle of friendship
Third circle: circle of participation
Fourth circle: circle of exchange

Figure 7–4 Circle of Friends. *Source:* Reprinted with permission from *Inclusion News,* © 1996. Inclusion Press.

circle, rather than having all the children sit facing the teacher. Some suggestions for topics at the first meeting include:

- What is a friend?
- What do you like to do with friends?
- How would you feel without friends?
- Have you ever had a day when you felt no one liked you?
- What could you do to help someone make friends?

The adult facilitators might have the students fill in their concentric circles at either the first or second session. Children who are uncomfortable sharing their circles should not be forced to do so. At the end of the session, review responses and post this paper somewhere in the classroom. It can be shared again at the beginning of the next circle meeting.

Consider letting the students come up with agenda items. Following a session on friendships and one on after-school activities, the students in one child's class decided they wanted to call her on the phone, visit her house to play after school, and have her join Brownies with the other second-grade girls. The teacher sent a letter to all the parents letting them know it was okay with the child's mother for the kids to call and to set up afternoon play times. Brownies proved more difficult, because the leaders were afraid to have someone join their troop who used a wheelchair and spoke only a few words. Classmates invited troop leaders to visit their class and join in a circle-of-friends activity designed to share the child's strengths and to answer questions. Her mother also participated. The outcome was that, after one year, the child had learned the Brownie pledge and the "Make New Friends" song. The troop had gained an extra leader, and they had a sleepover at the child's house in the spring (Malatchi, 1994a).

Educators who work with circle-of-friends activities note the following outcomes for *all* students who participate:

- increase in understanding and appreciation of all members of the class
- increase in listening skills
- development of group problem-solving skills
- increase in expressive language skills
- a feeling of belonging
- elevated self-esteem.

Additionally, teachers who engage in circle-of-friends activities often discover the following:

- Students are a resource in curriculum adaptations.
- Fewer classroom management problems occur when students feel empowered to share feelings and ideas.
- A feeling of community develops in their classrooms.
- Teachers develop a more holistic view of their students.

CELEBRATING DIVERSITY

In schools and classrooms where everyone is welcome and everyone belongs, there will be a diversity of abilities, cultures, and races. It is up to the adults to keep the issue of diversity an open one, and to celebrate diversity on an ongoing basis. For staff development workshops, PTA meetings, and classroom meetings, one way to promote the discussion, understanding, and celebration of diversity is through children's literature. This chapter began by mentioning four books by Eric Carle. Taking a new look at certain books written for children can open opportunities for discussions with adults, as well as children. The following books provide opportunities for the discussion of friendship, diversity (including multicultural), dreaming, and belonging. People of all ages can enjoy these books, and discussion questions and follow-up activities can be designed according to the age of the readers. Circle-of-friends activities might begin or end with the sharing of one of these books or many others that are available. Opening or closing a staff meeting or PTA meeting with one of these stories can stimulate thoughts of friendship, belonging, and diversity for adults, as well as children. Do adult attitudes need some adjustment? Try *The Sneetches* (Seuss, 1961). Are some students feeling isolated or friendless? Try *The Very Lonely Firefly* (Carle, 1995). Teachers might encourage a family member to read a story in their class and facilitate an activity. There are endless possibilities—just be creative! The following books (as well as many others) can be used with children and adults to promote partnerships, belonging, and diversity.

- *The Sneetches* (Seuss, 1961). This is an excellent example of the importance of celebrating diversity. Following World War II in 1953, Dr. Seuss wrote the tale of two groups of Sneetches. One group has stars on their bellies, the others do not. The group with stars are convinced that they are better than the other Sneetches and, as a result, exclude them from their parties and games. A variety of escapades occur while the Sneetches "without" try to become the Sneetches "with." This includes hiring someone to "fix" things, and paying all their money to this individual. By the last page, however, the Sneetches "decided that Sneetches are Sneetches and no kind of Sneetch is the best on the beaches. That day, all the Sneetches forgot about stars and whether they had one, or not, upon thars" (p. 24).
- *The Big Orange Splot* (Pinkwater, 1977). When adults and children need encouragement to dream, *The Big Orange Splot* is hard to beat. People of all ages enjoy the adventures of Mr. Plumbean as he tries to decide how to handle an orange splot that appeared on his house. His creativity and unusual approach upset his neighbors until, one by one, they begin to have their own dreams.
- *The Rainbow Fish* (Pfister, 1992). This is a wonderful book about the reciprocity involved in friendships. One of the most beautiful fish in the ocean is covered with sparkly scales that are the envy of other fish. The Rainbow Fish discovers the value of friendships and that to have a friend involves giving a part of himself. This is a very difficult choice until the fish tries it and feels so good about giving. "The Rainbow Fish shared his scales left and right. And the more he gave away, the more delighted he became" (p. 22).
- *Over the Deep Blue Sea* (Ikeda, 1992). Three children from diverse cultures have been close friends until they discover that their ancestors were enemies. Their friendship abruptly ends. It takes a crisis for these children to realize that friendship can overcome the damage caused by war or racial prejudice.
- *Tar Beach* (Ringgold, 1991). This powerful picture book brings up issues of race, dreams, family, community, and poverty—all in fewer than 30 pages of narrative and incredible illustrations. Faith Ringgold, the author and illustrator, is a noted quiltmaker whose works hang in the Guggenheim Museum in New York. In this, her first children's book, she weaves a tale about a little girl and the dreams she has on hot summer nights on a roof in Harlem. *Tar Beach* received the Parent's Choice Award in 1991.
- *Amazing Grace* (Hoffman, 1991). Support, independence, and achieving a dream are the key themes of this delightful book. A Reading Rainbow Selection, this book tells of Grace, an amazing, independent young girl who loves acting out the stories her grandmother tells her. When Grace discovers that her class play will be Peter Pan, she decides to audition for the lead role. She meets resistance from her classmates because she is a girl and she is black. With the support of her mother and grandmother, Grace rehearses for and wins the part of Peter. The play is a huge success, and even her classmates agree that Grace was amazing.
- *Tom's Fish* (Coffelt, 1994). Accepting others as they are and not trying to change them is the underlying theme of this picture book. Tom's favorite birthday present is a goldfish, Jessie. Jessie is a very unusual goldfish who can swim only upside down. Tom tries a variety of things to get Jessie to change and swim like other goldfish, but Jessie remains, happily, upside down. At the conclusion of the story, Tom realizes how *he* can change to accept and enjoy Jessie just the way he is.
- *Stellaluna* (Cannon, 1993). This book deals with acceptance, belonging, and welcoming. Separated from her mother as a baby, a young bat is raised by a

mother bird. This warm, moving story also addresses the issues of diversity, friendship, and the struggle to conform. When Stellaluna finally returns to her mother and the other bats, she maintains her friendship with the birds who were her family.

- *Who Belongs Here? An American Story* (Knight, 1993). This book, based on a true story, depicts the intolerance people often display to refugees. It is the story of Nary, who, with his grandmother, escapes from Cambodia to the United States where he believes life will be "better than heaven." He does find freedom and safety, but also finds that he is the object of cruel name calling and a desire on the part of some people that he go back to where he came from. The anecdotes throughout this book are an added bonus. They describe the experiences of other refugees and their contributions to American culture. Who would be here if we all went back to where we came from?

Including Carle's books, these are only 13 of over 100 books that lend themselves to group discussions (Malatchi, 1994b). While there are also valuable books that are specifically about individuals with disabilities, the books described here are recommended to be used in a proactive manner for children and adults in creating climates where diversity of all kinds is celebrated.

This chapter has looked at *hope, work, love,* and *belonging*—the words stressed in Eric Carle's "very" quartet. The issues addressed in this chapter are important for quality education for all learners and essential for building inclusive schools. The last two books in Carle's quartet (*The Very Quiet Cricket* and *The Very Lonely Firefly*) also speak about the quest to be heard, to have a voice in life, and be accepted by one's own community. If those of us who have chosen education as a career encourage families, colleagues, and ourselves to voice our dreams, share them, and find people to listen who care, our schools and communities will be filled with dream catchers, crickets will no longer be quiet, and fireflies won't be lonely. In the words of Dom Helder Camera: "If you dream alone, it is only a dream, but when you dream together, it is the beginning of reality" (Forest, 1991, p. 403).

REFERENCES

Brendtro, L., Brokenleg, M., & Van Bockern, S. (1990). *Reclaiming youth at risk: Our hope for the future.* Bloomington, IN: National Education Service.

Cannon, J. (1993). *Stellaluna.* New York: Harcourt Brace.

Carle, E. (1984). *The very busy spider.* New York: Philomel.

Carle, E. (1987). *The very hungry caterpillar.* New York: Philomel.

Carle, E. (1990). *The very quiet cricket.* New York: Philomel.

Carle, E. (1995). *The very lonely firefly.* New York: Philomel.

Coffelt, N. (1994). *Tom's fish.* New York: Harcourt Brace.

Falvey, M. (1996). *Inclusion News.* Toronto, Ontario, Canada: Inclusion.

Forest, M. (1991). It's about relationships. In L. Meyer, C. Peck, & L. Brown (Eds.), *Critical issues in the lives of people with severe disabilities* (pp. 399–407). Baltimore: Paul H. Brookes.

Forest, M., & Pearpoint, J. (1992). Common sense tools: MAPs and circles for inclusive education. In J. Pearpoint, M. Forest, & J. Snow (Eds.), *Inclusion papers: Strategies to make inclusion work* (pp. 40–56). Toronto, Ontario, Canada: Inclusion.

Giangreco, M.F., Cloninger, C.J., & Iverson, V.S. (1993). COACH: *Choosing options and accommodations for children.* Baltimore: Paul H. Brookes.

Hoffman, M. (1991). *Amazing Grace.* New York: Dial Books for Young Readers.

Ikeda, D. (1992). *Over the deep blue sea.* New York: Alfred A. Knopf.

Knight, M. (1993). *Who belongs here? An American story.* Gardiner, ME: Tilbury House.

Kubler-Ross, E. (1969). *On death and dying.* New York: Macmillan.

Malatchi, A. (1994a). ABC's of education: Parents as partners, the IEP process. *Four Runner, 10*(2), 4.

Malatchi, A. (1994b). Celebrating diversity: Books, books, books! Virginia Institute for Developmental Disabilities. Richmond, VA: Virginia Commonwealth University.

Martinez, C. (1990). A dream for myself. In R. Schalock (Ed.), *Quality of life: Perspectives and issues* (pp. 3–7). Washington, DC: American Association on Mental Retardation.

Maslow, A. (1970). *Motivation and personality.* New York: Harper & Row.

Moses, K. (1988). *Lost dreams and growth* [video]. Evanston, IL: Resource Networks.

Mount, B. (1992). *Person-centered planning.* New York: Graphic Futures.

Mount, B., & Zwernik, K. (1988). *It's never too early: It's never too late.* St. Paul, MN: Metropolitan Council.

O'Brien, J., & Lovett, H. (1996). What is person-centered planning? *Inclusion News.* Toronto, Ontario, Canada: Inclusion.

Orelove, F., & Malatchi, A. (1996). Curriculum and instruction. In F. Orelove & D. Sobsey, *Educating children with multiple disabilities: A transdisciplinary approach* (3rd ed., pp. 377–409). Baltimore: Paul H. Brookes.

Pearpoint, J., O'Brien, J., & Forest, M. (1995). PATH: *Planning alternative tomorrows with hope* (2nd ed.). Toronto, Ontario, Canada: Inclusion.

Pfister, M. (1992). *The rainbow fish.* New York: North-South.

Pinkwater, D.M. (1977). *The big orange splot.* New York: Scholastic.

Rainforth, B., York, J., & Macdonald, C. (1992). An ecological model of curriculum. In B. Rainforth, J. York, & C. Macdonald (Eds.), *Collaborative teams for students with severe disabilities* (pp. 69–104). Baltimore: Paul H. Brookes.

Riley, R. (1994). *Strong families, strong schools.* Washington, DC: U.S. Department of Education.

Ringgold, F., (1991). *Tar beach.* New York: Crown.

Romer, L.T., & Romer, M.A. (1995). Developing educational plans to support valued lifestyles. In N. Haring & L. Romer (Eds.), *Welcoming students who are deaf-blind into typical classrooms* (pp. 105–132). Baltimore: Paul H. Brookes.

Schaffner, C.B., & Buswell, B. (1992). *Connecting students: A guide to thoughtful friendship facilitation for educators and families.* Colorado Springs, CO: PEAK Parent Center.

Senge, P. (1990). *The fifth discipline: The art and practice of the learning organization.* New York: Doubleday/Currency.

Seuss, Dr. (1961). *The sneetches and other stories.* New York: Random House.

Snow, J. (1994). Dreaming and listening. In J. Snow, *What's really worth doing and how to do it: A book for people labeled disabled (possibly yourself)* (pp. 37–45). Toronto, Ontario, Canada: Inclusion.

Thousand, J., Villa. R., & Nevin, A. (1994). *Creativity and collaborative learning.* Baltimore: Paul H. Brookes.

U.S. Department of Education (1995). Educational placements of students with disabilities. *17th annual report to Congress* (pp. 13–37). Washington, DC: Author.

Villa, R., & Thousand, J. (1992). Restructuring public school systems: Strategies for organizational change and progress. In R. Villa, J. Thousand, W. Stainback, & S. Stainback (Eds.), *Restructuring for caring and effective education: An administrative guide to creating heterogeneous schools* (pp. 109–137). Baltimore: Paul H. Brookes.

Wilkins, D. (1995). *Nth Degree.* Luckey, OH: Author.

CHAPTER 8

Supporting Inclusive Education through Interagency Collaboration

Patrick H. Haley, Wyllys D. VanDerwerker, and Lissa A. Power-deFur

INTRODUCTION

Schools often struggle to place students with disabilities in more inclusive settings while trying to deal with the noneducational challenges the students may bring to the classroom. These challenges may include substance abuse within the home, truancy, juvenile delinquency, inadequate nutrition, parental unemployment, insufficient medical services, limited funds for prescribed medications, homelessness, or abuse and neglect.

This chapter reviews the importance of addressing educational issues while simultaneously attending to family, health, and mental health issues for certain children. Through a review of the mission of and services offered by various community-based agencies, this chapter helps educators to identify the role of interagency collaboration in the lives of children. Strategies for educators, community members, and parents are offered to establish and use the creative efforts and services of community agencies to support students with disabilities. Such community-based endeavors provide the necessary "wraparound" services to enable the student with disabilities and his or her family to experience success in school and in the community. For some students, this support is necessary to enable the student to return to the neighborhood school from a more restrictive setting and to be placed in an inclusive education setting. The chapter concludes with examples of how interagency collaboration supports a student's placement in the least restrictive environment.

THE ROLE OF INTERAGENCY COLLABORATION IN INCLUSIVE EDUCATION

"The challenge is to free ourselves from categorical programs and treat the whole child." Senator Edward Kennedy spoke those words (National Consensus Building Conference on School-Linked Integrated Services Systems, 1994, p. 2), which capture the importance of considering more than schooling when working with children and their families. Educators, by necessity, focus on the educational needs of the child. Many children's lives, however, are complicated by issues outside school. Categorical thinking (e.g., education, social services, mental health) and failure to treat the whole child will increase the chances that an inclusive placement will be unsuccessful for some children. Providing home-based support for children and families improves the success of the student's least restrictive placement in the regular school. "Addressing education or behavior problems without attending to family or health problems is seldom effective" (National Consensus Building Conference on School-Linked Integrated Services Systems, 1994, p. 9). Many children with disabilities who are educated in public schools concurrently receive services from other community agencies. Without collaboration among agencies, services may be duplicated, fragmented, or even at cross-purposes.

The overlap between the many agencies that serve children was made clear in a study conducted by the Virginia Department of Planning and Budget in response to the increasing cost of children's residential placements. In 1989, most of the students in publicly funded residential placements for children were served by more than one agency: 84% were served by juvenile justice, 57% by special education, 54% by social services, and 53% by mental health (Virginia Department of Planning and Budget, 1990). Analysis of placements revealed that the more than 14,000 cases receiving residential services from four public agencies represented fewer than 5,000 different children. The children had merely entered the residential placement system by one agency, then another, and then perhaps a third. Further, the type of service depended on the system by which the child entered the residential system (e.g., special education, social services, juvenile justice, mental health), with minimal involvement with the other agencies.

The need for interagency collaboration is perhaps clearest for students with serious emotional disturbance. The success of educational programs for students with emotional and behavioral disorders is poor; these students have the highest dropout rates, and after completing school, they have the poorest employment rates and the highest incarceration rates of all students with disabilities (Wagner, Blackorby, Cameto, & Newman, 1993). A higher percentage of students with emotional disturbance are placed in residential facilities than students with any other disability, except students with deaf-blindness (U.S. Department of Education, 1995).

The 1990 reauthorization of the Individuals with Disabilities Education Act (IDEA) included a new program in response to concerns about students with serious emotional disturbance. The *National Agenda for Achieving Better Results for Children and Youth with Serious Emotional Disturbance* (U.S. Department of Education, 1994) was the product of this planning. This report identified the magnitude of the problem associated with meeting the needs of children and youths with serious emotional disturbance and their families. Only 42% graduate from high school, in contrast to 50% of all youths with disabilities and 76% of the general population. Nearly 50% of students with serious emotional disturbance drop out of high school. Fewer than 17% are educated in general education classrooms, and 18% are educated outside their regular schools. Of students with serious emotional disturbance, 20% are arrested at least once before leaving school (in contrast to 9% of all students with disabilities and 6% of all students). This involvement with the criminal justice system continues, as 58% of youths with serious emotional disturbance are arrested within five years of leaving school, and 73% of those who drop out are arrested within five years (U.S. Department of Education, 1994). In addition, the *National Agenda* suggested that families are likely to be blamed for the student's disabilities and bear a significant financial burden to secure services for their children (U.S. Department of Education, 1994).

Youths with serious emotional disturbance generally receive an array of services from many different agencies and providers—services that may be overlapping or even competing. The services provided by education, mental health, substance abuse, child welfare, juvenile justice, and vocational agencies are all necessary to ensure the youths' success. However, without community-based, collaborative planning, the services may be fragmented, duplicative, and confusing. The agencies involved in serving these youths and their families must jointly plan and administer services.

The *National Agenda* established seven targets to achieve better results for children and youths with disabilities. Two of these reflect the importance of community-based services: Target 2, Strengthen School and Community Capacity; and Target 7, Create Comprehensive and Collaborative Systems (U.S. Department of Education, 1994). The report recognized that maintaining students with serious emotional disturbance in general education classrooms and regular schools requires the provision of an array of services in the schools and in other service delivery systems. Collaboration between the schools and mental health services was identified as one of the most positive approaches. A fundamental feature of success is the notion of services following the children and family, rather than the child and family following the services.

School-linked services have also been produced in response to efforts to improve integration of education, health, and social services for children. School-linked services are characterized by collaboration among schools, health care providers, and social service agencies; collaborative planning and governing of services; and provision of services at or near to schools (Center for the Future of Children, 1992). In some localities, community agencies have established a service delivery system within the public school system. The local health department may provide immunizations, medical, and dental care. The mental health agency may provide mental health counseling in the schools. Provision of such services within the schools precludes the need for out-of-school appointments and ensures that children keep their appointments. School-based services help the home and school fully understand the student's needs and ensure consistent application of intervention strategies.

As educators become more familiar with the flexibility and strengths of interagency collaboration, they find that collaboration is an important part of the inclusion supports developed for students who have a variety of disabilities and challenges outside the school. The following examples demonstrate this point.

- The creative efforts of an interagency team can provide parents of a three-year-old child with cerebral palsy the home-based therapy needed to ensure that toileting needs are addressed, thus removing toileting as an obstacle when the parents try to place the child in the neighborhood preschool/day care program. (See Chapter 9 for more information on inclusive services for preschoolers with disabilities.)
- A behavior specialist, often an employee of the local mental health and mental retardation agency, can help the school's effort to transfer improved behavior into community settings. The support provided by the behavior specialist can help the child function in the normalized settings that his or her parents frequent. The parents' increased comfort with their child's

behavior in public will result in an increase in opportunities for the child to accompany them.

- The health department can be supportive in providing staff training and on-site technical assistance to help a school team serve a child with special health needs. (See Chapter 16 for further information on children with special health needs.)
- The interagency team can help the parents and school personnel structure the home, school, and community supports needed to help an adolescent with severe mental retardation and behavior disorders return to the community from a residential center. In fact, many school divisions would be unable to return students to the district from residential settings without such support. The team approach, often available 24 hours per day, not only increases communication among all providers, but makes it easier to bring about changes in behaviors.
- Students who have been before the juvenile court and have a history of poor school performance can be successful in instructional environments when mental health counselors, juvenile probation officers, and home-based social services personnel all work together to help the student understand and use appropriate social and school behavior. These agencies are an integral part of the after-school supports the child needs to complete homework.
- Community agencies may provide structured summer activities for certain students with disabilities. Although these students may not need extended school year special education services, they will benefit from the supportive, organized programs offered by the parks and recreation program.
- Some special education students also receive foster care services through the local social services agencies. The success of the education placement and the foster care placement may rest on the child's ability to function within the neighborhood school. If a foster care placement is unsuccessful due to problems in the child's educational placement, the foster care placement may be changed, sometimes to a more restrictive setting. These more restrictive settings are often characterized by on-site education programs, thereby placing the child in a very restrictive educational program. Interagency planning and service coordination can provide the supports necessary at the school and for the foster parents, assisting in maintaining the placement in a less restrictive environment.
- Students who have physical disabilities can be more successful in inclusive environments when an interagency approach to education is used. The challenges the child faces in school are often similar to those he or she faces in the community. Physical obstacles that present challenges to inclusive school environments may be the same as those encountered in recreation or leisure environments. A knowledgeable interagency team can remove those obstacles in public environments, while the school staff members are responsible for the school environments.
- Students who come from homes where there is substance abuse, or other high-risk activity, may find it difficult to complete academic tasks in any classroom. The interagency team can identify the difficulties the child encounters at home and offer the support services needed to help the family provide structure and consistent parenting for the child. Services focusing on basic needs can go a long way toward improving the functioning level and effort a student brings to a classroom.

THE MOVEMENT TOWARD INTERAGENCY COLLABORATION

Local school districts that strive to maintain the student in the local school setting are often confronted with the need to offer many noneducational, ancillary services to maintain the student in the least restrictive environment. When school districts are unable to meet these needs in isolation, the use of interagency and intra-agency coordination, communication, and collaboration, and the integration of services are imperative.

As early as 1982, Johnson, McLaughlin, and Christensen suggested that interagency collaboration would improve services for children and youths with disabilities. They also noted the financial benefit of serving children within the community rather than in residential or day placements (Johnson, McLaughlin, & Christensen, 1982). During the 1980s, the juvenile justice system shifted its focus away from "status offenders" and "incorrigibles." A byproduct of this change in focus was an alarming increase in children and adolescents in the mental health system. As mental health providers worked to address the needs of these children, they began to realize that these needs should be addressed through an interagency approach. Stroul and Friedman (1986) first conceptualized a system of care for youths with emotional and behavior disorders. Their conceptual framework described a community-based system for children and their families that provided integrated services designed by an interagency team and coordinated by a case manager.

Ventura County, California, was a leader in changing how publicly funded agencies serve at-risk youth and their families. The project explored statutory and regulatory changes that fostered interagency cooperation, interagency protocols, and agreement. Efforts emphasized least restrictive and community-based alternatives for hard-to-place children (Jordan & Hernandez, 1990). During the late 1980s and early 1990s, efforts expanded into other parts of the country. In her analysis of state legislation promoting comprehensive services for students with serious emotional disturbance, Hill (1996) identified at least nine states that have created legislation to encourage and support comprehensive services. She identified certain core components: individualized services, family-focused services, a full array of services and interagency collaborative structure, community-based services, and flexible funding.

As professionals met across departments and agencies, they began to develop a new language—a language focusing on meeting the needs of children and youths and their families. This language embraces new concepts—child-centered, family-focused, comprehensive, community-based services; interagency planning; pooled funding; coordination and collaboration of services; case management; system of care; and family preservation and support. Providers recognized that comprehensive service delivery does more than refer children and families for services: it ensures that necessary services are received (Epstein, Quinn, Nelson, Polsgrove, & Cumblad, 1993; Knitzer, 1993; Melaville & Blank, 1991). Proponents of this approach distinguish between *cooperation* (e.g., referring the family to another agency) and *collaboration* (e.g., establishing common goals and working together to achieve these goals). Further, they argue that these services should be provided at the "front end," before crises occur (Melaville, Blank, & Asayesh, 1993). Referral to other agencies has not guaranteed the provision of services, often resulting in the proverbial "slipping through the crack."

The new interagency approach has been found effective, both in meeting the needs of students and their families' needs and in returning students to less restrictive educational and living environments. In her study of communities using a systems-of-care approach, Stroul (1993) found that children served in communities by interagency teams were less likely to be served in restrictive settings. Further, when these children were placed in a restrictive setting, placement was for shorter periods. Stroul also noted that school attendance and performance improved for students served by the interagency approach.

State-funded demonstration projects in Virginia provided interagency, community-based services in the least restrictive environment to children and youths with emotional and behavioral disorders. Evaluation results revealed that, after three years, more children remained in the community with a reduction in the frequency and duration of residential placements. In addition, local service providers noted an improvement in quality of services and treatment plans (Virginia Department of Mental Health, Mental Retardation, and Substance Abuse Services, 1994). Further, a study of the implementation of the Comprehensive Services Act, a statewide comprehensive, community-based service system, identified the following strengths of the act: improved collaboration and family involvement; community "ownership" of children, families, and services; and improved services to families and youths (Virginia Department of Mental Health, Mental Retardation, and Substance Abuse Services, 1995). Similar results have been identified in demonstration projects in Ohio and Vermont (Algarin & Friedman, 1991).

MAKING INTERAGENCY COLLABORATION WORK

Interagency collaboration is a mind-set and a philosophy, as well as an organizational process. Agencies recognize that certain goals cannot be met in isolation and that, in fact, agency-specific policies may become obstacles to shared decision making. Resources and authority are shared across agencies.

Interagency collaboration requires a commitment to flexibility. It challenges traditional "turf" issues that may arise when two or more agencies try to combine resources and efforts to reach a common goal. Interagency collaboration is based on establishing common connection, whereas interagency coordination is based on the principle of creating agreements. Collaboration sets the stage for service integration—promoting a broader, more inclusive environment. Interagency collaboration is a process where community agencies, both public and private, develop an outcome-oriented plan for the target population.

The experience of interagency initiatives across the country identifies certain key elements to success—success that improves outcomes for students and their families. These elements include: identifying stakeholders, creating a shared vision and philosophy, completing a needs assessment, nurturing and supporting teams, informing the community, and filling service gaps.

Identifying Stakeholders and Service Providers

A key component to developing effective interagency collaboration is to develop an understanding of the roles of various community agencies and the services provided. A simple review of a locality's telephone directory reveals a variety of public, private, federal, state, and local services providers who could become part of a support network for students with disabilities. Exhibit 8–1 provides a general overview of agencies and services frequently found in localities. Each locality will have its own collection of agencies and providers, and the missions and services may vary from those identified in Exhibit 8–1. One community may rely heavily on private service providers, while another community may rely solely on public agencies. (Information on the

Exhibit 8–1 Local Service Providers: Mission, Target Population, and Services

Agency	Mission	Target Population	Services
Public school	Provide appropriate education to all school-age children to promote an educated and employable citizenship	School-age and preschool-age children with disabilities	Academic and vocational instruction, special education and related services (e.g., counseling, occupational or physical therapy, transportation), extracurricular activities, career assessment, transition support
Public health	Provide public health services and programs	Local citizenry	Immunizations, medical care for indigent families, lead identification, health-related educational programs, may provide dental services, medical evaluations, hearing and vision screenings for public schools
Juvenile justice	Protect the public and provide the juvenile with opportunities to reform; may also include child welfare and domestic relations	Juvenile delinquents and status offenders and families	Local and state juvenile correctional facilities, group homes, restitution, counseling, mediation, law-related education
Mental health (and substance abuse services)	Provide assessment and clinical services for individuals with mental, emotional, and behavioral disabilities	Adults, adolescents, and children with mental health and substance abuse problems	Emergency/crisis intervention, outpatient services, intensive in-home services, specialized case management, respite care, day treatment programs
Social services	Protect children and families, provide welfare	Children, adults, families	Child protective services, foster care, adoption (including special needs adoption), welfare, Medicaid eligibility, employment services for eligible clients
Parks and recreation	Promote cultural, recreational, and leisure opportunities	Local citizenry	Neighborhood community centers, organized youth and adult activities, nature programs, indoor and outdoor recreational facilities
Vocational rehabilitation	Provide goods and services to help persons with disabilities obtain employment	Young adults and adults with disabilities	Assessment, guidance, counseling, work-related placement services, job-seeking assistance, personal assistance services, transportation, interpreter services, assistive technology, telecommunication devices
United Way Information and Referral Network	Provide reference services to identify programs for children and adults in communities	Local citizenry	Reference service providing contacts and referral guidelines
Private service providers	Provide specific services	Children and adults who meet criteria	Private education (including special education and related services), structured living arrangements, behavioral support
Public and private day care providers	Provide day care services	Preschool and school-age children	All-day and after-school care

Note: The services displayed are meant to be illustrative and may not include all services available in all settings.

relationship between the schools and other community-based agencies for transition to postschool employment education and independent living can be found in Chapter 14.)

Key stakeholders must be involved in developing a foundation and the guiding principles of a successful interagency system and philosophy. This group should include the leadership of community and private agencies, parents, local government, and funding sources. Stakeholders include agency heads who are trying to provide services on limited budgets, middle managers who work to address the limitations within current programs, and line staff who provide services on a daily basis. Involving the right people is fundamental to getting started in the right direction.

Educators who wish to embark on an interagency initiative to support their efforts to include students with disabilities should identify any agencies and providers in their community who provide services to these students. The first step is to gather information and create a picture of the current method of operation. This information includes the characteristics of the students who need services and a description of all agencies and organizations that provide services to these students. Exhibit 8–2 provides an example of the role played by other providers in the lives of students with disabilities. Note that the exhibit includes both existing and needed services. (A blank form is provided in Exhibit 8–3 for use by school personnel in replicating this chart for their own students.)

Many school districts are actively involved with community agencies through other interagency initiatives. These existing interagency teams may serve as springboards for this interagency initiative. School leaders should consider the interagency team supporting the early intervention component of special education (the local interagency coordinating councils required by Part H of IDEA), the linkages established through transition planning, the initiatives developed in response to the Safe and Drug Free Schools and Communities Act, or other locally developed safe school plans. (See Chapters 9 and 14 for more information on interagency activities in early intervention and transition.)

The contact with other agencies for the purpose of establishing interagency teams supporting students with disabilities should be made by the school district's leadership. The involvement and support of the district superintendent and school board are important for ensuring the commitment of other agencies. Working with service providers within the other agencies and obtaining their support will increase the likelihood of obtaining a commitment from the agency to participate.

Creating a Shared Vision and Philosophy

After stakeholders have been identified and have agreed to be participants in the interagency initiative, efforts should turn to the creation of a shared vision. Stakeholders need to take time to develop this vision, which embraces their philosophy for serving children in their community. This shared vision creates a climate and culture for change. With this comes a willingness to take risks, fail, reevaluate, and try again. A common ground of trust and beliefs must be reached to create a vision statement. Without this, a stakeholder may not share the vision, and that person or agency may undermine efforts, either by neglect or design.

Creating a vision involves identifying what the interagency teams want to accomplish, what the services will look like, and what the outcomes for children and families will be. The vision is supported by a philosophy and set of shared values that evolve over time. The following value statements are illustrative:

- Children with disabilities are best served in their community, living in their home and receiving an inclusive education in their neighborhood school.
- Collaboration of services and resources is best for the customer, the agency, and the public.
- Serving our children and their families is a responsibility of the total community.

Following the adoption of shared vision and values, teams should create specific goals to be accomplished. Most teams will establish primary goals related to improved outcomes for students and families, meeting the needs of the children and families within the community, and collaborative planning and service delivery by local professionals. Additional goals may include the following:

- to deliver services in a cost-effective manner
- to create partnerships among all service providers and partners, with commitment to teamwork
- to eliminate duplication of services
- to evaluate effectiveness of services
- to enhance existing programs and develop new ones, according to student and family needs

After goals are established, the stakeholders should develop a strategic plan and formalize interagency relationships.

Conducting a Needs Assessment

The creation of a common base of knowledge about the children and family in the community, the services available and services needed, and the nature of the services provided by each agency provides a framework for beginning collaborative efforts. The interagency team should conduct a needs assessment to identify service needs, gaps, and resources. Data showing demographics, trends, and the needs of specific educational and community populations help to focus interagency planning and set priorities. This information is also useful in gaining support from local and state policy makers and service providers.

Exhibit 8–2 Identifying Students Served by Multiple Agencies: Examples

Agency	Children					
	Mary A. (Age 10, Learning Disability)	John B. (Age 13, Mental Retardation)	Susan C. (Age 16, Traumatic Brain Injury)	Michael D. (Age 14, Emotional Disturbance)	Vanessa E. (Age 7, Emotional Disturbance)	Kevin F. (Age 16, Learning Disability)
Public schools	Anytown Elementary School; general education fourth-grade class, with consultant special education teacher	Anytown Middle School: five general education classes and one special education support class	Anytown High School	Regional day treatment program	Residential placement made with social services	Long-term suspension for drug violation; previously enrolled 100% in general education
Social services	Not applicable	Foster care	Welfare	Not applicable	Specialized foster care	Not applicable
Mental health	Family receives counseling	Not applicable	Not applicable	Mental health counselor works at day treatment program	Foster family receives services from a community mental health clinic	Substance abuse program
Juvenile justice	Not applicable	Not applicable	Ordered to attend school by court after school filed truancy petition	Not applicable	Family counseling ordered by juvenile court	Court-ordered substance abuse program after repeated arrests for driving while intoxicated
Health	Not applicable	Not applicable	Consultation with staff regarding medication, fatigue	Not applicable	Health care provider	Not applicable
Vocational rehabilitation	Not applicable	Not applicable	Participant in transition planning	Participant in transition planning	Not applicable	Enrolled him in job training program
Parks and recreation	Provider of gymnastics classes	Provider of swim team	Provider of teen club	Not applicable	Not applicable	Organize volunteer services for elderly
Private providers	Provider of after-school day care	Not applicable	Not applicable	Not applicable	Service provider	Not applicable
Needed services	Not applicable	Not applicable	Assistive technology to help with written/typed work	Structured after-school program	Prevention services for five-year-old sibling	Transportation to job

Note: Children cited are illustrative and are not intended to reflect any particular child.

Exhibit 8-3 Form for Identifying Students Served by Multiple Agencies

Agency	Children					
Public school						
Social services						
Mental health						
Juvenile justice						
Health						
Vocational rehabilitation						
Parks and recreation						
Private providers						
Needed services						

Needs assessments do not need to be difficult. The Communities That Care needs assessment model is one example of a research-based method of examining a community's resources and needs (Hawkins & Catalano, 1992). This model prescribes a process of community-based problem solving and planning. State and local public agencies often have needs assessments built into their annual plans. Schools should look to their biennial school plans or their special education plans. Other interagency teams may have conducted needs assessments. Many grant applications (e.g., Safe and Drug Free Schools and Communities Act, Juvenile Justice Delinquency Prevention Act) require local needs assessment. Municipalities often can provide data reflecting local demographics and trends. State agencies may collect statewide data that can be broken down by locality and used for needs assessment. Whatever the source, it is important to tie the needs assessment to the target population identified by the stakeholders.

Promoting, Developing, and Nurturing Teams

The leadership team (e.g., the agency heads) should provide a structure for how service delivery teams will receive and act upon referrals. Methods developed for "staffing" referrals should be field tested as forms, processes, and structures evolve. Since interagency collaboration generally requires additional staff meeting time, leadership should focus on keeping paperwork to a minimum, to reduce the additional time demands created by collaboration.

A key component to team planning for children and families is the assignment of a case manager.* The case manager is the one person who takes on the responsibility for communicating the interagency plan to all players; this person helps the child and family access the services and monitors the implementation of the plan. Without the case manager, it is not uncommon for services to become fragmented or duplicative. The case manager can identify the need to reconvene the interagency team if changes are necessary. The case manager is typically an agency employee; however, in some areas, parents are supported in their efforts to serve as case manager for their child.

---

*The term *case manager* is used in this chapter because this is the term frequently used by providers of services for youths and young adults with disabilities. This term may relate to the use of *case management* by Medicaid and other providers of services. The term *service coordination* is also used to describe similar services. This term is preferred by many consumers of services who believe that *case management* does not promote a partnership with the consumer. In addition, the concept of "managing a case" raises negative connotations in the minds of many consumers, providers, and advocates.

The leadership should ensure that a training plan for the teams and agency staff is developed and that training resources are secured. Team development is an important component of training; this enhances the team's capacity to work collaboratively and efficiently. Providing staff training across agencies helps all staff members develop common language and concepts. The information gathered during the needs assessment process should be used to tailor the training to the locality.

Teams, whether at the leadership level or the service delivery level, are not merely a collection of individuals. Teams reflect persons who work together toward a set of shared goals that are based on a common vision. Understanding the stages of team development that all teams experience is important. Teams will benefit from training and facilitation as they pass through various stages. Disagreement (and sometimes conflict) among team members is normal as teams develop, and reflects the team members' active involvement in the decision-making process. Teams frequently indicate that there is insufficient time to attend all team meetings. Leaders must ensure that this does not result in absenteeism at team meetings, as a full complement of team members must be involved in all decision making.

Informing the Community

Once the interagency support system is in place, leaders should "get the word out" to all persons involved with the lives of the students. This includes the teachers, administrators, and parents at the school(s) the students attend. A presentation to this group should answer questions about how interagency collaboration will help the child and affect educators. Questions about the roles of various agencies and professionals should be expected. The responses should maintain a focus on the shared vision—interagency support for children to enable them to live in their community and be educated with their peers. Similar presentations should be made to the staff in each agency, community groups, private providers, and parents affected by the interagency initiative.

Providing a Continuum of Services

As interagency service teams compare the identified service needs with the services available in the community, many gaps in the continuum of services will be identified. Often, creative problem solving and planning can identify a mechanism to provide the necessary service to an individual child. Frequently this can be accomplished by viewing the situation differently—as often happens when a number of persons are sitting at the table trying to solve a problem. However, there will be circumstances when pooled expertise and resources cannot create a necessary service from existing community programs. The interagency leadership must take responsibility for keeping track of these service gaps, and work to create the necessary services. The approaches used will vary considerably in different localities—from contracting with an out-of-community provider for local services to creating new publicly or privately operated programs.

INTERAGENCY COLLABORATION DOES MAKE A DIFFERENCE

There are many reasons why interagency collaboration is not routinely carried out in communities throughout the country. They range from lack of communication among the many public and private sector agencies, to lack of funds, to an inability of agencies to develop comprehensive solutions (Melaville et al., 1993). Exhibit 8–4 displays common barriers to interagency coordination and planning, with potential solutions. Communities with strong interagency teams generally find that the success of interagency collaboration outweighs the barriers, and they work to resolve barriers quickly.

Interagency collaboration can serve as a significant support for teachers as they help individuals with disabilities function in integrated environments. Students with disabilities are more likely to experience success in inclusive environments within public school classrooms if the locality focuses on integration of individuals with disabilities throughout the community. Through interagency collaboration, localities can provide a consolidated, unduplicated, cost-effective service delivery system. These services can include: social skills training groups, support networks, parent education, early intervention, nutrition education, sensitivity training, peer awareness activities, one-on-one behavioral support, home-based mental health services, summer activities aimed at maintenance of skills, and job experience and training programs. The case studies in Exhibits 8–5 through 8–8 provide examples of the supports that can be offered by interagency problem solving and service delivery.

Exhibit 8–4 Interagency Coordination and Cooperation: Barriers and Solutions

Issue	Issues That Affect Interagency Coordination and Cooperation	Potential Solutions
Legal	No authority to compel coordination or shared responsibility; target population(s) may be defined differently in statute.	Obtain coordination through commitment of agency or local governing body leadership. Cross-train all agency staff in definitions and eligibility criteria of target population(s).
Organizational structure	Complex, largely autonomous agencies with multiple management layers. Often difficult to identify responsible persons.	Obtain coordination through commitment of agency leadership and service providers simultaneously.
Turf	Agencies tend to protect their own employees, responsibilities, and time.	Conduct joint agency planning with the goal of minimizing time commitment.
Funding	Different, often competing, funding sources in federal, state, and local government. Funding is often limited. Other agencies frequently see education as the agency with the greatest resources, often to the detriment of their resources.	Modify funding requirements to increase flexibility in use. Pool funding when possible. Coordinate a multiagency effort to obtain additional funds. Train staff in sources of, uses of, and restrictions on funding.
Case management	Staffs in many agencies are not trained in case management skills, resulting in duplication or discontinuities in services.	Train all staff in case management.
Interdepartmental knowledge	Agency staffs often lack sufficient knowledge of other agencies and departments, their responsibilities, and their regulations.	Cross-train staffs in other agencies' missions, target populations, responsibilities, legal obligations.

Exhibit 8–5 Ricky

BACKGROUND INFORMATION

Ricky is a four-year-old student with a developmental disability who attends Head Start, with support from the early childhood special education teacher in the local school division. Ricky is aggressive with other students at the preschool, and the parents of other children have expressed their alarm. A behavioral support program was developed through collaboration between the early childhood special education teacher, a behavioral specialist from the mental health clinic, and the Head Start teacher. His attendance at preschool is poor, however, due to his parents' inability to provide transportation on a daily basis. This has resulted in minimal progress in his behavior.

The local health department nurse has been monitoring Ricky and his family since his birth, because of the high level of lead in the home. The family recently received an eviction notice, so it is unclear whether Ricky can remain in his current neighborhood or in this locality.

INTERAGENCY TEAM RESPONSE

Because Ricky has been served since the age of six months through early intervention interagency services, the family is known to most of the agencies on the interagency team. The team developed the following recommendations for Ricky:

- The local health department nurse who has been monitoring the family since infancy will assume the role of case manager, since she has a long-standing relationship of trust with the family.
- The department of mental health will provide home-based services to help Ricky's parents use the structured behavior management program being used in the Head Start program.
- The health department nurse will contact the family's neighborhood church to learn if the outreach program can help with transportation.
- The social services agency will meet with the family to obtain temporary housing assistance, identify the reasons for the recent eviction notice, and make referrals to other agencies, if appropriate. These services could include appointments with a group of retired business officials who volunteer to help persons in budgeting.

Exhibit 8–6 Robert

BACKGROUND INFORMATION

Robert is a 10-year-old student with mental retardation. He was attending his neighborhood public school until recently, when his aggressive behaviors escalated and he assaulted another student. He is currently receiving homebound instruction from a special education teacher while a reevaluation of the current individualized education program placement and services is made. The school division referred Robert and his family to the interagency team for assistance.

INTERAGENCY TEAM RESPONSE

The interagency team developed the following recommendations for Robert and his family:

- The assistant principal at the elementary school, who has been working with Robert's family since Robert first entered school, will serve as case manager.
- The mental health agency will offer counseling services to the family.
- A behavior specialist will visit Robert in his home to observe his behaviors and identify alternative strategies for addressing his aggressive behaviors. The specialist will work with the family to carry out these strategies in the home.
- Robert will return to his neighborhood school, with the assistance of a child aide. The aide will use the strategies identified by the behavior specialist.

Exhibit 8–7 Jason

BACKGROUND INFORMATION

Jason is a 15-year-old student with serious emotional disturbance. He attends the local high school. His performance in school has deteriorated in the last academic quarter. His teachers note that the deterioration is related to Jason's increased truancy.

Jason has a history of juvenile delinquency and recently stayed out late, violating his probation. He is at risk for commitment to a public or private juvenile corrections facility for continuing to violate specific parole restrictions imposed by the court. His father, who has custody, was recently incarcerated. No adult relative in the area is willing to help with Jason's care. The probation officer referred Jason to the interagency team before his court date, to have the team's recommendations available to the judge at sentencing.

INTERAGENCY TEAM RESPONSE

The interagency team developed the following services for Jason:

- Jason's probation officer will serve as case manager.
- The individualized education program team will review Jason's current placements to decide if his current course assignments are appropriate.
- Jason will go to the local mental health department with his probation officer to decide if counseling and/or a psychiatric evaluation is necessary.
- The probation officer will work with the local YMCA staff to develop a structured afternoon program, including a nightly exercise routine. A YMCA volunteer will drive Jason home each evening.
- The probation officer will process an application for a Big Brother through the local Big Brothers/Big Sisters program.
- The probation officer will find out the conditions associated with Jason's father's commitment.
- The social services department will meet with Jason's family members to identify support services necessary to provide a home for Jason. The social services department's foster care prevention personnel, in combination with mental health counselors, will help the relatives to carry out the plan.

Exhibit 8–8 Morty

BACKGROUND INFORMATION

Morty is a 14-year-old student with autism who is included in the local high school. He is an avid baseball fan and helps the junior varsity team manager. Morty has poor hygiene and wears dirty clothing on a daily basis. He displays many inappropriate behaviors during his interactions with others. Although Morty has no history of getting into physical altercations, he frequently uses abusive language. The principal has received many calls from parents of other students complaining about Morty's abusive language. The general education teachers have asked his special education teacher if the individualized education program committee could meet to discuss the need for Morty to return to the special education classroom. In addition, Morty was recently arrested for stealing coal from a coal car.

Morty's special education teacher believes that his inappropriate behavior is related to poor social skills and to the comments he is receiving from his peers related to his dirty and age-inappropriate clothing. The special education teacher discusses the requests from the general education teachers and her observation with the district's special education director, who makes a referral to the interagency team.

INTERAGENCY TEAM RESPONSE

The interagency team developed the following plans:

- The special education teacher, with the support of the special education director and school principal, will serve as case manager.
- The case manager will take Morty to the local church ministry clothing outlet to secure age-appropriate clothing. Funding will be provided by the school's parent/student/teacher organization.
- Morty will learn to wash his clothes at school in the

continues

Exhibit 8–8 continued

athletic area. A peer tutor will be identified to stay after school with Morty weekly to help him take care of his laundry.
- The local mental health agency will provide a behavior specialist to the school for two hours each per day for six weeks. The behavior specialist will shadow Morty and cue him when he encounters his peers.
- The special education teacher will meet with members of the baseball team to obtain their assistance in modeling appropriate comments.
- The court service worker who serves on the interagency team will check the status of Morty's arrest and

investigate the cause of the coal stealing. If this was in response to the need to heat his home, a referral will be processed through the department of social services for heating supplement funds.
- The special education teacher will explain the interagency support plan to the members of Morty's IEP committee. Additional interagency support may be requested if the IEP committee does not believe he can remain in an inclusive school environment. The interagency team, including the general education teachers, to discuss Morty's behavior and services provided.

CONCLUSION

Educators of students with disabilities will find it refreshing when other community agencies support the schools' efforts to educate students in their home school(s). It is in the community's best interest to work cooperatively when working with children and families. This collaboration will improve the student's performance in school and decrease the likelihood that the student will need to enter a more restrictive education program. Agencies can create the wraparound services necessary to support the student and his or her family and allow the child to stay within the school and community.

The support services offered through interagency collaboration not only help educators ensure a student's success in inclusive environments, they also increase the student's ability to be a member of the community. Because all students will one day leave the public education system, it is important that educators pursue every avenue to enable students to be included in their educational, living, and community environments. Educating students in their community can be accomplished with the support from local community agencies and providers.

REFERENCES

Algarin, A., & Friedman, R. (Eds.). (1991). *A system of care for children's mental health: Expanding the research base: Fourth annual research conference proceedings.* Tampa, FL: Florida Mental Health Institute, University of South Florida, Research and Training Center for Children's Mental Health.

Center for the Future of Children. (1992). *School-linked services.* Los Altos, CA: Author.

Epstein, M.H., Quinn, K., Nelson, C.M., Polsgrove, L., & Cumblad, C. (1993). Serving students with emotional and behavioral disorders through a comprehensive community-based approach. *OSERS News in Print, 5*(3), 19–24.

Hawkins, J.D., & Catalano, R.F. (1992). *Communities that care.* San Francisco: Jossey-Bass.

Hill, E. (1996). *Comprehensive services for students with serious emotional disturbance: An analysis of state legislation.* Unpublished doctoral dissertation, The College of William and Mary, Williamsburg, Virginia.

Johnson, W., McLaughlin, J., & Christensen, M. (1982). Interagency collaboration: Driving and restraining forces. *Exceptional Children, 48*(5), 395–399.

Jordan, D.D., & Hernandez, M. (1990). The Ventura planning model: A proposal for mental health reform. *Journal of Mental Health Administration, 17*(1).

Knitzer, J. (1993). Children's mental health policy: Challenging the future. *Journal of Emotional and Behavioral Disorders, 1*(1), 8–16.

Melaville, A., & Blank, M. (1991). *What it takes: Structuring interagency partnerships to connect children and families with comprehensive services.* Washington, DC: Institute for Educational Leadership.

Melaville, A., Blank, M., & Asayesh, G. (1993). *Together we can: A guide for crafting a pro-family system of education and human services.* Washington, DC: U.S. Government Printing Office.

National Consensus Building Conference on School-Linked Integrated Services Systems. (1994). *Integrating education, health and human services for children, youth and families: Systems that are community-based and school-linked.* Washington, DC: Author.

Stroul, B. (1993). *Systems of care for children and adolescents with severe emotional disturbances: What are the results?* Washington, DC: Georgetown University Child Development Center.

Stroul, B., & Friedman, R. (1986). *A system of care for children and youth with severe emotional disturbances.* Washington, DC: Georgetown University Child Development Center.

U.S. Department of Education. (1994). *National agenda for achieving better results for children and youth with serious emotional disturbance.* Washington, DC: Author.

U.S. Department of Education. (1995). *To assure the free appropriate public education of all children with disabilities: Seventeenth annual report to Congress on the implementation of the Individuals with Disabilities Education Act.* Washington, DC: Author.

Virginia Department of Mental Health, Mental Retardation, and Substance Abuse Services. (1994). *Comprehensive services for at-risk youth and families: Demonstration projects.* Richmond, VA: Author.

Virginia Department of Mental Health, Mental Retardation, and Substance Abuse Services. (1995). Service costs for Virginia's youth: Initial years of the Comprehensive Services Act. Richmond, VA: Author.

Virginia Department of Planning and Budget. (1990). A study of children's residential services. Richmond, VA: Author.

Wagner, M., Blackorby, J., Cameto, R., & Newman, L. (1993). What makes a difference? Influence on postschool outcomes of youth with disabilities. Menlo Park, CA: SRI International.

CHAPTER 9

Early Childhood Education

Mary Dunkle Voorhees, Tracy Landon, and Jaye Harvey

INTRODUCTION

This chapter addresses inclusion for preschoolers (ages three to five) with disabilities. First, preschool inclusion is defined and differentiated from school-age inclusion, with emphasis given to the importance of initiating inclusion early. Second, the chapter describes early childhood programs, provides examples of various inclusive program designs used in these programs, and describes components of quality inclusive early childhood programs. The chapter concludes by recommending guidelines for planning successful inclusion at the preschool level.

WHAT IS PRESCHOOL INCLUSION?

Inclusion is not an education issue: it is a lifestyle. Inclusion is going to story hour at the library, playing at the neighborhood playground, going to the pool when it is hot, and hanging around the mall when it is raining. It just makes sense that a child with a disability would also go to school with the children in the neighborhood. For my daughter, Katherine, inclusion is the opportunity to be inspired to try new skills. It is the chance to play and be a little girl after missing out on her babyhood [due to health problems]. It is the time to learn to live in the nondisabled world that she will live in as an adult. (Brittain, 1994, p. 5)

Preschool inclusion occurs when preschoolers who are eligible for special education and/or related services receive these services while they are enrolled full-time in general early childhood settings with same-aged peers without disabilities. These settings may be community based, such as private preschool programs, child care centers, Head Start,

and family day care programs, or they may be based in the public school, such as Title I preschool programs, school district–sponsored four-year-old programs, Head Start, and occupational child care programs in secondary schools. Meaningful inclusion involves much more than mere placement of preschoolers with disabilities in a general early childhood program (Bricker, 1995). For inclusion to be successful, all of the necessary supports must be provided so the child with disabilities forms friendships with peers, participates actively in all classroom activities, and accomplishes the individualized goals and objectives designed to meet his or her needs. According to Bricker:

Genuine inclusion means that during large circle time, the child with disabilities sits next to the other children, sings the songs, and participates in other planned activities to the fullest extent possible. . . . If the children go for a walk, the child in the wheelchair goes also. At story time, the child with the augmentative communication system contributes using his or her nonvocal mode of communication." (Bricker, 1995, p. 182)

Meaningful inclusion may not take place if critical supports—such as staff training, direct or consultative services from early childhood special education (ECSE) staff, modifications to the early childhood environment or activities, and specialized equipment and materials—are not provided.

School Age and Early Childhood Inclusion: A Major Difference

Because school attendance is mandatory for children beginning at age five or six in all states, children without disabilities are readily found within the public schools in kindergarten, elementary, middle, and secondary school settings. The operation of special and general education services by a common administrative agency greatly facilitates the inclusion of children with disabilities in those classrooms (Peterson, 1987). In contrast, while some preschool children without disabilities are educated in early childhood programs sponsored by local school divisions, most typically developing young children remain at home or are enrolled in community-based programs such as private preschool programs, child care centers, Head Start, and family day care homes. These programs typically are not readily accessible to public schools, as they are housed in separate facilities and operated by separate agencies that follow different program policies and schedules (McLean & Hanline, 1990). Therefore, a major difference between school-age and early childhood inclusion for public schools is the challenge of determining how to provide inclusive opportunities for preschoolers with disabilities when the school system does not provide programs for their typically developing, same-age peers (McLean & Hanline, 1990; Smith & Rose, 1991).

The Importance of Preschool Inclusion

(My child, Matthew) . . . at the age of 3, entered (a self-contained classroom) in the county's (ECSE) program. During that year, there was minimal improvement in any area. At the age of 4, Matthew was included in the Head Start program (with support provided by ECSE staff). At that time he had an (oral) vocabulary of 2 words and signed for about 10 objects. He had no self-help skills, very few social skills, and very poor motor skills. During the past year, we have been continually amazed at the progress Matthew has made. He currently has a 6 word (oral) vocabulary and his (signs have) increased almost to a normal vocabulary for his age. . . . His gross motor skills have also improved dramatically—he feeds himself; he is almost potty trained; and he cleans up after himself. Socially Matthew has learned to work in a group and (has begun to) play (and) share. If you could possibly see the changes that have occurred in Matthew you would understand why my husband and I feel this (inclusion) program is one of the best programs established for children. (K. Cooper, personal communication, January 29, 1996)

Beginning inclusion at the preschool level is crucial for several reasons. First, preschool children with and without disabilities who are educated together have opportunities to form friendships and to be better prepared for future inclusive experiences (Abraham, Morris, & Wald, 1991).

Researchers have found that preschoolers with disabilities in integrated settings establish friendships with peers without disabilities (Bussye, 1993; Green & Stoneman, 1989) and exhibit more appropriate social interactions and greater self-initiation than preschoolers with disabilities in segregated settings (Bussye, 1993; Esposito & Koorland, 1989). Strain (1990) found that a comparison of social outcomes for children in quality integrated settings to social outcomes for children in segregated settings heavily favors integration. Further, typically developing children attending inclusive settings display more favorable attitudes toward preschoolers with disabilities (Esposito & Peach, 1983) and an increased understanding and tolerance for differences (Ipsa & Matz, 1978; Radnovich & Houck, 1990). Second, children with disabilities in integrated settings exhibit gains in language, cognition, and play skills (Esposito & Koorland, 1989; Fenrick, Pearson, & Pepelnjak, 1984; Guralnick & Groom, 1988; Jenkins, Odom, & Speltz, 1989; Novak, Olley, & Kearney, 1980), and children without disabilities make typical developmental progress or, in some cases, even greater progress than would be expected in non-integrated preschool programs (Thurman & Widerstrom, 1990). Finally, initial placement settings are strong predictors of future placement settings (Edgar, Hegglelund, & Fischer, 1988). A study of subsequent placements of 328 preschoolers with and without disabilities found that children with disabilities whose first placements were in segregated settings were four times more likely to remain in segregated settings in the elementary years than the children who begin in mainstream settings (Miller, Strain, McKinley, Heckathorn, & Miller, 1993). Thus, an initial inclusive placement alone may result in future placement in general education settings (Miller et al., 1993).

PROGRAMS FOR PRESCHOOLERS WITHOUT DISABILITIES

To initiate an inclusive placement option in a general early childhood setting, partnerships must be established between ECSE and early childhood programs. Early childhood programs vary on many dimensions, including program purpose, schedule, and agency affiliation. Some programs, for example, focus on providing comprehensive services (e.g., educational, health, social services) with the goal of preventing school failure for at-risk children (e.g., Title I preschool programs, state early childhood program initiatives, Head Start). Others concentrate on educational enrichment for typically developing children (e.g., occupational child care programs in secondary schools, community-based preschool or nursery school programs). Still others, such as child care centers and family day care homes, focus primarily on providing child care services for working parents but may also include an educational component. All of these general early childhood programs, whether school or community based, are required by the Americans with Disabilities Act (1990) to make reasonable accommodations in policies, practices, and procedures to serve children with disabilities. This section provides specific information about each of these early childhood programs and discusses explicit issues related to serving children with disabilities within each program.

Head Start Programs

Head Start is a federal grant program, first authorized under the Economic Opportunities Act, for preschool children whose families fall below the federal poverty level. Local, nonprofit organizations operate Head Start programs in almost every county in the country. Federal money flows directly to local grantees, including government agencies, nonprofit agencies, and school divisions. Head Start programs may be classroom based, home based, or a combination of these. Comprehensive Head Start services include developmentally appropriate education, health services, parent involvement, social services, and cultural competence.

Increasingly, school districts are developing collaborative arrangements to provide ECSE services to children with mild to severe disabilities who are enrolled full or part time in Head Start programs. Federal regulations require that at least 10% of Head Start program enrollment be available for children with disabilities. Income eligibility requirements do not apply to this 10%, although some Head Start programs prefer to enroll families that meet the low-income requirement. The Head Start regulations (45 CFR Part 1308) published in the *Federal Register* on January 21, 1993, make the Head Start eligibility requirements regarding disabilities compatible with those of Part B of the Individuals with Disabilities Education Act (IDEA). Thus, the full range of Head Start services must be made available to children with disabilities and their families. Head Start regulations also mandate the development of interagency agreements with school districts.

Title I Preschool Programs

Title I programs are intended to improve the educational opportunities afforded children who are performing below grade level from families of low income. Title I (previously known as Chapter I) funding originates at the federal level through the Improving America's Schools Act. School divisions are awarded money based on a formula that takes into account the number of children in poverty. Children in "greatest need of special assistance" at the preschool, elementary, and secondary school levels are eligible for Title I services. This includes preschoolers with disabilities, as long as they reside in Title I attendance areas and meet the school district's "greatest need" standard. Title I funds may not be used to provide special education and related services. However, public school–based ECSE programs may develop collaborative agreements in a variety of ways to serve preschool children with disabilities in Title I preschool programs with special education and related services supplied through ECSE programs (Smith & Rose, 1993).

Community-Based Early Childhood Programs

Community-based early childhood programs are diverse. They may be educational or focus on child care, and they may be private for profit or private nonprofit. Some are licensed or regulated by state agencies (e.g., the department of social services, division of licensing programs) while others are not licensed. Community-based programs may also be accredited by national organizations such as the National Academy of Early Childhood Programs, affiliated with the National Association for the Education of Young Children (NAEYC). Community-based programs may be housed in recreation centers, private buildings, private homes, universities, churches, or school buildings. Program lengths vary from part time (e.g., three half days per week) to full time (e.g., five days a week, full day to coordinate with parent work schedules).

Licensed or regulated community-based early childhood programs must meet certain requirements. Specific program requirements are available from state or local licensing offices. National accreditation organizations focus more on recommended practices, thus offering quality assurance. In order to be accredited through the National Academy of Early Childhood Programs, for example, early childhood programs must complete a self-study and then demonstrate to outside validators that they use developmentally appropriate practices. School divisions may develop agreements with a wide variety of community-based early childhood programs to provide ECSE services to children with disabilities in early childhood settings.

Occupational Child Care Programs in Secondary Schools

Occupational child care programs within secondary schools are designed to train high school students for entry-level positions in child care. Programs typically include a laboratory training component, where students meet for blocks of time (such as two to three hours each day) in child care laboratories in school settings or community-based jobs through cooperative education agreements. Child care laboratories operate similarly to community-based early childhood programs, except that they have high school students as trainees.

ECSE programs in school divisions collaborate in a variety of ways with occupational child care programs. Some school divisions, for instance, locate ECSE classrooms at secondary schools or career centers to provide opportunities for full- or part-time placement of children with disabilities in the child care laboratory programs. High school students enrolled in programs such as these benefit tremendously by gaining first-hand experience in working with children with disabilities.

State and Local Early Childhood Program Initiatives

Nationwide, states and localities have initiated or are beginning to initiate early childhood programs. Many of these programs are designed for children who are at risk, while others serve children of school employees. For example, the 1994 Virginia General Assembly committed $10.3 million in grants to help localities reach unserved four-year-old children who are at risk for school failure. Similarly, some Virginia school divisions offer employee child care programs within public school buildings to meet the child care needs of public school staff. ECSE programs may develop agreements with these types of programs to serve children with disabilities.

PROGRAM DESIGN

Various program designs are used to provide ECSE services to children with disabilities who are enrolled in general early childhood settings. This section discusses two examples—collaborative and consultative models—and highlights critical issues related to initiating these programs.

Collaborative Models

In a collaborative program design, a group of children with disabilities (typically equal to a center-based or self-contained ECSE teacher's caseload) is enrolled in one or two early childhood programs. An ECSE teacher and assistant are based full time at the early childhood setting(s) to team teach, coach, learn from, and meet regularly with early childhood staff. Related service staff (e.g., occupational and physical therapists, speech-language pathologists) provide integrated therapy in the classrooms and participate regularly in team meetings. This model is similar to a coteaching model for school-age students.

Examples of collaborative models include the following:

- Up to 10 children who are eligible for special education services through Albemarle County (Virginia) Public Schools attend Westminster Child Care Center, a private, nonprofit program that rents space at Westminster Presbyterian Church in Charlottesville,

Virginia. One to three children with disabilities are enrolled in each of the five classes at the center. The ratio of children with disabilities to children without disabilities varies in each class, based on the level of support needed for each child with disabilities. An ECSE teacher and assistant are based full time at the center, and related service staff provide itinerant consultative and direct, classroom-based services.

- Up to eight children with disabilities are enrolled in two Title I First Steps classrooms in the Newport News (Virginia) Public Schools. The maximum ratio of children with disabilities to children without disabilities is 4:12 in each class. An ECSE teacher and assistant are located full time at the program and split their time between the two classes. One of them is in each classroom at all times. Related services are integrated into the classroom.

Consultative Models

In a consultative program design, children with disabilities are enrolled full time in early childhood programs with same-aged peers. An ECSE teacher and related service staff members (if applicable) travel from program to program to support early childhood staff and children with disabilities at multiple sites. ECSE staff roles may vary, based on the needs of the children with disabilities, their families, and the early childhood staff. For example, in one program the ECSE and related service staff may consult only with the early childhood staff; in another program they may provide direct, classroom-based services, as well as consultative services. The individualized education program (IEP) team determines the amount of direct service time needed to meet a child's identified needs and the amount of consultative time provided for the early childhood staff (e.g., weekly for one hour). When children with disabilities require more intensive support to succeed in a general early childhood setting, ECSE teaching assistants are placed in these settings. The ECSE teacher provides guidance and feedback to the assistant. This is similar to a consultative model at the school-age level.

Examples of consultative models include the following:

- Children with disabilities in Richmond City (Virginia) Public Schools, a large urban school district, may be enrolled full time in a variety of early childhood settings (e.g., the Richmond City Public Schools Head Start and Four-Year-Old programs and in community-based preschool programs or child care centers). An ECSE teacher and assistant serve 8 to 12 children, depending on the amount of direct and consultative support services that are specified on the children's IEPs. The teacher and assistant travel from program to program to provide direct support as needed and to consult with the early childhood staff. They also spend a large part of their time assisting the general education staff in making modifications or accommodations as needed (e.g., developing a communication system or picture schedule for a classroom). The early childhood and ECSE staff meet on a regular basis (e.g., weekly or biweekly), depending on staff and children's needs. Related service staff attend meetings once a month.

- Lee County (Virginia) Public Schools, a rural sparsely populated school division, enrolls up to 12 children with disabilities full time in five early childhood settings (e.g., Head Start, child care centers). One ECSE teacher and three teaching assistants provide support to these sites. ECSE staff are based full time at three of the sites where children with severe disabilities are enrolled. The ECSE teacher provides limited direct support and meets with the early childhood staff and ECSE assistants on a weekly basis.

Critical Issues in Program Design

Several critical issues must be addressed when designing a program based on either model. These issues include the ECSE and related service staff caseloads, classroom composition, placement of children with disabilities with same-age peers, and the merger of recommended early childhood and ECSE practices. Caseload requirements vary from state to state. Staff caseloads should take into consideration the severity of disability for each child, the number of hours of direct service as well as consultation time required, and travel time. In regard to classroom composition, a rule of thumb for school-age inclusive programs is to enroll natural proportions of children with disabilities—approximately 10% to 12% of the total school program. Experience at the preschool level, however, has not demonstrated that a specific number of children with disabilities should be enrolled in any classroom. Decisions should be based on the needs of the children with disabilities, characteristics of the children without disabilities, attitudes and training of the staff, support services available, and the ratio of adults to children (Cook, Tessier, & Armbruster, 1987). "The class size/ratio must be seen as fluid, not set, in order to accommodate the constant interaction of . . . [these] variables during the school year" (Johnson, Rogers, Johnson, & McMillan, 1993, p. 44). Chronologically age-appropriate placements, however, are recommended: "A four year old with severe impairments should be in a learning environment appropriate for typical four year olds with learning activities that match his unique needs" (Odom & McLean, 1993, p. 5). A final consideration in program design involves the ways early childhood and ECSE practices may be used together

in each component of quality inclusive programming. These components are described in detail in the following section.

COMPONENTS OF QUALITY EARLY CHILDHOOD INCLUSIVE PROGRAMS

When Katherine was a baby, I knew that she would have delays due to all her surgery and health problems, so I made a conscious effort to involve her with the neighborhood children so that she could see what the other children her age did. I did not know that this instinct was called inclusion. It seemed like a cruel joke that as she took her first steps and could participate on a new level, it was time to start preschool. For the first time in her life, she was a child with a disability rather than "Katherine who has some catching up to do." Although she made progress in school (in the ECSE class), my husband and I were concerned about the lack of role models and the kindergarten prep curriculum. In addition, she seemed to just sit whenever I was in class. I saw little participation or interaction. . . . This year Katherine attends half days at a NAEYC accredited child care center where several children from the neighborhood go. She has an itinerant special education teacher who collaborates with her early childhood teacher and receives physical, occupational, and speech therapies in the classroom. The difference has been dramatic. She came home the first day wanting to go to the potty. . . . She has become an enthusiastic artist and eats with a spoon. . . . Katherine is much stronger now and progressing with her gross motor skills. My very little child, who shied from physical contact with children a half foot taller, now greets her friends with a hug and combs her best friend's hair. . . . My husband and I believe that she will be able to live a "normal" life as long as she is allowed to live, learn, and play among her peers. (Brittain, 1994, p. 5)

Successful inclusive early childhood programs are demonstrating that a continuum of approaches that merge practices from the fields of early childhood education and ECSE is advantageous for all children. Different children, regardless of whether they have identified disabilities, learn best using varied approaches (Bredekamp & Rosegrant, 1992; Richarz, 1993). Relying on one approach with children from diverse backgrounds and with differing ability levels guarantees failure for some children (Katz, 1987). Several critical components of quality inclusive early childhood programs merge recommended practices from each field. These components focus on collaboration among staff and families (collaborative teaming, parent-professional partnerships) and on critical features in the design of the educational program for children (the classroom environment, social relationships, curriculum, and discipline techniques).

Collaborative Teaming

A successful inclusive early childhood program relies on collaboration among diverse staff and families. A recommended ECSE practice regarding staff collaboration is a cross-disciplinary approach where staff from different disciplines work as a team rather than individually (McLean & Odom, 1993). Similarly, a recommended early childhood practice is for all professionals who have educational responsibility for a child, along with the child's family, to share information to ensure the continuity of a child's educational experience (Bredekamp, 1987). Although this practice is recommended for a change in a child's program, one can assume that it would also apply to any situation where various professionals are working with a child (e.g., an inclusive program).

A collaborative team approach is consistent with these recommended practices, and this method has been used successfully in inclusive school-age programs (Fox & Williams, 1991; Rainforth, York, & Macdonald, 1992; Thousand & Villa, 1992) and early childhood settings (Voorhees, Aveno, & Landon, 1993). This approach provides a mechanism for diverse team members to communicate regularly; to share their discipline-specific skills and leadership, tasks, and responsibilities; and to participate in joint decision making. Inclusive programs typically establish classroom core teams and extended teams. Core teams consist of professionals involved in the classroom on a day-to-day basis. Although these teams may differ in various programs, they usually include early childhood and ECSE teachers and assistants. Core teams typically meet weekly to celebrate team accomplishments, discuss issues, and reach consensus on solutions to issues. Issues may involve general classroom concerns that affect all children (e.g., curriculum, class schedule, environment) and specific issues regarding individual children (e.g., adaptive equipment, behavioral concerns, IEP objectives). Families are invited to attend the portions of the meeting related to their children.

Extended teams include professionals (e.g., occupational and physical therapists, speech-language pathologists, audiologists, and vision specialists) who provide direct or consultative services to children with disabilities in the inclusive program. Because these professionals frequently are unable to meet weekly due to extensive caseload assignments, they typically attend classroom team meetings on a monthly basis. Other strategies are established, however, to facilitate more frequent communication. Extended team members, for example, may read weekly core team meeting notes and respond or meet individually with the early childhood or ECSE teacher, who then reports back to the core team. The purpose of extended teams is to address programmatic and child-specific issues and to support fellow team members (Fox & Williams, 1991; Rainforth et al., 1992).

Administrative support is required to ensure regular team meeting opportunities. Team meetings can be scheduled at various times depending on the program. In full-day programs, for instance, meetings often are held at nap time while a substitute or volunteer covers the classroom. In half-day programs, the meetings are in the morning before the children arrive or as soon as the children leave. If meetings are not held during designated work hours, programs should reimburse hourly staff for their extra time.

Collaborative teams do not develop spontaneously but require commitment and effort on the part of each team member to function effectively. Team members must first build trusting relationships with one another (Fox & Williams, 1991; Friend & Cook, 1992; Putnam, 1993). In addition, team members must clarify their new roles and responsibilities as these may vary based on the inclusive program design and the needs of staff, children, and families. Specific roles and responsibilities related to all aspects of the program (family communication, daily classroom responsibilities, assessment and monitoring of child progress) must be jointly defined (Kontos & File, 1993). Additionally, collaborative teams use a structured team meeting process to ensure that meetings are productive and efficient (Fox & Williams, 1991; Friend & Cook, 1992; Putnam, 1993). This involves strategies such as assigning meeting roles (e.g., facilitator, timekeeper, recorder), developing a meeting agenda with time limits for each item, and using group problem-solving strategies (e.g., brainstorming, consensus decision making) to encourage input and support for team decisions.

In summary, a collaborative team approach is one crucial component of an inclusive early childhood program. This approach provides a mechanism to encourage staff and family collaboration, resulting in a coordinated program that guarantees continuity for all children and families.

Parent-Professional Partnerships

The establishment of parent-professional partnerships is a second vital program component that reflects recommended practices in early childhood education and ECSE. Early childhood practices emphasize that families should be involved in every decision about their child's care and education. Early childhood teachers are viewed as responsible for maintaining regular communication with families to facilitate mutual sharing of information and insights about children's needs and development. Family involvement, such as observing and participating in their child's classroom and attending parent conferences, is encouraged (Bredekamp, 1987).

Similarly, ECSE practices emphasize the family's decision-making role in all aspects of their child's program (Vincent & Beckett, 1993). In ECSE programs, however, the family rather than the child may be viewed as the focus of service (Fox, Hanline, Vail, & Galant, 1994). In a family-centered approach, emphasis is placed on providing a range of services to support the family rather than on family participation in the program. Services, therefore, are geared to meet the needs of the family as they relate to the child's development (McWilliam & Strain, 1993). For example, school districts that choose to use individualized family service plans (IFSPs) for their three-to-five-year-olds may include family-identified needs related to medical, housing, or transportation services on a child's IFSP (Fox et al., 1994).

Early childhood education and ECSE practices used together provide opportunities for families of children with disabilities and families of children without disabilities to socialize, receive support, and participate in the same activities. Emphasis is placed on giving families with children with disabilities the same opportunities as other families in inclusive settings. For example, families are invited to visit the early childhood program, receive a parent handbook, tour with the director, and ask questions about the program before deciding whether it is an appropriate placement for their children. ECSE staff may accompany the parent(s) on the visit if requested. The program offers multiple ways for families to be involved in advisory, decision-making, training, and advocacy activities of the early childhood program (e.g., advisory board, inclusion planning team, inservice training) and in their child's educational program (e.g., observing and participating in their child's classroom, going on field trips, attending parent meetings or workshops on topics of interest to all families, or attending parent conferences). All parents are invited to participate but may choose their own methods. The family's level of involvement is expected to change over time, and at times the family may choose not to be involved. Staff members respect these choices.

Regular communication with families is maintained through methods they have selected. Early childhood, ECSE, and related service staff discuss ways to coordinate their communication. For example, ECSE and related service staff may schedule joint parent conferences with the early childhood teacher during the same times that conferences are offered to all families, or they may use a system in which all staff can exchange information with the family by writing in a notebook that the child brings to and from school. Further, staff are knowledgeable about community resources and help families gain access to appropriate resources (e.g., respite care, mental health, or recreation programs) based on family-identified needs.

Early childhood staff are involved as joint partners in any additional activities that are required in regard to ECSE services. For example, ECSE, related service, and early childhood staff work together with families to plan and conduct joint assessments and develop the IFSP or IEP. Early childhood staff attend IEP meetings and any additional meetings required. Staff recognize and support the family's role as primary decision makers for their child in all aspects of the child's education (e.g., determining high-priority educational goals). ECSE and related service staff also serve as resources to assist early childhood staff in meeting the needs of children and families without identified needs in the program. For example, the ECSE teacher may provide guidance and assistance in regard to a child who has challenging behaviors but is not eligible for special education services. The merger of recommended early childhood education and ECSE practices results in a program that accommodates the needs of all children and families.

The Classroom Environment

In addition to components related to staff collaboration and family involvement in high-quality, inclusive early childhood programs, there are several components related to the educational program for children. One of these is a well-designed classroom environment. Recommended early childhood practices, such as the use of learning centers and child-size furniture, provide the foundation for providing a developmentally appropriate classroom design. ECSE-recommended practices build on these early childhood practices by focusing on ways to adapt the classroom to meet the needs of children at varying ability levels, including children with and without disabilities. A merger of these practices is described below.

An effective approach for organizing the classroom space is to divide it into individual, clearly defined learning centers that focus on specific activities. Centers are designed to integrate learning in the major areas of child development: cognition (e.g., thinking, reasoning, questioning, experimenting), language/literacy, physical development (e.g., gross and fine motor skills), social-emotional development (e.g., interpersonal relations), and creative expression. Recommended centers include: sand and water, science and nature, blocks and construction, literacy (which includes books, a writing area, and a listening area), table toys (small manipulatives), rainy-day gross motor play (when outdoor play is not feasible), housekeeping/dramatic play, art, and a quiet area (where a child can go to be alone). Centers are separated by low shelves, dividers, or other means (e.g., area rugs or changes in the floor surface from carpet to tile). Clear, unobstructed paths lead children from one center to another without disruptions to other centers. Quiet areas, such as the literacy area, are located next to other quiet areas, such as table toys. Noisy areas, such as blocks, are located near other noisy areas, such as dramatic play. Centers are located near appropriate classroom fixtures (e.g., art is near the sink). Classroom fixtures and furniture are child-sized (Dodge, 1988; Vergeront, 1987).

Adaptations are made to the environment if necessary to promote active engagement and independence in young children. Entryways to centers or pathways between them, for example, are widened as necessary to accommodate a child using a walker or wheelchair. Tactile cues are provided throughout the classroom (e.g., gluing blocks on a sign at the entryway to the block center) to help children who are visually impaired to locate centers. The classroom schedule and rules are posted in picture and written form, and concrete methods such as carpet squares or drawings indicating the number of children allowed to play in a center at one time are used to assist children with challenging behaviors (Campbell, 1992; Osborne, Kniest, Garland, Moore, & Usry, 1993). Adapted furniture such as chair inserts, corner chairs, or prone boards are provided to assist children with physical disabilities to take part in classroom activities. The least intrusive equipment and adaptations are used to ensure that children are not singled out from their peers. An effort is made to ensure that children with disabilities are at the same height as their peers in table, floor, and standing activities. For example, to sit at the same level as his or her peers, a child who needs physical support would use an adapted chair that sits flat on the floor (e.g., a floor sitter) during a floor activity such as circle time rather than sitting in a wheelchair at a higher level.

A large variety of materials is available to meet the developmental needs of the children within the classroom: books of varying lengths and complexity, puzzles with different numbers and sizes of pieces, realistic play materials, and materials that promote more abstract or creative play (Bredekamp, 1987). The ECSE teacher and related service staff assist with selecting and adapting appropriate materials to meet the needs of children with disabilities. For example, commercially available materials, such as magnet blocks, Mr. and Mrs. Potato Head with Velcro pieces, and toys that light up or that have highly contrasting colors are used. Adaptations can be made to toys, such as gluing knobs or cork stoppers to puzzle pieces or adding foam grip bike handles or curlers over paintbrush handles, to make them easier to grasp (Osborne et al., 1993). When special materials are necessary, they are functional and age-appropriate. Switches, for instance, are used to modify age-appropriate toys and tape recorders so children with motor difficulties can easily activate them. Electronic communication devices or picture communication systems can be used to provide ways for children who are nonvocal to communicate with adults and peers in the classroom. The children without disabilities also are attracted to these materials, which encourages their interaction with children with disabilities.

A quality, inclusive early childhood environment also provides a consistent, predictable schedule of classroom routines. The schedule includes a balance of teacher-directed and child-initiated activities; active and quiet activities; and individual, small-group, and large-group activities. The amount of time in teacher-directed, large-group activities (e.g., circle or story) is kept to a minimum, with child-initiated activities (e.g., learning centers, outdoor play) forming a substantial part of the day (Bredekamp, 1987). Adaptations are made to existing routines within the daily schedule to ensure successful participation by all children. For example, concrete objects are routinely used as props for circle and story to assist children with limited sight or challenging behavior; children with hearing impairments are seated in close proximity to the activity leader; and children who have difficulty paying attention during large-group times are given the choice of going to the quiet area or taking a permissible break. Adaptations are also made to the routines themselves when needed. For example, Westminster Child Care Center (in Charlottesville, Virginia) began serving meals in classrooms on the first floor when the second-floor cafeteria proved inaccessible to children with physical disabilities.

Social Relationships

Another significant component of an inclusive early childhood program is the social environment, which includes adult-child interactions and child-child social interactions within the classroom. Recommended early childhood practices encourage adults to enrich children's social skills development by providing a responsive environment based on developmentally appropriate interactions. These interactions are guided by "adults' knowledge of age appropriate behaviors in children balanced by adults' awareness of individual differences among children" (Bredekamp, 1987, p. 9).

Recommended ECSE practices also recognize the adult's role in providing a positive, nurturing social environment that is responsive to individual children's needs and supportive of the development of positive social skills (McEvoy & Yoder, 1993). Many children with disabilities, however, do not spontaneously acquire appropriate social skills through play (McEvoy & Yoder, 1993) or develop friendships with their peers simply by attending an inclusive program. This is because they either lack the skills to interact (e.g., the ability to initiate or respond to peers) or because they have other behaviors that interfere with their abilities to interact appropriately (Gresham & Evans, 1987). This is a major concern; in response to the question, "What skills do children learn in school that are most likely to lead to successful adjustment in adult life?" social skills is almost always the answer (Strain, 1985). As a result, ECSE practices emphasize ways to promote social interaction between children with disabilities and their peers in inclusive settings. ECSE research identifies a number of effective strategies to promote interaction, including environmental, curricular, peer-mediated, and child-specific approaches.

A quality, inclusive early childhood program uses early childhood guidelines as a basis for creating a favorable social environment. Adults model appropriate interactions (e.g., using age-appropriate language with children with disabilities); interact with children frequently showing affection, interest, and respect; and support the initiation of friendships (Bredekamp, 1987). Most young children learn positive social behaviors and form friendships as a direct result. In addition, ECSE practices are employed to benefit children with or without disabilities who do not naturally form friendships. In these cases, staff and families collaborate to select the most normalized, least intrusive, but most effective strategies. For example, staff may structure the environment in the following ways:

- *Encourage the proximity of children with social difficulties and other children.* Use small, well-defined play spaces, smaller tables in the classroom; plan seating where children with and without disabilities sit side by side (McEvoy & Yoder, 1993; Odom & Brown, 1993).
- *Make available social toys.* Provide dress-up clothes, puppets, toy vehicles, sand and water toys, a record player/records, blocks, wagons, seesaws, kiddie cars, and jungle gyms (Hendrickson, Strain, Tremblay, & Shores, 1981; Odom, Hoyson, Jamieson, & Strain, 1985).
- *Provide theme-related prop boxes.* Fill these boxes with objects that encourage interaction among children in the classroom (e.g., a picnic basket, tablecloth, paper plates, plastic spoons and forks) (Rogers-Warren & Wedel, 1980).

Staff may also use curricular activities to promote interaction between children with and without disabilities. Activities that are particularly conducive to promoting the development of social skills include the following:

- *Affection activities.* These include a discussion about friendship and use familiar songs or games that have been adapted to encourage children to display feelings of affection toward their peers (McEvoy, Twardosz, & Bishop, 1990). For example, the song "If You're Happy and You Know It" is rephrased to include directions to children, such as pat each other on the back and give a hug.

- *Cooperative activities.* These require two or more children to work together in a coordinated way to reach a common goal, such as keeping a ball on an uplifted parachute (Goffin & Tull, 1988).
- *Dramatic role-playing activities.* Children are given roles, a story line, and props (Goldstein & Gallagher, 1992). Familiar stories with repetitive lines, such as "The Three Bears," provide ideal materials for reenactment. Adaptations are made so that children who are nonverbal have other ways to participate (e.g., gesturing or using an electronic communication device with preprogrammed story parts).

Peer-mediated intervention is another approach to facilitating child-child social interaction. Children without disabilities are taught ways to initiate and sustain interaction with their less socially skilled classmates (Odom & Strain, 1984). Often these peer-mediated interventions are considered more effective than teacher-directed attempts, because peers are able to monitor children's social behaviors more consistently (Greenwood, Carta, & Kamps, 1990) and because teachers may inadvertently interrupt ongoing social exchanges (Chandler, Fowler, & Lubeck, 1992). In peer-mediated approaches, adults first identify socially skilled children who are eager to follow adult directions, are willing to continue attempts at interaction even when faced with a socially unresponsive playmate, and who attend preschool regularly (Odom & Strain, 1984). Next, adults use modeling and role-playing techniques to teach these children how to initiate interactions with children with disabilities. Initiations that result in higher response rates are taught, such as sharing a toy spontaneously, asking others to share their toys, offering or asking for assistance, organizing play, giving compliments, showing physical affection, and asking questions (Hendrickson, Strain, Tremblay, & Shores, 1982). The children are also taught to recognize the various communicative forms used by children with disabilities to initiate (such as a facial expression, a look, or pointing) and to understand the importance of responding appropriately based on a child's communicative purpose (e.g., by responding to a request for attention or acknowledging a child's refusal to participate) (Rainforth et al., 1992). Next, staff support the children's persistent use of these strategies by providing feedback and encouragement (Hendrickson et al., 1982). Additionally, when the children with disabilities do not respond, staff assist by prompting the children with disabilities to respond (Strain & Odom, 1986). The ultimate goal is for peers to use these strategies naturally during future social exchanges with children with disabilities.

Additional strategies (e.g., incidental teaching and prompting/guiding) involve teaching specific skills to children with disabilities to promote social interaction. In incidental teaching, the teacher prompts children to initiate social interaction with one another or models how to initiate social interaction during unstructured activities, such as free play (Odom & Brown, 1993). Teacher prompting is similar to incidental teaching in that the teacher gives a series of prompts to a child to encourage social behavior; however, prompting, which may include a physical prompt (e.g., a gesture or hand-over-hand assistance) is done to encourage a child to respond to as well as to initiate interaction with another child (Odom & Brown, 1993). This strategy is more intrusive than incidental teaching because the teacher is at greater risk of interrupting play by using a physical prompt, which consequently could take the child's attention away from his or her peers.

In summary, the interests and needs of each child are considered as teachers select strategies to promote social interaction in their classrooms. The combined use of recommended early childhood and ECSE practices ensures that staff are able to meet the needs of every child in the classroom.

The Curriculum

The curriculum is an important component of an inclusive early childhood program. Curriculum includes the content that is taught and methods for identifying and teaching the content to each individual (Wolery & Sainato, 1993). Recommended early childhood practices, as described in *"Guidelines for Appropriate Curriculum Content and Assessment in Programs Serving Young Children Ages 3 through 8"* (National Association for the Education of Young Children and National Association of Early Childhood Specialists in State Departments of Education, 1991), emphasize two dimensions of the developmental appropriateness of the curriculum: age and individual appropriateness. Curriculum is age appropriate when knowledge of typical child development is used to plan experiences that are based on the ages of the children in the classroom. Curriculum is individually appropriate when it is responsive to individual differences such as personality, unique growth patterns, and learning styles (Bredekamp, 1987). The early childhood curriculum is based on broad program goals and objectives. The teacher individualizes these objectives through regular observation of each child to determine the child's needs, strengths, and interests.

An inclusive early childhood program uses a developmentally appropriate curriculum as its foundation. ECSE practices are used to complement early childhood education practices to meet the individualized needs of each child in the classroom (Wolery & Fleming, 1993). Early childhood programs develop weekly lesson plans focusing on a thematic unit (e.g., families, winter, tools). General program goals (e.g., expanding verbal communication skills) and related objectives (e.g., recalling words in a song or fingerplay or following directions) are taught within daily theme-based activities. Program goals and objectives address the following areas of development: physical (which includes gross and fine motor skills), social-emotional, cognitive (which includes math, science, and social studies), language and literacy, creative expression, and health/safety/nutrition (Bredekamp & Rosegrant, 1992). The early childhood teacher facilitates children's learning by setting up the environment to elicit children's initiation and then identifying and elaborating on their interests (Fox et al., 1994). Particular attention is given to the process through which children learn, what the teachers will do to promote learning, and the context in which teaching and learning will occur (Fox et al., 1994).

The ECSE teacher works as a team with the early childhood teacher, the family, and related service staff (if applicable) to adapt curriculum as needed for any child, including children without disabilities. Children's individual characteristics are considered in planning adaptations or modifications to activities and in providing support to ensure that all children are able to participate (Bredekamp & Rosegrant, 1992). As required by federal law (IDEA), the development and implementation of an IEP for each child with disabilities is one aspect of the individualization process. IEP development may include a family interview and observation of the child in typical routines by the family, early childhood teacher, and ECSE staff to determine priority skills with present and future utility. Skills that are targeted are designed to make the child successful in the early childhood program, at home, and in the community, such as operating a switch to activate toys and a tape recorder or choosing foods, activities, or playmates. The IEP serves as the backbone for meaningful instruction and ongoing assessment of the child with disabilities.

Early childhood, ECSE, and related service staff (when applicable) meet regularly to discuss how to implement the IEP for a child with disabilities within daily activities. Discussion focuses on the most appropriate routines and activities in which to teach the objectives, appropriate teaching strategies, and ways to record progress. IEP objectives are taught in multiple child-initiated, play-based activities (e.g., learning centers, outdoor play) and teacher-directed activities (e.g., circle and story) within children's daily routines (Bricker & Cripe, 1992). Activities are selected that naturally require the child to perform the skill and that ensure that, by performing the skill, the child will become more independent within the routine. For example, the objective, "to make choices between two foods, activities, or playmates" may be taught at snack or lunch, at the beginning of learning centers when the child makes an activity choice, or when getting ready to go outdoors and the child chooses a walking partner.

It is critical for the team to select the most appropriate teaching strategies for each child. Teaching strategies—including child-initiated, teacher-guided, and teacher-directed strategies—fall on a continuum from least to most intrusive and may be classified based on the level of teacher involvement required (Bredekamp & Rosegrant, 1992). Characteristics and examples of each type of strategy are depicted in Exhibit 9–1.

All three types of strategies are used in inclusive early childhood programs. The goal is to select the least intrusive strategy that provides the child with the most control and results in efficient learning of the objective (Wolery & Sainato, 1993). Instructional decisions are based on consideration of the classroom environment, schedule, or activity; the materials used; and response adaptations (Wolery & Fleming, 1993). For example, one child may learn to pour his or her juice without spilling simply by being provided the opportunity to pour from a pitcher at snack time; another child may learn by watching the teacher or other children model how to pour; another child may need oral directions from the teacher to learn most efficiently; another child may need a lid on a pitcher to assist in pouring or a pitcher with a spout that can be pushed to fill the cup.

Another recommended practice in early childhood education and ECSE involves the documentation of each child's progress. For typically developing children, records are collected on the child's progress in relation to the broader program goals and objectives. These records are evaluated by comparing them to a child's previous progress or to a curriculum standard. To ensure that an objective is met, however, ECSE staff must demonstrate that a child has attained mastery of an objective at the criterion specified on the child's IEP. The use of a portfolio is one way to merge early childhood education and ECSE practices. Progress can be documented by observing a child's performance and by collecting permanent products for the portfolio. Observational techniques include the use of anecdotal notes, running records, teacher reflections, checklists or inventories, responses to questions or requests, rating scales, parent input, and other child progress monitoring forms. Observations can focus on spontaneous performance or may involve asking the child to engage in a specific activity. Products include writing samples, drawings and other art samples, audiotapes of children retelling or dictating stories, videotapes of story reenactment or play, photographs of large projects, completed projects, and logs of books read to children (Grace & Shores, 1991). Records are collected in chronological order and filed by area of development in each child's portfolio.

In conclusion, recommended early childhood education practices are the cornerstone of quality, inclusive early childhood programs. However, recommended ECSE practices are also essential to ensure that the curriculum is individualized to meet the needs of all children.

Discipline Techniques

The final major component of an inclusive early childhood program involves the use of positive discipline techniques. With this approach, adults guide children to regulate their own behavior and develop self-control. Positive discipline techniques focus on preventing problems before they occur; teaching children appropriate alternatives to their inappropriate behavior; and using simple, concrete explanations of what the children can do to solve their own problems. Adults can encourage children to talk about what has

Exhibit 9–1 Teaching Strategies

Strategy	Characteristics	Example
Child-initiated	Relies on the child's spontaneous initiations and/or responses and occurs in child-selected activities in the child's natural environment.	A child is putting a difficult, multipiece puzzle together; the teacher acknowledges the child's effort and encourages her to keep trying. (*Acknowledgment*)
Teacher-guided	Prearranged and flexible; occurs in the child's natural environment; the teacher offers assistance when necessary by enriching and extending the child's play.	A child walks to the teacher and holds out a painting apron; the teacher waits; the child says, "On"; the teacher assists. (*Naturalistic time delay*)
Teacher-directed	Carefully structured; controlled by the teacher; does not occur spontaneously; often requires a single, correct student response.	The teacher molds a child's hand to form the sign "more" followed by giving the child more juice; the teacher gradually reduces her level of physical support. (*Graduated guidance*)

happened and to generate alternative ways to behave in the future (for example, a teacher may say, "I see two children were fighting for the purple paint and it spilled; what can you do the next time you both want to use the purple paint?"). The teacher can also provide a choice of acceptable alternatives to the misbehavior and ask the child to select one (for example, a child who refuses to sit at the table for a snack may be asked, "Do you want to sit in the red chair or the blue chair?"). Adults may redirect children to alternative behaviors (for example, a child climbing on a shelf may be reminded, "The shelf is used to store our toys; if you want to climb, then climb on the climbing structure."). Always, the focus is on respecting children's autonomy and their right to behave in different but acceptable ways (National Association for the Education of Young Children, 1986).

Positive behavioral support is recommended for use in ECSE. Although the end result of using positive behavioral support is the same as that of positive discipline—behavioral change through education—the methods can be very different. Instead of focusing on encouraging the child (or children) to solve the problem, adults focus on identifying the purpose that a child's misbehavior serves and developing a teacher-directed plan to reduce the child's misbehavior and to teach the child alternative, more adaptive ways to meet his or her needs (O'Neill, Horner, Albin, Storey, & Sprague, 1990). Teacher intervention is done quickly, calmly, neutrally, and consistently. Teachers use planned body language, few words, and agreed-upon strategies to respond to, reduce, and replace the misbehavior with an adaptive behavior (Landon, Voorhees, Aveno, & Sydeman, 1993).

An inclusive early childhood program uses positive discipline as the basis for fostering self-control in all children. When children's behavior is simply inappropriate, reflecting a "normal deviance," then it can be prevented or responded to with a positive discipline strategy. An adult can spend time talking with a child and guiding the child to an alternative, more acceptable behavior. Behavior is *inappropriate* if it is harmful to the child or others (e.g., hitting or scratching self or others), abusive to materials (e.g., throwing books on the floor), or interferes with acceptance by others (e.g., whining, stereotyped behavior like body-rocking or mouthing objects, screaming during instructional time). Improvement would lead to more positive interactions with peers or others (Janney, Black, & Ferlo, 1989).

Behavior is *challenging* if it requires immediate attention due to extreme property damage (e.g., window breaking) or extreme physical harm to the child or others (e.g., self-injurious behavior such as head-banging, biting or hitting oneself, or extreme aggression toward others) (Janney et al., 1989). Challenging behavior needs to be prevented or stopped quickly (Landon et al., 1993). Recommended ECSE practices involve the use of a systematic plan that

addresses the child's reason for using the challenging behavior (O'Neill et al., 1990). The plan specifies ways to reduce or prevent the behavior of concern, staff response to the behavior, and strategies to teach the child acceptable alternative behavior. Chapter 15 offers further discussion of approaches for dealing with challenging behavior.

In summary, many recommended practices for early childhood education are effective at preventing and reducing misbehavior exhibited by children with disabilities. Conversely, some children without identified needs exhibit behavior that falls outside typical accepted ranges. In cases where children hurt themselves or others, or cause extreme property damage, ECSE practices can be extremely effective at reducing the challenging behavior and teaching children an alternative means of communication. Consequently, merging recommended practices from early childhood programs and ECSE helps to meet the emotional needs of all the children in an inclusive program.

PLANNING FOR SUCCESSFUL IMPLEMENTATION

Although advocates have called for preschool inclusion since the 1970s, the movement to achieve inclusive preschools has been disappointing (Demchak & Drinkwater, 1992). Controversy surrounds preschool inclusion (Campbell, 1991) and, consequently, many local school districts have yet to initiate these programs (Laski, 1991). Even though recommended practices encourage inclusion at the preschool level (DEC Task Force on Recommended Practices, 1993), local school divisions are reluctant to institute inclusive placement options because of organizational challenges such as financial issues, transportation, and early childhood and ECSE program policy differences. Additionally, while substantial research is available to guide instructional practices within inclusive early childhood programs, little research is available on ways to initiate and sustain these programs (Peck, Furman, & Helmstetter, 1993).

Many initially successful inclusive early childhood programs are not sustained because preliminary steps are not taken to gain support from all the key stakeholders—administrators, educators, families, related service staff—and to involve them in planning for inclusion. Systematic planning and *a community sense of ownership* are central to the success and longevity of preschool inclusion (Peck et al., 1993). Thus, ECSE programs in local school divisions must form grassroots initiatives with existing early childhood programs to plan for inclusion options that are compatible with local priorities. The following section describes 15 steps to guide teams as they plan for and initiate quality inclusion options for preschoolers with disabilities (see Exhibit 9–2). These planning steps were originally devel-

Exhibit 9–2 Planning Steps for Inclusion at the Preschool Level

---

INITIAL STEPS

Complete these steps sequentially, beginning at least 12 months before program implementation:

Step 1: Form a preschool inclusion planning team.
Step 2: Educate the team about inclusion.
Step 3: Visit quality inclusive early childhood programs.
Step 4: Recommend potential inclusive option(s) to expand current ECSE placements.
Step 5: Gain approval from school division and early childhood administrators for inclusive option(s).

SUBSEQUENT STEPS

Complete these steps concurrently in accordance with local needs:

Step 6: Identify barriers to initiating the approved inclusive option(s).
Step 7: Recommend job revisions and criteria for staff selection.
Step 8: Gain support from key stakeholders.
Step 9: Develop a program philosophy and goals.
Step 10: Provide ways for ECSE, early childhood, and related service staff to learn about one another's programs.
Step 11: Conduct a series of inservice training sessions on recommended practices in inclusive programs.
Step 12: Develop contracts and policies to support the program philosophy and goals for the inclusive program.
Step 13: Develop a process for making individualized placement decisions in the least restrictive environment.
Step 14: Conduct ongoing evaluations and use results for program improvement.
Step 15: Provide orientation activities.

---

oped by Voorhees et al. (1993), through the Systematic Inclusive Preschool Education Project, funded by the U.S. Department of Education. The steps are based on a review of the research regarding critical preparation and planning issues for inclusive school-age and early childhood programs (Alessi, 1991; Johnson et al., 1993; Peck et al., 1989) and the authors' personal experiences in initiating inclusive preschool programs. Voorhees, Landon, and Harvey (1995) expanded and modified these steps through the Virginia Department of Education's Integrated Placement Options for Preschoolers (IPOP) project, funded by Federal Part B Preschool money. These revised steps were then piloted by eight Virginia school divisions and collaborating early childhood education programs. Many additional school districts then used the steps to initiate inclusive placement options.

The planning steps are designed to be completed over a two-year period by a preschool inclusion planning team. Year 1 is devoted to planning prior to offering a new placement option. Planning continues in year 2, while the inclusive program is implemented. Some schools and communities may take longer to complete these planning steps if more than one new option is to be offered. Although the planning steps may seem overwhelming, they are completed over a period of time by a team of people. In addition, planning is proactive; fewer problems arise in a new program when planning occurs prior to implementation.

Step 1: Form a Preschool Inclusion Planning Team

The first step in planning for inclusive programs for preschoolers with disabilities involves two tasks: (1) obtaining administrative approval to form a preschool inclusion planning team, and (2) forming the team. Teams include representatives of all groups of stakeholders that might be affected by preschool inclusion: families, teachers, assistants, and administrators. Team tasks include making recommendations regarding inclusive options that could be offered and conducting the necessary planning steps to implement these options.

Special education administrators, ECSE teachers, and parents, for example, may work to obtain administrative approval to organize a preschool inclusion planning team and facilitate team meetings. The first step of planning is to determine the existing procedures within a school division for forming a team and to obtain permission to develop the preschool inclusion planning team. It is useful to prepare written materials regarding the purpose of forming a team, the rationale for and benefits of preschool inclusion, and the steps a team will take to plan for inclusion. These may be presented formally to school boards or in informal meetings with superintendents or other appropriate high-level administrators.

Once approval for forming a team is obtained, those who proposed the team complete several tasks to prepare for monthly preschool inclusion planning team meetings. First, a list is developed of potential inclusion planning team members from the school division, community agencies, and regular early childhood programs, keeping in mind that the optimum size for a team (or subteam) is 7 to 10 people. The list should include the following:

- school division representatives (e.g., families of preschool children with disabilities, the special education director, ECSE coordinators, principals of schools where ECSE classes are located, teachers and paraprofessionals in ECSE, and related service staff)
- community agency representatives from agencies that serve or could serve young children with disabilities (e.g., IDEA Part H local interagency coordinating councils, local departments of social services and health, agencies providing contracted related service staff)
- early childhood program representatives (e.g., preschool or child care board members, directors, teachers and assistants, and families of children without disabilities)

Next, proponents of the team determine meeting logistics such as how to invite stakeholders to the first meeting, when and where the meeting should occur, and how to motivate people to attend. Serving refreshments or a meal and providing child care usually increase attendance. A structured, collaborative team meeting process should be selected for use in team meetings. Teams that use such a process are more efficient, make decisions by consensus, and end meetings with a written record of their work. Final tasks involve assigning a liaison to share information with important ex officio team members (e.g., the superintendent, representatives from the school board, and the district transportation director). The liaison shares team meeting notes, draws attention to team actions, and solicits input. It is imperative that a school division administrator be available to elicit advice from the school division's attorney regarding legal or policy issues that may affect the team's decisions.

Step 2: Educate the Team about Inclusion

Beginning a quality, inclusive preschool program is a challenging task. To make the required changes, team members must believe strongly in the value of inclusion, understand the importance of planning and the significance of their involvement, and be knowledgeable about recommended practices in inclusive early childhood programs. Therefore, a second planning step involves gaining the team's support for inclusion and educating team members about inclusive programs for preschoolers with disabilities. The persons spearheading the team plan initial meetings by

determining the agenda, handouts, participatory activities, and who will present the information. Important initial meeting content includes the following:

- an overview of the planning steps and the team's purpose
- the educational, philosophical, legal, and financial rationales for preschool inclusion
- the benefits of inclusion for children, direct service staff, administrators, and families
- the definition, critical features, advantages, and disadvantages of various types of inclusive placements for preschoolers
- guidelines for merging recommended early childhood and ECSE practices in early childhood inclusion programs
- the process of change and the specific organizational and programmatic changes required to develop inclusive options for preschoolers

Step 3: Visit Quality Inclusive Early Childhood Programs

Seeing inclusion in action is a critical step in planning—"A picture is worth a thousand words!" Thus, following the completion of educational activities, the team visits various quality inclusive programs. The ECSE coordinator at the state department of education should be able to provide recommendations. The team then determines which members will visit these programs. The selected members schedule visits, making sure to do the following:

- arrange classroom and, if possible, team meeting observations
- schedule time to talk to administrators; early childhood, ECSE, and related service staff; and parents of children with and without disabilities in the program, asking program participants to identify the benefits of inclusion and the challenges they encountered and how they addressed them
- collect written program materials, including program descriptions, contracts or interagency agreements, and job descriptions

During a regularly scheduled preschool inclusion planning team meeting, team members describe the programs they visited, emphasizing their perceptions of the advantages and disadvantages of providing the option(s) observed.

Step 4: Recommend Potential Inclusive Option(s) To Expand Current ECSE Placements

Once team members have visited inclusive programs in other schools and communities, they recommend which options to offer and develop a timeline for implementation. The team identifies potential early childhood education sites that are interested in collaborating with the school district to include children with disabilities. The list begins with early childhood programs in the school division (e.g., Head Start, Title I preschool programs, occupational child care programs) and then includes effective early childhood programs in the community. The team agrees upon a procedure for contacting potential sites to determine their receptivity to collaboration. When contacting programs, the team may want to ask whether they have enrolled children with special needs in the past and, if so, to describe their experiences.

After developing a list of interested sites, the team considers how to assess the quality of these sites. In small communities, team members may visit all of the early childhood programs in the area, talk personally with the program directors, and use an observation guide to assess program quality. In larger communities, the team may limit contacts to programs that are accredited by the National Academy of Early Childhood Programs or other accrediting organizations. Some large communities conduct surveys or use a request for proposal (RFP) process to identify interested sites that meet specific standards of quality set by their locality. Sites are asked to provide program-specific information such as tuition rates, number of classrooms, staff/child ratios, and staff qualifications. Final selection is made after team representatives observe programs and determine their quality.

The team also determines the approximate number of children who will be eligible for ECSE services in the upcoming school year. The team verifies the current ECSE enrollment and number of children who will be exiting the program at the end of the current school year, and estimates the number of children who will enter the program from infant/toddler services and from new referrals. It is important to collect this information to coincide with the school board's budget development process, because a projected increase in enrollment will mean that additional ECSE staff will need to be hired. These added employees could staff a new collaborative or consultative inclusion site. If ECSE enrollment will remain the same or decrease, then current resources could be reallocated by closing a self-contained classroom and assigning the ECSE staff the new role of working in the inclusive early childhood program. If the latter option is selected, it is important to consider the willingness of the ECSE staff to change roles.

The next critical task for team members is to contact families to share information about potential inclusive placements and to determine families' interest in this type of educational setting. Letters, surveys, home visits, and phone calls are all appropriate methods of contact. It is imperative to explain to parents that if these options become available, parents will be involved in determining their child's placement through the IEP meeting.

The team is then prepared to achieve consensus regarding which inclusive option(s) to initiate next year and in subsequent years. No matter which option the team selects, a modest beginning is recommended to ensure the inclusive program's success. Unless there is ample staff support, it is best to plan for and implement only one option the first year and plan to offer additional options in following years. Larger divisions may want to pilot a new inclusive option in one administrative area rather than in the entire division to prevent planning from being overwhelming. Similarly, school divisions that are implementing site-based management may choose to pilot an inclusive option at one school site.

Step 5: Gain Approval from School Division and Early Childhood Administrators for Inclusive Option(s)

Once the team has decided which inclusive option(s) to initiate, they then must gain approval from school and early childhood officials for the proposed option(s). This involves determining the district's procedures for approval of new programs and tailoring the following tasks to fit these procedures. The team must gain approval from upper-level school administrators (e.g., principals, special education director, superintendent, and school board) for the recommended inclusive option(s). This may entail developing a detailed written proposal. Most proposals include the planning steps that have been accomplished, the recommended inclusive options, and the rationale for and benefits of these options. Once the team secures district approval, they share their next planning steps and elicit school administrators' concerns. These concerns are addressed in future team meetings.

If the proposed option involves community early childhood programs, another task is to gain approval from relevant administrators (and board members, if applicable) for the proposal. It will be helpful to emphasize the benefits of collaboration to children, staff, and families in the early childhood programs as well as to the school district. As before, the early childhood program administrator's concerns are identified and taken to the team for solutions. If representatives from the selected collaborating early childhood program(s) have not served on the preschool inclusion planning team, the team should be expanded to include them. New members receive written materials about the team's purpose and past activities.

Once the inclusion planning team has gained administrative approval to begin the recommended option(s), 10 additional steps must be completed to ensure the inclusive program's success. The order in which they are completed should be based on local needs and concerns. Many of these steps should be completed concurrently.

Step 6: Identify Barriers to Initiating the Approved Inclusive Option(s)

The identification of barriers and solutions to initiating the approved options is a critical planning step. By addressing the team's concerns before the concerns become realities, roadblocks are avoided. Numerous organizational barriers must be addressed prior to providing ECSE services to children with disabilities in general early childhood settings. These include issues regarding funding, transportation, supervision of ECSE staff, and early childhood and ECSE program policy differences. The team should develop a list of specific local barriers.

Typical barriers that arise in regard to funding include the issues of tuition payment and separation of church and state. If the team recommends collaboration with a community-based early childhood program that charges tuition, then the school division's responsibility regarding tuition payment will inevitably become an issue. The Office of Special Education Programs at the U.S. Department of Education has stated that Federal Part B preschool and other Part B money may be used to pay tuition if placement in the early childhood setting is needed to provide a free and appropriate public education (FAPE) to a child as determined by the IEP (Wessel, 1989). The question of payment, therefore, relates to determination of what is a FAPE in the school division. School districts have used a variety of sources to fund tuition payments. In addition to federal special education dollars, scholarships provided by the early childhood program and funds from agencies such as state and local departments of social services and the United Way have been used. Additionally, school districts have established agreements with early childhood programs to provide in-kind contributions such as additional staff, staff training, materials, and integrated related services in lieu of tuition payments or for reduced tuition rates.

A second funding issue may arise if the team recommends paying tuition for children with disabilities to attend a church-based early childhood program. In general, government funds may not be used to support church functions. As a result, school divisions in which the only quality programs are housed in churches will need to address this issue. Many school districts are collaborating with early childhood programs located in churches that can document the absence of religious affiliation (i.e., the program is operated by a separate board other than a church board, the preschool rents space from the church, the curriculum does not include religious instruction, and the program does not claim religious exemption for tax purposes.) The team may need to consult with the school board attorney to assist with this issue, as local policies and practices vary.

Transportation can become a major barrier if the team recommends collaboration with a community-based program. If an IEP committee determines that a general early childhood setting is the most appropriate placement, then the school district is responsible for providing transportation to services described in the IEP. Often it is difficult for the district to arrange for transportation to additional sites. Some school divisions have been able to provide transportation through use of a county car instead of a special education bus. Other districts have used the community-based program's transportation system or reimbursed parents for their mileage.

There are several comprehensive sources of information regarding organizational barriers and potential solutions (Smith & Rose, 1991, 1993; Strain & Smith, 1993). The team should review these for guidance. The team then needs to brainstorm regarding the best solutions for the locality. The process of identifying barriers or concerns and bringing them to team meetings for discussion and resolution continues throughout the planning and implementation of inclusive programs.

Step 7: Recommend Job Revisions and Criteria for Staff Selection

Job descriptions must be modified to include the duties associated with the new inclusion program. This enables the team to develop selection criteria to identify the most qualified staff to serve children in the new placement site. School division and early childhood administrators will be able to identify the procedures to modify job descriptions to make them applicable to employment in inclusive programs and to develop staff-selection criteria. An initial task is to gather current job descriptions of ECSE teachers and assistants, early childhood teachers and assistants, and therapists, and modify them to reflect new staff roles and responsibilities required in the inclusion program. Attending weekly team meetings, for example, may not be a part of existing job expectations. Staff who may work in the new inclusive program should be invited to provide input about job revisions.

Staff selection criteria should include general specifications such as flexibility and the ability to work cooperatively with other adults, as well as specific criteria for each staff position. Competency in using an integrated therapy approach, for example, is an important criterion for related service staff. The team may also be involved in developing sample job announcements, letters soliciting staff interest in inclusion, and sample interview questions. The team then shares recommended job descriptions and staff-selection criteria with person(s) within the school division and with collaborating early childhood administrators responsible for hiring/selecting staff. Once final descriptions and criteria have been agreed upon, the most qualified staff can be interviewed and selected according to school and early childhood program procedures. It may be helpful to share the revised job description with interested applicants, have them visit an inclusive program like the one to be initiated, and visit the collaborating programs during the interview process.

Step 8: Gain Support from Key Stakeholders

Information about the inclusive placement option(s) is shared with stakeholders, and then concerns are elicited and resolved. This step must be completed prior to beginning the inclusion program. Key tasks include generating a list of the stakeholders in need of information about the inclusive option(s) (e.g., families, administrators, and direct service staff), determining the information to be shared (e.g., the rationale and benefits of inclusion and a description of the new option), and identifying persons responsible and deadlines for information sharing. Information can be shared through phone calls, individual or group meetings, and questionnaires. Whatever method is used, it is important to elicit stakeholders' concerns and/or perceived barriers to inclusion and to record concerns in writing. The team may want to ask stakeholders for their ideas about how to address their concerns, explaining that the preschool inclusion planning team also will generate potential solutions. Actions taken to address a particular concern are shared with the person(s) who raised the concern.

Step 9: Develop a Program Philosophy and Goals

Families, staff, and administrators in the collaborating ECSE and early childhood programs will want to develop a shared program philosophy (or mission) and goals for the inclusive program. This step begins with selecting a process either to develop the vision or to revise current missions and program goal statements to address issues related to the new inclusion program. Families, staff, and administrators are invited to provide input into the development of the new program philosophy and goals. Once this is accomplished, the team can use the program philosophy and goals during team meetings to guide program decisions, develop/revise policies, and so forth. For example, if a goal is collaborative staff planning, then a policy may be needed to require staff to meet weekly. It may be necessary to refine these initial statements following the completion of inservice training and firsthand experience with inclusion. The refined philosophy and goals may then be used to develop collaborative agreements or contracts, update policies, and make future decisions about the inclusion program.

Step 10: Provide Ways for ECSE, Early Childhood, and Related Service Staff To Learn about One Another's Programs

To foster collaboration among early childhood, ECSE, and related service staff in inclusive programs, another cru-

cial planning step is to encourage staff members to learn about the practices of other staff members. Once they understand their colleagues' practices, staff members can develop programming that meets the needs of all the children. Diverse professional practices should be presented to staff. It may be helpful to ask those regularly involved in the classroom (early childhood and ECSE teachers and paraprofessionals; speech-language pathologists; physical and occupational therapists; and volunteers) to identify what they desire to learn about one another's practices. Additionally, the team should recommend ways for staff to learn about their colleagues' programs. Conducting observations and interviews, attending program meetings or workshops, and exchanging verbal or written information may be useful.

Step 11: Conduct a Series of Inservice Training Sessions on Recommended Practices in Inclusive Programs

The team plans for, schedules, and provides inservice training and follow-up technical assistance to program participants. Joint training on early childhood and ECSE recommended practices will give staff from diverse backgrounds a common foundation for developing quality early childhood inclusion programs. Everyone—early childhood and ECSE administrators, teachers and teaching assistants, related service staff, and volunteers—should participate in inservice training. Families should be invited to attend also. Training should begin before the children with disabilities enter the program.

The team asks program staff to identify inservice training needs, preferred times and locations for training, and preferred training methods. A needs assessment or a self-study related to implementation of recommended practices, for example, can be used to identify training needs. The team may decide to develop an instrument or to use a commercially available one. The Creative Curriculum Self-Assessment and Observation Form (Dodge, 1991) or the Early Childhood Environment Rating Scale (Harms & Clifford, 1980) may be useful. A survey of potential training methods—such as attending workshops, viewing videotapes, reading articles, or observing specific features of a quality program in action—can be used to help participants identify ways they learn best.

Based upon the collected information, the team selects topics and training methods, and schedules inservice training on the days and times preferred by potential training participants. The team also arranges logistical details (e.g., convenient location, food to be provided, babysitting services, and compensation of staff who attend after work hours). Finally, the team considers ways to provide follow-up technical assistance to assist staff in applying the information presented at the inservice training. Follow-up strategies could include the following: checklists; peer coaches, mentors, or models; a facilitator to assist with implementation; evaluation tools that specify the use of these practices; regular team meetings where staff discuss classroom issues; and written inservice training materials. Persons responsible for facilitating these follow-up activities should be identified.

Step 12: Develop Contracts and Policies To Support the Program Philosophy and Goals for the Inclusive Program

To clarify the responsibilities of the collaborating ECSE and early childhood programs, it is necessary to develop policies and a contract to support the new inclusive option. The newly developed program philosophy and goals should guide the development of these documents. The team may be involved in several ways. First, the team can identify appropriate procedures for developing or revising contracts and policies and obtain permission to do so from school division and early childhood administrators. Second, the team can suggest new policies and/or revise current ones to realize the program philosophy and goals. If applicable, the team can help to develop a formal contract between the collaborating programs, specifying each program's responsibilities related to accomplishing the program philosophy and goals. Issues to be addressed in the collaborative agreement may include the services provided by each agency, supervision of staff and children, insurance coverage, tuition, transportation, and staff roles and responsibilities. Some teams have developed an administrative contract that includes information about the financial and legal responsibilities of each agency, and a direct service contract that specifies issues related to the educational program (e.g., direct service staff responsibilities). Further, the team must obtain approval for the agreement or contract from the appropriate division and early childhood administrators. The contracts or policies should be amended as new concerns arise during the planning year and during the first year of program implementation.

Step 13: Develop a Process for Making Individualized Placement Decisions in the Least Restrictive Environment

It is critical to develop a consistent process for IEP committees to make individualized placement decisions in the least restrictive environment. Smith and Rose (1993) assert that "parents and professionals should have a full range of placement options from which to make individual placement decisions," and that "all placement options should be of sufficient quality to result in the delivery of appropriate and effective special education and related services." Once

these criteria are met, then "placements should be made individually for each child—tailoring the location and services to meet the individual needs and preferences of the child and family" (p. 77).

Smith and Rose (1993) provide sample placement procedures and forms that may be used to guide decisions about the least restrictive environment for ECSE services. It may be useful for the team to review these materials when developing a local placement process. Administrative approval will be needed for IEP teams to use this process as they make children's placement decisions. Strategies to provide the least restrictive environment for all children will need to be developed, particularly if the new inclusion program is an appropriate placement for more preschoolers than there are spaces available. Inclusion may not be successful if children are placed in sites that do not use effective practices, where staff have not had training, and where coordinated policies are not in place between the ECSE and early childhood programs. Legally, however, any child within the school division must have access to services in the least restrictive environment to meet his or her needs. Determining a way to address this issue during the initiation of the inclusive options is a challenging task for the preschool inclusion planning team. It is not legal for a school division to develop exclusion criteria for placement based on age or type or level of disability. Some communities have addressed this dilemma by piloting the inclusive option in one geographical area of the division and providing access to children who live in that area. Other districts have given priority of placement based on child and family needs. For example, a family who needs full-time day care services receives priority for their child's IEP placement in a day care setting. Being honest with families and involving them in developing creative strategies is the best policy. Families should be apprised of the team's goal to develop additional options so all children will be served in the least restrictive environment.

Step 14: Conduct Ongoing Evaluations and Use Results for Program Improvement

To provide data to help decision makers make ongoing improvements to the inclusive program, the team must evaluate the impact of the new program on various stakeholder groups. Programs are most successful when improvements are based on informed decisions. First, the team determines the purpose of the evaluation. Families, staff, and administrators may be asked what information they would like to have about the program's impact. The superintendent, for example, may want cost-effectiveness data; the special education director may want information about child progress and parent satisfaction; and families may want peer-acceptance information. Next, the team identifies evaluation participants. If the team wants to determine parent satisfaction, for example, then families of children with and without disabilities in the inclusive program should be evaluation participants. Once these decisions are made, the team can select or develop evaluation methods and instruments and assign staff to collect data. Interviews, questionnaires, cost-benefit analyses, standardized tests, and portfolios may all be useful.

The preschool inclusion planning team also addresses confidentiality matters and develops an evaluation timeline. Typically, some evaluation instruments are administered at the beginning and at the end of the year to provide before-and-after comparisons; others are administered just at the end of the year; and others are administered throughout the year. Once the evaluation activities have been completed and the results summarized, the team uses the results to make program improvements and to provide feedback to program participants.

Step 15: Provide Orientation Activities

A final crucial planning step is for the team to recommend orientation activities to be offered for children with disabilities and their families at the new program's onset. The team may suggest that ECSE staff and families share specific information about the children with disabilities (e.g., children's strengths, preferences, use of adaptive equipment) with early childhood staff before implementing the program. Or the team may develop guidelines to facilitate ongoing communication among families, staff, and administration in the early childhood and ECSE programs. Asking families to identify preferred staff contact persons

and methods of communication such as written notes, phone calls, home visits, and team meetings is important, as is identifying one person to be responsible for coordinating communication between the direct service providers in the inclusion program and the early childhood and ECSE administrators.

The team also may suggest preenrollment activities to facilitate a smooth transition to the inclusive program. For example, each child with disabilities could visit his or her next classroom with ECSE staff and family members prior to attending the new program full time. It may be advantageous to hold a team meeting following the visit, to elicit and address questions, concerns, and barriers. Also, an introductory packet that includes the paperwork needed by the collaborating programs could be developed for all parents.

CONCLUSION

Although forming a team and completing these planning tasks require time and commitment, it truly is worth the effort. Inclusion programs that experience sustained success have clearly articulated philosophies and use highly collaborative planning and decision-making processes; programs that fail are planned and implemented by administrators or special education staff alone, without the involvement of the early childhood professionals and families (Peck et al., 1989; Peck et al., 1993). Implementing a sound planning process increases the chances of developing a successful inclusion program for preschoolers. The efforts of a full year of planning will make a lifetime of difference to the preschoolers with and without disabilities in the community.

REFERENCES

Abraham, M.R., Morris, L.M., & Wald, P.J. (1991). *Project APIP integrated preschool classroom.* Washington, DC: George Washington University.

Alessi, R.V. (1991). ODDM: The gentle bulldozer. *Quality Outcomes-Driven Education, 1*(1), 11–18.

Americans with Disabilities Act of 1990, 42 U.S.C.A. § 12101 *et seq.*

Bredekamp, S. (1987). *Developmentally appropriate practice in early childhood programs serving children from birth through age 8.* Washington, DC: National Association for the Education of Young Children.

Bredekamp, S., & Rosegrant, T. (1992). Reaching potentials through appropriate curriculum: Conceptual frameworks for applying the guidelines. In S. Bredekamp & T. Rosegrant (Eds.), *Reaching potentials: Appropriate curriculum and assessments for young children* (pp. 28–42). Washington, DC: National Association for the Education of Young Children.

Bricker, D. (1995). The challenge of inclusion. *Journal of Early Intervention, 19*(3), 179–194.

Bricker, D., & Cripe, J. (1992). *An activity-based approach to early intervention.* Baltimore: Paul H. Brookes.

Brittain, H. (1994). Integration bright spots. *Early Childhood Special Education Technical Assistance Center Newsletter, 16,* 5.

Bussye, V. (1993). Friendships of preschoolers with disabilities in community-based child care settings. *Journal of Early Intervention, 17,* 380–395.

Campbell, P.H. (1991). An essay on preschool integration. In L.H. Meyer, C.A. Peck, & L. Brown (Eds.), *Critical issues in the lives of people with severe disabilities* (pp. 437–477). Baltimore: Paul H. Brookes.

Campbell, P.H. (Ed.). (1992). *Preschool integration network training manual.* Akron, OH: Children's Hospital Medical Center of Akron, The Family Child Learning Center.

Chandler, L.K., Fowler, S.A., & Lubeck, R.C. (1992). An analysis of the effects of multiple setting events on the social behavior of preschool children with special needs. *Journal of Applied Behavior Analysis, 25,* 249–263.

Cook, R.E., Tessier, A., & Armbruster, V.B. (1987). *Adapting early childhood curricula for children with special needs.* Columbus, OH: Charles E. Merrill.

Cooper, K. (1996). Letter to Pennington Gap (Virginia) Head Start Program.

Demchak, M.A., & Drinkwater, S. (1992). Preschoolers with severe disabilities: The case against segregation. *Topics in Early Childhood Special Education, 11*(4), 70–83.

Division for Early Childhood Task Force on Recommended Practices (1993). *DEC recommended practices: Indicators of quality programs for infants and young children with special needs and their families*. Pittsburgh, PA: Division for Early Childhood/Council for Exceptional Children.

Dodge, D.T. (1988). *The creative curriculum for early childhood*. Washington, DC: Teaching Strategies.

Dodge, D.T. (1991). *A guide for supervisors and trainers on implementing the creative curriculum for early childhood*. Washington, DC: Teaching Strategies.

Edgar, E., Hegglelund, M., & Fischer, M. (1988). A longitudinal study of graduates of special education preschools: Educational placement after preschool. *Topics in Early Childhood Special Education, 8*(3), 61–74.

Esposito, B.G., & Koorland, M.A. (1989). Play behavior of hearing impaired children: Integrated and segregated settings. *Exceptional Children, 55*, 412–419.

Esposito, B.G., & Peach, W.J. (1983). Changing attitudes of preschool children toward handicapped persons. *Exceptional Children, 49*, 361–363.

Fenrick, N.J., Pearson, M.E., & Pepelnjak, J.M. (1984). The play, attending, and language of young handicapped children in integrated and segregated settings. *Journal of Early Intervention, 3*, 57–67.

Fox, L., Hanline, M.F., Vail, C.O., & Galant, K.R. (1994). Developmentally appropriate practice: Applications for young children with disabilities. *Journal of Early Intervention, 18*(4), 243–257.

Fox, T.S., & Williams, W. (1991). *Implementing best practices for all students in their local school*. Burlington, VT: Vermont Statewide Systems Support Project.

Friend, M., & Cook, L. (1992). *Interactions: Collaboration skills for school professionals*. White Plains, NY: Longman.

Goffin, S.G., & Tull, C.Q. (1988). Ideas! Encouraging cooperative behavior among young children. *Dimensions of Early Childhood, 16*(4), 15–18.

Goldstein, H., & Gallagher, T.M. (1992). Strategies for promoting the social-communicative competence of young children with specific language impairment. In S. Odom, S. McConnell, & M. McEvoy (Eds.), *Social competence of children with disabilities* (pp. 189–213). Baltimore: Paul H. Brookes.

Grace, C., & Shores, E. (1991). *The portfolio and its use: Developmentally appropriate assessment of young children*. Little Rock, AR: Southern Association on Children Under Six.

Green, A.L., & Stoneman, Z. (1989). Attitudes of mothers and fathers of nonhandicapped children toward preschool mainstreaming. *Journal of Early Intervention, 13*, 292–304.

Greenwood, C.R., Carta, J.J., & Kamps, D. (1990). Teacher-mediated versus peer-mediated instruction: A review of educational advantages and disadvantages. In H.C. Foot, M.J. Morgan, & R.H. Shute (Eds.), *Children helping children* (pp. 177–205). Chichester, England: Wiley.

Gresham, F.M., & Evans, S.E. (1987). Conceptualization and treatment of social withdrawal in the schools. *Special Services in the School, 3*, 37–51.

Guralnick, M.J., & Groom, J.M. (1988). Peer interactions in mainstreamed and specialized classrooms: A comparative analysis. *Exceptional Children, 54*, 415–425.

Harms, T., & Clifford, R.M. (1980). *Early childhood environment rating scale*. New York: Teacher's College.

Head Start Performance Standards, 45 CFR, 1308 (1993).

Hendrickson, J.M., Strain, P.S., Tremblay, A., & Shores, R.E. (1981). Relationship between toy and material use and the occurrence of social interactive behaviors by normally developing preschool children. *Psychology in the Schools, 18*, 500–504.

Hendrickson, J.M., Strain, P.S., Tremblay, A., & Shores, R.E. (1982). Interactions of behaviorally handicapped children: Functional effects of peer social initiations. *Behavior Modifications, 6*, 323–353.

Improving America's Schools Act, 20 U.S.C. § 6301 *et seq.* (1994).

Individuals with Disabilities Education Act, 20 U.S.C. § 1400 *et seq.* (1991).

Ipsa, J., & Matz, R.D. (1978). Integrating handicapped preschool children within a cognitively oriented program. In M.J. Guralnick (Ed.), *Early intervention and the integration of handicapped and nonhandicapped children* (pp. 167–190). Baltimore: University Park Press.

Janney, R., Black, J., & Ferlo, M. (1989). *A problem-solving approach to challenging behaviors* (U.S. Department of Education Grant No. 600-86-300358). Syracuse: Syracuse City School District.

Jenkins, J.R., Odom, S.L., & Speltz, M.L. (1989). Effects of social integration of preschool children with handicaps. *Exceptional Children, 55*, 420–429.

Johnson, L.G., Rogers, C.K., Johnson, P.A., & McMillan, R.P. (1993). *EC-SPEED model program conference: A summary of conference proceedings*. Columbus, OH: Ohio Department of Education.

Katz, L.G. (1987). Early education: What should young children be doing? In S.L. Kagan & E.F. Zigler (Eds.), *Early schooling: The national debate* (pp. 151–167). New Haven, CT: Yale University.

Kontos, S., & File, N. (1993). Staff development in support of integration. In C.A. Peck, S.L. Odom, & D.D. Bricker (Eds.), *Integrating young children with disabilities into community programs: Ecological perspectives on research implementation* (pp. 169–186). Baltimore: Paul H. Brookes.

Landon, T., Voorhees, M.D., Aveno, A., & Sydeman, J. (1993). Fostering self-control: Using nonaversive behavior management and positive discipline. In A. Aveno (Ed.), *Inclusive preschool partnerships: A guide for making them work*. Charlottesville, VA: University of Virginia, Department of Curriculum, Instruction, and Special Education.

Laski, F.J. (1991). Achieving integration during the second revolution. In L.H. Meyer, C.A. Peck, & L. Brown (Eds.), *Critical issues in the lives of people with severe disabilities* (pp. 405–421). Baltimore: Paul H. Brookes.

McEvoy, M.S., Twardosz, S., & Bishop, N. (1990). Affection activities: Procedures for encouraging young children with handicaps to interact with their peers. *Education and Treatment of Children, 13*(2), 159–167.

McEvoy, M.A., & Yoder, P. (1993). Interventions to promote social skills and emotional development. In *DEC recommended practices: Indicators of quality programs for infants and young children with special needs and their families* (pp. 77–81). Pittsburgh, PA: Division for Early Childhood/Council for Exceptional Children.

McLean, M., & Hanline, M.F. (1990). Providing early intervention services in integrated environments: Challenges and opportunities for the future. *Topics in Early Childhood Special Education, 10*(2), 62–77.

McLean, M., & Odom, S.L. (1993). Practices for young children with disabilities: A comparison of DEC and NAEYC identified practices. *Topics in Early Childhood Special Education, 13*(3), 274–292.

McWilliam, R.A., & Strain, P.S. (1993). Service delivery models. In *DEC recommended practices: Indicators of quality programs for infants and young children with special needs and their families* (pp. 40–46). Pittsburgh, PA: Division for Early Childhood/Council for Exceptional Children.

Miller, L.J., Strain, P.S., McKinley, J., Heckathorn, K., & Miller, S. (1993). *Preschool placement decisions: Are they predictors of future placement?* Pittsburgh, PA: Research Institute on Preschool Mainstreaming.

National Association for the Education of Young Children. (1986). *Helping children learn self-control: A guide to discipline.* Washington, DC: Author.

National Association for the Education of Young Children and National Association of Early Childhood Specialists in State Departments of Education. (1991). Guidelines for appropriate curriculum content and assessment in programs serving children ages 3 through 8. *Young Children, 46*(3), 21–38.

Novak, M.A., Olley, J.G., & Kearney, D.S. (1980). Social skills of children with special needs in integrated and separate preschools. In T.M. Field, S. Goldberg, D. Stern, & A.M. Sostek (Eds.), *High risk infants and children: Adults and peer interactions* (pp. 327–346). New York: Academic.

Odom, S.L., & Brown, W.H. (1993). Social interaction skills interventions for young children with disabilities in integrated settings. In C.A. Peck, S.L. Odom, & D.D. Bricker (Eds.), *Integrating young children with disabilities into community programs: Ecological perspectives on research and implementation* (pp. 39–64). Baltimore: Paul H. Brookes.

Odom, S.L., Hoyson, M., Jamieson, B., & Strain, P.S. (1985). Increasing handicapped preschoolers' peer social interactions: Cross-netting and component analysis. *Journal of Applied Behavior Analysis, 18,* 3–16.

Odom, S.L., & McLean, M. (1993). Establishing recommended practices for programs for infants and young children with special needs and their families. In *DEC recommended practices: Indicators of quality programs for infants and young children with special needs and their families* (pp. 1–10). Pittsburgh, PA: Division for Early Childhood/Council for Exceptional Children.

Odom, S.L., & Strain, P.S. (1984). Classroom-based social skills instruction for severely handicapped preschool children. *Topics in Early Childhood Special Education, 4*(3), 97–116.

O'Neill, R.E., Horner, R.H., Albin, R.W., Storey, K., & Sprague, J.R. (1990). *Functional analysis of problem behavior: A practical assessment guide.* Sycamore, IL: Sycamore.

Osborne, S.C., Kniest, B.A., Garland, C.W., Moore, D.D., & Usry, D.O. (1993). *Special care curriculum and trainer's manual: A resource for training child caregivers.* Lightfoot, VA: Child Development Resources.

Peck, C.A., Furman, G.C., & Helmstetter, E. (1993). Integrated early childhood programs: Research on the implementation of change in organizational contexts. In C.A. Peck, S.L. Odom, & D.D. Bricker (Eds.), *Integrating young children with disabilities into community programs: Ecological perspectives on research and implementation* (pp. 187–206). Baltimore: Paul H. Brookes.

Peck, C.A., Richarz, S.A., Peterson, K., Hayden, L., Minear, L., & Wandschneider, M. (1989). An ecological process model for implementing the LRE mandate. In R. Gaylord-Ross (Ed.), *Intervention strategies for persons with handicaps* (pp. 281–297). Baltimore: Paul H. Brookes.

Peterson, N.L. (1987). *Early intervention for handicapped and at-risk children.* Denver: Love.

Putnam, J. (1993). *Cooperative learning and strategies for inclusion: Celebrating diversity in classrooms.* Baltimore: Paul H. Brookes.

Radnovich, S., & Houck, C. (1990). An integrated preschool: Developing a program for children with developmental handicaps. *Teaching Exceptional Children, 22*(4), 22–26.

Rainforth, B., York, J., & Macdonald, C. (1992). *Collaborative teams for students with severe disabilities: Integrating therapy and educational services.* Baltimore: Paul H. Brookes.

Richarz, S. (1993). Innovations in early childhood education: Models that support the integration of children of varied developmental levels. In C.A. Peck, S.L. Odom, & D.D. Bricker (Eds.), *Integrating young children with disabilities into community programs: Ecological perspectives on research and implementation* (pp. 83–108). Baltimore: Paul H. Brookes.

Rogers-Warren, A.K., & Wedel, J.W. (1980). The ecology of play materials on social play. *New Directions for Exceptional Children, 1,* 1–24.

Smith, B.J., & Rose, D.F. (1991). *Identifying policy options for preschool mainstreaming. Policy and practices in early childhood special education series.* Pittsburgh, PA: Research Institute on Preschool Mainstreaming, Allegheny-Singer Research Institute.

Smith, B.J., & Rose, D.F. (1993). *Administrator's policy handbook for preschool mainstreaming.* Cambridge, MA: Brookline.

Strain, P.S. (1985). Programmatic research on peer-mediated interventions. In B.H. Schneider, K.H. Rubin, & J.E. Ledingham (Eds.), *Children's peer relations: Issues in assessment and intervention* (pp. 193–206). New York: Springer-Verlag.

Strain, P.S. (1990). LRE for preschool children with handicaps: What we know and what we should be doing. *Journal for Early Intervention, 14,* 291–296.

Strain, P.S., & Odom, S.L. (1986). Peer social initiations: Effective intervention for social skills development of exceptional children. *Exceptional Children, 52,* 543–551.

Strain, P.S., & Smith, B.J. (1993). Comprehensive educational, social, and policy forces that affect preschool integration. In C.A. Peck, S.L. Odom, & D.D. Bricker (Eds.), *Integrating young children with disabilities into community programs: Ecological perspectives on research and implementation* (pp. 209–222). Baltimore: Paul H. Brookes.

Thousand, J.S., & Villa, R.A. (1992). Collaborative teams: A powerful tool in school restructuring. In R.A. Villa, J.S. Thousand, W. Stainback, & S. Stainback (Eds.), *Restructuring for caring and effective education: An administrative guide to creating heterogeneous schools* (pp. 73–108). Baltimore: Paul H. Brookes.

Thurman, S.K., & Widerstrom, A.H. (1990). *Infants and young children with special needs: A developmental and ecological approach* (2nd ed.). Baltimore: Paul H. Brookes.

Vergeront, J. (1987). *Places and spaces for preschool and primary (indoors).* Washington, DC: National Association for the Education of Young Children.

Vincent, L.J., & Beckett, J.A. (1993). Family participation. In *DEC recommended practices: Indicators of quality programs for infants and young children with special needs and their families* (pp. 19–25). Pittsburgh, PA: Division for Early Childhood/Council for Exceptional Children.

Voorhees, M., Aveno, A., & Landon, T. (1993). Planning for inclusive preschool programming. In A. Aveno (Ed.), *Inclusive preschool programs: A guide for making them work.* Charlottesville, VA: University of Virginia, Department of Curriculum Instruction and Special Education.

Voorhees, M.D., Landon, T.L., & Harvey, J. (1995). *Integrated placement options for preschoolers: A planning guide.* Richmond, VA: Virginia Department of Education.

Wessel, M. (1989). *Policy clarification letter.* Washington, DC: U.S. Department of Education, Office of Special Education Programs.

Wolery, M., & Fleming, L.A. (1993). Implementing individualized curriculum in integrated settings. In C.A. Peck, S.L. Odom, & D.D. Bricker (Eds.), *Integrating young children with disabilities into community programs: Ecological perspectives on research and implementation* (pp. 109–132). Baltimore: Paul H. Brookes.

Wolery, M., & Sainato, D. (1993). General curriculum and intervention strategies. In *DEC recommended practices: Indicators of quality in programs for infants and young children with special needs and their families* (pp. 50–57). Pittsburgh, PA: Division for Early Childhood/Council for Exceptional Children.

CHAPTER 10

Strategies for Including Students in Elementary School Programs

Johnna R. Elliott

INTRODUCTION

The public elementary school is a rich and complex place filled with the energy of many minds coming together to create and to learn. It is the place where children embark on a challenging series of experiences. During the six years most students spend there, they learn to read, write, and calculate numbers. They learn about the Earth and the people who live here. Children paint and dance, sing and play, talk and listen, and learn how to learn. From the first day they enter school, children begin to learn something else of great significance. They learn to develop relationships with people outside of their immediate family. Their world expands as they start to figure out how they fit into this large and complicated social milieu.

Most children come to elementary school with mental and physical attributes that allow them to be academically successful and socially competent. Other children face certain challenges, or disabilities, that require educators to make adjustments in instruction. Public schools are becoming increasingly interested in learning ways to make these adjustments so that all children can be educated together (Ford et al., 1989; Stainback, Stainback, & Moravec, 1992).

From 1991 to 1993, this author was afforded the opportunity to work as an *inclusion specialist* in three elementary schools in a rural area of southwest Virginia. These schools were committed to retrieving children with moderate and severe disabilities from segregated, centralized, self-contained programs and bringing them home to their community schools to be educated among their peers and neighbors. The job entailed determining what these students needed and then working with school staff to meet those needs within the context of the general education classroom. Other students with learning and emotional difficulties were returned to the general classroom as well. Special education staff worked alongside classroom teachers to provide assistance and support. Together, all staff members became committed to serving children in this way. Many of the strategies and examples included in this chapter are drawn from this experience.

This chapter is intended as a practical road map to guide teachers and administrators over a bumpy road filled with potholes and surprises. It is not intended as a blueprint for restructuring elementary schools. Rather, the chapter describes procedures for determining what skills a student in an inclusive setting might need to learn and provides an array of strategies teachers might use to accommodate and instruct these learners. Three things must be present for these strategies to be successful. First, school staff must listen closely to parents and communicate with them openly and often. Second, school administrators must understand the special education process and assume a position of leadership as changes are made and problems arise. Third, teamwork is a critical factor. Effective inclusive practices happen only when school staff support one another through the easy times and the rough spots.

THE STUDENTS SERVED IN ELEMENTARY SCHOOL PROGRAMS

All children have special needs. Overall, about 10% of children in public schools are given special education labels because their learning styles fall outside of the norm. The

I would like to thank the students, families, and staff of Elliston-Lafayette Elementary School, Shawsville Elementary School, and Riner Elementary School in Montgomery County, Virginia, for their support, patience, and assistance. I would also like to thank Chris Burton and Cyndi Pitonyak for their friendship and inspiration in my work and in my life.

label requires that educators spend extra time planning for and documenting progress. As we offer all students the opportunity to receive special education services within the context of general education classes, we open the door to some who have unique learning styles and needs. No one person can be the expert on every type of learning style; there will always be a place for specialists in the classroom. For inclusive practices to be successful, however, all teachers must be willing to give every student a chance. Inclusion means that students with conditions such as autism, mental retardation, or physical disabilities may be members of a general education classroom. The attitudes with which these students are received by their special and general education teachers often determine the success or failure of the placement.

CASE STUDIES

Throughout the chapter, many suggestions are offered for adapting elementary school curricula and materials. To help clarify these suggestions, examples are provided based on the educational experiences of three students. These particular students were selected because their learning needs are complex. Their composite experience covers a period of kindergarten through fifth grade, affording the opportunity to examine content from each grade level.

Carl

Carl came to kindergarten at age six, after spending two years in an early childhood program for students with multiple disabilities. Carl had cerebral palsy, a winning smile, and a strong will. He was able to stand for short periods of time, use a palmar grasp (i.e., functional use of digits was emerging), and say parts of a few words. He could also use sign language to communicate "drink" and "more." Severe allergies made Carl uncomfortable most of the time; he usually had itchy arms and a runny nose. This discomfort, coupled with his difficulty communicating his needs, led to frequent, severe behavioral outbursts (e.g., tantrums and crying). Carl enjoyed interacting with his classmates but was often aggressive toward them. He pulled hair, pinched, and scratched to initiate and terminate interactions with others and to escape from task demands. Carl was able to sit on the toilet for a short time, but rarely used it for its intended purpose. He was also resistant to eating, which led to nutritional concerns.

Joni

Joni entered second grade at her home school after attending a segregated class for students with moderate mental retardation located in a town 30 minutes away. She was a sweet-natured, shy eight-year-old with Down syn-

drome. Joni was able to perform many self-help skills independently. She could read and write her name and could scribble on paper. She was able to follow two-step directions but often chose not to do so. She learned her way around the building easily and particularly enjoyed the playground and cafeteria. She had difficulty with transitions from one activity to another; once she began an activity, she often did not want to stop. At first, she was resistant to participating in many activities and following school and classroom rules.

Chelsea

Chelsea arrived at fourth grade in her home school after spending much of her school career in a self-contained class for students with mental retardation 25 miles away in another town. She was a funny, lively young lady who was quite social and made friends quickly. Due to cerebral palsy, her speech was often unintelligible, her vision was impaired, and her fine and gross motor skills were not fully developed. She needed assistance with personal management skills and in navigating the building and school grounds. She scribbled with writing tools and could use silverware in a cumbersome way. She could not draw, write, or cut. At first, staff assumed Chelsea had mental retardation. Soon, it was discovered that she could make fairly sophisticated, near grade-level responses if given enlarged, written options to choose from. She was able to use a letter board to spell out responses if a helper sat with her and steadied her arm. By the end of fifth grade, she was performing many academic skills on grade level, with adaptations. Chelsea received occupational, physical, and speech therapy.

Other Examples

Throughout the chapter, additional examples are provided as they relate to students with other types of disabilities. These examples are intended to spark ideas about ways to work with the curriculum. It is important to realize that no single strategy is always appropriate for a certain type of student. Instruction must always be individualized to meet the needs of the particular student, regardless of the student's educational label.

STAFFING FOR SUCCESS

Effective inclusive instruction can be provided only when programs are properly staffed. As students with disabilities are scheduled into general education classes, care must be taken to ensure that they have the support they need to be successful. Much of this support will come from specialists (teachers and therapists who specialize in a particular area such as learning disabilities, mental retardation, speech-language pathology, emotional and behavioral support, or reading) or aides (personnel hired to provide services under the direction of a specialist). The amount of time a student requires from a specialist will probably not change with inclusive services. For example, a student with a mild learning disability may require "resource-level" services. That student may require one hour of individualized reading instruction daily, which means that a specialist must be available for one hour each day during a time when reading instruction is occurring. A student with more significant learning challenges may require "self-contained level" services (i.e., assistance for more than 50% of the day). This could mean that the student requires instruction from a specialist during language arts and math activities and support from an aide during science and social studies activities. Such an arrangement would require a much larger time commitment from the specialist each day. Supporting students in this way generally requires scheduling students with similar service needs into the same classroom so that the specialist can assist several students at the same time.

Efficient use of staff will vary, depending on the size of the school. Larger schools (e.g., with six or more classes at each grade level) may need to cluster students with disabilities into three of those classes at each grade level. In these cases, a special education teacher should be assigned to provide instruction for each grade level. Smaller schools may be able to staff several grades with one specialist. Instructional aides can provide a significant amount of support but must consult with the specialist regularly. It is generally best to avoid assigning an aide to a particular student. If a student requires ongoing assistance, the aide should usually be assigned to that child's classroom and encouraged to work with all students as much as possible. Occasionally, a one-to-one aide may be necessary for a student with particularly challenging behaviors. Although this may appear costly at first, it is generally a reasonable arrangement because it allows the child to remain in his or her community, attend regular classes when possible, and receive intensive instruction. In addition, it is usually much less costly than sending the child away from home to an alternative program.

Some students with moderate or severe disabilities require assistance from a specialist throughout the day. If these students are attending their home schools with their same-age peers, they will naturally be spread out among schools and grade levels. These students can generally be served effectively by a specialist who works as a consultant to the general education teacher along with a classroom aide. This *consulting teacher*, or *inclusion specialist*, acts as the case manager for these students. He or she manages the individualized educational program (IEP), works with the family, provides specific instructions concerning appropriate instructional techniques, coordinates related services,

works with outside agencies, provides some direct service, trains the aide, and adapts materials.

PROCESSES FOR IDENTIFYING APPROPRIATE INSTRUCTIONAL OBJECTIVES

Once students with disabilities have access to general education settings, it is critical to make the most of their instructional time. It is important to select goals and objectives that make sense within the context of the general education classroom. For students with mild disabilities, this is relatively simple. Many standardized and criterion-referenced assessments that lead to appropriate instructional programs are available commercially. For students with more severe disabilities, teachers must rely less on these instruments and more on a combination of processes. These processes include analysis of a student's abilities, preferences, and limitations; family issues and concerns; and the context in which the student participates.

An Ecological Approach to Curriculum Development

Examining the environments with which a person interacts and identifying skills all people need in order to be independent in those environments is called an ecological approach to curriculum development (Nietupski & Hamre-Nietupski, 1987). This approach has long been recognized as the most effective method of designing functional curricula that focus on teaching meaningful life skills to students with significant disabilities within natural environments (Brown et al., 1979). Ford et al. (1989) and Giangreco, Cloninger, and Iverson (1993) have designed curriculum guides that bring this process to the school setting to assist teachers in designing functional programs based on age-appropriate normalized school environments. However, meaningful goals and objectives for students with moderate or severe disabilities may change, depending upon the specific classroom and the particular activities that occur there. It is helpful to allow these students about one month to become acclimated to the class before developing or revising IEPs. Once students become familiar with daily routines, staff should analyze specific activities to determine the degree to which the student is able to participate in them. Staff should identify and teach skills that will allow the student to increase participation in general class activities.

This process worked well for Joni, essentially a nonreader, who began second grade by sitting in the back of the group during reading instruction and attending to the teacher about 20% of the time. The teacher selected stories from basal texts or novels that Joni did not fully understand. However, after careful observation and planning by the consulting teacher, Joni achieved numerous academic and social benefits from participating in the lesson. The following IEP objectives were developed for Joni and implemented by the general education teacher or aide during reading instruction:

1. During reading group activities, Joni will learn to sight-read two functional vocabulary words per week. (These were added to the larger vocabulary list. Joni practiced them with the aide prior to large-group instruction.)
2. Joni will increase the amount of time she is able to participate in large-group listening activities from 3 minutes to 20 minutes. (The teacher gave Joni a variety of little jobs throughout the lesson that helped her maintain her interest and feel a part of the group.)
3. During writing activities, Joni will write her name, the date, and assigned words or brief sentences on her worksheet. (The aide assisted Joni in completing this while the teacher monitored all students' work.)
4. Joni will read a two- to three-sentence summary of daily stories (no more than 15 words, comprised mainly of her sight words) with the assistance of a peer or aide. (This summary was prepared by the consulting teacher prior to the lesson.)

Through this process, Joni's reading skills improved rapidly during the year. It was apparent that she was highly motivated by the attention of her peers.

The IEP Process

The IEP process is the most important tool for establishing working relationships with parents of children who have disabilities. Because the majority of these children are identified as needing special education services during elementary school, it is critical that these early experiences be positive. Schools that are committed to inclusive services must be careful not to force this service delivery option on parents. As placements are discussed, committee members must be particularly willing to listen to parental concerns and address them openly. Most parents have legitimate questions about the nature of instruction and supervision in inclusive settings. They are entitled to thoughtful and thorough answers (see Chapter 7 for further discussion of parental involvement).

Activity-Based Planning

If the committee believes that the student can be served within the context of the general classroom, then skills should be referenced to the general curriculum and classroom activities. For example, consider a third grader who is able to recognize 50% of first-grade sight words. If the committee believes that learning the rest of the first-grade sight words is appropriate, then they might explain that these words will be mixed in with the general weekly spelling list, written on index cards to be reviewed for homework, and incorporated into daily writing assignments that are directed and monitored by the special education teacher.

For children with more severe disabilities, many IEP objectives will likely focus on functional skills targeted through the ecological assessment. Traditionally, an ecological assessment targets skills across four areas: domestic (or personal management), leisure, vocational, and community. The most important functional skills for elementary-aged students are generally in the area of personal management. Toileting, grooming, mealtime skills, and dressing are often areas where these students require direct instruction. When describing this instruction to the parents, it is important to emphasize how it fits into the natural class routine, while maintaining the student's personal dignity. Consider the case of Carl. His personal management abilities were quite limited. During the IEP process, the following objectives were developed:

1. Carl will wash his hands independently using soap, water, and a paper towel after snack and lunch, five consecutive days.
2. Carl will brush his teeth with some assistance after lunch, in a private area, daily, according to a task analysis, five consecutive days.
3. Carl will sit on a toilet in a private area three times per day according to a schedule and urinate in the toilet one time daily, four of five consecutive days.
4. Carl will consistently feed himself finger foods during snacks and lunch, five consecutive days.
5. Carl will use his walker within the classroom and building (including transition in and out of walker) with supervision.
6. Carl will zip and unzip his backpack and his jacket (with adapted pulls) independently, four of five days.

Note that all of the skills specify when and where they will be taught within the normal routine of the day. Two of these skills, toileting and brushing teeth, were judged to necessitate privacy. The kindergarten class had its own bathroom. However, because toileting and toothbrushing sessions generally lasted 20 minutes and required a teacher present, the committee decided to use the more privately situated bathroom in the health clinic. It is important to note here that *inclusion* does not mean that students can never have private, individualized instruction. However, if skills can fit naturally into the general class routine, then that is typically where the instruction should occur.

Accommodations

Typically, special educators provide two types of services to students with disabilities: (1) instruction (i.e., skills students should learn to perform as directed by IEP goals and objectives) and (2) accommodations (i.e., supports and services provided for students to help them succeed).

Accommodations are appropriate when it becomes evident that a student will not be able to learn to perform a skill in the same manner as other students. They range from allowing a student to use a calculator on math problems to providing assistance in the bathroom. When students with significant disabilities were served exclusively in self-contained programs, many accommodations were typically assumed. However, when planning for inclusive services, it is important to articulate them on the IEP so that the entire team is aware that they are necessary and must be provided.

Consider the accommodations developed by the IEP committee to support Carl during his kindergarten day. Notice how they differ from instructional objectives in that they are things done for Carl rather than things Carl must learn to do.

1. Carl will receive the physical assistance, such as hand-over-hand prompts or help in standing or walking, necessary to help him partially participate in all activity routines.
2. Carl will be provided with a variety of choices of activities during appropriate classroom activity routines using pictures of activities and people.
3. Peer interactions will be monitored in all settings. Peers will be advised as to Carl's abilities and difficulties. Strategies for interactions will be specifically taught to all students in both informal and formal situations.
4. All seating will be modified as necessary so that Carl is stabilized and positioned in a manner similar to his peers.
5. If Carl becomes upset, he will be given the opportunity to take a break from the activity until he is judged to be ready to return. Breaks might include walks in the building or outside, or being held.
6. Carl's behavior will be monitored. If difficulties arise, his team will adjust his positive behavioral support plan according to ongoing analyses of the functions of his behavior (see Chapter 15).
7. Carl will be closely monitored in all situations to prevent him from physically harming others or himself (see companion objective below).
8. Cold wet compresses will be applied to Carl's allergic skin reactions.
9. Carl's medications will be monitored. Behavioral changes will be reported to his mother as needed.
10. A privacy area for diapering and toilet training will be provided.
11. Carl's team will meet weekly to discuss progress and needs.

It may be very appropriate to include instructional objectives that target the same areas. For example, in accommodation 7, while it is important to prevent Carl from scratching a classmate, it is also necessary that he be taught appropriate interaction skills. Therefore, the following objective was included elsewhere on the IEP:

> Carl will use his hands in appropriate ways when interacting with peers using prevention and redirection strategies as demonstrated by the special education teacher.

Although the consulting teacher led the educational team in planning for Carl, most accommodations were provided by an aide. This team found it helpful to have several aides trained to work with Carl, which is a valuable practice that permits great flexibility for school teams.

During her fifth-grade year, Chelsea was able to participate in all academic activities as long as certain accommodations were made. The specialist helped Chelsea's teachers learn to make these adaptations. The adaptations were articulated on the IEP as follows:

1. Chelsea will participate in all academic activities by using her letter-number board, computer, and/or adapted written materials, with the assistance of a facilitator to support her upper arm as she spells and points.
2. Print materials will be enlarged so that letters are at least one-quarter of an inch high and modified so that a limited amount of material appears on any one page. Items will be double spaced. Answer choices will be provided beneath each item. As much as possible, worksheets will resemble those of the other students.
3. Long or complex assignments, tests, and study guides will be shortened and/or simplified to reflect the main idea of the material.
4. Assignments will be read to Chelsea by a teacher, aide, or fluent peer. At least 25% of the time, the reader will assist Chelsea in pointing to text as it is read.
5. Chelsea will have access to her letter-number board at all times and in all settings.
6. Peer interactions will be monitored in all settings. If Chelsea's participation in any setting, academic or social, is limited due to ineffective peer interactions, formal and/or informal peer-training strategies will be employed to enhance peer relationships.
7. Chelsea will have a daily peer buddy to assist her with reading and completing appropriate assignments, and to help with other duties, as determined by peer-planning activities.
8. During small-group activities, Chelsea will have a specific role as determined by herself, her peers, or

staff. Staff will monitor the group to ensure that she makes a meaningful contribution to the group.

9. If Chelsea is unable to complete an assignment due to fatigue or other reasons, she will be allowed to take a short break.

10. During cutting activities, Chelsea will use loop scissors with hand-over-hand assistance from an adult.

Peer Planning

When students with obvious disabilities enter the general education classroom for the first time, children and staff are naturally curious. Who is this person? Why does he look or act so differently? What can I expect from her? Can he play with us? Can she learn?

When one's experiences with people who have disabilities have been limited, these are reasonable questions that warrant thoughtful, respectful attention. Forest and Lusthaus (1989) have developed two strategies to help educators provide meaningful information about individuals with disabilities. These two strategies, Circles of Friends and the McGill Action Planning System, can be used to help peers understand the abilities and needs of a new student (see Chapter 7 for a discussion of these strategies). They are also helpful in determining more effective ways of supporting students. Each of these strategies requires that one or more class lessons be taught by the person who knows the student best. If the IEP committee believes that peer planning could be helpful for a student, then it should be included on the IEP as an accommodation. If possible, the student's permission should be obtained prior to the class lesson, and the student should be given the chance to participate.

Determining Placement

Placement decisions are always made by the IEP committee. A fundamental hallmark of inclusion is that special education is a service, not a person or place. At the IEP meeting, the team must look at individual services the student needs and consider where they can be most appropriately provided. In keeping with the directive of least restrictive environment, the fundamental questions are: (1) Can this service be provided in a general education setting? and (2) What type of assistance will the student need in order to participate in each activity? The answers to these questions should reflect student needs, not availability of staff. A school system committed to providing inclusive services will work to staff programs once placement determinations are made. It is important to review placement options with parents. If the committee is leaning toward a general education placement with supports and services, it is important to explain exactly what this would look like and how adjustments can be made within that setting.

Program-at-a-Glance

Once the IEP is developed, the committee must be certain that all people who will work with the student are aware of the program. Information contained in the plan may have relevance in art, music, physical education, the media center, and the cafeteria. Therefore, the case manager should provide these specialists with an overview of the student's program. An excellent way to do this is to summarize the IEP in a one page Program-at-a-Glance (Giangreco et al., 1993). This document should highlight instructional objectives, accommodations, relevant social and behavioral issues or plans, and any special information such as medications, adaptive equipment, and medical concerns. In reviewing the program with pertinent staff, the case manager should remind them of the confidential nature of the information.

INSTRUCTION IN THE GENERAL EDUCATION SETTING

Elementary school classrooms are set up in a variety of ways. Special education teachers must be aware of the nuances of different instructional models when designing inclusive programs for students with disabilities. Some models easily lend themselves to multilevel instruction, while others pose more challenges. However, it is possible to provide inclusive instruction regardless of the educational model when staff are flexible.

Graded, Grouped by Age

Carl's kindergarten class was an example of a graded, grouped by age program, in which students move through one grade each year and are grouped so that all students are approximately the same age. Because age is the main criterion for membership, students have a wide range of abilities. In Carl's class, his teacher designed instruction so that all students could work through activities at their own levels. As a result, students achieved different goals within the context of the same activity. A typical math lesson focused on sorting a variety of small objects into groups, based on one or more given characteristics. While some students quickly completed the task according to several given characteristics, others completed only one set. Carl's objective was to pick up individual objects with his fingers and place them in a can. The teacher's flexible criterion for success for all students made it easy to individualize for a student at this most basic level.

Graded, Grouped by Ability

Many schools tend to "level" students, which means to place students with similar ability levels together in a class for all or part of the day. This type of tracking can pose challenges for inclusive education. The tendency may be to place children with disabilities in lower-level classes, closest to their perceived ability. This may be appropriate for some students who require intensive assistance in order to complete assignments. However, students with moderate and severe disabilities generally require an adapted curriculum. A higher-level curriculum is often as easy to adapt as a lower-level one. Often, in placement decisions, teacher acceptance and flexibility are more important than the level of the class.

Nongraded, Multiaged Groups

Some primary school programs are nongraded. Students enter school and remain with a group of students until their teachers believe they are socially and academically ready to move to a graded class. Children in these programs tend to group themselves according to individual interests and skills. Children with disabilities fit nicely into these settings, because age and ability vary widely. Individual differences are the norm, rather than the exception.

Collaboration

When students with disabilities receive instruction in the regular classroom, specialists and general educators must become partners. The nature of this partnership is unique in every instructional setting, depending on the needs of the students and the work styles of the staff. (Chapter 3 provides an overview of staff roles and responsibilities in inclusive settings.) In addition, it is important for all members of the team to possess certain characteristics. Each team member must be flexible and willing to try new things with the support of the team in spite of the initial discomfort that may accompany the effort. For example, Carl's speech-language pathologist became discouraged with his progress during isolated direct instruction in articulation and functional sign language; Carl was unhappy and uncooperative with her lessons. She discovered that this instruction was much more effective when she used peer tutors and provided instruction within the context of free-play activities. The speech-language pathologist was initially uncomfortable with this change from a clinical setting; however, with support from the team, she soon realized it was more effective. The kindergarten teacher was flexible and scheduled free play according to the speech-language pathologist's schedule. Both teachers changed their typical ways of operating to accommodate Carl. The result was a remarkable improvement in Carl's language skills.

Another characteristic important for successful collaboration is open communication. Team members must feel they can share information and concerns in an open and honest way. In turn, each member must feel that his or her concerns are heard and valued by the team. Scheduling a common planning time where all team members come together periodically is one good way to provide a forum for communication. Another technique is for specialists to put programs in writing and to share them with all team members.

Individualizing Instruction in the General Education Classroom

Once the team decides to provide special education services in the general education classroom, staff must decide how to provide those services most effectively. There are a variety of ways to organize instruction, depending on student needs.

One-to-One Instruction

One-to-one instruction might be the best choice for teaching skills that other students do not need to learn. For example, Joni benefitted from one-to-one instruction when she began an intensive reading program and when she received math instruction on the computer.

One-to-one instruction can be provided in a private part of the room or at the student's table or desk. Care must be taken not to distract other students who are involved in a different lesson. If the room is crowded, noisy, or too distracting, one-to-one instruction may be most effective in another place such as the media center, conference room, or a resource area.

Parallel Instruction

Parallel instruction is sometimes used when special and general education teachers are coteaching. They may divide the class into several groups to work on a subject in different ways. Chelsea's teachers realized that some students were able to complete reading assignments at home; they came to class prepared to discuss the selections. Other students were not good independent readers able to complete assignments at home; they needed oral reading instruction at school. Because Chelsea was not able to attend to small print well enough to be an independent reader, she joined the oral reading group and listened to the novels as they were read aloud.

Another way that parallel instruction is used is when one teacher works with a small group on a specific skill area while the other teacher conducts large-group instruction. For example, a teacher might present the procedures for multiplying two-place numbers, then assign and monitor a follow-up practice activity. The other teacher might pull a small group aside to practice multiplication tables, a lead-up skill to two-place multiplication.

Integrated Instruction

Integrated instruction is used when the goal is to teach one skill within the context of another. It is a highly effective strategy for helping students feel that they are part of the class. In addition, participation in the ongoing activity is often highly motivating for students because they are reinforced by their peers. Integrated instruction often requires that materials be adapted for the student. Joni increased her vocabulary through integrated instruction that was provided during language arts and content instruction. While other students were reading text, Joni was learning to identify pictures in the books. She began by pointing to items in pictures and later learned to say the names of many of those items. During math lessons, Joni focused on identifying digits while others were learning calculations. During writing assignments, she learned to copy her name, the date, and a few sight words onto her paper. In each case, she was able to use the same materials as her classmates, but toward a different goal.

Alternative Individualized Schedules

In some cases, a student may be unable to follow the typical general education schedule. Children who are extremely active or who have severe behavioral difficulties may fall into this category. They may be able to be members of a class, but may require alternative individualized schedules for part of their day. Alternatives such as built-in, noncontingent breaks, several short lessons rather than one long lesson, access to a private place to calm down, the option of taking a walk, time at the computer, or a shortened day are all examples of schedule alternatives that may enable a child to be a part of the general classroom for the rest of the day.

Additional Staff Support for Individualized Instruction

All of these strategies require staff in addition to the general classroom teacher. Although special education teachers and aides will likely provide most of the extra support, other specialists may pitch in to provide assistance as well. Specialists from programs such as reading, gifted education, and English as a Second Language, who traditionally pull students out for services, might consider ways to integrate their content into the classroom. Therapists, volunteers, peer tutors, and specialty teachers in the building may also be sources of additional support.

ADAPTING THE ELEMENTARY SCHOOL CURRICULUM

A major key to successful inclusion of all students in general education settings is effective adaptation of the curriculum. To adapt the curriculum is to change it in a way that makes it meaningful and relevant to a particular student. Adaptations are limited only by the imagination and the amount of time teachers have to bring to the task. In the section that follows, components of the typical elementary school curriculum are described. Each component is followed by a brief discussion of ways the content can be adapted, and ideas for teaching according to the modifications. This section in no way represents the only way to adapt materials. It is meant to spark ideas across the curriculum from kindergarten through fifth grade. (Further information on adapting curriculum is found in Chapter 6. Chapter 18 further addresses adaptations for students with reading disorders.)

Language Arts

The core of the elementary school curriculum is language arts instruction. Reading and writing skills are usually taught for at least two hours each day at every grade level. Most schools teach these skills through a highly structured basal text series, a whole-language approach, or a combination. Although whole-language allows for easier individualization, either approach can be adapted for students with disabilities.

Basal reading programs are carefully developed according to student reading level. They tend to include specific vocabulary, a reading passage, questions for discussion, and follow-up worksheets or activities that focus on language skills such as vocabulary development, grammar, punctuation, and phonics. Classes may spend two to three days on each lesson. Basal reading lessons can be adapted in a variety of ways, depending on a student's reading ability. The teacher might add a few sight words to the vocabulary list to assist beginning readers. The reading passage can be rewritten at the student's level, and worksheets can be modified so that the student has repeated practice with sight words and vocabulary at his or her level. The student might enjoy reading the modified story aloud or reading it to parents as homework. A nonreader may listen as the story is read orally, hold vocabulary cards up as classmates read them, answer simple questions such as character names, draw or cut and paste pictures to illustrate parts of the story, or bring and share related resources from the library for enrichment.

A whole-language approach to language arts instruction differs significantly from basal readers. Froese (1991) defines whole language as a "child-centered literature-based approach to language teaching that immerses students in real communication situations whenever possible" (p. vii). Students read novels, dictate stories, write letters and poems, act out parts of novels, and engage in a variety of related projects and activities. Language skill lessons are embedded into activities as teachers notice skill deficits. Activities tend to be less competitive, as students progress at their own levels. Activities based on this approach are easily modified for students at any level.

As students move through the grades, novels become more complex. Some students might have difficulty following complex stories. Chelsea used a story-frame strategy to participate in these reading activities. As the class read the novel aloud, she made a booklet to accompany the text. At the end of each chapter, she identified the main characters, the setting, and one action that occurred. This was recorded on a page in her booklet. Chelsea illustrated the action by copying, gluing, or drawing a picture on the page. By the end of the novel, her booklet contained one page for each chapter. She had a record of the novel to share with the class and her family. A more elaborate version of this story-frame strategy can be used for students with learning disabilities who need a concrete method for a chapter-by-chapter review of the characters, action, and other aspects of novels.

Creative writing is a hallmark of whole-language instruction and is emphasized as early as kindergarten. Individually, students are encouraged to write letters, keep journals, and write their responses to literature. Students work at their own levels and are evaluated on individual progress. Most students with disabilities can work easily within this model. The specialist can evaluate each piece of writing and work individually with the student to increase his or her skills. Students who are not able to write independently will require accommodation. A student who is able to talk might dictate to a scribe (e.g., a teacher, aide, or peer) who transcribes the student's words. Students who are unable to talk may use gestures, signs, or pictures to communicate to a scribe. Carl had a photograph album of important people and places in his life. During writing activities, he pointed to a picture. His scribe recorded the name of the picture, then asked Carl a series of "yes" or "no" questions to add detail. Carl practiced his functional sign language while participating in the activity. He used rubber block stamps to record his name on each of his writing assignments.

Students who are unable to write using pencils or pens may complete their writing assignments on a computer. Increasingly, elementary schools rely on computer-based programs for significant portions of writing instruction. These programs typically consist of a variety of activities designed to teach keyboard configuration as well as creative writing. Standard hardware and software can often be modified to allow students with a range of abilities to participate in computer-based writing instruction. Software that reads aloud words and sentences as they are composed is becoming increasingly popular as computers with speech output are becoming more affordable. Carl enjoyed working on the computers after word-processing software was installed that enlarged letters on the screen. Some software contains graphics that can be added to text to increase interest and stimulate writing ideas. Screens can also be enhanced by specialized overlays that magnify the text.

Handwriting

Elementary school students spend a fair amount of time learning to write legibly. As is evident by most adult handwriting, this is not an easy skill to acquire and maintain. Students who have difficulty learning to write may benefit from a few simple accommodations easily provided during large-group instruction. Darkening lines with a marker or using paper with a raised bottom line can help students with poor vision or perceptual problems stay on the line. Art supply or teacher stores carry a variety of templates that can be used to help students practice forming letters correctly. A piece of tape anchoring the paper to the table is often a helpful accommodation. While many students have difficulty learning to write in cursive, others find it easier than printing. If a student is struggling with one style of writing, it should be decided whether it is necessary for the student to learn both methods. It may be helpful to consult with an occupational therapist to evaluate the need for adaptive equipment or alternative positioning.

As a result of physical limitations, some students will never put pencil to paper to produce written language. If the student is cognitively capable of interpreting print, this handwriting instruction time might be used for parallel instruction on keyboarding. Students with poor vision may appreciate enlarged letter stickers on the keys. Students who are unable to use standard keyboards can benefit from the variety of expanded and alternative keyboards currently on the market. Students with the most severe disabilities may not be able to produce or understand written language. Alternative activities such as using a name stamp to label work, pasting pictures to paper, or practicing with an augmentative communication system might be appropriate during these lessons. This may also be a good time to take students aside for personal care needs or other activities that require individual attention.

Spelling

Many students with learning disabilities have enormous difficulty learning to spell. Rote memorization activities often fail to meet their needs. Beginning around second grade, some students may benefit from structured, small-group practice on words they have misspelled during weekly writing assignments. Pairing students to quiz one another, designing procedures where students fill in missing letters to complete words, and providing specialized homework activities will help students improve spelling skills. If a "spelling group" is formed, an open-door policy that allows any student in the class to participate will help prevent any stigma that may be attached to segregated instruction. This group might be taught by specialists from Title I (formerly Chapter I), special education, or English as a Second Language programs. Allowing these students to use spelling dictionaries and spell checkers is another reasonable accommodation as they move up through the grades.

Some students may never become competent spellers. In fact, spelling may never be an appropriate instructional objective for them. Instead, appropriate related goals for these students will probably range from understanding the functional meanings of words they hear frequently to sight-reading a limited vocabulary. However, these students will likely have other skill needs that can be addressed within the context of spelling instruction. These might include speech and language goals, fine motor skills, and behavioral and participation objectives. Following are samples of some ways these skills have been integrated into spelling activities for students of varying ability levels across the elementary grades:

- Prespelling activities
  - Put word cards on a special wall as needed.
  - Hold up word cards as peers spell them during drills.
  - Imitate letter sounds as students practice phonics.
  - Point to letters on a letter board as an assistant or peer transcribes the message.
  - Practice writing name and date on a prewritten list of spelling words.

- Choosing words
  - Provide an alternative list of functional words; print these words on the board beside the general list; have the student copy and practice saying or reading them; discuss their meaning.
  - Target a few of the general words and highlight them; lightly dot them onto the writing paper if necessary; direct the student to practice tracing, copying, and/or reading them.

- Learning the words
  - Modify word searches so that words are in left-right pattern and are easy to find.
  - Match pictures to words (using either the same list or an adapted list).
  - Use letter stamps to print one or more words on the paper.
  - Identify the initial letter in each word.
  - Say the word as someone else pronounces and writes it.
  - Select or circle a word from a choice of two when it is named.
  - Point to the words on the board as the teacher calls them out.

  - Type the general list or an adapted list on the computer (large print programs are available).
  - Draw or find a picture representing an adapted list of words. (Copy pictures from magazines to make a picture and word book.)

Math

Elementary school children learn functional skills involving money and time management, arithmetic computation, and reasoning skills through a variety of math curricula. In the early grades, many programs employ a hands-on, activity-based approach to teaching skills such as counting, sorting, and categorizing objects, and recognizing and creating patterns. This approach is usually accompanied by creative, artistic activities involving patterns and numbers, or use of follow-up worksheets or a textbook. Typically, as students move up through the grades, teachers increasingly use activities from a text. Enrichment exercises such as logic, reasoning, and memorization games, as well as computer programs, help students to learn these concepts.

Children who have difficulty navigating the standard math curriculum sometimes report that they see little relevance between math skills and their lives. "Why do I have to do this; I'll never use it" is a phrase almost every math teacher has heard more than once. An important task for the specialist in this situation is to design meaningful, applied activities that illustrate the relevance of the concepts in real-life situations. Another important task is to work with the existing curriculum and find ways to supplement it to meet individual needs. Following is a list of ways this instruction might be provided within the context of the general classroom. Although the specialist and general educator might choose to divide tasks in a variety of ways, most are ideas the specialist can use to supplement the curriculum.

- While the general education teacher provides whole-group instruction, the specialist monitors students' work at their seats, assisting as needed, and noting common errors to address in future lessons.
- The specialist teaches students alternative ways to calculate (e.g., use of a calculator, finger counting systems) or uses specialized curricula.
- The specialist conducts a "prelesson" session to give some students prior practice on the day's work.
- The specialist locates and conducts activities and games that will enrich lessons.
- The specialist maintains an "enrichment" center where students can practice math skills during unstructured times.
- The specialist reviews and instructs students in the use of computer software that reinforces skills.

- Following whole-group instruction by the general education teacher, the specialist provides direct follow-up instruction to selected students.
- The specialist designs and conducts "fact drills," such as addition facts and multiplication tables.
- While the general education teacher conducts the lesson, students come to the specialist to be assessed on skill proficiency.
- The specialist prepares individualized homework assignments for selected students. For example, Joni was often assigned to bring X number of items to school the next day.
- The specialist might design special class jobs involving applied math skills for individual students. For example, Chelsea collected and sorted ice cream money from students daily. She made change and delivered the items at the end of the day.

Some students with more severe disabilities may never become proficient with traditional math programs. However, they may benefit from functional math instruction. The *Syracuse Community-Referenced Curriculum Guide* (Ford et al., 1989) provides an excellent process for designing functional time and money programs. In addition, students can benefit from practicing developmental math skills within ongoing class activities. A careful analysis of typical classroom activities yields a wealth of opportunities to provide functional skill instruction within the context of the lesson. Consider the following typical developmental skills and ideas for incorporating them into general class activities:

- *Sorting and categorizing*—collecting materials at the end of a lesson and putting them into their proper bins; sorting manipulatives as others are completing more advanced skills
- *One-to-one correspondence*—passing out materials, giving out treats, filing papers
- *Rote counting*—counting the number of problems on a paper, number of students in each group, number of students buying lunch each day
- *Number recognition/identification*—using any text or worksheet for the purpose of locating and naming digits; identifying the date
- *Grasp-release*—picking up manipulatives; placing them on the table so a peer can count them
- *Coin identification*—collecting lunch money; purchasing a snack from a vending machine; acting as class "banker"
- *Telling time*—matching a picture of a clock face with the wall clock at key transitional times during the day

Science, Social Studies, and Health

Teachers generally devote a total of one to two hours per day to science, social studies, or health instruction. In elementary grades, instruction is often activity-based, making it fairly easy to accommodate a variety of learning styles. Many teachers use projects that can be completed through a variety of modalities (e.g., collages, drawings, written work, oral reports). Students who have difficulty with print may require oral reading and/or assistance in completing writing assignments. Often, a peer can provide this assistance.

Students with more significant learning problems may require an adapted curriculum in the content areas. The first step in adapting a lesson is to review the specific content and determine the main idea. For example, in a unit on the solar system, the special and general education teachers may decide that a particular student mainly needs to know how to identify the sun, moon, and Earth and to understand that we live on Earth. Once this decision is made, the specialist takes each planned activity and adapts it to focus on these few facts. The student might work with other concepts, but instruction occurs only around the main idea. A bottle of erasure fluid, a pair of scissors, tape, and a photocopy machine are the tools necessary to adapt any worksheet. Irrelevant, sometimes distracting materials can be easily eliminated. When adapting materials in this way, students appreciate it when their adapted worksheet looks similar to those of their peers.

Specialty Classes

Art, music, and physical education enrich the elementary school curriculum and offer an environment that easily accommodates students with disabilities. Students with mild disabilities can almost always function in these classes without intervention or, at most, with minimal accommodations and/or consultation from a therapist or adaptive physical educator. Students with more severe disabilities can partially participate in all or most activities with adequate consultation and planning. Partial participation means analyzing the student's abilities and the activity to determine which steps of the activity the student can complete and what level of assistance will be needed. For example, many kindergarten art activities involve cutting, gluing, and coloring. Carl's teachers realized that he was not able to do any of these things. Therefore, activities were adapted so he could tear paper instead of cut with scissors, pat down materials that were preglued, and use crayons with full physical assistance. In music and physical education, his aide and his peers provided the physical assistance needed to partially participate in all movement-based activities by holding him at the waist and guiding his hands as necessary. Consultation with an adaptive physical education teacher is helpful when planning ways that students can partially participate in physical education activities.

Specialty classes are excellent settings for physical and occupational therapists and speech-language pathologists to provide consultation or direct services to students. These specialists can provide the team with ideas about movement, positioning, adaptive equipment, and communication skills that will enhance student participation in specific class activities. For example, a student may be highly motivated to learn the sign for "more" if requesting more paint during art class, another song in music, or another turn on the swings. Students with multiple disabilities often require augmentative communication and specialized positioning or mobility equipment. They may find these classes, which often are fairly exciting, to be interesting places to practice using this equipment. For example, Carl learned to use his wheeled walker rapidly by moving around the hardtop on the playground with encouragement from his peers.

Skill Matrixing

Careful and thoughtful planning is necessary to include students with the most severe disabilities in general classes while simultaneously teaching them developmental, functional, communication, and social skills. In addition to the strategies listed above, it may be helpful to develop a skill matrix where instruction in basic skills is referenced to the daily classroom schedule. This matrix can serve as a planning tool or as a tracking system to ensure that skills are addressed daily. It can also be modified for use as a data collection instrument by coding a student's progress in the appropriate block (for example, I = independent performance; PP = physical prompt was required; V = verbal prompt was required). Exhibit 10–1 describes Carl's typical kindergarten schedule. IEP objectives are recorded across the top. A check indicates when during the day that objective can naturally be taught. Of course, many skills such as gestural and verbal communication and appropriate behavior should be taught during all activities. A partial list of Carl's objectives illustrates how many opportunities he had to practice each skill each day (see Exhibit 10–2 for a blank skill matrix form).

Exhibit 10–1 Carl's Kindergarten Schedule and Skill Matrix

IEP Objectives (Partial List)

Daily Activity Schedule	Share materials with a peer.	Play with three toys independently.	Tear and pat down preglued paper.	Sign "more," "finished," "eat," "drink," "bathroom," "yes," and "no."	Identify objects/pictures by pointing/gesturing.	Wash hands.	Sit on toilet three times a day, urinate at least once.	Hold and drink from a cup.	Stand unsupported by people (OK to hold on to table/chair).
Arrival, hang coats, seats	✓	✓		✓	✓			✓	✓
Group time, pledge, announcements, jobs				✓	✓				✓
Morning calendar/ applied math	✓			✓	✓				
Language centers (activities change daily)	✓	✓	✓	✓	✓	✓	✓		✓
Math manipulatives	✓		✓	✓	✓				✓
Lunch				✓	✓	✓		✓	
Rest/story				✓	✓			✓	
Play time or physical education	✓	✓		✓	✓				✓
Art, music, or media center	✓	✓	✓	✓	✓				✓
Snack				✓	✓	✓	✓	✓	
Go home on the bus				✓					✓

Note: Checks (✓) indicate that the skill can be taught during the corresponding activity.

Exhibit 10–2 Blank Activity and Skill Matrix Form

IEP Objectives

Daily Activity Schedule									

Data Collection Code:
Note: Checks (✓) indicate that the skill can be taught during the corresponding activity.

CONCLUSION

The strategies reviewed in this chapter should provide a reference for the practical daily task of including students with disabilities in elementary school programs. It is critical to expect that every inclusive classroom will look and feel unique. Inclusion is not so much an educational model as it is a philosophy of openness and a willingness to try things in new and different ways. The very nature of embarking on this type of creative venture means that people will likely make mistakes.

These mistakes will become the learning tools needed to strengthen and improve programs. Communities committed to inclusive schools must realize this and work to support one another through the process.

REFERENCES

Brown, L., Branston, M.B., Hamre-Nietupski, S., Pumpian, I., Certo, N., & Gruenewald, L.A. (1979). A strategy for developing chronological age appropriate and functional curricular content for severely handicapped adolescents and young adults. *Journal of Special Education, 13*, 81–90.

Ford, A., Schnorr, R., Meyer, L., Davern, L., Black, J., & Dempsey, P. (1989). *The Syracuse community-referenced curriculum guide for students with moderate and severe disabilities*. Baltimore: Paul H. Brookes.

Forest, M., & Lusthaus, E. (1989). Promoting educational equity for all students: Circles and maps. In S. Stainback, W. Stainback, & M. Forest (Eds.), *Educating all students in the mainstream of regular education* (pp. 43–55). Baltimore: Paul H. Brookes.

Froese, V. (Ed.). (1991). *Whole-language: Practice and theory.* Needham Heights, MA: Allyn and Bacon.

Giangreco, M., Cloninger, C., & Iverson, V. (1993). *COACH: Choosing options and accommodations for children: A guide to planning inclusive education.* Baltimore: Paul H. Brookes.

Nietupski, J., & Hamre-Nietupski, S. (1987). An ecological approach to curriculum development. In L. Goetz, D. Guess, & K. Stremel-Campbell (Eds.), *Innovative program design for individuals with dual sensory impairments* (pp. 225–253). Baltimore: Paul H. Brookes.

Stainback, S., Stainback, W., & Moravec, J. (1992). Using curriculum to build inclusive classrooms. In S. Stainback & W. Stainback (Eds.), *Curriculum considerations in inclusive classrooms: Facilitating learning for all students* (pp. 65–84). Baltimore: Paul H. Brookes.

CHAPTER 11

Middle School: A Naturally Inclusive Environment

Kathleen Jamison, Ramona D. Kroll, and Janet R. Shelburne

INTRODUCTION

The movement to create developmentally responsive programs in special education paralleled the restructuring of junior high schools to provide systems of support for young adolescents. Together, the two reforms create a naturally inclusive environment for young adolescents between the ages of 10 and 14. Middle school offers general and special educators the opportunity to function collaboratively as a team, centered in the belief that all children can learn and that diversity should be celebrated. Inclusion practices fit well within the middle school environment, where extremes are normal, where growth is dynamic, and where the need to be alike and find common ground is critical to self-esteem.

This chapter provides an overview of characteristics, needs, and effective teaching practices for middle school–age children with and without identified disabilities. The middle school environment—philosophy, structure, and climate—is discussed as a framework for understanding inclusion in middle school. The characteristics of young adolescents are described, followed by a presentation of a variety of strategies and techniques to support successful inclusion of students with disabilities. Personal vignettes from middle school teachers are offered to illustrate ideas and suggestions.

MIDDLE SCHOOL ENVIRONMENT: PHILOSOPHY, STRUCTURE, AND CLIMATE

William M. Alexander, fondly recognized as the father of the middle school (McEwin, 1992), emphasized the importance of developmentally responsive schools for young adolescent learners. Alexander (1971) recommended that the middle school concept focus on the period of growth between childhood and adolescence. As a spokesperson for middle-level education, he advocated for separately organized schools that meet the needs and characteristics of this population.

The educational reform known as middle school restructuring is accomplished by changing the scheduling of curriculum and organization of the junior high school. Changing the name of a junior high school does not create a middle school. Exhibit 11–1 compares the middle school model and the traditional junior high model. Middle schools are organized according to the educational and developmental needs of young adolescent learners.

Approximately 25% of schools across the country are designed as middle schools, with the most common grade span being grades six through eight (Epstein & MacIver, 1990). This grade span allows middle school educators to put more emphasis on active learning and student participation. Incorporating the team approach allows even large middle schools to keep students from feeling lost. This grade span uses interdisciplinary teaming more than any other grade combination. The precise grade-level organizational pattern of a school, however, is less critical to meeting the needs of this age group than the educational philosophy that is the structural foundation of middle school (Kohut, 1988). Exemplary middle school programs may use a variety of grouping strategies: multiage grouping, developmental grouping, heterogeneous grouping, or homogeneous grouping. Therefore, flexibility in teachers and administrators is crucial. No single arrangement is best or right for all situations.

The National Middle School Association sets forth the rationale and philosophy for middle school through the position paper, *This We Believe* (1995). This document articulates the critical components of middle school:

- knowledgeable educators, committed to young adolescents between the ages of 10 and 14

Exhibit 11–1 Comparison of Junior High Departmentalization and Middle School Teaming

Junior High Departmentalization	Middle School Teaming
5 classes shared by coincidence	2 to 4 teachers with shared student/community
Curriculum departments located on same halls	Teams located in same proximity
Schedules fixed according to bell schedule, with mass rush of all grade levels in halls simultaneously	Block scheduling—teams stagger release time around instruction time with no bells; halls are quieter with fewer students
Homogenous and tracked grouping	Heterogenous grouping
Cut system of athletics; most resources allocated for a few children	Inclusive athletics; all who want to participate may
Teachers trained in one or two subject areas	Teachers trained in child development across disciplines
Teachers departmentalized	Team teaching
Counselors mainly deal with scheduling and orientation	Counselors work with children and oversee advisory programs

- a balanced curriculum based on adolescent needs, with curricular options and individualized instruction
- a range of organizational arrangements and the flexibility to meet needs with wide range of exploratory activities for enrichment, socialization, and interest development
- varied instructional strategies based on the learner's characteristics and interest with balanced attention to personal development, skills, and effective use of appropriate knowledge
- comprehensive advising and counseling, offered by classroom teachers and guidance counselors
- continuous progress for students with ongoing assessment, feedback, and goal setting
- evaluation procedures compatible with adolescent needs, using a wide range of alternative assessments
- interdisciplinary teams with common planning periods to maximize team efficiency and collaboration
- positive school climate characterized by collaboration between teachers and administrators.

These elements of the middle school structure and philosophy work equally well for children with and without disabilities.

An inclusive middle school will evoke a positive school climate. Respectful, harmonious interaction among staff members is facilitated by a leader (the principal) who is open to change and who promotes an encouraging, yet businesslike, atmosphere that fosters success. In such an inviting environment, parents and community members are readily accepted, included, and respected. Involvement of parents in the process of education, involvement of the school in the community, and involvement of the community in the school are paramount. Young adolescents have a special need to belong and to be accepted as valued members of the community and school, laying the foundations for community pride and citizenship. In school, such support can be evi-

denced by displaying student work; organizing student jobs; giving students a voice in decision making; and creating opportunities for celebration of team, grade, or school successes. These activities provide opportunities for ownership and belonging. Developing a community of learners within the classroom and within the school sets a positive climate for learning—a climate as important as the learning itself.

Middle schools are different from elementary and high schools in their philosophy, internal and external structure, and student body. Differences among students are greater during their middle school years than at any other time in their lives. Dramatic and extensive physical, intellectual, emotional, and social changes occur unpredictably and at varied times and rates. This is magnified for students with disabilities, for whom self-esteem and social skills often remain ongoing issues.

General and special education teachers, related services personnel, and teaching assistants who choose to work with adolescent learners between the ages of 10 and 14 need to understand these students' needs, strengths, and interests and to hold high expectations for them. It takes a special level of commitment and genuine desire to teach this age group and a thorough understanding of adolescent growth and development to be successful. Successful middle schools hire diverse staff with a myriad of teaching styles, personality types, age ranges, interests, and skills to meet the needs of this broad range of learners.

MIDDLE SCHOOL TEACHING TEAMS

Middle schools are usually larger than the elementary schools that feed into them. It is important that general and special education teachers and related services personnel develop good skills in communication and collaboration. Special educators traditionally have developed expertise in targeting areas of difficulty within a curriculum, analyzing and adapting instructional materials and teaching strategies, developing individualized education programs (IEPs), and creating appropriate behavioral support systems. Most general educators have extensive knowledge about curriculum, learning stages and skill sequencing, and large-group management. Related services personnel can provide support in oral and written language, communication (speech-language pathologists), and fine and gross motor skills (occupational and physical therapy). All skills are necessary for teaming to be effective.

On inclusive teams, teachers' roles are defined by collaborative interaction. Through collaboration, educators can minimize the need for the traditional special education pull-out approach for students evidencing academic or behavioral difficulties. These students can receive needed instruction, curricular modifications, or early behavioral intervention as needs arise. General education students benefit from the additional support and enrichment activities provided with the expertise of two teachers.

Teams can be designed by grade level to ensure that all core subjects are taught within each team. Team size can vary from two to five teachers. Ideally, for sixth-grade students first entering middle school, a two-teacher team reduces teacher contact, transition time, and organizational difficulty. The two-person core team enhances flexibility, blocking of content, community building, and communication. These aspects of teaming are advantageous for all students, and especially are supportive of the student with disabilities. As students progress through middle school grades, the number of core teachers may increase, preparing students for high school. Many criteria are used in team selection for the student being included. These include the personalities of the teachers, their teaching styles, and flexibility.

Staff in Montgomery County, Virginia, Public Schools surveyed general and special educators regarding what their needs were from other teachers on the team as they began to work together. Exhibit 11–2 presents the needs that teachers

---

Exhibit 11–2 What Middle School Teachers Need To Implement Inclusion

General education teachers need special education teachers to:

- stay in class for the entire period or block unless there is an emergency
- participate in creating team rules based on middle school philosophy, then follow them
- be familiar with content being taught
- prepare for class as a team partner using best practices for young adolescents
- know teacher expectation and middle school state standards of mastery before content is taught; negotiate if different criteria are needed
- offer input into creating lessons and developing units based on current research and best practice
- teach class collaboratively
- modify or adapt curriculum based on student needs, using predetermined and communicated IEP objectives as a framework and agreed-upon ranges for spontaneous modifications
- prepare additional "packet" or learning center on student independent work level for emergencies
- offer input into grading and/or checking of work following ongoing assessment practices for middle school
- set consistent team time when special education issues can be addressed
- clarify strategies being used; evidence them as best practice for the child
- set up a team notebook that is available to the team for reference

Special education teachers need general education teachers to:

- provide state and local curricular guidelines in content area
- provide range of objective expectations for consideration when modifying content
- include special education teacher in planning of units and setting criteria
- accept the IEP as a legal document and offer input into its development
- accept accommodations and modifications as outlined in the IEP
- understand that special students need academic adaptations and modifications to access information just as students in wheelchairs need ramps to access facilities; think of the academic adjustments as the "ramps of the mind"
- offer input or suggestions for improving modifications
- use common sense to provide on-the-spot modifications to reduce frustration
- provide copies of lesson plans prior to the lesson
- set aside a team time or team day to discuss special education issues
- be tolerant of emergency situations and IEP parent needs that might pull a special educator away from class
- invite special education teacher's input into all major team decisions
- agree to disagree and still be okay with team members; the issues are legal, not personal
- accept diverse ideas and be willing to try something different when status quo isn't working
- build a community where all students belong, where middle school diversity is celebrated
- accept that individualized assessment is not "less"

Source: Reprinted with permission from *Middle School Inclusion Survey,* © 1993, Montgomery County Schools.

identified as necessary to work as a team carrying out inclusion successfully.

Many middle schools actively use instructional assistants as part of the inclusion team. The instructional assistants work with students with disabilities in many different classrooms. They often are placed on several teams and grade levels and may report to more than one special education teacher. Because the special education teacher needs to be informed of what happens in all academic classes where instructional assistants support students with disabilities, a tracking system is important. Practical, form-based record-keeping systems encourage consistency across teachers, classes, and grade levels. One way to achieve this communication is the use of a notebook that encourages the instructional assistant to record necessary information. A tracking system notebook (Jamison & Parker, 1993) developed for Montgomery County (Virginia) Public Schools is outlined in Exhibit 11–3.

Another use of a notebook is to maintain a log of necessary information in each classroom. The model student notebook (Jamison, 1991), a three-ring binder, is used in inclusive classrooms in middle school. It is developed and monitored by the special education teacher or instructional assistant. After the system is in place, volunteer students can be trained to monitor the notebook. The notebook serves as reference for missing assignments, daily classwork, homework assignments, and handouts. It is designed for student access and, therefore, confidential information is not maintained in this notebook. Exhibit 11–4 presents the outline for the model student notebook.

Before staff can creatively implement an inclusive middle school environment, training in inclusive education and in the team-building process is essential. General and special educators and related services personnel should be offered a variety of workshops and the opportunity to visit middle schools where inclusive programming is practiced. Teachers can then be responsible for training instructional assistants at their sites. Training of teachers and administrators should focus on team building, staff roles and responsibilities, collaborative planning and communicating, behavioral supports, and curriculum modifications and adaptations. It is essential to include training for instructional assistants who will be working with students individually and in small groups in an inclusive classroom. Use of a general training handbook can be of great assistance in training instructional assistants. Key elements are presented in Exhibit 11–5. (A variety of staff development activities can be found in Chapter 19.)

ACCOMMODATING ADOLESCENT DEVELOPMENT IN INCLUSIVE MIDDLE SCHOOLS

Young adolescents are, by the very nature of their rapid growth and development, a diverse student population. The adolescent's physical transformation is compounded by the

---

Exhibit 11–3 Instructional Assistant Tracking System Notebook

SECTION 1: OVERVIEW CHARTS (ADAPT BLANK MATRIX CHART TO MEET NEEDS)

Homework check sheet: matrix to reflect correct copying, completing, or turning in of assignment using student name and date assigned

Graded-items check sheet: matrix to track completion of items to be graded by student name

Accommodations: matrix of student names and IEP accommodations needed in classes

IEP goals: matrix of student names and objectives from short-term IEP objectives

Testing accommodations: matrix to reflect student names and accommodations for specific standardized testing given routinely or required by state

SECTION 2: COMMUNICATION AND OBSERVATION

Issue action: problem-solving chart divided into columns for: (1) issue or problem, (2) action that includes steps toward resolution and follow-up date, and (3) who takes responsibility (e.g., person or agency)

Phone log/meeting log: any available preferred log

Academic observation log/student assessment log: Exhibit 11–8

Academic organizational checklist: Exhibit 11–13

Behavioral observation log: Exhibit 11–10

Incident report: any available one used in locale; include antecedent behavior

SECTION 3: TRAINING INFORMATION

Professional information: memos, notes, inservice handouts, articles

Resource materials: strategies, curriculum, suggestions for modifications and accommodations

Specific directions: school, caseload, staff

Source: Reprinted with permission from K. Jamison and P. Parker, *Consulting Teacher Handbook,* © 1993, Montgomery County Schools.

Exhibit 11–4 Model Student Notebook

This is a three-ring binder system of organization, developed and monitored by a special education teacher or assistant. This notebook is designed for student access; therefore, no confidential information should be maintained in the notebook. After the system is in place, responsible volunteer students can be trained to update the notebook on a daily basis in the following areas:

- classroom assignments copied onto daily assignment sheet
- homework assignment and test schedule copied onto homework sheet
- notes from the board placed under appropriate subject heading
- handouts or project information placed under appropriate subjects

SECTION I: ASSIGNMENTS AND ACTIVITIES

- daily classroom activities and assignment sheet (a blank weekly calendar works nicely)

- homework assignment sheet (one used by team)
- long-term calendar (monthly or for grading period)

SECTION II: CONTENT-SPECIFIC INFORMATION

- class notes and worksheets
- quizzes and tests
- project/activity descriptions

SECTION III: CLASSROOM INFORMATION

- classroom rules and expectations
- grading policy
- buddy system/peer helpers
- group lists
- job responsibilities

Source: Reprinted with permission from K. Jamison, *Model Student Notebook*, © 1991, Montgomery Country Schools.

social, cognitive, and emotional changes occurring in development. Students in the middle school have been referred to as people who often have little more than chronological age in common.

Middle school students, with and without disabilities, need to find ways to belong appropriately. This need is magnified by their seeming opposite needs for self-exploration and self-definition. With an oversensitivity to body and self-awareness, young adolescents need to establish a sense of who they are and what they can do. They need time alone to sort out rapid changes and indulge in deep thought about themselves. They need time with peers and with adults to test out and talk about their discoveries while forming a sense of identity. Middle schools that have an inclusive philosophy offer student-centered programs that provide structure and opportunities to channel rapid changes in body, mood, and mind for all students, including those with disabilities.

Young adolescents need caring adults who can offer individualized attention, support, and advocacy on an ongoing basis throughout the entire middle school experience. They need regular interaction with a small group of peers who become a familiar support community. A guidance program based on proactive self-exploration and prevention is necessary to meet affective needs of middle school students in healthy ways. Many middle schools use a teacher-advisory program to respond to these needs. In this program, one teacher meets a group of students and leads discussions that focus on values, self-awareness, conflict resolution, and peer-related issues. This teacher can also be a contact person for support and an advocate for students' academic and personal welfare. Although the program is often coordinated through the guidance office, faculty and staff across the school usually facilitate the small groups. This approach promotes the acceptance of students with disabilities and the development

Exhibit 11–5 General Training Handbook: Instructional Assistants

- Job description: mission and context
- Job activities: child-specific duties, classroom duties, and tools and equipment
- Job qualifications and work performance outline
- Job responsibilities: ongoing training, recordkeeping, communication, confidentiality, attending inclusion meeting, contact between related services and special education teacher, on-the-spot and global modifications

- Student needs: confidentiality, hygiene, level of supervision, peer planning and involvement, in-class support, pull out from the class
- Tips for working in the classroom
- Behavior management suggestions
- Overview of exceptionality categories

Source: Adapted with permission from K. Colley, L. Daniels, D. Eaton, and R. Hansen, *Instructional Aide Handbook*, © 1994, Montgomery County Schools.

of social skills for all students. The middle school vignette about Michael (Exhibit 11–6) provides an excellent example of the impact a teacher advisory group can have.

The ability to make choices is an important part of an adolescent's developing independence. However, opportunities to make choices and express preferences are often absent from middle school programs for students with disabilities. Students receiving special education, along with their peers, experience a sense of accomplishment through exercising choices. It is important that teachers maintain sensitivity to student needs for choices and the associated risk taking and occasional failure. Middle school teachers need to encourage independent and interdependent behavior rather than the learned helplessness that often comes from the lack of choices. The middle school vignette about Jay (Exhibit 11–7) illustrates the success that can follow giving a student the ability to choose topics.

Teachers need to help students manage choices in academic settings. The teacher's consistent response to choices is important. If a student chooses to waste time that results in taking the teacher's or classmates' time, a natural consequence would be to require time back from the student's bank of preferred choice time (e.g., lunch, library, hall time between classes, or after school). If students interrupt others or talk while working, interfering with the rights of others to learn, then silent lunch might be an appropriate consequence. Often strategies offered by the special education teacher can work successfully with students who have recurring motivational or work-completion problems. Periodic academic observation offers valuable information in assessing student performance and developing academic plans. Exhibit 11–8 displays a student assessment log that is useful for recording observations. The middle school vignette about Jeff in Exhibit 11–9 is an example of the positive impact of providing choices to a student with disabilities.

Adolescents seek increased independence and self-direction, yet they need the security provided by structure and clear limits. Appropriate structure makes it possible for young adolescents to experience competence and achievement (Dorman, Lipsitz, & Verner, 1985). Middle school students challenge authority, spurred by their ability to see multiple causes and effects. Although students are able to participate in defining and establishing workable rules to live by, they need adult monitors so they do not become overwhelmed by that freedom.

Classroom time can be structured to accommodate the common behaviors of middle school students and prevent problem behavior. Because young adolescents vacillate from extreme energy to times of inactivity, they need a variety of activities that include physical exertion, quietness, and wiggle room. This can be related to erratic hormonal response, rapid physical growth, and preoccupation with emotional issues. Adult sensitivity in response to these critical issues can make a difference between student success and student failure. To promote needed flexibility while respecting set boundaries, teachers can engage students in sports and physical education, provide scheduled breaks, and identify places where they can be noisy and active (using outdoors whenever possible). Students also respond well when teachers give them "extras" such as extra time with friends, computer time, time with a well-liked teacher, or library time.

Exhibit 11–6 Middle School Vignette: Michael

I was the inclusion teacher on Michael's team his sixth-grade year in middle school. Sixth grade can be a difficult transition period for many early adolescent students and was especially difficult for Michael, who has severe intellectual limitations and a serious seizure disorder. Michael also had many challenging behaviors that did not encourage positive peer relationships.

I taught one advisory period each morning. These advisory periods were planned by the guidance department, and all sixth-grade students on every team, general and special education, were involved in them. Michael was scheduled into my advisory class, along with 12 general education students.

During September advisory class, Michael often barked and meowed very loudly, disrupting the lesson. I moved to his desk, continuing to teach the daily lesson, and tried to involve him in what we were discussing. Several weeks went by before I figured out what Michael needed. One day during class I walked over to Michael while he was barking loudly. I continued to teach the lesson as the other 12 students' eyes followed me to see what was going to happen. I gently placed my hand on Michael's cheek and rubbed as I taught. He stopped barking! He rubbed the back of my hand with his face. The class was stunned! What had happened? I finished the lesson standing near Michael.

Over the next several weeks, whenever Michael began to bark or meow, I walked over to him and gently rubbed his cheek. He instantly stopped and became engaged in the advisory lesson by asking questions and sharing stories about what he had done last night as all the students did. By the middle of October, Michael quit barking and meowing. I didn't need to walk over and stand by him again. The other students in the advisory class knew that Michael had interesting stories to contribute. Michael knew that he was an important member of our class and that we would wait for him to share his stories. We all learned to practice being patient with one another. We all saw the power that listening to one another gives.

Exhibit 11–7 Middle School Vignette: Jay

One of my most challenging teaching experiences occurred during the year one of my sixth-grade students was a boy with Tourette's syndrome. Jay used very loud vocalizations, mostly repeating profanities, and a loud grunt. I found it very difficult to teach with this noise occurring in the classroom most of the time. Many of my students had known Jay in elementary school and could tune out his outbursts better than I could. My resource teacher gave me helpful hints about techniques to use to help quiet Jay's vocalizations. Sometimes these worked. Sometimes they did not.

My team worked with Jay's mother and the doctor to get a medication change. This medication helped greatly to diminish the outbursts. Nevertheless, as I got to know Jay better, I discovered two special methods that enabled me to help Jay to have a good school year. The first thing I found out about Jay was that he was a wonderfully dramatic reader, and that he did not vocalize when he was reading. The second discovery was that he loved social studies.

Jay loved to visit the school library and the public library. I sometimes assigned him topics to research based on the content we were studying. At other times, he selected topics in which he was interested to research. He sometimes had time to share his information with the class, and sometimes he just made his report to me. I kept filmstrips and an individual viewer for him to use on various topics of interest to him when he was having a really bad day. He also liked to create projects. I kept a variety of activities from which he could choose that correlated with our topics of study. These projects provided hands-on activities that helped him stay focused.

I believe his most successful experience in school that year was when he had the main role in a Greek play that my reading class presented as part of our unit on Greek history. I knew he was talented enough with his reading to perform splendidly. I was just not sure what would happen with the vocalizations. On the day of the performance, he was nervous and vocalized some profanity at the beginning of the play, but once he got into his part, he was a big success in the role.

Having Jay included on our team was not always successful. There were days when nothing seemed to work with him. It took a tremendous effort by all the members of our team to help Jay be part of the general school program.

If I have learned one thing after 27 years of teaching, it is that success comes in small steps. I believe that Jay had many small steps of success that sixth-grade year, and so did our team.

Students with disabilities who exhibit inappropriate behaviors at school may need adult monitoring to cope with the middle school environment and its freedom. Behavioral observation logs can be used effectively by teams to identify inappropriate behaviors. Identification and recognition of behavior patterns are the first steps in behavioral planning. Exhibit 11–10 is an example of a behavioral observation log used by Montgomery County, Virginia, Public Schools.

Young adolescents with disabilities, like their peers, are very concerned about fitting into their peer group. As a result, it is important that behavior management techniques and discipline be age appropriate. Behavioral supports should be developed with a student's dignity in mind. Choices should be provided, and consequences should be natural and fit into the middle school routine.

Individualized behavioral plans should reflect school and classroom discipline standards. Rules should be clearly posted to offer a visual reference point for students. In addition, daily changes should be graphically organized and posted. Teachers should ensure that transitions between activities are quick and smooth. Predetermined auditory and visual cues are useful for responding to inappropriate behaviors, as is providing the child a choice between predetermined alternatives.

Some students with disabilities require a positive behavior support plan. The team working with the student should be involved in developing this plan. A behavior support plan for students at the middle level could address the challenging behavior, its frequency, and its purpose; strategies tried and their success; possible reinforcers; information on the choices the student has during the day; and potential new strategies. (Chapter 15 offers further information for melding schoolwide discipline and individual supports for students with disabilities.)

One approach for dealing with behavior problems in a middle school is "Bounce" (Edwards, Jamison, & Kroll, 1993). Bounce is an alternative intervention used with students, with or without disabilities, whose behaviors interfere with their learning and the learning of others. The Bounce setting is created for students with recurrent problematic behaviors. It provides a tight support system around a child, provides opportunity for responsible action, and offers social consequences for inappropriate social behavior. It is designed to give students strategies to be alert to antecedent conditions or behaviors, to self-monitor, and to choose to redirect behavior. Bounce encourages an expedient return to the classroom after students have been removed for disruptive behavior. Exhibit 11–11 provides more detailed information about the Bounce program.

ACADEMIC EXPECTATIONS

Middle school programs furnish a broad-based, comprehensive academic program, with a wide range of experiences. Academic emphasis at this age can focus easily on interdisciplinary presentation of skills and knowledge. Interdisciplinary units or thematic units make learning more

Exhibit 11–8 Student Assessment Log

Name: _____   Date: _____

Subject: _____   Time: _____

Period: _____

	P	N	A	G	E
1. Attends class regularly — 1					
2. Attends class on time — 2					
3. Class preparation — 3					
4. Homework completed — 4					
5. Listens to class presentations — 5					
6. Participates in class activities — 6					
7. Follows instructions — 7					
8. Follows class rules — 8					
9. Class work completed — 9					
10. Works collaboratively — 10					
11. Appropriate social interaction — 11					
12. Appropriate level of activity — 12					

P = Poor, N = Needs improvement, A = Average, G = Good, E = Excellent

ANECDOTAL REFLECTION:

1. Describe specific (today) academic concerns.

2. List/describe any ongoing academic concerns you may wish to address with your team.

Teacher: _____   Team: _____

Source: Reprinted with permission from K. Jamison and P. Parker, *Consulting Teacher Handbook,* © 1993, Montgomery County Schools.

relevant to the learner by connecting the desired content and skills to an idea that the learner finds interesting. Drawing across disciplines to develop units of study can provide a broad reference continuum from which to connect learning. This technique helps students connect the content related to a central topic that repeats itself across the day in different subjects. This is especially beneficial to the students with disabilities who need extended time and exposure to ensure understanding. Using a variety of teaching methods, strategies, and learning materials in the classroom also assists teachers to meet varied learning styles and needs. Exhibit 11–12 offers a menu of teaching strategies that have been effective with middle school students.

Students at this age benefit from opportunities for kinesthetic experiences in learning. They need to master basic math concepts and computation skills, reading, writing, problem solving, critical thinking, and study skills. The curriculum must emphasize both process and product, leaving room for self-exploration and self-definition. Using multi-level, multimodal approaches designed as best practice for

Exhibit 11–9 Middle School Vignette: Jeff

I had been a one-on-one aide only one year when I was assigned to work with Jeff in a sixth-grade inclusion classroom. Nothing, however, could have prepared me for the challenges that were ahead in working with Jeff. Jeff is a loving boy who is also severely mentally retarded with challenging behaviors. I had been told horror stories about his challenging behaviors during the previous school year when I visited the elementary school in the spring to meet Jeff and his teachers. He was in a room with his aide much of the time where he acted out and slept.

My main goal for the sixth grade was to help Jeff make behavior choices that would allow him to stay in the inclusion classrooms. I wanted to help Jeff become socially accepted by his new teachers and fellow classmates. Constant modeling of appropriate behavior, high expectations, and stubbornness on my part soon helped Jeff. He was staying in most of his classes daily. He was making tremendous academic and social progress.

I developed a system of breaks or play time. He adapted very well to this system. For example, he knew that if he did 30 minutes of math, then he could listen to his tapes for 15 minutes. I found that the activities he enjoyed most were good bargaining tools. If, for example, he refused to go to social studies, he lost his free game time. Natural consequences seemed to work well: "You take my time, you give me your time."

I truly believe that including all students in the general classroom is important. With much love, time, and determination on my part, Jeff became part of the entire student population.

all middle school students is a natural best practice for students with disabilities.

The achievement of middle school students fluctuates from rapid progress, to plateaus, to regression. As a result, no single systematic approach or style of teaching works effectively at all times with all students. Students enter middle school with a rich background of knowledge and experience. Linking what students know to what they are doing in school provides avenues for personal, meaningful construction of knowledge. Further, student participation in setting learning goals gives them an investment in their learning. It is also motivating to give students the opportunity to monitor their own progress. Exhibit 11–13 is a self-monitoring checklist that can be used to facilitate independence.

Individualized assessment is important for students with disabilities in middle school. Alternative methods of assessment could include: portfolios, projects, individualized learning contracts, oral presentations and testing, computer-generated tasks, kinesthetic testing (e.g., building, dancing, body movement), and art.

As middle school students progress from sixth through eighth grade, teachers demand more independent performance. Sixth-grade teams are usually made up of two teachers who provide a nurturing transitional environment from the elementary school. Academic expectations, though differentiated and appropriate, are less independent and less weighted than at the eighth-grade level.

MIDDLE SCHOOL COURSES

Content Courses

Many middle schools are introducing advanced classes (e.g., math and foreign language), available for high school credit, to meet the needs of some high academic achievers. Some middle school enthusiasts believe that academic pursuit of high school level classes at increasingly younger ages creates unnecessary pressure at a most critical developmental cycle. However, when such classes are worked into the master schedule with maintenance of middle school philosophy, there is little compromise to the overall program. If, for example, general math classes are raised to algebra for credit as the only math alternative in middle school, inclusion teachers will have more obvious differentiation in curricular adaptations for students in special education who need general math skills. Math labs and special math classes could be options that result in a pendulum swing to more restrictive placement for greater numbers of students at the middle school level. Teachers must be creative in exploring options.

Elective Courses

Elective courses provide a range of choice based on interest and aptitude. Early middle school years usually provide the opportunity for students to try out different electives. Most middle schools offer some form of "exploration" during the early years, providing students with the opportunity to explore a variety of fine and related arts. This is especially important for students who have not chosen a year-long elective such as band or chorus. As students move toward the eighth grade, they usually have semester options in fine arts and practical arts. These elective classes are important for students with disabilities, because they provide hands-on experiences in learning and are success oriented by nature. They also provide integrative support to content teachers during interdisciplinary units by assisting in areas such as cooking, music, singing, and computer-generated information.

Career Exploration

Students begin the process of preparing for the world of work during the middle school years. Career awareness and

Exhibit 11–10 Behavioral Observation Log

Name: _____   Date: _____

Subject: _____   Time: _____

Period: _____

		P	N	A	G	E
1. Interaction with peers	1					
2. Interaction with teachers	2					
3. Appropriate comments to others	3					
4. Response to touch/bump by peers	4					
5. Control of anger/negative feelings	5					
6. Does not provoke others	6					
7. Does not fight with peers	7					
8. Follows class/school rules	8					
9. Level of aggression to teacher	9					
10. Appropriate level of noise	10					
11. Self-controlled behavior	11					
12. Appropriate level of activity	12					

P = Poor, N = Needs improvement, A = Average, G = Good, E = Excellent

ANECDOTAL REFLECTION:

1. Describe current behavioral concerns.

2. List/describe any ongoing behavioral concerns you may wish to address with your team.

Observer: _____   Title: _____

Source: Reprinted with permission from K. Jamison and P. Parker, *Consulting Teacher Handbook,* © 1993, Montgomery County Schools.

exploration activities are equally valuable to students with disabilities and the general student population. Career activities can be offered through unit studies that include multi-level, multimodal activities for divergent learners. These may include: games, computer exploration, field trips, guest speakers, job shadowing, observing, and recording. In addition, organization of a job corps with custodial, cafeteria, or clerical staff provides valuable experience. (Chapter 13 presents further information on vocational education, and Chapter 14 reviews the importance of transition planning for students with disabilities.)

PLANNING STUDENTS' PLACEMENT AND SERVICES

The key to a successful middle school inclusive education program is the appropriate placement of each student with disabilities. Decisions about how to distribute special education students across teams to maintain appropriate coverage and natural proportions are the nuts and bolts of placement. Special education teachers should be assigned to cover needs of students and to connect with the fewest number of teams possible. Placing special education teachers on

Exhibit 11–11 Bounce Program

What: Support (not punitive)

Redirection (not disruptive)

Social Skill Instruction (of disruptive behavior)

Why: To provide creative alternatives for students who need behavior intervention

Where: Specific room in school designated for this purpose

Who: Staff person, such as paraprofessional, trained in process with experience in working with behavioral needs, e.g., previous aide in special education classroom

When: Available across the entire day except for one predetermined, designated period used for paperwork and follow up

How many: Two students per team (regular or special education) chosen by team teachers, including special education teacher

Process: Team participation is voluntary; varied meeting times provided to increase participation

- Profile on each student selected by the team sent to Bounce staff person, to include what behavioral interventions work and don't work, IEP information, and other information
- Meeting set with team, guidance, Bounce staff person, and student to review student needs and Bounce parameters: how to get to Bounce, responsibilities while in Bounce, and student accountability to use strategies taught

Procedure: Teacher makes decision whether Bounce or administrative action is appropriate for a disruptive offense; both disciplinary action and Bounce should not be assigned for the same offense.

- Checklist (simplified referral) filled out and sent with student to Bounce—This is the "ticket" to Bounce that includes date, time, teacher, cause of outburst.
- Student goes to Bounce, goes through process, and returns to class as soon as possible with return "ticket"

Room Structure: Set up in four stations to include:

- Cool down journal or drawing: student writes down frustration, feelings, opinions related to the problem.
- Hands-on art or craft: student reviews journal writing and discusses with Bounce person possible strategies to use while "creating" with art medium of choice, e.g., clay, paint, origami.
- Quiet listening and self-talk: student restates the strategies chosen to avoid repeating the behavior while relaxing, listening to music.
- Positive journaling: student writes a statement in ego journal (Dembrosky, 1988) to end on a positive statement about self.

Tips:

- Relaxing music playing in the background, e.g., largo Baroque
- Room organized and visually inviting
- Stations remain in same place each time to offer predictability
- Bounce staff person to use soft tone of voice and understanding demeanor; building trust is imperative to the success of the process
- Written documentation kept on each visit in child's folder to include follow-up plan

Philosophy: The philosophy is based on the need for students who have recurrent emotional reactions to be provided with an immediate cool down time that has redirection and follow up. The goal is for students to learn the following new behaviors:

- Admitting that there is a problem: Do I need help?
- Defining the problem: What did I do?
- Taking ownership in the negative effect the behavior has on life: What did I want?
- Learning strategies that can effect change: What can I do to make it different?
- Practicing these strategies: How/when can I check for success?
- Evaluating how strategies are working: Is my behavior improving?

Source: Adapted with permission from J. Edwards, K. Jamison, and R. Kroll, *Therapeutic Bounce,* © 1994, Montgomery County Schools.

a team is most desirable. This maintains a holistic approach that reflects middle school philosophy. If the school population is small, it may be necessary to assign the special education teacher by grade. Either approach allows the teachers to modify, adapt, and provide accommodations for a manageable range of curricula.

Each student should be assigned to a special education teacher who serves as the student's case manager. In this way, when a student receives services from many staff persons, one person will be knowledgeable about the student's progress and performance in all settings.

The task of assigning students to various classes is best

Exhibit 11–12 Teaching Strategies

VISUAL MODE	AUDITORY MODE	KINESTHETIC MODE	METHODS OF ASSESSMENT
semantic mapping	tape recordings	exhibits	
graphic overviews	oral reading	games and puzzles	observation
Venn diagrams	asking questions	projects	anecdotal records
flow charts	choral reading	field trips	portfolio
timelines	videos	plays	test
outlining	filmstrips	role playing	projects
posters	lecture	manipulatives	role playing
photographs	explanation	demonstrations	drama
transparencies	discussion	constructing a mobile	participation
flash cards	debate	building a model	ongoing grading
models	musical selection		process grading
charts			product grading
graphs			quizzes
color coding			
highlighting			
boxing in or underlining			
filmstrips			
videos			
bulletin boards			
banner			

Exhibit 11–13 Organizational Checklist

1. Have I prepared for this class? Have I:
   ____ Read all assigned materials?
   ____ Reviewed all class notes?
   ____ Written down questions I have about the material?
   ____ Asked the teacher for help on difficult material?
   ____ Reviewed homework assignments?

2. Do I have the following materials for this class? Do I have:
   ____ Notebook?
   ____ Pencil/pen?
   ____ Textbook?
   ____ Completed homework?
   ____ Additional required materials?

3. Am I ready for class to begin?
   ____ Is my textbook on the desk in front of me?
   ____ Are my paper and pencil on the desk to take notes?
   ____ Are all other materials put away?
   ____ Am I seated quietly at my desk?
   ____ Is my mind focused on the class I am in now?

4. Did I complete all work and assignments?
   ____ Did I complete all class assignments?
   ____ Did I ask questions?
   ____ Did I turn in all important class work?
   ____ Did I take clear notes?
   ____ Did I write down all assignments?

5. Is my work organized?
   ____ Is my notebook neat?
   ____ Can I find things easily?
   ____ Have I put class information in correct section?
   ____ Is my notebook free of trash?

Source: Adapted with permission from Montgomery County Schools In-Service Handout, *Organizational Checklist,* © 1994 Montgomery County Schools.

completed by a team, including the lead special education teacher(s) and the guidance counselor. Middle school staff will find the following steps to be helpful in planning for the next school year:

- *Step 1:* Counselors or lead special education teachers collect information from IEPs, current teachers, and feeder elementary schools. This should include information on strategies that have worked successfully and those that have not been successful.
- *Step 2:* A needs-placement matrix is developed and displayed on a large piece of paper. All classes, services, and supports are listed across the top of the page in columns, e.g., reading, math, speech, occupational therapy.
  - *Step 2A:* The students are listed in each row. Checks are made in each column to identify the classes, services, and supports each child requires.
  - *Step 2B:* The amount of service is color coded (e.g., pink for students with more than 80% of special education services; yellow for students with 50% to 79% special education services; blue for 20% to 49% special education services; and green for consultation, less than 20% special education services).
  - *Step 2C:* Identify the staff support needed with circles, squares, and triangles (e.g., mark classes, services, or supports that require a special education teacher with a circle; those that require an instruc-

tional assistant with a box; those that require related service personnel with a triangle).
- *Step 3:* A tentative number of teachers, instructional assistants, and related service personnel for each grade level is identified.
- *Step 4:* General and special education teacher and teacher assistant assignments are made, matching staff with student needs and numbers.
- *Step 5:* Sixth-grade teachers and teacher assistants visit feeder schools to meet with current teachers and meet the students. Upper-grade staff meet with lower-grade staff.

CONCLUSION

Young adolescents, both with and without disabilities, need opportunities to try out physical, social, emotional, and cognitive abilities to discover their skills and aptitudes. As they begin to think about connections between current achievement and future roles, they search out opportunities to succeed. To provide these opportunities, middle schools need to be structured, organized, and caring.

Middle school structure enhances inclusive education. Community-building activities, team teaching, and differentiated instruction are essential components of restructured middle schools and inclusive programming. Incorporating best practice brings about change and growth that can be as challenging as it can be rewarding. What better place to evidence this process than in an inclusive middle school that is stretching to reach its potential.

REFERENCES

Alexander, W. (1971). How fares the middle school? *National Elementary Principal, 51,* 8–11.

Colley, K., Daniels, L., Eaton, D., & Hansen, R. (1994). *Instructional aide handbook.* Unpublished manuscript. Christiansburg, VA: Montgomery County Public Schools.

Dembrosky, C.H. (Ed.). (1988). *Affective skill development for adolescents: Self-esteem.* Lincoln, NE: Affective Skill Development.

Dorman, G., Lipsitz, J., & Verner, P. (1985). Improving schools for young adolescents. In S.A. Williams & R.P. Murphy (Eds.), *Developing successful middle schools* (pp.15–20). Bloomington, IN: Phi Delta Kappa Center for Education, Development, and Research.

Edwards, J., Jamison, K., & Kroll, R. (1993). *Bounce.* Unpublished manuscript. Christiansburg, VA: Montgomery County Public Schools.

Epstein, J.L., & MacIver, D.J. (1990). The middle grades: Is grade span the most important issue? *Educational Horizons, 19,* 88–94.

Jamison, K. (1991). *Model student notebook.* Unpublished manuscript. Christiansburg, VA: Montgomery County Public Schools.

Jamison, K., & Parker, P. (1993). *Consulting teacher handbook.* Unpublished manuscript. Christiansburg, VA: Montgomery County Public Schools.

Kohut, S. (1988). *The middle school: A bridge between elementary and high schools.* (2nd ed.). Washington, DC: National Education Association.

McEwin, K.C. (1992). William M. Alexander: Father of the American middle school. *Middle School Journal, 23*(5), 32–38.

National Middle School Association. (1995). *This we believe.* Columbus, OH: Author.

CHAPTER 12

Inclusion in the Secondary School

Judy K. Montgomery

Inclusion is an educational belief that grants all students equal membership in their school community. All students should learn together while being provided with the support services needed to help them succeed. It is belonging first—not bargaining later. (L. Eshilian, Whittier High School, Whittier, CA, personal communication, 1994)

INTRODUCTION: FOUR STUDENTS AND INCLUSIVE EDUCATION

In this chapter, the stories of four students are presented to exemplify inclusive education. Todd and Janice began high school with experiences in inclusive middle schools. Todd was familiar with a resource program for many years. Janice left the special class for the general education program when her parents requested a more natural social environment. Chris and Lisa, on the other hand, encountered high school and full inclusion on the same day. For each of these students, the school supports and inclusive practices used to enable their placement were individualized. Inclusion in the secondary school is like so much of high school experiences—a series of individual stories and the people who live them.

Students Who Were Included before High School

Todd

Todd is a 15-year-old student at a large urban high school. He has been identified as a student with exceptional needs and has received special education services of various types for the past six years. He is in a general education English class and receives academic support from the resource teacher, the speech-language pathologist, and four peer tutors in his class. The peer tutors volunteered to help Todd and two other students this year for service points.

Psychological and academic testing revealed that Todd has a Wechsler full-scale IQ score of 81 and a 15-point spread between his verbal and performance scores, with performance much higher. He was on medication for attention deficit hyperactivity disorder (ADHD) for four years, but has been taken off it this year with no ill effects.

Todd has learning disabilities in the areas of reading, oral and written language, and organizational skills. He has a short attention span (about 8 to 10 minutes), and great difficulty composing his thoughts on paper. His conversational vocabulary is limited, and he writes short, stilted sentences. His writing is slow and labored, with many erasures, cross-outs, and re-starts. His knowledge and use of punctuation, capitalization, and other mechanics of writing are sporadic at best. He usually loses interest before he gets to proofreading or editing his work. He reports that his fingers cramp when he writes, and that this affects his pitching for the school's baseball team.

Todd reads at the fourth-grade level. He occasionally reads for pleasure, especially high-interest books such as adventure stories or science fiction at his level (or above his level, if he has seen the movie).

Todd is very good in math and can do grade-level work. He can grasp the operations and the relationships between numbers quickly. However, he rarely turns in work because he either fails to write down the assignment, does it and loses it, or simply forgets to finish the work he begins in class. He can explain the processes and even helps others at times. He needs to have word or story problems read to him to complete the assignment.

Todd has many friends, is athletic, and is very social. He is led easily by others and takes risks that others only talk about doing. He often shows poor judgment, can get angry quickly, and blurts out his feelings when he is frustrated or feels he has been made to look foolish.

Todd is becoming more sensitive about what he can and cannot do in his English class; he is aware that most, but not all, students turn in more written work than he does. He likes the teacher, and several of his best friends from baseball are in the class. He has started to read the assigned novels; however, he is genuinely confused by the vocabulary and the length of the passages, and he cannot recall what the teacher wants him to do when he finishes a chapter. Todd wants to compile a portfolio of his written work for this class to please the teacher, but he cannot think of what to write without his cooperative learning group starting him off. He works best with a group of four students who are both friends and tutors.

Todd is like so many students in high school who struggle with academics, social acceptance, and the label of learning disabilities. The freedom of high school, daily schedules, and the responsibility to learn on his own tax Todd's poorly developed organizational skills. How can inclusion make a difference for him?

Janice

Janice is a 14-year-old student with Down syndrome, some visual problems, and a keen interest in music. She entered high school with her classmates from a local feeder junior high school at the end of eighth grade. She wants to pursue her interests in music, make money with an after-school job at a day care center, and eventually live in an apartment on her own in the same large city where she lives now with her parents. She is the fifth child in the family and has observed many years of older siblings attending high school, holding jobs after school, going to social and athletic events, graduating, and leaving home for college or jobs and families of their own. She has a sense of her own multiple roles that exceeds the maturity level of many students in her high school. She is the youngest sister, an aunt, a musician, a student worker, and a person with disabilities. She has attended the annual Convention of the Down Syndrome Congress for the past five years and knows many young people her age with the same type of disability.

Janice's achievement scores are more indicative of her skill level than her IQ testing. She reads at the third-grade level and can write simple sentences. Her oral language is much more advanced, so her dictated work is at a seventh- or eighth-grade level. She can engage in a conversation about American presidents, the Civil War, or the Industrial Revolution, because these topics were covered in her history courses in junior high. She memorized what she considered the important elements on the periodic table in science. She reads fiction books at the fourth-grade level with some help from friends and loves books on tape.

Janice has a vast collection of records, audiotapes, and compact discs (CDs). She has joined a music club for persons with disabilities that meets every other week, and she began the CD lending library at her church with the help of her older brother. On a weekly basis, after Sunday services, she keeps track of which CDs are out on loan and for what length of time. This has been a great vehicle to improve her socialization skills.

In high school, Janice takes three music classes, typing and keyboarding on the computer, U.S. history, physical education, introduction to human development, study hall, and Spanish. Her schedule changes each semester, with a goal of completing high school in four or five years with a certificate of completion and several new job-related skills. Janice is a part of her individualized educational program (IEP) team each year and often stops in to see the guidance counselor assigned to her.

Janice has one older brother in high school and three friends she has known for many years. They help her during the day and may eat lunch with her, include her when they go to an after-school spirit rally, or walk home through the regional park to watch the drill team practice. She needs assistance in U.S. history from her cooperative learning group and turns in adjusted assignments determined by the counselor and her teacher. She can do all typing assignments on her own and keeps a portfolio of her speed drills, typing forms, and written work. This is graded by the teachers and self-graded in a grading session at the end of each report card period. She uses a word-processing program available at the school.

Janice has a poor sense of time and expects others to keep track of her appointments and responsibilities. She does not write down assignments, cannot recall that she has a report due, and walks very slowly to class—often arriving late, smiling and waving at her classmates when she enters the class. This behavior was accepted the first semester she was in high school; subsequently, Janice was counseled that she would receive detentions to be made up after school if her tardiness continued. She still gets many detentions for tardiness and late work. When she is too late for her after-school job, where she works three days a week, she breaks down in tears and complains that she will get in trouble because the teachers "gave her detentions." Discussion is continuing on what other methods might be used to motivate Janice.

Students Who Were Included for the First Time in High School

Christopher

Christopher, a 10th grader, experiences cerebral palsy, moderate learning disabilities, and periodic hospitalizations for heart problems and asthma. He is considered in fragile medical health. Many of his learning struggles can be traced to his erratic attendance at school, his limited upper-body fine motor coordination, and his medications for asthma and heart dysrhythmia. He likes school but also likes to stay home where much less is demanded of him.

He was in a special education class for elementary and middle school. He made minimal progress but gradually improved as he got older and began to experience more positive interactions at school with peers than he did staying home. He has had only three teachers in his previous schools, often staying in the same room for many years. He built a close personal relationship with his last teacher and calls him "Daddy" sometimes. It was hard for him to leave middle school.

He learned to use a computer word-processing program because his writing was impossible to read, and handwriting fatigued him greatly. He can read and write at the fifth-grade level, likes to read for pleasure, and loves books on sports or military topics. Chris moved into an inclusive high school not because he was seeking a change, but because things changed around him. The high school closest to his home completely converted to an inclusive environment and welcomed students from many parts of his district. He could walk to school with his peers and neighbors and liked the idea of being in school sports with them.

Chris would take physical education classes all day if he had his way. Instead, he is the boys' sports equipment manager for two sports, which requires that he take gym for two classes to assist the coach and inventory the equipment. He has learned to use the computer inventory program and the game scheduler.

He repeated the first math class he took in high school in order to improve his grade, and he takes a math study hall in the special education support room the hour before and the hour after general math. He is taking an English novel class this year and helps with the school newspaper as part of his English assignment. Chris has great gaps in his knowledge base for science and social studies, and he is an observer in the biology class this year. He is basically auditing the class in preparation for taking it next year.

Most students think of Chris as slightly clumsy rather than as a person with cerebral palsy. He seems uninterested in learning more about himself, his disability and abilities, or his skills for a future job. He does not have actual peer tutors and few students knew him before high school, but he accepts help easily, sometimes even when he does not need it. He has had only one asthma attack and no hospital stays for his heart problems since beginning high school a year ago, and he seems to be in better health overall. His attendance is good, and he tries most of the work at school. He turns in very little work, however, and there is almost no follow-through at home. Chris can continue in high school until age 22 and is likely to do so, according to his parents. Arranging his schedule each year is a challenge for his IEP

team; he is not yet an active participant in the decision-making process, and prefers that classes and teachers do not change from semester to semester—especially his sports equipment manager jobs.

Students who are included in high school for their first nonsegregated experience face the rigors of a high school curriculum and the sudden change of environment at a highly vulnerable age. Like Chris, some of them let school just flow around them, with little social contact and limited plans for the future. They suffer from a lack of adult supervision all the time and accomplish very little on their own. Some struggle with the work or are highly anxious about changes in place, people, expectancies, and daily activities. At times, a morning-only academic program is suggested, and afternoons are spent in community work programs. This is being done less often in inclusive high schools but may be incorporated for the 18- to 22-year-old students who lack the appropriate peer group in high school. (D. Hunter, Chapman University, Orange, CA, personal communication, 1996)

Lisa

Lisa was given the label of autism when she was three years old. She is now a junior in high school, taking honors English and math classes, and riding the city bus to school each day. She has no speech; she screams when she is upset or excited; and she bites her arms and hands and, on occasion, those of her mother and peer tutors. She takes a full load of classes at a comprehensive high school of 3,000 students. This year, she is taking economics, honors English, math, chemistry, physical education, and health and family living. Lisa writes opinion pieces and poetry often and has had two letters to the editor published with her picture in the *Los Angeles Times*. Her current interest is Caesar Chavez and his approach to social justice for farm workers in central California. She uses facilitated communication with the assistance of seven peer tutors during the school day.

Lisa began school at the age of four in a self-contained class of six students with autism, pervasive developmental delay, and/or severe emotional disturbance. She remained with them until she was seven, and then enrolled in another self-contained class of nine students—five with autism and four others with severe mental retardation and developmental disabilities. She showed no signs of reading or understanding print until the eighth grade when facilitated communication was used. She was taught the hand-over-hand method of pointing to letters on a board to spell her name and the names of items in class. She "learned" to spell every word the first time it was spelled for her, and soon it was evident that she had been reading for a long time. She wanted to "write" using the new method every day. She required someone, almost anyone, to hold her at the wrist.

Later, she needed a touch at the shoulder, and now it helps her print on a portable keyboard device if the peer tutor holds her clothing at her shoulder or holds a hand above or near her right shoulder.

Lisa struggles with her behavior daily. She writes in her computer journal that sometimes the autism seems to win the day, and sometimes she does. She often writes out apologies to her teachers or classmates for what she calls "obnoxious" or "atrocious" behavior. This usually includes screaming, pounding the table, or growling in class. She goes from class to class with a peer, teacher, or instructional aide, as moving from one environment to another remains a frustrating barrier for her. Some days she cannot enter a classroom and screams and pulls back from the door repeatedly. Students in her classes are aware of her behaviors, interact with her when she will allow it, and often receive notes from her when she cannot make contact with them any other way. She works on homework five to six hours a night and has few other interests. She is learning to catch and throw a ball this year—a very difficult task for her—and is still compelled to run water from a faucet over her hands and arms many times during the day.

Lisa requested a MAPs (Making Action Plans) strategy session when she was 16 to decide what college she should attend. The meeting was called and took place in her home. Twenty-two people who knew Lisa personally and professionally attended the meeting and went through the standard eight questions of a MAPs session (e.g., Who are you and what are you doing today? What are your gifts? What are your dreams and goals? What are your nightmares and fears? See Chapter 7 for greater detail on the process.). Four students from her class were there. She said her greatest fear was that autism would ultimately win the "fight inside" her and no one would know who she is. She wanted to live near home after high school and to attend college. She said she was afraid to go to college because she was so short and people would laugh at her. She has taken a college preparatory track in high school and will have enough science, math, and language courses to enter a major university. She asked to take the Preliminary Scholastic Aptitude Test (PSAT) with the rest of the juniors who had signed up. She has written a letter to see if she can take the Scholastic Aptitude Test (SAT) with extended time and a facilitator due to her autism.

Clearly, Lisa—a student with severe disabilities without previous experience in inclusive settings—is an unusual example of what can happen in the high school setting. She stepped from no literacy to advanced skills, from self-contained classrooms to a comprehensive high school campus, from no friends to being surrounded by age-appropriate peers. She continues to have emotional outbursts, highly unusual behavior, and setbacks as she struggles with who she is. Critics of facilitated communication have observed

her progress to independent typing; they wonder if she knew how to read and type years before and simply waited to display her literacy until high school. Her tutors are not students in her own classes, so they do not know the work she is doing and serve only as her physical support to type. She is unable to take the classes many students in inclusive high schools take—drama, physical education, music, art, ceramics, etc.—due to severe coordination problems and a genuine lack of interest on her part.

It is experiences like Lisa's that make educators realize that a student's degree of disability is not a reliable predictor of success in an inclusive high school.

THE SECONDARY SCHOOL: AN ENVIRONMENT FOR INCLUSION

What does inclusion look like in secondary education? It is decidedly different than elementary school—as it should be. High school marks a passage for every student. The day is spent differently, social contacts are frequent and intense, and teachers view students as passing through on the way to their adult lives. Todd exemplifies the fully included high school student—with the ups and downs, highs and lows that are commonly experienced to one degree or another in high school. In many ways, high school is a more conducive educational environment for inclusion than other educational and social settings. There are more options for students, a larger pool of people for interaction, and a greater number of solutions for the challenges each student brings.

This chapter features the lives of high school students who have been fully included in two categories. The first set of students was included at least four years before they entered high school; the second group of students was included for the first time in high school. The experiences of and strategies for working with these two groups of students are quite different.

Interestingly, the division is not between students with severe disabilities and students with mild to moderate disabilities, as one might anticipate. The success of students in inclusive settings has less to do with their disabilities and much more to do with their age-appropriate friendships and natural supports (Montgomery, 1995; Schumacher & Deshler, 1995). Students who have been included in elementary school are often well equipped, as are their peer supports, to handle high school. Students without that background must develop curricular strategies and friendships simultaneously. It can be done, but it takes more team planning and often a greater length of time before the student is successful. Students in both groups experience many of the same benefits of inclusive education, however, and research findings indicate that it is never too late to begin (Hoskins, 1995).

The Language of Inclusive Schools

Using people-first language is an important first step in designing inclusive schools at all levels. People-first language is much more than trying to be politically correct. It reminds us that the students we are talking about are people first and not primarily disability categories. Thus, we say *students with* cerebral palsy or autism, rather than "cerebral palsied kids" or "autistic people." Students who use people-first language acknowledge that some of their peers have Down syndrome, and are not "Down's kids." Unfortunately, the media are replete with examples of offensive and judgmental language describing individuals with special needs. We often read of "victims" of spina bifida or students who "suffer from autism." Students experience, rather than suffer, developmental disabilities or hearing loss. People use wheelchairs—they are not confined to them. As professionals eliminate these derogatory terms from their language, students will do the same, adding dignity to the social communication directed toward peers and colleagues who experience disabilities. "Handicapism," like ageism and sexism, is not a part of today's inclusive school.

The Culture of High School

High school—either a three- or four-year arrangement—is a special time in the educational journey. Compulsory education laws were established for children up to age 16 (or higher) in this country after child labor laws prevented children from working in the factories of the new industrial age. At first, educators were at a loss about what to teach in the four years that suddenly followed eighth grade. Was there really new material and curriculum that students "needed" in this new extension of education called high school? Should students return to previous concepts and go into greater depth—in history, science, and European fiction? Should teachers find new subjects to teach, such as languages and political science? Should students be taught about the world of jobs in business, typing, and woodworking classes? Should they be prepared for another form of education—college—previously available only to families of position and wealth? Eventually, all of these ideas were incorporated into the high school curriculum, and all students attended through age 16, 17, or 18. They went for a variety of reasons—college preparation for some, job skills for others, and social contacts for almost everyone.

This range of purposes for continued education meant that large, comprehensive high schools became diverse communities, with two or three "tracks" for students. Unlike elementary schools, students attended for different reasons and had different end points to reach within their four-year programs. There is an individualism in high school that lends itself well to inclusion.

An oft-stated adage is that "high school teachers teach subjects, not students." To some degree, this is true, and quite appropriate. Each teacher is a subject or discipline expert. Students enter selected subject areas to study for a period of time, the length dependent on the student's individual educational goals. True to the culture of high school, each teacher is there to offer a small piece of a comprehensive program. While some high schools may have developed a more student-driven curriculum than the one described here, a majority are still organized to allow students to "mix and match" their way toward graduation. The curriculum is not helter-skelter, but merely multifaceted, allowing the student to make choices beyond the required subjects.

This multioption concept can be very useful for an inclusive high school. Todd, for example, moves from less favored classes to personally selected ones every 47 minutes. Before high school, he struggled with being in the same classroom for long periods of time and completing work others had chosen for him. In high school, he can be in an inclusive environment with age-appropriate peers, taking classes with college-bound students, although his goal is a certificate of completion. The option of meeting the requirements for a diploma remains open for him, as well as postsecondary education. Todd's choices are much greater in high school than they were in grade school.

There are other advantages to inclusive practices inherent in the culture of high school. Some gifted students in high school are skilled mentors and mature peer tutors, frequently able to grasp the content of the curriculum in the first presentation. Due to the recursive nature of the school curriculum, by high school many students are revisiting aspects of curriculum for the second or third time (e.g., U.S. geography, the scientific method, famous people in history). This means that they can handle the new information quickly and connect it to prior knowledge, leaving time for them to teach it to other students. Teaching information to someone else is one of the most powerful ways to remember it, and even reconstruct it at a higher cognitive level (Ellis & Hunt, 1993). For example, the Future Teachers of America club in the high school is one of the best sources of tutors for fully included students. These aspiring teachers are outstanding tutors and often can spare the time (e.g., during study halls) to be skillful tutors.

Another advantage of high school is the wide range of classes offered. Many students discover that, finally, they can make real choices regarding the classes that matter to them. In previous years, teachers made the choices, or there were no real choices because all students had to eventually take all classes.

School Size, Staff, and Standards

Janice is a good example of a student who enters high school with interests, friends, and skills that can be recognized in the adolescent years. She has had inclusive family experiences and community involvement and can help plan her own program. Janice can enter a comprehensive high school with little extra support and probably be a functioning member of her school in a short time. Keeping expectations and standards high for her can be a challenge, as students and teachers can be easily engaged with her social skills and warm personality. She will need to be pushed to take more challenging classes and stretch herself.

The sheer size of most high schools is an advantage, although this may be well disguised, initially. A school of 1,500 students may seem large for organizing a student's personal schedule, but it has potential natural supports in every class. Students with disabilities have access to many assistants, and many personalities and styles of support. The size of a high school also enables students to "fit in" in many different ways. It is hard work to stand out in a large high school; so much is going on every day that one must be truly unique to make a ripple in this large pond!

The instructional staff in high schools—though often preoccupied with discipline, crowd control, and content—are highly independent instructors who often solve problems and meet challenges every day in their classes with little or no contact with other teachers. Although there are teacher-teams, much of the day-to-day decision making is assumed by individual teachers. One teacher's expectations are merely the standard for that class and that period of time. Another teacher may hold to a totally different standard. This range of approaches—relatively rare in elementary and middle school settings—can provide incredible flexibility for designing the IEP and creating a personalized course of study in high school. Some uniformity may be helpful at times, but the range of approaches is a high school's true strength.

The movement from class to class allows great freedom for students—a step toward the real-life situations ahead for them. The protective climate of elementary and even middle schools is replaced with a genuine sense of what adult life will be like. The consequences of being late for class, for example, are essentially the same for all students, prompting Janice's sporadic, but positive behavior changes after she discovered how detentions limited her after-school social life and work time. In many ways, the continuation of segregated special education classes for students in high school is a great disservice to them.

EMBEDDING INCLUSION IN THE STRUCTURE OF SECONDARY SCHOOLS

Inclusive high school programs are designed to fit within the structure of the school: same class periods; choices for electives; physical education requirements; and optional extra periods for cocurricular activities such as band, orchestra, clubs, and newspaper. Three arrangements are listed below: supported services room, three-choice support schedule, and the house option (Montgomery, 1994).

The *supported services room* combines all the personnel and unit resources available to a school in one room. A school may have, for example, three resource teachers, two special class teachers, five instructional aides, a half-time speech-language pathologist, a half-time psychologist, and a half-time nurse. All of these specialists have their desks and files in one room, and students are scheduled to come to the support room during the day. Support teachers are there different times of the day, depending on their schedules for coteaching, counseling, and other instructional support activities. All personnel share all the students who have services through an IEP. Thus, a student receives services from the staff member who is scheduled at a certain time; it may or may not be the person who assessed the student for a service. This role-release format allows students to be scheduled to meet their needs, and they are not dependent upon the travel or administrative convenience needed by staff who have many responsibilities. Teachers are aware of all the students who have identified special needs, not just the ones on their caseload. Students may have support in their classroom through a coteaching arrangement or direct services. Staff must learn to rely on the expertise of their colleagues, and to trust that students can reach goals in many different ways (Rojewski, 1996).

The *three-choice support schedule* uses three choices for each student with special needs, rather than the traditional two choices—required and elective. The third choice is the subject area plus support—such as English support or math support. This support takes place in the special education classroom and occurs the hour before the regularly scheduled class, the hour after the regularly scheduled class, or both. In this way, the student can receive preteaching, reteaching, or both to facilitate learning in a required class. Students with special needs must be scheduled into a program that includes a regular homeroom and one to two electives, plus required classes that are preceded or followed by time in the special education room. Note that this is not a special education class that students leave to go "out to regular education." Quite the opposite, it is a third option for students who need support. Exhibit 12–1 displays a typical schedule for a student in this arrangement.

The *house option* is referred to as "houses" or "tribes" or a similar term describing an arrangement in which students are assigned to a large student grouping and remain with these assigned groups throughout high school. These groupings consist of 100 to 200 students with four to five teachers, and a counselor or support educator. Often, one special education teacher and an aide are assigned as well, and students with special needs make up about 10% of the group (10 to 20 students). Each house has a name; elects a gov-

Exhibit 12–1 Typical Third Option Schedule

Period One	Supported Math
Period Two	Math
Period Three	Supported Math
Period Four	Music
Period Five	English
Period Six	Supported English
Period Seven	Creative Dramatics
Period Eight	Physical Education

Note: The next semester, the student might require less support in math and add another class, or not take a math class at all and add Experiments in Chemistry with one period of support and one other class in computers.

erning body, which includes the mentor coordinator; and handles all of its own decisions, social events, and competitions with other houses. Teachers remain with the students throughout the three or four years of high school and serve as their advisors and guides. Students with special needs are assigned to classes within the house, and natural supports and peer assistance are developed by the house for each member. All students within a house are responsible for their own activities and well-being as well as for the other members of this school family. Teachers have a common planning time, and they know the same group of 100 plus students for an extended period of time. This arrangement builds highly efficient problem-solving techniques, in which students and teachers can brainstorm new approaches that help the student and the house members.

SCHEDULES FOR STUDENTS AND STAFF

Scheduling students into classes each year is a critical component of comprehensive high schools. The larger the student population and the greater the number of class choices available, the larger the task of matching students with classes. Many schools have replaced hand scheduling with computers, speeding up the process considerably. Schools of 1,000 or more students who change classes more than three times per day require about three days devoted to scheduling by computer each semester. Although software programs vary, each one allows educators to set their own class-conflict criteria. These criteria identify class conflicts of time, subject, room, teacher, level, or any other variables entered by the schedulers.

Inclusive schools typically follow one of two approaches in scheduling, depending upon the amount of time, options, and experience they have with computer-assisted scheduling. One approach is to hand schedule all students with special needs first; the second approach is to schedule all students together, allowing all class conflicts to be resolved by

hand. High schools report no particular advantages to either approach; they merely need to make the decision whether to put extra time in before or after the computer scheduling is completed. It is a good idea to try both approaches, since choosing a system perceived to be superior may improve staff attitudes about scheduling even though the actual work involved is unchanged.

Another variable has been added to scheduling by inclusive high school teams who wish to create planning times. An extra 15 to 30 minutes can be created at the beginning of each day as an extended homeroom period. If 3 minutes is taken from six time periods, 18 minutes can be set aside each day for teacher planning time. All teachers can plan during this time, and many can plan together for their inclusive classroom responsibilities. This extra period of time for everyone guarantees some student bonding time, a chance for announcements or special events, and a built-in study hall every day before classes begin for those who need it to complete work or study for a test. The real bonus is added when teachers in one grade level take over classes in another grade level—creating groups of students in their homerooms—for one trimester, semester, or grading period. Teachers cover their colleagues' classes during this homeroom/study time so that an entire grade level of teachers can plan together every morning for approximately eight or nine weeks. This type of scheduling makes coteaching possible, builds in team planning, and encourages monitoring and instructional adjustments as requested. When creating schedules, inclusive schools build in a planning time for everyone in the high school setting. Although it can also be done at elementary grade levels, this planning time is one of the definitive markers of successful inclusive schools at the secondary level.

ASSESSMENT AND TESTING PRACTICES IN SECONDARY PROGRAMS

Secondary education features more tests, assessments, and barrier measurements than all eight previous years of schooling. Students take many internal tests (e.g., grade-level standardized tests, physical education qualifiers, and honor society qualifiers) and external tests (e.g., PSAT, SAT, and language competency exams).

Students with exceptional needs in inclusive schools must deal with these barrier tests to the extent appropriate for each individual. The various tests and the student's graduation goals are planned during the IEP meeting, beginning in the middle school years. All the team members and the student and his or her family members can take part in the discussion and weigh the advantages of various exams or standards. Accommodations and modifications should be discussed and planned for. Student IEPs may also address test-completion skills for those students with a goal of succeeding on barrier tests. Student goals often change from meeting to meeting as the student experiences more or less success in school. Students with learning disabilities usually have lower expectations for themselves than typical high school students (Rojewski, 1996). This self-assessment adjusts several times during the high school experience as students attempt new classes, different levels of academic support, more cocurricular activities, and work-study programs.

The IEP should delineate the adjusted graduation standards; attainment of credits, diploma options, and appropriate examinations; and planned completion process. For some students, graduation is a feasible goal in five years or more, instead of the usual four. For others, a certificate of completion or special education diploma is more appropriate. Sometimes a minimal number of units or credits is required for a diploma, certificate of completion, or similar accounting such as Carnegie Units. Transition planning will accompany this graduation planning, addressing community experiences, employment, and postschool adult living, in addition to instruction. Chapter 14 offers further discussion of transition.

INCLUSIVE PRACTICES IN HIGH SCHOOL PROGRAMS

Many different inclusive practices are used in high schools. A few examples are illustrated in the student stories in this chapter. Six practices are discussed below:

1. literacy as a focal point
2. episodic learning activities
3. technology
4. grading options and measuring progress
5. grouping strategies
6. coteaching

Literacy As a Focal Point

Literacy, as broadly defined, is reading, writing, spelling, listening, and thinking (Montgomery, 1994). Literacy is the main emphasis of elementary education but is often abandoned if students have not exhibited reading skills by the end of fourth grade. Yet, for some students, the purpose and functions of literacy are not clear until much later in their academic careers. The literature on adult illiteracy has shown that many persons are able to learn to read much later in life, often taught by untrained volunteers, when the functions and uses of literacy take on new and intensified meaning. Students who are nonreaders in high school face severe limitations in educational and vocational options after formal schooling ends. Literacy can remain a goal for many students with severe disabilities throughout high school, increasing the emphasis on meaningful print in classes,

schedules, maps, charts, graphic arts, designs, patterns, logos, cocurricular activities, social events, leisure activities, and life work skills.

Inclusive high schools refocus students on literacy skills and anticipate that many who used reading and writing to a very limited degree before will increase their comprehension and reliance upon print materials. The typical high school student reads and writes more in the last four years of school than in all the previous years combined. It makes sense that the student with disabilities should have the same increased literacy experiences in high school.

Todd, Janice, Chris, and Lisa all had literacy goals and objectives on their IEPs for high school. All of them made significant gains in literacy in the formative high school years when reading, writing, spelling, listening, and thinking skills were intensified in their interactions with their peers. (See Chapter 18 for further discussion of accommodations in the general education classroom that support students with reading difficulties.)

Episodic Learning Activities

There are two fundamentally different ways to learn a new verbal task: episodic and semantic (Baddeley, 1990). From birth to the age of nine years or so, all children are episodic learners. Learning takes place when the child actively engages in an activity (e.g., learning to skate by skating, learning to fish by fishing, learning to play chess by moving the pieces around the board). Children cannot learn simply by watching someone else; they must try and fail several times until they can claim it as one of their skills. This is time consuming, and requires lots of hands-on materials, supervision, and guided practice. It is also a lot of fun!

After the age of nine or so, children can learn through semantic methods. That is, they can learn from reading about something, asking questions, watching a video, interviewing someone else, and so forth. Their learning potential is extended greatly, because they can learn from the experiences of others and do not have to do it all themselves. At school, this means the curriculum can expand beyond community helpers and math that can be seen and touched, into studies of countries, cultures, and concepts that cannot be verified by touching them or engaging in the activity. The semantic learner can move swiftly from one new learning experience to another and read stories, reports, and fact books to verify what is assumed from one source to another.

Some students with disabilities remain at the episodic level of learning well into high school or beyond. They must physically verify new learning by actively doing something—growing the plant when studying the life cycle of vegetation, jumping the broad jump five times and measuring the distance of each jump to determine the number that means an average jump, or making a medieval castle out of construction materials to absorb the idea of construction of offensive and/or defensive fortifications for armies on foot. The episodic learners will need opportunities to learn and demonstrate their new understandings with such activities. The entire class does not need to engage in the same activity. It may be a single group, a representative from each work group, or even one or two students who create something that other students are learning about through research. In this way, their activity can be shared with the whole class and serve as an extension activity for some and a critical learning activity for others.

Episodic learning activities include music, art, painting, field trips, locating materials and artifacts, costumes, drama, and construction of models or schema. Activities can cross disciplines and be completed in multiple classes, or they can be completed within one class, depending upon the planning time devoted to this practice. Teachers have found that episodic learning activities are easier to do the second time, when time and materials can be estimated from experience.

Chris and Janice both benefited greatly from episodic learning activities in the classroom.

Technology

Most high schools have a wide range of technology. This can boost the opportunities for inclusive practices. Audiovisual equipment, computers, management information systems, and interactive media can extend the classroom into the immediate community and the world. Some technology will be valuable at the individual level, providing augmentative and alternative communication systems for students who cannot speak or write due to a disability. Some technology will speed up the reading and writing process for students who are unable to search for words easily, have a limited vocabulary, edit poorly, spell poorly, can attend for short periods of time, or turn in very few written products.

Using technology in the classroom can involve some students who do not respond without it or would not be motivated without it. Nonreaders can follow the textbook material if there are passages of print on audiocassettes, videotapes of the concepts presented in the book, or CD ROM or hypercard stacks with graphics available. This technology can be critical in classes that are heavily content loaded, where a student with mild learning disabilities cannot keep up with the volume of work or the quick jumps from topic to topic. Many teachers use the technology to highlight the important points in the readings and hold non-reading students responsible for only the material in videos or audios that they can review again before a test. Other teachers have students prepare content-based technology for a class project instead of a written report, so that it can be used with students in the class who cannot read or write.

Lisa used technology to respond in the classroom and to complete her homework. Chris used several software programs in school that were purchased for him or designed for him by the students in the computer classes as their projects.

Grading Options and Measuring Progress

Grading in inclusive high schools is probably one of the greatest barriers educators have to overcome (Montgomery, 1994). Grades take on new meaning in high school. They are no longer merely a number or letter for parents to ascertain progress compared to the rest of the class. In high school, grades determine if a student is eligible for athletics, assembly programs, schoolwide honors, extracurricular activities, college acceptance, scholarships, and eventually job interviews and letters of recommendation. Grades suddenly matter. There is little time left to earn them, and each year brings the student closer to the point after which low grades can no longer be averaged out by other high grades. Should students with disabilities be held to the same standards for grades? The answer is . . . sometimes.

For some students, adjustments to the grading practice will be needed. The most important part of grading practices for students in inclusive high schools is careful recording of the modifications on the IEP. This statement allows the team to modify in any way that suits the needs of the student, teachers, and the school. Without this statement, grades can be misinterpreted as following the same criteria as the rest of the high school. If adjustments are not needed, the statement is unnecessary.

Modifications can be made in a number of different ways (Montgomery, 1994). Some schools use pass/no pass for students. Others use averaged grades that reflect a grade from the special education support teachers and another grade from the classroom teacher. These are averaged, and the student is awarded a grade that reflects both effort and achievement. Another popular method is a percentage system that assigns a certain percentage of the grade to each task that makes up the grade. For example, attendance could be 30% of the grade, the project 5%, answering questions in class 25%, and the highest quiz score 20%, with homework as the remaining 20%. This breakdown could correspond to what the student is most capable of handling so that actual progress could be counted. The percentages are changed each report card period if needed, so that students can gradually increase their levels of responsibility. Classes have different percentage systems, depending on the types of work expected and the student's performance level.

Some high schools like to use a daily student grade. At the end of each class, a grade is recorded for the student reflecting his or her work during that period of time. This gives the student a new opportunity each day to exceed his or her performance of the previous day. If the grading period is 45 days, the student will receive 45 individual grades that may reflect several very poor days as well as several excellent ones. This start-over-with-a-clean-slate approach can make a difference for students with erratic behavior and a tendency to give up when things start to slide for them.

Group grades are possible in some classes. If students work in groups, they can each give a grade to the other person(s) in their group in a confidential envelope to the teacher. The teacher can add a grade of his or her own and average the grades, to assign a grade (or all the grades) to the student. This technique is typically used for all the students in the class. In this way, students are more responsible to their peers. The pressure of knowing that their peers are grading them can make a big difference in high school.

Contracts are excellent ways to measure progress and award grades in high school. This method has been used in postsecondary programs for students with learning disabilities in college. Students make an appointment with the teacher or professor, bringing a rubric that includes the work already outlined for class and a suggested modification of it for a negotiated grade. For example, the teacher requests five written book reports, a written out-of-class project, one field trip write-up, three quizzes, and a research project with a partner in the class on an assigned topic. The student can propose that he will do two written book reports; complete the out-of-class project; take all three quizzes but count only the two best scores; have the field trip write-up be a map, chart, or diagram; and do the three extra graphics for someone else's research project in class. The student would complete all of this for a grade of C. If he did all of the work, he would not receive a grade less than C; if he did not, he would receive a C-, D, or F. If he exceeded the teacher's expectations for this contract, he could receive a grade higher than a C. This is an empowering technique; it requires some advance work with counselors, mentors, or teachers and some "selling" on the part of the student. The altered rubric is attractive to some teachers because it can be negotiated back and forth until it is acceptable to both parties. It has an extra element of fairness, because it can be offered to anyone in class who wants to design an individual rubric for themselves and present it to the teacher for agreement. This method is highly effective for students who seem overwhelmed by the work until they feel they have some control over the outcome.

In the student examples given earlier, Lisa received individual contract grades, while Todd and Janice used percentage systems.

Grouping Strategies

Classes can be grouped internally using three methods: skill groups, friendship groups, and random groups.

Skill groups are composed of all the students who cannot perform the needed skill. This is the most common way for teachers to group. Each group of three to six students is assembled based on what they cannot do. Although it is easy to target the instruction, it is labor-intensive on the part of the teacher, who must move from group to group without the benefit of any of the participants modeling for others.

Friendship groups are composed of students who have selected one another as learning partners. The class is told to divide into groups based on who the students want to work with. Tasks are assigned to students who enjoy working with one another, like the social time it affords, and will work hard to stay in the room and stay engaged rather than be separated from their buddies. In each group, some students are quite good at a task, while others need help. Students typically help one another to get the work done so that they can stay together as long as possible, especially if the teacher states that this activity will occur more often or every week if it is successful. It is one of the best ways to accomplish work that seems insurmountable when students are struggling with it alone.

There are disadvantages of friendship groups, too. These groups create a very noisy, social environment. Some time will be spent in chatter instead of work. Some students may not be picked for friendship groups, and they may wander around by themselves or work alone. This may happen to students with special needs and cause additional problems in class. Some teachers stay active in the process of selecting friendship groups and ask students to be in the teacher's group; or they may ask a few sensitive students ahead of time to look around and ask unattached students to join their group. Done often, the friendship groups coalesce in different ways, and many students are included in ways teachers did not anticipate.

The *random group* approach is also effective for students of all skill levels. The teacher decides ahead of time who should be in each group. Students are matched for skills, tasks, and products so that there is a mixture of talents in the group to accomplish as much as possible. The random group only *looks* random to the students; in fact, it is carefully planned. Sometimes the teacher calls out names for the group; sometimes students are given words to match up, pieces to add to a riddle or puzzle, or some type of content-based "tag" to use to seek out their group mates. This approach requires considerable advanced planning by the teacher but results in highly coordinated work groups that use the talents of all students. After a few tries, a highly effective combination of students can be drawn together for the remainder of the semester.

Grouping strategies in inclusive schools tend toward friendship and random groups, and rely less on skill groups and total group instruction. Lisa was unable to work in skill groups and preferred to work alone most of the time. She could handle random groups if she was told exactly what her role was each time. She frequently lost patience with other students in the group and got angry at herself, biting her hands and growling. Todd loved friendship groups and worked extra hard to be seated near a friend or be placed in a group with friends. Janice seemed to work equally well with all types of grouping, but needed the group to help her complete any assigned work. Students often did her work for her, until they began using group grading techniques.

Coteaching

One of the most effective strategies for inclusive schools is coteaching, or team teaching (Dalheim, 1994). Teachers can combine their expertise in the same classroom and provide an ideal learning environment for all students. Some teachers like to use a "one teach, one drift arrangement," with one teacher providing instruction and the second supporting student work by being in the classroom to assist students directly. Some like to use station or parallel teaching, in which groups of students are organized around topics or projects, with teachers moving back and forth to provide instruction to small groups of students. Everyone has greater access to the teacher in this model, and students who need support—regardless of whether they have disabilities—can receive it easily.

Some teachers like to teach side-by-side in the classroom, holding a dialogue for students to see and hear, responding to cues and ideas from one another, and building on the excitement that two people can provide for a whole class (Ciborowski, 1992). When a special educator and general educator coteach, students can benefit from the instructional expertise of the special educator and the discipline expertise of the general educator. Different teaching styles can be accommodated with time, and students gain from another adult's approach to the same topic in the same class.

Team teaching, in any one of the forms listed here, takes planning, trust, and a willingness to give up control of some aspects of the classroom. Coteachers say that this method becomes easier as the subject matter is better known to both teachers. Modifications can be made on the spot for students, and teachers can model alternative ways of knowing for the class. This results in grading and measuring progress in new and more authentic ways.

A LOOK INSIDE AN INCLUSIVE HIGH SCHOOL CLASSROOM

Using two teachers in a coteaching situation changes the class dynamics significantly. Consider the following example from a class of 45 secondary school students. Four students in the class have been identified with special needs, including Michael with a severe asthmatic condition,

Rachel with moderate cerebral palsy who uses a walker, and Carol and Tuan—two students with mild to moderate developmental and learning disabilities. This conforms to the notion of natural proportions in the environment with approximately 10% of the students in a class with exceptional needs. Of course, many more students in this inclusive environment benefit from support in the curriculum offered by the coteachers (Hobson & Shuman, 1990). The general education teacher is a curriculum expert in U.S. history, while the special educator is highly skilled in alternative strategies and instructional support. This combination offers support to a wide variety of students and uses the strengths of the teachers and the class as a whole. The required curriculum remains the same, while the instructional strategies incorporate approaches, materials, and products that the students with special needs can use. A lesson on the causes of the American Revolution can be appreciated through the following sample of the students' interactions with one another and the dialogue with the teachers.

> *General Education (GE) Teacher:* For homework last night, you read Chapter 10 in the textbook. What do you think the author meant in that chapter? Why do you think the English king demanded that the taxes be collected in the New World and then sent to the House of Lords?

> *Rachel:* I think he misunderstood the colonists' intentions. The King thought they would be returning to England some day and would support the government and the maintenance of the army.

> *James:* Clearly, the King hadn't visited the colonies. He would have sensed the spirit of separateness and independence they already felt.

> *Carol:* I think the King should come to visit the new England. Then he would like the colonists and not fight them.

> *Special educator (SE):* Carol has an idea. Why didn't the King make a visit? Was it possible? Do a one-minute "quick share" with your neighbor and talk about this idea. Write your ideas down so you will remember them for our discussion.

> *(One to two minutes pass while students talk to one another, some in twos and some in larger groups while they remain in their seats. Tuan gets up and goes over to sit near a friend. They talk.)*

GE: Okay, one minute is up. We'll do a "whip around" to share our ideas. Be ready to respond quickly or to point to someone else who can take your turn.

GE walks up and down rows and points to students randomly as ideas are expressed. James and Carlos give answers. Danielle points to someone else when it is her turn. She repeats what that person says as her turn. At other times, she gives an answer on her own.

Tuan: The King could never visit. It would take months to come over on a boat and meet people here. There were no telephones, either. That's crazy.

SE: What would happen to his kingdom if he was gone for a year or more?

Carol: Some other king would take over his country.

Tricia: These people were not communicating. They didn't even have good ways to pass news back and forth across the ocean. Either they were going to have to agree to be separate countries, or they were going to have to fight it out.

Jason: The colonists were really bummed about the taxes. They were not going to send their money to England. It wouldn't matter who decided to visit them.

GE: I hear you saying that two causes of the Revolutionary War might be a lack of a means of communication and taxation without representation. The colonists were willing to fight to decide those issues if they had to.

SE: Did the author give us any hints about where the war was likely to be fought? Who would send troops where? What do you think? Why? One of the essay questions on the Friday quiz will center on these issues. Take 10 minutes now and practice writing a cogent statement of the forces at work here. Those of you who wish to can draw a chart or graph and be ready to defend it. The map skills group needs to come to the front of the room to work out their answers with Mrs. M. now. As soon as you finish your written argument, begin reading the assignment for tomorrow on pages 238–245. If you are an assigned tutor for this week, plan to get together with your tutoring partner. Service points for tutoring will be collected at the end of the week. Any questions? Okay, begin.

This actual classroom scene reveals a number of strategies to advance curriculum and increase the likelihood that students with special needs will acquire new understanding and new learning in an inclusive environment. The coteachers used questioning the author (Viadero, 1994), alternative products (Montgomery, 1995), quick share (Montgomery, 1995), "whip around," peer tutoring, and open-ended questioning designed to teach, not to test the students (Viadero, 1994). Secondary school teachers know their subject material well and can structure and restructure their questioning sessions to help all students to find meaning in facts and content. This is critical for students who are nonreaders and cannot access the information from the textbook. Although lessons and strategies vary each day, teachers and students actively support each other's learning, and the curriculum remains intact (Hardin & McNelis, 1996). Teachers supporting one another and keeping standards high for all students require creative teaching, and continual monitoring and adjusting for individual needs. All students in this class were able to demonstrate their new learning on the Friday quiz. The products ranged from well-crafted, written essays, to symbol charts, to dictated sentences.

ARE YOU USING INCLUSIVE PRACTICES IN YOUR HIGH SCHOOL?

A series of questions that form the basis for a self-assessment of a school's inclusive practices through the eyes and ears of a teacher or administrator is found in Exhibit 12–2. The questionnaire is divided into sections on *what we say, what we do, and what we believe.* The self-assessment can be used several times to provide a benchmark of where a particular high school program is at one point, and where it is after implementing new strategies or scheduling.

The first two sections of the self-assessment refer to teacher and staff actions, and the third section is an assessment of values and beliefs. The number of "yes" answers should gradually increase in the first two sections as schools move toward more inclusive programming. The third section is designed to encourage open discussion on controversies associated with inclusive education—issues focused on beliefs, values, and personal experiences with high school students. The questions in this section do not have right or wrong answers; instead they serve as a barometer of feelings, attitudes, and comfort level within inclusive high schools. A staff person may want to address one statement each month at a staff meeting, or during an inservice or planning day. Responses from students—both general and special education—would also be revealing.

Exhibit 12–2 Are We Using Inclusive Practices? Participant Self-Assessment

Please respond by marking YES or NO for each statement. Add up the number of YES responses and write the score at the bottom. Do not write your name on the assessment.

WHAT DO WE SAY?

Y   N   Do students and staff in your building use people-first language at all times?

Y   N   Do clerical staff in your building use people-first language at all times?

Y   N   Do all the teachers, support staff, and clerical staff act and talk as though they were responsible for all the children in your building?

Y   N   Can *most* of the teachers in your building describe inclusion as an educational concept?

Y   N   Can *most* of the teachers in your building describe three or more inclusive practices that they use in their classrooms?

Y   N   Could *all* teachers and support personnel name at least two students in their building who have moved from more restrictive to less restrictive environments?

Y   N   Do you have a clearly articulated vision for your school that celebrates all children's gifts, and is it boldly printed in a highly visible place in your school?

WHAT DO WE DO?

Y   N   Do at least 50% of your classrooms include students who would have been in self-contained settings two or more years ago?

Y   N   Are there teacher (or adult) organized programs in your building designed to teach students to be effective peer tutors?

Y   N   Are included students in your building serving on the student council, involved in school-wide student government, writing for the school newspaper, or taking part in any aspect of site-based management or student management teams?

Y   N   Do the teachers and staff at each grade level keep track annually of students from your community who are educated in other schools?

Y   N   Have your general and special education staff agreed on appropriate grading systems for all students in your building?

Y   N   Are there five or more books, articles, or teacher instruction guides about inclusion in the teachers' workroom or lounge today?

Y   N   Are all students in your building within two chronological years of the rest of the students in their assigned classes?

WHAT DO YOU BELIEVE?

- What do you believe about assessment procedures? Do you believe they are more damaging than helpful to students?
- What do you believe about the cost of educating children with special needs? Do you believe that it costs more? Less?
- What do you believe about the skills of general educators and special educators in working with students with exceptional needs? Do you believe that these two groups of educators are equally skilled?
- What do you believe to be the effect of the use of categorical labels for children? Do you believe they inevitably have negative consequences?
- What do you believe about children learning from other children and learning from adults? Do you believe they learn more quickly from other children?
- What do you believe about the choices parents should be given about special or general education placements for *all* their children?

Inclusive practices require constant vigilance, updating, and individualization to be useful to the staff and students in that school. High schools have an opportunity to enlarge the world for a student with disabilities and to extend a warm welcome into an inclusive community. The high school should serve all students equally—as the final step out of compulsory educational preparation and into the world of work or postsecondary programs.

REFERENCES

Baddeley, A.D. (1990). *Human memory: Theory and practice.* Oxford, England: Earlbaum.

Ciborowski, J. (1992). *Textbooks and the students who can't read them.* Cambridge, MA: Brookline.

Dalheim, M. (Ed.). (1994). *Toward inclusive classrooms* (Teacher to Teacher Series). Washington DC: National Education Association.

Ellis, H.C., & Hunt, R.R. (1993). *Fundamentals of cognitive psychology* (5th ed.). Madison, WI: Brown & Benchmark.

Hardin, D.E., & McNelis, S.J. (1996). The resource center: Hub of inclusive activities. *Educational Leadership, 53*(5), 41–43.

Hobson, E., & Shuman, R.B. (1990). *Reading and writing in high schools* (Analysis and Action Series). Washington DC: National Education Association.

Hoskins, B. (1995). *Developing inclusive schools.* Bloomington, IN: CASE Research Committee.

Montgomery, J.K. (1994, September/October). Supporting inclusive education: Program models, classroom practices, grading options. *The Special Edge.* Sacramento, CA: California Department of Education.

Montgomery, J.K. (1995). *Facing the challenge of inclusion: A resource guide for teachers.* Torrance, CA: The Education Center.

Rojewski, J.W. (1996). Educational and occupational aspirations of high school seniors with learning disabilities. *Exceptional Children, 62*(5), 463–476.

Schumacher, J.B., & Deshler, D. (1995). Secondary classes can be inclusive, too. *Educational Leadership, 52*(4), 50–51.

Viadero, D. (1994). Why textbooks often baffle students. *Education Week, 13*, 31–34.

CHAPTER 13

Vocational Education: Options To Meet the Varying Needs of Students

Diane C. Elliott, Pamelia Luttrull, and Sharon H. deFur

Senior English teacher: So Bill, what are your career plans for next year?

Bill (who had played varsity basketball): I think I will play professional basketball. But, if that doesn't work out, I'll get a full-time job that pays well.

INTRODUCTION

Teachers often face students with unrealistic or undefined career goals. Teachers of students with disabilities can only wonder how much success their students with low academic abilities, and little or no work experience, will have in their future. Vocational education can be the path that allows these students to learn the necessary skills to be successful in the adult working world. Including students with disabilities in vocational education not only offers students important employment skills, but also provides experiences that build confidence and a sense of self-worth. Vocational training and high school work experience correlate positively with success in the adult world (Kohler, 1994). By law, vocational education must be offered to students with disabilities in the least restrictive environment, with students receiving needed accommodations, supports, and supplemental services.

Increasingly, students with disabilities are participating in vocational education. This fact offers promises of increasingly skilled workers with disabilities—but, with the opportunity, come challenges. The high skills demanded in the general education curriculum transfer to vocational education. So as the standards increase for all students, there is a risk of widening the gap between students with disabilities and students without disabilities. This chapter explores the opportunities and the challenges of including students with disabilities in vocational education programs.

VOCATIONAL EDUCATION AS AN INCLUSION OPPORTUNITY

Legislative History

Educators and administrators may find the evolution of the participation of students with disabilities in vocational education instructive in understanding current policies and practices of inclusion in vocational education. The purpose of vocational education is to prepare students for lifelong learning, to provide skills for gainful employment, and to teach the general academic skills needed to be successful in the adult world. Vocational education, espousing these purposes, began with the Smith-Hughes Act of 1917. A long history and policy of trade, agriculture, and manual training preceded this act and influenced an evolving educational philosophy, which was that the United States wanted educated workers and not just skilled laborers. The Smith-Hughes Act established a partnership among federal, state, and local governments in the administration of vocational education programs that continues today. Thus began the role of federal policy in regulating vocational programs (Sarkees-Wircenski & Scott, 1995).

Forty-six years later, students with disabilities were formally offered access to vocational training in response to the Vocational Education Act of 1963. This law stipulated that people with disabilities could be included in vocational training with nondisabled peers, and it required that specific moneys be directed for this purpose. In reality, little funding was used to promote vocational education for special populations as a result of this legislation. Nonetheless, the Vocational Education Act of 1963 established legal access to training programs for all people according to their interests, needs, and abilities. The law served primarily to focus attention on the need to provide vocational education opportunities for people with academic, socioeconomic, or other disabilities (Sarkees-Wircenski & Scott, 1995). In an effort to ensure that students with special needs receive vocational education, policy makers required that states set aside funds to provide vocational training for those who were disabled or disadvantaged in the Vocational Education Act Amendments of 1968 (P.L. 90-576). Furthermore, these amendments discouraged separate programming for students with disabilities or for students who were disadvantaged. Thus, vocational education policy for students with disabilities has a long legislative history of promoting inclusive educational settings.

Two other laws that were passed in the 1970s strengthened the participation of students with disabilities in vocational education. Access to vocational education programs by students with disabilities was supported by the Education for All Handicapped Children Act (P.L. 94-142) in 1975. By law, the general education environment became the instructional environment of choice unless a student's needs suggested a more restrictive setting. Two years earlier, Section 504 of the Rehabilitation Act Amendments (P.L. 93-112) was signed into law. This law made exclusion from programs, such as vocational education, a violation of civil rights. Any program that received federal funds was subject to the requirements of this law; failure to comply threatened the loss of federal funding. Following the enactment of this law, the number of students with disabilities in vocational education programs increased by 66% from 1973 to 1978 (Clark & Kolstoe, 1990).

Several subsequent pieces of legislation extended these basic rights. The Carl D. Perkins Vocational Education Act (P.L. 98-524) of 1984 provided assurances that special populations would be allowed equal access to vocational education with the provision of accommodations or supplemental services necessary for success. The Perkins Act was also designed to improve the quality of vocational education programs with the goal of providing students with the marketable skills needed to improve productivity and promote economic growth (Sarkees-Wircenski & Scott, 1995). In 1990, this law was amended and renamed the Carl D. Perkins Vocational Education and Applied Technology Act (P.L. 101-392). The requirement to set aside funds for special populations was eliminated in this legislation. This act challenged states to increase the academic and technical standards of vocational education for all students, including students with disabilities.

The Americans with Disabilities Act of 1990 (ADA) (P.L. 101-336) changed the potential employment outlook for people with disabilities. ADA guarantees equal opportunities for persons with disabilities in employment, public accommodations, transportation, state and local government services, and telecommunications. ADA expanded the civil rights requirements gained under Section 504 to include the private sector. Thus, the policies regarding opportunities for individuals with disabilities from the 1960s through the 1980s came together to ensure access to training and employment.

Furthermore, the Education for All Handicapped Children Act was amended in 1990 and renamed the Individuals with Disabilities Education Act (IDEA) (P.L. 101-476). Significantly, this act established the requirements for transition planning, including the development of employment objectives, instruction, and community experiences for students age 16 and older (and younger, when appropriate). Vocational education has been a prominent factor in the transition planning efforts for youths with disabilities (for more information about transition and inclusive education, see Chapter 14). Exhibit 13–1 summarizes related federal legislation that supports the participation of students with disabilities in vocational education programs.

Education policy is ever-changing. In the mid-1990s, Congress is attempting to consolidate federal employment training policies and funding. Vocational education legislation will change again. Nonetheless, the civil rights gained for individuals with disabilities are established as essential components of all future legislation. Advocates, however, must continue to monitor legislative changes to ensure that past assurances and protections remain.

Vocational Education Options

Vocational education traditionally involves a variety of formats representing seven occupational clusters: home economics; industry and trade; business education; agriculture; marketing; health occupations; and technology education. Vocational education can focus on defined skills such as typing, bookkeeping, or life-management classes, or it can offer comprehensive training through a completer program (a program that takes two or three years to complete in a curriculum sequence) in a variety of technical skill areas such as auto mechanics, electronics, or multimedia productions.

Vocational programs, planned carefully, offer multiple exit stages that correlate with the student's aptitudes, interests, and long-term goals. For example, in a drafting program, two years of training at the high school level will give the student basic knowledge in civil, architectural, or mechanical engineering. The student would be able to enter the work force with knowledge of all the rules and regulations of drafting. An articulated two-year, postsecondary training program in the drafting sequence would enable the student to receive more specialized training in mechanical or architectural design, and to strengthen drafting skills. The student would then have the option of continuing with a

Exhibit 13–1 Selected Federal Legislation Supporting Participation in Vocational Education for Students with Disabilities

Year	Law	Overview
1963	Vocational Education Act (Public Law 88-210)	Stipulated that people with disabilities could be included in vocational training with nondisabled peers
1968	Vocational Education Act Amendments of 1968 (Public Law 90-576)	Set aside funds to provide vocational training for those who were handicapped or disadvantaged
1973	Rehabilitation Act Amendments of 1973, Section 503 and 504 (Public Law 93-112)	Section 503 requires employers receiving federal contracts to take affirmative action for individuals with disabilities; Section 504 prohibits discrimination on the basis of disability
1975	Education for All Handicapped Children Act (Public Law 94-142) (renamed IDEA in 1990)	Stipulates a free and appropriate education for all youths with disabilities
1984, 1990	Carl D. Perkins Vocational Education Act (Public Law 98–524); Carl D. Perkins Vocational Education and Applied Technology Act (Public Law 101-392)	Provides assurances that special populations would have equal access to vocational education with accommodations necessary for success
1990	Americans with Disabilities Act (Public Law 101-336)	Guarantees equal opportunities for persons with disabilities in employment, public accommodations, transportation, government services, and telecommunications
1990	Individuals with Disabilities Education Act (Public Law 101-476)	Mandates transition planning for students receiving special education who are 16 or older; such planning must include employment objectives, adult living objectives, instruction, and community experiences
1994	School to Work Opportunities Act (Public Law 103-239)	Provides funding for states to plan to develop school-to-work programs within high schools that include school-based learning, work-based learning, and connecting activities; specifies that students with disabilities must be included in programs funded under this act

four-year university program where the student could study to become an engineer. Vocational education can fully prepare students for successful and productive work experiences and rewarding careers. Today, vocational education prepares students to enter employment immediately upon leaving public school or to continue their education and training in postsecondary settings.

Of concern is the finding that students with disabilities may not access the full range of vocational program options (Lombard, Hazelkorn, & Neubert, 1992). Lombard et al. (1992) found that students with disabilities are most likely to enroll in technology education occupational clusters or in consumer education occupational clusters and least likely to enroll in health occupations or marketing. These choices may limit the employment options or advancement for students. Educators must ensure that vocational preparation choice is based on the student's aptitudes and interests in combination with the employment outlook of the adult community where the student will live and work. Too often, students with disabilities have been placed in vocational preparation classes based on space availability or the flexibility of the instructor.

Vocational Youth Organizations As Inclusion Opportunities

Social integration and full community participation symbolize success for adults with disabilities. In the school culture, extracurricular activities, service opportunities, and organizations provide experiences that promote the development of social and leadership skills. Students with disabilities are poorly represented in these school opportunities; when asked, they often report feeling disengaged from the social and organizational culture of schools. Vocational youth organizations offer a chance to counter this sense of isolation. Self-advocacy, self-awareness, and self-determination exemplify critical skills for success as adults for youths with disabilities.

Student organizations associated with vocational classes can help students acquire leadership, citizenship, occupational skills and knowledge, and public speaking skills. Skill competitions through student organizations enable students to perform activities studied in the classroom, thereby reinforcing their learning experiences. Becoming a member of a vocational student organization can provide the opportunity for students to develop a sense of belonging, meet new friends, and develop social skills. Vocational teachers can help students get involved by picking up on a student strength and encouraging the student to compete in a skill competition. High schools and vocational centers have various student organizations, and many require student participation as part of the vocational training. State and national organizations can help local school divisions start a local chapter of a particular student vocational organization. A list of related youth organizations is provided in Exhibit 13–2.

Keeping Up with Technological Advances

Challenges exist for vocational administrators in maintaining effective and up-to-date vocational education pro-grams. Businesses want future employees to be fully trained and ready to work. Maintaining current programs and information on employment trends is a continual challenge for vocational educators. Vocational advisory councils advise vocational education staff on programming issues as well as needs in specific job areas. Vocational education advisory councils consist of professional school staff, local employers, and business and industrial leaders. Other sources include parents, individuals with disabilities, and chamber of commerce members (Sarkees-Wircenski & Scott, 1995). The ongoing contact between school and business allows educators to keep their finger on the pulse of the community and current trends in employment.

In this technological age, when equipment can become obsolete within months of its initial appearance on the market, vocational educators may be forced by economics to use outdated equipment or technology. Consequently, vocational educators and policy makers continue to explore how to use on-site training at business and industry sites, where youths can be trained in the environment in which they may work. As a result, schools are increasingly looking to community work experiences and business partnerships for all students; these may become the classroom settings of the future in vocational training programs.

To be effective in guiding vocational transition planning, secondary teachers of students with disabilities must keep

Exhibit 13–2 Vocational Education Youth Organizations

NATIONAL SERVICES AREAS	YOUTH ORGANIZATIONS
Home economics	Home Economics Related Occupations (HERO) Future Homemakers of America (FHA)
Trade and industrial	Vocational Industrial Clubs of America (VICA)
Business education	Future Business Leaders of America (FBLA) Office Education Association (OEA) Future Secretaries of America (FSA) Future Data Processors (FDP)
Agriculture	Future Farmers of America (FFA) National Postsecondary Agricultural Student Organization (NPASO)
Marketing and distributive education	Distributive Education Clubs of America (DECA)
Health occupations	Health Occupations Student Association (HOSA)
Technical education	Technical Education Clubs of America (TECA) American Industrial Arts Student Association (AIASA)

Note: For more information about vocational student organizations, contact your local or state director of vocational education.

abreast of which jobs will be in demand in the future. State employment services prepare regular reports on the employment outlook by region and by state. In offering students with disabilities vocational education, some students may require a program that does not demand acquisition of all the competencies for the program area. For example, tire repairer, muffler installer, lube technician, and brake repairer are all jobs that can be "cut-out" from the auto mechanics competencies. However, before training a student in such specific skill areas, the teachers (special educators and vocational educators), parents, and student should work with local employment agencies to determine the need for such skilled workers.

A CONTINUUM OF INCLUSIVE VOCATIONAL EDUCATION

Similar to special education, vocational education options for students with disabilities span a continuum from full inclusion and participation in regular vocational education, with or without supports, to separate vocational special educational programs. In accordance with the student's individualized educational program (IEP), decisions regarding vocational education placement and programs are made in concert with the least restrictive environment principles. IEP decision making regarding vocational education can be effective only to the extent that the composition of the team reflects persons knowledgeable about the vocational education placement options and the demands of those settings, and to the extent that the team has adequate data about the needs, interests, preferences, and aptitude of the student and his or her future employment plans.

Regular Vocational Education without Special Education Support

One full inclusion option for students with disabilities in vocational education is for students to participate in vocational training programs and to follow the curriculum as designed without any alterations or adaptations. Many special education students, with adequately developed academic skills, can be successful in these programs. Being a vocational completer (i.e., completing the total sequence of courses for a vocational area) yields a vocational certificate from the program. Vocational education completers enjoy a higher probability of employment in their field of training. Fully inclusive models provide other advantages to the student. For example, most vocational programs provide either formal or informal assistance in placing students who have successfully completed their training into full-time or part-time jobs. This assistance in the employment search may include a job-placement program or job referral through the vocational instructor's contacts or recommendations.

Full inclusion classes provide students with close simulations of a real work environment. Another advantage is that students are provided the greatest level of socialization available with their peers who do not have disabilities. These characteristics promote the social integration skills that assist full participation in the adult work community.

Regular Vocational Education with Special Education or Related Services Support

Not all students with disabilities can be successful in a regular vocational program without modifications. The independent academic or behavior demands of the vocational program may exceed the student's proficiency due to his or her disability. For example, the text used in the class may prove too difficult to read and understand for some students with a significant reading disability, or the material may be presented at too fast a pace for students who take a longer time to master or integrate concepts. Although these students may have the aptitude for the technical vocational skill, their disability interferes with their demonstrating performance-based knowledge.

Special education accommodations or related services supports may provide the means to gain access to the general vocational curriculum for these students. These accommodations or related services would be developed as part of the student's IEP. Examples of accommodations include peer note taking, assessment accommodations, books on tape, peer tutoring, paraprofessional support, behavior management support, and assistive technology. IEP teams determine the need for specific accommodations, based on the student's present level of educational performance and long-term goals.

Changes in classroom and material content can be made, with input provided by the vocational education teacher. The vocational education teacher should assume the responsibility of instructing students in vocational content. The special education teacher can help the vocational teacher with the modification of instruction, texts, and tests to suit the individual needs of the student.

Technology is an ever-growing area. Assistive technology consists of devices that can remove or reduce barriers or obstacles to physical or cognitive performance. Technological advances include low-technology devices, such as a splint to enable a student to hold a tool correctly, and high-technology devices, such as voice-activated (instead of keyboard run) computers and electronic communication systems. The IEP team can seek consultation with specialists such as occupational or physical therapists, rehabilitation engineers, or technology specialists to provide guidance regarding the use of assistive technology.

Some vocational education programs have the luxury of employing a vocational support resource teacher. This professional often offers supplemental skills instruction, tutorial support, remediation, and vocational counseling to students with special needs, including students with disabilities. In addition, this professional can coordinate with special educators and other general educators in the planning and implementation of students' IEPs. Students may receive direct instructional support from the resource teacher, or the resource teacher might coteach with the vocational instructor. This professional possesses competencies that span both vocational education and special education.

Hazelkorn and Lombard (1991) recommend that special educators provide direct vocational instructional support strategies. They argue that this approach benefits vocational education teachers and has a positive effect on successful vocational education outcomes for students with disabilities. They cite supports within the vocational classrooms such as: "(a) attending class with students, (b) giving further explanations or demonstrations of activities, (c) assisting during lab sessions, and (d) providing hands-on help" (p. 15). These authors also cite three other collaborative techniques that have been effective for students with disabilities: cooperative learning, tutoring, and competency-based curricula.

Team teaching between vocational educators and special educators offers instructor support for the student with a disability. In this model, the vocational educator and the special educator work together to plan lessons and activities. In addition, the special education teacher may work directly with the students, giving further explanation or direct assistance with class activities. Having a second teacher in the room frees the vocational education teacher to work directly with students who need extra help mastering vocational competencies. A bonus benefit is that the special education teacher learns valuable information about the vocational curriculum by being present in the classroom, and the vocational teacher learns strategies for working with students with disabilities. Students benefit by having two teachers assist with the lessons. The stigma of special education is removed when both teachers work together side-by-side. This model allows for both professionals to use their areas of expertise—special educators in the learning process and vocational educators in their area of specialty.

Another model that includes two adults in the classroom is the use of a paraprofessional in the vocational class. A paraprofessional in the vocational classroom extends support to students and may allow the vocational teacher greater flexibility. Some students may actually require one-on-one support by an aide. For example, students with emotional or severe learning difficulties may profit from having an adult work one-on-one in the classroom with them. The paraprofessional can offer academic support by repeating or explaining instructions. The assistant can help the student stay on task, redirect behaviors, and provide immediate reinforcement or consequences. However, if appropriate, the IEP committee should develop a plan to decrease the student's dependence on a full-time aide and to help the student gain an acceptable level of independence for vocational education. The committee should discuss this plan for increased independence each time it meets.

Although paraprofessionals provide support to classroom instructors and students, they are not trained educators. In addition, teachers are seldom prepared with the skills to best use or to supervise paraprofessionals. Administrators can assist by establishing staff development for teachers and paraprofessionals to address these competency deficits; administrators can also facilitate the development of policies and procedures for supervising and role development between teachers and paraprofessionals. It is critical for the teacher and the paraprofessional to define roles and responsibilities within the classroom. A teacher and a paraprofessional who develop a rapport and recognize each other's role in a student's education form a winning team for educators and students.

Regular Vocational Education with Modified Competencies

In that vocational education is competency-based, the curriculum lends itself to systematic modification. Competencies can be identified and clustered for related occupations or occupational subsets. "Helper" or "cut-out" programs in vocational education can be created for students who do not have the academic ability to master all the competencies necessary to be certified in a vocational area, but who do have the skills to master some of the competencies. A helper program involves students in a program such as masonry, which does not have job titles to cut out from the competencies but has positions as a mason's helper. A person in a food service program may not have the skills to be a chef but could follow a program designed to be a cake decorator, salad bar attendant, or sandwich maker. Students would be instructed in the specific competencies required to be successfully employed in these areas.

Vocational Special Education

Separate vocational special education classes or programs are options for students whose disabilities are so severe as to require a different vocational curriculum than technical skill preparation. These vocational special education programs often focus on work-adjustment skills, employability skills, and vocational exploration. These programs alone do not represent integrated education. They are usually costly to maintain because of the required smaller class size, which results in duplication of instructors, physical setups, and equipment. Nonetheless, vocational special education programs provide many students with significant disabilities an opportunity to develop the prerequisite work behaviors and social skills, job-seeking skills, and job-keeping skills; too often the development of these skills is not integrated as a vital component of the regular vocational education program.

Least restrictive environment issues must be addressed before the IEP team recommends a separate vocational special education program. The argument in favor of vocational special education programming may be substantiated if it is a step in a process toward an inclusive, community-based vocational experience. Educators and IEP teams who decide to offer vocational special education in a separate setting need to address the next step toward community integration that this setting will promote.

Community-Based or Business Cooperative Instruction

Generalizing the skills taught in a classroom has long been an educational problem that in-the-field training helps to overcome. In-the-field training for vocational education includes community work experience with business or industry. Work experience options include paid, competitive employment; supported employment; and extended employment. Work experience for evaluation and training purposes may also include unpaid options. Students may participate in unpaid work experiences without violating the Fair Labor Standards Act if those experiences are for evaluation, exploration, or training for a limited amount of time; if an employee relationship is not established; and if the employer does not benefit in any way from the student performing within the business. Students may also volunteer as a way of exploring work experiences, but schools cannot require students to offer their labor services voluntarily. Educators are advised to consult the Fair Labor Standards Act in developing community-based or business cooperative programs. Students with disabilities who are participating in community-based work-experience programs must have these programs described in their IEPs.

Vocational education has offered all students opportunities to work and gain on-the-job training skills in business for many years through cooperative education or other work-study programs. Likewise, work-experience programs were implemented for students with mental retardation through vocational rehabilitation prior to the passage of the Education for All Handicapped Children Act of 1975. Interestingly, the follow-up research of the past decade of young adults with disabilities reveals that high school work experience, particularly paid work experience, correlates highly with employment after school exit. These facts, in combination with the requirement under IDEA that transition plans address community experiences, have resulted in an increase in the availability of community-based work experience to many students with disabilities. These vocational training options

afford an opportunity for individualized training designed around a student's needs, interests, and preferences.

Paid employment with school instruction can be provided through vocational classes such as marketing, office training, or trade and industrial training programs. Students, with or without the help of family members and friends, may find their own jobs, or special education personnel can facilitate the job search. A vocational rehabilitation counselor can assist in a job search for students who are eligible for vocational rehabilitation services. Paid employment in a business or industry has many benefits. For example, paid employment does not necessarily need formal agency or school supports. It also offers training in an environment that maximizes the student's level of independence. School personnel instruct and provide necessary supports (such as assisting with procedural problems on the job or helping a student think through social issues). Teachers can also facilitate communication between the employer and student when an issue arises. The greatest benefit occurs when the employer, the educators, and the student collaborate to identify needed skills and competencies to master while on the job.

Adolescents and young adults with emotional and behavioral problems face tremendous challenges in making successful employment transitions; the employment outcomes for these young adults are comparable to young adults with severe cognitive and physical limitations (Virginia Department of Education, 1993). According to Sitlington and Frank (1990) and Smith (1992), the traditional educational approach to preparing students with emotional disabilities has not been successful. In their research on postsecondary employment for students with emotional disabilities, Siegel, Robert, Waxman, and Gaylord-Ross (1992) found that when these students were afforded classroom instruction matched to on-the-job training, 40% of the students were successfully employed. Work programs offer a renewed promise for these youths, in that these programs are particularly positive learning experiences for students with behavioral problems.

In community-based, work-experience programs such as work-study or on-the-job training, the primary responsibility for instruction commonly belongs to the special education teacher, a work-study teacher, a cooperating community-based organization, vocational rehabilitation personnel, or a combination (Sarkees-Wircenski & Scott, 1995). Work-study consists of spending part of the day in the classroom and part of the day at a paid job under the supervision of the employer. The teacher periodically visits the work site to check on student progress. On-the-job training provides education and training experiences at a job site either for or without pay.

Frequently, school administrators express concern regarding the liability for students with disabilities working off campus. In establishing such programs, insurance and liability issues should be cleared through the school's insurance policy to ensure that students are covered in case of an accident. If a student is not employed by the business or industry where he or she is placed, then the student is not covered under the business's workers' compensation insurance policy; students involved in community work-experience programs should carry the extra school insurance typically offered to all students in the fall. Some special education programs provide this insurance coverage as a matter of course for participating students.

Transportation to and from work sites should be checked with school division policy. Options may include: students provide their own transportation, the school provides bus or car transportation, the student takes public transportation, volunteers with the school system provide transportation, a job coach provides transportation, or transportation is provided through any other creative and safe alternatives. Students with IEPs cannot be required to pay transportation costs if the community-based work experience is a part of the student's free and appropriate public education.

There is a strong argument that community-based instruction represents full inclusion and integration into the adult world (see Chapter 14). For some students, it also represents a first opportunity to experience success and pride in work.

Supported Employment Training

Supported employment offers people with severe disabilities the opportunity to perform meaningful work and receive pay. Supported employment is an appropriate option for those individuals with labels of mental retardation of varying degrees or with physical or sensory disabilities, autism, traumatic brain injury, or a history of mental illness.

Support is provided through a job coach or natural supports. A job coach works closely at the job site with primary responsibilities for teaching the student with disabilities (employee) to perform work tasks correctly with increasing speed and accuracy. The job coach may function secondarily in promoting self-discipline, discussing work problems, and correcting mistakes (Hagner, 1992). The employer often views the job coach as a positive presence within the workplace, because the employee is provided the immediate accessible support needed (Kregel, 1994). A job coach has a critical role in helping the worker with a disability identify, choose, and access needed supports.

According to Callahan (1992), an increasing number of researchers, supported employment specialists, and social commentators have urged the use of natural supports rather than supports from outside the natural setting for supported employment. A natural support is something or someone already present in the work environment that can be used to increase or sustain an employee's performance. An example of a natural support is an employee who notifies the worker who cannot tell time when the break is over. Natural supports are not necessarily specially constructed for an employee with a disability, but these supports can be identified where they occur naturally within the work culture (Moon, Inge, Wehman, Brooke, & Barcus, 1990). Natural supports on a job site may include providing more systematic support from supervisors than a worker without disabilities would receive, or assigning a mentor employee to help train the worker with a disability. A mentor employee is typically a veteran coworker who is willing to assist the worker with a disability in the daily routine as well as teach the "ins and outs" of the workplace, particularly the pattern of social interactions that already exists (Hagner, 1992). Helping a supported employee to be accepted and to be a social part of the workplace is difficult unless one of the following takes place: the mentor already works in the environment; if the mentor does not already work in the environment, he or she fits in quickly with the existing staff or is able to obtain the assistance of a veteran employee (Hagner, 1992).

Acquiring the social skills necessary to participate in the give and take of a work environment is as essential as learning how to perform the duties of the job. The use of a mentor employee can be of great help. Social skills are the key to a good interaction when dealing with people. By learning not only the skills of a trade, but also job-seeking and job-keeping skills, students will be better prepared to get and keep a job (Benz & Halpern, 1993). Such skills could include interviewing; handling personality conflicts; using appropriate language, dress, and manners on the job; and learning proper procedures for leaving a job.

Extended Employment Training

Extended employment, or sheltered workshop, is the most restrictive of work options. Extended employment is not provided through the public schools, but through outside agencies such as rehabilitation commissions, mental health and mental retardation agencies, or paid vendors. Sheltered workshops contract with local businesses and industries to provide production work for the employees at the shelter and occasionally in work enclaves. Workshop employment is provided at a site with constant supervision, and wages are paid on a piece-rate basis (i.e., workers are paid according to the amount of product produced). Typically, workers' earnings are minimal and insufficient to provide any level of independence. Many workshops now provide work sites that are outside the sheltered setting. Increasingly, these work settings are adopting a supported employment model for their workers. Sheltered workshops remain a choice in the vocational preparation continuum but, as with all special education considerations, IEP teams should identify the least restrictive environment when recommending extended employment training as a postsecondary employment outcome.

CHALLENGES TO INCLUSIVE VOCATIONAL EDUCATION PRACTICES

Disability-related education policy has promoted access to the general curriculum of education, including vocational education. Participation of students with disabilities in vocational education has increased over the past two decades. In Virginia, for example, approximately half of all secondary-aged students with disabilities participate in some form of vocational education (deFur, Getzel, & Kregel, 1995). Although greater access is evidenced by the increasing numbers of students with disabilities being served, there are still challenges that can prevent students with disabilities from receiving the maximum benefit of vocational education participation.

Erroneous assumptions about the demands of vocational education often contribute to failures for students with disabilities who participate in vocational education. For example, Evers and Bursuck (1994) reported that a common assumption that vocational education programs require a lower literacy level is not well-founded; in fact, technical classes require basic academic skills that are comparable to, or in some cases exceed, general academic classes. The authors concluded that students with academic learning disabilities will, in all probability, require support services to succeed in these classes.

Parents, students, and educators sometimes perceive vocational education as a second-class program, inferior to the general academic program. It may be necessary to convince them that vocational education promotes high standards for the student. Ask them to consider what comes to mind when they hear the term *vocational education*. Then ask them to consider the synonyms for *vocational* and the synonyms for *education*. Using Exhibit 13–3, ask them to combine any word in the first column with any word in the second column. Ask them to describe their reactions to these combinations.

Many of the combinations evoke strong and positive images (e.g., "professional literacy," "career direction," "employment scholarship," "specialist training"). Literally thinking in different terms may change one's perceptions of vocational education. Families sometimes create barriers to vocational programming for their son or daughter with a disability because they do not perceive vocational education as providing a route to the desired adult outcome for their child. This synonym exercise or other informational guidance may assist in transition counseling for families and students with disabilities where vocational education represents the educationally appropriate transition instruction and families remain resistant to this alternative.

Necessary Instructional Competencies for Vocational Educators

A common concern of vocational educators and special educators alike is that vocational educators have little, if any, training in providing instruction to students with disabilities. In fact, not all vocational instructors have training in instructional methods. In some states, the instructor's years of expertise in his or her chosen field can substitute for formal educational pedagogical training. This may present a problem when instructors need to modify instruction, worksheets, tests, and assessments. The vocational teacher may need assistance or inservice training in how to develop alternative methods of teaching and assessment.

Uncertainty about educating students with disabilities can create anxiety on the part of the vocational educator. For inclusive vocational education settings to be successful, special education teachers should be available and collaborate with the vocational educator throughout the school year and provide instructional support when needed. Collaboration is an important competency to develop for vocational and special educators.

Vocational teachers may need an opportunity to explore curriculum options, modifications and accommodations, individualized instruction, alternative grading and assessment, and safety concerns, as well as develop a basic understanding of the general characteristics of how specific disabilities might affect educational instruction. For example, students with hearing impairments may need preferential seating and visual cues; students with mental retardation

Exhibit 13–3 Synonyms for Vocational Education

VOCATIONAL	EDUCATION
• Business	• Direction
• Career	• Schooling
• Trade	• Guidance
• Vocation	• Instruction
• Job	• Training
• Occupation	• Knowledge
• Professional	• Learning
• Employment	• Literacy
• Work	• Scholarship
• Responsibility	• Exploration
• Specialist	• Coaching
• Enterprise	• Development

may need tasks analyzed and may need to be instructed in more discrete segments with more opportunities for practice; and students with learning disabilities who have the cognitive skills to achieve may need alternative instruction or evaluation methods. Of equal importance is for vocational teachers to understand that the instructional needs for students with disabilities also differ within disability categories and that each student's instruction requires individualization.

Increasingly, it is important for vocational teachers of students with disabilities to be familiar with the provision of transition services. With the advent of the School to Work Opportunities Act of 1994 comes an expectation that transition programs for all students will include school-based learning, work-based learning, and connecting activities. Educators need the competencies to implement programs that incorporate these concepts.

Curriculum Issues

Kohler, DeStefano, Wermuth, Grayson, and McGinty (1994), in analyzing the process for identifying exemplary transition programs for youths with disabilities, cited key elements of exemplary programs. Of note is the high frequency with which career/vocational training was cited as an exemplary practice for transition programs. Among the most frequently cited program areas were vocational assessment, supported employment services, secondary curriculum that includes employability skills, mainstreamed vocational programs, special vocational programs, secondary curriculum that includes on-the-job training, and career education experiences.

By surveying secondary-aged students with mild disabilities from one school setting and their teachers, Karge, Patton, and de la Garza (1992) identified the important curricular considerations for transition services for these students. Furthermore, they found that the secondary curriculum for these students with mild disabilities did not sufficiently address the following vocationally related areas:

- job-search skills
- job-maintenance skills
- job-related functional academics
- transportation skills
- paid jobs in the community before graduation
- counseling for postsecondary options
- self-advocacy skills for job and community

Banks and Renzaglia (1993) presented the need for curricula that prepare students for community work experience or other work experiences to focus on core skills that are generalizable. For older students, they stated: "The curriculum . . . should focus on the refinement of work and work-related skills as they specifically relate to the job site selected for employment after graduation" (p. 7).

Banks and Renzaglia (1993) described the need for community-based vocational experiences for students with moderate to severe disabilities at various age levels. Although the authors did not promote the traditional community experiences at the elementary level, they proposed that activities at that level can support prevocational skill development. Activities such as classroom jobs, office assistance, and cafeteria assistance offer opportunities to develop appropriate work attitudes and behaviors. Career awareness should be an integral part of elementary instruction for all students, including students with disabilities.

Developmentally, middle school is a time of career exploration. According to Banks and Renzaglia (1993), community-based work experiences should begin in middle school for students with moderate to severe disabilities. These experiences could include spending time in several jobs where situational assessment (i.e., observation) data could be collected. The result is a narrowing of job-training options that can then be successfully provided during high school.

The high school years can represent a vocational training period in the vocational education continuum. Community-based work experiences or work experiences in some format are essential for youths with disabilities. Researchers who conducted longitudinal studies found that paid employment during high school correlates with postschool employment success (Halpern, Doren, & Benz, 1993). For youths who have employment as a transition goal, these vocational experiences are a critical component of their secondary education. However, Halpern et al. (1993) argued that vocational work experiences must be relevant to emerging careers and not just an opportunity to earn money and experience the world of work. They suggested that apprenticeships that develop technical skills offer an opportunity to improve the relationship between vocational training and career development.

Job placement symbolizes an end goal in the career development option. However, this goal requires that all adults—including adults with disabilities—revisit the career development continuum, as they will be forced to improve work-related skills or even to change careers. Secondary vocational programs attempt to identify job-placement options for students, but American programs often lack that work connection. The School to Work Opportunities Act of 1994 promotes connecting activities with the intended outcome of improving job-placement options for all youths exiting high school vocational programs. For youths with disabilities, who enjoy an entitlement to transition planning, job placement should be a definite goal during the last few years in secondary education. Job placement in competitive employment represents full community inclusion. Providing this experience while the student is still receiving special education allows for support as needed, the coordination of goals with the employment setting, the provision of job follow-along, and ongoing skill development. The probability of long-term success (i.e., continued employment in this setting) increases with an effective assessment of the job site, matching the demands of that setting to the skills of the youth with a disability.

Safety

Vocational teachers express legitimate concerns regarding safety issues. Students with disabilities who experience difficulty with behavioral and impulse control, as well as those with visual, hearing, and physical disabilities, challenge vocational educators to create settings that are safe, educational, and appropriate. Special educators play a major role in creating successful settings. Matching the skills and goals of the student to the vocational setting is the first step in addressing these concerns. In addition, students with and without disabilities should be required to pass safety tests before operating equipment. Providing educational, technological, or behavioral supports where there are skill discrepancies is a second step to meet safety concerns. Educational supports may include peer partners or a paraprofessional, as well as resource instruction. Technological supports may mean equipment modification that increases safe operation for a specific student. Specialists (e.g., vocational rehabilitation specialists for the blind, audiologists, occupational or physical therapists) can be valuable in identifying or recognizing actual limitations as well as in creating appropriate accommodations. For example, the audiologist can identify if the student who is hard of hearing can hear a warning signal and, if not, recommend the use of a visual or tactile warning signal. Behavioral supports may include written behavior contracts or other systems of behavior management.

Grading

Vocational education teachers question how students with disabilities who are working in regular vocational education curricula should be graded. Questions include: "Are these students held to the same standard as peers without disabilities?" "If I grade a student based on his IEP goals, he may get an A, but his work is not comparable to my students without disabilities. Does this student get full credit for mastering only part of the competencies?" These represent legitimate questions, particularly in the current era of accountability. Vocational education teachers sometimes complain that their curriculum is being watered down by the participation of students with disabilities and the accommodations that must be made. They have concerns regarding compromising on the competencies required for students to complete the class. Philosophically, they want to hold the student with a disability to the same standard as students without disabilities.

There is an additional problem of weakening the competencies to the point where the student is actually unprepared to work in a satisfactory manner in his or her chosen field. Does anyone really want a nurse who mastered only 65% of the necessary competencies? Or a carpenter who can build a plumb wall 75% of the time? In order to combat this problem, teachers must ensure that the testing measures, materials presented, and methods of instruction are modified rather than the competencies themselves. If it is necessary to modify the competencies, then optional training ("helper" programs or "cut-outs" described previously) should be considered. These concerns must be addressed if students with disabilities are to be included in vocational education classes.

In establishing grading policies, one must identify the values and beliefs that will drive these decisions. The goal of vocational education is to prepare students to work and experience success in their vocation of choice. Educators must maintain comparable standards to apply to students with disabilities or run the risk of not adequately preparing the student to work, experience success, and achieve independence as a competent worker. At the same time, students with disabilities are entitled to reasonable accommodations, which may include modifying how the students are evaluated.

Because vocational education is competency based, differential grading for a student in a vocational class, theoretically, should be less difficult. Competency lists may be generated by the vocational education advisory board or the vocational teacher, or they may be state-standardized. Competency-based teaching is similar to basing instruction on the IEP. The terminal objective (or goal, as it is referred to in IEPs) represents the long-term goal; this goal is then followed by a series of enabling objectives. Since the curriculum is goal-oriented and built upon ascending competency development, it is possible to work with the students who can grasp the concepts of the curriculum quickly and to instruct students who take longer to master individual goals and objectives. Competency-based vocational instruction lends itself to individualizing instruction. Students with disabilities, nevertheless, should be expected to master each competency. Grading could be based on the degree to which each competency is achieved. Adopting this grading policy for all students, not just students with disabilities, would be a bold educational reform.

Grading practices may vary, depending on where on the continuum of vocational education the student with a disability receives his or her instruction. For example, for students who are participating in assistant programs where the IEP defines that the student will acquire only 50% of the competencies, the school division has the latitude to award the student half or quarter credit. Thus the transcript would reflect the rate at which the student is gaining competencies toward a vocational completion program. Students could receive the letter grade relevant to their acquisition and mastery of the competencies.

Grading—for all students—always carries subjective value judgments in spite of attempts to make grading objective. For vocational educators, grading will become less of an issue when the purpose of the student's vocational program is clear, and when the standards for the chosen vocational program are maintained.

Assessment

Modifying assessment is one of the most common accommodations listed on a student's IEP. IEP teams need to examine the appropriateness of the accommodation to the vocational program. For example, extended time on testing is a frequently given accommodation. However, some vocational standards are based on timed responses (e.g., words per minute typed or word processed or the efficient completion of technically related tasks). IEP teams must examine the relationship between the suggested accommodation and the student's long-term employment objectives. Appropriate assessment accommodations should reflect the demands for independence in the student's future employment setting.

Accommodations could include changing the directions for designing and administering tests. Test directions that are short, simple, and typed permit students to comprehend the instructions and review as needed. Test administration modifications may include allowing students to test in an alternative environment and allowing extra time for students who have difficulty with reading and comprehension. Modifications in test construction may mean having extra space on the paper for the student to work the math problems without having to rewrite them, placing all of the matching items on the same page, and avoiding words such as *not, never, always,* and *except* in true-false items (Wood, 1992). (Chapter 6 provides additional suggestions for accommodations and modifications.)

Vocational education offers an opportunity to implement performance-based assessment—that is, an assessment where the student physically demonstrates the acquisition of vocational technical or manual skills. Performance tests can measure a student's ability to complete a task without the limitations of reading and writing. They represent a more authentic test of the student's ability to perform the demands of a vocational skill.

VOCATIONAL EVALUATION AS A FOUNDATION FOR EFFECTIVE INCLUSION PRACTICES

Making an appropriate match between the student's needs, interests, preferences, and aptitudes with a vocational education program eliminates many of the challenges in providing vocational education to students with disabilities. A match involves assessing the student, the instructional setting, and the future employment options. Vocational evaluation or vocational assessment offers the opportunity to make this match. Using the information from these assessments in developing IEPs opens the door to appropriate vocational education placements.

Vocational evaluation information provides vital student career-counseling data. Making a vocational education placement decision solely on student interest without adequate counseling or substantiating information can be problematic. Students sometimes identify an area for training without adequate information. For example, a student may think she wants to train in an area such as masonry, only to discover later that she does not want to get dirty in her future job.

Vocational information can be gained from a comprehensive evaluation, or from classroom-administered tests or observations. A comprehensive vocational evaluation usually includes a formal assessment completed by a vocational evaluator; vocational assessment is often less formal, while not necessarily less systematic. Assessment can be informal surveys, tests, or interviews (or a combination of these methods) completed by classroom teachers and guidance counselors. The evaluation and assessment data should be used to help the student make informed choices regarding training and employment, and to help develop goals and objectives for the IEP and the transition plan (Sitlington, 1994).

Vocational Evaluator Professional Skills

Employment requirements and training of vocational evaluators vary widely from state to state (Nolte, 1994). School-based vocational evaluators may be former special education teachers, vocational resource support teachers, or guidance personnel, particularly in systems that have no specific position requirements. Some school systems employ a certified vocational evaluator (certified by the Commission on Certification of Work Adjustment and Vocational Evaluation Specialists). School systems that do not employ personnel to conduct vocational evaluations may work in cooperation with their vocational rehabilitation services agency to conduct comprehensive student evaluations.

A vocational evaluation that is completed by a certified vocational evaluator should be multidisciplinary and incorporate information from individuals involved with the student. Leconte (1994) identifies some of those individuals who should be involved: teacher (special, vocational, general), counselor, psychologist, employer, and physical or occupational therapist. The vocational evaluation report should provide relevant information addressing the student's current performance levels, what he or she needs to learn to accomplish vocational goals, and what teaching techniques are most likely to help the student meet his or her identified goals (Hicks, 1994). To ensure that IEPs include appropriate vocational education program objectives and services, vocational evaluation reports must always be reviewed as part of the IEP process. Vocational evaluators must offer reports that are readable and easily translatable to the IEP process.

Vocational Evaluation Practices

Consider the example of a 17-year-old student with mental retardation in his third year of high school. Sam has no history of competitive employment and to date has made no future employment or independent living plans. The IEP team identified that Sam needed the services of a vocational evaluator to help formulate adult employment and living objectives for his transition plan. The vocational evaluation report for Sam depicted in Exhibit 13–4 provides the IEP team with transition goals and objectives for the upcoming year. Based on this report, the IEP team recognizes that, for Sam, the inclusive vocational education program will be community-based work exploration and experiences. Sam may also be able to explore vocational options within the general vocational education programs offered in his high school; however, because many of his interest and aptitude areas are not a part of his high school curriculum, he will need to spend time observing workers (job shadowing) in these fields in the community.

Exhibit 13–4 Sample Vocational Evaluation Report

Name: Sam
Referral Source: IEP referral
Exceptionality: Mental retardation

Date of Evaluation: 2/6/96
Date of Birth: 1/2/79
Chronological Age: 17 years, 1 month

REFERRAL INFORMATION AND GENERAL OBSERVATIONS

Sam was referred for a vocational evaluation by the IEP team to assist in identifying his vocational interests, skills, aptitudes, and technical-related academic achievement levels. Referral information stated that Sam has an agreeable nature and a desire to please, making it difficult to determine his true employment preferences. His teacher reported that he is cooperative, pleasant, and gets along well with others, but that he has immature social adaptive skills. Sam is easily led, very distractible, and in need of ongoing supervision to stay on task. His teacher reported that he can follow easy directions and learns best by doing. The IEP team requested that recommendations be made regarding instructions in specialized vocational, independent living skills or community experiences Sam would need; they also requested assistance in identifying an appropriate employment objective.

During the initial interview, Sam said he did not know what he would like to do for a job. He reported that when he is home, he likes to cut wood, cut grass, wash the car, clean up, and rake leaves. He reported previous work experience through the community-based vocational instruction program at the local motel, where his job duties included picking up trash, vacuuming, folding towels, and cleaning windows. This school year, his placement is at a church where he does general cleaning tasks. Most of his work experiences have been in the general housekeeping area.

Sam responded to questions quickly and spoke very fast during the interview. He reported that keyboarding is his favorite class with the comment, "I'm a good typist." He also reported that he comes to school every day and gets good grades. When asked if he has any learning problem that he knows of, he indicated that he "has no trouble in school." Sam did not demonstrate a true understanding of his strengths or weaknesses.

PHYSICAL CAPACITIES

Referral information and discussion with Sam revealed no physical limitations or medical problems that would interfere with his ability to work. Most work was completed from a seated position, but he also demonstrated the capacity to work while standing. Sam is clearly right-handed.

The greatest barrier to Sam's ability is his distractibility and limited concentration. He certainly possesses the energy and ability to perform work involving at least sedentary to medium physical demands. His stamina is such that he should be able to maintain work behaviors for half-day placements this upcoming year. Given Sam's age and proximity to post-school transition, an appropriate goal would be increasing his work stamina to a whole day.

continues

Exhibit 13–4 continued

INTERESTS

Sam's vocational interests were measured using the Reading-Free Vocational Interest Inventory. One of his highest interests is in the area of animal care (a preference for activities concerned with feeding, watering, sheltering, exercising, and grooming animals, and cleaning quarters and equipment). Sam has not had an actual experience in this area. Animal care occupations include pet shop attendant, dog groomer, animal caretaker, and stable attendant. These represent viable employment options for this community.

Another high-interest area was laundry service (a preference for occupations involving dry cleaning, laundering, pressing, ironing, dyeing, and repairing of clothing, furnishings, and accessories in commercial laundries, dry cleaners, launderettes, or private households). Laundry service occupations include laundry laborer, dry cleaner, and launderette attendant. There are some similarities with Sam's past community experiences and these expressed interests. Sam could shadow or have work experiences in the local laundry and dry cleaners this year.

DIRECTION FOLLOWING

Direction	Yes	No
Follows simple one-step verbal instructions.	X	
Follows complex verbal instructions.		X
Follows simple diagrams.		X
Follows complex diagrams.		X
Follows simple written instructions.	X	
Follows complex written instructions.		X

Sam's understanding of spoken English, as measured by a screening test of single-word receptive vocabulary, reflects skills typically seen in preschool or kindergarten-age children; nonetheless, these scores are consistent with his cognitive ability. (Sam previously received speech therapy as a related service.) His score on this screening test supports his need for spoken instructions to be phrased using very simple vocabulary. During his evaluation and the observation at his community-based placement, Sam performed relatively well when instructions were repeated and demonstrated. He occasionally needed hand-over-hand instructions and responded well to this approach. Sam will need concrete and visual cues for multistep tasks with physical demonstration when he is learning the task.

TECHNICAL-RELATED ACADEMIC SKILLS

Based on reports and the results of a screening of Sam's reading recognition and arithmetic abilities, Sam's skills are comparable to students in elementary school. Using quick screening tools, his reading recognition, reading comprehension, and his arithmetic skills are comparable to students who are in second or third grade. Sam is able to perform math computations involving simple addition and subtraction, multiplication that does not involve regrouping, and simple division. Although these skills are low, they indicate that he can use functional academic skills and instruction and that he could apply these skills on the job. Once a job training option has been selected, Sam should be instructed in the related academic competencies for that field.

JOB-SEEKING/JOB-KEEPING SKILLS

Sam responded verbally to questions related to appropriate work behaviors; from this he demonstrated a general understanding of proper behaviors necessary to maintain employment. Sam should continue to develop these skills and should be given opportunities to respond and react to multiple job-keeping demands.

WORK SAMPLES

Sam was also exposed to three job categories through participating in work samples. Sam successfully, but not independently, completed the cook and baker job sample with the assistance of the

continues

Exhibit 13–4 continued

evaluator. He expressed an enjoyment of this work sample. Functionally, it would be appropriate to develop instructional goals in the area of cooking and general meal preparation.

On the information processing work sample, Sam completed the letter, number, and letter/number combination entry tasks with 100% accuracy. He entered information from completed purchase orders into the computer with 88% accuracy. His errors were due to impulsivity (not checking to make sure he had entered the information accurately prior to going on to the next section). Instructions were modified for Sam, with the instructions being administered prior to each section rather than all at the beginning. Under these circumstances, Sam completed this job sample independently.

On the office services work sample, Sam's accuracy in sorting mail improved with additional instruction and practice. The errors made on all of these office-related tasks appeared to be due to working quickly and not taking the time to check his work.

Based on these three work sample sets, it is clear that Sam should continue to develop information-processing skills; skills in this area will translate across multiple employment options. Sam should be taught self-monitoring strategies that will help him aim for accuracy and not speed in detail work.

Work Behavior		Asset	Marginal	Limitation
1.	Personal hygiene/grooming and dress	X		
2.	Punctuality	X		
3.	Conformity to rules and regulations	X		
4.	Acceptance of supervisory authority	X		
5.	Acceptance of constructive criticism	X		
6.	Frustration tolerance	X		
7.	Reaction to unpleasant or monotonous task	X		
8.	Works on assignment persistently	See comments		
9.	Works independently			X
10.	Follows directions		X	
11.	Attention		X	
12.	Distractibility			X
13.	Planning and organizational abilities			X
14.	Work speed	X		
15.	Work quality	See comments		

WORK BEHAVIOR RATING COMMENTS

Sam demonstrated some positive work-related behaviors as reflected in the above list. He consistently displayed a positive and cheerful attitude and was cooperative in attempting assigned tasks.

In terms of behaviors that may interfere with his ability to perform job tasks effectively and efficiently, Sam was easily distracted and displayed poor organizational, reasoning, and problem-solving skills. He sang, hummed, and talked to himself almost continuously during his assessment, although this was not observed at the community-based instruction job site.

Sam did not appear to be easily frustrated and/or affected by obstacles to the completion of work. For example, when sorting mail, he simply did not sort the pieces that he was confused about. Upon completion of the task, he was encouraged to request assistance when he was unsure of a task.

Sam requires consistent supervision while working because of his inability to remember or follow through with multiple-step instructions. This significantly restricts his ability to work independently. Instructionally, continued emphasis on the development of appropriate social skills is warranted.

COMMUNITY-BASED JOB SITE OBSERVATION

Sam is currently working Tuesday and Thursday mornings as part of the school district's community-based instruction program. With supervision, he works at a church where he vacuums, sets up chairs, sweeps, straightens up, cleans the bathroom, and mops the floor. He has been working at this

continues

Exhibit 13–4 continued

site since November of this school year. Sam is aware of his specific job duties and the routine involved and is able to work fairly independently (but still requires constant supervision). However, he needs intermittent reminders and suggestions related to the various tasks he performs. For example, when setting up rows of folding chairs, he needed reminders to set the chairs close enough to touch each other and where to start a new row. He occasionally seeks assistance from the teacher who accompanies him to the job site, but it almost appears as though he is seeking approval/positive reinforcement rather than assistance with the tasks.

SUMMARY AND RECOMMENDATIONS

Sam demonstrates skills and aptitudes consistent with eventual competitive employment with supports. He displays a high energy level, positive attitude, motivation, and is consistently cooperative. He does need to work on asking questions when tasks are unclear or when he has forgotten instructions. He is receptive to suggestions to alter his work methods to perform tasks more efficiently.

The information gathered during Sam's evaluation is consistent with referral reports. He requires constant supervision to stay on task and is very distractible. He follows simple verbal instructions and does best when those instructions are accompanied by a demonstration.

Sam's academic abilities are minimal, but functional to the extent that he can read simple labels for directions, warnings, etc. He could most likely follow very simply phrased written instructions and could benefit from them to learn new tasks (in combination with verbal instructions, demonstration, etc.).

Sam's vocational interests are still not well defined. He states that he likes the cleaning work he performs but that he does not know what he would like to do for a job once he completes school. Job tasks for which he indicated a liking on a vocational interest inventory were in the areas of animal care and laundry service. During the evaluation, he performed best on tasks involving typing and/or data entry as well as the cleaning work he performs at his community-based instruction job site. In general, he will perform best on jobs that do not require higher-level problem solving, reasoning skills, or independent judgment, and in which the duties remain relatively unchanged from day to day.

Instructionally, Sam will benefit from continuing to improve his functional skills such as making change, using a ruler, cooking (reading recipes, making liquid and dry measurement, following written instructions), following a schedule, and using community resources. Additionally, continued discussion regarding the importance and benefits of working and earning wages would be helpful. Sam needs to work on self-advocacy skills, such as asking for help and understanding his disability.

It is recommended that Sam continue with his present community work placement, with the addition of a systematic and planned effort to decrease the amount of supervision provided; his progress should be charted to determine his ability to perform the work independently in that situation.

To help Sam formulate adult employment objectives, school and community experiences should be provided to increase his occupational awareness. These include observing and shadowing in various classes at the vocational center, job shadowing at actual work sites, and additional work experiences through the community-based instruction program at school. Sam's current vocational placement appears to be consistent with his abilities. Other suggested jobs that are consistent with his aptitudes include the following: laundry worker I; folder (laundry); stable attendant; dishwasher, machine; kitchen helper. Supported employment would be an appropriate employment objective for Sam.

Vocational Evaluator

Collaborating with Vocational Evaluators and Educators for Inclusive IEP Planning

Vocational education teachers or vocational evaluators seldom participate in the development of IEPs (deFur et al., 1995). However, vocational education teachers or evaluators can identify the setting and curriculum demands of programs and improve the match with the skills and interests of the student. This effort allows the special education program to address any discrepancies in skills. Logistically, coordination between special education and vocational education is complex, but this is a key aspect of inclusion in vocational education programs (Hazelkorn & Lombard, 1991; Weisenstein, Stowitschek, & Affleck, 1991).

IEP committees include the student and his or her family, who will help design vocational education objectives and approaches. Vocational evaluation can provide valuable data on which to make these planning decisions. When considering initial vocational education placement, the following factors should be considered:

- Review the vocational evaluation and answer these questions: What are the student's interests, skills, desires? Does the student have an employment objective?
- Describe the student's present level of performance and answer these questions: Will the student's academic levels be compatible with the program suggested? Is the student prepared for the academic demands of this program? For example, can the student who is interested in carpentry use a ruler accurately? What special instruction is needed to achieve vocational goals?
- Discuss the student's career-exploration activities and answer these questions: Has the student experienced a variety of vocational options? (These options can be provided through job and/or class shadowing, computer exploration, or work samples during a vocational evaluation.) Are community experiences needed?
- Does the student have the necessary prerequisite courses to participate in the training areas? For example, if placement in a data entry program is considered, has the student successfully completed a keyboarding class? Will the student need specialized instruction in these areas?
- Are modifications in the course objectives and curriculum necessary? Are modifications needed to make the classroom, shop, and work sites accessible? Are these modifications and accommodations reasonable given the student's disability and the expectations the student will encounter in the adult world?
- Are jobs available in the local area for people trained in this specific skill?

This information can be recorded from records, recent assessments, or observations in a format like the one presented in Exhibit 13–5. These data can be incorporated into the present level of educational performance on students' IEPs and used in the development of transition goals and objectives in employment, instruction, and community experiences.

IEP decision making is a critical first step to success in vocational education programs. Vocational evaluation or assessment data must drive these decisions. In some schools, when vocational personnel cannot attend IEP meetings, instructors provide special educators with a description of the setting demands of the vocational classroom. This, along with evaluation data, can be compared to the present level of educational performance demonstrated by the student. With this information, decisions can be effectively made regarding the appropriateness of specific vocational programs, or accommodations can be identified that may facilitate entry in those programs.

For students who are in a regular vocational class where coteaching with a special educator or vocational resource teacher is not an option, communication among the professionals is critical. Vocational educators must keep the special educator informed if the student is not progressing satisfactorily. An IEP meeting can be held and the program or supports changed if needed. Likewise, communication is two-way; the special educator must monitor progress and offer support as needed. Collaborative efforts are essential for students with disabilities to participate successfully in inclusive vocational education programs.

Exhibit 13–5 Factors IEP Teams May Consider When Considering Vocational Education Placements

Student's Name _____   Date _____

Vocational evaluation results (interests, skills, desires, employment objectives):

Level of performance:

continues

Exhibit 13–5 continued

Exploration experiences and needs:

Prerequisite courses completed and needed:

Necessary academic and physical modifications and accommodations:

Employment outlook:

CONCLUSION

Vocational education includes many of the ingredients sought after by special education programming. It is competency-based, which allows for individualization; it is performance-based, which allows for a variety of ways to demonstrate competency attainment; it is experiential in instruction, which provides the concrete presentations and feedback needed by many students with disabilities; it is a satisfying learning experience, where failures only represent new learning opportunities and successes are obvious and genuine; and instructionally, it develops meaningful skills that can be used to accomplish employment goals and develop adult independence. Importantly, vocational education also offers students with disabilities an education in inclusive environments, including the community, the classroom, and the world of business. Effective vocational education inclusion practices begin and end with collaboration between special and vocational educators and evaluators in conjunction with the student, the family, and the community.

REFERENCES

Americans with Disabilities Act of 1990, Pub. L. No. 101-336.

Banks, R., & Renzaglia, A. (1993). Longitudinal vocational programs: A review of current recommended practices for individuals with moderate to severe disabilities. *Journal of Vocational Rehabilitation, 3*(3), 5–16.

Benz, M.R., & Halpern, A.L. (1993). Vocational and transition services needed and received by students with disabilities during their last year of high school. *Career Development for Exceptional Individuals, 16*, 197–209.

Callahan, M. (1992). Job site training and natural supports. In J. Nisbet (Ed.), *Natural supports in school, at work, and in the community for people with severe disabilities* (pp. 257–276). Baltimore: Paul H. Brookes.

Carl D. Perkins Vocational Education Act of 1984, Pub. L. No. 98-524.

Carl D. Perkins Vocational Education and Applied Technology Act of 1990, Pub. L. No. 101-392.

Clark, G.M., & Kolstoe, O.P. (1990). *Career development and transition education for adolescents with disabilities.* Boston: Allyn and Bacon.

deFur, S., Getzel, L., & Kregel, J. (1995). *Transition services outcomes: Virginia's Project UNITE.* Unpublished manuscript.

Education for All Handicapped Children Act of 1975, Pub. L. No. 94-142.

Evers, R.B., & Bursuck, W. (1994). Literacy demands in secondary technical vocational education programs: Teacher interviews. *Career Development for Exceptional Individuals, 17*, 135–143.

Hagner, D.C. (1992). The social interactions and job supports of supported employees. In J. Nisbet (Ed.), *Natural supports in school, at work, and in the community for people with severe disabilities* (pp. 217–239). Baltimore: Paul H. Brookes.

Halpern, A.S., Doren, B., & Benz, M.R. (1993). Job experiences of students with disabilities during their last two years in school. *Career Development for Exceptional Individuals, 16*, 63–73.

Hazelkorn, M., & Lombard, R. (1991). Designated vocational instruction: Instructional support strategies. *Career Development for Exceptional Individuals, 14*, 15–26.

Hicks, P.A. (1994). Vocational assessment and planning: School psychology's opportunity for role diversification. *Vocational Evaluation and Work Adjustment Bulletin, 27*(4), 143–148.

Individuals with Disabilities Education Act of 1990, Pub. L. No. 101-476.

Karge, B.D., Patton, P.L., & de la Garza, B. (1992). Transition services for youth with mild disabilities: Do they exist, are they needed? *Career Development for Exceptional Individuals, 15*, 47–68.

Kohler, P., DeStefano, L., Wermuth, T., Grayson, T., & McGinty, S. (1994). An analysis of exemplary transition programs: How and why are they selected? *Career Development for Exceptional Individuals, 17*, 187–202.

Kohler, P.D. (1994). On the job training: A curricular approach to employment. *Career Development for Exceptional Individuals, 17*, 29–39.

Kregel, J. (1994, Fall). Natural supports and the job coach: An unnecessary dichotomy. In K. Inge (Ed.), *Rehabilitation Research and Training Center Newsletter*, Richmond, VA: Virginia Commonwealth University.

Leconte, P.J. (1994). Vocational appraisal services: Evolution from multi-disciplinary origins and applications to interdisciplinary practices. *Vocational Evaluation and Work Adjustment Bulletin, 27*(4), 119–127.

Lombard, R., Hazelkorn, M., & Neubert, D. (1992). A survey of accessibility to secondary vocational education programs and transition services for students with disabilities in Wisconsin. *Career Development for Exceptional Individuals, 15*, 179–188.

Moon, M.S., Inge, K.J., Wehman, P., Brooke, V., & Barcus, J.M. (1990). *Helping persons with severe mental retardation get and keep employment.* Baltimore: Paul H. Brookes.

Nolte, D. (1994). Interdisciplinary approach to vocational evaluation/assessment from a secondary education perspective. *Vocational Evaluation and Work Adjustment Bulletin, 27*, 141–142.

Rehabilitation Act Amendments of 1973, Pub. L. No. 93-112.

Sarkees-Wircenski, M., & Scott, J. (1995). *Vocational special needs.* Homewood, IL: American Technical.

School to Work Opportunities Act of 1994, Pub. L. No. 103-239.

Siegel, S., Robert, M., Waxman, M., & Gaylord-Ross, R. (1992). A follow-along study of participants in a longitudinal transition program for youths with mild disabilities. *Exceptional Children, 58*, 346–356.

Sitlington, P. (1994). Vocational evaluation and assessment in special education. *Vocational Evaluation and Work Adjustment Bulletin, 27*(4), 136–140.

Sitlington, P., & Frank, A. (1990). Are adolescents with learning disabilities successfully crossing the bridge into adult life? *Learning Disability Quarterly, 13*, 97–111.

Smith, J. (1992). Falling through the cracks: Rehabilitation services for adults with learning disabilities. *Exceptional Children, 58*, 451–460.

Virginia Department of Education. (1993). *Demographics of students exiting special education.* Richmond, VA: Author.

Vocational Education Act of 1963, Pub. L. No. 88-210. Vocational Education Act Amendments of 1968, Pub. L. No. 90-576.

Weisenstein, G., Stowitschek, J., & Affleck, J. (1991). Integrating students enrolled in special education into vocational education. *Career Development for Exceptional Individuals, 14*, 131–144.

Wood, J. (1992). *Adapting instruction for mainstreamed and at-risk students.* New York: Macmillan.

CHAPTER 14

Transition Planning with an Inclusive Philosophy

Sharon H. deFur and Douglas L. Russell

HISTORICAL OVERVIEW OF TRANSITION POLICY AND PRACTICE

A Trend toward Inclusion

Legislation championing community integration of individuals with disabilities has been predominant for the past two decades. National and state policies now promote the integration of youths with disabilities into the mainstream of educational and community programs. Furthermore, the Americans with Disabilities Act of 1990 (ADA) intends to increase access to private employment and public services for people with disabilities and makes such equal access a civil right.

Consequently, the expectation should be that the "community"—that is, the community of school, work, and leisure—contains people of diverse backgrounds, including people with disabilities. But, in reality, this expectation represents a shift in paradigms for society and for families of youths with disabilities. Such changes do not come easily, for they require a switch in beliefs and philosophy, or, at the least, an alignment of stated values with intentions. Embracing an inclusive philosophy that recognizes youths and young adults with disabilities as an integral part of the community is the *foundation* for integrated transition planning.

Completion of secondary education and entrance into the adult world as productive and contributing members of society represent the primary goal of public education (Kohler, 1994). During the past two decades, special educators and disability policy advocates have promoted this goal as one that applies to all students, including students with disabilities. During this period of advocacy, an initiative now called *transition* emerged as a process to promote successful postschool outcomes for youths and young adults with disabilities.

Many might argue that transition from high school to work does not represent a new concept to special education, but just a new term with a broadened perspective. For example, during the 1960s and 1970s, community work-experience programs were commonplace for students with mental retardation, and a close alliance existed between vocational rehabilitation and education programs. Traditionally, though, these programs were separate from the mainstream of education. Postschool employment outcomes for students with mental retardation typically were in sheltered workshops; young adults with more severe disabilities were often placed in day-activity placements or were institutionalized. Young adults whose disabilities were sensory, physical, or hidden (such as learning disabilities or emotional disabilities) attempted to enter the adult community through traditional means, but frequently faced architectural, social, and other discriminatory barriers. Segregation in school and community life was the norm.

In the early 1980s it became apparent that past disability legislative initiatives had not resulted in full community participation for youths and young adults with disabilities. A generation of students and their families had grown up with access to the community of school and education. Yet, the promise of education seemed broken as youths with disabilities and their families realized that entitlements ended with public education, that adult systems did not provide a guide through the maze of services, and that integration into the community remained evasive. Public testimony and follow-up studies reported rather dismal outcomes in terms of employment, postsecondary education, and independent living (Chadsey-Rusch, Rusch, & O'Reilly, 1993; Neubert, Tilson, & Ianacone, 1989; Peraino, 1992; Sitlington, Frank, & Carson, 1990; Virginia Department of Education, 1994; Wagner et al., 1991). Education and rehabilitation policy makers and advocates for people with disabilities examined these data and responded with new policy directives promoting interdisciplinary transition services and planning.

Policy Responses

Schools are social institutions and are often implicitly or explicitly appointed as places to initiate social policy. In the case of students with disabilities, the least restrictive environment clauses of special education laws and regulations speak to the intention that, to the extent possible, classrooms are to be adapted to include students with disabilities. Removal from the "regular educational community" should occur only when absolutely necessary for the student to benefit from education. For the past two decades, general education classrooms and neighborhood schools have been the place for social integration of students with disabilities, thus raising a generation of young adults without disabilities who accept—or, at least, do not fear—people with disabilities (Staub & Peck, 1994). For a young adult with a disability to graduate from school and then enter a segregated existence not only contradicts this educational-social policy, but promotes an economic policy of dependence. Recognizing the continuation of segregation in the adult lives of graduates with disabilities, policy makers once again looked to the schools and disability education policy to combat these contradictory outcomes. In 1990, the Education for All Handicapped Children Act of 1975 (P.L. 94-142) was amended and renamed the Individuals with Disabilities Education Act (IDEA). IDEA represents landmark legislation mandating that youths with disabilities have needed transition services included in their individualized education programs (IEPs).

Section 602 of IDEA states that the IEP for each student, beginning no later than age 16 (and at a younger age, if determined appropriate), must include a statement of the needed transition services, including, if appropriate, a statement of each public agency's and each participating agency's responsibilities, linkages, or both, before the student leaves the school setting (IDEA).

Furthermore, in Section 602, the IDEA legislation defines *transition* as a coordinated set of activities for a student, designed within an outcome-oriented process, which promotes movement from school to postschool activities, including: postsecondary education, vocational training, integrated employment (including supported employment), continuing and adult education, adult services, independent living, and community participation. The coordinated set of activities must be based on individual student needs; take into account student preferences and interests; and include instruction, community experiences, development of employment, and other postschool adult living objectives. When appropriate, the coordinated set of activities must include instruction regarding daily living skills as well as functional vocational evaluation.

IDEA transition policy clearly promotes the role of education in the preparation of youths with disabilities for their roles as adults living within the community. Community integration outcomes are the presumption of each of the components of transition policy.

Employment Outcomes

Past follow-up studies found that youths with disabilities do not have a similar rate of employment as youths without disabilities; moreover, youths with disabilities who are employed are frequently underemployed (Chadsey-Rusch et al., 1993; Neubert et al., 1989; Peraino, 1992; Sitlington et al., 1990; Virginia Department of Education, 1994; Wagner et al., 1991). Consequently, the definition of *transition services* includes a coordinated set of activities that promote movement to integrated employment outcomes, including supported employment. These activities or strategies involve the development of postschool employment objectives, as well as specialized instruction or community experiences that increase the likelihood of reaching these long-term inclusive employment goals. Transition planning for employment outcomes is based in the following beliefs: all people have vocational interests and abilities; vocation has a broad definition that includes volunteering and exploration as well as paid work; and the community is the desired location to learn and demonstrate vocational skills and interests. All IEPs of students with disabilities, 16 years of age and older, must address needed transition services that will promote movement toward the student's employment goals, including functional vocational assessment when appropriate.

Adult Living Outcomes

Follow-up studies have found that youths with disabilities continue to remain dependent on their families longer and that these youths are not as likely to participate socially within their community as their peers without disabilities (Chadsey-Rusch et al., 1993; Neubert et al., 1989; Peraino, 1992; Sitlington et al., 1990; Wagner et al., 1991). Barriers such as a lack of housing, financial planning, transportation, self-advocacy, and other independent living skills contribute to this situation. The framers of the IDEA legislation responded by requiring that IEPs address needed transition services in the establishment of adult-living goals. IEPs are also expected to address the instruction or community experiences needed to achieve these goals. For some students, these goals and objectives address independent living skills, as well.

Postsecondary Education Outcomes

Transition services also include activities that promote movement into postsecondary education environments that may include continuing education or vocational training as well as higher education. Follow-up studies report that few students with disabilities enroll in any type of postsecondary education program, and many of those who do enroll do not complete their training (Chadsey-Rusch et al., 1993; Neubert et al., 1989; Peraino, 1992; Sitlington et al., 1990; Virginia Department of Education, 1994; Wagner et al., 1991). Many students, anxious to shed their special education label, fail to seek the supports and services available to them in postsecondary education settings; others are unaware of the process to obtain such services. Long-term education and training goals must be considered in developing transition activities.

Is Every Transition Service for Every Student?

Not every student needs transition services for postsecondary education, employment, and adult living. However, regulations require that each of these transition service areas—employment, adult living, instruction, and community experiences—be considered for every student who receives special education. The law dictates that the IEP team support and justify *not* offering a service when the team determines that this service area is not necessary, based on the student's needs, interests, and preferences. The long-held assumption that students with hidden disabilities do not face barriers in adult life is a myth (deFur & Reiff, 1994). Identifying long-term goals and discussing the demands to achieve those goals clarifies services that may be needed.

Who Participates in Transition Planning?

Transition planning requires an interdisciplinary perspective, both conceptually and legally. Planning for school exit implies that the players who will be responsible for postschool transition activities should be part of the IEP planning team. First and foremost, the IDEA regulations specify that the student must be a part of this planning, requiring that the student be invited to participate in the IEP transition meeting(s). Furthermore, if, for some reason, the student is unable to attend, educators are expected to ensure student involvement through other means. These could include informal interest inventories, student interviews, or preplanning conferences with the student prior to the IEP meeting.

Families are also integral to postschool plans, as they often become the facilitators of services and activities once youths leave school. Parents are long-time members of IEP teams, and it is necessary to advise them as to who else is now joining this team, including their son or daughter.

Adult service agencies and community organizations provide options for many youths with disabilities exiting schools, and increasingly these adult agencies have some options for services that overlap with education. Therefore, IEP meetings must invite or involve those adult service providers who might be paying for or providing transition services to youths while they are in school or after they exit school. Exhibit 14–1 lists examples of these agencies and organizations.

Emerging Definitions

The Council for Exceptional Children's Division on Career Development and Transition put forth a position on transition that further delineates the intention to prepare youths with disabilities to be full community participants (Halpern, 1994). This position paper defines transition as follows:

> Transition refers to a change in status from behaving primarily as a student to assuming emergent adult roles in the community. These roles include employment, participating in post-secondary education, maintaining a home, becoming appropriately involved in the community, and experiencing satisfactory personal and social relationships. The process of enhancing transition involves the participation and coordination of school programs, adult agency services, and natural supports* within the community. The foundations for transition should be laid during the elementary and middle school years, guided by the broad concept of career development. Transition planning should begin no later than age 14, and students should be encouraged, to the full extent of their capabilities, to assume a maximum amount of responsibility for such planning. (p. 117)

A direct relationship exists between a goal for full participation in society for young adults with disabilities and the transition policy of IDEA. Believing that success is measured by integration into the adult community means that the demands of that community must be considered in preparing the student for those adult roles. Inclusive transition planning and services are directed to this preparation

---

*Natural supports means coordinating the resources available within the workplace to enable a person with a disability to participate inclusively. For example, ride-sharing is a natural support many people use; co-workers can provide support in learning new skills, giving feedback, and reinforcing work and social accomplishments.

Exhibit 14–1 Agencies and Community Organizations That Are Adult Service Providers

- vocational rehabilitation
- mental health services
- mental retardation services
- job training services
- employment services
- independent living services
- Social Security Administration
- ARC (formerly known as the Association of Retarded Citizens)
- local advocacy organizations
- employment services organizations
- parks and recreation departments
- housing agencies
- transportation agencies
- social services
- health agencies

and keep community participation as the foundation for decision making. This means, as Stephen Covey, author of *The Seven Habits of Highly Effective People* (1989), says: "Begin with the end in mind."

SETTING TRANSITION GOALS WITH AN INCLUSIVE PHILOSOPHY

Defining an Inclusive Philosophy

Interestingly, in the original discussion of transition in the early 1980s, employment was seen as the quintessential outcome for transition. Will's original transition model outlined in *Bridges from School to Work Life* (1984) discussed only employment outcomes. In some ways, the work site was being attributed with the same social policy powers to influence integration as public education had been entrusted with. The implication was that putting people with disabilities into work sites with people without disabilities would result in full community participation. Unfortunately, these outcomes have not occurred.

Halpern (1985) criticized Will's model as narrow and presented an alternative model that included integration into the community, of which employment was a part, as the desired outcome. By 1994, Halpern suggested that achieving goals for meaningful personal and social relationships may be the most important of all transition outcomes. Likewise, Chadsey-Rusch and Heal (1995) suggested that social integration outcomes relate to a positive quality of life, including work. On the topic of integration, Hagner and DiLeo (1993) stated:

> Although it is true that physical presence is a necessary condition for social belonging to a diverse

community it is not a sufficient one. . . . [Integration] means being included as an insider in the social group and participating in the customs and rituals that symbolize membership. (pp. 36–37)

These premises challenge educators and disability professionals to broaden their perspective of the successful outcomes for youths with disabilities and complicate thinking about what efforts must be made to achieve the true goals of community integration.

Covey's advice to "begin with the end in mind" symbolizes the essence of school-to-postschool transition planning; believing that the end is full community participation establishes the foundation for an inclusive philosophy. Syzmanski (1994) asserted that "transition programs must be built on the firm belief that people with disabilities are members of the community, whose contributions and participation are important and valued" (p. 406). Chadsey-Rusch and Heal (1995) suggested that interventions to promote social integration must be two-pronged. One prong is more familiar to educators: improving the skills of the youth with a disability to participate socially in work and community environments; the other prong is developing interventions that change the behaviors and attitudes of the nondisabled community and workplace. This second prong requires educators to venture outside the realm of tradition to take some bold moves, such as offering disability awareness training to employers or community members, challenging community settings that prohibit participation, or developing natural supports within these environments. Transition planning with an inclusive philosophy means taking risks and implementing activities that address each of these social integration prongs.

Student-centered transition planning questions the traditional role of educators controlling the education planning process. An adult, using the resources and supports available, may choose to participate (or not to participate) in the life of the community. If the end in mind includes young adults with disabilities who exercise choice and control in decisions in their lives and who advocate for themselves within their community, then youths must be given opportunities to act accordingly. One task of education is to prepare youths to choose their level of participation as young adults, realizing that these choices may require supports and resources. Transition planning with an inclusive philosophy means preparing youths and their families for community participation, knowing the options and knowing the supports. Sometimes, it means allowing choices that might contradict one's own philosophy.

Transition Curriculum

Developmentally, adolescents begin to acquire a work identity during their early teen years. This stage represents a time when youths begin some career exploration. Interests in careers begin to emerge, youths hold part-time employment, academic and cocurricular talents are expressed and cultivated. High school is, at least, a partially differentiated curriculum designed to match interests, aptitudes, and long-term goals. In many European countries where school-to-work transitions are part of the educational system, secondary education programs are highly differentiated. Adolescents are tracked into vocational training or preparation for university, based on academic skills. In contrast, education in the United States maintains a philosophy of equal opportunity for university preparation throughout the secondary education experience. In the United States, education systems are very successful at transition planning for college for those students who plan to attend, but perform poorly in preparing students for the world of work and community participation.

Given these circumstances, what should be the transition curriculum for youths with disabilities? Where should this curriculum be delivered? Clark, Field, Patton, Brolin, and Sitlington (1994) described the transition curriculum as a life-skills instruction approach. These authors stated that a life-skills instruction approach means "a commitment to providing a set of goals, objectives, and instructional activities designed to teach components and skills needed to function successfully in life" (p. 126). They described these skills as those that "relate to functioning as a family member, good neighbor and citizen, worker, and functioning participant in the community" (p. 125). They stated that "the first consideration for where life skills should be taught should be general education settings and the community" (p. 129).

As stated earlier, an inclusive transition philosophy means preparing with the end in mind. Adopting a life-skills approach for transition curriculum is critical to this preparation. For many students with disabilities, this means instruction in the community where the student will live and work as an adult. Community-based instruction in integrated settings is inclusive education. Accomplishing transition goals for many students means leaving the school grounds and receiving instruction within the community. There may be a semantic argument that community-based programs where students leave the general education setting are "pull-out" programming for youths with disabilities. To counteract this assumption, educators can make bold moves such as developing integrated, community-based programs for all students who need life-skills instruction for their transition planning, or educators can accept that inclusive education takes place in many settings.

Adolescence—A Transition Enigma

Secondary education, the initiation of transition planning, and adolescence all coincide. For teens with disabilities, inclusive educational practices may seem to conflict with the feelings and reactions they are having developmentally, although education in segregated settings is not necessarily the better alternative. However, transition planning with an inclusive philosophy anticipates these developmental stages and the concomitant emotions, challenges, and opportunities this developmental stage offers.

Self-consciousness happens to be a pervasive characteristic of this age. In a qualitative study of high school students with learning disabilities, Guterman (1995) found that students strongly believed that a negative stigma is attached with being labeled as "learning disabled." These students with learning disabilities did not want help in their general education classes, fearing that this attention would make the stigma worse. Adolescents with disabilities are in a "damned if you do, damned if you don't" situation; they may fail academically if they stay in classes without help, yet they are taunted if they go to pull-out programs for help. Neither alternative promotes successful transition outcomes. Transition planning with an inclusive philosophy helps students weigh the pros and cons of where their education takes place; education with an inclusive philosophy searches for ways of reducing the stigma of supports in any setting.

The purpose of transition planning is to offer students choice and control, including skills in self-advocacy and self-determination. Again, developmental characteristics may create conflict in promoting these skills. For example, rejection of adult advice is a typical characteristic of adolescents. Yet Wehmeyer (1993) found that teens with disabilities rely more on authority than on their own beliefs. Teenagers tend to debate, often for the sake of debating, but teens with disabilities frequently lack the social skills to enable acceptable adult-student debate. Adolescents often engage in overthinking and are overwhelmed by the choices. Wehmeyer (1993) found that youths with disabilities have high anxiety about the decision-making process.

Clearly, youths with disabilities need developmental experiences to foster their maturity; some may need direct instruction in areas such as self-advocacy, communication, or social skills. Inclusive settings offer opportunities for social participation and observation of other students without disabilities also reacting in these developmental stages.

Educators must attend to the individual instructional needs that students with disabilities have and realize that a traditional academic approach may not meet the direct instructional needs of some students. A traditional academic approach may be appropriate for students whose long-term goal is college or vocational-technical training, even though many of these students need life-skills instruction. Clark et al. (1994) stated: "Response to this concern must involve curriculum considerations and not just an instructional environment or instructional strategy response" (p. 132). The instructional curriculum for transition must include life-skills instruction focused on employment and adult living. Many commercial and teacher-developed curricula can assist in these instructional strategies.

Adolescent development characteristics reflect an expected set of behaviors and attitudes. These change with the experiences that come with ongoing development. Educators cannot control these developmental characteristics, but they can control the environment and climate where all students are educated. The challenges are (1) to create an inclusive curricular environment that includes life-skills instruction for *all* students—one that accommodates for the special needs of youths with disabilities; and (2) to create an inclusive setting where individualized instruction is the norm for all students rather than the exception, where family and natural supports are identified for all students, and where all students choose to exercise their curricular options in appropriate community and classroom settings.

The Transition Process

There are five phases for transition planning that, to some degree, parallel stages of career development. These are assessment, exploration, training, placement, and future transitions. Each of these phases offers the opportunity to promote an inclusive philosophy and inclusive practices in the transition services and activities provided.

Assessment

Student assessment provides the baseline for transition planning and gives information regarding strengths, needs, and aptitudes. Traditional assessment focuses on a student's academic or vocational strengths and weaknesses; in essence, it follows a deficit model. Assessment for transition with an inclusive philosophy should take a holistic view and look not only at the student, but also at the anticipated inclusive environment and the supports needed for achieving success in this environment.

For example, authentic (or portfolio) assessment offers an opportunity to integrate traditional evaluation and performance-based assessment yielding information about the student. Teachers can collect these data through life-skills instruction activities. Authentic assessment includes observation and documentation of products and problem solving and focuses on the individual student, a primary consideration for transition planning (Armstrong, 1994). Menchetti and Bombay (1994) suggest that person-centered planning, which is also student-centered, offers assessment data that can be critical to developing transition goals. (See Chapter 7 for more detailed information about person-centered planning.) In addition, this holistic approach creates an opportunity to assess the resources and needed family supports, including any cultural inclusion considerations, to promote

community integration for the youth with a disability (Harry et al., 1994). In some cases, IEP teams use a person-centered planning approach to identify transition goals, objectives, and services.

Chadsey-Rusch and Heal (1995) recommended that work settings be assessed regarding support for social integration in work environments. Jobs, classrooms, and communities represent settings where students with disabilities participate. Each of these settings contains certain social, skill, and behavior expectations or demands. Setting demand analysis provides information about the anticipated environment. Observation and evaluation of the setting in light of the student's strengths and weaknesses allow one to identify accommodations and natural supports necessary for the student to be successful. The need to train those people who work within the setting can be identified, as well as direct instructional needs for the student.

Assessment for transition is a dynamic, continuing process. Although assessment represents the first step in transition planning, assessment is ongoing throughout the transition period.

Exploration

Exploration consists of a time of establishing preferences. For the transition process, students need to explore where and at what they might want to work, where they might want to pursue further education, and where they might want to live and play. Youths with disabilities often do not have as many natural opportunities for exploration as their nondisabled peers. For example, some may not babysit, mow lawns, volunteer in the community, travel independently, participate in community recreation, or interact with the many other ways in which youths without disabilities explore their future vocational and recreational options. Transition planning with an inclusive philosophy ensures that these opportunities are directly offered in appropriate ways.

Employment-exploration opportunities could include community-based work experiences, job shadowing, mentoring, internships, informational interviews, and other opportunities to interact within real work settings. (See Chapter 13 for more information on these vocational programs for youths with disabilities.) Adult living exploration opportunities could include simulated housekeeping activities or visiting housing settings; setting up adult business transactions such as bank accounts and loans; acquiring medical services; and receiving instruction in self-advocacy. Recreation options include participating in community leisure and neighborhood social events.

Training

Training provides youths with the qualifications to participate in further education, acquire employment, and participate as independently as possible in adult life. As described previously, transition training considers each of these areas in the creation of a life-skills curriculum in secondary education. Altering the traditional academic curriculum may be necessary to achieve long-term goals. Altering the instructional environment to include the community may also be necessary to promote postschool inclusive expectations for the student and the community.

Placement and Future Transitions

Long-term transition goals focus on outcomes in education, employment, and adult living. The ultimate test of effective transition lies in where young adults with disabilities "land" once they leave school and whether they continue to advance in their adult development. Integrated outcomes are the goal—integrated employment, housing within the community, and participation in the life of the community. Halpern's (1993) quality-of-life framework includes physical and material well-being, performance of adult roles, and personal fulfillment. These are the ends to have in mind as transition planning begins.

Planning for Postsecondary Employment in an Inclusive Environment

Integrated employment outcomes (part-time or full-time employment) include supported employment. Transition planning for employment should include goals and objectives toward the appropriate and desired employment setting for the individual. Some people believe that goals for postsecondary education eliminate the need for long-term employment goals; participating in postsecondary education delays entry into the work world but does not eliminate the need to address employment goals.

The annual goals for transition in the area of employment should address instructional and community experiences—the life skills that will increase the student's likelihood of moving into an integrated employment setting at

school exit. For example, a positive relationship between working during high school and postschool employment exists (Chadsey-Rusch et al., 1993; Neubert et al., 1989; Peraino, 1992; Sitlington et al., 1990; Wagner et al., 1991). Community work experience and volunteer opportunities in integrated settings while in school create the groundwork for postschool employment and participation in these settings. Jamie's case study described in Exhibit 14–2 illustrates transitional employment instruction in a community-based setting.

Depending on the disability, a variety of supports may be necessary prior to and during the community work experience. Accommodations, natural supports, and assistive technology should be identified and coordinated for all students who require these types of transition special education services. Accommodations and other supports vary from person to person. A person who uses a wheelchair may need architectural accommodations, whereas a person with mental retardation may require some job coaching and ongoing support from coworkers.

Delivery of employment-related transition services should include activities that take place within the classroom, home, neighborhood, and community. These activities could include, but are not limited to, vocational assessment, career exploration, vocational education, and job placement. Some students may need instruction in job-readiness skills. Jeffrey, the student described in the case study in Exhibit 14–3, has IEP transition goals, objectives, and services that will help him identify his employment objectives and improve his employability skills.

In addition, social skills training and self-advocacy skills are critical to workplace success. The workplace represents a primary site for social integration for adults; the importance of developing social integration skills for the individual and the provision of supports for social integration on the job cannot be emphasized enough. Also as adults, people with disabilities must be able to advocate for themselves. In employment settings, they will be expected

---

Exhibit 14–2 Case Study of Jamie: Planning for Postsecondary Employment

Jamie is an 18-year-old student with moderate cognitive disabilities. Jamie, her family and significant others, and her IEP team have come to an agreement that Jamie's transition plan should include a school exit goal of entering employment when she leaves school in three years. This year, to prepare for this outcome, Jamie will receive instruction in the field of nursing home care assistant (a career in which she has both an expressed interest and aptitude as identified through vocational assessment). Jamie's vocational instruction will take place on site at a local nursing home (inclusive community environment), where the employer and members of the nursing home staff will participate in implementing the goals and objectives of Jamie's IEP. Jamie's rehabilitation counselor has agreed to train the nursing home staff and administrators in using natural supports and in helping Jamie integrate into the work culture. Because Jamie has difficulty monitoring time, the IEP team has identified an assistive-technology adaptation for Jamie. She will wear a watch with an alarm that beeps every 15 minutes, giving her the assistive technology that helps her remember to move from one resident to another. Jamie's IEP team will meet at least annually to review goals and objectives.

Exhibit 14–3 Case Study of Jeffrey: Developing Employment Objectives and Employability Skills

Jeffrey is a 16-year-old student whose disability has a mild impact on his cognitive learning abilities. He hopes to attend college when he finishes high school, but he wants the option of working before leaving high school. Jeffrey has difficulty with social skills and with attending to tasks. At his IEP meeting, he expressed a great deal of concern that he has not worked at a summer job and that he is not certain about what area he would like to develop job skills. Jeffrey will participate in a school-based vocational assessment; he and his IEP team will use the information to decide what vocational instruction he should receive. Jeffrey agreed to take responsibility for participating in activities to improve his social skills, specifically in work settings, through a self-advocacy group offered through a local learning disabilities association. Jeffrey's self-advocacy goals include leading his next IEP meeting. He will participate in the schoolwide employment shadowing program with supports given as needed. Jeffrey's family agreed to work with the local job-training agency to find Jeffrey a summer job.

to identify their needs for reasonable accommodations, request natural supports when appropriate, and exercise their rights if required. The transition curriculum must address these issues to promote community integration for students who leave school.

Families play a critical role in setting long-term employment goals and implementing the transition curriculum to support those goals. Most students with disabilities find their jobs using the family-friend network rather than through public agencies (Benz & Halpern, 1987; Hasazi, Gordon, & Roe, 1985). Families influence career decisions by their statements and their actions. It is helpful for the family and educational team to work together on an inclusive transition plan. Discussing long-term goals with families beginning when children enter special education creates a future focus. All parents have a hard time letting go of their children as their children become young adults. For families with disabilities, this time requires additional preparation and successful experiences to build confidence in their sons' and daughters' independence. Inclusive education and community participation throughout school can help in this preparation.

School and business partnerships are becoming increasingly common in communities. Vocational education has a history of working with local businesses in cooperative education ventures. With the School to Work Opportunities Act of 1994, more localities are including these partnerships as part of the transition model for all students. These partnerships represent an opportunity for integrated employment options for youths with disabilities. Collaborating across the system in developing these partnerships is critical to promoting an inclusive philosophy for employment transitions.

Special educators and rehabilitation personnel can provide training for businesses to work with youths with disabilities as employees. Training in establishing natural supports, facilitating social integration into the workplace, and making reasonable accommodations will increase the likelihood of success for young employees with disabilities.

Planning for Postsecondary Education and Training in an Inclusive Environment

Most secondary schools focus on college preparation; thus, postsecondary education represents the transition program for most of the young adults in the United States. College or university training is seldom offered in segregated settings. (In the United States, Gallaudet remains one of the few universities that serve a specific population of students with disabilities.) In fact, approximately one-half of high school students with disabilities view postsecondary education as a viable option for them (deFur, Getzel, & Trossi, in press). Nonetheless, very few young adults with disabilities enter or complete postsecondary education or training (Wagner et al., 1991). Inadequate academic, social, and personal preparation of students with disabilities by secondary education, coupled with the student's lack of knowledge, skill, or willingness to access postsecondary supports, underlies this problem (deFur et al., in press).

When youths with disabilities and their families set long-term educational goals of attending college or university, it is imperative that the instruction that the youths receive prepares them both academically and socially. Obviously, they must meet the academic requirements and develop skills of independence in academic preparation such as study skills and test taking. Students should be able to explain their disability and relate it to instructional needs. Students should be able to understand the rights available to them regarding equal access and reasonable accommodations. Youths need opportunities to practice these self-advocacy skills with their high school teachers and counselors prior to school exit. Youths should know the accommodations they will need to be successful in postsecondary settings; these accommodations must be reasonable in terms of the setting demands of college and university. Students need to know where and how to access the supports offered to them through the college and university system. These supports are often found in offices in student counseling centers or in student support services. Supports include tutors, note takers, assistive technology readers, and word processors, as

Exhibit 14–4 Case Study of Ted: Planning for Postsecondary Education at College

Ted is a 17-year-old student with a severe hearing loss. Ted has good oral skills, but also uses American Sign Language (ASL). He relies on an ASL interpreter to understand spoken language in the classroom. At the IEP meeting, Ted expressed that he wants to go to public state college to study history and government with a long-term goal of becoming a lawyer. Ted's academic program has been consistent with this goal, and he has been successful in earning diploma credits and passing all state competency requirements. He has taken a study skills and test-taking class through a special education program. Ted's guidance counselor agreed to arrange for Ted to take the SATs,

with time extensions as needed and an interpreter for oral directions. This year Ted agreed to take on the responsibility of working with his general classroom teachers regarding the use of the interpreter and a peer note taker. His family agreed to take Ted to visit college campuses, including the student support services on campus. Ted will continue to work on his speech and speech reading with the speech-language pathologist to increase his ability to interact with the hearing public. He will be referred to the summer-orientation program at the local community college where he can have an opportunity to experience college life firsthand.

well as interpreters, physical accommodations, and so forth. Readily available services at colleges and universities may differ; matching the student and the postsecondary institution is very important (deFur et al., in press). The case study of Ted, described in Exhibit 14–4, illustrates the importance of developing academic, social, and communication skills that are required for college.

Preparation for the social and time-management aspects of postsecondary education can be facilitated by campus visits or by asking speakers with disabilities to come to the secondary school. It is becoming more common for colleges and universities to offer orientation classes for young adults with disabilities as well as without disabilities.

Colleges and universities are not the only education options for youths with disabilities. Technical training, continuing education, apprenticeships, and adult education also represent viable options. Bob, described in Exhibit 14–5, will have a seamless transition to vocational training and employment. Students with disabilities are entitled to special education through age 21 (or older, depending on state regulations). Some secondary programs offer transition services for older students at community college sites, thus

enabling students to be in age-appropriate, inclusive settings while continuing to receive special education support. Also, many community colleges and some four-year colleges have established curricula that provide training or vocational certificates for young adults whose disabilities typically would prevent them from participating in such an academic setting. Adult services can also support these training programs when students have a clear vocational goal. Transition planning with an inclusive philosophy means considering all students as lifelong learners and helping youths with disabilities and their families to plan for these educational outcomes.

Planning for Adult Living in Inclusive Settings

Although employment and education contribute to the quality of a person's life, how and where a person lives and plays within the community may be of greater importance. Adult living outcomes include such things as living in a residence of choice, having transportation options, planning for financial and medical needs, participating in the community in recreation and leisure activities, and achieving

Exhibit 14–5 Case Study of Bob: Planning for Postsecondary Vocational Training

Bob is a 19-year-old student with mild cognitive disabilities. Bob has been in training as a carpenter's assistant in the vocational carpentry program at his local high school and has completed half of the competencies for certification. At his last IEP meeting, Bob indicated that he is anxious to graduate with his peers. The guidance counselor and the vocational education teacher described how the high school and the local community college have worked together to create seamless technical training programs. The IEP team agreed to provide Bob with special education tutorial services daily while he continued his vocational training on the local community

college campus; this collaborative colocated program between the public schools and the community college allows this special education support to be available until Bob reaches the maximum age of eligibility for special education. The rehabilitation counselor agreed to help with the remainder of community college finances for Bob. Because Bob is working part time and receives Social Security, a PASS (program to achieve self-sufficiency) will be developed to purchase the tools he will need for the community college training program. Bob will participate in the summer orientation to the college campus life.

Exhibit 14–6 Case Study of Liza: Planning To Participate Fully As an Adult in the Community

Liza is a 20-year-old student with physical disabilities and moderate cognitive disabilities who is entering her last year of public education. When she finishes school, Liza wants to live with a friend from her class who will also be graduating. Since the age of 18, Liza has been receiving Social Security. Liza will be participating in a supported employment program, and the IEP team will be helping the rehabilitation counselor develop a PASS (program to achieve self-sufficiency) so that Liza will keep her benefits as she works. Liza will join the high school service club this year; she and her service club mentor will be volunteering in an inclusive third-grade class. Liza's family attends a local church. Liza will attend the young adult group meetings; a peer from this group agreed to give Liza a ride in her van to the meetings. Liza and her family and Liza's friend's family will meet with the mental retardation services case manager to explore how to obtain supported living funds for the two friends to live together when they graduate. Adult living curriculum skills for Liza this year will focus on independent-living skills in cooking, self-care, communication, and housekeeping.

independent living skills or supports such as self-care or supported care. Achieving goals for adult living creates a foundation that allows individuals to work and learn new skills.

IEP goals and objectives for young adults with disabilities in these areas reveal the depth of long-term commitment to full community integration by transition planning teams. Many young adults with disabilities have skills to work, but lack the necessary transportation or funds for child care to work. Some may have not learned how to manage their medical needs or to request reasonable accommodations for themselves. Many young adults would like to live more independently. Unfortunately, few independent living options are available. Most group homes have waiting lists. Further, group homes are usually defined for people with a certain disability and do not offer supported living for persons wishing to choose their housemate based on friendship. Liza, as described in the case study in Exhibit 14–6, and her friend will have the opportunity to exercise the choice of housemates and to live as independently as possible in a home or apartment.

To counteract these factors, youths and families, in partnership with IEP teams and adult service case managers, should identify individual support needs and develop a plan for achieving these goals. These plans may require advocacy for the development of new and alternative living options. Educators must become familiar with, and link with, those agencies and organizations that provide the support and planning to realize these postsecondary outcomes (see Exhibit 14–1). System resources (people and funds) are limited, so educators and families must develop creative alternatives to explore.

The unspoken curriculum (that is, the extracurricular activities, the social structure, and the climate of a school) also has a role to play in actualizing adult living goals. Youths with disabilities, regardless of the severity of the disability, seldom have a place in the "power and influence structure" of their school or home community. They are less likely to be involved in extracurricular activities where true social relationships are formed. Friendships are perhaps the most significant quality-of-life indicator. While IEPs cannot mandate friendships or goals to increase the number of friends, transition planning with an inclusive philosophy will include creating the structure that allows friendships and social relationships to develop. John's case study, as described in Exhibit 14–7, illustrates some ways in which these experiences can be structured by IEP teams.

Families have an essential role in planning for adult living in inclusive settings. Contemplating adult living goals often creates angst for families as they decide to let go of, or reduce, their caretaker role for their children. Letting youths drive or travel independently, live on their own, manage their own finances, and establish their own independent role in the community represent a major step for families. Remember that many times throughout their child's life, families revisit the stages of grief they may have felt upon first learning that their child had a disability; perhaps no stage is as intense as the experience of having the child leave the protective state of schooling. Discussions about adult living outcomes prompt these emotions in families. Sensitivity to these emotions is critical in helping families and young adults with disabilities make choices within an inclusive philosophy.

CONCLUSION: ADOPTING AN INCLUSIVE PHILOSOPHY FOR TRANSITION

Personal commitment and communication among parents, students, educators, and adult service providers are essential to actualizing an inclusive philosophy for transition. One of the top 10 critical competencies for a transition specialist is to be able to "identify and implement strategies to facilitate acceptance and integration of young adults with disabilities in employment and community environments" (deFur & Taymans, 1995, p. 44). School administrative support for inclusive practices and for

Exhibit 14–7 Case Study of John: Developing Friendships, Self-Advocacy, and Independent Living Skills

John is a 17-year-old in foster care with a visual impairment, seizure disorder, and an emotional disability. John has lived in this community for only one year. John is working toward a standard high school diploma. He has excellent verbal skills. He is receiving counseling services from the school psychologist and mobility and orientation training from the vision teacher. At his IEP meeting, John indicated a desire to live in the city with friends when he graduates, but he currently is dependent on others for transportation, money management, and household care skills. At his most recent IEP meeting, the social services agency case manager offered to fund John's participation as a summer camp "counselor in training" as one step to improve his independent living skills and social interactions. In school, John agreed to join the debate team as a way to develop self-advocacy skills and friendships. John's curriculum will include instruction in using the city bus system to travel around the city and other independent living skills. John's foster family agreed to work with him to establish a bank account and credit. They also agreed to have him talk with his doctor to increase John's understanding of his seizure disorder and the medicine he takes to control it. Finally, John's foster family and the social service agency agreed that John will continue to receive foster care services until he is established within the community as a young adult.

appropriate transition curriculum will allow educators to act on their beliefs of promoting full community integration as adults (Janney, Snell, Beers, & Raynes, 1995; Miller, Frita, & Littlejohn, 1995). For the goals of community integration to be achieved, it is insufficient for only educators to hold this philosophy and these beliefs. Adult services, community organizations, and businesses must share this inclusive philosophy as well. Administrative support at each organizational level is an essential beginning (Griffin, 1994).

Transition and inclusion hold similar philosophical foundations. If one truly believes that education should prepare students to live and work in the community, then one must believe in the principles of school-to-postschool transition and the principles of inclusion. What must be reconciled is how and where these beliefs are translated into action on behalf of students. Adopting an inclusive philosophy for transition planning means framing each educational decision in the context of the principles given below. When planning or implementing transition services for youths and young adults with disabilities, service providers should ask themselves if the action in which they engage on behalf of the individual with a disability promotes one or more of these principles:

- Youths and young adults with disabilities have a right to live and work within the community.
- Youths and young adults with disabilities can learn the life skills to live and work within the community to the best of their ability.
- Youths and young adults with disabilities have a right to appropriate educational experiences that promote their successful transition into adult lives.
- Youths and young adults with disabilities can develop an ability to evaluate themselves and to exercise choice and control in their lives.

Inclusive practices have become the accepted educational model for children and youths with disabilities. Translating this model to the community remains a challenge, but one that holds promise. Assistive technology, expanding economies, heightened expectations, and a generation of youths who have been educated together create the backdrop for an adult community that embraces diversity of ability as the community of choice for the future.

REFERENCES

Americans with Disabilities Act of 1990, Pub. L. No. 101-336.

Armstrong, T. (1994). *Multiple intelligences in the classroom*. Alexandria, VA: Association for Supervision and Curriculum Development.

Benz, M., & Halpern, A. (1987). Transition services for secondary students with mild disabilities: A statewide perspective. *Exceptional Children, 53*, 507–514.

Chadsey-Rusch, J., & Heal, L.S. (1995). Building consensus from transition experts on social integration outcomes and interventions. *Exceptional Children, 62*, 165–187.

Chadsey-Rusch, J., Rusch, F., & O'Reilly, M. (1993). Transition from school to integrated communities. In P. Kohler, J. Johnson, J. Chadsey-Rusch, & F. Rusch (Eds.), *Transition from school to adult life: Foundations, best practices, and research directions* (pp. 1–29).

Urbana-Champaign: University of Illinois, Transition Research Institute.

Clark, G., Field, S., Patton, J., Brolin, D., & Sitlington, P. (1994). Life skills instruction: A necessary component for all students with disabilities: A position statement of the Division on Career Development and Transition. *Career Development for Exceptional Individuals, 17*, 125–134.

Covey, S. (1989). *The seven habits of highly effective people*. New York: Simon and Schuster.

deFur, S., Getzel, E., & Trossi, K. (in press). Making the postsecondary education match: A role for IEP planning. *Journal of Vocational Rehabilitation*.

deFur, S., & Reiff, H. (1994). Transition of youths with learning disabilities to adulthood: The secondary education foundation. In P. Gerber &

H. Reiff (Eds.), *Adults with learning disabilities* (pp. 99–100). Andover, MA: Andover Medical.

deFur, S., & Taymans, J. (1995). Competencies needed for transition specialists in vocational rehabilitation, vocational education, and special education. *Exceptional Children, 62*, 38–51.

Education for All Handicapped Children Act of 1975, Pub. L. No. 94-142.

Griffin, C. (1994). Organizational natural supports: The role of leadership in facilitating inclusion. *Journal of Vocational Rehabilitation, 4*, 296–307.

Guterman, B.R. (1995). The validity of categorical learning disabilities services: The consumer's view. *Exceptional Children, 62*, 111–124.

Hagner, D., & DiLeo, D. (1993). *Working together: Workplace supported employment and persons with disabilities*. Cambridge, MA: Brookline.

Halpern, A.S. (1985). Transition: A look at the foundations. *Exceptional Children, 57*, 479–486.

Halpern, A.S. (1993). Quality of life as a conceptual framework for evaluating transition outcomes. *Exceptional Children, 59*, 486–498.

Halpern, A.S. (1994). The transition of youth with disabilities into adult life: A position statement of the Division on Career Development and Transition. *Career Development for Exceptional Individuals, 17*, 115–124.

Harry, B., Grenot-Scheyer, M., Smith-Lewis, M., Park, H., Xin, F., & Schwartz, I. (1994). *Developing culturally inclusive services for individuals with severe disabilities*. Unpublished manuscript. College Park, MD: University of Maryland.

Hasazi, S.B., Gordon, L., & Roe, C. (1985). Factors associated with the employment status of handicapped youth exiting high school from 1979–1983. *Exceptional Children, 53*, 455–469.

Individuals with Disabilities Education Act of 1990, Pub. L. No. 101-476.

Janney, R.E., Snell, M.E., Beers, M.K., & Raynes, M. (1995). Integrating students with moderate and severe disabilities into general education classes. *Exceptional Children, 61*, 425–439.

Kohler, P. (1994). On the job training: A curricular approach to employment. *Career Development for Exceptional Individuals, 17*, 29–40.

Menchetti, B.M., & Bombay, H.E. (1994). Facilitating community inclusion within vocational portfolios. *Assessment in Rehabilitation and Exceptionality, 1*, 212–222.

Miller, M., Frita, M., & Littlejohn, W. (1995). Effective planning for inclusion: Who does what? *Case in Point, 9*(1), 10–15.

Neubert, D.A., Tilson, G., & Ianacone, R.N. (1989). Postsecondary transition needs and employment patterns of individuals with mild disabilities. *Exceptional Children, 55*, 494–500.

Peraino, J. (1992). Post-21 follow-up studies: How do special education graduates fare? In P. Wehman (Ed.), *Life beyond the classroom: Transition strategies for young people with disabilities* (pp. 21–70). Baltimore: Paul H. Brookes.

School to Work Opportunities Act of 1994, Pub. L. No. 103-239.

Sitlington, P., Frank, A., & Carson, R. (1990). *Iowa statewide follow-up study: Adult adjustment of individuals with mild disabilities one year after leaving school*. Des Moines: Iowa Department of Education.

Staub, D., & Peck, C. (1994). What are the outcomes for nondisabled students? *Educational Leadership, 52*(4), 36–40.

Syzmanski, E. (1994). Transition: Life-span and life-space considerations for empowerment. *Exceptional Children, 60*, 401–410.

Virginia Department of Education. (1994). *Demographics of students exiting special education in Virginia* (House Document No. 14). Richmond, VA: Virginia General Assembly.

Wagner, M., Newman, L., D'Amico, R., Jay, E., Butler-Nalin, P., Marder, C., & Cox, R. (1991). *Youth with disabilities: How are they doing?* Washington, DC: U.S. Department of Education.

Wehmeyer, M. (1993). Perceptual and psychological factors in career decision-making of adolescents with and without cognitive disabilities. *Career Development for Exceptional Individuals, 16*, 135–146.

Will, M. (1984). *OSERS programming for the transition of youth with disabilities: Bridges from school to work life*. Washington, DC: Office of Special Education and Rehabilitative Services.

CHAPTER 15

Including Students with Behavioral Challenges: Blending Schoolwide Discipline and Individual Supports

K. Brigid Flannery, Jeffrey R. Sprague, and Anne W. Todd

INTRODUCTION

Most discussions about inclusion eventually turn to the question, "What about students with behavioral problems?" Students who hit or fight with their peers, talk out, disrupt others, or defy teacher requests present the most substantial barriers to participation in the general education program. What systems are needed to provide effective support to these students? How much will it cost? How do schools develop the expertise to respond to antisocial and disruptive behavior? Can we include all students with challenging behavior? This chapter provides some guidance and answers to these questions.

This chapter discusses the need for integrated approaches to address challenging behavior in schools and outlines foundations for a proactive, schoolwide plan to provide a safe, orderly learning environment for all students. Next, the chapter describes the four major systems necessary to provide effective support for students with challenging behavior, outlining critical assessment and development activities and procedures for implementing each system. Finally, the chapter discusses issues related to liability and safety.

The activity that is the subject of this chapter was supported in whole or in part by the U.S. Department of Education, Grant Nos. H029N30003 and H133B2004. However, the opinions expressed herein do not necessarily reflect the position or policy of the U.S. Department of Education, and no official endorsement by the department should be inferred.

The authors would like to acknowledge the work of Rob Horner, George Sugai, Geoff Colvin, Tim Lewis, Rick Albin, and Rob O'Neill, which served as a basis for this chapter.

The Need for System-Based Approaches To Address Problem Behavior in Schools

Disruptive and antisocial behavior is increasing in frequency and intensity in our schools (Walker, 1995). Students who use physical and verbal aggression, commit vandalism, carry weapons, defy adult requests, or engage in self-destructive behavior (e.g., hit themselves, abuse alcohol or drugs) are the most likely to be excluded from the regular school program via suspension, expulsion, or referral to special education or alternative education (Reichle, 1990). These students prompt the most teacher requests for assistance (Bulgatz & O'Neill, 1994; Horner, Diemer, & Brazeau, 1992; Sprague & Rian, 1993) and often account for nearly half the office referrals in a given school (Hall, Horner, & Ard, 1995; Walker, 1995). If these patterns of behavior go unchecked, students with challenging behavior will likely drop out of school (U.S. Department of Education, 1994) and become adults with antisocial lifestyles that include criminal behavior, domestic abuse, alcohol and drug use, and other personal adjustment problems (APA Commission on Youth Violence, 1993; Walker, Colvin, & Ramsey, 1995).

The landscape of our schools is changing rapidly. More students are from culturally diverse backgrounds, are unprepared to enter school, and present learning and behavioral challenges (Knitzer, 1993; Knitzer, Steinberg, & Fleisch, 1990; Stevens & Price, 1992). In addition, shrinking support for public education results in fewer supports for teachers (e.g., time, materials, expert support) and larger class sizes. Each of these elements increases the complexity of the challenge to include all students in the regular school program.

Traditional systems of school discipline respond to students with challenging behavior by punishing or excluding them (Mayer & Sulzer-Azaroff, 1990; Walker et al., 1995). Sadly, the punishment and exclusion strategies such as office referral, detention, suspension, and expulsion are among the least effective responses to disruptive and antisocial behavior (Lipsey, 1992). Using these methods without effective skill instruction and preventive support can result in *increases* in aggression, vandalism, truancy, tardiness, and dropout rates (Mayer & Sulzer-Azaroff, 1990).

Understanding the Challenge

Disruptive and antisocial behavior poses a serious challenge to inclusive education. To successfully include the widest range of students with challenging behavior, schools must change traditional practices and develop new approaches to support and empower teachers. Schools should provide an environment that promotes prosocial behavior for students and adults. Successful school improvement to support students with challenging behavior requires a broad-based foundation (Sugai & Horner, 1994; Walker et al., 1995).

The Foundation for Including Students with Challenging Behavior

Before embarking on a large-scale effort to develop effective, proactive teacher and student support systems, personnel should consider the variables that will contribute to successful change. Most students in a given school behave appropriately with universal interventions such as schoolwide rules and reinforcement systems. Approximately 10% to 15% of the total school population who challenge schoolwide rules (students with and without identified disabilities) will be successful with extra supports such as skill teaching, self-management systems, and appropriate consequences (Todd, Horner, Vanater, & Schneider, in press). Finally, a small group of approximately 3% to 7% of students will need some form of intensive, individualized behavioral support to succeed and be included in the general education program (Walker et al., 1995). Without adequate political support, resources, and staff commitment, any effort to improve behavioral support is doomed to fail (Mayer, 1995). Nevertheless, few schools have all the resources and supports required for widespread, rapid change. Developing and maintaining systems to support students with challenging behavior will require commitment and a period of time (generally a few years). Figure 15–1 presents an overview of the foundation outlined in the following sections.

Improving Behavioral Support As a Schoolwide Priority

Schools must strive for quality services with limited resources and support. As such, it is unlikely that schools can approach all possible improvement efforts at once.

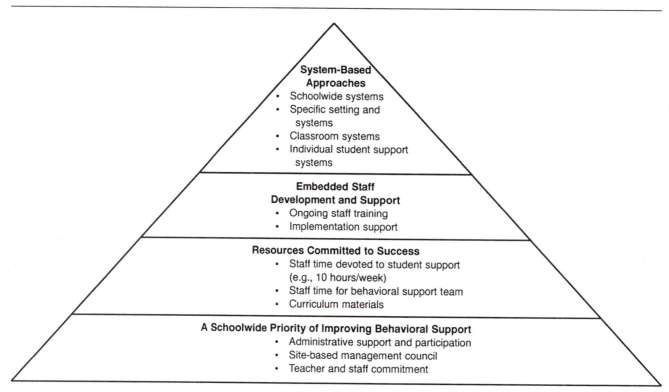

Figure 15–1 The foundation for including students with challenging behavior

Adapting curriculum, improving math and reading instruction, providing arts and music, and delivering services for other at-risk students will require time, resources, and commitment. Improving behavioral support procedures to include a wider range of students with challenging behavior should be among the *top three priorities* for action. Active administrative support and leadership should be evident through presentations to staff, active participation and attendance at planning meetings, a commitment to data collection (e.g., discipline referrals, suspensions, expulsions), and a visible presence in the school building. In a school's site-based management teams (e.g., parents, teachers, and administrators), the inclusion of students with behavioral challenges should be an integral part of the school-improvement plan and reflected in budgetary allotments. Teachers and staff in the building must show commitment to the effort by volunteering for work groups, agreeing to participate in training activities, and implementing change.

Committing Resources To Ensure Success

Words and written plans must be backed with the resources needed to provide effective support to students and teachers. A good index of behavioral support capacity in a building of 400 students is approximately 10 hours per week of expertise devoted to providing individualized student supports (e.g., teacher consultation, observations, program development, training). This time may all come from one person or may be spread across a few people (e.g., special education teachers, consultants, or teacher facilitators from general education). In-building expertise is preferable. In addition to focused staff resources, the team and system-based approaches described in this chapter assume that *all* building staff will allot time for planning, implementing, and evaluating behavioral support activities. It is advisable to integrate many of these activities with universal school-improvement and safe-schools initiatives designed for all students, thus avoiding a major additional burden to staff. If successful inclusion of students with behavioral challenges is truly a school priority, then administrators must ensure that resources meet the above recommendations. A final commitment involves development and application of curricula. It is useful to deliver instruction for all students on core prosocial behaviors (Walker et al., 1995), peer mediation (Shepherd, 1994), empathy (Embry, Flannery, Vasonyi, Powell, & Atha, in press), and a host of situation-specific behaviors in the school. Application of this content may require purchase of materials or staff time to develop in-house training materials and formats.

Providing Effective Staff Development and Support

Application of new procedures and revision of existing structures require a program of effective staff development and support. Schools will change if given support for team-based training within the school and active involvement of administrators in the training, and if there is long-term commitment to the process (Sugai, Horner, Todd, Colvin et al., 1995). Training and support needs to do more than simply add novel information through inservice training such as one-day workshops or conferences. Effective staff development *embeds* policy, training activities, and evaluation within the ongoing operation of the school (Albin, Horner, & Walker, 1993). Embedded staff development focuses on frequent, short, in-house training sessions that are delivered by in-house staff as much as possible. Training also should include opportunities for staff to observe and coach one another (Showers, 1990) as they learn to carry out new practices.

Developing Systems-Based Approaches

A comprehensive, integrated system of schoolwide and individualized procedures for teaching and enforcing rules for appropriate behavior can both prevent and reduce rates of disruptive and antisocial behavior (Colvin, Kameenui, & Sugai, 1993; Colvin, Martz, DeForest, & Wilt, 1995; Nelson & Colvin, 1995; Sugai & Horner, 1994; Todd et al., in press). The following sections describe the features of systems that affect *all* students and staff (schoolwide), those designed to address specific-setting issues such as the cafeteria or hallways, classroom procedures, and individual-student support procedures.

THE FOUR ESSENTIAL SYSTEMS FOR PROVIDING EFFECTIVE SUPPORT

There are several central themes in developing a comprehensive, positive behavioral-support system in any school. First, strategies must be responsive to all students, not just to one class or category of students such as students with emotional behavioral disorders, students at risk, or students with severe disabilities (Sugai & Horner, 1994). Second, strategies should focus not only on individual students, but on the whole school. Building individual plans for all students is overwhelming. The focus on schoolwide systems reduces the number of individual plans. Third, the process for developing behavioral-support plans must include those staff who carry out the plan, and must be responsive to their values and their experiences and to the unique routines within the school (Albin, Lucyshyn, Horner, & Flannery, 1996; Colvin et al., 1993; Todd et al., in press). Throughout this chapter, the term *staff* refers to a broad range of individuals including, but not limited to, counselors, general and special education teachers, paraprofessionals, parents, volunteers, administrators, and others. Finally, the system should strive to accommodate the increased challenges presented by students who typically are served in more restrictive settings.

George Sugai, Robert Horner, and their colleagues have identified four systems for providing and implementing comprehensive, positive behavior-support services: (1) schoolwide systems, (2) specific-setting systems, (3) classroom systems, and (4) individual-student systems (see Figure 15–2) (Sugai, Horner, Todd, Colvin et al., 1995; Sugai, Horner, Todd, & Sprague, 1995). The critical features common to all systems are as follows:

- The system is for *all* students.
- Student expectations are simple, clear, and known by all.
- Students are taught appropriate behavior.
- Positive behavior is recognized and rewarded.
- A continuum of consequences for problem behavior exists.
- Student behavior is actively monitored.
- Procedures for emergencies and crises are in place.
- Regular feedback is provided to staff and students.

Schoolwide Systems

Schoolwide systems provide the structure and procedures that affect all students and personnel within the school. The primary purposes are to provide guidance and support for the majority of students who want to do a good job and to provide staff with an overall plan. A schoolwide system defines the basic rules of the school based on the districtwide rules, provides plans to define those rules, and pro-

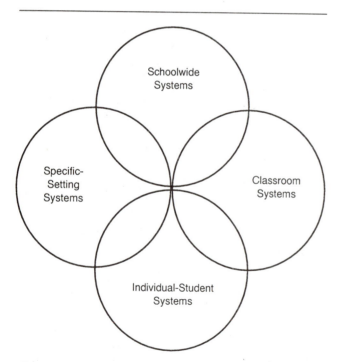

Figure 15–2 Effective behavioral support in schools. *Source:* Reprinted from *Comprehensive, Positive Behavior Support,* Field-Initiated Grant Application, R. Horner, G. Sugai, J. Sprague, and A. Todd, September 1995.

vides feedback systems (both rewards and corrections). If the schoolwide system is working, students can describe acceptable and unacceptable behavior; staff are consistent in how they define and implement school rules; administration and staff act in concert in implementing the rules; staff directly teach students the rules; students are rewarded for following rules more than they are punished for failing to follow them; and, above all, the number of office referrals and the number of students involved in problems (office referrals) is low (typically less than 15% of the total population).

Schoolwide systems allow schools to shift toward more positive, proactive, and preventive support systems that include all students and staff. The schoolwide system is more durable and effective if a school team develops it and it has the active support and involvement of a school administrator. It is efficient and, if done well and consistently, effective with most students. Staff should not be discouraged or disappointed, however, if some students show no response to the schoolwide discipline system.

Specific-Setting Systems

Sometimes there are unique requirements for specific settings because of different routines, contexts, expectations, and people. The uniqueness of the setting often results in a lack of consistency of supervision and feedback, which increases opportunities for students to engage in problem behaviors. Features of these settings that may affect a student's behavior include the physical layout, variety of adults providing supervision, numbers of students, types of demands, and degree of choice. Specific-setting systems provide the structure and procedures associated with specific times (e.g., before or after school) and places (e.g., cafeteria, playground, hallways, and bus arrival/departure areas).

Classroom Systems

The third system focuses on those structures and procedures that teachers use to support and teach individuals or groups of students. These procedures are consistent with the schoolwide rules but focus on what happens and how things happen in a specific teacher's classroom. Typically, teaching styles differ across classrooms because of the values, experiences, and routines of the teacher. Each classroom-management plan must fit and support the unique features of the teacher, but must also be grounded in the schoolwide rules. Moreover, variables such as the number and diversity of students, task and curricular demands, and the physical layout of the classroom may influence the behavioral expectations. Expectations and plans that align closely with the existing routines, performance goals, and strategies of the classroom are most successful.

Individual-Student Systems

The fourth system focuses on those students for whom the schoolwide, specific-setting, and classroom systems are not enough. These students will need individualized, comprehensive, behavioral-support plans to be successful in school. Although the number of students in this group tends to be small (3% to 7% of all students in the school), the impact of their behavior on classrooms, specific settings, and the school as a whole is significant (Sugai, Horner, Todd, Colvin et al., 1995). These students require more than 70% of the staff's time and result in more than 35% of the office referrals (Sugai, Horner, Todd, Colvin et al., 1995). Individual-student support systems focus on proactive plans of support based on functional assessments that assist staff who have regular contact with the students. An individual-student support system can include such things as a team support structure, functional assessment of behavioral support, individually designed instruction, and behaviorally based interventions. Schoolwide systems, features of schoolwide rules, and specific-setting and classroom routines must be embedded into the individual support plan. For example, in schools using a schoolwide program for students to monitor their own behavior, staff value individual-student support plans that focus on teaching students to be "self-managers."

USING ASSESSMENT RESULTS TO IMPROVE STUDENT SUPPORT

The approach to including students with challenging behavior depends on the size of the school, the types and number of problems (found from the schoolwide assessment), and the capacity of the staff and administration. Many schools have teams established for supporting individual students who encounter academic problems. The approach of this chapter mirrors that approach for supporting students with behavioral challenges.

There are four steps for effecting change, whether it is at the level of the system or the individual student. These include:

1. Establish a team.
2. Conduct an assessment.
3. Design a plan of support.
4. Implement, monitor, and revise the plan.

These four steps are based on the foundations and systems laid out earlier in this chapter. The process should be systems-driven, team-based, and proactive. The steps schools can take to establish each of the four systems are discussed below.

Step 1: Establish a Team

There is no single way to design the team structure that supports the four systems: schoolwide, specific settings, classroom, and individual support. What is important is that a school approaches assessment, implementation, and problem solving through teamwork (Colvin et al., 1995; Sugai & Horner, 1994). Most schools have a schoolwide team (e.g., teacher-support team, teacher-assistance team, behavior-support team) and teams for students who need individual support plans. Schools also may have a subteam (ad hoc committee) to deal with specific settings such as the cafeteria or playground, because the schoolwide team may not represent the staff in those settings (e.g., part-time staff or parent volunteers) or may have too much to do. Schools are encouraged to look at existing teams to see if one or more team can be redesigned to support these systems (Sugai & Horner, 1994). If more than one team is developed, a member of each additional team should serve on the schoolwide team to establish continuity and maintain communication.

Whatever the overall structure, each team within the school should have several critical features:

- Action plans are built from an assessment of the problem.
- Action plans are team driven.
- Administrators actively participate in team meetings.
- At least one member of each team participates in the schoolwide team to establish a natural communicative link between teams.
- Teams meet regularly (weekly or biweekly).

Schoolwide Team

The first step is to form a schoolwide team that establishes goals, processes, and procedures for all four systems within the school. Developing a schoolwide team is important because it integrates schoolwide discipline and individual-support procedures. Collective membership of the schoolwide team should have active administrative participation (e.g., principal), behavioral expertise, and a balance of general and special educators. The schoolwide team is responsible for conducting a schoolwide assessment; for developing a school-improvement plan based on the assessment; and for implementing the plan, monitoring progress, and making ongoing revisions to the plan. Schoolwide teams work most effectively if they meet weekly.

Specific-Setting Team

The schoolwide team may implement the tasks associated with this system, or a specific-setting team may be established. This may be necessary when the schoolwide team is very busy or does not include individuals from the specific settings. For example, the plan for the playground may involve only the playground supervisors and a representative or two from the teaching staff. If a specific-setting team is established, at least one member should be a member of the schoolwide team to maintain communication and consistency. Once the rules and expectations are established and the plan is developed, a specific-setting team may not be necessary. Instead, the ongoing monitoring and revision can occur through the schoolwide team.

Classroom Team

As the number of students increases, so does the range of diversity, abilities, and learning styles. Classroom teachers with concerns about student behavior will need help in assessing the problems, identifying the type of data to be collected, collecting the data, and designing a plan to resolve the classroom issues. The school should develop procedures for teachers to obtain such support from the schoolwide team or others. For example, the schoolwide team could establish regular opportunities (once or twice a month) for classroom teachers to discuss strategies for topics, including curriculum adaptations, classroom management, and teaching prosocial skills. Another alternative would be to discuss these topics at grade-level team meetings on a regular basis. The purpose is to encourage an ongoing dialogue between classroom teachers so that management and teaching strategies shift to meet the needs of each group of students.

Individual-Student Team

Even with each of the previous systems in place, some students need individual, comprehensive, positive behavioral-support plans. Often, the schoolwide team is the forum for staff to request assistance initially with individual students, but another team may be appropriate. The referring person should be asked about his or her concerns, what general strategies were previously used, and where problems occurred or did not occur. An example of the information necessary for referring an individual student is provided in Exhibit 15–1.

A team also should be established for each individual student (e.g., action team, student-support team). This team is responsible for developing the individualized plan and providing support. The referral information helps identify who should be members of an action team for each individual student. The action team can have any number of members, but must include at a minimum: the teacher, the student, a family member, and a schoolwide team representative. All other staff who interact with the student on a regular basis should be encouraged to participate. It is important to have people with technical knowledge (e.g., counseling, assessment, behavioral technology) and those who know and have rapport with the student (Todd et al., in press). Members can participate in a variety of ways, from participating in general discussions to gathering the assessment data and developing the plan.

Step 2: Conduct an Assessment

The systems of support within a building must be integrated to form one comprehensive system. However, establishing more than one system at a time is difficult due to limited time and resources. Assessment and evaluation should help determine where to start implementation of a schoolwide system. A schoolwide assessment and evaluation will give school teams information on existing discipline policies and procedures, referral patterns, school safety routines, components of procedures that are currently working or not working, and targeted areas for improvement. Figure 15–3 provides information on specific areas of assessment for each of the four systems.

Assessment results illustrate four typical patterns of problem behavior (discipline), with each different pattern requiring different solutions (Sugai, Horner, Todd, & Sprague, 1995). Understanding the different patterns and the different solutions is a key to understanding the logic behind the schoolwide systems approach (see Exhibit 15–2).

Pattern 1: Many Teachers, Many Students, Many Problems, and Many Situations

When assessment of the school identifies discipline (or problem behavior) issues involving numerous incidents and

---

Exhibit 15–1 Critical Features for Referring a Student to a Teacher Support Team

- Provide a brief statement of the current problem. Identify specific problem situations, problem behaviors, and expected behaviors.
- What consequences have been tried to date for correcting the problem behaviors?
- What has been tried to date to teach the expected behaviors?
- What has been tried to date to change the situations in which the problem behaviors occur?
- When is the problem behavior most and least likely to occur?
- What do you think the student may gain from engaging in the problem behaviors?
- Is there an appropriate behavior that the student could use that would make the problem behavior unnecessary?

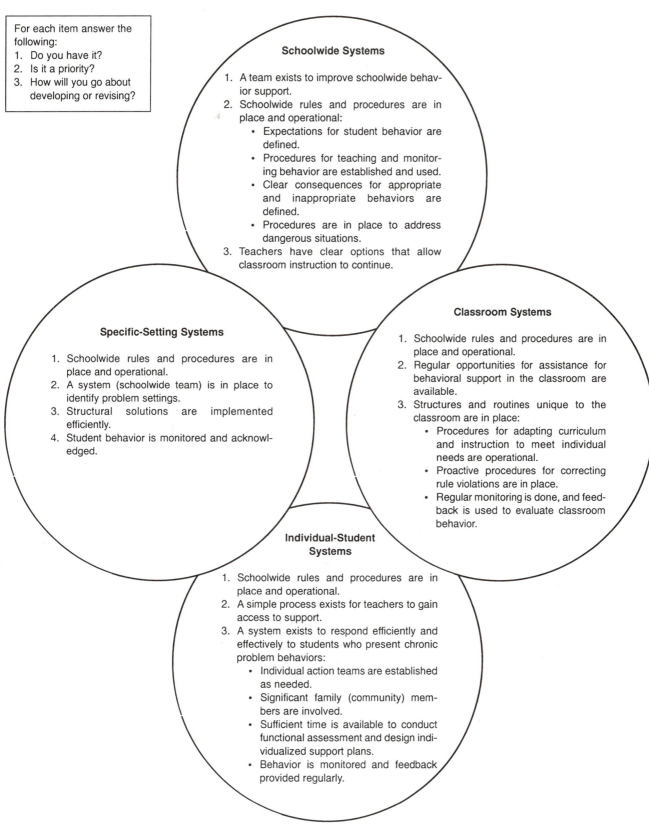

For each item answer the following:
1. Do you have it?
2. Is it a priority?
3. How will you go about developing or revising?

Schoolwide Systems

1. A team exists to improve schoolwide behavior support.
2. Schoolwide rules and procedures are in place and operational:
   - Expectations for student behavior are defined.
   - Procedures for teaching and monitoring behavior are established and used.
   - Clear consequences for appropriate and inappropriate behaviors are defined.
   - Procedures are in place to address dangerous situations.
3. Teachers have clear options that allow classroom instruction to continue.

Specific-Setting Systems

1. Schoolwide rules and procedures are in place and operational.
2. A system (schoolwide team) is in place to identify problem settings.
3. Structural solutions are implemented efficiently.
4. Student behavior is monitored and acknowledged.

Classroom Systems

1. Schoolwide rules and procedures are in place and operational.
2. Regular opportunities for assistance for behavioral support in the classroom are available.
3. Structures and routines unique to the classroom are in place:
   - Procedures for adapting curriculum and instruction to meet individual needs are operational.
   - Proactive procedures for correcting rule violations are in place.
   - Regular monitoring is done, and feedback is used to evaluate classroom behavior.

Individual-Student Systems

1. Schoolwide rules and procedures are in place and operational.
2. A simple process exists for teachers to gain access to support.
3. A system exists to respond efficiently and effectively to students who present chronic problem behaviors:
   - Individual action teams are established as needed.
   - Significant family (community) members are involved.
   - Sufficient time is available to conduct functional assessment and design individualized support plans.
   - Behavior is monitored and feedback provided regularly.

Figure 15–3 Assessing and evaluating your school. *Source:* Adapted from *Preventing Violent Behavior through Effective Behavioral Support*, Field Initiated Studies Educational Research Grant, R. Horner, G. Sugai, J. Sprague, and A. Todd, June 1996.

Exhibit 15–2 Patterns Linked to the Four Systems

SCHOOLWIDE • many staff • many students • many problems • many times and settings	**SPECIFIC SETTINGS** • many staff • many students • specific times and settings • specific problems
CLASSROOM • many students • few staff/few classrooms • low academic success • inconsistent problems	**INDIVIDUAL STUDENTS** • few students • few staff • repetitive problems • requests for removing students

many different students, the solution is to improve the schoolwide discipline procedures and policies. In one school, for example, 45% to 50% of the students were involved in office referrals (or problem incidents) during a three-month period, and the incidents were of a widely varying nature. If staff attempt to respond to such a problem with individual student discipline strategies (e.g., punishment for rule violation), the result is often an overload of the system. When many students are getting into trouble, the problem is with the *schoolwide system*, not the students.

Pattern 2: Many Students, Many Staff, Specific Problems at Specific Times or Places

When assessment identifies a specific setting that accounts for a large proportion of problem behaviors, the solution is to improve the plans and expectations for the specific setting. Often, the specific setting refers to the cafeteria, washrooms, halls, or playground. The architectural features of a school often influence problems in specific settings. When a specific setting results in a disproportionate number of problem incidents, focusing on the structural features of that setting is important. Too often staff attempt to address each incident as an independent event and to focus on each student in the context of independent events. There are simply too many students and too many events to deal with each problem independently. Problems are more likely to occur when lack of adult supervision or the architectural features of the school create frustrating demands. For example, the presence of 50 students and one adult who does not rotate around the area on the playground creates a high probability for problems. If unmonitored, student bathrooms become more likely sites for problem behaviors. Requiring 300 students to enter a small door for lunch at the same time leads to problems. Generally isolated pockets within a school that are difficult to monitor are often problem locations.

Assessment that identifies problems centered around specific times or settings (e.g., cafeteria, bus loading), and in which many different students and teachers are involved, suggests the need to revise, teach, and provide feedback (both positive and negative) for the *specific-setting routines* and to establish behavioral expectations for students and staff.

Pattern 3: Many Students, Few Teachers, Low Academic Success, Inconsistent Problems

When assessment reveals many incidents occurring in specific classrooms, the solution is to improve the classroom-management and support plans in those individual classrooms. As in specific settings, too often staff try to address each incident as an independent event, and to focus on each student in the context of independent events. For example, if many students are not completing their homework assignments, it may be that students cannot see the assignment as posted or cannot hear the teacher's directions, or that staff have not notified parents about homework assignment expectations. Remedies to these problems are to clarify and follow through with classroom expectations. Other problems could be the result of lesson presentation style. If several students become disruptive after 30 minutes of lecture, then those students probably need an alternative to listening to long lectures, or the teacher could adapt the presentation style to encourage more active listening skills. Assessment that reveals problems, poor academic outcomes, and inconsistent referrals from a few classrooms suggests changes in specific *classroom management* and curricular adaptations.

Pattern 4: Few Students, Few Teachers, Repetitive Problems, Requests for Removing Students

When assessment identifies a small number of students who account for a large number of problems, the solution is to improve the individual support systems for those few students. Unlike the other three patterns, the response is not structural but individual. These students need additional resources and individualized support plans.

The challenge in designing individual support plans is to use resources efficiently and creatively to provide the support that allows each student with chronic problem behaviors to be successful, and also to provide the safe, educational context that allows other students (and teachers) to be successful. When assessment results in a small number of students (fewer than 10%) producing more than 25% of the problems, a small number of teachers reporting problems, requests for removal of certain students, or requests for more support to handle these students, the solution is to address *individual-student support* through support plans based on the results of the functional assessment.

To develop a support plan for an individual student, additional assessment information is needed about the student and his or her interaction with the environment. During the last decade, there has been a reemphasis on understanding when, where, and why a specific student engages in problem behaviors before actively developing a behavioral support plan (Sprague & Horner, 1995). Procedures known as *functional assessments* have been developed to address this need. Functional assessment procedures describe the relationship between the environment, physiological and psychological events affecting a student, problem behaviors, and desired student outcomes. During the past few years, considerable attention has been paid to conducting functional assessments in schools (Carr, Robinson, Taylor, & Carlson, 1990; Durand, 1990; Horner, O'Neill, & Flannery, 1993; Wacker et al., 1990).

A functional assessment involves careful observation of the individual to determine when and why the behavior occurs. Students perform these problem behaviors for a reason, and often it is to "get something" (e.g., teacher or peer attention) or to get out of an undesirable situation (e.g., tasks that are too hard). Through interviews with the student and with people who know the student well, information can be gathered about strategies that have or have not worked, medical information, the student's daily schedule, what the student likes or does well, and how the student communicates. Not only can a team gather information about the student between 8 A.M. and 3 P.M., but it may want to consider what happens outside of the school day. Setting events (e.g., lack of sleep, no breakfast, fight with a mother before school) may influence these behaviors and should be considered as part of the assessment (Dadson & Horner, 1993; Horner, Vaughn, Day, & Ard, 1996). Observations conducted in the settings where the behavior is most likely and least likely to occur validate the information gathered through interviews. They also help to define clearly the behavior of concern, events that predict its occurrence, and what function the behavior serves. A variety of tools have been developed to gather information through interviews, observations of the student, or specially designed situations (Carr et al., 1994; Dunlap & Childs, in press; Dunlap, Kern-Dunlap, Clarke, & Robbins, 1991; Dunlap & Kern, 1993; Durand & Crimmins, 1988; Lewis, Scott, & Sugai, 1994; Reed, Thomas, Sprague, & Horner, 1995).

A functional assessment should result in a summary statement that provides information on three things: (1) description of the problem behaviors, (2) predictors, and (3) consequences for behaviors. The summary statement should answer the questions: "What is this behavior?" and "Why is the person doing it?" The precision with which this is done will influence the comprehensiveness of the assessment and thus the effectiveness of the behavioral-support plan. Exhibit 15–3 provides illustrative information from several students' functional assessments, and Exhibit 15–4 is a blank form.

Because some students perform the same problem behavior for several different reasons or functions, it is easy to organize the summary statements around the functions as opposed to individual behaviors. For example, if the student uses several behaviors (e.g., hitting, yelling out) to get attention of his or her peers, then develop an intervention based on "getting attention," rather than on each behavior. If the same student has a group of behaviors (e.g., hitting, striking out) that are used to get out of undesired situations, treat those as a group. This will help in developing behavioral support plans based on the function of the behaviors (why the student does the behavior) rather than each problem behavior.

Step 3: Design a Plan of Support Based upon Rules and Expectations

Schoolwide

The schoolwide team should develop a short list of rules that describe the desired behavior or actions of students and support teaching and learning within the school. The most efficient strategy to develop new rules is for the schoolwide team to draft rules and share these with staff for discussion and approval. If the school already has rules, the team should review them for simplicity and clarity. Limiting the number of rules to three to five will help students and staff remember them and increase the likelihood of their implementation. Rules should be written using only a few words and in language simple enough to allow any student, staff, or parent to apply them to any school situation.

All students and staff must clearly understand what each rule means and use the rules to guide their behavior. For example, "Be safe" is concise and simple, but it may be interpreted differently by people in different situations. Defining expectations for each rule helps clarify what the rule means. For example, "Be safe" in school may mean: keep hands, feet, and materials to yourself; stay within the boundaries of the school grounds; and walk, don't run, in the building. It is helpful to provide students and staff with

Exhibit 15–3 Functional Assessment: Predictors, Behaviors, and Consequences

PREDICTORS	PROBLEM BEHAVIORS	CONSEQUENCES
What important events, places, or activities tend to be associated with the behavior? What appears to set off the behavior?	*What do the problem behaviors look like?*	*What does the person gain or avoid when he or she displays these behaviors? Why does this behavior work?*
Given difficult tasks or teacher corrections	Silas blurts out rude statements, uses impolite words, swears	to avoid engaging in work
Given independent work times	Silas fiddles with materials rather than doing the work	to get the teacher's attention
When in the classroom and peers tease her	Marie whines, pounds, is aggressive to others, and leaves	to get out of the situation
Given writing tasks that need to be edited or teacher correction on written work	Cindy puts her head down and does not talk	to get out of making written corrections, to avoid writing

Source: Reprinted from *Guidelines for Students with Specialized Health Care Needs,* Virginia Department of Health.

a set of examples that span the range of situations they may encounter. This will help them not only to remember the rule but to know when to apply it. Some examples of rules and expectations are provided in Exhibit 15–5.

The schoolwide plan should focus on what the consequences will be if students do not follow the rules and also provide a balance in emphasis on rules, expectations, and problem behaviors. The plan must provide opportunities for students to be taught the rules, be coached, and receive positive feedback for following the rules. Similar to teaching academic skills, several strategies are necessary to ensure that students learn the rules and how to follow them. Some sample strategies are presented in Exhibit 15–6. Implementation can be enhanced in the following ways:

- providing a title to the strategy or award (e.g., the Gotcha Award, Good Citizen)
- identifying what students will receive (e.g., trophy, certificate, privilege)

Exhibit 15–4 Form for Functional Assessment: Predictors, Behaviors, and Consequences

PREDICTORS	PROBLEM BEHAVIOR	CONSEQUENCES
What important events, places, or activities tend to be associated with the behavior? What appears to set off the behavior?	*What do the problem behaviors look like?*	*What does the person gain or avoid when he or she displays these behaviors? Why does this behavior work?*
1.		
2.		
3.		
4.		

Exhibit 15–5 School Rules and Expectations

KENNEDY ELEMENTARY SCHOOL

1. Be safe.
   - Walk in the halls and classrooms.
   - Keep hands, feet, and materials to self.
   - Do not carry knives or weapons.
   - Stay within school boundaries.
2. Be respectful.
   - Listen to the person talking.
   - Use polite words.
   - Wait your turn to talk.
   - Use words instead of your body to resolve differences.
3. Follow directions of all school adults.

WASHINGTON MIDDLE SCHOOL

1. Cooperate with others.
   - Settle differences by using words.
   - Use polite words.
   - Manage yourself.
2. Respect the rights and property of others
   - Ask to borrow materials from others.
   - Return borrowed materials to owner or storage spot.
   - Keep materials and body to self.
3. Maintain a safe and orderly environment.
   - Clean up materials when finished.
   - Report accidents/messes to adult.
4. Behave in a healthy manner.
   - Wash hands before leaving restroom.
   - Wash hands before meals.

Exhibit 15–6 Strategies for Schoolwide Acknowledgment of Acceptable Behavior

---

- Turn in names of students who follow rules appropriately and hold random drawings each week for "honored students."
- Provide a certificate of achievement to students on a quarterly basis.
- Acknowledge students in the school newspaper for following rules and expectations.
- Provide a button or sticker to students "caught" following rules or expectations. Certificates can be saved and used for buying school store supplies or snacks.
- Award lunch with the principal if. . . .
- Award extra recess or break time to groups of students.

- clearly defining criteria for who is eligible, how often it is awarded, and how many students may receive it
- presenting the award publicly (e.g., at an assembly, over the loudspeaker, on a board outside the office) (Colvin & Sugai, 1993)

The schoolwide team should determine the best process or format to provide information about expectations to all staff, students, parents, and others. This can be done by holding student and staff meetings and publishing the rules in the school bulletin or parent/student handbook. There are many different ways to distribute information, and often the method is determined by how things are done in a particular school.

Specific Settings

Expand the schoolwide rules or develop behavioral expectations for specific settings to build clarity and consistency for staff, parents, and students. The key to addressing specific problem settings is to focus on the structural features of the setting that led to problems. The solution often lies in altering variables such as the following:

- Revising student schedules so that all students are not moving about at the same time.
- Shifting staff supervision assignments and roles.
- Teaching rules and behavioral expectations to students and staff for each setting.
- Providing specific feedback to students and teachers on a regular basis.
- Making changes in the physical layout of the school (e.g., providing fencing and lighting, opening double doors).

Consequences must be developed for appropriate behavior, as well as problem behavior. The consequences developed must be ones that the staff can live with and deliver efficiently. The team must consider the number of staff available, supervisory skills of the staff, number of students, and the types of problems (individual or groups) in each setting. Staff should monitor the infractions to provide feedback to the others on the effectiveness of the system.

Last, the team should develop and clarify the roles and responsibilities of the staff involved. Students need initial information and instruction about the expected behavior within each setting. This involves the use of similar strategies to those described for the schoolwide system. Once initiated, the students and staff need ongoing feedback and reminders regarding the expectations within these settings. Exhibit 15–7 illustrates a specific-setting plan. This plan, which is for an elementary school's lunch, is one page and formatted so that critical information is easily available.

Classrooms

The key to addressing incidents in classroom settings is to focus on clearly defined classroom rules that are

Exhibit 15–7 Specific Setting Plan: An Example of Lunch

LUNCH
Leroy Elementary
1995–1996

Goal: Students will be self-managers by receiving, eating, and cleaning up lunch in a safe, respectful, clean, and timely manner.

Rules and Behavioral Expectations:

1. Be safe.
   - Walk single file facing forward.
   - Hold tray with two hands.
   - Eat when seated in classroom.
2. Be respectful.
   - Keep hands, feet, and objects to self.
   - Use a quiet, inside voice.
   - Face forward and keep line moving.
   - Follow classroom rules, even when the teacher is out of the room.
3. Follow directions of all school adults.

Consequences for Appropriate Behavior:

- Students will receive positive feedback from supervisors and teachers.

Consequences for Infractions:

- First infraction: Teacher states the rule and redirects the student.
- Second infraction: Student takes a three- to five-minute break at the back of the room. After the break, student talks with teacher about what to do differently next time.
- Third infraction: Student takes lunch to time-out area.

Evaluation and Monitoring:

- Teachers will provide monthly lunch report to schoolwide behavior support team coordinator.
- Schoolwide behavior support team will summarize reports and give a monthly update at staff meetings.

Teacher Responsibilities:

- Teachers will teach, model, and practice appropriate assembly procedures and expectations in their classrooms, throughout the year.

Supervisor Responsibilities:

- All available teachers will monitor students in the hallways and classrooms.
- Supervisors will notify the classroom teacher when a student goes to time-out area.

---

consistent with schoolwide rules. Teachers should provide opportunities for teaching, practicing, and monitoring the procedures and routines. Teaching the rules and expectations is critical, as is adapting the presentation style to encourage and support all styles of learning. Solutions often include the following: clarifying rules and expectations, providing consistent implementation and feedback for classroom routines and expectations, and using curriculum adaptations and teaching strategies in different ways to support diverse learning styles and rates.

Individual Students

A behavioral support plan is based on the summary statements from the functional assessment. The plan describes the procedures for teaching prosocial behaviors that conflict with and replace the problem behaviors. These procedures should take into consideration the experience, values, and skill level of the individuals who will implement the plan (Albin et al., 1996). Three steps for developing a support plan include: (1) describe how and why the current environment is supporting the behaviors (Horner et al., 1993),

(2) develop alternative behaviors that replace the problem behaviors (Horner & Budd, 1985), and (3) develop potential strategies for teaching and maintaining new behaviors. For example, for each summary statement developed from the functional assessment, one could ask these questions: "Given this situation, if the student does what we want him to do, does he get/avoid what he wants?" and "What would be a better (more socially accepted) way for him to get/avoid what he wants when he performs the problem behaviors?" (Todd et al., in press).

In order to teach the alternative behaviors, the action team identifies strategies it will use. These strategies might include changing the curriculum, rescheduling, restructuring the environment, as well as teaching the student how to request help and manage homework assignments. The action team should consider several questions once it understands the problem as clarified through the assessment:

- What are ways to prevent the problem behavior from occurring?
- What can be done to increase the desired/expected behavior?
- What should happen when the desired behavior occurs?
- What should happen when problem behavior occurs?

Support plans should include teaching sessions so the student can learn some new strategies, feedback and coaching sessions to check in and see how implementation is going, and—of course—a plan for when things don't go as planned. Finally, the action team should develop a plan to be used in extreme situations when the safety of the individual or others is in jeopardy. Even with a well-developed plan, there will be times when it is not successful. It is best to be prepared for these times by identifying when this may occur and what strategies will be used to quickly reduce the intensity or the frequency of the behavior. For example, what if the student suddenly becomes violent toward himself or others? Or leaves the school grounds? Being prepared for these events helps to reduce injury and chaos in a school. If all other plans are in place and being used, an emergency plan should rarely be needed. If the emergency plan is used frequently, it is an indication that the individual-support plan for that student should be reviewed and redesigned.

Whenever possible, individual-support plans should align with and emphasize the schoolwide, specific-setting, and classroom rules and expectations. Samples of components of behavior-support plans are provided in Exhibit 15–8.

Exhibit 15–8 Examples of Behavioral Support Plan Components

SUMMARY STATEMENTS: BEHAVIORS AND FUNCTIONS	ALTERNATIVE/DESIRED BEHAVIOR	STRATEGIES
• When John is in situations where he is likely to make errors and be corrected, he whines, pounds, throws, and hits to avoid the task or situation.	• Ask for help. • Ask for a break.	• Provide individual teaching sessions to teach John to ask for help or take a break before pounding, throwing, or hitting something. • Teacher attends to whining by reminding John that this is a time when he could ask for help or a break.
• When presented with a situation where a desired activity or object is made unavailable (peer will not share item, preferred item won't work), Mark whines, throws, and hits to get what he wants.	• Use words rather than whine, hit, or throw.	• Teach to talk rather than whine, throw, or hit. • Teach negotiation routine to students, including Mark's peers.
• When Kendra is in situations where she is likely to be teased and taunted (recess, lunch, large-group situations) by peers, she hits and punches to get out of the situation and to get adult attention.	• Use problem-solving approaches. • Ask for help.	• Provide role-play situations. • Have "talk" time with adult prior to the difficult situations.

Step 4: Implement, Monitor, and Revise the Plan

Schoolwide, Specific Settings, and Classrooms

There are three steps in implementing any of these systems: (1) teach, (2) supervise, and (3) follow up (Colvin, Martz, DeForest, & Wilt, 1995). Like acquisition of any new skill, practice builds fluency. In *teaching,* the teacher or supervisor works with the student before the student is in a situation to use the rule or expectation. Long-term results depend on time spent in the beginning on defining, practicing, and understanding rules and expectations. The teacher should explain the rules or expectations, use verbal rehearsal, role-playing, or practice. It is important to teach students to discriminate between appropriate and inappropriate behaviors. Students can be expected to perform successfully only when they understand and know what to do and how to do it. At first, teachers may find themselves using some of their academic teaching time to explain, teach, and remind students about behavioral expectations. Over time, because of fewer disruptions, this proactive approach will result in increased time to instruct students in academic areas.

During *supervision,* students should be provided the opportunity to demonstrate the rule (e.g., be respectful) in the natural environment under the watchful eyes of teachers or other staff. Critical to this step is the teacher's or supervisor's moving around the students to provide encouragement, prompts, and corrections (Colvin, Martz, DeForest, & Wilt, 1995).

The last step in implementation is *follow up.* Once the student has demonstrated an ability to follow the rules and expectations, the student should be allowed more independence. However, feedback, encouragement, reinforcement, and prompts are continued. These steps can be implemented grade level by grade level, class by class, and during schoolwide assemblies.

It is critical to gather information about how implementation of a system is working to ensure ongoing change. Information can be gathered from sources such as referrals, injuries to staff and students, emergencies, awards for appropriate behavior, and parent complaints. Watch for patterns that indicate a need for a change in or reclarification of the rules and expectations.

Individual Students

Individual students should be taught, coached, and provided with feedback. This may require individual sessions, as well as opportunities in the natural environments. To effect sustainable change, it is critical to monitor and revise the plan as needed. No plan will last forever; as the student changes and grows, so do the environments, situations, and expectations. The addition of a new student to a group or class can have an impact due to new interactions, rate of delivery of instruction, opportunity for

reinforcement, or turns at responding. One of the responsibilities of the action team coordinator is to continue collecting information on student progress and discuss it with the team. Often the target student can help collect information through a self-management strategy. However it is gathered, it is critical that information be collected regularly rather than waiting until there is a crisis. Specific information to be gathered will vary from student to student, but might include such measures as periods of the day without incident, implementation of the self-management card, number of office referrals, and number of absences.

Keeping It Going

Systems described in this chapter work together to improve the capacity of schools to include students with problem behaviors. Although a school may decide to begin by focusing on one system more than others, all are important. Schools need to develop a schoolwide team and assess the school systems. Patterns from assessment information and staff interest will determine the focus for each school. Schools should put the systems in place at a pace that is responsive to building needs but not overwhelming to staff. As each system becomes stable, the schoolwide team can review the assessment for another system and develop a plan of improvement.

Once something is in place, it is easy to assume that it will keep on going; yet this rarely works for long. Systems must be fine-tuned, based on change in students and staff and other community issues. A glance at assessment information may reveal that things are fine except at certain times of year. In this case, adding some "booster" programs during those months may be necessary when referrals are high (e.g., December, May). Celebrate successes. Encourage staff to take the time to "pat themselves on the back" for the work they have done and the benefit this has been to students.

IS IT POSSIBLE TO INCLUDE ALL STUDENTS WITH SERIOUS CHALLENGING BEHAVIOR?

This section outlines critical procedures that every school should have in place to accommodate the small group of students with serious challenging behavior. These include special concerns and procedures for students with disabilities, responding to physical aggression, and school security and crisis response.

Working with Students with Disabilities

Students with disabilities require special consideration in areas of discipline. Many believe that these students are exempt from discipline procedures applied to the general student population, but this is not so (Heumann & Hehir,

1995). As concern about weapons in schools increases, this issue is especially critical (Stephens, 1995). Chapter 4 provides an overview of the main provisions of special education law. The following section focuses on how the law affects students with problem behavior.

The key decision point in dealing with students with disabilities who perform problem behaviors is *whether the behavior is related to the disability*. If the student's behavior is determined to be related to the disability, then the school must document the use of preventive, positive measures such as those described in this chapter. In addition, the school is responsible to properly train and support teachers who carry out the procedures. Any procedure that is unique to the student must be reflected in the student's individualized education program (IEP).

Students with disabilities may be suspended from school for up to 10 school days without prior determination of the relationship between the problem behavior and disability if the school team determines that more drastic measures are needed or safety is involved. If the school team recommends that a student be removed for more than 10 days, there must be evidence that the behavior was *not* related to the disability. That student must still receive educational services. With proper notification to the family, the school team may also initiate a change of placement (to another program or building).

Federal guidelines from the Safe and Gun Free Schools and Communities Act (Jackson, 1995) require a one-year expulsion if a student (including students with disabilities) brings a firearm to school. These guidelines allow the chief administering officer of a local school district to modify this requirement on a case-by-case basis. The IEP team may recommend alternative disciplinary and educational programming in accordance with special education law.

It is strongly recommended that clear policies and procedures regarding students with disabilities be developed and distributed before the beginning of each school year and renewed annually to prevent the occurrence of serious challenging behavior. These procedures obviously need to be consistent with federal and state regulations. The National School Safety Center publishes a variety of sample policies and procedures related to student discipline.* In addition, many state education agencies can provide assistance to school personnel.

Responding to Physical Aggression

Any form of challenging behavior presents the possibility of injury to staff and students or property damage. Preventive

procedures and responses to violent and criminal behavior are critical. Staff who work with students who are or may be physically violent should be trained in safe and effective physical management procedures (Oregon Technical Assistance Corporation & Oregon Mental Health and Developmental Disabilities Services Division, 1996). A variety of methods are available and provide reasonable protection from liability during use. Staff should *never* use physical management procedures with a physically aggressive student without proper training. This training must include procedures for diffusing situations early so the student does not "lose face" and escalate to dangerous behavior. It is critical to keep in mind that staff will be more likely to use a restraint or hold if taught to do so. Consistent with any plan of support, ongoing training and monitoring are critical to prevent overuse or misuse of these serious procedures.

Developing Procedures for School Security and Crisis Response

All students and teachers have a right to be protected against foreseeable criminal activity; student violence that adequate supervision can prevent; dangerous individuals who are admitted to the school without proper clearance; and school administrators, teachers, and staff who have been negligently hired, retained, or trained (Rapp, Carrington, & Nicholson, 1987). The best deterrent to most criminal activity is active supervision and visual monitoring of public areas in the school building (Crowe, 1990). Defining supervision responsibilities in all specific-setting plans, monitoring and providing feedback, and ensuring consistent adult (teachers, assistants, others) presence are effective strategies for continued, active, and effective supervision.

The school's physical plant and surroundings also need to be considered. These considerations include the location of the campus, the school grounds, and the buildings and classrooms (Stephens, Butterfield, Arnette, James, & Kenney, 1994). The location of the school in its community or neighborhood may influence the likelihood of violence or crime due to proximity to certain businesses, traffic patterns, or neighborhood activities (e.g., drug dealing or vandalism). The school grounds should be assessed regarding ease of illegal trespassing or intrusion by dangerous individuals. School buildings themselves can either promote or deter certain types of unwanted behavior (Crowe, 1990). School personnel should assess the building for features such as ease of visual surveillance, number of open-access doors, security systems, communication with the main office, and restrooms. Developing plans for specific school areas is necessary (e.g., playground, auditorium, or bus loading) (Sugai & Horner, 1994).

---

*National School Safety Center, Pepperdine University, 24255 Pacific Coast Highway, Malibu, CA 90263.

Many risk factors affecting school safety are present in the surrounding community. Poverty, family distress, crime, drugs, and criminal activity may be traced to the homes of students, other community members, and the immediate neighborhood surrounding the school. As such, community agencies such as the police, church groups, social services, and the local media must be involved in school security planning and application. Increasingly, schools employ police personnel (school resource officers) to provide supervision within and around school campuses and to serve as instructors regarding drug abuse and violence prevention. School resource officers can provide a range of services, the least of which may be to help children develop an understanding and trust of law enforcement personnel (Barry, 1995). Schools using school resource officers must include the officer in the behavior-support plans.

A good way to detect gaps in school security is to work with local law enforcement personnel to review school policies and procedures. Cooperative agreements between school and law enforcement personnel can help prevent many unfortunate incidents and reduce complications when they happen. Cooperation with police also is essential if a student commits a crime on campus. For any criminal offense, it is recommended that law enforcement personnel be involved. School personnel should not attempt to act as police or fail to report a crime a student has committed (Stephens, 1995).

Training Staff and Students

A comprehensive plan for training and informing staff and students will be needed for each procedure outlined in this section. Schools routinely practice fire drills, and other emergency response behaviors are worthy of similar approaches. For example, some schools practice "earthquake" drills, where students quickly move under their desks. This drill is a safety signal for the teachers to get students to a safer place if a hostile intruder is in the building. Teachers need clear methods for communicating with the principal's office regarding dangerous events occurring in a particular part of the building. Without training and information, each staff person responds differently to dangerous events. Many of these responses may not be in the best safety interest of children or adults and could make the situation worse.

Evaluating and Monitoring Overall School Safety

The schoolwide team should take responsibility for organizing regular evaluation and monitoring and providing this feedback to students, staff, and parents. Exhibit 15–9 provides an outline of a school safety assessment (Sprague & Colvin, 1996) to aid in planning and ongoing evaluation. Other measures may be incorporated into ongoing school improvement plans as needed.

Exhibit 15–9 Risk and Protective Factors Affecting School Safety and Violence

RISK FACTORS	PROTECTIVE FACTORS OR RESPONSE PLANS
• illegal weapons • vandalism • student transiency (i.e., changes in school enrollment) • graffiti • gang activity • truancy • student suspensions and expulsions • students adjudicated by the court • parents withdrawing students from school because of safety concerns • child abuse in the home • trespassing on school grounds • acceptance of diversity • poverty • crimes (e.g., theft, extortion, hazing) • illegal drug and alcohol use • fights, conflict, and assault • bullying, intimidation, and harassment • deteriorating condition of the physical facilities in the school	• opportunities for extracurricular programs and sports activities • professional development and staff training • crisis and emergency response plans • consistently implemented schoolwide discipline plans • student support services in school (e.g., counseling, monitoring, support team systems) • parent involvement in school (e.g., efforts to enhance school safety, student support) • student preparation for crises and emergencies • supervision of students across all settings • suicide prevention/response plans • student participation and involvement in academic activities • positive school climate for learning • response to conflict and problem solving • collaboration with community resources • high expectations for student learning and productivity • effective student-teacher relationships

Source: Adapted with permission from J. Sprague and G. Colvin, *The Oregon Conference Monograph,* Vol. 8, pp. 95–102, © 1996, George Sugai.

Schools are changing. Disruptive and antisocial behavior is increasing. Traditionally, schools have responded to students with problem behaviors on an individual basis and most often through use of punishment and exclusion. No school system has the capacity—resources or political support—to provide individual support plans to the increasing number of students with disruptive behaviors. Instead, schools are encouraged to adopt a preventative approach by developing as a team a schoolwide behavior support system. This system should be based upon development and implementation of clear rules, expectations, and reinforcement for all students. Putting this system in place will allow the staff time to focus on the small numbers of students who may require intensive, individual behavior support.

REFERENCES

Albin, R.W., Horner, R.H., & Walker, H.M. (1993). *Building capacity for positive behavior management: Embedded inservice training.* Unpublished manuscript.

Albin, R.W., Lucyshyn, J.M., Horner, R.H., & Flannery, K.B. (1996). Contextual fit for behavioral support plans: A model for "Goodness of Fit." In L.K. Koegel, R.L. Koegel, & G. Dunlap (Eds.), *Positive behavioral support: Including people with difficult behavior in the community* (pp. 81–98). Baltimore: Paul H. Brookes.

American Psychological Association, Commission on Youth Violence. (1993). *Violence and youth: Psychology's response.* Washington, DC: Author.

Barry, B.J. (1995, Fall). Education is everyone's business. *School Safety,* 16–17.

Bulgatz, M., & O'Neill, R.E. (1994). *Teachers' perceptions and recommendations concerning students with challenging behaviors in the regular classroom: An initial survey.* Unpublished master's thesis. University of Oregon, Eugene.

Carr, E.G., Levin, L., McConnachie, G., Carlson, J.I., Kemp, D.C., & Smith, C.E. (1994). *Communication based intervention for problem behavior: A user's guide for producing positive change.* Baltimore: Paul H. Brookes.

Carr, E.G., Robinson, S., Taylor, J.D., & Carlson, J.I. (1990). *Positive approaches to the treatment of severe behavior problems in persons with developmental disabilities: A review and analysis of reinforcement and stimulus-based procedures* (Monograph of The Association for Persons with Severe Handicaps No. 4).

Colvin, G., Kameenui, E.J., & Sugai, G. (1993). Reconceptualizing behavior management and school-wide discipline in general education. *Education and Treatment of Children, 16*(4), 331–349.

Colvin, G., Martz, G., DeForest, D., & Wilt, J. (1995). Developing a school-wide discipline plan: Addressing all students, all settings, and all staff. In A. Deffenbaugh, G. Sugai, & G. Tindal (Eds.), *The Oregon Conference: Monograph* (pp. 169–172). Eugene: University of Oregon.

Colvin, G., & Sugai, G. (1993) *Curriculum for establishing a proactive school-wide discipline plan: Project Prepare.* Eugene: University of Oregon College of Education, Behavioral Research and Teaching.

Crowe, T.D. (1990, Fall). Designing safer schools. *School Safety,* 9–13.

Dadson, S., & Horner, R.H. (1993). Manipulating setting events to decrease problem behaviors: A case study. *Teaching Exceptional Children, 25,* 53–55.

Dunlap, G., & Childs, K.E. (in press). Intervention research in emotional and behavioral disorders. An analysis of studies from 1980–1993. *Behavioral Disorders.*

Dunlap, G., & Kern, L. (1993). Assessment and intervention for children within the instructional curriculum. In J. Reichle & D. Wacker (Eds.), *Communicative approaches to the management of challenging behavior* (pp. 177–203). Baltimore: Paul H. Brookes.

Dunlap, G., Kern-Dunlap, L., Clarke, S., & Robbins, F.R. (1991). Functional assessment, curricular revision, and severe behavior problems. *Journal of Applied Behavior Analysis, 24,* 387–397.

Durand, V.M. (1990). *Severe behavior problems: A functional communication training approach.* New York: Guilford.

Durand, V.M., & Crimmins, D. (1988). Identifying the variables maintaining self-injurious behavior. *Journal of Autism and Developmental Disorders, 18,* 99–117.

Embry, D., Flannery, D., Vasonyi, A.J., Powell, K.E., & Atha, H. (in press). A theoretically driven school-based model for early violence prevention. *American Journal of Preventive Medicine.*

Hall, S., Horner, R.H., & Ard, W.R. (1995). *Office referrals: Patterns for elementary and middle schools.* Eugene: University of Oregon.

Heumann, J., & Hehir, T. (1995, April 26). *Questions and answers on disciplining students with disabilities* (OSEP-95-16). Washington, DC: U.S. Department of Education, Office of Special Education and Rehabilitative Services.

Horner, R.H., & Budd, C.M. (1985). Teaching manual sign language to a nonverbal student: Generalization of sign use and collateral reduction of maladaptive behavior. *Education and Training of the Mentally Retarded, 20*(1), 39–47.

Horner, R.H., Diemer, S., & Brazeau, K. (1992). Educational support for students with severe problem behaviors in Oregon: A descriptive analysis from the 1987–1988 school year. *Journal of the Association for Persons with Severe Handicaps, 17*(3), 154–169.

Horner, R.H., O'Neill, R.E., & Flannery, K.B. (1993). Building effective behavior support plans from functional assessment information. In M. Snell (Ed.), *Instruction of persons with severe handicaps* (4th ed.) (pp. 184–214). Columbus, OH: Macmillan.

Horner, R.H., Vaughn, B.J., Day, H.M., & Ard, W.R. (1996). The relationship between setting events and problem behavior. In L.K. Koegel, R.L. Koegel, & G. Dunlap (Eds.), *Positive behavioral support: Including people with difficult behavior in the community* (pp. 381–402). Baltimore: Paul H. Brookes.

Jackson, J.E. (1995, November 3). *Revised gun-free schools act guidance* (Memorandum). Washington DC: US Department of Education, Office of Elementary and Secondary Education.

Knitzer, J. (1993). Children's mental health policy: Challenging the future. *Emotional and Behavioral Disorders, 1*(1), 8–16.

Knitzer, J., Steinberg, Z., & Fleisch, B. (1990). *At the school house door: An examination of programs and policies for children with behavioral and emotional problems.* New York: Bank Street College of Education.

Lewis, T.J., Scott, T.M., & Sugai, G. (1994). The problem behavior questionnaire: A teacher based instrument to develop functional hypotheses of problem behavior in general education classrooms. *Diagnostique, 19*(2-3), 103–115.

Lipsey, M.W. (1992, October). *The effects of treatment on juvenile delinquency: Results from meta-analysis.* Paper presented at the meeting of the National Institutes of Mental Health on Potential Applicants for Research To Prevent Youth Violence, Bethesda, MD.

Mayer, G.R. (1995). Preventing antisocial behavior in the schools. *Journal of Applied Behavior Analysis, 28,* 467–478.

Mayer, G.R., & Sulzer-Azaroff, B. (1990). Interventions for vandalism. In G. Stoner, M.K. Shinn, & H.M. Walker (Eds.), *Interventions for achievement and behavior problems* (pp. 559–580). Washington, DC: National Association of School Psychologists.

Nelson, R., & Colvin, G. (1995). School-wide discipline: Procedures for managing common areas. In J. Marr, G. Sugai, & G. Tindal (Eds.), *The Oregon Conference Monograph* (Vol. 7, pp. 109–120). Eugene: University of Oregon, College of Education, Oregon Behavioral Research and Teaching.

Oregon Technical Assistance Corporation and Oregon Mental Health and Developmental Disabilities Services Division. (1996). *The Oregon intervention system: Community program.* Salem, OR: Author.

Rapp, J.A., Carrington, F., & Nicholson, G. (1987). *School crime and violence: Victim's rights.* Malibu, CA: National School Safety Center and Pepperdine University.

Reed, H., Thomas, E., Sprague, J.R., & Horner, R.H. (1995). *Research project: Student guided functional assessment.* Unpublished master's thesis, University of Oregon, Eugene.

Reichle, J. (1990). *National working conference on positive approaches to the management of excess behavior: Final report and recommendations.* Minneapolis: University of Minnesota, Institute on Community Integration.

Shepherd, K.K. (1994). Stemming conflict through peer mediation. *The School Administrator, 51,* 14–17.

Showers, B. (1990). Teachers coaching teachers. *Educational Leadership, 47*(7), 43–48.

Sprague, J.R., & Colvin, G. (1996). Is your school safe? Do you have an adequate plan? In A. Deffenbaugh, G. Matis, & C. Neudeck (Eds.), *The Oregon Conference Monograph* (pp. 95–102). Eugene: University of Oregon, College of Education, Oregon Behavioral Research and Teaching.

Sprague, J.R., & Horner, R.H. (1995). Functional assessment and intervention in community settings. *Mental Retardation and Developmental Disabilities, 1,* 89–93.

Sprague, J.R., & Rian, V. (1993). *Support systems for students with severe problem behaviors in Indiana: A descriptive analysis of school structure and student demographics.* Unpublished manuscript, Indiana University, Bloomington.

Stephens, R.D. (1995). *Safe schools: A handbook for violence prevention.* Bloomington, IN: National Education Service.

Stephens, R.D., Butterfield, G.E., Arnette, J.L., James, B., & Kenney, K. (1994). *School crisis and response: NSSC resource paper.* Malibu, CA: National School Safety Center, Pepperdine University.

Stevens, L.J., & Price, M. (1992). Meeting the challenge of educating children at risk. *Kappan, 74*(1), 18–23.

Sugai, G., & Horner, R.H. (1994). Including students with severe behavior problems in general education settings: Assumptions, challenges, and solutions. In J. Marr, G. Sugai, & G. Tindal (Eds.), *The Oregon Conference Monograph* (pp. 102–120). Eugene: University of Oregon, College of Education, Oregon Behavioral Research and Teaching.

Sugai, G., Horner, R.H., Todd, A., Colvin, G., Lewis, T., & Sprague, J.R. (1995). *Assessing behavioral support in schools.* Unpublished manuscript.

Sugai, G., Horner, R.H., Todd, A., & Sprague, J.R. (1995). *Effective behavioral support: Teacher support for students with chronic problem behaviors.* Unpublished manuscript.

Todd, A., Horner, R.H., Vanater, S., & Schneider, C. (in press). Working together to make change: An example of positive behavioral support for a student with traumatic brain injury. *Education and Treatment of Children.*

U.S. Department of Education. (1994). *Sixteenth annual report to Congress on the implementation of Public Law 94-142: The Education for All Handicapped Children Act.* Washington, DC: Author.

Wacker, D.P., Steege, M.W., Northup, J., Sasso, G., Berg, W., Reimers, T., Cooper, L., Cigrand, K., & Donn, L. (1990). A component analysis of functional communication training across three topographies of severe behavior problems. *Journal of Applied Behavior Analysis, 23,* 417–429.

Walker, H. (1995). *The acting-out child: Coping with classroom disruption.* Longmont, CO: Sopris West.

Walker, H., Colvin, G., & Ramsey, E. (1995). *Antisocial behavior in public schools: Strategies and best practices.* Pacific Grove, CA: Brookes/Cole.

CHAPTER 16

Students with Special Health Care Needs

Dianne Koontz Lowman

It's frightening. I guess the one thing that we at our center believe [is] that children are children first. So even though we get really nervous and upset, we want for kids to be treated as kids. And we wanted the whole time for Fred to have the opportunity to come to school. (Lowman, 1994, p. 67)

Fred* was referred to the early childhood special education (ECSE) program at the age of three and was being discharged from the hospital for the first time since his birth. He was on a ventilator, had a tracheostomy, was fed through a nasogastric tube, and received dialysis at night. Fred was a bright child with a great smile and quick sense of humor. Fred's parents wanted him to attend the ECSE program in the local elementary school. As the opening quotation suggests, Fred's teacher also wanted him to attend school. But she was afraid.

INTRODUCTION

Children with special health care needs have unique needs compounded by extreme medical conditions (Sirvis, 1988). Some terms used to describe this population are: children who are technology-dependent, medically fragile, or chronically ill. The definition used in this chapter is as follows:

---

*The quotations used in this chapter were gathered during a qualitative study of teachers of students with special health care needs. The experiences of one student, Fred, are used to illustrate many of the points. I first met Fred in the hospital when he was two and one-half years old. Later I had the opportunity to visit Fred's ECSE classroom as he was preparing for the transition to kindergarten. Today, Fred is a full member of a first-grade class in his home school. I would like to thank Fred's family for allowing me to learn from their story.

Children with special health care needs are children with a chronic condition and/or who require technology or ongoing support to prevent adverse physical consequences (Bruder, 1990; Lowman, 1994; Virginia Departments of Education & Health, 1995). Children with special health care needs may or may not require special education services. (Lowman, 1994; Sirvis, 1988)

Because the causes of special health care needs may be varied, the health-related needs of children within the educational setting may be categorized according to the level of services or supports required, as illustrated in Exhibit 16–1. Children with the most extensive need for supports in the educational setting are those children who require continuous, ongoing specialized health care procedures. Examples of these supports may be the continuous use of a mechanical ventilator or the continuous administration of oxygen. Other children require intermittent, specialized health care procedures, usually for procedures such as gastrostomy feedings or clean intermittent catheterization. These procedures may be performed one or more times during the school day. The final category of children with special health care needs includes those children who require episodic services. These services may be needed for uncontrolled seizures, unstable diabetes, or poorly controlled asthma. It is important to note that many children who have a medical condition, such as diabetes or asthma, do not require specialized health care procedures within the educational setting. While there are many students in school with health care needs, the focus of this chapter is on the students described in Exhibit 16–1—students who have special health care needs who require specific intervention within the educational setting. Health-related procedures such as those described in Levels A, B, and C can be diffi-

Exhibit 16–1 Levels of Services Required by Children with Special Health Care Needs

LEVEL A

Children with one or more conditions who require *continuous*, ongoing specialized health care procedures. These procedures include but are not limited to:

- mechanical ventilation
- continuous administration of oxygen
- continuous cardiopulmonary monitoring
- combination of procedures such as tracheostomy care and sucking and gastrostomy feeding

LEVEL B

Children who require an *intermittent* specialized health care procedure. These procedures include but are not limited to:

- nasogastric feedings
- gastrostomy feedings

- oral feedings where a documented risk of aspiration exists
- oral, nasal, and pharyngeal suctioning
- tracheostomy care
- urinary catheterization
- ostomy care
- medication via injection, inhalation, or complex regimens

LEVEL C

Children with identified conditions of unusual severity who require *episodic* specialized services due to the potential for a medical crisis. These conditions include but are not limited to:

- uncontrolled seizure disorders
- unstable diabetes
- poorly controlled asthma
- allergies with a history of anaphylactic shock
- severe immune deficiency

Source: From *Report of the Departments of Education and Health. Report on the Needs of Medically Fragile Students to the Governor and the General Assembly,* Senate Document No. 5 (p. 5) by Virginia Departments of Education and Health, 1995, Richmond, VA: Commonwealth of Virginia.

cult for school personnel to accommodate in the educational setting.

Children with special health care needs such as those described in Levels A and B represent a relatively new population of students in general education classrooms (Knight & Wadsworth, 1994; Lowman, 1993; Mulligan-Ault, Guess, Struth, & Thompson, 1988; Virginia Departments of Education & Health, 1995). There are no precise data on the number of students with special health care needs who are receiving or who require educational services (Lehr, 1990). A 1995 survey of all 1,800 public schools in Virginia showed that 8,500 students (less than 1% of the total school population) met the definition of special health care needs presented in Exhibit 16–1 (Virginia Departments of Education & Health, 1995). A study of ECSE teachers in Virginia in 1994, for example, indicated that 14.5% of the teachers conducted gastrostomy feedings, 7.7% suctioned tracheostomies, and 6.8% performed catheterizations during the school day (Lowman, 1993).

Because the inclusion of children with special health care needs in general education classrooms is relatively new, school personnel have typically not been prepared to meet their specialized needs. Many preservice university and college teacher training programs have not prepared teachers to deal with complex health care needs in the classroom (Fauvre, 1988; Lehr, 1990; Sciarillo, Draper, Green, Burkett, & Demetrides, 1988). Preparation of personnel is discussed in greater detail later in this chapter.

When faced with including students with special health care needs into the classroom, many classroom teachers voice an initial fear:

> I worried the entire summer about catheterizing a student. I felt unqualified to perform a medical procedure for which I was never trained and certainly never wanted to perform. . . . However, after having been trained . . . and receiving reassurance, I found the procedure to be much less intimidating than I had imagined, much to my relief. (Lowman, 1993, p. 455)

As this comment illustrates, teachers are initially afraid of the unknown aspects of teaching children with special health care needs. After opportunities to get to know the child and to become comfortable with the health-related procedures are provided, the comfort level of teachers improves.

BENEFITS OF INCLUSIVE EDUCATION

Benefits for the Student with Special Health Care Needs

In an article that focuses on the integration of children with special health care needs into the home and community setting, Revell and Liptak (1991) summarized the possible effects of chronic illnesses on children. The impact of a special health care need on the child may be restricted growth and development, frequent hospitalizations, painful or embarrassing treatments, the inability to participate in peer activities, and the unpredictable course of the illness. Attendance in a general education classroom may give the child with special health care needs a chance to practice developmental skills, an opportunity that may be restricted when the child is in a medical or homebound setting. For example, Fred's teacher noticed his eye-hand coordination was delayed. The teacher speculated that the tracheostomy, connecting tubes, and extended time in a hospital bed limited Fred's ability to look down at his hands and practice tasks involving eye-hand coordination. Fred's teacher and the occupational therapist worked to elevate a working surface, making it easier for Fred to look at his hands while completing fine motor tasks. In addition, attendance in a full-day class at his neighborhood school helped build Fred's stamina and tolerance of motor activities.

Children with special health care needs are frequently overprotected because of the serious nature of their needs. Attendance in the general education classroom setting gives these children opportunities to explore and try new skills, to develop independence and self-sufficiency, and to achieve mastery (Fauvre, 1988). Attendance in a general education classroom also provides opportunities for social-emotional development and for interaction with peers. According to Sherman and Rosen (1990):

> Adult stimulation does not compare with the interactions and socialization of other children. Children entering school with [tracheostomies] are enchanted with their peers and are clearly delighted to meet others like themselves. Socialization and language development are key objectives in a program and seem especially needed by children who experience fewer play opportunities as a result of their health problems. (p. 361)

A second-grade teacher of a student on a mechanical ventilator described the student's social interactions with the other students in the room: "[Andy] has the same feelings as a normal child. Like little Andy was sending love letters to little girls. So you know he has the same feelings as anyone else, he just cannot get his words out" (Lowman, 1994, p. 239).

Benefits for Other Students

Often other students in the school do not exhibit the same initial fears as adults. In a qualitative study of the perceptions of ECSE teachers, the majority of the teachers reported that the other students in the school reacted in a positive, kind, and caring manner toward the child with special health care needs (Lowman, 1994). Close contact with children with special health care needs allows students to become comfortable with health-related issues. One preschool teacher described the following situation, showing how comfortable children can feel with equipment used by a classmate with special health care needs.

> One of the little boys that really plays with Robert a lot . . . [and Robert were] pushing each other in the wagon, and Robert's oxygen came undone. And [the other child] said "Stop, stop Robert." And he stopped and went and plugged him back up. He's that adjusted to it. (Lowman, 1994, p. 161)

The opportunity to explore the medical equipment is important to reduce students' fears and help answer questions about specific health-related procedures (Goldberg, 1994; Knight & Wadsworth, 1994). In one kindergarten classroom, five-year-olds explore medical equipment in the dramatic play area. Children have a chance to answer the telephone, listen to each others' hearts, get shots, or have breathing treatments (using donated equipment). Each child has his or her own face mask, so "we don't catch germs from each other." This type of dramatic play is important to "help them cope with the things that worry them. . . . Injuries, accidents . . . are worries for children." When one child in this classroom had to have his tonsils out, his mother reported that the experiences in school prepared him for his operation without undue anxiety (Goldberg, 1994, p. 35).

THE ROLE OF TEAM MEMBERS

Team cooperation in the preparation for students with special health care needs is absolutely critical (Lowman, 1994; Sobsey & Cox, 1996). Input is needed from the parents, the school staff (administrators, teachers, assistants, school nurse, and other related service personnel), the discharge nurse from the hospital, health care professionals from the local health department, the Medicaid Technology Waiver* case manager, and representatives from the medical equipment vendor. Equally important is the provision of networks of support for personnel involved in the daily inclusion of children with special health care needs into the educational setting (Lowman, 1994). The supports provided by this network might include comradery, mutual and emo-

---

*The Medicaid Technology Waiver program allows Medicaid to reimburse for private duty nursing provided in the child's home on either a continuous basis or as a respite for the primary caregiver. The waiver allows Medicaid eligibility to be determined as if the child was receiving services in an institution. To meet the target population for this waiver, the child (age birth to 21 years) must need both a medical device to compensate for the loss of a vital body function and substantial and ongoing nursing care to avert death or further disability.

tional support, construction, and information. Fred's teacher described the importance of support from other school personnel as she prepared for Fred's transition to her class:

> Usually we tried to have two people go together [to visit Fred at home] because in the beginning it was really emotional, and it was very hard to go by yourself. . . . You would go one week and he would be doing so well and we would be so excited. And then you would go back and he wasn't doing well at all . . . . The first year we lived with the threat that the phone would ring and that Fred would be dead. (Lowman, 1994, p. 68)

Fred's teacher valued the emotional support she received from staff such as the classroom paraprofessional, the school principal, and the speech-language pathologist.

The family is a critical member of the planning team. The elements of family-centered care presented in Exhibit 16–2 remind professionals in the school system about the important role of parents in the lives of children with special health care needs (Shelton, Jeppson, & Johnson, 1989). These elements illustrate several critical points. First, many service providers enter and leave; it is the family that will remain constant throughout the child's life. Children with special health care needs and their families may have endured numerous hospitalizations and interactions with professionals before the child comes to school; Fred was not released from the hospital until he was almost three years old. He had two extended hospitalizations before entering kindergarten. Second, school personnel need to recognize the importance of offering opportunities for family-to-family support. School personnel, however empathetic, can never know exactly what it is like to live daily with life-and-death issues. Another parent who has been

through similar experiences can offer valuable support. Third, it is important not to let the school personnel assume the role of the parents. When Fred first came to school, he had a personal nurse. Fred's teacher consulted the nurse about a new walker for Fred:

> I asked the nurse, did she think we should send the walker home. And she said, "Oh I don't think so. Their house is little and they probably won't be able to use it." Yet when his mom came to pick him up she said, "I'd really like to take that home." (Lowman, 1994, p. 81)

In this instance, Fred's teacher was letting the school nurse assume the role of the parents. It is important to remain in constant contact with the parents on all decisions regarding health care needs. (See Chapter 7 for further discussion of family involvement.)

Another important member of the team may be the school nurse. However, provision of school health services in the educational setting is a complex issue (Chomicki & Wilgosh, 1994). As described by Sobsey and Cox (1996), most states have either nurse practice acts that restrict the administration of health-related procedures to nurses, with no provision for delegating responsibilities, or ambiguous laws regarding what nursing functions can be carried out by others. The role of the school nurse, at this time, varies greatly depending on each state's nurse practice act (Virginia Departments of Education & Health, 1995). Readers are encouraged to contact the public school administrator in charge of school health services (e.g., the medical director, director of school nurses, director of pupil personnel, principal) in their school district to determine what role the school nurse can play in planning for students with health care needs.

Exhibit 16–2 The Elements of Family-Centered Care

- recognizing that the family is the constant in the child's life while the service systems and personnel within those systems fluctuate
- facilitating parent/professional collaboration at all levels of care:
  - care of an individual child
  - program development, implementation, and evaluation
  - policy formation
- honoring the racial, ethnic, cultural, and socioeconomic diversity of families
- recognizing family strengths and individuality and respecting different methods of coping
- sharing complete and unbiased information with parents on a continuing basis and in a supportive manner
- encouraging and facilitating family-to-family support and networking
- understanding and incorporating the developmental needs of infants, children, and adolescents and their families into service delivery systems
- implementing comprehensive policies and programs that provide emotional support to meet the needs of families
- designing accessible service delivery systems that are flexible, culturally competent, and responsive to family-identified needs

Source: Adapted with permission of the Association for the Care of Children's Health, 7910 Woodmont Avenue, Suite 300, Bethesda, MD 20814, from *Family-Centered Care for Children with Special Health Care Needs* by T.L. Shelton, E.S. Jeppson, and B.H. Johnson, © 1989.

Personnel from outside the school system may be directly involved in planning for students with complex health care needs. When the student has recently been hospitalized, the transition nurse from the hospital may provide valuable information about the child's background, medical needs, and specific health-related procedures. In other cases, personnel from the local health department can provide information and training in the administration of specific health-related procedures. If the child is eligible for the Medicaid Technology Waiver program, the Medicaid Technology Waiver case manager can serve as a service coordinator between the medical community, the equipment representatives, and the school personnel. In some cases, representatives from the medical equipment companies provide the training associated with the equipment. Many school divisions have involved members of the local rescue squad and fire department in planning for storage of equipment (e.g., where oxygen is found in the school building), evacuating during fire drills, and training in the administration of specific health-related procedures.

Members of the team from the school system may be varied, depending on the needs of the children. Administrators ultimately have the responsibility for arranging and coordinating services and personnel, and set the tone for acceptance of children with special health care needs. The principal of Fred's elementary school traveled to the hospital to meet Fred and to receive information from the medical staff. This principal was also trained in all health-related procedures the classroom staff would be administering; he stated that he wanted to know what his teachers and assistants were doing. Classroom teachers and assistants are most often the persons who administer the specific health-related procedures in the educational setting. In the study in Virginia (Virginia Departments of Education & Health, 1995), these classroom personnel performed health-related procedures more frequently than any other group of school personnel (school nurses, related services personnel, or non-professional staff). In a 1988 study of teachers of students with severe disabilities, teachers were identified as most often responsible for implementing health-related procedures in the classroom (Mulligan-Ault et al., 1988). Related service personnel are also involved in the administration of health-related procedures. For example, in some school systems, the occupational therapist and/or the speech-language pathologist are the backup personnel trained to conduct gastrostomy tube feedings. In Fred's school, a respiratory therapist was on staff to work with several children throughout the school. Other school systems have employed licensed practical nurses (LPNs) as classroom assistants.

Parette and Holder-Brown (1992) explored the role of the school guidance counselor in providing services to children with complex health care needs. They suggested that guidance counselors are in a unique position to work with members of the medical and the educational communities, as well as to provide access to community resources. School counselors also support the psychosocial needs of the family as they deal with the day-to-day stresses of coping with complex medical problems.

Darrow, Carleton, and Stephens (1993) discussed the important role of physical educators for students who are chronically ill. They summarized research that found that postsecondary status of individuals with chronic health impairments correlated more significantly with psychosocial factors than with intelligence or severity of disability. Physical educators are in a perfect position to facilitate social-emotional development through the cooperative activities of physical education. These authors suggested strategies for physical educators regarding the social development of students during the elementary and secondary years.

School transportation directors should work more closely with teachers, guidance counselors, and administrators when children with special health care needs are placed in neighborhood schools (Harrington-Lueker, 1991). The school transportation staff needs direct information about children's medical needs as does the school staff. "Involving the transportation staff directly in the IEP [individualized education program] and in staff training sessions on everything from feeding tubes to tracheostomies could well mean a safer ride" (Harrington-Lueker, 1991, p. 28).

The members of the team will vary, based on the needs of the student, the classroom staff, and the family. As can be seen from the previous section, there are many resources both within and outside of the school system. It is important for one member of the school team to be responsible for the coordination of efforts and resources. This point of contact may vary, depending on the individual school system; some systems use an administrator (e.g., the building principal or supervisor), a health care professional (e.g., the school nurse), or classroom staff (e.g., the classroom teacher).

SCHOOL AND STAFF PREPARATION

Preparation of Staff and Students

Many teachers initially voice fear about receiving students with special health care needs, or about having to perform health-related procedures for which they perceive they are not adequately prepared. Two of the most common concerns voiced by classroom teachers are: (1) What if I do something wrong? Am I liable? and (2) What are the school system's policies concerning what I am being asked to do?

In addressing the issue of liability, there are few published court decisions that address personal liability for injuries to students with special health care needs. Points to consider include: discretionary function immunity, sovereign immunity, and *in loco parentis* (R. Hegner, personal communication, December 6, 1995; Virginia Departments of Education & Health, 1995; Virginia Department of Health, in press). Exhibit 16–3 provides a description and overview of each doctrine. The critical aspect of protecting oneself against liability is *negligence*, which is the careless failure to do what a reasonable person would do. "It is important for administrators, teachers, nurses, and all staff to be aware of their roles and responsibilities, and to receive adequate training to fulfill these responsibilities" (Virginia Departments of Health & Education, 1992, p. 288). Risk prevention (to protect oneself from the charge of negligence) includes the following:

- documentation
- education and training for staff
- being alert to "product notices" (attending to warning labels on equipment)
- being alert to trends and taking steps to prevent future occurrences (Virginia Departments of Health & Education, 1992, p. 288)

Documentation and training for staff are addressed below, in the section on the development of the health services plan.

When teachers ask about school policy regarding educating students with special health care needs, they usually discover that there is no written policy or procedure for the inclusion of children with special health care needs into school settings (Lowman, 1994; Virginia Departments of Education & Health, 1995). A survey of local school divisions by the Virginia Departments of Education and Health (1995) revealed that only 12 of the 80 school divisions responding had guidelines regarding the administration of health-related services. Local school systems are often left to develop local policies and procedures without guidance from the state (Virginia Departments of Education & Health, 1995). See the Suggested Reading at the end of this chapter for a list of the resources from several states that have developed written policies and procedures.

Many localities are currently involved in the development of local policies and procedures regarding the inclusion of students with special health care needs. A critical component of these policies and procedures must be the training for personnel in the administration of health-related procedures (Bennett, Haley, Smith, & Valluzzi, 1993; Lehr, 1990; Lowman & Rosenkoetter, 1994; Sherman & Rosen, 1990; Sobsey & Cox, 1996; Virginia Departments of Education & Health, 1995). Specific information on training in the administration of health-related procedures is addressed later in this chapter in the section on the development of the health services plan.

If not prepared, other teachers and staff in the school building will react in a negative, curious, or frightened man-ner to the inclusion of students with special health care needs. To be successful, training in the administration of specific health-related procedures should include the following components:

- Training should take place before the child enters school.
- Training should be provided by a health care provider with the parent.
- Training should be child-specific.
- Everyone who may be responsible for providing emergency care should be trained, including backups in case of staff absences.
- The training should include an opportunity for supervised practice and documentation of competency.
- Time lines should be established for regular review and retraining on the health-related procedures. (Virginia Departments of Education & Health, 1995, Appendix D, pp. 3–4)

To meet the need for general inservice training for school personnel, an inservice program was developed by the Oregon Health Sciences University and the University of Washington (Bennett et al., 1993). The Medically Fragile Inservice for Related Service Teams (M-FIRST)* project provided competency-based training via four training events each year followed by individually developed activities carried out by participants in their home work site. Technical assistance was provided by the project. The M-FIRST training competencies included:

- management of medical conditions in the school setting
- grief and loss
- managing transitions
- working with families
- interdisciplinary team processes
- functional approaches to providing educational services
- safety measures
- legal issues
- clinical issues

*The M-FIRST project was conducted collaboratively by the University Affiliated Programs at the Oregon Health Sciences University, Child Development and Rehabilitation Center, and the University of Washington, Child Development and Mental Retardation Center, along with the Departments of Education in Oregon and Washington. The address for the Child Development and Rehabilitation Center of the Oregon Health Sciences University is P.O. Box 574, Portland, Oregon 97207-0574. The address for the Child Development and Mental Retardation Center of the University of Washington is CTU WJ-10, Seattle, Washington 98195.

Exhibit 16–3 Liability Issues

Factors for school divisions to consider when developing local school policy for determining who will provide specialized health care procedures in the educational setting include:

- Section 504 of the Rehabilitation Act of 1973
- Individuals with Disabilities Education Act
- Nurse Practice Act
- Third-party payment
- *Legal liability issues.* In addressing the issue of personal liability, there are few published decisions that address school district liability for injuries to students who have special health care needs. In one case, *Nance v. Matthews*, 622 So. 2d 297 (Ala 1993), 20 IDELR 3, a student brought a suit for damages against a school principal, school nurse, and special education aide. The complaint was based on the negligent supervision of training of the aide by the principal, nurse, and special education director, as well as the aide's negligent failure to catheterize the student. The principal, nurse, and special education director were protected by discretionary function immunity from liability for negligent supervision.

- *Sovereign immunity.* One possible defense in a negligence suit is the doctrine of sovereign immunity. This doctrine protects governmental agencies and employees who commit acts of negligence while performing acts within the scope of their employment. Sovereign immunity applies only to negligent acts, not intentional or malicious acts. The doctrine of sovereign immunity for governmental employees has been partially or completely eliminated by legislative or judicial decisions in some states. Consult the local school board attorney regarding the issue of liability, including the defense of sovereign immunity.
- *In loco parentis.* In determining who is qualified to dispense medication or conduct health care procedures, some school divisions have relied on the legal doctrine of *in loco parentis*, which means "in place of the parents." Historically, the doctrine empowered school officials to exercise the same control over students at schools that parents could exercise at home. Many legal and societal events over the past three years have led educators, attorneys, and judges to change their views of *in loco parentis*. Consult the local school board attorney before relying on this doctrine.

Source: From *Guidelines for Students with Specialized Health Care Needs*, by Virginia Department of Health, in press, Richmond, VA: Virginia Department of Health.

- team leadership
- team support (Bennett et al., 1993, p. 34)

Trainers frequently need to document the ability of the person(s) trained to complete the procedure in an efficient and safe manner. The trainer should use this documentation to decide if the person can administer the procedure independently. The Documentation Checklist for Gastrostomy Bolus Feeding in Exhibit 16–4 is one example of appropriate documentation that can be used during training in the administration of a specific health-related procedure (Caldwell, Todaro, & Gates, 1989; Haynie, Porter, & Palfrey, 1989). Resources such as the ones listed in the Suggested Reading are available to help school systems in this documentation.

General inservice for school staff is important in introducing staff to health-related procedures that are new to them. However, this inservice alone is not sufficient. Giangreco, Dennis, Cloninger, Edelman, and Schattman (1993) conducted a qualitative analysis of the experiences of general education teachers who had a student with severe disabilities in their class. Transformations, such as changes in the teachers' attitudes and involvement with the students, came about gradually with direct involvement with the stu-

dent. According to Fred's teacher, the other faculty members in Fred's school did not seem to be bothered by the presence of health-related procedures:

> There is a little boy in the first grade who is also on oxygen. One teacher said, "You just get used to it." The principal says they have a wider comfort zone because [they] are around it. And [they] are not ignorant of it, so [they] are not so uncomfortable with the whole thing. (Lowman, 1994, p. 79)

In Fred's school, staff were not frightened by health-related procedures because they had direct involvement with the procedures over a period of time.

It is important to prepare the other students in the class by giving them a chance to ask questions and to handle, play with, and experience medical equipment (Goldberg, 1994; Lowman, 1994). One child care teacher prepared a classroom of four-old-years for the arrival of a child who did not use her arms and who was fed through a gastrostomy tube. The teacher explained how the new student worked with her feet, and encouraged the other children to try to use their feet to play, color, glue, etc. (Lowman, 1994). Fred's teacher explained Fred's special health care needs to the other children in her class:

Exhibit 16–4 Documentation Checklist for Gastrostomy Bolus Feeding

	Demonstrations		Return Demonstrations			
	Date	Date	Date	Date	Date	Date
A. State name and purpose of procedure						
B. Preparation						
1. Complete at _____ time(s)						
2. _____ Amount (cc)						
_____ Formula/feeding (type of feeding)						
3. Feeding to be completed in _____ minutes						
4. Position for feeding _____						
5. Identify potential problems and appropriate actions						
C. Identify supplies:						
1. Catheter _____ (size) _____ (type)						
Balloon size _____cc						
a. Small port plug						
b. Feeding port						
2. Clamp and plug						
3. 60-cc catheter-tipped syringe						
4. Formula at room temperature						
5. Small glass of tap water						
D. Procedure:						
1. Wash hands thoroughly.						
2. Gather equipment.						
3. Position child and explain procedure.						
4. Remove plug from feeding tube.						
Child-Specific: Steps 5–11 should be prescribed for each child						
5. Check for proper placement of tube. Attach syringe and aspirate stomach contents by pulling plunger back.						
6. Measure contents.						
7. Return stomach contents to stomach.						
8. If stomach contents are over ____cc, subtract from feeding.						
9. If more than _____ cc, hold feeding.						
10. Pinch or clamp off tube.						
11. Remove syringe.						
12. Attach syringe without plunger to feeding port.						
13. Pour formula (room temperature) into syringe (approx. 30–40 cc).						

continues

Exhibit 16–4 continued

	Demonstrations		Return Demonstrations			
	Date	Date	Date	Date	Date	Date
14. Release or unclamp tube and allow feeding to go in slowly.						
15. When feeding gets to 5-cc marker, add more formula.						
16. Continue procedure until the feeding is completed.						
17. Allow about 30 minutes to complete feeding (the higher the syringe is held, the faster the feeding will flow).						
18. Lower the syringe if feeding is going too fast.						
19. Make feeding like meal time. Young children may suck on a pacifier.						
20. Flush tube with ____ cc of water when feeding is complete.						
21. Pinch off tubing, remove syringe, close off clamp.						
22. Allow child to remain in feeding position for minimum of one-half hour after feeding.						
23. Wash syringe with soap and warm water and put in home container.						
24. Report any problems to parents.						
25. Document procedure and problems in log.						

Checklist content approved by:

_____   Date _____
Parent/Guardian Signature

_____   Date _____
Administrator

_____   Date _____
Health Care Professional

Source: Adapted with permission from T.H. Caldwell, A.W. Todaro, and A.J. Gates, *Community Providers Guide: An Information Outline for Working with Children with Special Health Care Needs,* and M. Haynie, S.M. Porter, and J.S. Palfrey, *Children Assisted by Medical Technology in Educational Settings: Guidelines for Care,* © 1989, Children's Hospital.

Fred needs a tube to breathe because his lungs don't work as well as yours and mine. The nasogastric tube was the biggest thing for them; they just couldn't understand why he didn't want to eat. And we just laughingly said, "Well, the way we feel about that tube is the way that he feels about food." (Lowman, 1994, p. 78)

Fred's teacher tried to find a way the children could relate to Fred's health-related needs to help them understand his special needs.

Preparation of Environment

Beyond preparation of the staff and students, the physical environment also needs to be examined and modified if necessary. Modifications might be as simple as determining a way to hang the feeding bag or adjusting the time the class has lunch. Modifications may also be on a larger scale. A second-grade teacher moved the desks from her classroom when a student in a wheelchair with a portable ventilator was not able to move between the rows of desks. Instead of rows of desks, she used centers and learning areas.

Management of oxygen also needs special consideration. Fred was connected to a machine that manufactures oxygen. Fred's teacher said the machine was hard to get used to initially, because it was so noisy. Putting a rug under the machine helped reduce the noise level in the classroom. The staff and children learned to walk around and over the tubing to Fred's oxygen:

> So we have a little machine in our room that makes oxygen and . . . he has real long blue tubing so he can get all over the room . . . everyone has learned to be careful of it. Certainly we've stepped on it a million times. It's pretty flexible. . . . We've broken [the joints] but we just replace them. . . . All the children, including one little boy who has to hop on his hands and knees, have learned to lift his feet when he goes over the tubing. (Lowman, 1994, p. 75)

It is especially critical to note any modifications that will be needed in the transportation arrangement. It is important to include transportation representatives in the planning and training before the student enters school. Components to consider might be how to secure oxygen cylinder, presence of bus assistant, air temperature inside the bus, etc. For example, because of Fred's tracheostomy, the bus driver was careful to warm the bus thoroughly before picking him up. On very cold mornings, Fred was picked up one hour later than usual to give the air a chance to warm.

HEALTH SERVICES PLAN

Many sources have shown that the development of a written plan of care would assist in the provision of health-related services in the classroom setting (American Academy of Pediatrics, 1990; Fauvre, 1988; Lowman, 1994; Lowman & Rosenkoetter, 1994; Sobsey & Cox, 1996; Virginia Departments of Education & Health, 1995). Documentation is critical to protect the child and the school personnel. Exhibit 16–5 includes a sample format for the health services plan (Lowman, 1994; Lowman & Rosenkoetter, 1994; Virginia Departments of Education & Health, 1995). Development of this plan is recommended for all health-related procedures described in Exhibit 16–1. School divisions are encouraged to use and adapt this form as appropriate. Suggested content for the health services plan is discussed below.

Effective Dates

The team developing the health services plan should decide the effective dates of the plan. Because health needs can change frequently and quickly, it is recommended that the health services plan be a document separate from the individualized education program (IEP) or individualized family service plan (IFSP). This would avoid having to call another IEP meeting to make a change in health-related procedures. Some school systems staple the completed health services plan to the IEP document. This plan should be completed *before* the child comes to school or the center. Because health needs can change frequently, this plan should be developed at a meeting *separate* from the IFSP/IEP meeting. In addition, staff should plan to review the health services plan frequently and make revisions after a major illness or hospitalization.

Members of the Planning Team

The specific members of the planning team will vary, depending on the needs of the child, the staff, and the family. Members could include the parents or guardian, the child (if appropriate), the service coordinator, the primary teacher, the class paraprofessional, the school administrator, the special education administrator, other related service staff as appropriate (speech-language pathologist, occupational therapist, physical therapist), the school nurse or school health contact person, the transportation director, the transition nurse from the discharging hospital or the local health department, the Medicaid waiver case manager, and a representative from the equipment company. It is important for one person to be responsible for the coordination of documentation and resources.

Description of the Child's Medical Condition

This section should contain a complete description of the child's current medical condition, including relevant medical history and the child's needs for growth and development, and the effect of the medical condition on the child's performance in school. It is not necessary to provide the child's complete medical history, but rather medical information that is relevant to educational planning and the school setting. The school's medical or health staff, or staff from the health department, will be helpful in reviewing medical reports and determining the effect of the child's medical condition on the child's performance in school.

Strategies To Support the Child in the School Setting

Based on information from the medical components, the team will identify activities in which the child may participate or any adaptations or modifications that will be needed. For example, if the child has a tracheostomy, he or she may need to avoid contact with particles such as sand, powder, or lotion. If the child requires gastrostomy feedings in school, it will be necessary to plan to store formula and hang the feeding bag.

Exhibit 16–5 Health Services Plan

Student: _____

Parents: _____

This Health Services Plan will be in effect from_____ to_____.

Members of planning team:

Description of child's medical condition:

Strategies to support the child in the school or center-based setting:

Feeding and nutritional needs:

Transportation arrangements:

Medication to be dispensed, amount, time, and person administering:

Where and when the procedure(s) should be performed:

Who will perform the procedure(s):

Training that is to take place prior to the child entering class:

Schedule for review and monitoring of training:

Emergency procedures:

Plan for absences:

We have participated in the development of this health services plan and agree with the contents:

_____   _____
Parents/Guardian   Date

_____   _____
School Administrator   Date

_____   _____
Health Care Professional   Date

_____   _____
Teacher   Date

_____   _____
                                                                                              Date

_____   _____
                                                                                              Date

Source: Adapted from *Integrating Preschoolers with Complex Health Care Needs into Early Childhood Special Education Programs: The Teacher's Perspective*, by D.K. Lowman, 1994, unpublished doctoral dissertation, University of Virginia, Charlottesville. Copyright 1994 by Dianne Koontz Lowman. Reprinted by permission.

Feeding and Nutritional Needs

The plan should describe the child's current diet, feeding modifications needed, oral-motor interventions, fluid intake requirements, food allergies, and food likes and dislikes if applicable. Many children with severe oral-motor feeding problems will have a more detailed feeding plan that could be referenced in this section.

Transportation Arrangements

If the child is eligible for special education services, transportation arrangements will be specified on the IEP. This section should address whether specific accommodations will be needed for the child to be transported safely (e.g., training for the bus driver, an assistant on the bus). Many questions arise concerning the transportation of oxygen on a school bus, which should be resolved through the local school district's policy.

Medication To Be Dispensed, Amount, Time, and Person Administering

School systems have guidelines for the administration of medication in the school building; persons should refer to school division guidelines for specific information concerning who will administer medication and the required documentation. This section should include the type of medication, dosage, timing, and procedures of dispensing. In addition, this section should address the effect of the medication on the child's performance in school and procedures to follow if the medication is not ingested.

Where and When the Procedure(s) Should Be Performed

This section should address the location, frequency, and time of day involved with completing the health procedure(s). The type of health-related procedure will determine where the procedure should be performed. A child can receive gastrostomy feedings during lunch in the cafeteria with the other children. On the other hand, clean intermittent catheterization should be performed in a private bathroom. The child's needs may also dictate where procedures should be performed. For example, Fred did not like to have his tracheostomy suctioned; he cried, coughed, and gagged. This procedure was embarrassing for him and was performed in private.

School Personnel Who Will Perform the Procedure(s)

The school administrator will be responsible for determining who will perform each health-related procedure. The specific qualifications of the individual needed to perform the procedures should be considered. The need for support personnel such as paraprofessionals can also be considered at this time.

Training before the Child Enters Class

A critical component of the health services plan is training. "The key to increased competence and comfort is training" (Lehr, 1990, p. 141). This section should list in detail who will be providing the training and how often the training will be monitored and reviewed. Initial training should be provided by a health care professional (i.e., school nurse, public health personnel, transition nurse from hospital). The parents should be consulted and work with the health care provider to provide the training in the administration of health-related procedures.

Schedule for Review and Monitoring of Training

Include timelines for regular review and retraining for the administration of health-related procedures. Some localities suggest reviewing training every six months; other localities suggest reviewing and retraining once a year. It is also important to review the administration of a health-related procedure immediately when the child's medical needs change.

Emergency Procedures

Dealing with an emergency is scary for most school personnel. The emergency plan should be specified in detail. It should describe how the child typically reacts, if known, and list specifically what to do, who to call, and the order in which people should be notified. Decide where copies of the emergency plan will be posted and stored. The school administrator should notify the local rescue squad about the health-related procedures and the location of the child in the school building.

Plan for Absences

Outline the plan for dealing with instances when the person responsible for conducting the health-related procedure is absent. There should always be at least one backup person trained in the administration of the specific health-related procedure. There should also be a plan if both persons trained are absent on the same day. Discuss a plan for what to do if the child is absent from school for an extended period and home-based instruction is required. Discuss a plan for receiving current medical information before the child returns to school from an extended illness or hospitalization.

Individualizing the Plan

The health services plan presented in this chapter is one way to provide documentation to protect the child, the teacher, the school, and the parents. All health services plans do not need to be as extensive as the plan outlined in this chapter. Fred's plan was long and detailed because of the numerous health-related procedures that had to be conducted in school. The components of the health services plan will be based on the individual student's health-related needs. For example, if a child has an emergency plan for a severe asthma attack, the plan may be a one-page document. The planning team, based on the child's health-related needs, will determine the specific contents of the health services plan.

CONCLUSION

Despite their initial fears, teachers describe the positive aspects of including children with special health care needs into their classrooms. As one teacher confirmed: "I feel it's part of the job. I feel like that's why I'm here. . . . It's their right to be part of my class. They have their own right to an education" (Lowman, 1994, p. 166). Another teacher emphasized that it is important to see "the child as a child and not the oxygen." A third teacher stressed that it is important to view a student with special health care needs as a person, and not get wrapped up in the overwhelming impact of all the tubes (Lowman, 1994, p. 213). Fred's teacher summarized her experiences having Fred in her classroom: "[Fred] is just another little person in our room. We are all learning the special things he can teach us. We miss him when he is absent. He is a child first" (Lowman, 1993, pp. 455–456).

REFERENCES

American Academy of Pediatrics. (1990). Children with health impairments in schools. *Pediatrics, 86,* 636–638.

Bennett, F.C., Haley, P., Smith, G., & Valluzzi, J. (1993). Inservice programs for related services teams serving medically fragile children. *OSERS News in Print,* 31–35.

Bruder, M.B. (1990, October). *Children with complex health care needs: Issues in policy and personnel preparation.* Paper presented at the International Early Childhood Conference on Children with Special Needs, Albuquerque, NM.

Caldwell, T.H., Todaro, A.W., & Gates, A.J. (Eds.). (1989). *Community provider's guide: An information outline for working with children with special health care needs.* New Orleans, LA: National MCH Resource Center, Children's Hospital.

Chomicki, S., & Wilgosh, L. (1994). Obtaining health care for individuals with intellectual impairments: A literature review. *Physical Disabilities: Education and Related Services, 13*(2), 55–69.

Darrow, D., Carleton, W., & Stephens, S. (1993). Physical education intervention for the chronically ill and disabled. *Delta Kappa Gamma Bulletin, 59*(2), 29–34.

Fauvre, M. (1988). Including young children with "new" chronic illnesses in an early childhood education setting. *Young Children, 43*(6), 71–77.

Giangreco, M.F., Dennis, R., Cloninger, C., Edelman, S., & Schattman, R. (1993). "I've counted Jon": Transformational experiences of teachers educating students with disabilities. *Exceptional Children, 59,* 359–372.

Goldberg, E. (1994). Including children with chronic health conditions: Nebulizers in the classroom. *Young Children, 49*(2), 34–37.

Harrington-Lueker, D. (1991). Special buses: It's up to local boards to regulate transportation for special education. *The American School Board Journal, 178*(4), 27–28, 43.

Haynie, M., Porter, S.M., & Palfrey, J.S. (1989). *Children assisted by medical technology in educational setting: Guidelines for care.* Boston, MA: Project School Care, The Children's Hospital.

Knight, D., & Wadsworth, D.E. (1994). Guidelines for educating students who are technology dependent. *Physical Disabilities: Education and Related Services, 13*(1), 1–8.

Lehr, D.H. (1990). Preparation of personnel to work with students with complex health care needs. In A.P. Kaiser & C.M. McWhorter (Eds.), *Preparing personnel to work with persons with severe disabilities* (pp. 135–151). Baltimore: Paul H. Brookes.

Lowman, D.K. (1993). Preschoolers with complex health care needs: A survey of early childhood special education teachers in Virginia. *Topics in Early Childhood Special Education, 13*(4), 445–460.

Lowman, D.K. (1994). *Integrating preschoolers with complex health care needs into early childhood special education programs: The teacher's perspective.* Unpublished doctoral dissertation, University of Virginia, Charlottesville.

Lowman, D.K., & Rosenkoetter, S. (1994). Creating successful transition for children with complex health care needs: New friends on the journey. In S.E. Rosenkoetter, A.H. Hains, & S.A. Flower (Eds.), *Bridging early services for children with special health care needs and their families: A practical guide for transition planning* (pp. 181–196). Baltimore: Paul H. Brookes.

Mulligan-Ault, M., Guess, D., Struth, L., & Thompson, B. (1988). The implementation of health related procedures in classrooms for students with severe multiple impairments. *Journal of the Association for Persons with Severe Handicaps, 13,* 100–116.

Parette, H.P., & Holder-Brown, L. (1992). The role of the school counselor in providing services to medically fragile children. *Elementary School Guidance and Counseling, 27*(1), 47–55.

Revell, G.M., & Liptak, G.S. (1991). Understanding the child with special health care needs: A developmental perspective. *Journal of Pediatric Nursing, 6*(4), 258–267.

Sciarillo, W.G., Draper, S., Green, P., Burkett, K., & Demetrides, S. (1988). Children with specialized health needs in the special education setting: A statewide technical assistance approach. *Infants and Young Children, 1,* 74–84.

Shelton, T.L., Jeppson, E.S., & Johnson, B.H. (1989). *Family-centered care for children with special health care needs.* Washington, DC: Association for the Care of Children's Health.

Sherman, L.P., & Rosen, C.D. (1990). Development of a preschool program for tracheostomy dependent children. *Pediatric Nursing, 16*(4), 357–361.

Sirvis, M. (1988). Students with special health care needs. *Teaching Exceptional Children, 20*(4), 40–44.

Sobsey, D., & Cox, A. (1996). Integrating health care and educational programs. In F.P. Orelove & D. Sobsey, *Educating children with multiple disabilities: A transdisciplinary approach* (3rd ed.; pp. 217–251). Baltimore: Paul H. Brookes.

Virginia Department of Health. (in press). *Guidelines for students with specialized health care needs.* Richmond, VA: Author.

Virginia Departments of Education and Health. (1995). *Report of the Departments of Education and Health. Report on the needs of medically fragile students to the Governor and the General Assembly of Virginia* (Senate Document No. 5). Richmond, VA: Commonwealth of Virginia.

Virginia Departments of Health and Education. (1992). *School health guidelines*. Richmond, VA: Author.

SUGGESTED READING

BOOKS

Batshaw, M.L., & Perret, Y.M. (1992). *Children with disabilities: A medical primer* (3rd ed.). Baltimore: Paul H. Brookes.

Graff, J.C., Ault, M.M., Guess, D., Taylor, M., & Thompson, B. (1990). *Health care needs for students with disabilities: An illustrated medical guide for the classroom*. Baltimore: Paul H. Brookes.

Rosenkoetter, S.E., Hains, A.H., & Flower, S.A. (1994). *Bridging early services for children with special health care needs and their families: A practical guide for transition planning*. Baltimore: Paul H. Brookes.

Urbano, M.T. (1992). *Preschool children with special health care needs*. San Diego, CA: Singular Publishing Group.

MANUALS

Caldwell, T.H., Todaro, A.W., & Gates, A.J. (Eds.). (1989). *Community provider's guide: An information outline for working with children with special health needs*. New Orleans, LA: National MCH Resource Center, Children's Hospital.

California Department of Education. (1990). *Guidelines and procedures for meeting the specialized physical health care needs of pupils*. Sacramento, CA: Author.

Epstein, S.G., Taylor, A.B., Halberg, A.S., Gardner, J.D., Walker, D.K., & Crocker, A.C. (1989). *Enhancing quality: Standards and indicators of quality care for children with special health care needs*. Boston: New England SERVE.

Haynie, M., Porter, S.M., & Palfrey, J.S. (1989). *Children assisted by medical technology in educational settings: Guidelines for care*. Boston: Project School Care, The Children's Hospital.

Heller, K.W., Alberto, P.A., Schwartzman, M.N., Shiplett, K., Pierce, J., Polokoff, J., Heller, E.J., Andrews, D.G., Briggs, A., & Kana, T.G. (1990). *Suggested physical health procedures of students with special needs*. Atlanta, GA: Georgia State University.

Kluge Children's Rehabilitation Center. (1992). *The strawberry connection guide to supporting families of children with feeding tubes*. Charlottesville, VA: Author.

Mountain Plains Regional Resource Center and the Utah State Office of Education. (1992). *Guidelines for serving students with special health care needs*. Salt Lake City: Utah State Office of Education.

Parent Educational Advocacy Training Center and the ARC of Northern Virginia. (1993). *Taking charge: A parent's guide to health care for children with special needs*. Alexandria, VA: PEATC.

Tamari, P., Kempf, B., & Woodward, E. (Eds.). (1991). *Information and resource directory for children with special health care needs*. Selden, NY: Starting Early Childhood Division of Developmental Disabilities Institute.

Virginia Department of Health. (in press). *Guidelines for students with specialized health care needs*. Richmond, VA: Author.

West Virginia Department of Education. (1990). *Basic and specialized health care procedure manual for West Virginia Public Schools*. Charleston, WV: Author.

NEWSLETTERS

ACCH News

[Published bimonthly by the Association for the Care of Children's Health, 7910 Woodmont Avenue, #300, Bethesda, MD 20814, 301-654-6549]

Catch Quarterly

[Published by the American Academy of Pediatrics, 141 Northwest Point Boulevard, P.O. Box 927, Elk Grove Village, IL 60009-0927]

Families and Disability Newsletter

[Published three times a year by the Beach Center on Families and Disability at the University of Kansas, 3111 Haworth Hall, Lawrence, KS 66045, FAX 913-864-5323]

Springboard

[Published by the Center for Children with Chronic Illness and Disability, Box 721-UMHC, Harvard Street at East River Road, Minneapolis, MN 55455]

REPORTS: RESEARCH, TECHNICAL, PROCEEDINGS

Caldwell, J.H., Sirvis, B., Todaro, A.W., & Accouloumre, D.S. (1991). *Special health care in the school*. Reston, VA: Council for Exceptional Children.

Joint Task Force for the Management of Children with Special Health Care Needs. (1990). *Guidelines for the delineation of roles and responsibilities for the safe delivery of specialized health care in the educational setting*. Reston, VA: Council for Exceptional Children.

Koop, C.E. (1987). *Surgeon General's report: Children with special health care needs* (DHHS Publication No. HRS/D/MC 87-2). Rockville, MD: U.S. Department of Health and Human Services.

National Center for Education in Maternal and Child Health. (1990). *Children with special health needs: A resource guide*. Washington, DC: The National Maternal and Child Health Clearinghouse.

U.S. Congress, Office of Technology Assessment. (1987). *Technology-dependent children: Hospital v. home care—A technical memorandum* (OTA-TM-H-38). Washington, DC: U.S. Government Printing Office.

CHAPTER 17

Educating Students Who Are Deaf and Hard-of-Hearing

Brenda Chafin Seal

INTRODUCTION

Deaf education is the oldest branch of special education in the United States. From 1812 to 1850, at least 10 state legislatures throughout the country appropriated funds to build "asylums" for the education of "deaf and dumb" persons (Gannon, 1981). These schools were established within each state, generally in remote or rural areas. Children who enrolled in these schools primarily were those who were born deaf and failed to develop spoken language, those commonly referred to as deaf and dumb. In each state, however, some parents refused to send their deaf children away to school. A few of these parents sent their children to local schools—some successfully, others without success. Many children who were deaf or hard-of-hearing were not educated at all. This trend continued throughout the 19th century and for the first three-quarters of the 20th century.

Although this chapter focuses on children who are educated in their local schools, it is important to point out that schools for the deaf—private and public, day and residential—educate at least 21% of the nation's deaf students. According to the U.S. Department of Education's (1994) annual report to Congress, approximately 61,000 students with hearing impairment, ages 6 to 21, were educated in the United States in 1992–1993. Among those students attending local schools, 27% were enrolled in general education classes, 21% were taught in resource rooms, and 31% attended separate classes for students with hearing impairment. In our country, there is not and there has never been a single type of placement, either residential or local, that has served all of a state's or locality's deaf and hard-of-hearing students.

Educating students who are deaf and hard-of-hearing in inclusion programs is controversial. Some experts in deafness have embraced the philosophy of inclusive education, advocating full membership in a general education classroom; full ownership by both special and general educators of the student's education; and provision of supplemental services that are part of, rather than isolated from, the curriculum. Others have rejected inclusion as poor practice for students with significant hearing loss. The purpose of this chapter is to explore issues that affect the education of deaf and hard-of-hearing students and to provide practical knowledge for making inclusion decisions for these students. This chapter is written from a personal philosophy that is itself *inclusive* of all educational options for all children who come to the educational process bearing the distinction of being deaf or hard-of-hearing.*

HISTORICAL PERSPECTIVES

The prevalence of deafness in children has remained relatively stable over the past 150 years. Although severe and profound hearing losses are considered a low-incidence disability, the addition of moderate and mild hearing losses raises the prevalence of childhood hearing loss to about 20% (Berg, Blair, Viehweg, & Wilson-Vlotman, 1986). The incidence of fluctuating hearing loss is difficult to obtain; many children experience temporary hearing loss with ear infections and other illnesses. Recent estimates project that another 56,000 children under the age of 6, those most likely affected by fluctuating hearing loss, should be

---

*Current terminology acknowledges that hearing loss occurs in degrees of severity. Those children whose loss precludes the development of spoken language are generally referred to as *deaf.* Those whose hearing loss affects but does not prevent the development of spoken language are called *hard-of-hearing*. Use of the terms *deaf* and *hard-of-hearing* as adjectives is common to current literature and practice, and it should not be interpreted negatively.

included in the incidence figures for hearing impairment (Schildroth & Hotto, 1995).

A variety of acquired and congenital disorders can cause hearing loss in children, and despite improved medical interventions, a decrease in the prevalence of deafness has not occurred. In fact, the rubella epidemic of 1963–1965 nearly tripled the number of children born deaf during that two-year period (Moores, 1987). Since then, spinal meningitis (Bess & Humes, 1990) has become the most common postnatal cause of deafness in young children. Other acquired losses result from bacterial and viral infections and from ototoxic drugs, but their incidence is low. Congenital causes include several syndromes, such as Down syndrome, that have hearing loss as a secondary characteristic. About 33% of all children who have hearing loss have additional disabling conditions: learning disabilities, mental retardation, cerebral palsy, visual impairment, behavioral disorders, and developmental delays (Karchmer, 1985). Hearing loss is exacerbated by these conditions, so that educational concerns are multiplied, not merely added to the child's profile. At least 90% of congenitally deaf children are born to hearing parents (Schein & Delk, 1974). About 50% of their deafness is inherited (with 40% recessive, 10% dominant, and 1 to 2% sex-linked transmission) (Moores, 1987). The other 50% have unknown causes.

When the majority of deaf children attended schools for the deaf, deaf adults played a prominent role in their education. Even schools that were "oral" and prohibited sign language often had deaf adults who signed in the residential environments. American Sign Language (ASL), first brought to this country by Thomas Hopkins Gallaudet in the early 1800s, was passed on from these deaf adults to deaf children. As a result, the residential school and ASL have become a social-educational institution that is central to the Deaf culture.*

For many years, ASL was viewed as an inferior gestural system. It was first described as a rule-governed language in 1960 (Stokoe, 1960); later analyses have brought increased acceptance of ASL into educational environments. About 67% of deaf and hard-of-hearing children use sign language. Not all sign language users, however, use ASL. Several other sign systems that attempt to code spoken English were introduced in the early 1970s (Gustason, Pfetzing, & Zawolkow, 1980). These Manually Coded English systems are different from ASL in their grammatical structure, but they rely heavily on vocabulary from ASL. Hearing and deaf signers who move comfortably between ASL and English systems usually borrow from both, such that a Pidgin Sign Language has emerged. Pidgin Sign is most commonly used between hearing and deaf individuals.

The 1970s also brought a dramatic shift to the prior trend of sending deaf and hard-of-hearing children to schools for

the deaf. Legislation of the 1950s and 1960s that prohibited racial segregation was followed by legislation of the 1970s and 1980s that prohibited segregation of individuals with disabilities. In addition, the rubella epidemic of the 1960s occurred at a time when Head Start and other early intervention programs were being promoted (Moores, 1987). The resulting trend of placing young deaf and hard-of-hearing children in their local schools quickly spread to mainstreaming older deaf students. Schools for the deaf experienced declining enrollments and a change in their student population. Students who had multiple handicapping conditions and those who did not have strong family support systems were more likely to attend residential schools. Those who were "just deaf" and those with a strong family support system were more likely to be enrolled in their local schools.

The placement options for deaf and hard-of-hearing students that existed over the next 20 years (Brill, 1978; Moores, 1987) came from the system of special education services proposed by Deno (1970). This menu is sometimes depicted with two inverted triangles, one presenting the progressive severity of hearing loss, and the other the prescribed placements and support services (see Figure 17–1). Proponents of inclusion discourage placing a student according to a preexisting design; they recommend, instead, fitting the design to the student.

Since the 1970s, educators, parents, and deaf adults have voiced many concerns about the education of students with hearing loss. Concerns about the least restrictive environment, erosion of the Deaf culture, and the increasing complexity of students' educational needs led Congress to establish a Commission on Education of the Deaf through the Education of the Deaf Act of 1986. The Commission's report (1988) included 52 recommendations for improving the "unsatisfactory" quality of education for hearing-impaired students. The Commission's report was also fundamental in inspiring the Office of Special Education and Rehabilitative Services, the National Association of State Directors of Special Education, and the Conference on Educational Administrators Serving the Deaf (with input from the National Association of the Deaf) to join forces to improve education of students who are deaf and hard-of-hearing. Their project, sometimes referred to as the Deaf Education Initiatives Project (Pugh & Hicks, 1995), represents the first multiple-agency effort to address education of deaf and hard-of-hearing students.

CURRENT ISSUES SURROUNDING THE PHILOSOPHY OF INCLUSIVE EDUCATION

Medical versus Cultural Perspective

Fundamental to many concerns surrounding inclusion of deaf and hard-of-hearing students are two perspectives: medical and cultural. The medical perspective focuses on

*The word Deaf is generally capitalized when it refers to culture.

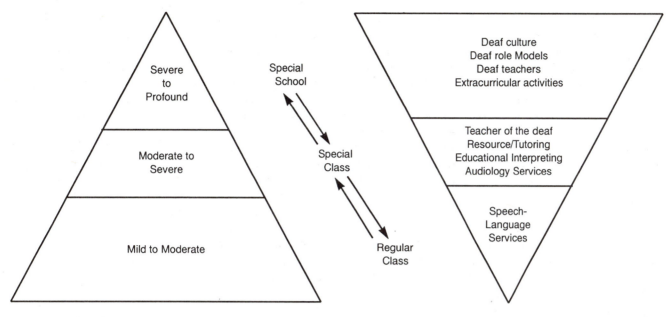

Figure 17–1 Severity of hearing loss and traditional placement options

efforts to "fix" children with hearing loss. Hearing parents who suspect hearing loss frequently begin a medical trail to determine "what's wrong with" their child. Once the hearing loss is diagnosed, amplification and early intervention quickly follow. Technological advances enable the fitting of powerful hearing aids for some deaf children and the surgical implantation of electrodes into the cochleas of others. (Currently, cochlear implants are recommended for only those children who are at least two years old and show no potential benefit from other amplification.) Results are varied, with some children showing little or no gain in hearing and others showing improved hearing and language development. Increasing numbers of parents pursue implant surgery to restore hearing in their children (Owens & Kessler, 1989). Improved hearing with amplification or with surgery is more likely to occur when the loss is less severe, yet the medical perspective supports all efforts to reduce the impact of hearing loss on the child's development.

The cultural perspective views deafness as *different*, not disordered. Deaf individuals are different from hearing individuals—in their language, in their values, and in the way they perceive the world. Members of the Deaf culture may work and live in the hearing world, but their personal and social lives center around others who are Deaf. Their difference is not minimized; instead, it is pronounced—much like the differences of other minorities are pronounced. And, like some minorities that seek to protect their members from perceived threats, the Deaf culture has become more visible in its protectionism. The Deaf President Now campaign at Gallaudet University in 1988 is an example of a large-scale effort to preserve the identity of the Deaf culture. On a smaller, sometimes more personal, scale are Deaf adults who admonish professionals for influencing hearing parents in decisions to "fix" their deaf babies. The same admonishments are also given to educators who try to minimize hearing loss and *include* a deaf child in a classroom with hearing children. Proponents of the cultural perspective believe that the student's difference warrants a special education with other students who are deaf and with teachers and support service personnel who are educated in deafness. Hallahan and Kauffman (1995), in arguing against inclusion, recommended that educators take heed from the Deaf community and its value of culture. They advocated that enabling a child to embrace his or her difference and to identify with others who share the difference is a more promising educational practice than attempting to reduce the disability as undesirable.

Most college programs today continue to approach deafness as a disorder, as a pathology that prevents normal development of spoken language. The alternative perspective, the cultural perspective, has only recently been recognized and presented in training programs. Today's graduates of deaf education, speech-language pathology, and audiology programs should be informed about both perspectives. Informed educators are critical to decision making about placement.

Bilingual-Bicultural Education

Another frequently debated issue in inclusion of deaf and hard-of-hearing children is the bilingual-bicultural, or "bi-bi," issue. This issue, with some of its tenets grounded in the medical-cultural dichotomy, is also philosophical. Proponents of bilingual-bicultural education believe that deaf and hard-of-hearing children are better served in early childhood programs and in kindergarten through 12th grade when they are provided access to both the Deaf culture and the larger hearing culture. This dual access boils down to education in two languages: ASL and English. The Bilingual Education Act and its 1981 Amendment provided that children of "limited English proficiency" be taught in their native language by teachers who are sensitive to their cultural heritage. Johnson, Liddell, and Erting (1989) recommended that deaf babies be provided ASL as a first language and that ASL be the formal language for teaching English as a second language. Disagreement over this sequence has been voiced by many educators who respond that hearing parents rarely have knowledge of or skill in ASL to make it a feasible first language. Short of encouraging hearing parents to find surrogate deaf parents, educators must recognize that deaf children born into a hearing culture are likely to have more exposure to English, spoken or signed, than to ASL.

Local educators provide students with access to both ASL and English through several bilingual models (e.g., Luetke-Stahlman, 1983). In sequential bilingual models, hearing parents may be encouraged to learn sign language and pair it with spoken language, fostering all modes of communication development in their deaf child. (The use of all communication methods with deaf children is referred to as the *Total Communication philosophy*.) As the child becomes older (e.g., in middle school), ASL is introduced, possibly in a class or unit on Deaf studies or by deaf speakers who encourage immersion into the Deaf culture. If, however, the deaf child has deaf parents, the sequential model reverses its order, with the assumption that the child enters school with ASL as his or her native language and must then be taught English as a second language, using ASL as a basis for learning the second language. In other bilingual models, deaf students may be exposed to both ASL and English at the same time. A deaf teacher who uses ASL may be paired with a hearing teacher assistant who uses spoken and signed English. Conversely, a hearing teacher who uses English signing may be paired with a deaf teacher assistant, who uses ASL. Both languages are used in the classroom throughout the school day (Mueller-Vollmer, 1990).

To date, there are no efficacy studies on the success of these models. In discussing second-language learners, Schiff-Myers (1992) stressed the importance of the comprehensiveness of the first language and learning that first language during the critical language-learning period (between birth and five years of age). According to Schiff-Myers, the higher the linguistic development in the child's first language, the better his or her second language learning, whether that language is English, ASL, Spanish, or Japanese. In fact, the increasing numbers of deaf and hard-of-hearing children whose parents use a language other than English and ASL raises additional concerns for educators. In the United States, with at least 17% of deaf students from African American cultures, 16% from Hispanic American cultures, and a growing percentage from Asian (4%) and other (3%) cultures (Schildroth & Hotto, 1995), the challenge to schools to be bilingual is more realistically a challenge to be multilingual-multicultural in programming.

Educational Interpreters

Critical to the education of deaf and hard-of-hearing students in integrated classes is the use of interpreters. Professional interpreters for deaf adults have been common for about 30 years. The use of educational interpreters for children is a recent phenomenon, however, brought on by the entry of deaf students in local schools and the efforts of the schools to meet the students' communication needs. The field of educational interpreting is probably the most rapidly growing deafness-related discipline today. While universities and colleges continue to close their low-enrollment deaf education programs (Craig & Craig, 1993), federal training grants are funding more college and university interpreter training programs (Patrie, 1994; Schrag, 1991). Two-thirds of the graduates of these programs enter educational interpreting positions (Schrag, 1991).

The issues surrounding an "interpreted" education (Winston, 1995) are complex. First of all, no single method or system is used by all interpreters. Because the majority of deaf students use sign language, sign language interpreters are most common. Some deaf students require ASL interpreters, but many require English sign language interpreters (or "transliterators," for a verbatim translation from English to sign and from sign to English). Another group of deaf and hard-of-hearing students does not sign at all; they rely on cued speech transliterators to access spoken language. Cued speech is a system of handshapes and movements that represent the sounds of spoken language (Cornett, 1967). Cued speech enables some students to speech-read what is being said. Cued speech is not a language but a supplement to spoken language. Still another group of students relies on oral interpreters to access spoken language. Oral interpreting involves silently reproducing the spoken language used by a speaker who is difficult to speech-read. The interpreter conveys the mood and intent of the message with expression and natural gestures (Castle, 1994). Oral interpreting is less common than either cued speech or sign language interpreting.

Several issues surround educational interpreting: the qualifications of educational interpreters, the shortage of qualified interpreters, the impact of unqualified interpreters on a student's education, ethical issues associated with an interpreter imparting the content and style of another person's instruction, role conflicts that some interpreters experience in serving as the primary resource for deafness and as a teacher aide. A National Task Force on Educational Interpreting studied many of these issues. Its report, *Educational Interpreting for Deaf Students* (Stuckless, Avery, & Hurwitz, 1989), and the 1992 Amendments to the Education of the Deaf Act (P.L. 102-421), have brought many of these issues to our attention. Knowledge of these issues is important, especially given that the primary tool for implementing inclusion for deaf students today is to provide them an educational interpreter (Winston, 1995).

Despite the current number of interpreter training programs in the United States (at least 70 in 1996), there continues to be a shortage of qualified educational interpreters, especially in rural areas (Maroney, 1995). This shortage is exacerbated by low salaries that often accompany the positions. Nationally certified, freelance interpreters can easily earn higher salaries working part time. Schools that offer low wages, with no benefits or possibility for promotion, are not attractive to these interpreters. Administrators who find it difficult to recruit and retain qualified interpreters may hire unqualified interpreters. Parents and teachers must then decide if an unqualified interpreter is better than no interpreter at all. Some states have taken steps to ensure that the "highest qualified professional" is hired in schools. In Virginia, for example, mandated qualifications for interpreters (Virginia Department of Education, 1994) have led to higher standards, but have not eliminated the shortage of qualified educational interpreters.

Determining whether an educational interpreter is indeed qualified is challenging to most school administrators. Even interpreters who present credentials (e.g., state association or the Registry of Interpreters for the Deaf) may not have an educational background or knowledge of the demands of educational settings. Being able to interpret at a level that is commensurate with a child's cognitive-linguistic level requires much more than skill at signing or cueing or mouthing the language. Educational interpreters must *understand* the language used by teachers and the language that is unique to the curriculum. Cokely, Baker-Shenk, Isham, and Colonomos (1992) reported that regardless of skill level, an interpreter cannot interpret what he or she does not understand. The demands of the educational environment, then, require the interpreter to present complex language in a way that enables the student to learn. Imagine the constraints of interpreting a foreign language, advanced algebra, behind-the-wheel driver education, or sensitive sexuality topics in family life education, and doing so all in the same day. Interpreter training programs routinely provide training in the interpreter's role, ethical conduct, and professional status, but not in the language of academic instruction (Diane, 1995). Those interpreters who aspire to

excellence for themselves and for their student consumers study to learn the material they are expected to interpret.

Challenges that deaf and hard-of-hearing students experience when they attempt to learn through an interpreter can also be overwhelming. Trying to understand the spoken language of 20 or 30 people when it is represented through the hands and face of the interpreter, finding a social role in a peer group when a third party is involved, and learning to be solely responsible for academic material while relying on the knowledge and skill of another person to deliver the material, are all problematic, even for mature students. Add to these challenges the reliance on a single sensory channel throughout a six-hour day. Learning through an interpreter is extremely fatiguing (Winston, 1995).

In spite of all these challenges, however, more deaf and hard-of-hearing students are being educated in their local schools with educational interpreters. Some of these students struggle to learn, in spite of having qualified interpreters, and some succeed, perhaps because of qualified interpreters. No magical formula exists that enables educators to predict success of a deaf or hard-of-hearing student in an integrated setting, with or without an interpreter. Educators must approach each student with the broadest possible knowledge base in order to make decisions that lead to the best possible education.

IMPLEMENTING SUCCESSFUL INCLUSION

Defining Success

"Successful" inclusion programs are defined differently by different constituencies. Parents, school personnel, and students may view a single education placement from different, even conflicting, perspectives. Parents who are satisfied that their son or daughter is receiving a quality education in an integrated setting are likely to view inclusion positively. Day-to-day judgments about the qualifications of teachers, the delivery of supplemental services, and their child's projection of satisfaction are commonly used to gauge success. While these judgments are subjective, their validity should not be taken lightly; a successful education program is dependent upon parental support and involvement.

Subjective judgments are also made by students who are deaf or hard-of-hearing; these generally receive more attention as the student becomes older. The primary student who projected contentment may show discontent when, at about the fourth grade, he or she becomes self-conscious at being the only deaf student in the class. Parents may be shaken by the changes in their child and look for changes in the program to which they can attach the unhappiness. It is possible that the characteristics that made the placement successful when the student was younger are still intact, but that changing needs of the student make the program no longer appropriate.

Subjective judgments about the success of an inclusive education program are made by school personnel, too. Teachers who have positive experiences with a deaf or hard-of-hearing student may view inclusion positively, while those who have negative experiences may view inclusion negatively. Administrators who fill their interpreting positions with qualified interpreters may view their programs as successful, while administrators who struggle to find interpreters may think their programs are unsuccessful. The bottom line is that the success of an inclusive placement for a deaf or hard-of-hearing student is difficult to define, different according to who is defining it, and subject to change from one day to the next. What constitutes success for one student (e.g., As and Bs on the report card, graduation with a diploma, acceptance into college) can sharply contrast with what constitutes success for another (e.g., development of independent living skills, successful transition to a vocational program, positive self-regard). The U.S. Department of Education's 16th annual report to Congress (1994) reported that 56% of hearing-impaired students graduated in 1992 with a diploma; another 17% graduated with a certificate of completion, 13% dropped out, 2% reached age 22, and 12% had an unknown status. Those students who graduated with a diploma had a grade-point average of 2.3. These data are important only in that they caution us about the importance of determining for each student the goals of the placement and determining the criteria used to judge success in reaching the goals.

At the administrative level, successful inclusion may be determined by more general and objective measures, especially demographic and program data. Demographic data should include: number (and percentage) of students eligible for hearing-impaired services; number (and percentage) who matriculate from grade to grade; number (and percentage) of reentry students; number (and percentage) who graduate, who receive a certificate of completion, who pass minimum competency or literacy tests, who score within a given percentile on achievement tests, who meet their individualized education program (IEP) goals, who enter postsecondary educational programs; and any other meaningful data that profile the students. Program data should include: number of teachers certified in hearing disorders or deaf education, general education teachers, educational audiologists, speech-language pathologists, interpreters, and other staff who work with the students; student-to-staff ratios; professional development experiences on the needs of deaf and hard-of-hearing students offered to the staff; number of teachers who enroll in continuing education courses relevant to deafness (including sign language classes); and systematic evaluations of the needs of the teachers and staff who work with deaf and hard-of-hearing students.

Large school systems that have established programs for students with hearing loss are better able to gain access to demographic and program data than small systems enrolling their first deaf student. Large systems are also more likely to provide multiple placement options for deaf and hard-of-hearing students and individually prescribe the appropriate option for each student. Multiple options also afford large school programs more flexibility in moving a student from one option to another when change is recommended. Whether successful large-scale models can offer administrators on small-scale levels any hope for replication is doubtful. Striving for successful inclusive education at any level, however, is about meeting individual needs. As such, large and small school systems alike should approach inclusion by focusing on how to deliver to the individual student the best possible educational program. At least three areas within the educational program are critical to successful inclusion: (1) administrative support, (2) general educator competencies, and (3) support personnel competencies.

The Program: Administration

In systems where site-based management provides the leadership, the building principal is often the individual responsible for inclusion. The supportive administrator puts students' needs first (with meaningful assessment data), gives teachers a choice to participate, provides adequate resources (including a variety of service options), evaluates the program on an ongoing basis, provides ongoing professional development, and engages the teachers in development and assessment of the school's inclusion philosophy (Vaughn & Schumm, 1995). This administrator not only offers leadership to achieve inclusion but also knows about the needs of deaf and hard-of-hearing students, and the resources and options necessary to meet their needs. This knowledge is not immediately acquired, but is achieved over time through several efforts, as depicted in Exhibit 17–1.

The Program: General Education Teachers

Competencies needed for teaching deaf and hard-of-hearing students have been detailed (Sass-Lehrer, 1983). More than 70 competencies have been isolated that teachers are expected to demonstrate in their work with deaf and hard-of-hearing students. One of the critical debates surrounding inclusive education involves the assumption that general education teachers must demonstrate these same competencies—that they must learn a prescribed list of additional skills in order to deal with their special students (Smelter, Rasch, & Yudewitz, 1994). In traditional special education programs, only the special educators are expected to have skills in a given specialty. In an inclusion program,

Exhibit 17–1 Strategies That Administrators Use in Supporting Inclusion for Deaf and Hard-of-Hearing Students

- Make use of existing print and nonprint resources (e.g., this book, related periodicals, and computer-accessed discussion groups and bulletin boards).
- Consult with other administrators who have programs for students with hearing loss, especially residential school administrators.
- Recognize the need for and secure assistance in hiring and evaluating interpreters (e.g., interpreting referral agencies, lead interpreters from other schools) (Seal, 1995).
- Encourage community-based involvement, especially involvement of members of the deaf community.
- Ensure that demographic and program data are complemented with individual student assessment data.

however, general educators are expected to acquire knowledge of deafness and the communication and educational needs of their deaf and hard-of-hearing students, just as they are expected to acquire knowledge of the cultural, behavioral, and learning needs of all students in their classrooms. No one expects the general education teacher to gain the depth of knowledge demonstrated by teachers with special degrees and experiences. Learning and teaching are processes, and, as such, require time. It takes time to learn the strengths and weaknesses of each student and time to plan and coordinate teaching goals and strategies with the teacher of the deaf, the interpreter, and other support staff. It also takes time to adapt instructional activities to meet students' needs. In fact, at least two related competencies are critical for general education teachers who have deaf or hard-of-hearing students in their classroom: competencies in time management and in instructional management.

Time is a critical variable in successful teaching. A common observation made by practicum students who have placements in both deaf and integrated classrooms is that the pace of teaching is noticeably slower for students in deaf classrooms. This observation, that teaching special students requires more of a teacher's time, reducing contact time with other students, is the source of much inclusion controversy (Smelter et al., 1994). Teachers who are conscious of how their instructional time is allocated and how they use their time to engage students in learning (Goodman, 1990) are teachers who have an upper hand on teaching, regardless of the labels their students may wear. Even these talented teachers, though, may be surprised at the additional time required for a student who has a hearing loss. These teachers learn that every auditory message that accompanies a visual message (like those found in books, worksheets, maps, overheads, computer screens, videotapes, filmstrips, etc.) requires the child with a hearing loss to attend *sequentially*, not simultaneously. The deaf student

who attends with an interpreter and the hard-of-hearing student who attends to the teacher's face require extra time to gain access to information that hearing children acquire with dual sensory systems. Several time-management strategies are listed in Exhibit 17–2.

General education teachers who are effective in instructing special students are also competent at adapting the socioemotional, behavioral, and physical environments of their classroom, and their planning and instruction (Wood, 1992). Several strategies that can assist teachers to adapt are listed in Exhibit 17–3.

The Program: Special Educators and Support Staff

A third program area that is critical to successful inclusion involves the special educators and support staff who bring special knowledge to the general education environment. Speech-language pathologists, teachers of the deaf, educational interpreters, and audiologists have knowledge of deafness that must be shared with general educators (see Table 17–1). This knowledge may encompass information about the Deaf culture, communication methods, hearing aids and auditory training systems, methods for observing and teaching social skills, guidelines for selecting and rewriting texts, methods for using note takers and taking notes, knowledge of the impact of multiple disabilities on student learning, knowledge of telecommunication devices, educational films and videotapes from the National Captioning Institute, and so on. In successful inclusion programs, special educators and support staff share their knowledge with teachers who have special knowledge about course content and curriculum. This sharing occurs in

Exhibit 17–2 Strategies That Assist General Educators in Time Management

- Before addressing the class, gain students' visual attention from an established locus in the room.
- Provide descriptive statements before, not during, instructional demonstrations.
- Pause to facilitate a shift in attention from the teacher or interpreter to the book, transparency, computer monitor, map, etc.
- Sequence hands-on activities during the instructional phase (e.g., "This activity has four steps. First we will sort all the shapes by color.").
- From an established locus in the room, repeat student comments, questions, and answers that are directed to the whole class.
- Provide time frames that define an activity's beginning and end (e.g., "Each group will need about 10 minutes to create its rebuttal.").

Exhibit 17–3 Strategies That Help General Educators Adapt to the Needs of Deaf and Hard-of-Hearing Students

---

THE SOCIOEMOTIONAL ENVIRONMENT

- Embrace all communication differences in the classroom.
- Welcome all support staff (e.g., interpreters, speech-language pathologists) as integral members of the classroom.
- Learn to use name signs to address deaf and hearing students.
- Encourage all students to use signs for basic courtesies and greetings.
- Consult with the special educators or support staff when questions about the socioemotional environment arise.

THE BEHAVIORAL ENVIRONMENT

- Provide structured guidelines for classroom communication (e.g., only one speaker at a time, hands raised before responding).
- Establish roles in group work (e.g., one student serves as recorder, another as reporter, monitor, evaluator).
- Establish a protocol for entering and exiting the classroom, for making the transition from one activity to another, for moving from one station to another, etc.
- Consult with special educators or support staff when questions about the behavioral environment arise.

THE PHYSICAL ENVIRONMENT

- Arrange desks and tables for maximum visual access.
- Reduce ambient noise with carpets, drapes, and bulletin boards.
- Ensure appropriate lighting and adjust lighting as needed.
- Establish a central locus from which to address the class.
- Learn how to use microphone of auditory training system, to accommodate distance for personal hearing aids, to troubleshoot hearing aid feedback, etc., as needed.
- Consult with special educators or support staff when questions about the physical environment arise.

THE INSTRUCTIONAL ENVIRONMENT

- Capitalize on strategies that engage students in active learning.
- Present oral assignments with written supplements.
- Provide consistency in the language of directions.
- Provide consistency in testing protocol.
- Provide multiple evaluation methods (e.g., pass-fail, mastery criterion).
- Consult with special educators or support staff regarding instructional materials and methods that may need to be adapted or when questions about instruction arise.

---

both formal meetings and informal gatherings, in cooperative planning and troubleshooting conferences, and in small-group and schoolwide inservice sessions. In successful programs, the stronger the special education teachers are in their special knowledge, and the stronger the general educators are in their special knowledge, the better the opportunities for sharing. The better the opportunities for sharing, the better the education for the student.

The Student: Psychoeducational Profile

Several student areas are important when implementing a successful inclusion program; these include the student's psychoeducational, communication, and social profiles. In traditional approaches, when a deaf student was determined to have average intelligence and good oral communication and social skills, decisions about placement were rather "cut-and-dried." The more "hearing-like" the students, the more likely they were to be mainstreamed and to receive fewer special services. The special education continuum illustrated in Figure 17–1 guided placement and instructional decisions. The contrast that an inclusion program offers is that knowledge about the student's psychoeducational, communication, and social profiles is used to determine the degree to which special services are added to, not subtracted from, the student's placement.

The student's psychoeducational profile generally focuses on both cognitive ability and academic achievement. Ability tests traditionally investigate verbal and performance intelligence. It is not unusual for students with hearing loss to demonstrate a verbal-performance gap on intelligence tests. In fact, some educators tend to dismiss verbal IQ scores as inappropriate representations of deaf students' cognitive skills. Other educators who view the educational environment as a verbal environment place high value on verbal scores. Regardless of attitude toward the tests, educators should use IQ scores for the teaching information they provide. Students who score high on performance and low on verbal measures of intelligence are more likely to benefit from *doing* rather than *listening* or *reading* to learn.

Achievement test scores are also part of the student's psychoeducational profile. Most achievement tests are designed for and enable a comparison with hearing students. The Stanford Achievement Test provides normative data for students who are hearing impaired; in 1993–1994, the test was administered to 15,000 deaf and hard-of-hearing students across the country (Holt, 1995). On the average, a one-to-two year achievement gap separates deaf and hearing students in the primary grades. This gap begins to widen at about the fourth grade when achievement scores plateau for the average deaf student. Future educational gains are

Table 17–1 Shared Specialties in Teaching Deaf and Hard-of-Hearing Students

Specialized Knowledge	Teacher of the Deaf	Educational Interpreter	Speech-Language Pathologist	Educational Audiologist	General Educator
Hearing Loss	■	■	■	■	
Amplification	■		■	■	
Deaf Culture	■	■			
Social Skills	■	■	■		
Communication Methods	■	■	■		
Classroom Acoustics	■		■	■	
Visual Accessibility	■	■			
Telecommunication/ Assistive Devices	■			■	
Adapting Texts and Materials	■				■
Curriculum					■
Student Assessment	■	■	■	■	■

minimal; the gap between hearing and deaf students widens, with achievement and degree of hearing loss negatively correlated (Paul & Quigley, 1990). Many theories have been offered to explain these performance patterns: the tests are culturally and linguistically biased against minority children (and deaf and hard-of-hearing children are in a linguistic minority); poor reading skills prohibit deaf students from demonstrating actual learning on the tests; and deaf and hard-of-hearing students do not learn at the rates that hearing students learn. None of these theories has been validated through research, and educators must be careful not to make decisions about individual students on the basis of any of these theories. Rather, careful analysis of all achievement measures, including grades, should be used to determine a student's learning strengths and weaknesses.

Students with hearing loss consistently perform better on tests of mathematics than on tests of language and reading (Paul & Quigley, 1990). Average gain, as reported on the Stanford Achievement Test for students from 10 to 18 years of age, is 2.5 grade levels in math and 1.1 grade levels in reading. The average reading level at 18 years is 3.7; the average math level is 6.2. Knowledge of a student's comparative performance is important in educational decisions. Students who fall two or more grade levels below their peers at the elementary level are at risk for even lower per-

formance in middle and high school. These students frequently need small-group or individual instruction (options that may be more common in deaf schools, self-contained classes, or resource classes), options that should be part of an inclusive program. Providing multiple options and being alert to changing profiles that require changes in programming are critical to successful inclusion.

The Student: Communication Profile

A wide range of abilities and disabilities is evident in the communication profiles of deaf and hard-of-hearing students. In general, communication disabilities parallel type, etiology, and severity of hearing loss. Students with mild and moderate conductive losses are more likely to use and understand spoken language, while students with severe and profound sensorineural losses are more likely to use sign language. Within each category of hearing loss, however, there also exists a wide range of skills, with some deaf students demonstrating complete independence and others requiring interpreters when communicating with hearing peers and teachers. Some students with moderate hearing losses communicate well in group and individual settings, with hearing and hearing-impaired partners; other hard-of-hearing students demonstrate limited communication skills in all contexts. No single list of characteristics can be used to describe the variety of communication skills likely to be found among students who are deaf and hard-of-hearing.

A wide range in communication skills requires an equally diverse range in service delivery options. The speech-language pathologist—in consultation with parents, audiologists, teachers of the deaf, classroom teachers, and interpreters—identifies strengths and weaknesses in a student's use of hearing; mode of communication; and use, content, and form of language. Intervention is then prescribed according to individual strengths and weaknesses. Intervention may necessitate any one or combination of these options: (a) one-on-one services in a pull-out or in a classroom setting, (b) small-group instruction with selected hearing and/or hearing-impaired peers, (c) whole-class instruction on working with an interpreter, (d) team teaching in which all teachers focus on a particular communication skill, and (e) indirect services that may include periodic observations and/or routine consultations with teachers in monitoring the student's communication performance. Intervention also varies according to the student's needs at different ages. Older students, for example, may reject pull-out services that they enjoyed at younger ages, and the student with complex disabilities may benefit from short-term services that move to the job site when he or she enters a work transition program.

Different service-delivery options often require negotiations with parents and teachers. Parents typically request individual services for their child's speech and may judge the entire educational program by the amount of time allocated to speech in the IEP. In a study of speech-language pathologists who serve students with hearing loss, Otis-Wilborn (1992) reported that, in spite of the growing need for speech-language pathologists to work collaboratively with other teachers in improving their students' communication skills, the average student with a hearing loss continues to receive two or three 15- to 30-minute pull-out therapy sessions weekly. Speech-language pathologists and teachers should discuss with parents the relative merits of decreasing time in isolated sessions and increasing time to work on classroom communication.

The Student: Social Profile

The development of social skills occurs during the formative years, and the child moves from dependence on parents to a dependence on peers for experiences that lead to social competence. The relationship between a young deaf child and his or her parents is critical to the early stages of social development. Hearing parents are likely to struggle through certain crisis periods when their child's hearing loss is identified (Luterman, 1979). If sign language is chosen for the child's communication development, then parents must begin a period of language learning that may be met with limited success. Although hearing loss itself does not cause delays in social development (Schloss & Smith, 1990), it may limit communication that hearing parents use to convey social rules to their child. In contrast, those few deaf children who learn ASL from their deaf parents may enter school with better social skills than deaf peers who have limited communication with their hearing parents.

Once in school, children enter a period of interpersonal bids and negotiations for friendships. In discussing social competence and communication skills, Gallagher (1993) described two types of friendships: those that involve being accepted by one's peers (having a sense of inclusion within a social circle) and those that involve chumships or close friends (having a sense of personal equality and reciprocity with another). Young children who have limited communication skills are less likely to be valued by play partners. Elementary children who are unable to rely on their communication skills to negotiate status within their peer group may feel less socially competent than their peers who express themselves well in peer interactions. Many deaf adolescents have described their social lives in mainstream environments with terms of "loneliness, rejection, and isolation" (Lane, 1995, p. 279).

Proponents of mainstreaming argued for 20 years that interacting with hearing peers gives deaf and hard-of-hearing students experiences to develop social skills needed to function in a hearing world. In a report that focused on placement and social experiences, Mertens (1989) reported that students who graduated from deaf schools reported more positive social experiences in high school than those who graduated from mainstream programs. Mainstreamed students who identified negative experiences reported feeling isolated as the only deaf student in their school or grade. In contrast, mainstreamed students who identified positive social experiences reported several features common to their placements: they had close friends, their peers learned to sign and fingerspell, their interpreters encouraged interaction and deaf awareness, they participated in extracurricular activities, and they had strong parental support.

Educators should use this information about social development and needs of deaf and hard-of-hearing students in their decisions about placement and provision of supplemental services. Deaf students who have few social experiences with hearing peers and no opportunities for social experiences with deaf peers may benefit from visitations, exchange programs, and on-line electronic (or pen-pal) communication opportunities with deaf students in other schools. They may also benefit from attending deaf schools themselves. Inclusive schools recognize that their own supportive communication about different educational placements is critical to the success of any decision.

Checklist for Decision Making

A successful inclusion program is based on individual needs. It is unlikely that the same program or services will be appropriate for any two students. Programs and services must be evaluated regularly to ensure that they meet students' changing needs. A list of basic questions, however, should guide decisions about placement and intervention for all students (see Exhibit 17–4).

CASE STUDIES

The following three cases are offered to represent the wide range of variables that affect successful inclusion decisions. While these cases are real, details have been changed to protect the anonymity of those involved.

Darren: He Did It!

When he was 13 months old, Darren suffered a high fever over several days. Within days, his mother suspected he was deaf and, by 15 months, his severe-to-profound hearing loss was diagnosed. He was fitted with his first hearing aids just weeks later. His parents, both well edu-

cated, enrolled him in individual speech-language therapy at a university speech and hearing center; they enrolled themselves in the John Tracy Clinic Correspondence Course designed for parents of deaf babies. By age two, Darren was participating two days a week in the university preschool program for deaf students and enrolled in private speech-language therapy. The prognosis for learning spoken language without sign language or cued speech continued to be positive throughout his early learning years. At age five, he entered kindergarten at his local school, a decision made after his parents consulted the audiologists; speech-language pathologists; university supervisors; preschool teachers; and the school's teacher of the deaf, speech-language pathologist, and principal. Darren's mother also began taking courses in reading and deaf education.

Darren continued in regular classes throughout his elementary years. During the first through fourth grades, he worked with the teacher of the deaf in her resource room, sometimes before school to avoid missing critical segments of classroom instruction. The teacher of the deaf worked closely with his classroom teachers, often preteaching new units before they were introduced. Each year, the principal asked her to identify teachers whose communication and instructional styles were conducive to Darren's learning

---

Exhibit 17–4 Questions for Successful Inclusion

PSYCHOEDUCATIONAL PROFILE

- What are the student's cognitive skills?
  - How does the student perform on formal measures of intelligence?
  - Is there a gap between the student's verbal and performance scores?
  - What are the student's cognitive strengths? Cognitive weaknesses?
- How does the student perform on measures of academic achievement?
  - What are the student's learning strengths? Learning weaknesses?
  - Do the student's grades accurately reflect learning?
- What changes have occurred since the last evaluation?
- What strategies, adjustments, and personnel are needed for current learning needs?

COMMUNICATION PROFILE

- What type of hearing loss does the student have?
  - What is the severity? What amplification systems are used?
  - Is amplification useful in personal communication? Classroom communication?
  - What is the hearing status of the parents?

- What type of communication does the student use?
  - Does the student's communication vary with different partners? In different educational contexts (small group, large group)?
  - What are the student's communication strengths? Weaknesses?
- What changes have occurred since the last evaluation?
- What strategies, adjustments, and personnel are needed for current communication needs?

SOCIAL PROFILE

- What are the social skills of this student?
  - How does the student perform on measures of social development?
  - Does the student interact with others who are hearing? With others who are deaf or hard-of-hearing? With younger or same-age peers? With teachers? With interpreters?
  - What are the student's social strengths? Weaknesses?
- What changes have been observed in the student's social development since the last evaluation?
- What strategies, adjustments, and personnel are needed for current social needs?
- What are the parents' desires? The student's desires?

needs. Darren also received individual speech-language services twice weekly.

In the fifth grade, Darren's teacher of the deaf was assigned to another school. As a result, conferences with classroom teachers replaced her instruction with Darren. This new pattern continued when he moved to middle and high school. Darren continued one-on-one services from the speech-language pathologist, but direct services continued to involve only periodic conferences. In Darren's senior year, he rejected all support services. "This is something I have to do by myself, without depending on others," he shared with his parents and school personnel. Darren graduated, pursued a bachelor's degree, and later earned a master's degree in international studies. Today, his career involves frequent travel to foreign countries; although he still does things by himself, his mother said that he now uses oral interpreters and text-telephones when he travels abroad.

When interviewed about her son's education, Darren's mother reported that the success of inclusive education was the result of hard work and extensive networking on the part of excellent teachers and support professionals, and exceptional drive and a good sense of humor on Darren's part. She shared that his competitive personality (he ranked second on the tennis team), his core of lifelong friends, and his intense love of reading were also important to his success.

Brandon: He's Much Happier at the Deaf School

Brandon was born deaf to hearing parents. His profound sensorineural loss, of unknown origin, was diagnosed at 15 months. He was fitted with hearing aids at 17 months, and his parents enrolled in a parent-infant program that involved home visits from a teacher of the deaf. The visiting teacher began sign language instruction with them when Brandon was 18 months old. The county school system encouraged Brandon's enrollment in their hearing-impaired preschool when he turned two. He received speech services from a speech-language pathologist and auditory training sessions from the county's audiologist, and his parents received weekly sign language instruction from the preschool teacher. This programming continued until Brandon turned five and enrolled in his local school. The itinerant teacher of the deaf worked closely with his kindergarten teacher, teaching her basic signs and how to use an auditory training system. A sign language interpreter was also hired. The itinerant teacher and speech-language pathologist alternated their schedules to be in the classroom, facilitating Brandon's communication with his classmates, teacher, and interpreter. Although the schedules changed over the next four years, the same supplemental services—speech-language therapy, resource instruction, audiological monitoring, sign language interpreting—were maintained. His annual evaluations and report cards showed progress. His parents continued to learn, too, in summer family camps at the school for the deaf 30 miles away.

At the summer camp after his fourth grade, Brandon met Jonathon. The two became best friends. Jonathon's deaf parents invited Brandon to spend a week with them at their home. When Brandon returned home, he announced that he wanted to go to the deaf school like Jonathon. Brandon's parents spent the next several weeks talking with their local school's special education director and individuals who had worked closely with Brandon. Their decision to transfer him to the school for the deaf was finalized when they learned that the county would transport him daily and that reentry to his home school could occur at any time, that their sign instruction could continue, and that the itinerant teacher would visit Brandon periodically to assess the transfer.

Four months later, Brandon's mother reported that he had made many friends at the new school, that he had had his first sleepover, and that he was captain of the soccer team. When asked about his academic progress, she said that homework at the deaf school was less than he had been used to, and because he was reading two grade levels above his classmates, his teacher was supplementing his work with books he would have had at his old school. She said that Brandon was much happier at the deaf school than he had been in his local school.

Esther: So Far, So Good

Esther lost her hearing at 18 months from spinal meningitis. Her parents enrolled her in a university speech and hearing clinic at 20 months; at 24 months, she received a cochlear implant. Postsurgery audiometric responses revealed a moderate-to-severe hearing loss. From 26 months to age five, she attended four speech-language sessions a week at the clinic and two sessions a week with the local school system's teacher of the deaf. She was also enrolled in a preschool class at a local church; the teacher of the deaf observed routinely and made recommendations to the teachers based on her observations. Esther's parents first chose cued speech for Esther's oral language learning (at 30 months); at four years, the teacher of the deaf recommended the addition of sign language for difficult concepts. At five, Esther enrolled in a local kindergarten. She continued to receive services at the university, one-on-one instruction with the teacher of the deaf, and one-on-one speech therapy from the speech-language pathologist. A cued speech/sign language interpreter-aide was hired for kindergarten and for first grade. Esther's IEP called for cued speech interpreting for new vocabulary and English Sign Language interpreting for all other communication. The interpreter attended the university sessions with Esther to learn cued speech. A new interpreter was hired when Esther was in second grade; a third interpreter was hired when she was in fourth grade and continues to be Esther's interpreter in the fifth grade. The IEP has remained consistent regarding the interpreter's use of both cued speech and sign language.

Although Esther often uses signs and fingerspelling with her interpreter and best friend, her primary communication method includes spoken language. In the first month of the fifth grade, she reported that she did not need the interpreter when she was in her group. Her teacher uses what she calls mini-lessons; whole-class instruction occurs in 10-minute segments and the students then go to assigned groups to work on activities associated with the lesson. The interpreter remains available, assisting the teacher with group management and observing Esther for any signal to interpret.

Esther's school work is good. She earns *A*s on her report card; recent Iowa Test of Basic Skills scores placed her at grade level in math and science and above grade level in all other areas. She communicates with her teacher and peers without the interpreter but uses her interpreter when the teacher speaks to the whole class. The interpreter sometimes repeats Esther's phrases or sentences when others have difficulty understanding. Despite these successes, her parents are concerned about the turnover of educational interpreters.

Each interpreter has had a different style and skill level. Her parents worry that middle and high school years will be more demanding and that consistency in interpreting will be more essential. This anticipation of future demands and careful planning to meet Esther's future learning, communication, and social needs suggest continued inclusion success, even with changing players.

CONCLUSION

Several themes characterize the successful inclusion programs for Darren, Brandon, and Esther. These same themes summarize the contents of this chapter: (1) inclusive education programs for students who are deaf and hard-of-hearing are not about a single placement; (2) supportive administrators and competent teachers are critical to success; (3) the networking of special educators and support staff requires sharing specialized knowledge and skills with others involved in the student's program, including parents; (4) changes in psychoeducational, communication, and social profiles of each student require dynamic programming that values its own assessment as critical to success.

REFERENCES

Berg, F., Blair, J., Viehweg, S., & Wilson-Vlotman, A. (1986). *Educational audiology for the hard of hearing child.* Orlando, FL: Grune & Stratton.

Bess, F.H., & Humes, L.E. (1990). *Audiology: The fundamentals.* Baltimore: Williams & Wilkins.

Bilingual Education Act. (1981). Amendment to Title VII of the Elementary and Secondary Education Act of 1965. In *A compilation of federal education laws.* Washington, DC: U.S. Government Printing Office.

Brill, R.G. (1978). *Mainstreaming the prelingually deaf child: A study of the status of prelingually deaf children in various patterns of mainstreamed education for hearing-impaired children.* Washington, DC: Gallaudet University.

Castle, D.L. (1994). Oral interpreter certification: The history and the need. *Interpreter Views, 11,* 1, 14.

Cokely, D., Baker-Shenk, C., Isham, W., & Colonomos, B. (1992). *Interpreters on interpreting: Interpreter models and process* [Video]. Burtonsville, MD: Sign Media.

Commission on Education of the Deaf. (1988). *Toward equality: Education of the deaf, a report to the President and Congress of the United States.* Washington, DC: U.S. Government Printing Office.

Cornett, R.O. (1967). Oralism vs. manualism: Cued speech may be the answer. *Hearing and Speech News, 35,* 6–9.

Craig, H., & Craig, W. (1993). Schools and programs in the United States. *American Annals of the Deaf, 138,* 191–204.

Deno, E. (1970). The cascade of special education services. Bulletin. *Exceptional Children, 39,* 495.

Diane, K. (1995). Call it what it is: K–12 interpreting versus academic interpreting. *Interpreter Views, 12,* 12, 28.

Gallagher, T.M. (1993). Language skill and the development of social competence in school-age children. *Language, Speech, and Hearing Services in Schools, 24,* 199–205.

Gannon, J.R. (1981). *Deaf heritage: A narrative history of deaf education.* Silver Spring, MD: National Association of the Deaf.

Goodman, L. (1990). *Time and learning in the special education classroom.* Albany: State University of New York.

Gustason, G., Pfetzing, D., & Zawolkow, E. (1980). *Signing exact English.* Los Alamitos, CA: Modern Signs.

Hallahan, D.P., & Kauffman, J.M. (Eds.). (1995). *The illusion of full inclusion.* Austin, TX: Pro-Ed.

Holt, J.A. (1995). Efficiency of screening procedures for assigning levels of the Stanford Achievement Test (Eighth Edition) to students who are deaf or hard of hearing. *American Annals of the Deaf, 140,* 23–27.

Johnson, R.E., Liddell, S.K., & Erting, C.J. (1989). *Unlocking the curriculum: Principles for achieving access in deaf education* (Gallaudet Research Institute Working Paper 89-3). Washington, DC: Gallaudet University.

Karchmer, M.A. (1985). A demographic perspective. In E. Cherow, N.D. Matkin, & R.J. Trybus (Eds.), *Hearing-impaired children and youth with developmental disabilities: An interdisciplinary foundation for service* (pp. 36–56). Washington, DC: Gallaudet University.

Lane, H. (1995). The education of deaf children: Drowning in the mainstream and the sidestream. In D.P. Hallahan & J.M. Kauffman (Eds.), *The illusion of full inclusion* (pp. 275–287). Austin, TX: Pro-Ed.

Luetke-Stahlman, B. (1983). Using bilingual instructional models in teaching hearing-impaired students. *American Annals of the Deaf, 128,* 873–877.

Luterman, D. (1979). *Counseling the communicatively disordered and their families.* Boston: Little, Brown & Company.

Maroney, E. (1995). Quality interpreter shortage in rural educational settings. *Interpreter Views, 12,* 17, 27.

Mertens, D.M. (1989). Social experiences of hearing-impaired high school youth. *American Annals of the Deaf, 134,* 15–19.

Moores, D.F. (1987). *Educating the deaf: Psychology, principles, and practices.* Boston: Houghton Mifflin.

Mueller-Vollmer, P. (1990). Balancing ASL and TC in the classroom. *Perspectives in Education and Deafness, 8,* 16–17.

Otis-Wilborn, A. (1992). Developing oral communication in students with hearing impairments: Whose responsibility? *Language, Speech, and Hearing Services in Schools, 23,* 71–77.

Owens, E.O., & Kessler, D.K. (1989). *Cochlear implants in young deaf children.* Boston: College-Hill.

Patrie, C.J. (1994). Educational interpreting: Who leads the way? *Interpreter Views, 11,* 1, 19–20.

Paul, P.V., & Quigley, S.P. (1990). *Education and deafness.* White Plains, NY: Longman.

Pugh, G., & Hicks, D. (1995). Deaf education initiatives project: A response to the challenge. *Journal of Childhood Communication Disorders, 17,* 5–8.

Sass-Lehrer, M. (1983). Competencies critical to teachers of hearing-impaired students in two settings. *American Annals of the Deaf, 128,* 867–872.

Schein, J., & Delk, M. (1974). *The deaf population of the United States.* Silver Spring, MD: National Association of the Deaf.

Schiff-Myers, N.B. (1992). Considering arrested language development and language loss in the assessment of second language learners. *Language, Speech, and Hearing Services in Schools, 23,* 28–33.

Schildroth, A.N., & Hotto, S.A. (1995). Race and ethnic background in the annual survey of deaf and hard of hearing children and youth. *American Annals of the Deaf, 140,* 96–99.

Schloss, P.J., & Smith, M.A. (Eds.). (1990). *Teaching social skills to hearing-impaired students.* Washington, DC: Alexander Graham Bell Association for the Deaf.

Schrag, J. (1991). *Special education in the 1990s. Educational interpreting: Into the 1990s. Conference Proceedings.* Washington, DC: Gallaudet University.

Seal, B.C. (1995). Evaluating the educational interpreter. *Interpreter Views, 12,* 17, 38.

Smelter, R., Rasch, B., & Yudewitz, G. (1994). Thinking of inclusion for all special needs students? Better think again. *Phi Delta Kappan, 76,* 35–38.

Stokoe, W. (1960). *Sign language structure: An outline of the visual communication systems of the American deaf. Studies in linguistics.* (Occasional Papers No. 8). Washington, DC: Gallaudet University.

Stuckless, R., Avery, J., & Hurwitz, T.A. (1989). *Educational interpreting for deaf students: Report of the National Task Force on Educational Interpreting.* Rochester, NY: National Technical Institute for the Deaf.

U.S. Department of Education. (1994). To assure the free and appropriate public education of all children with disabilities. *16th Annual Report to Congress on the Implementation of the Individuals with Disabilities Education Act, Section 16.*

Vaughn, S., & Schumm, J.S. (1995). Responsible inclusion for students with learning disabilities. *Journal of Learning Disabilities, 28,* 264–270, 290.

Virginia Department of Education. (1994). *Regulations Governing Special Education Programs for Children with Disabilities in Virginia.* Richmond, VA: Author.

Winston, E.A. (1995). An interpreted education: Inclusion or exclusion? *Interpreter Views, 12,* 11, 35.

Wood, J.W. (1992). *Adapting instruction for mainstreamed and at-risk students* (2nd ed). New York: Macmillan.

CHAPTER 18

Students with Dyslexia and Other Reading Disabilities

Virginia L. McLaughlin and Carol S. Beers

INTRODUCTION

The thought of educating students with severe reading disabilities alongside peers of the same age in general education classrooms troubles many parents and professionals. They worry about whether inclusion is a realistic alternative for those with limited reading and written communication skills. How can students receive the intensive instruction that they need in large, heterogeneous groups? How will they keep up in the content subject areas? How will they fit in with their peers? Wouldn't the students be better served in programs specifically for those with dyslexia?

The questions are not easily answered, but informed deliberations generally focus on six important considerations:

1. the nature of dyslexia or severe reading disabilities
2. recognition of placement as only one dimension of an educational program
3. curricular priorities for a specific student
4. feasibility of accommodations within the general education classroom
5. provision of appropriate support for teachers
6. decision making based on the needs of each individual student.

Each of these considerations is discussed in the sections that follow.

THE CHALLENGE OF SEVERE READING DISABILITIES

Since the passage of the Education of Handicapped Children Act in 1975 (P.L. No. 94-142), federal regulations have included dyslexia as one of the conditions encompassed under the definition of learning disabilities (U.S. Department of Education, 1977). The term *learning dis-*

abilities is, therefore, more broadly based than the term *dyslexia*. As defined by the interdisciplinary National Joint Committee on Learning Disabilities (1994), learning disabilities is a general term that refers to a heterogeneous group of disorders manifested by significant difficulties in the acquisition and use of listening, speaking, reading, writing, reasoning, or mathematical abilities. These disorders are intrinsic to the individual, presumed to be due to central nervous system dysfunction, and may occur across the life span. In this definition, as well as the definition used in federal regulations, there are exclusionary clauses that specify that the disability is not the result of poor instruction, low intelligence, or socioeconomic deprivation. *Learning disabilities* is thus the generally accepted and encompassing term for a variety of specific disabilities, including significant disorders manifested in reading.

Throughout this chapter, the authors use the term *reading disabilities*, because it is more broadly defined and more inclusive than the term *dyslexia*. The term *dyslexia* is sometimes used to refer to a smaller number of students who cannot learn to read in normal classroom situations. Professionals who favor the term *dyslexia* tend to focus on neurological correlates of the disability (Flowers, 1993; Orton, 1925; Rooney, 1995). The authors prefer the term *reading disabilities*, because it focuses more on educational implications than on presumed neurological dysfunctions.

Typical characteristics associated with students who manifest reading disabilities include: delayed language development, sequencing difficulties, gross motor problems, left-right confusion, attention problems, memory deficits, reduced reading rates, and written language deficits (Spafford & Grosser, 1996). Prevalence estimates for reading disabilities vary, depending upon definition. Hynd and Cohen (1983), for example, estimated that dyslexia affects up to 5% of our school population; however, Harris and Sipay (1990) suggested that the rate may be closer to 10 to 15%. Lyon (1991) noted that the figure may be as high as 20%. For the broader category of learning disabilities, there has been a clear increase in the percentage of students identified across the country. In 1989, the U.S. Department of Education reported that only 4.41% of the school population was classified as learning disabled; in 1994 that figure had increased to 10.25%. According to Spafford and Grosser, at least half of these students experience reading disabilities.

Students with reading and other learning disabilities are being served primarily in regular schools and in regular classrooms. Approximately 25% of students with learning disabilities are educated full time in regular classes, and 54% receive some pull-out services in resource rooms (U.S. Department of Education, 1994). Only 20% are educated in separate classes and even fewer (1%) in special schools. Although the momentum for more inclusive service delivery continues to grow, even the current pattern indicates that the vast majority of students with reading disabilities are already in general education programs. The question, then, is not whether they should be there, but how to ensure that students with severe reading disabilities are effectively educated in inclusive environments.

PLACEMENT VERSUS PROGRAM

Too often, debates about inclusion mistakenly focus on place rather than program. Details about instruction and support (*what* is provided) are often overshadowed by the issue of placement (*where* it is provided). The legal principle of least restrictive environment (LRE) states that to the maximum extent appropriate, students with disabilities are to be educated with their peers who do not have disabilities. Unfortunately, this critical principle is sometimes interpreted too narrowly. "Educated with" is reduced to a matter of physical proximity—being present in the mainstream—and falls far short of the intent for an appropriate education.

Those who advocate for more inclusive programs do so with the conviction that appropriate education always aims to maximize independent functioning in present and future environments. The optimal settings for the development of academic, social, and vocational competencies necessary for functioning in real-world environments are the real-world classrooms, the real-world schools, and the real-world communities. Because acquisition and practice in self-contained settings typically do not generalize well to more inclusive settings, proponents argue that students should be in the inclusive natural environments in the first place.

But just being there is hardly enough. A well-conceived program that promotes effective instructional and social interactions is required if students with diverse needs are expected to learn together successfully. The following quote supports the notion that, as important as it is, place is but one feature of a complete program:

> We believe, first and foremost, that the very great majority of students with disabilities can receive an appropriate education in general education, including general education classrooms, if those programs and classrooms are designed to provide individualized instruction. . . . Placement in general education should ensure that students receive appropriate curricula, instructional methods, recurring evaluation, supplementary services and aids, related services, and facilitation of relationships and friendships with other students. (Turnbull, Turnbull, Shank, & Leal, 1994, p. 123)

For students with severe reading disabilities, inclusive settings are preferred, for all of the reasons discussed here and in Chapter 1 of this book. But inclusion is only justified when approached as a complete program, not as an isolated issue of place. As Slavin, Karweit, and Madden (1989) concluded following a comprehensive review of effective programs, "The *setting* within which remedial or special education services are provided makes little difference. What does matter is the quality of the *programs* implemented within the setting" (p. 355).

Characteristics of Effective Reading Programs

Quality programs for students with reading disabilities are most likely to occur in settings that incorporate effective schooling practices shown by research to foster overall positive student achievement, attitudes, and social behavior (Cotton, 1995). Such strong classrooms, schools, and districts tend to offer greater advantages for inclusion. Beyond these general characteristics, there are additional concerns specific to quality reading programs. Pikulski (1994) identified the following 11 features as critical to program success:

1. a reading program that coordinates instruction in the general education classroom with any pull-out services
2. provision of additional time for quality instruction
3. individual or very small group instruction
4. focus on prevention and early intervention
5. simple texts for early intervention
6. repeated reading to build fluency
7. instruction in phonemic awareness, phonics, and word patterns
8. daily writing activities
9. ongoing assessment of student progress
10. communication between home and school
11. professionally prepared, accomplished teachers

Educators and parents may find Pikulski's list of features helpful for judging the appropriateness of available program options or for planning program modifications.

CURRICULUM PRIORITIES

If inclusion involves the entire educational program and not merely a student's placement, then the curriculum—*what* is taught—must be recognized as a pivotal consideration for planning inclusive programs. Nearly all other decisions flow from the determination of the curricular priorities for an individual student. Indeed, the heart of the individualized education program (IEP) is the specification of goals and objectives as the curricular targets judged by the IEP team to be most important for the particular learner in the given year.

The standard or general education curriculum is the appropriate initial frame of reference for IEP development. Pursuit of this curriculum is truly least restrictive for students with reading disabilities, for it maintains graduation, diploma, and postsecondary options (Laycock & Korinek, 1989). The general education curriculum with its full range of academic and vocational education offerings is the curriculum of choice for most students with reading disabilities. This standard curriculum can be adapted for specific student needs by emphasizing selected components, adjusting the pace of the curriculum, or modifying instructional delivery. To the extent that the standard curriculum can be individualized appropriately for students with severe reading disabilities, inclusion is a viable approach.

Individualization sometimes requires supplementing the standard curriculum to address additional critical needs for students with reading disabilities. IEPs for these students may include specific goals and objectives for learning strategies or study skills, social and behavioral skills, and functional living skills. For adolescents, IEPs include specific transition components to prepare students for successful transitions from high school to postsecondary education, the adult community, and work settings. Although these curriculum goals extend beyond the explicit standard curriculum, they can still be addressed within the general education setting. In fact, many contend that the naturally occurring environments with age-appropriate peers are the most appropriate settings for helping students acquire and maintain important functional skills (Stainback & Stainback, 1992). By adapting and supplementing the standard curriculum, most students with reading disabilities can be served effectively in inclusive programs.

Importance of Oral Language

Throughout the standard general education curriculum, oral language development is emphasized. Although important for all students, attention to oral language development is especially critical for students with reading disabilities. Reading is a language process closely connected with language processes used in speaking and listening, as well as in writing. Students' proficiency with semantic, syntactic, and phonemic systems will affect how easily they learn to read. A student who has a good vocabulary and understands the conventions of word order and word combinations in standard oral English may more easily make a transition to the more representational world of print. Corson (1984) speculated that the benefits of this transition may be seen more readily in the latter stages of literacy development than the earlier stages.

In addition to helping students make the transition from oral language into print, there are other equally important reasons to incorporate oral language opportunities into reading instruction. Barnes (1976) investigated the role of oral language in problem solving and found that students who were encouraged to talk as they attempted to solve problems were more successful. Oral language is an important rehearsal for later thinking processes. Corson (1984) emphasized that it is only through hearing and trying out words that young children acquire the words necessary for engaging in abstract thought. And last, oral language in a classroom allows students regularly to confront other students with viewpoints other than their own. Oral language, then, becomes an important tool for problem solving, a medium for changing thought, and a mechanism for learning others' points of view. Rich use of oral language in classrooms where students have severe reading problems must, therefore, be a critical component of the curriculum.

Whole-Language or Phonics

Concerns about the appropriateness of inclusion for students with severe reading disabilities intensify when advocates of whole-language approaches and advocates of phonics debate the relative merits of these alternatives for teaching reading. Based upon comprehensive review of research on early reading achievement, Smith (1994) found abundant evidence regarding the positive effects of teaching even the most basic phonic skills. But the selection of whole-language or code-emphasis approaches does not have to be an either-or decision. Systematic decoding instruction can be coordinated or integrated with a meaning-emphasis approach that immerses students in literature. Indeed, this coordinated approach may prove most effective for students with severe reading disabilities (Adams, 1990; Vellutino, 1991).

Example of an Early Intervention Curriculum: Reading Recovery

Reading Recovery is an intensive tutorial program for first graders, which is designed to *prevent* children from experiencing reading difficulties. Based upon the significant work of Marie Clay (Clay, 1979, 1982, 1985, 1990, 1991), this program helps students learn strategies for approaching text so that they can become independent readers and writers functioning within an average group of their first-grade classroom. When students reach this point, they are released by the Reading Recovery teacher. Unlike other programs, Reading Recovery does not promote long-term dependency on assistance outside the classroom.

This type of program is not intended as a "cure" for more severe reading disabilities; however, the intensive, early intervention prior to labeling enables many students at risk of reading failure to succeed without additional specialized services. Programs like Reading Recovery thus reduce the overidentification and misidentification of reading disabilities. These programs also have features that can be adapted for students who do have identified reading disabilities and are served in general education and resource classes.

Students who are identified for participation in Reading Recovery are usually functioning within the bottom quartile of their class. Extensive assessment draws upon the classroom teachers' observations as well as students' performance on a variety of tasks. First graders, for example, may be asked to identify letters, read a list of high-frequency words, write all the words they know, respond to a specially constructed book in order to determine their understanding about the conventions of print, and write a sentence that the teacher has dictated.

Once students are identified for Reading Recovery, teachers who have been specially trained for Reading Recovery build fast-paced lessons around individual children's strengths. Daily 30-minute tutoring sessions focus on children's responses to actual reading and writing tasks. Through the teacher's careful and reflective observations, children learn a variety of strategies necessary for reading, such as word-by-word matching, moving left to right across print, using a return sweep, searching for cues, self-monitoring, and self-correction. In each lesson, the student rereads several familiar stories, composes and writes a brief story or message, and is introduced to a new book. Throughout each lesson, the teacher responds to the child's performance and progress. In this way, the child is supported at a very critical stage of literacy development.

There is much evidence to suggest that Reading Recovery makes a difference. In New Zealand, for example, Clay (1990) reported figures to indicate that fewer than 1% of the students in the program need further assistance. These students are typically referred for special education and may be identified as having reading disabilities. Pinnell (1990) reported similar results from the Ohio project where Reading Recovery was first introduced in a systematic way. Years after these children were discontinued from Reading Recovery, they were following a normal grade progression and able to work with their age peers. Replications of these studies are continuing in various other sites, and comparisons with other intervention programs have been favorable (Pikulski, 1994; Pinnell, Lyons, DeFord, Bryk, & Seltzer, 1994).

Most importantly, Reading Recovery has had a systematic effect on the culture of schools. In schools where there are strong Reading Recovery programs, there are also changes in the behaviors and attitudes of primary teachers. Teachers in these settings gradually modify their classrooms to allow for immersion in real reading and real writing with more flexible instructional groupings. Gradually, there are changes in beliefs about children. Because teachers see the lowest functioning children returning to their classrooms as readers, they begin to have less rigid notions about who can learn to read and write. They begin to realize in a very meaningful way that all children can become literate, given the right support and environment.

Example of Supplementary Curriculum: Strategy Instruction

Although the causes of learning disabilities are frequently debated, the term itself conveys the crux of the problem—a disability in learning. Students with learning disabilities are often viewed as having poor strategies for approaching the complex requirements of academic tasks. These students function as inefficient learners because they lack strategies, choose inappropriate strategies, and/or generally fail to engage in effective self-monitoring behavior (Reid, Hresko, & Swanson, 1991). This interpretation of learning disabilities has led to the development of intervention approaches that focus on explicit teaching of learning strategies to help students learn and perform more successfully. Strategy instruction has been demonstrated to be very effective in promoting such skills as reading comprehension, listening comprehension, note taking, memory for content, essay writing, and test taking (Scruggs & Mastropieri, 1993). Although there are many variations of strategy instruction for students with learning disabilities (Graham, Macarthur, Schwartz, & Page-Voth, 1992; Pressley & Associates, 1990; Rooney, 1989; Scruggs & Mastropieri, 1993), perhaps the best known is the Learning Strategies Intervention Model developed at the University of Kansas Institute for Research on Learning Disabilities (e.g., Deschler, Alley, Warner, & Schumaker, 1981; Ellis, Deschler, Lenz, Schumaker, & Clark, 1991).

Learning strategies have been defined as techniques, principles, or rules that enable a student to solve problems and complete tasks independently (Ellis & Lenz, 1987). The strategies incorporate cues to help students use certain cognitive and metacognitive processes. For example, there are specific strategies to help students acquire and comprehend new information, others to assist with memory and organizational skills, and still others to facilitate oral and written expression and test taking. Many strategies include self-questioning and self-monitoring steps that engage metacognitive processes. The steps of each strategy are the steps of a validated problem-solving process applied to a common academic problem. To promote recall and application, first-letter mnemonics are used to refer to the specific steps of a strategy. Presented in Exhibit 18–1 are examples of three widely used strategies: LISTEN Strategy; DEFENDS: A Writing Strategy for Defending a Position; and RAP: A Paraphrasing Strategy for Reading Comprehension.

Teachers use the following eight-step approach to instruct students in the use of learning strategies:

1. Pretest and obtain student commitment to learn the strategy.
2. Describe the strategy.
3. Model the strategy.
4. Establish fluency through verbal rehearsal of the strategy.
5. Provide practice and feedback using materials at the student's own level.
6. Provide advanced practice and feedback.
7. Posttest and obtain student commitment to generalize use of the strategy.
8. Promote use of the strategy in different learning and content settings.

Strategies instruction is particularly effective with adolescents in middle and secondary schools as they deal with more advanced subject matter and increased expectations for independent performance.

Examples of Alternative Specialized Curricula: Orton-Based Reading Programs

More highly specialized curriculum options are sometimes recommended for students who demonstrate the most severe reading disabilities. Many of the remedial approaches specifically designed for students with dyslexia are based upon the early work of Orton that was later adapted by Stillman, Gillingham, and Slingerland (Rooney, 1995). Although many variations exist, Orton-based approaches share certain characteristics: instruction centers on phonological awareness; approach is highly structured, carefully sequenced, and multisensory; and approach incorporates extensive drill and practice (Rooney, 1995).

These characteristics of Orton-based approaches necessitate one-to-one or very small group instruction, and they

Exhibit 18–1 Selected Learning Strategies

LISTENing Strategy
L = Look at the speaker.
I = Idle your motor.
S = Sit (stand) up straight.
T = Tell yourself to pay attention.
E = Engage your brain.
N = Note why you are listening.

DEFENDS: A Writing Strategy for Defending a Position
D = Decide on exact position.
E = Examine the reasons for the position.
F = Form a list of points that explain each reason.
E = Expose position in the first sentence.
N = Note each reason and supporting points.
D = Drive home the position in the last sentence.
S = Search for errors and correct.
   S = See if it makes sense.
   E = Eject incomplete sentences.
   A = Ask if it's convincing.
   R = Reveal *COPS* errors and correct.
      C = Capitalization
      O = Overall appearance
      P = Punctuation
      S = Spelling
   C = Copy over neatly.
   H = Have a last look.

RAP: A Paraphrasing Strategy for Reading Comprehension
R = Read a paragraph.
A = Ask yourself what were the main ideas and two details.
P = Put main idea and details in your own words.

Source: LISTENing Strategy courtesy of Dr. Jeanne Bauwens. DEFENDS and RAP reprinted with permission from A Component Analysis of Effective Learning Strategies for LD Students, *Learning Disabilities Focus,* Vol. 2, No. 2, pp. 94–107, © Lawrence Erlbaum Associates, Inc.

are typically implemented in special schools, special classes, or other pull-out settings. Critics of these programs point to the lack of a convincing research base, overfocusing on areas of deficit, insistence on discrete sequential steps that may impede higher-level instruction, and delayed exposure to content subjects as limitations of Orton-based approaches. In general, the highly specialized remedial programs that require removal of students from the mainstream are more justified as intensive early intervention for young children with the clear aim of returning students to more inclusive settings as soon as possible (Pikulski, 1994; Slavin, Karweit, & Madden, 1989).

INSTRUCTIONAL ACCOMMODATIONS

After curricular priorities are established, issues related to *instruction*—the delivery of the curriculum—must be addressed. Effective instruction for students with reading disabilities begins with good teaching in the classroom. All that educators have learned about effective teaching practices continues to apply. When teachers are already incorporating best practices, the needs of most students with reading disabilities can be met with some reasonable modifications.

Effective reading instruction is not something that occurs only during reading or English classes but throughout the day, as students are exposed to a variety of reading tasks. Whenever students are required to read texts, it is important that instruction is structured around three phases—before-reading, during-reading, and after-reading activities. This is especially important for students with reading disabilities, because they require additional support to be successful.

Before-reading instruction builds a student's readiness (or schema) before reading a text. Students may be actively involved in making predictions, asking questions, or organizing information about the topic or text they are about to read. The purpose of a before-reading activity is to activate the students' schema for the topic, which is accomplished by engaging them in discussion about the text to be read. Before students approach text, they should have some general idea about what they do or do not know about its contents. Oral language is a primary vehicle for these activities. *During-reading* instruction helps students to remain actively involved with the text by prompting them to rethink their predictions or questions from the prereading phase. Students may be engaged in discussion with teachers or they may follow study guides that facilitate their understanding. Instruction *after reading* encourages students to revisit and revise the predictions, hypotheses, and opinions that they had prior to reading the text. Effective instruction during this phase also encourages students to validate, in some way, their final interpretations and conclusions about the text.

Examples Using Narrative Text

Strategies for instruction before reading, during reading, and after reading can be used effectively at all levels with students who have reading disabilities. This section provides selected examples of two effective strategies for application with narrative text—story impressions and story maps. These strategies are easily implemented in general education classes and provide much-needed support for students with reading disabilities.

Story Impressions

Story impressions are a mechanism for introducing concepts to students in a meaningful context. McGinley

and Denner (1987) developed this procedure as a strategy for building anticipatory sets. The teacher first gives a general introduction to the story by saying, "Today we're going to make up what we think this story could be about." Then, the teacher introduces word clues to the story—a list of important vocabulary words from the story about to be read. The students read the clues with assistance as needed and are asked to brainstorm ideas to connect the clues. Using the word clues, the students then compose a jointly written story that is recorded by the teacher. During this phase, the students are actually generating hypotheses about the nature of the text that they will be reading. Misconceptions about vocabulary are corrected at this time. As the students read the assigned story silently, they note ways the text is similar to or different from their own story. After reading the story, students review the similarities and differences with their original story. The teacher asks them to rewrite their story, using the same vocabulary introduced before reading, to reflect the actual text that they read. This approach to story impressions thus provides an important framework for enhancing decoding and comprehension skills.

Exhibit 18–2 illustrates the benefits of this approach with students who demonstrate reading disabilities. Students in the class were given the following list of vocabulary words: *Brian*, *Mark*, *fair*, *clown*, *make-up*, *enough*, *Mr. Taylor*, *mirror*, *wig*, *nose*, and *task*. Exhibit 18–2 shows the stories that a group of fourth- and fifth-grade students wrote before and after reading a text.

Exhibit 18–2   Before Reading and after Reading Stories Dictated by Fourth-Grade Students with Severe Reading Disabilities

---

BEFORE READING STORY

Brian and *Mark* are going to the *fair*. They are going to see a *clown* with *make-up* on. There were *enough* clowns like *Mr. Taylor*. Mr. Taylor needed a *mirror* to put on his *wig* and his big red *nose*. *Brian* and *Mark* help Mr. Taylor with his *task* to be a clown.

AFTER READING STORY

Brian and *Mark* saw Mr. Taylor. Mr. Taylor asked the boys to go to the *fair*. At the fair, they saw a clown putting *make-up* on people. The clown put a *wig* and *nose* on them. When they looked in the *mirror* at themselves, they laughed. The clown asked the boys to help him with his *task* at 1:00 P.M. We don't know if the boys have enough time to help.

Story Maps

Another useful strategy for facilitating the reading of narrative text is a story map. The use of story maps to help students understand the pivotal aspects of a story is especially effective in aiding comprehension of students in special education and compensatory settings (Gurney, 1987; Idol & Croll, 1987). Based on the work of cognitive psychologists who found that students routinely use their knowledge of how stories are structured to help them remember important details, a story map provides a graphic representation of story grammar (Gerstein & Dimino, 1989). While the elements of story grammar vary, depending upon which system is used, most systems share the following features: characters, setting, problems, events, and solutions. In story map instruction, students are asked to fill in blank forms that have elements of the story designated. See Figure 18–1 for an example of a story map created by a fourth-grade student with reading disabilities.

Bergenske (1987) suggested several key steps to help students use story mapping. In the first step, the teacher explains the basic elements of a story: title, characters, setting, problem, events, and resolution. In the second step, students analyze familiar stories, such as "Three Billy Goats Gruff," by underlining different parts of the story or filling in story maps. In the third step, the teacher gives students narrative story guides, which are story frames with key elements of the story missing (see Exhibit 18–3). In the final step, students learn to write stories using the necessary elements.

One variation of story mapping involves applications with cooperative learning groups. A jigsaw activity, for example, may have different "expert" groups of students reading different sections of the story to compose various aspects of the story map. As an alternative, different "expert" groups may identify different elements of the story grammar.

Another variation of a story map is a *predictogram* (Exhibit 18–4). In a predictogram, students are presented a list of key words or phrases that they will encounter in the

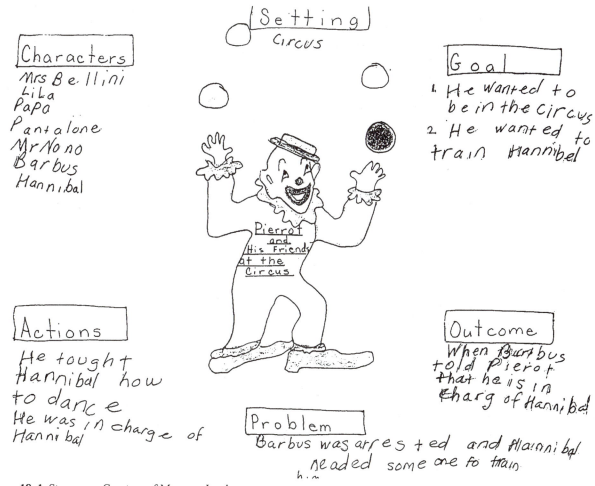

Figure 18–1 Story map. Courtesy of Maureen Jacobs.

Exhibit 18–3 Narrative Story Guide

LITTLE FOX

Little Fox was tired because he and his people had been traveling by foot. Now they rested on the _____. But _____ did not like the plains because _____
_____
_____.

Little Fox had a dream. In the dream, he rode _____. When he woke up, he talked to _____, a wise man. Little Fox wanted to know what the dream meant. Owl Man told him to _____.

Little Fox went across the plains. He fell asleep in _____. When he woke up, he saw _____ racing across _____. They looked like _____. One came over to him. Little Fox remembered his dream about riding _____, so he knew what to do.

First he dropped _____. Then he put _____. He then said to the animal "_____." The animal was a _____. Little Fox called him Red Snow because _____. The horse was important to the Indians because _____.

story. Students are then asked to predict whether the words will be used to denote characters, the setting, the problem, events, or the resolution. An important follow-up activity with students is to ask them to make changes after they have read the story.

Examples Using Nonfiction Text

Because students with reading difficulties often have the most difficulty in social studies or science classes, it is equally important for students to have instruction that emphasizes before-, during-, and after-reading strategies when they read nonfiction. Texts in these classrooms are very different from the texts in a reading classroom; the vocabulary is often very specialized, the writing style is usually more dense and compact, there is a heavy reliance on nonprint visual information, there are specific organizational writing patterns, and the material is targeted for a higher reading level. For these reasons, teachers in inclusive classrooms must make maximum use of strategies that acti-

Exhibit 18–4 Predictogram Used with Eighth-Grade Student

The following are names, ideas, and things that are important in the story "The Tree That Loved a Girl." Place each word under the heading where it belongs:

return	homesick
Polly	love
message	baby
village	mourn
oak tree	necklace

CHARACTERS	SETTING	PROBLEM
_____	_____	_____
_____	_____	_____
_____	_____	_____

GOAL	EVENTS	RESOLUTION
_____	_____	_____
_____	_____	_____
_____	_____	_____

vate students' prior knowledge and assist them in making connections between what they know and what they do not know. While there are many strategies that can be used for this purpose, graphic organizers and study guides are described as two examples.

Graphic Organizers

Graphic organizers are versatile tools for helping students understand and retain critical concepts. Because graphic organizers provide a more concrete representation of facts and relationships, they are particularly helpful to students who have reading disabilities. Visual representations may include pictures and diagrams, as well as graphs and charts. Some familiar graphics include sequence chains, cycles, Venn diagrams, compare/contrast matrices, story maps, fishbone maps, spider maps, and concept webs. Graphic organizers may be used in virtually any content area, for any level of difficulty, and at all stages of a lesson—from teacher presentation through guided and independent practice to evaluation of learning outcomes (Lovitt, 1989).

Graphic organizers are particularly flexible tools. Teachers can easily differentiate lessons for students with reading disabilities by providing learners with graphic organizers at the appropriate level of difficulty. For example, students who have serious written language problems may be given a completed graphic organizer to enable them to follow the teacher's presentation. Other students may be given a partially completed graphic to structure their note taking during the presentation. The most advanced students may be given a blank graphic for them to complete through independent note taking. The goal is to establish expectations for increased independence.

When teachers use graphic organizers, their presentations tend to be clearer and easier for students to follow. The creation and completion of these organizers model effective organizational and critical-thinking skills. Graphic organizers are appealing to students and heighten their interest and motivation. New information can be linked to prior knowledge through these visual depictions. Recall increases as students are more actively engaged in learning.

A *semantic map* is a graphic organizer that activates and builds on students' prior knowledge. The map itself is a diagram that helps students see how words and concepts are related to one another. Generally, they involve some type of brainstorming session in which students are asked to verbalize their associations to different topics. Semantic maps can also be used before reading a passage. When used in this way, they become an organizational framework for categorizing students' prior knowledge about the subject at hand. They may also be used during or after reading to help students organize information about the text (Heimlich & Pittelman, 1986). Semantic mapping has been found to be effective with students with learning disabilities (Sinatra, Berg, & Dunn, 1985). Figure 18–2 depicts a semantic map that was used after students with reading disabilities read a story about the American Revolutionary soldier.

Study Guides

A similarly versatile approach involves the use of study guides for presentation, practice, and assessment activities. Whereas graphic organizers convey relationships through visual representations, study guides accomplish the same purpose through outlines, questions, or summary statements. Study guides provide a logical structure and focus for both teachers and students, highlight critical information, and facilitate student involvement in learning (Lovitt, 1990). Suitable for content and learners at any level, study guides are useful at all stages of a lesson. As an advanced organizer, a study guide may be used to preview key concepts prior to a presentation or reading. During the lesson, the study guide provides a helpful reference for tracking comprehension. Students may complete practice activities independently or in groups by responding to study guide questions. Study guides are also useful for homework and test preparation.

The three-level study guide (Herber & Barron, 1973) is one type of study guide that is useful for students with reading difficulties. This particular guide provides a mechanism for students to sort out the most important information in a text. The construction of the three-level study guide requires the teacher to ask "What are the key concepts and understandings that I want students to have?" and "Why?" Once a teacher has answered these questions, he or she may begin constructing this guide at three levels—literal, interpretive, and applied. The teacher usually constructs levels one and two (the literal and interpretive levels) simultaneously in order to ensure a good fit between the facts presented in level one and the interpretation of these facts in level two. The last level is developed as the teacher asks "What are the possible applications of this material?" Exhibit 18–5 gives an example of a three-level study guide that was used with students with reading disabilities after they had read the same passage on the American Revolutionary soldier mentioned above.

Most basal series and textbooks provide study guides for students that can be adapted for a variety of uses. Like graphic organizers, study guides can easily and discretely be individualized for learners with different needs. The amount of reading and writing can be tailored to students' skill level. For example, response demands can vary from short essays for advanced students to fill-in-the-blank or matching items for students with more severe reading disabilities. Additional cues, such as page numbers or word banks, can be added as needed.

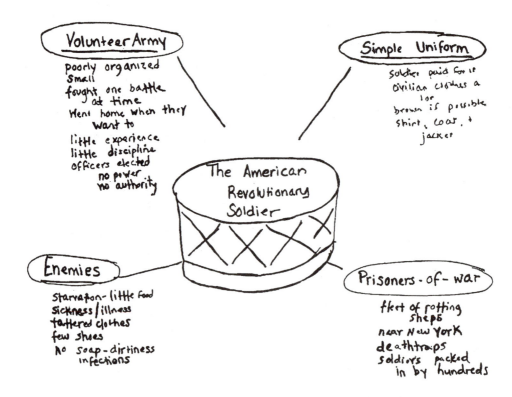

Figure 18–2 Semantic map

Exhibit 18–5 Three-Level Study Guide

THE AMERICAN SOLDIER OF THE REVOLUTIONARY WAR

I. Mark the following statements as true (t) or false (f).
_____ 1. The American Revolution began over 300 years ago.
_____ 2. American soldiers were poorly trained.
_____ 3. Officers were men of power and authority.
_____ 4. Officers were elected by their men.
_____ 5. Soldiers earned less than $7.00 per month.
_____ 6. During winter, many soldiers died of disease.
_____ 7. Food was not a major problem in the winter.
_____ 8. The British turned rotting ships into prison camps.

II. Check the statements that are true. Indicate on which page you found the answer.
_____ 1. The American soldier of the Revolutionary War was a well-polished fighting machine. (page _____)
_____ 2. Soldiers were responsible for buying their own uniforms. (page _____)
_____ 3. Washington's armies were not mobile during the winter because of the lack of strength of the troops. (page _____)
_____ 4. Prisoners taken by the American soldiers were treated well. (page _____)

III. Contrast the hardships suffered by the American soldiers during the winter of 1776 to those suffered by our soldiers during Operation Desert Storm in the heat of the desert. Which soldiers do you believe suffered worse? Why?

Selection of Accommodations

Given the complex and unique nature of reading disabilities, there are no formulas for adapting instruction. Specific adaptations must be planned to meet the individual student's needs. A problem-solving orientation can help teachers systematically choose adaptations that are most likely to be successful. A problem-solving approach involves analysis of the teacher's expectations for the class in a particular lesson, assessment of the student's strengths and weaknesses, consideration of alternative teaching strategies, selection of a specific strategy, and continuous monitoring of the student's performance during implementation. The aim is to improve the match between the instructional program and individual student's learning needs. To support the problem-solving process, instruments such as the Intervention/Transition Checklist (Wood, 1992) may be helpful. This checklist facilitates analysis of the characteristics of mainstream settings alongside an analysis of the student's present performance levels in corresponding categories. The format makes it easier to determine exactly where mismatches occur and the types of adjustments that should be made to enable a student to be more successful.

Typical accommodations for students with disabilities include enhancing content learning through listening, modifying oral presentations, adapting reading tasks, enhancing written responses, involving peers and cooperative learning, using computers and assistive technology, adjusting time demands, modifying the classroom environment, promoting self-management, modifying assignments and tests, and using responsive grading practices (Smith, Polloway, Patton, & Dowdy, 1995). The idea is to choose the few specific accommodations that are most likely to make a difference for the student. Modification of instruction in this systematic way promotes higher-level student functioning and also allows teachers to select accommodations that are feasible and manageable in their classrooms. Only by making adjustments in a systematic way can educators and families determine the appropriateness and effectiveness of specific interventions.

Use of Computers and Assistive Technology

Continual advances in technology and greater access to technology in the schools have created new opportunities to individualize the educational programs of students with reading disabilities. Computers offer alternative formats for instruction, extensive access to information beyond printed text, and enhanced capabilities for reading and written expression.

Early applications of computer-assisted instruction were primarily for drill and practice. Although some of these programs provided useful reinforcement of basic skills in language arts and mathematics, their impact on educational programs was limited. The proliferation of drill and practice software for all types of skill development at all levels has made it difficult for teachers and parents to recognize quality programs. Okolo identifies the following features of drill and practice software as particularly desirable for students with learning disabilities:

- programs that provide high rates of responding relevant to the skill to be learned
- programs in which graphics and animation support the skill or concept that is being practiced
- programs in which reinforcement is used sparingly and approximates the type of reinforcement schedule that students encounter in the classroom
- programs in which reinforcement is clearly related to task completion or mastery
- programs in which feedback helps students locate and correct their mistakes
- programs that store information about student performance or progress that can be assessed by the teacher at a later time
- programs with options for controlling features such as speed of problem presentation, type of feedback, problem difficulty, and number of practice trials (Okolo, 1993, p. 117)

Computers enable students with reading disabilities to obtain unlimited informational resources to supplement and extend what they are able to glean from printed texts. Through CD-ROM technology, for example, students can use encyclopedias and other reference materials in multimedia formats. As more schools and homes are connected to the Internet and World Wide Web, students will be able to gain access to multimedia from the best libraries, museums, and other sources around the globe. Although teachers are just beginning to explore the uses of these new technologies, there is great potential for enriching instructional opportunities for students who are less able to benefit from printed text because of severe reading disabilities.

Finally, computers provide important tools for helping students with reading disabilities compensate for their problems with reading and written expression. This compensatory or assistive technology offers a means by which to circumvent weaknesses while capitalizing on strengths (Raskind & Higgins, 1995).

Word processing, perhaps the most widely used application, is a versatile system for both instruction and communication. Raskind notes that "the 'freedom to make errors' and easily alter and manipulate text may serve to release persons with written language deficits from the 'mechanical' aspects of writing and enable them to redirect their efforts toward the 'meaning' of their written communication, as well as to help reduce the anxiety or fear associated with writing" (1994,

p. 153). Spell-checkers and grammar-checkers are standard components of most word-processing systems and provide further support for students with disabilities.

Speech synthesis or computer voice output systems add another dimension to personal computers (PCs). With screen-reading software, speech synthesizers "read" text displayed on a screen. Optical character recognition (OCR) systems have the additional capacity to read text that is scanned into a computer. BookWise (Xerox Imaging Systems, 1993) is an example of a PC-based interactive system that scans books and other printed materials, converts the text to synthesized speech, highlights the text, and reads it aloud. Teachers and students can tailor BookWise to individual abilities and learning styles through the selection of reading material; the adjustment of reading speed; and the focus on word, phrase, or sentence reading.

Technology thus offers new possibilities for both remedial and compensatory approaches to reading disabilities. The potential of technology is heightened when its usage is clearly linked to curricular goals for the student and applications are well integrated into the classroom.

PROVISION OF SUPPORT

Delivery of the IEP for students with reading disabilities in general education classrooms with appropriate curricular and instructional accommodations necessitates ongoing support for the professionals involved. Support for effective inclusion begins with a comprehensive program for professional development involving teachers, specialists, administrators, and support staff. An effective staff-development program is essential to ensure that school personnel have adequate understanding of the needs of students with reading disabilities and necessary skills to adapt educational programs effectively. Additionally, professionals need preparation for working together collaboratively. Successful staff-development programs integrate attention to the priorities of the schools and the needs of professional staff (Fullan, 1990; Gall & Vojtek, 1994). Staff development should be a continuous process and incorporate multiple approaches appropriate for adult learners. Some of the approaches well suited to staff development for inclusion include presentations and demonstrations by colleagues already engaged in inclusive service delivery; school and classroom visits to observe effective inclusion practices; and the use of case methodology to simulate challenges likely to be encountered (McLaughlin & Boerio, 1995). Those who advocate for inclusion (e.g., Bauwens & Hourcade, 1995; Friend & Cook, 1992) emphasize that an effective, ongoing program for staff development is an essential condition for success.

Teachers who serve students with reading disabilities must be able to access more personalized support beyond staff development. To implement the IEP and to address new challenges that arise, teachers often need help in planning and problem solving. This type of indirect support is frequently provided by assistance teams or individual consultants. Recent models of indirect support emphasize a collaborative style of interaction that differs from the more traditional expert approaches in that it is voluntary; demands parity among participants; is based upon mutual goals; and requires sharing of decision making, resources, and accountability (Friend & Cook, 1992). One of the most widely used structures for collaborative support is assistance teams. A core team, usually comprised of three classroom teachers, responds to a teacher's request for assistance by helping him or her to focus on a clear goal, generate appropriate intervention strategies, and develop an action plan to address specific learning and behavior problems of students (Chalfant & Pysh, 1989). In many schools, child study or resource teams have adopted this problem-solving approach and function like assistance teams. Whereas assistance teams involve small groups, consultation is typically a one-on-one interaction between a teacher and a specialist (e.g., a reading specialist, learning disabilities resource teacher, speech-language pathologist). The collaborative consultative process is similar to assistance teaming in that it involves support for planning and problem solving to address a specific concern. Classroom teachers who work with students with reading disabilities may gain new ideas and skills, as well as additional collegial support through these indirect services.

Assistance teams and collaborative consultation are described as *indirect* services because they provide support to the teacher, enabling him or her to work more effectively with the students. At times, teachers need more *direct* support in the form of collaborative teaching or coteaching. In this approach, the classroom teacher and a specialist have joint responsibility for planning, delivering, and evaluating instruction in the general education setting (Bauwens & Hourcade, 1995). In serving students with reading disabilities, the coteacher in the classroom may be a reading specialist, a learning disabilities teacher, or a speech-language pathologist. Having two professionals with complementary expertise in the classroom allows for more extensive accommodations in curriculum, instruction, evaluation, and behavior management.

No single collaborative arrangement can meet the varied needs and preferences of the professionals who serve students with reading disabilities. Each school should provide an array of opportunities for collaborative support that can be accessed by individuals on an as-needed basis. The types of support most critical to success will depend upon the unique needs of the student with reading disabilities, the expertise and comfort level of the teacher, the nature of the subject matter, and the challenges presented by the mix of students in a given class.

EXAMPLE OF COMPREHENSIVE SUPPORT: SUCCESS FOR ALL

Since the early 1980s, researchers at Johns Hopkins University have been developing, evaluating, and replicating a comprehensive approach to restructuring elementary schools entitled Success for All. A primary objective has been to create curricular and instructional methods for use in heterogeneous classes as an alternative to ability grouping of classes, remedial pull-out programs, and special education (Slavin, Stevens, & Madden, 1988). Success for All programs focus on the early grades (kindergarten through sixth-grade) with the intent of preventing learning problems in the first place and then recognizing and intervening immediately when academic deficits are observed. The Success for All program has been widely replicated in more than 300 schools in 24 states with positive results (Madden, Slavin, & Karweit, 1993; Slavin, 1996; Stevens & Slavin, 1995). In longitudinal studies, the need for special education placements was cut in half (Slavin, 1996).

Central to the Success for All model is the integration of instruction by special education resource teachers and Chapter I remedial reading teachers using either coordinated pull-out tutorial sessions or coteaching in the general education classroom. Key components include prekindergarten and kindergarten programs, family support and integrated services, and extensive staff development and support (Slavin, Madden, & Dolan, 1994).

The reading program used in Success for All is Cooperative Integrated Reading and Composition (CIRC). CIRC combines identified best practices in cooperative learning, reading, and writing instruction. Specifically, the CIRC program features three elements: basal-related activities, direct instruction in reading comprehension, and integrated language arts/writing. Students work in heterogeneous teams throughout all of these activities.

For the basal-related activities, students use whatever texts or other reading materials are used in the school. Teacher-led reading groups meet for about 20 minutes each day. When students are not working with a teacher, they are engaged in partner reading, story-related writing, vocabulary practice, story retelling, or spelling activities. Partner checking is built into daily routines, and tests are used to

---

Exhibit 18–6 Case Study of an Elementary Student: Joey

As a kindergartner, Joey began to exhibit difficulties with naming letters and their sounds. By the end of the year, he was significantly behind in his expressive language skills and could name only a few letter sounds. He was referred to the school's child study committee and, after a full evaluation, it was determined that he had significant weaknesses in auditory processing. As a child with learning disabilities, he began his first-grade year receiving reading services in a learning disabilities resource room for one hour daily. He also received services with a speech-language pathologist for 30 minutes weekly. Despite frequent communication between home and school and close monitoring of his program, Joey's progress was minimal. At his annual IEP review, his teachers and his mother agreed that his special education services should be increased for the following year.

In second grade, arrangements were made for a second-grade teacher and the learning disabilities specialist to coteach in Joey's second-grade classroom. Direct reading services continued to be provided in a pull-out resource room setting. Close coordination of services between the cotaught classroom and the resource room was a high priority to ensure that the instruction in both settings was related. In the general education classroom, a literature-based approach to reading instruction was used. The coteachers were also able to focus on other skills to help Joey succeed in the classroom. For example, both teachers worked together to promote skill development in attending to oral instruction, following directions, and requesting clarifying information when needed. Although Joey made much progress in the second grade, by the end of the year he was still reading one and one-half years below grade level. Because more improvement had been seen in second grade than ever before, however, the annual review committee decided to continue the same arrangement that utilized resource pull-out and cotaught classroom service delivery for the following year. All parties agreed to meet after the first grading period of third grade to reevaluate his placement.

The learning disabilities specialist began an intensive one-on-one phonetic-based corrective reading program at the beginning of Joey's third-grade year. In an effort to integrate services more fully for Joey, the speech-language pathologist began working with the learning disabilities specialist. Instruction was provided in the resource room using the materials Joey was already using for reading instruction. This allowed Joey to experience repeated readings of the same materials, which helped improve his reading fluency. By the time the IEP committee reconvened at the end of the first grading period, Joey had made considerable progress in reading. No changes were made in his program and, by the end of the school year, Joey's reading fluency was on grade level.

When planning for fourth grade begins, special consideration should be given to the issue of Joey's weak reading-comprehension skills. Although reevaluation of Joey's eligibility for special education indicated that he no longer requires speech-language services, it may be necessary to consult the speech-language pathologist from time to time to ensure generalization of skills. Whatever the final decision regarding services for Joey, continuing support will be vital to sustain his continued academic progress.

Exhibit 18–7 Case Study of a High School Student: Christy

Christy's severe word recognition problems were first detected in the primary grades when, despite high average cognitive ability, she was unable to master basic decoding skills for reading. After she was found eligible for special education, Christy received services in a self-contained learning disabilities class for four years. Although Christy acquired some limited phonological awareness, she functioned no higher than a mid-third grade level in reading.

During middle school, Christy was mainstreamed for all of her content subjects and received additional reading instruction and support from the learning disabilities resource teacher. Her program focused on the development of learning strategies and compensatory skills to support her functioning in her general education classes.

As she advanced to high school, both Christy and her parents favored a fully inclusive program. As a ninth grader in high school on a block schedule, Christy is now taking algebra, biology, world geography, and English. As part of her IEP, her teachers meet regularly to discuss Christy's progress and to share ideas about effective accommodations.

The learning disabilities resource teacher consults with Christy's biology and algebra teachers and assists them as needed. The teachers prepare study guides, allow Christy to tape lectures, encourage peer support in class, and permit Christy to take tests in the resource room if she needs additional assistance with reading and composition. Christy may also seek extra tutoring support from the resource teacher as needed.

Coteaching support is provided for Christy's English and world geography classes. The reading specialist coteaches with Christy's English teacher, and the learning disabilities specialist coteaches with her geography teacher. In English, coteaching permits smaller groups for parallel instruction in vocabulary, comprehension, and writing skills. In geography, the learning disabilities teacher typically introduces new vocabulary and models and monitors note taking, while the general education teacher presents new content and conducts review activities. In both cotaught classes, graphic organizers and study guides are provided for Christy and any other students who need additional support. Cooperative learning groups are used frequently to keep students actively engaged. Christy completes written assignments on a word processor. She submits a first draft along with a final version for which she has used both spell-check and grammar-check. In some instances, Christy and her teachers have negotiated alternative assignments.

Christy is maintaining a C average for the year in the college preparatory curriculum. She and her parents are planning for her to go to college and are investigating schools that provide high levels of support for students with learning disabilities.

monitor performance at regular intervals. Direct instruction in reading comprehension is provided at least once every week, and students read independently from trade books of their choice for homework every evening. The language arts and writing curriculum involves writers' workshops, skills instruction, informal and formal peer and teacher evaluations, and celebration of students' work.

STUDENT-BASED DECISION MAKING

After weighing all of the considerations about the appropriateness of inclusion, judgments ultimately must center on the specific and unique needs of the individual student. Together, families and professionals must define through the IEP a program best suited to the priorities for the student at a particular point in time. Inclusion does not have to be an either-or phenomenon. In fact, the major professional organizations such as the Council for Exceptional Children (CEC, 1993), the Council for Learning Disabilities (CLD, 1993), the National Joint Committee on Learning Disabilities (1993), and the Orton Dyslexia Society (1994) have formalized position statements that support appropriate inclusion but reaffirm the need for a full continuum of placement options. (These position statements can be found in Appendix A.) CLD's position statement includes the following:

> One policy that the Council *cannot support* is the indiscriminate full-time placement of *all* students with LD in the regular education classroom, a policy often referred to as "full inclusion." . . . Program placement of each student should be based on an evaluation of the student's individual needs. The Council *cannot support* any policy that minimizes or eliminates service options designed to enhance the education of students with LD that are guaranteed by the Individuals with Disabilities Education Act. (CLD, 1993, p. 595)

A variety of placement alternatives should be available to be tailored to specific student needs. Many students with reading disabilities may be served in general education settings for the majority of the school day but receive direct services in a pull-out program for one or two periods. Some may be served in self-contained classes for a short period of time during their school careers and then make the transition to inclusive programs. Occasionally, students who have been functioning in inclusive programs require some concentrated pull-out support. As the case studies in Exhibits 18–6 and 18–7 illustrate, students' needs change across time. The goal, however, remains the same—*to the maximum extent possible*, students with reading disabilities should be educated with their nondisabled peers. What we deem possible is more likely to be limited by our capacity as educators to envision and deliver appropriate support than by the abilities and disabilities of the students we serve.

REFERENCES

Adams, M.J. (1990). *Beginning to read: Thinking and learning about print.* Cambridge, MA: MIT.

Barnes, D. (1976). *From communication to curriculum.* London: Penguin.

Bauwens, J., & Hourcade, J. (1995). *Cooperative teaching: Rebuilding the schoolhouse for all students.* Austin, TX: Pro-Ed.

Bergenske, D.M. (1987). The missing link in narrative story mapping. *The Reading Teacher, 41,* 333–335.

Chalfant, J.C., & Pysh, M.V.D. (1989). Teacher assistance teams: Five descriptive studies on 96 teams. *Remedial and Special Education, 10*(6), 49–58.

Clay, M.M. (1979). *Reading: The patterning of complex behavior* (2nd ed.). Auckland, New Zealand: Heinemann Educational.

Clay, M.M. (1982). *Observing young children: Selected papers.* Portsmouth, NH: Heinemann Educational.

Clay, M.M. (1985). *The early detection of reading difficulties* (3rd ed.). Auckland, New Zealand: Heinemann Educational.

Clay, M.M. (1990, April). *Reading Recovery in the United States: Its successes and challenges.* Paper presented at the Annual Meeting of the American Educational Research Association, Boston, MA.

Clay, M.M. (1991). *Becoming literate: The construction of inner control.* Portsmouth, NH: Heinemann Educational.

Corson, D. (1984). The case for oral language in schooling. *Elementary School Journal, 84*(4), 458–467.

Cotton, K. (1995). *Onward to excellence. Effective schooling practices: A research synthesis 1995 update.* Portland, OR: Northwest Regional Educational Laboratory.

Council for Exceptional Children. (1993). *Policy on inclusive schools and community settings.* Reston, VA: Author.

Council for Learning Disabilities. (1993). Concerns and a reaction to full inclusion of all students with learning disabilities in the regular classroom. *Journal of Learning Disabilities, 26*(9), 594–596.

Deschler, D.D., Alley, G.R., Warner, M.M., & Schumaker, J.B. (1981). Instructional practices for promoting skill acquisition and generalization in severely learning disabled adolescents. *Learning Disabilities Quarterly, 4,* 415–421.

Education of Handicapped Children Act, Pub. L. No. 94-142 (1975).

Ellis, E.S., Deschler, D.D., Lenz, B.K., Schumaker, J.B., & Clark, F. (1991). An instructional model for teaching learning strategies. *Focus on Exceptional Children, 23,* 1–23.

Ellis, E.S., & Lenz, B.K. (1987). A component analysis of effective learning strategies for LD students. *Learning Disabilities Focus, 2*(2), 94–107.

Flowers, D.L. (1993). Brain basis for dyslexia: A summary of work in progress. *Journal of Learning Disabilities, 26*(9), 575–582.

Friend, M., & Cook, L. (1992). *Interactions: Collaboration skills for school professionals.* New York: Longman.

Fullan, M.G. (1990). Staff development, innovation and institutional development. In B. Joyce (Ed.), *Changing school culture through staff development: 1990 ASCD Yearbook* (pp. 3–25). Alexandria, VA: Association for Supervision and Curriculum Development.

Gall, M.D., & Vojtek, R.O. (1994). *Planning for effective staff development.* Eugene: University of Oregon.

Gerstein, R., & Dimino, J. (1989). Teaching literature to at-risk students. *Educational Leadership, 46*(5), 53–57.

Graham, S., Macarthur, C., Schwartz, S., & Page-Voth, V. (1992). Improving the compositions of students with learning disabilities using a strategy involving product and process goal setting. *Journal of Learning Disabilities, 58,* 322–334.

Gurney, D.E. (1987). *Teaching mildly handicapped high-school students to understand short stories using a story grammar comprehension strategy.* Unpublished doctoral dissertation, University of Oregon, Eugene.

Harris, A.J., & Sipay, E.R. (1990). *How to increase reading ability* (9th ed.). New York: Longman.

Heimlich, J.E., & Pittelman, S.D. (1986). *Semantic mapping: Classroom applications.* Newark, DE: International Reading Association.

Herber, H.L., & Barron, R.F. (Eds.). (1973). *Research in reading in the content areas: Second year report.* Syracuse, NY: Syracuse University.

Hynd, G.W., & Cohen, M. (1983). *Dyslexia: Neuropsychological theory research and clinical differentiation.* New York: Grune & Stratton.

Idol, L., & Croll, V. (1987). Story mapping training as a means of improving reading comprehension. *Learning Disabilities Quarterly, 10,* 214–230.

Laycock, V., & Korinek, L. (1989). Toward least restrictive curriculum for behaviorally disordered adolescents. *Programming for Adolescents with Behavioral Disorders, 4,* 11–25.

Lovitt, T. (1989). *Constructing graphic organizers: An instructional packet to accompany the video production.* Salt Lake City: Utah Teacher Resource Center.

Lovitt, T. (1990). *Study Guides: An instructional packet to accompany the video production Study Guides.* Salt Lake City: Utah Teacher Resource Center.

Lyon, G.R. (1991). *Research in learning disabilities.* Bethesda, MD: National Institute of Child Health and Human Development.

Madden, N.A., Slavin, R.E., & Karweit, N.L. (1993). Success for all: Longitudinal effects of a restructuring program for inner-city elementary schools. *American Educational Research Journal, 30*(1), 123–148.

McGinley, W.J., & Denner, P.R. (1987). Story impressions: A prereading/writing activity. *Journal of Reading, 31,* 248–253.

McLaughlin, V.L., & Boerio, L. (1995). *Program leadership for serving students with disabilities: Instructional modules and case materials.* Richmond, VA: Virginia Department of Education.

National Joint Committee on Learning Disabilities. (1993). Providing appropriate education for students with learning disabilities in regular education classrooms. *Journal of Learning Disabilities, 26*(5), 330–332.

National Joint Committee on Learning Disabilities. (1994). Learning disabilities: Issues on definition, a position paper of the National Joint Committee on Learning Disabilities. In *Collective perspectives on issues affecting learning disabilities: Position papers and statements.* Austin, TX: Pro-Ed.

Okolo, C.M. (1993). Computers and individuals with mild disabilities. In J.D. Lindsey (Ed.), *Computers and exceptional individuals* (pp. 111–124). Austin, TX: Pro-Ed.

Orton Dyslexia Society. (1994). Position statement on inclusion. Baltimore: Author.

Orton, S.T. (1925). "Word-blindness" in school children. *Archives of Neurological Psychology, 14,* 581–615.

Pikulski, J.L. (1994). Preventing reading failure: A review of five effective programs. *The Reading Teacher, 48*(1), 30–39.

Pinnell, G.S. (1990). Success for low achievers through Reading Recovery. *Educational Leadership, 48*(1), 581–615.

Pinnell, G.S., Lyons, C.A., DeFord, D.E., Bryk, A.S., & Seltzer, M. (1994). Comparing instructional models for the literacy education of high-risk first graders. *Reading Research Quarterly, 29*(1), 9–39.

Pressley, M., & Associates. (1990). *Cognitive strategy: Instruction that really improves children's academic performance*. Cambridge, MA: Brookline.

Raskind, M.H. (1994). Assistive technology for adults with learning disabilities: A rationale for use. In P.J. Gerber & H.B. Reiff (Eds.), *Learning disabilities in adulthood: Persisting problems and evolving issues* (pp. 152–162). Boston: Andover.

Raskind, M.H., & Higgins, E.L. (1995). Reflections on ethics, technology, and learning disabilities: Avoiding the consequences of ill-considered action. *Journal of Learning Disabilities, 28*(7), 425–438.

Reid, D.K., Hresko, W.P., & Swanson, H.L. (1991). *A cognitive approach to learning disabilities*. Austin, TX: Pro-Ed.

Rooney, K. (1989). Independent strategies for efficient study: A core approach. *Academic Therapy, 24*(4), 383–390.

Rooney, K.J. (1995). Dyslexia revisited: History, educational philosophy, and clinical assessment applications. *Intervention in School and Clinic, 31*(1), 6–15.

Scruggs, T.E., & Mastropieri, M.A. (1993). Special education for the twenty-first century: Integrating learning strategies and thinking skills. *Journal of Learning Disabilities, 26*(6), 392–398.

Sinatra, R., Berg, D., & Dunn, R.S. (1985). Semantic mapping improves reading comprehension of learning disabled students. *Teaching Exceptional Students, 17*, 310–314.

Slavin, R.E. (1996). Neverstreaming: Preventing learning disabilities. *Educational Leadership, 53*(5), 4–7.

Slavin, R.E., Karweit, N.L., & Madden, N.A. (1989). *Effective programs for students at risk*. Needham Heights, MA: Allyn and Bacon.

Slavin, R.E., Madden, N.A., & Dolan, L.J. (1994). Whenever and wherever we choose: The replication of Success for All. *Phi Delta Kappan, 75*(8), 642–647.

Slavin, R.E., Stevens, R.J., & Madden, N.A. (1988). Accommodating student diversity in reading and writing instruction: A cooperative learning approach. *Remedial and Special Education, 9*, 60–66.

Smith, C.R. (1994). *Learning disabilities: The interaction of learner, task, and setting* (3rd ed.). Needham Heights, MA: Allyn and Bacon.

Smith, T.E.C., Polloway, E.A., Patton, J.R., Dowdy, C.A. (1995). *Teaching students with special needs in inclusive settings*. Needham Heights, MA: Allyn and Bacon.

Spafford, C.S., & Grosser, G.S. (1996). *Dyslexia: Research and resource guide*. Needham Heights, MA: Allyn and Bacon.

Stainback, S., & Stainback, W. (Eds.). (1992). *Curriculum considerations in inclusive classrooms: Facilitating learning for all students*. Baltimore: Paul H. Brookes.

Stevens, R.J., & Slavin, R.E. (1995). The cooperative elementary school: Effects on students' achievement, attitudes, and social relations. *American Educational Research Journal, 32*(2), 321–351.

Turnbull, A.P., Turnbull, H.R., Shank, M., & Leal, D. (1994). *Exceptional lives: Special education in today's schools*. Columbus, OH: Merrill.

U.S. Department of Education. (1977). Implementation of Part B of the Education of the Handicapped Act. *Federal Register, 42*, 42474–42518.

U.S. Department of Education. (1989). *Eleventh annual report to Congress on the implementation of the Individuals with Disabilities Education Act*. Washington, DC: U.S. Government Printing Office.

U.S. Department of Education. (1994). *Sixteenth annual report to Congress on the implementation of the Individuals with Disabilities Education Act*. Washington, DC: Author.

Vellutino, F.R. (1991). Introduction to three studies on reading acquisition: Convergent findings on theoretical foundations of code-oriented versus whole-language approaches to reading instruction. *Journal of Educational Psychology, 83*, 437–443.

Wood, J.W. (1992). *Adapting instruction for mainstreamed and at-risk students*. New York: Merrill.

Xerox Imaging Systems. (1993). *BookWise*. Peabody, MA: Author.

CHAPTER 19

Staff-Development Activities

Susan Mongold

INTRODUCTION

Because the purpose of staff development is to facilitate an individual's learning, understanding the factors that affect the level and amount of retention is important when designing the activity. Adults learn through semantic methods, such as from asking questions or watching a demonstration or video. (See Chapter 12 for discussion of semantic and episodic learning.) When a staff-development presentation involves only reading or traditional lecture, the individual learns but retains only a small amount of the new information. Involving the individual through discussion, small-group activities, and demonstrations significantly increases the amount of new information retained (Kemp, Morrison, & Ross, 1994).

Any chapter or topic from this book could be presented to a group combining lecture and presentation methods. The presenter could prepare either participant handouts or overhead transparencies stating the main points. If the presenter remains open to audience discussion or embeds questions for the audience into the text of the lecture, the traditional lecture can be enhanced. This type of presentation would raise the learner's retention rate, but not to the level that can be reached with application.

In this chapter, specific learning objectives have been drawn from each of the preceding chapters, followed by suggestions on how to involve the audience in learning.

Information is provided on the recommended target audience, purpose, required time frame, and materials needed for the activity. The target audience for these activities is school personnel—teachers, administrators, and support and related services staff. (See Exhibit 19–1 for a list of staff-development activities discussed in this chapter.)

Depending upon a school division's identified training or program needs, these activities can be combined to facilitate the development of common terminology, understanding, program development, or implementation of inclusive education programs in schools. As the school broadens its base of support to include community leaders from business, organizations (e.g., advocacy and support groups, churches), other government agencies, and private and public service providers (e.g., Big Brothers/Big Sisters, United Way), the information in this book and the activities in this chapter can be used to develop the common ground necessary for cooperation and collaboration.

Each staff-development activity has several basic assumptions: (1) the facilitator will adjust the suggested activity to fit the group size; (2) the focus of the activity will be narrowed or broadened depending upon the variety of disciplines represented and the experience of those in attendance; and (3) the methodology of combining an understanding of new information with an application of that understanding increases the participant's retention.

The facilitator's experience in providing staff-development training is important. While the facilitator does not need to be an expert in staff development, knowledge of adult learning principles and basic group facilitation skills is necessary. The resources found at the end of the chapter may be useful in preparing staff-development training. To be successful, the facilitator should remember that adults want the staff-development activity to be useful and easily applied to their current situation, new information and skills

Aspen Publishers, Inc., grants permission for photocopying for limited personal or internal use. This consent does not extend to other kinds of copying, such as copying for general distribution, for advertising or promotional purposes, for creating new collective works, or for resale. For information, address Aspen Publishers, Inc., Permissions Department, 200 Orchard Ridge Drive, Suite 200, Gaithersburg, Maryland 20878.

Exhibit 19–1 List of Staff-Development Activities

Activity 1.1—Creating a definition	Activity 12.1—Inclusive practices in secondary school
Activity 2.1—Having a common vision	Activity 13.1—Vocational education
Activity 2.2—Involving stakeholders	Activity 14.1—Transition planning with an inclusive philosophy
Activity 3.1—Beyond visioning: The plan	Activity 14.2—Setting measurable transition goals
Activity 4.1—The continuum of least restrictive environment decisions	Activity 15.1—Behavioral supports
Activity 4.2—Court interpretation of a least restrictive environment	Activity 15.2—Addressing problem behavior
Activity 5.1—Financing the cost of inclusion	Activity 16.1—Developing health services training
Activity 6.1—Adapting curriculum	Activity 17.1—Working with students who are deaf and hard-of-hearing
Activity 6.2—Applying strategies to our curriculum	Activity 17.2—Working with interpreters and hearing devices
Activity 7.1—Sharing dreams	Activity 18.1—Working with students with reading disabilities
Activity 7.2—Gathering information	
Activity 8.1—Identifying needed supports and resources	Note that not all of these activities need to be conducted in a specific order. Facilitators are encouraged to pick and choose the activities that are best suited for the target audience and goals of the local school division and community. Activities that should be conducted before another activity are noted in the discussion of the activity itself.
Activity 8.2—Identifying *your* stakeholders	
Activity 8.3—Building on current partnerships	
Activity 9.1—Preschool and inclusion	
Activity 10.1—Strategies for elementary inclusion	
Activity 11.1—Middle school characteristics	The facilitator should follow appropriate copyright procedures before reproducing any tables or figures for distribution.
Activity 11.2—Middle school adolescence	

should be introduced to build upon the adults' current experience base, and adults wants to be allowed to express themselves and then make their own decisions. The activities in this chapter incorporate these principles of adult learning.

In addition, the facilitator should understand group facilitation skills. This includes a basic understanding of using open-ended questions, encouraging participants to answer one another's questions, managing a hostile or talkative participant (e.g., through seating arrangements or proximity to the facilitator), and using materials (e.g., participant handouts or an easel chart) to provide visual aids of the content being presented. The resources listed at the end of the chapter may be helpful in preparing to lead a staff-development activity.

In the same vein, the facilitator's experience with inclusive education is important to the success of staff-development training. In general, the audience expects the facilitator to be a content expert. Facilitators who are not content experts should invite cofacilitators or guest speakers who are content experts to present the content. The facilitator's role is to assist the audience in learning new skills or information.

ACTIVITY 1.1—CREATING A DEFINITION

Target Audience

All educators (teachers and administrators), parents, students

Audience Size

Up to 20 persons

Purpose

To define inclusion; to identify the current supports and barriers to inclusion (within the school division)

Time

60 to 75 minutes

Materials

- Easel paper, stand, and markers
- Tape or push pins
- Copies of Exhibit 1–2

Facilitator Preparation

Copy Exhibit 1–2.

Instructions

Divide participants into groups of two or three persons. Give each group 10 minutes to develop a definition of inclusion and write it on easel paper. Post all definitions.

Distribute copies of Exhibit 1–2 to the participants. Compare and contrast the participants' definitions and the definitions of inclusion from the handout. Facilitate a discussion around these definitions. Facilitation questions could include: Which definitions from the handout most closely match our definitions? How do the differences between our definitions and the definitions from the handout influence the success of inclusive programming? Why are the definitions so different? Ask participants if they want to change their definition as a result of the discussion. If so, allow five minutes for the revision.

Continuing the activity, ask participants to describe what inclusion would look like in their school. (Answers could include: child attends neighborhood schools, child experiences and environment vary, support structures are classroom based and generic, diversity is valued and embedded within curriculum.) Make a list of what is said, using the easel paper and markers. Post as necessary.

Once the group has defined inclusion, ask them to think individually of at least two supports and two barriers to implementing inclusion in a school. Allow no more than five minutes. After five minutes, ask for participants to volunteer to share their ideas. Keep track of the ideas using two easel pages—one with the header "supports" and the other with the header "barriers." Solicit ideas from the group until all ideas are posted. Encourage discussion and clarity as the ideas are shared.

Conclude the discussion by asking the participants to look at the list of supports and barriers. Determine if any of the supports can change any of the listed barriers.

ACTIVITY 2.1—HAVING A COMMON VISION

Target Audience

School stakeholders (school personnel involved in planning and implementing inclusive education)

Audience Size

Up to 30 persons

Purpose

To identify the relationship between inclusion and other school reform initiatives in this district

Time

45 minutes

Materials

- Easel paper, stand, and markers
- Tape or push pins
- Chapter 2

Facilitator Preparation

Participants need to read Chapter 2 before activity.

Instructions

Ask participants to identify recent or current education reform and restructuring efforts in their school district. List on easel paper and post. Split participants into small groups of three to four people. Ask the small groups to identify the characteristics of the reform effort and the similarities of these characteristics to inclusion. Allow the small groups 10 minutes.

After 10 minutes, ask the small groups to share their ideas. Record ideas on easel paper and post. Facilitate a discussion around the following questions: Why do we need to work together on school reform initiatives? Who does this include? Who would be involved in linking inclusion to other school reform efforts? Create a master list on easel paper.

Facilitator Note

This activity could serve as the way to create an invitation list for a follow-up vision development workshop for stakeholders. If the purpose of the activity is to create a stakeholder list, keep a list of stakeholders as they are named, with the name of person who made the suggestion. This might be helpful in determining who invites the stakeholder.

ACTIVITY 2.2—INVOLVING STAKEHOLDERS

Prerequisite

Activity 2.1 should be a prerequisite if stakeholders include persons implementing other school reform initiatives.

Purpose

To model collaboration and program implementation by jointly planning a vision development workshop

Time

60 minutes

Materials

- Easel pad, stand, and markers
- Tape or push pins

Facilitator Preparation

Administrative support is necessary for this activity to move forward. While this activity results in a work plan, the process of developing the work plan should model the techniques and process that will be used to develop a vision. Because a consultant is often viewed as a neutral party, consider using an external facilitator to lead this planning session. Good sources for an external facilitator include state departments of education, local universities, and other organizations that may have grants for systems changes. The facilitator selected should have knowledge of special education and inclusion.

Instructions

Outline the steps of a vision planning workshop (from selecting a date and location, to invitations, RSVP, and follow up, setting the agenda, facility arrangements, meeting minutes, and more). Ask the group to brainstorm about the steps involved. As a step is suggested, write it in large letters on a single piece of copy paper and tape it to the wall. Keep this up until about five pages are displayed. Work with the group to arrange the pages in chronological order. Continue taking steps from the group, writing them on copy paper, and posting them in the appropriate chronological place.

As the items are rearranged, redefined, and discussed, expand the notes to include smaller steps under each task. Finally, create a task list of everything to be done.

The final step in this workshop is to ask participants to sign up to implement the plan. The vision of restructuring the school with the help of peers, constituents, and community will not become a reality unless all participants commit to implementation.

ACTIVITY 3.1—BEYOND VISIONING: THE PLAN

Target Audience

School stakeholders

Audience Size

15 to 30 persons

Purpose

To understand the issues in planning, implementing, and evaluating inclusion at the school level

Time

90 minutes

Materials

- Index cards of three different colors
- Chapter 3
- Exhibit 19–2

Facilitator Preparation

Using Exhibit 19–2, write the planning statements on one color index card, the implementation statements on another color index card, and evaluation statements on a third color index card. Participants must read this chapter prior to this activity. Participants should have a copy of the chapter with them at the activity.

Instructions

Randomly distribute the index cards. Ask the card holders to read their card statements and look up the statement in Chapter 3. The card holder should write, in his or her own words, a statement that briefly describes the issues or considerations. (With a smaller group, this is done individually. With a larger group, this is done in pairs.) Allow 10 to 15 minutes for participants to complete this.

Exhibit 19–2 Planning and Implementation

PLANNING
- Articulate values and develop the vision.
- Listen to the people affected by the change.
- Provide transformative experiences.
- Plan for bringing students to their neighborhood schools.
- Meet with parents and prepare IEPs.
- Consider staffing and physical resources.
- Resolve transportation needs.
- Teach skills needed for the change process.

IMPLEMENTATION
- Develop the master schedule.
- Develop instructional teams.
- Adjust policies and procedures.
- Develop a solution-oriented approach to problems.
- Teach skills needed for inclusive instruction.

EVALUATION
- Create process to evaluate outcomes.
- Is the vision growing as the team grows?
- Are the policies and procedures working to move vision to reality?
- What skills do we need to continue to teach?
- Are our outcomes still relevant?

After 10 to 15 minutes, reconvene the group and ask the planning card holders to share first. Discuss as needed. Continue with the implementation cards and, finally, the evaluation cards.

Then create three small groups to take one set of cards (planning, implementation, or evaluation). Allow each group 30 minutes to identify a process to get started in its education community. This involves translating the concepts from Chapter 3 to action steps for that school. After 30 minutes, ask the groups to share the identified process, starting with the planning stage. As groups present, allow the other small groups to ask questions, obtain clarification, and enhance the process.

Facilitator Note

The product created during this activity can become the first draft of a work plan for the school. If this is a goal of this staff-development activity, the facilitator should serve as the note taker.

ACTIVITY 4.1—THE CONTINUUM OF LEAST RESTRICTIVE ENVIRONMENT DECISIONS

Target Audience

School stakeholders, special education faculty

Audience Size

10 to 25 persons

Purpose

To identify and place on a continuum the placement and options that should be available to students with disabilities; to apply the factors that guide a least restrictive environment decision for each individual

Time

90 minutes

Materials

- String or chalk
- Tape
- Ten feet of wall or chalkboard
- Blank paper
- Markers
- 5- x 8-inch index cards

Facilitator Preparation

Prepare continuum wall prior to start of activity.

Instructions

Create a 10-foot line on the wall (using either string and tape or chalk on a blackboard). Distribute the blank paper and markers. Ask participants to work in groups of two or three. Each small group should make a list of school and community placement and service options, ranging from general education to residential placements. As participants rearrange and settle in to work, encourage them to be very specific in the placement descriptions and to be sure to include the use of supplemental aids and services as part of the placement description. Allow the small groups 10 minutes to generate their lists.

After 10 minutes, call the groups to attention and establish one end of the continuum (line on wall) as general education and the other end as residential placement. Ask for a volunteer to read one option from his or her list. The facilitator writes the placement option on an index card. Ask the large group to determine where along the continuum line to tape the specific placement option. Tape the card in that spot.

Repeat this process, taking placement options from various groups and taping the option along the continuum, until all options are posted. The facilitator may need to make adjustments to ensure that all the options fit and can be read or as the group of participants decide to move the option. As variations of previously mentioned options are offered, a different color ink can be used to add these variations to the same (or additional) index card.

Once all options are posted, the facilitator should review the factors that determine least restrictive environment (e.g., closeness to home, environment meets a child's specialized learning needs).

After reviewing these factors, the facilitator returns to the continuum of placement options. Starting at the residential end of the continuum, discuss each placement option, answering one or more of the following questions: What special needs of children can be met in this environment? What challenges might this placement option present to a child's development? What are the services and supports that are necessary to move to the next place on the least restrictive environment continuum? How could these needs be met in a general education classroom? The facilitator should emphasize that the IEP team needs to make decisions for each child on an individual basis, using questions like these.

ACTIVITY 4.2—COURT INTERPRETATION OF A LEAST RESTRICTIVE ENVIRONMENT

Prerequisite

Activity 4.1

Purpose

To understand how the court rulings influence the interpretation and implementation of least restrictive environment

Time

60 minutes

Materials

- Appendix B–4
- String or chalk
- Tape
- Ten feet of wall or chalkboard
- Blank paper or index cards
- Markers

Facilitator Preparation

Create signs to post along the continuum created in Activity 4.1 for each court case described in Appendix B–4. For example, in the case of *Daniel R.R. v. State Board of Education*, the facilitator would have three cards or papers. The three cards would describe Daniel, Daniel's parents' placement request, and the school's placement position.

Instructions

To expand Activity 4.1, include case-based court interpretations found in Appendix B–4. Apply the court interpretations to the continuum of placement developed by the participants.

Use the continuum created in Activity 4.1 to demonstrate the type of placement options the child was in or was recommended to be in, the placement options sought, and the factors that influenced the court decision. With each court case described, place the prepared signs along the continuum. Ask participants to determine where to position the placement option along the continuum. Discuss the decision of the court (outcome) and how the outcome affects the definition of least restrictive environment and inclusion.

Facilitator Note

This activity could be combined with Activity 1.1. Participants could examine how their definition of inclusion could be affected by these court rulings.

ACTIVITY 5.1—FINANCING THE COST OF INCLUSION

Target Audience

School administrators, teachers, related service staff (special education administrators with knowledge of special education financing in the district should be included in this activity)

Audience Size

15 to 25 people

Purpose

To identify the costs and funding sources for implementing inclusion

Time

45 minutes

Materials

- Chapter 5
- Easel pad, stand, and markers
- Tape or push pins

Facilitator Preparation

Be sure all participants have read the chapter prior to participating in this activity.

Instructions

Ask the participants to determine the potential costs of implementing inclusive education in this district. The participants should consider personnel, staff development, transportation, facilities, materials and equipment, residential placement, and legal consultation. Write the answers on easel paper and post.

Ask the participants to determine the funding sources that could support their efforts for inclusion. Encourage discussion and application to the specific school division. Write the answers on easel paper and post.

Continue the discussion by asking participants to brainstorm a list of persons who have a vested interest in these costs or the financing of the costs, specifying the stakeholders in the community.

Conclude the discussion by asking the participants to consider how this information (costs and stakeholders) will affect new programs being started in the local school. As a group, create a plan for identifying costs that may need to be addressed and strategies for addressing these needs.

ACTIVITY 6.1—ADAPTING CURRICULUM

Target Audience

Teachers of any grade level, other school personnel (e.g., administrators, related service staff)

Audience Size

15 to 20 people

Purpose

To identify specific strategies to use when adapting curriculum

Time

60 minutes

Materials

- Guest speaker or panel presenters
- Index cards

Facilitator Preparation

Participants will need to read the chapter prior to this activity. While reading the chapter, participants should make a note of their questions about adapting curriculum in their classroom. Participants should bring the question(s) to the staff-development activity. Give participants an index card on which to write their questions. This activity uses a panel presentation of one or more experts in adapting existing curriculum. Curriculum specialists with experience adapting curriculum for disabilities may be identified in this or a neighboring school district. College or university faculty and state education agency personnel may also be resources.

Instructions

The guest speaker or panel members present a 15-minute overview of general principles of adapting curriculum. This presentation is followed by a facilitated discussion between the audience and guest speaker/panel. To encourage discussion, the facilitator can start with questions like: What have you found to be the biggest challenge to adapting curriculum? How have you worked with teachers to overcome this challenge? How can teachers help one another in the process of adapting curriculum? Or the facilitator could collect the questions developed by participants during the chapter reading and use these questions to guide discussion.

ACTIVITY 6.2—APPLYING STRATEGIES TO OUR CURRICULUM

Target Audience

Teachers in the same school or of similar grade levels from different schools

Audience Size

6 to 12 people

Purpose

To apply strategies for adapting curriculum

Time

60 to 90 minutes

Materials

- Copies of Exhibit 6–2
- Subject matter experts (The panel should reflect the subject areas of particular interest to the participants, drawing from those discussed in Chapter 6: language arts, math, science, health, social studies, art, music, physical education.)

Facilitator Preparation

Participants should read the chapter prior to this activity and have the chapter with them at this session. Participants should also bring an existing lesson plan (for one topic or activity). Participants in this activity include subject matter experts (e.g., math, science) who can work with participants in topical groups.

Instructions

Group the participants based on the content area of the lesson plan they brought (content groups). Have the subject matter expert sit with the appropriate group. (Or, if only one curriculum specialist is used, let the group know he or she will regularly circulate among the groups.)

Distribute copies of Exhibit 6–2. Instruct the participants in the content groups, working first in pairs, to apply the handout ideas to their lesson plans. Allow 10 to 15 minutes for the pairs to complete this.

In the content groups, ask the pairs to share their situation and new ideas with the other content group members. The content group members can serve as consultant teachers and offer suggestions and support. The subject matter expert or curriculum specialist can help people get started, help people think about new ideas, and serve as a consultant. Allow 10 minutes per participant (e.g., if each content group has four participants, allow 40 minutes for sharing).

ACTIVITY 7.1—SHARING DREAMS

Target Audience

Teachers, school administrators, related service staff, and others from a single school

Audience Size

10 to 25 persons

Purpose

To understand the circle of emotions experienced by the family of a child with a disability; to apply that understanding to teacher/administrative practices

Time

60 minutes

Materials

• Exhibit 19–3

Facilitator Preparation

Copies of Exhibit 19–3

Instructions

Using Exhibit 19–3, ask participants to define each emotional stage. Under each stage, ask participants to share their ideas about natural and imposed triggers that may activate this emotion. Possible answers drawn from Chapter 7 include natural triggers (financial issues, medical expenses, transitions, milestones, developmental stages) and imposed triggers (unrealistic recommendations or predictions, assessment and evaluation, descriptions of what the child cannot do or how far behind the child might be developmentally). Encourage participants to share voluntarily when these types of triggers have touched their lives or the life of someone they know.

Split the participants into two small groups (or four small groups, depending upon overall group size). Have one group answer the question, "How does understanding the shattered dreams circle and the triggers help me to work with families?" Ask the other group to answer the question, "What barriers do we (teachers) or our school put up to keep families and children with disabilities from dreaming or sharing their dream with us?"

Allow the groups about 20 minutes to discuss these questions. After 20 minutes, ask the two groups to share their answers. Encourage discussion between the groups.

ACTIVITY 7.2—GATHERING INFORMATION

Target Audience

School teachers, administrators, related service staff, and others from a single school

Audience Size

10 to 15 persons

Exhibit 19–3 Circle of Emotions

	Denial	Anger	Anxiety	Fear	Bargaining	Guilt	Depression	Acceptance
Definition								
Natural Triggers								
Imposed Triggers								

Purpose

To understand and practice implementing the MAPs (making action plans) and/or PATH (planning alternative tomorrows with hope) processes

Time

60 to 90 minutes (*Note*: Actual implementation of either MAPs or PATH takes two hours; this is a simulation so it will move more quickly.)

Materials

- Chapter 7
- Name tags
- Markers

Facilitator Preparation

Participants should read Chapter 7 prior to this activity. They should focus on the instructions to the appropriate process (MAPs or PATH). A decision to implement either MAPs or PATH alone or to conduct a two-part activity (first implementing MAPs and then implementing PATH) must be made before this activity begins. Be sure that participants understand that this will be a role-play activity where everyone participates.

Instructions

Reviewing Chapter 7, the facilitator points out that: MAPs is a tool to gather information about the child, family, class, or team. This information is used to facilitate inclusion of children with disabilities into the classroom. PATH is a tool used to create a common goal or vision of where a person is today and where the person wants to be in the future. This information can be used to develop a plan for getting to that point in the future.

Ask for two participants to volunteer to be the school representative and family member working as a team to arrange for the MAPs process. (For PATH, three volunteers are needed: a graphic recorder, a guide, and a pathfinder.) The two volunteers should carry out their roles as outlined in Chapter 7 (select participants to role play family members, school personnel, and the "star" of the MAPs process). Name tags can be worn so the audience can keep the various roles straight. Continue this activity by following the directions on how to conduct either the MAPs or PATH process. Encourage participants to stay in character to help build their understanding of the value of dedicating the time to this type of engagement with the family.

ACTIVITY 8.1—IDENTIFYING NEEDED SUPPORTS AND RESOURCES

Target Audience

School teachers, administrators, related service staff, and others

Audience Size

Up to 20 to 30 persons

Purpose

To identify possible supports and resources within the community for students with disabilities

Time

75 minutes

Materials

- Four case studies provided by either the facilitator or participants

Facilitator Preparation

Prepare easel paper using Exhibit 19–4 as a guide. Prepare four case studies using Exhibits 8–5 through 8–8 as a guide.

Instructions

Divide the participant group into four smaller groups. Distribute the four case studies, one to each small group. Allow 20 minutes for the small groups to read the case study and develop answers.

The small group should determine (1) what supports the school division would need to include the student in an inclusive education program and (2) what community groups are possible resources for the necessary support.

After 20 minutes, ask each small group to share the identified supports and the possible resources for those supports. The facilitator should track these on several easel pages, using the format illustrated in Exhibit 19–4. Continue developing the list as each group reports its information. Record duplicate supports needed with check marks by the item and add the identified resources to that row.

As a large group, examine the list of possible supports needed and resources. Identify any of the resources that are currently in place and working with the school division, and mark those with a colored marker. Expand the discussion by asking general questions such as: "Are there other community supports we have not identified?" "Do we have chil-

Exhibit 19–4 Easel Page Format

Identified Support	*Possible Resources*

dren in our school who could currently benefit from these types of services?"

ACTIVITY 8.2—IDENTIFYING *YOUR* STAKEHOLDERS

Prerequisite

Activity 8.1

Target Audience

School teachers, administrators, related service staff, and others

Purpose

To expand the discussion and apply to a specific community or project

Time

30 to 45 minutes

Materials

- Local phone book
- Any locally developed information and referral listing of local human service providers and agencies
- Note paper

Instructions

This activity is an expansion of Activity 8.1. After completing Activity 8.1, ask for a volunteer to take notes. Once the note taker is ready, facilitate a group discussion asking questions including: (1) If our school division were to identify a needed program, what community stakeholders should we involve in the program development? (2) How would we involve stakeholders?

The note taker should make a list of community stakeholders, using the resources to help trigger ideas and identify addresses or correct titles. The facilitator should point out that the list of resources identified in the case study activity reflects the list of stakeholders who should be involved in school program development.

ACTIVITY 8.3—BUILDING ON CURRENT PARTNERSHIPS

Prerequisites

Activities 8.1 and 8.2

Target Audience

School teachers, administrators, related service staff, and others

Purpose

To continue the expansion of Activities 8.1 and 8.2 and discuss current partnerships in the locality

Time

45 minutes

Materials

- Easel pad, stand, and markers
- Exhibit 8–4

Facilitator Preparation

Copy of Exhibit 8–4

Instructions

Since most school divisions are already participants of various interagency teams and/or community groups, it may be useful to identify these teams and their scope. Ask the participants to identify (1) Which of these community groups are currently working on known collaborative projects? (2) Where do these groups overlap in such a way that they could support additional program development or implementation? (3) Based on the stakeholders identified in the case study activity, which of these groups could be expanded? (4) What new groups could be invited to participate and why? Discuss these answers and record as appropriate.

Distribute Exhibit 8–4 and continue the discussion asking questions such as the following: Which of these issues is a concern in our education community? How can we apply the potential solution to our education community?

Facilitator Note

These foundation activities can be used to include community stakeholders in the planning process for inclusion program development. This chapter's activity, combined with one or more activities from introductory chapters addressing specific disabilities or programs, could be used to establish the common understanding of needs and programs.

ACTIVITY 9.1—PRESCHOOL AND INCLUSION

Target Audience

Elementary school teachers, administrators

Purpose

To understand the difference between preschool and school-age inclusion programs and the value of preschool inclusion; to identify the early childhood education programs in the community that prepare children for school

Time

45 minutes

Materials

- Chapter 9
- Blank paper

Facilitator Preparation

The participants should read the chapter before this activity.

Instructions

Discuss the difference between preschool and school-age inclusion programs. Points to make include: (1) school attendance is mandatory for all school-age children, preschool attendance is not, and—as a result—there is no cohort of age-peers within the schools; and (2) the community's preschool programs that children often attend may not be readily accessible to public schools.

Facilitate a discussion by asking the large participant group: What are the benefits for the children, parents? What are the educational objectives for children involved in the programs that demonstrate cooperation and collaboration between early childhood special education and early childhood staff?

Continue this activity by asking each individual participant to use blank paper (distributed by facilitator) to write down the names of as many community preschool programs that provide inclusion opportunities for preschool children with disabilities. Allow participants five minutes.

Generate a list on easel paper of all the programs identified by participants. Reviewing this list, ask the participants to identify the programs that involve both early childhood and early childhood special education staff. As programs that involve both types of staff are identified, mark them with a check on the easel paper.

Conclude this activity by facilitating a discussion around the differences in these preschool programs. Discussion questions include the following: (1) For the programs that have a check (both types of staff), are the costs to families higher? (2) Does the school's program differ from those without collaboration between staff?

ACTIVITY 10.1—STRATEGIES FOR ELEMENTARY INCLUSION

Target Audience

Elementary school teachers, administrators, related service and support staff

Audience Size

15 to 20 persons

Purpose

To learn general principles and strategies for successful elementary inclusion programs

Time

60 minutes

Materials

- Chapter 10
- Student information contributed by participants
- Exhibit 10–2

Facilitator Preparation

Participants should read Chapter 10 prior to this activity. Participants should also bring one student record with them to this staff development activity. If actual or illustrative student records are used, ensure appropriate confidentiality. This activity includes presentations by one or more subject matter experts to discuss each area (consulting teacher model, team process). The presenters should review Chapter 10 before working with participants.

Instructions

In 25 minutes or less, subject matter experts explain the following points: (1) they explain the benefits of using a consulting teacher; (2) they explain that learning goals and skill development objectives for children with disabilities are compatible with the context of the general classroom environment; (3) they explain that the skills to be addressed are prioritized through team process; and (4) they identify resources and accommodations.

The facilitator should split the room into groups of three. Ask one participant in each group to share information about a specific student. Allow each group 20 minutes to discuss the student's history and current daily schedule. Complete Exhibit 10–2. Based on the presentation, the small group should answer the following questions: What process should be followed to assess the skills of this student? Who should be involved in assessment and instruction? What are some suggestions for accommodations or resources? Conclude by writing IEP objectives, marking the matrix with a check when there is a match between the objective and the daily activity. After 20 minutes, ask each small group to share with the experts the student history and their answers. The facilitator should moderate a discussion, based on the case study results and input from the subject matter experts.

Facilitator Note

More time may be needed for certain topics, especially if the school staff are not familiar and comfortable with consulting teacher, team process, and accommodations.

ACTIVITY 11.1—MIDDLE SCHOOL CHARACTERISTICS

Target Audience

Middle school teachers, administrators, related service and support staff

Audience Size

16 to 20 persons

Purpose

To understand how the characteristics of middle school complement successful inclusive education programs

Time

45 minutes

Materials

- Easel chart, stand, and markers
- Tape or push pins

Facilitator Preparation

Participants should read Chapter 11 before participating in this activity.

Instructions

Ask participants to list the characteristics of middle school. When identifying the characteristics of middle school, participants should consider the contrasts between middle, elementary, and high school. As participants identify characteristics of middle school, the facilitator should write them down on the easel paper and post as necessary. The facilitator should use the easel paper to track the answers. Answers from the chapter include: adolescent needs to consider in curriculum design, varied instructional strategies, counseling and advice offered to adolescents, positive school climate.

Once the large group has generated a list of characteristics, review each item by asking: Is this a characteristic of middle school, successful inclusion programs, or both? What is the relationship between this characteristic and inclusive education? Is this characteristic true of our school? How can this characteristic of our school be applied to all students?

Facilitate discussion, taking notes on easel paper as needed.

ACTIVITY 11.2—MIDDLE SCHOOL ADOLESCENCE

Prerequisite

Activity 11.1

Purpose

To compare and contrast the characteristics of adolescents that require special attention from middle school faculty with the characteristics of students in special education who need individualized attention

Time

60 minutes

Materials

- List of middle school characteristics generated in Activity 11.1
- Easel paper, stand, and markers
- Tape

Facilitator Preparation

Post the list of characteristics generated in Activity 11.1 as a reference.

Instructions

Split the large participant group into three or four small groups. Using the characteristics identified in Activity 11.1, ask each small group to answer the following question: (1) How is this characteristic of a middle school adolescent similar to the needs of an adolescent with a disability? Ask the group to give an example. Be sure each small group has a recorder and presenter designated. Allow 20 minutes.

After 20 minutes, have the small groups create a list of characteristics of adolescents. To stimulate discussion within each group, participants should answer questions such as the following: What are the similarities between the needs of an adolescent with a disability and those of a middle school adolescent? How do we address needs of middle school adolescents in our school? How can these approaches help us work with students with disabilities?

Facilitate sharing between the small groups.

ACTIVITY 12.1—INCLUSIVE PRACTICES IN SECONDARY SCHOOL

Target Audience

Secondary school teachers, administrators, related service staff, and others

Audience Size

15 to 28 persons

Purpose

To understand inclusive practices in high school programs; to apply these practices to case examples

Time

90 minutes

Materials

- Exhibit 19–5
- Exhibit 19–6

Facilitator Preparation

Copy the exhibits.

Instructions

Split the large participant group into four small groups (3 to 7 people). Distribute Exhibit 19–5, one to each group. Instruct the small groups to read a case study and answer the following questions: How would you work with this student? What approach would you use? What concerns would you have? Allow each group 30 minutes.

After 30 minutes, ask each group to review their case briefly and share the tools or techniques they would use to work with the student. After all groups have shared their ideas, distribute Exhibit 19–6, which summarizes the tools used for these students as described in Chapter 12.

Encourage each group to compare and contrast this list with their ideas for working with the student. Facilitate a discussion using questions such as: What tools or techniques did you describe that are similar to the ones listed on this handout? What tool(s) listed on the handout would you not be able to use? Why?

Exhibit 19–5 Case Studies of Secondary Students

TODD

Todd is a 15-year-old student at a large urban high school. He has been identified as a student with exceptional needs and has received special education services of various types for the past six years. He is in a general education English class and receives academic support from the resource teacher, the speech-language pathologist, and four peer tutors in his class. Psychological and academic testing revealed that Todd has a Wechsler full-scale IQ score of 81 and a 15-point spread between his verbal and performance scores, with performance much higher. He was on medication for attention deficit hyperactivity disorder (ADHD) for four years but has been taken off it this year with no ill effects.

Todd has learning disabilities in the areas of reading, oral and written language, and organizational skills. He has a short attention span (about 8 to 10 minutes), and great difficulty composing his thoughts on paper. His conversational vocabulary is limited, and he writes short, stilted sentences. His writing is slow and labored, with many erasures, crossouts, and restarts. His knowledge and use of punctuation, capitalization, and other mechanics of writing are sporadic. He usually loses interest before he gets to proofreading or editing his work. Todd reads at the fourth-grade level and occasionally reads for pleasure, especially high-interest books like adventure stories or science fiction.

Todd is very good in math and can do grade-level work. He can grasp the operations and the relationships between numbers quickly. However, he rarely turns in work because he fails to write down the assignment, does it and loses it, or simply forgets to finish the work. He needs to have word or story problems read to him.

Todd has many friends, is athletic, and is very social. He is led easily by others, and takes risks that others only talk about doing. He often shows poor judgment, can get angry quickly, and blurts out his feelings when he is frustrated or feels he has been made to look foolish. Todd is becoming more sensitive about what he can and cannot do in his English class; he is aware that most, but not all, students turn in more written work than he does. He works best with a group of four students who are both friends and tutors.

LISA

Lisa was given the label of autism when she was three years old. She is now a junior in high school, taking honors English and math classes, and riding the city bus to school every day. She has no speech; screams when she is upset or excited; bites her arms and hands and, on occasion, those of her mother and peer tutors. She takes a full load of classes: economics, honors English, math, chemistry, physical education, health, and family living. Lisa writes opinion pieces and poetry often and has had two letters to the editor published with her picture in the *Los Angeles Times*. She uses facilitated communication with the assistance of seven peer tutors during the school day.

She began school at the age of four and was in self-contained special education classes until middle school. She showed no signs of reading or understanding print until the eighth grade, when facilitated communication was used. She was taught the hand-over-hand method of pointing to letters on a board to spell her name and the names of items in class. She "learned" to spell every word the first time it was spelled for her, and soon it was evident that she had been reading for a long time. She wanted to "write" using the new method every day. Now she needs a peer tutor only to hold her clothing at her shoulder or hold a hand above or near her right shoulder.

Lisa struggles with her behavior daily. She writes in her computer journal that sometimes the autism seems to win the day, and sometimes she does. She often writes out apologies to her teachers or classmates for what she calls "obnoxious" or "atrocious" behavior. This usually includes screaming, pounding the table, growling in class, or pulling back from the door of the classroom repeatedly. Students in her classes are aware of her behaviors, interact with her when she allows it, and often receive notes from her when she cannot make contact with them any other way. She works on homework five to six hours a night and has few other interests.

A MAPs—making action plans—strategy session was completed when Lisa was 16 to decide on college attendance. Twenty-two people who knew Lisa personally and professionally participated. She wanted to live near home after high school and to attend college. She said that she was afraid to go to college because she was so short and people would laugh at her. She has taken a college preparatory track in high school. She plans to take the PSAT and has written a letter to see if she can take the SAT with extended time and a facilitator.

CHRISTOPHER

Christopher, a tenth grader, experiences cerebral palsy, moderate learning disabilities, and periodic hospitalizations for heart problems and asthma. He is considered in fragile medical health. Much of his learning struggles can be traced to his erratic attendance at school, his limited fine motor coordination, and his medications for asthma and heart dysrhythmia. He likes school, but also likes to stay home, where much less is demanded of him.

He was in a special education class for all of elementary and middle school. He made minimal progress, but gradually improved as he got older and began to experience more positive interactions at school with peers than he did staying home. He has had only three teachers in his previous schools, often staying in the same room for many years.

He learned to use a computer word processing program as his writing was impossible to read, and it fatigued him greatly. He can read and write at the fifth-grade level, likes to read for leisure, and loves books on sports or military topics. Chris would take physical education classes all day if he had his way. Instead, he is the boys' sports equipment manager for two sports,

continues

Exhibit 19–5 continued

requiring that he take gym for two classes to assist the coach and inventory the equipment. He has learned to use the computer inventory program and the game scheduler.

He had repeated the first math class he took in high school in order to improve his grade and takes a math study hall in the special education support room the hour before and the hour after general math. He is taking an English novel class this year and helps with the school newspaper as part of his English assignment. Chris has great gaps in his knowledge base for science and social studies, and is an observer in the Science of Biology class this year, in preparation for taking it next year.

His attendance is good and he tries most of the work at school. He turns in very little work, however, and there is almost no follow-through at home. Chris can continue in high school until age 22 and is likely to do so, according to his parents. Arranging his schedule each year is a challenge for his IEP team as he is not an active participant in the decision-making process yet and prefers that classes and teachers do not change from semester to semester, especially his sports equipment manager jobs.

JANICE

Janice is a 14-year-old student with Down syndrome, some visual problems, and a keen interest in music. She entered high school with her classmates from a local "feeder" junior high school at the end of eighth grade. She wants to pursue her interests in music, make money with an after-school job at a day care center, and eventually live in an apartment on her own in this same large city she lives in now with her parents. She is the fifth child in the family.

Janice's achievement scores are more indicative of her skill level than her IQ testing. She reads at the third-grade level and can write simple sentences. Her oral language is much more advanced, so her dictated work is at a seventh or eighth-grade level. She can engage in a conversation about American presidents, the Civil War, and the Industrial Revolution, as these topics were covered in recent history courses. She reads fiction books at the fourth-grade level with some help and loves books on tapes.

Janice takes three music classes, typing and keyboarding on the computer, U.S. history, physical education, introduction to human development, study hall, and Spanish. Her schedule changes each semester, with a goal of completing high school in four or five years with a certificate of completion and several new job-related skills. Janice is a part of her IEP team each year and often stops in to see the guidance counselor assigned to her.

Janice has one older brother in high school and three friends she has known for many years. They help her during the day and may eat lunch with her, or include her in after-school social activities. She needs assistance in U.S. history from her cooperative learning group and turns in adjusted assignments determined by the counselor and her teacher. She can do all typing assignments on her own and keeps a portfolio of her speed drills, typing forms, and written work. She uses a word processing program available at school.

Janice has a poor sense of time and expects others to keep track of appointments and responsibilities for her. She doesn't write down assignments, can't recall that she has a report due, and walks very slowly to class, often arriving late, smiling and waving at her classmates when she enters the class. This behavior is no longer accepted and Janice receives after-school detentions when she is tardy and her work is late.

Exhibit 19–6 Summary of Secondary School Inclusive Practices

TODD

- Moves from less favored classes to personally selected ones every 47 minutes.
- IEP includes literacy goals and objectives.
- Uses percentage grading systems in all classes.
- Works well with a friendship group.

JANICE

- Uses after-school detention as consequence for being late to class.
- IEP includes literacy goals and objectives.
- Benefits from episodic learning experiences in the classroom.
- Uses percentage grading systems.
- Works well with all groups and needs the group to help her complete the assignment using group-grading techniques.

CHRISTOPHER

- Uses three-choice support scheduling.
- IEP includes literacy goals and objectives.
- Benefits from episodic learning experiences in the classroom.
- Uses software programs in school.

LISA

- IEP includes literacy goals and objectives.
- Uses technology in the classroom and to complete her homework.
- Uses a contract for grade in some classes.
- Works well in random groups if she is told exactly what her role is.

ACTIVITY 13.1—VOCATIONAL EDUCATION

Target Audience

Middle and secondary school teachers, administrators, related service staff, parents

Audience Size

15 to 40 persons

Purpose

To understand the perspectives of vocational education, vocational evaluation, special education, and employment counseling in offering inclusive vocational education opportunities

Time

90 minutes

Materials

- Panel of presenters

Facilitator Preparation

This activity uses a panel. The panel should include a vocational educator and a secondary special educator. In addition, it would be useful to include a vocational evaluator and an employment or rehabilitation counselor. Each panel member should read Chapter 13 prior to the activity. The vocational education panel member should emphasize vocational competencies, safety issues, and program options. The special education panel member should emphasize adapting curriculum, team teaching, and the consultative model. The vocational evaluator should emphasize the purpose of a complete evaluation and of working together as a team to evaluate and plan for vocational options. The employment/rehabilitation counselor should emphasize the local job market, work skills, and behavior being sought in the community.

In addition, the facilitator should ask participants to bring at least one question about a student they have known to this staff-development program. The questions should relate to vocational evaluation and education for the student.

Instructions

Introduce panel members and topic to the audience. Throughout the presentations, the facilitator should serve as moderator for questions.

Conclude the panel by asking questions such as: What have you found to be the biggest challenge to moving a child with special needs into a vocational education pro-gram? How have you worked to overcome this challenge? What can this panel suggest as alternatives?

ACTIVITY 14.1—TRANSITION PLANNING WITH AN INCLUSIVE PHILOSOPHY

Target Audience

Middle school and secondary school teachers and administrators, support staff, related service staff

Size

10 to 20 persons

Purpose

To understand the issues of transition planning; to apply this understanding to case examples

Time

75 minutes

Materials

- Chapter 14

Facilitator Preparation

Participants should read Chapter 14 before activity.

Instructions

Refer participants to Chapter 14. Facilitate a discussion of the chapter content by asking questions like: What did you find to be the most important point of the chapter? What part of the transition process do you find the most challenging? The most rewarding?

Split the large group into three smaller groups. Assign each group either placement, secondary education, or adult living options case examples (from Chapter 14). (There are two case examples for each of the three option types. With a larger group, split the three groups in half and assign one group placement options for Jamie and the other group placement options for Jeffrey. Repeat with secondary education and adult living options.)

Ask each group to identify the following: (1) Who are the educators and specialists working with the student? (2) How are their activities coordinated? Are their goals congruent? (3) How can assessment and exploration be used to determine this student's options? (4) What else might be considered for this student to enable his or her successful transition past school? Allow each group 20 minutes to answer the four questions.

After 20 minutes, reconvene the group. Have each small group share the case example and their answers to the four questions. Discuss as a large group.

Conclude the case example review by asking the large group: (1) How can the process of case examination be replicated for students in school? (2) What other information would teachers need to start the assessment process for students?

ACTIVITY 14.2—SETTING MEASURABLE TRANSITION GOALS

Target Audience

Middle school and secondary school teachers, related service staff

Size

10 to 20 persons

Purpose

To understand how to set measurable goals and identify the responsible agency/person

Time

60 minutes

Materials

- Case studies from Chapter 14, or participants can use current student records

Facilitator Preparation

If actual or illustrative student records are used, ensure that appropriate confidentiality issues are addressed.

Instructions

Have participants work in pairs. Using either the case studies from Chapter 14 or actual student records, have the pairs do the following: (1) read the case study/student records; (2) identify the transition issue(s); (3) select two of the transition issues and write goals and objectives that address each one. For each goal and objective, the person/agency responsible, desired outcome, time frame, and outcome measure should be identified. Allow the small group 20 to 30 minutes to complete this assignment.

Once the groups are done, ask for a group to volunteer to share their goals/objectives with the large group. Using

the information presented in Chapter 14, examine the goal, objective, desired outcome, measurement used to identify when the goal is met, and responsible person/agency. Continue this process with all groups on a voluntary basis.

Stimulate discussion by asking questions such as the following: How is transition planning similar/different from the IEP process? How are the goals/objectives/measurable outcomes similar/different from the statements found on an IEP? Who else (agency or community representatives or other school staff) should be involved in setting these goals/objectives?

ACTIVITY 15.1—BEHAVIORAL SUPPORTS

Target Audience

Teachers, administrators, related service and support staff

Audience Size

10 to 25 persons

Purpose

To identify the source of behavioral problems

Time

45 minutes

Materials

- Blank easel paper (large)
- Markers
- Tape
- Blank copy paper
- Preprinted easel paper

Facilitator Preparation

Create a preprinted easel page that says: (1) schoolwide system, (2) classroom setting, (3) individual student system, (4) specific-setting systems. Participants should read Chapter 15 before this activity.

Instructions

Ask the participants to give examples of behavior problems they have experienced. The facilitator should write the examples on the easel paper, posting as necessary. Once at least 10 behavior problems are posted, split the room into three groups.

Referring to the easel chart listing the four systems of behavioral support, ask the small groups to identify which of the four is the source of the problem (e.g., is the behavior problem schoolwide? classroom? individual? or setting-specific?). Allow the groups 15 minutes to complete this activity.

After 15 minutes, reconvene the participants. Taking each behavioral example one at a time, ask the groups to identify the source. When group answers differ, encourage the groups to explain their choices. Use these differences to discuss the varying degrees of importance that can be placed on each of the settings.

ACTIVITY 15.2—ADDRESSING PROBLEM BEHAVIOR

Target Audience

All school personnel

Audience Size

Unlimited

Purpose

To understand options on working with a behavior problem

Time

60 minutes

Materials

- Panel members
- Copies of the school code of conduct

Facilitator Preparation

Select panel members who are knowledgeable about the school's code of conduct. Panel members should represent both special education and general education.

Instructions

Introduce topic and panel. Briefly review the school code of conduct. Ask participants to describe a behavioral problem they are having that they want to understand how to handle better. Participants do not need to identify individual students, teachers, or administrators. The facilitator should note these behavioral problems on easel paper.

After participants have shared behavioral problems, the panel members should select one problem to role play. The panel members will play the role of a review team assessing the behavior problem by determining: (1) how the school code of conduct addresses the behavior; (2) if the behavior is a violation of the code, how the IEP should address the behavior; and (3) what changes could be made in the edu-

cational program or services that would address the behavior. After the role play, the facilitator moderates a question-and-answer period.

This is repeated for several role plays, choosing behavior problems that are listed on the easel page.

ACTIVITY 16.1—DEVELOPING HEALTH SERVICES TRAINING

Target Audience

All personnel who have contact with students with special health needs

Audience Size

Unlimited (single school)

Purpose

To discuss concerns about working with students who have medical involvement; to turn the concerns into a list of specific training needs

Time

45 minutes

Materials

- Easel pad, stand, and markers
- Tape

Facilitator Preparation

Cofacilitate this activity with a school nurse. Participants should read Chapter 16 prior to this activity. Ask participants to bring an example of a health problem they have encountered.

Instructions

Facilitate a large-group, open discussion of the concerns participants might have about meeting the needs of children with medical involvement. Use the examples of health problems that participants have encountered to generate this list. Write the concerns on easel paper and post as the list grows. Allow about 30 minutes for large-group discussion/brainstorming.

Start with the first item on the list and ask the participants: What strategy could be used to address this health concern? What training could be provided that would make this concern become a strength of our school? Who should receive training? Assign a recorder to take notes. Ask these questions for every item on the list.

After reviewing all concerns, have the note taker briefly review the concerns and training plan.

ACTIVITY 17.1—WORKING WITH STUDENTS WHO ARE DEAF AND HARD-OF-HEARING

Target Audience

Teachers, administrators, related service and support personnel

Audience Size

10 to 20 persons

Purpose

- To understand the factors behind traditional placement options for deaf students
- To understand the issues around inclusive programs for students who are deaf or hard-of-hearing (e.g., from medical versus cultural perspectives, need for individual assessment
- To apply this understanding to identified concerns

Time

60 minutes

Materials

- Figure 17–1
- Exhibit 17–4
- Content expert (e.g., teacher of the deaf, educational audiologist, speech-language pathologist)
- Participants' concerns

Facilitator Preparation

Schedule content experts. Have participants write on index cards their concerns when working with students who are deaf and hard-of-hearing.

Instructions

Distribute Figure 17–1. Emphasize the following points: (1) educating students who are deaf and hard-of-hearing in inclusion programs has unique controversies (e.g., medical versus cultural perspective); (2) the determination of least restrictive environment for students who are deaf and hard-of-hearing includes different issues than for students with other disabilities, based on family and community culture (e.g., residential deaf school is the preferred placement for many members of the Deaf community); and (3) the unique supports and services required by students who are deaf and hard-of-hearing (e.g., educational interpreters with knowledge of class vocabulary and skills in the student's signing system; functioning hearing aid, auditory trainer, or cochlear implant; note taker).

Distribute Exhibit 17–4. Emphasize the following points: (1) a student's cognitive, communication, and social profile are part of the individual needs assessment that must be assessed when determining placement; and (2) this type of assessment includes more than the traditional placement options based on the severity of the hearing loss.

Using the index cards listing participants' concerns about working with students who are deaf or hard-of-hearing, facilitate a discussion between participants and content experts. When discussing placement options, ask questions about the support available to the student, general education teacher, administrator, and parents.

ACTIVITY 17.2—WORKING WITH INTERPRETERS AND HEARING DEVICES

Target Audience

Teachers, related service staff, instructional assistants, and administrators who work directly with a deaf or hard-of-hearing student who uses an educational interpreter, hearing aids, or an auditory trainer or who has a cochlear implant

Audience Size

10 to 15 persons

Purpose

To understand how to work with educational interpreters, hearing aids, and cochlear implants (if applicable)

Time

60 minutes

Materials

- Panel of presenters

Facilitator Preparation

Select up to three panel members—an educational interpreter working in this school division, a supervisor of programs for students who are hearing impaired, and an educational audiologist.

Instructions

Introduce topic and panel members. Allow the panel members approximately 45 minutes (15 minutes each).

After the presentation, serve as moderator for questions. Follow the question-and-answer session with a demonstration. For example, the panel members can role play an interpreting situation (e.g., audiologist is the science teacher teaching acoustics, the supervisor is the hearing-impaired student, the educational interpreter interprets). Once the demonstration is over, ask the panel members to discuss important points and problems (noise, lighting, vocabulary, educational instructor's knowledge of the topic).

ACTIVITY 18.1—WORKING WITH STUDENTS WITH READING DISABILITIES

Target Audience

All teachers in a single school building

Size

12 to 18 persons

Purpose

To understand the characteristics of effective reading programs; to determine how instructional accommodations support effective reading programs

Time

90 minutes

Materials

- Chapter 18
- Copies of Exhibit 19–7

Facilitator Preparation

Copy Exhibit 19–7. Ask participants to read Chapter 18 before this activity. Participants should bring the chapter with them to this activity.

Exhibit 19–7 Characteristics of Effective Reading Programs

- coordinates instruction in the general education classroom with pull-out services
- provides additional time for quality instruction
- provides individual or very-small group instruction
- focuses on prevention and early intervention
- uses simple texts for early intervention
- uses repeated reading to build fluency
- provides instruction in phonemic awareness, phonics, and word patterns
- requires daily writing activities
- provides ongoing assessment of student progress
- emphasizes communication between home and school
- uses professionally prepared, accomplished teachers

Instructions

Distribute and review Exhibit 19–7.

Split the large group into three small groups. Assign each small group one of the following assignments:

- *Group 1:* Discuss placement versus program options for students with dyslexia and learning disabilities. Discuss the following question: Why is it more important to look for match between the reading program and the reading deficit?
- *Group 2:* Discuss an effective reading program. Discuss the following question: What are the characteristics of effective reading programs? Remind this group that Chapter 18 contains information relevant to this discussion.
- *Group 3:* Let each teacher offer a reading approach or accommodation to a reading method that they have used successfully (brag time). Each group member should contribute one item. For each area of strength, the teachers should discuss how they can support one another in learning a new skill.

After 20 minutes, reconvene the three groups. Ask each group to share the highlights of their discussion.

REFERENCE

Kemp, J.E., Morrison, G.R., Ross, S.M. (1994). *Designing effective instructions.* New York: Macmillan College.

RESOURCES

Farrah, S.J. (1990). Lecture. In M.W. Galbraith (Ed.), *Adult learning methods: A guide for effective instruction.* Malabar, FL: Robert E. Krieger.

Sheal, P.R. (1994). *How to develop and present staff training courses.* (2nd ed.) London: Kagan Page.

APPENDIX A

Policy and Position Statements

309

American Federation of Teachers Resolution on Inclusion of Students with Disabilities (1994)

AFT Resolution on the policy known variously as inclusion, full integration of students with disabilities, the regular education initiative, unified system, or inclusive education.

Whereas there is no legal mandate or consistent definition for "inclusion," let it be known that for AFT policy we define inclusion as the placement of all students with disabilities in general education classrooms without regard to the nature or severity of the students' disabilities, their ability to behave and function appropriately in the classroom, or the educational benefits they can derive;

Whereas the mission of the public schools and of the AFT is to provide high standards, rich and challenging classroom experiences, and maximum achievement for ALL students, including students with disabilities as well as nondisabled students in general education classes;

Whereas public schools, particularly in urban areas, already are facing severe burdens because of the inequities in funding that plague them, overcrowding, the persistent social problems that surround them, and demands that they resolve the immense problems that students bring to school, severely reducing the schools' ability to provide a high-quality educational program for any student;

Whereas two years before the 20th anniversary of the passage of the Education for All Handicapped Children Act (P.L. 94-142), Congress' continuing cynicism in funding the mandates of the law at under 10% of costs instead of the 40% promised has compromised schools' ability to provide appropriate services to students with disabilities, and has placed even greater strains on education generally by requiring that higher and higher percentages of funding go to special education;

Whereas inclusion is being championed as the only placement for all students with disabilities by a movement of some advocacy groups—in the face of opposition from the parents of many students with disabilities and many respected advocates for the disabled—when there is no clear evidence that inclusion is appropriate or provides an educational benefit for all students with disabilities, and no clear evidence of its benefit for the other students;

Whereas there are deep concerns about the high percentage of minority children in some classes for students with disabilities and inclusion is viewed by some advocates and parents as the only means of getting minority children out of those classes;

Whereas inclusion is being adopted by a large number of local school boards, state departments of education, legislators, and other policy makers all over the country as a means to save money by placing all students with disabilities in general education classrooms and curtailing special education supports and services;

Whereas inclusion is being adopted in contradiction to the mandates of P.L. 94-142 and the Individuals with Disabilities Education Act (IDEA, the revision of P.L. 94-142) that require students to be evaluated and, based on individual needs, assigned to the "least restrictive environment" (LRE) that exists within a continuum, or range, of placements;

Whereas even when students with disabilities are appropriately placed, general and special education staff who work with them are not receiving the training they need that they are entitled to by law;

Whereas the federal law and court decisions forbid school districts from removing disruptive students with disabilities from programs for more than 10 days a year, and require that, in the absence of school district and parental consent to an interim placement or a court order, such stu-

Courtesy of the American Federation of Teachers, Washington, D.C.

dents "stay put" in the class while their placement is being evaluated and adjudicated;

Whereas the existing federal legislation limits the ability of teachers to challenge legally inappropriate placements of students with disabilities in general education classrooms;

Whereas insufficient medical personnel are employed by school districts to care for medically fragile children under existing circumstances, and inclusion would place these students in medical danger and increase the responsibilities of teachers and paraprofessionals;

Whereas inclusion threatens to overwhelm schools and systems that are already extremely vulnerable—particularly in areas with great poverty and social needs—by placing additional responsibilities on teachers, paraprofessionals, and support professionals, thus threatening the ability of schools to meet the educational needs of all students;

Whereas students with disabilities have frequently been placed in programs that failed to serve their needs to meet high educational standards, fueling the desire of their parents to have their children in general education classrooms even when such placements are not appropriate;

Resolved that the AFT continue to seek high, national achievement standards for education, applicable to ALL students, disabled and nondisabled alike;

Resolved that the AFT oppose inclusion—that is, any movement or program that has the goal of placing all students with disabilities in general education classrooms regardless of the nature or severity of their disabilities, their ability to behave or function appropriately in the classroom, or the educational benefits they and their general education peers can derive;

Resolved that the AFT denounce the appalling administrative practices that have accompanied the inclusion movement. These include, but are not limited to, placing too many students with disabilities in individual general classrooms; placing students with disabilities in general education classrooms without services, professional development, or paraprofessional assistance; refusing to assist teachers who are having problems meeting the unique needs of students with disabilities; and changing individual educational programs (IEPs) en masse so that students with disabilities may be placed in general education classrooms without supports and services and irrespective of the appropriateness of the placement;

Resolved that the AFT seek alliances with organizations that support the continuum of alternative placements and the educational placement of students with disabilities within the least restrictive environment appropriate to the individual needs of the students;

Resolved that the AFT seek with its allies to reopen P.L. 94-142 and IDEA, convincing Congress both to recognize in the law the high costs and complex problems of special education, and to respond by providing:

1. full funding for all of its mandates
2. a 5-year reauthorization of the laws for educating students with disabilities—just as every other education act requires—to realize the benefits of new hearings and discussions of problems that arise
3. the legal right for teachers to attend the IEP meetings of children they teach; the right to appeal inappropriate placements; and the right to be fully represented during due process hearings without reprisal (i.e., intimidation, coercion, or retaliation for being a child advocate); and the right to be involved in the assessment of delivery of services, staff training, and availability of resources to ensure the effectiveness of the program as intended by Congress
4. the reauthorization and enforcement of the continuum of placements, which includes mainstreaming as an existing alternative strategy within the range of services for students with disabilities
5. that criteria for placement in general education require the proximate ability of students to function appropriately both academically and behaviorally when supplementary aids and services are provided by the district
6. support for districts in maintaining consistent discipline policies for ALL students who disrupt classrooms or engage in dangerous behavior
7. reauthorization of and insistence on comprehensive professional development
8. negation of court decisions concerning students with disabilities that are detrimental to educational programs—such as the "stay put" provision, limitations on the discipline of students with disabilities, and decisions that favor inclusion
9. for limitations on the number of students with disabilities in self-contained and general classrooms

Resolved that the AFT seek with its allies to address the problem of the high percentages of minority students in special education; and

Resolved that the AFT renew our long-standing commitment to meeting the needs of ALL students for high standards, rich and challenging classroom experiences, and maximum achievement, whatever their educational placements might be.

American Speech-Language-Hearing Association Inclusive Practices for Children and Youths with Communication Disorders (1996)

It is the position of the American Speech-Language-Hearing Association (ASHA) that an array of speech, language, and hearing services should be available in educational settings to support children and youths with communication disorders. The term *inclusive practices* best represents this philosophy. The *inclusive-practices* philosophy emphasizes serving children and youths in the least restrictive environment that meets their needs optimally. Inclusive practices consist of a range of service-delivery options that need not be mutually exclusive. They can include direct, classroom-based, community-based, and consultative intervention programming. Inclusive practices are based on a commitment to selecting and designing interventions that meet the needs of each child and family. Factors contributing to the determination of individual need include the child's age, type of disability, communication competence, language and cultural background, academic performance, social skills, family and teacher concerns, and the student's own attitudes about speech, language, and hearing services.

ASHA recognizes that the provision of speech, language, and hearing services in educational settings is moving toward service-delivery models that integrate intervention with general educational programs, often termed inclusion. Inclusion has numerous strengths, including natural opportunities for peer interaction, and available research suggests cautious optimism regarding its effectiveness in promoting communication abilities and skills in related developmental domains. ASHA believes that the shift toward inclusion will not be optimal when implemented in absolute terms. Rather, the unique and specific needs of each child and family must always be considered.

The broad goal of inclusive service delivery should be compatible with continued recognition of the individual's unique needs and concerns. Inclusive practices are recommended as a guide in the development of intervention programming for children and youths with communication disorders.

Source: Reprinted with permission from Inclusive Practices for Children and Youths with Communication Disorders: Position Statement and Technical Report, *Asha,* Vol. 38, Suppl. 16, © 1996, American Speech-Language-Hearing Association.

Children and Adults with Attention Deficit Disorders Position on Inclusion (1993)

CHADD believes that every child in America is entitled to a free and appropriate public education. The needs of many children are adequately met through regular education and placement in the regular classroom. There are times, however, when regular education staff is not sufficient to ensure that all children succeed in school. Access to a continuum of special education placements and services is especially important for many children with disabilities. This ensures their right to receive a free and appropriate public education designed to meet their unique needs and which facilitates their achievement in school.

There was a time in America when a free and appropriate public education was not guaranteed by law. Indeed, it was not all that long ago that children with undetected disabilities languished unnoticed in classrooms, and parents of children with identified disabilities were frequently told that their children could not be educated in the public schools because no special education services were available. That all changed with the passage in 1975 of Public Law 94-142, which CHADD considers to be a benchmark in meeting the educational needs of all children.

Since renamed the Individuals with Disabilities Education Act (IDEA), this landmark legislation, among other things, mandates:

- a free and appropriate public education in the least restrictive environment designed to meet the unique needs of children with disabilities
- the right to a comprehensive, multidisciplinary assessment
- a team approved individualized education program (IEP) that includes current functioning levels, instructional goals and objectives, placement and services decisions, and procedures for evaluation of program effectiveness
- the availability of a continuum of special education services and placements appropriate to the child's specific learning needs
- procedural safeguards to ensure that the rights of children with disabilities and their parents are protected

The principles embodied in the IDEA are as valid today as they were when P.L. 94-142 was passed 18 years ago. The problems facing the education of children with disabilities in public schools are not the result of the act, but rather its incomplete implementation. While it may be true that there are some children who are being excluded from the regular education classroom without sufficient reason, it is equally true that many children with attention deficit disorders (ADD) and other disabilities continue to be denied access to an appropriate range of special education and related services and settings.

We believe that the concept of inclusion should reflect society's commitment that every child be educated in the environment that is most appropriate to that child's identified needs. CHADD supports inclusion defined as education that provides access to appropriate support and remediation at every level to facilitate each child's ability to participate and achieve. The environment in which these services can best be delivered depends on the needs of the individual student.

Many children with disabilities are educated successfully in regular classrooms with appropriate accommodations and supports. However, others require alternative environments to optimize their achievement. CHADD supports this continuum of services and placements. As state and federal governments proceed with the reform of public

Courtesy of Children and Adults with Attention Deficit Disorders, Plantation, Florida.

education, they must ensure that schools continue to be required to accommodate to the individual needs of children with disabilities by providing a variety of options in support of the right of each child to a free and appropriate education.

Children with attention deficit disorders, like children with other disabilities, can exhibit a range of impairment, thus requiring a continuum of educational services. For some children with attention deficit disorder, screening and prereferral adaptation in the classroom may be all that is needed. For others, it will be necessary to refer for a more comprehensive assessment that could lead to a formalized IEP process. Children with attention deficit disorders have diverse needs and will require enhanced teacher preparation in identification, as well as the planning and implementation of a variety of intervention and instructional strategies.

As Congress debates education reform, let it not lose sight of the integrity of the principles embodied in IDEA. Specifically, we recommend:

- a continued recognition of the importance of the availability of a continuum of special education services and placement settings designed to meet the individual needs of each child with a disability

- increased monitoring of the mandated practices and procedural protections contained within the IDEA to ensure better compliance with the law
- maintenance of the integrity of funding streams for special education to ensure that we do not return to the days when a public school could tell a parent of a child with a disability that the school cannot "afford" to provide special education and related services
- a renewed commitment to preservice and inservice teacher training and staff development so that all educators can completely recognize the educational needs of all students and, when necessary, make appropriate accommodations and referrals for comprehensive assessments
- stronger collaboration between regular and special education teachers

Adherence to the principles embodied in IDEA will ensure that all children are included in the federal mandate for a free and appropriate public education. We welcome the opportunity to continue to be part of the education reform movement.

Council for Exceptional Children Policy Regarding Inclusive Schools and Community Settings

The Council for Exceptional Children (CEC) believes all children, youths, and young adults with disabilities are entitled to a free and appropriate education and/or services that lead to an adult life characterized by satisfying relations with others, independent living, productive engagement in the community, and participation in society at large. To achieve such outcomes, there must exist for all children, youths, and young adults a rich variety of early intervention, educational, and vocational program options and experiences. Access to these programs and experiences should be based on individual educational need and desired outcomes. Furthermore, students and their families or guardians, as members of the planning team, may recommend the placement, curriculum option, and the exit document to be pursued.

CEC believes that a continuum of services must be available for all children, youths, and young adults. CEC also believes that the concept of inclusion is a meaningful goal to be pursued in our schools and communities. In addition, CEC believes children, youths, and young adults with disabilities should be served whenever possible in general education classrooms in inclusive neighborhood schools and community settings. Such settings should be strengthened and supported by an infusion of specially trained personnel and other appropriate supportive practices according to the individual needs of the child.

POLICY IMPLICATIONS

Schools

In inclusive schools, the building administrator and staff with assistance from the special education administration should be primarily responsible for the education of children, youths, and young adults with disabilities. The administrator(s) and other school personnel must have available to them appropriate support and technical assistance to enable them to fulfill their responsibilities. Leaders in state/provincial and local governments must redefine rules and regulations as necessary, and grant school personnel greater authority to make decisions regarding curriculum, materials, instructional practice, and staffing patterns. In return for greater autonomy, the school administrator and staff should establish high standards for each child, youth, and young adult, and should be held accountable for his or her progress toward outcomes.

Communities

Inclusive schools must be located in inclusive communities; therefore, CEC invites all educators, other professionals, and family members to work together to create early intervention, educational, and vocational programs and experiences that are collegial, inclusive, and responsive to the diversity of children, youths, and young adults. Policy makers at the highest levels of state/provincial and local government, as well as school administration, also must support inclusion in the educational reforms they espouse. Further, the policy makers should fund programs in nutrition, early intervention, health care, parent education, and other social support programs that prepare all children, youths, and young adults to do well in school. There can be no meaningful school reform, nor inclusive schools, without funding of these key prerequisites. As important, there must be interagency agreements and collaboration with local governments and business to help prepare students to assume a constructive role in an inclusive community.

Courtesy of the Council for Exceptional Children, Reston, Virginia.

Professional Development

And finally, state/provincial departments of education, local educational districts, and colleges and universities must provide high-quality preservice and continuing professional development experiences that prepare all general educators to work effectively with children, youths, and young adults representing a wide range of abilities and disabilities, experiences, cultural and linguistic backgrounds, attitudes, and expectations. Moreover, special educators should be trained with an emphasis on their roles in inclusive schools and community settings. They also must learn the importance of establishing ambitious goals for their students and of using appropriate means of monitoring the progress of children, youths, and young adults.

Division for Early Childhood of the Council for Exceptional Children Position on Inclusion (1993)

Inclusion, as a value, supports the right of all children, regardless of their diverse abilities, to participate actively in natural settings within their communities. A natural setting is one in which the child would spend time had he or she not had a disability. Such settings include but are not limited to home and family, play groups, child care, nursery schools, Head Start programs, kindergartens, and neighborhood school classrooms.

DEC believes in and supports full and successful access to health, social service, education, and other supports and services for young children and their families that promote full participation in community life. DEC values the diversity of families and supports a family-guided process for determining services that are based on the needs and preferences of individual families and children.

To implement inclusive practices DEC supports: (a) the continued development, evaluation, and dissemination of full inclusion supports, services, and systems so that options for inclusion are of high quality; (b) the development of preservice and inservice training programs that prepare families, administrators, and service providers to develop and work within inclusive settings; (c) collaboration among all key stakeholders to implement flexible fiscal and administrative procedures in support of inclusion; (d) research that contributes to our knowledge of state-of-the-art services; and (e) the restructuring and unification of social, education, health, and intervention supports and services to make them more responsive to the needs of all children and families.

Courtesy of the Division for Early Childhood, Pittsburgh, Pennsylvania.

Division for Learning Disabilities of the Council for Exceptional Children Position on Inclusion: What Does It Mean for Students with Learning Disabilities? (1995)

WHAT IS THE LAW

- Free, appropriate public education is required by law for students with specific learning disabilities.
  - IDEA, The Individuals with Disabilities Education Act
  - 504, Section 504 of the Vocational Rehabilitation Act
- Availability of a continuum of placement options is required by law.
  - *Special classes* provide intensive, highly individualized instruction.
  - *Resource help* provides specific skill instruction daily or several times each week focused on individual needs.
  - *Consultation* and/or in-class support provides assistance to general education teachers who have students with learning disabilities (LD).
  - *Accommodations* and modifications in the general classroom provide the minor support needed for individuals to meet group expectations.
- *Mainstreaming and inclusion are not in federal statutes or regulations.*
- Placement in a least restrictive environment (LRE) is required by law.
- The LRE for a particular student with LD is the combination of settings in which (1) interactions with students without disabilities and with the curriculum and instruction they receive is maximized, and (2) opportunities are made available for specific, intensive educational service to meet the unique needs of that child. For example:
  - Without using a word processor in his fourth-grade class, Leon's ability to express his good ideas would be restricted by his inefficient and poorly formed handwriting; the LRE for Leon may be the general education class with accommodations.
  - Without intensive daily help Maria's severe reading and writing disabilities will restrict her academic success; the LRE for Maria may be the general education classroom with curricular modifications, and with one or more hours daily in the special education classroom.

MODEL POLICIES

- An individualized educational plan [sic] (IEP) should ensure parent and/or student participation in establishing placement, related services, and student goals.
- A student's needs, not a district, school, or personal philosophy, should determine that student's placement.
- Options across the continuum should be available to meet the needs of individuals with disabilities. For example:
  - Mark's inability to remember math facts requires that his sixth-grade teacher select appropriate time for Mark's use of a calculator.
  - Anna's specific needs and IEP require that an LD specialist guide her in an intensive, small-group setting for three hours per week.
- Related or supportive services should be available based on individual student need.
- *If a continuum of service options is not available to individual students with specific learning disabilities, the intent of IDEA is not being met.*

Note: The National Association for the Education of Young Children also supports this position on inclusion.

Courtesy of Division for Learning Disabilities of the Council for Exceptional Children.

- State and local budget allocations and reimbursements should be categorical, based on the recognition that students with LD often require specialized programs, personnel, and resources.
- Teacher competencies, certification standards, and licensure criteria should identify specific professional skills that are critical to effective teaching of students with learning disabilities.

IMPLICATIONS FOR PRACTICE

- The teacher in a regular classroom setting cannot provide the specific and/or intensive instructional services appropriate for some students with LD.
- Students with LD who are placed in general education classrooms will need consultation, support services, and/or direct services from an LD specialist at varying points in their school careers to be successful.
- Determination of the appropriate placement option must be made in conjunction with development of the IEP.
- General education teachers can assist students with LD by using appropriate instructional practices, accommodations, and auxiliary aids in the classroom.
- Personnel who possess specialized skills in learning disabilities must be available to assess learning and guide general education teachers in determining appropriate accommodations, adaptations, and aids.
- Special education and general education professionals must work actively with each family and student to maximize integration with peers and independence at home, in school, and in the workplace.
- *A range of programs, personnel, and service options must be available to permit selection based on individual student needs.*
- The different professional competencies possessed by LD specialists and general education personnel are both needed to achieve positive educational outcomes for all students with LD.
- The annual IEP review must ensure a free, appropriate public education for each individual student with LD.

SOME CURRENT PHILOSOPHIES

- *Mainstreaming* and the *Regular Education Initiative* (REI) encourage the participation of students with learning disabilities in general education classes to the extent it is appropriate to meet their needs.
- *Inclusion* and *inclusive schools* refer to the placement of students with disabilities in general education classrooms or buildings.

- *Full-inclusion* is used by some to refer to the full-time placement in general education classrooms of *all* students with disabilities.
- *A "full-inclusion" program, as defined by its advocates, provides placements ONLY in general education classes for students with learning disabilities.*
- In practice, the terms *mainstreaming, inclusion,* and *full inclusion* are often used interchangeably.

RESEARCH FINDINGS

- Although statistics indicate that more than 80% of students with LD are in general education classrooms, the data refer to all students with LD who spend *any* time in general education classrooms.
- *There is no validated body of research to support large-scale adoption of full inclusion as the only service delivery model for ALL students with LD.*
- Past reports of studies focused on how well students with LD adapted in general education settings were often based on preliminary findings or partial reports.
- Studies comparing the academic progress of students with LD across various settings or program delivery models have tended to produce inconclusive results.
- Recent studies of the progress of students with LD in mainstream settings have shown that *some* students with LD can manage the mainstream curriculum if general education teachers implement accommodations and redesign the instructional environment.
- Recent studies have also shown that many students with LD still need intensive, individualized instruction to achieve significant academic growth.
- Recent studies of the social benefits of including students with LD in the mainstream have produced mixed results.
- Several large-scale, federally funded studies targeting the issue of inclusion are still in progress.

DLD ACTION

- DLD continues to monitor research on model programs and to disseminate information on best practices.
- DLD continues to lobby for the preservation of the services necessary to provide access to learning for students with LD. Our position includes a commitment to categorical assessment, a continuum of service options, and the use of the IEP to plan and monitor services.

RESOURCES

Garnett, K. (1995). *Thinking about inclusion and learning disabilities: A teacher's guide*. Available from CEC/DLD (Stock No. D5140).

Joint Committee on Teacher Planning for Students with Disabilities. (1995). *Planning for academic diversity in America's classrooms.* Available from the University of Kansas Center for Research on Learning, Lawrence, KS.

Kauffman, J.M., & Hallahan, D.P. (Eds.). (1995). *The illusion of full inclusion: A comprehensive critique of a current special education bandwagon.* Austin, TX: Pro-Ed.

Special issue on inclusion. (1995, Summer). *Journal of Special Education, 29*(2).

Learning Disabilities Association of America Position Paper on Full Inclusion of All Students with Learning Disabilities in the Regular Education Classroom (1993)

The Learning Disabilities Association of America, LDA, is a national, not-for-profit organization of parents, professionals, and persons with learning disabilities, concerned about the welfare of individuals with learning disabilities. During the 1990–91 school year 2,117,087 children in public schools in the United States were identified as having learning disabilities. This is more than 50% of the total number of students identified in all disability categories.

Full inclusion, full integration, unified system, inclusive education are terms used to describe a popular policy/practice in which all students with disabilities, regardless of the nature or the severity of the disability and need for related services, receive their total education within the regular education classroom in their home school.

The Learning Disabilities Association of America does not support full inclusion or any policies that mandate the same placement, instruction, or treatment for *all* students with learning disabilities. Many students with learning disabilities benefit from being served in the regular education classroom. However, the regular education classroom is not the appropriate placement for a number of students with learning disabilities who may need alternative instructional environments, teaching strategies, and/or materials that cannot or will not be provided within the context of a regular classroom placement.

LDA believes that decisions regarding educational placement of students with disabilities must be based on the needs of each individual student rather than administrative convenience or budgetary considerations and must be the results of a cooperative effort involving the educators, parents, and the student when appropriate.

LDA strongly supports the Individuals with Disabilities Education Act (IDEA), which mandates:

- a free and appropriate public education in the least restrictive environment appropriate for the students' specific learning needs
- a team-approved individualized education program (IEP) that includes current functioning levels, instructional goals and objectives, placement and services decisions, and procedures for evaluation of program effectiveness
- a placement decision made on an individual basis and considered only after the development of the IEP
- a continuum of alternative placements to meet the needs of students with disabilities for special education and related services
- a system for the continuing education of regular and special education and related services personnel to enable these personnel to meet the needs of children with disabilities

LDA believes that the placement of *all* children with disabilities in the regular education classroom is as great a violation of IDEA as is the placement of *all* children in separate classrooms on the basis of their type of disability.

LDA urges the U.S. Department of Education and each state to move deliberately and reflectively in school restructuring, using the Individuals with Disabilities Education Act as a foundation—mindful of the best interests of all children with disabilities.

Courtesy of Learning Disabilities Association of America.

National Association of Elementary School Principals Position Statement on Inclusion (1994)

The National Association of Elementary School Principals (NAESP) urges school systems to provide educational programs that will permit all children to develop their abilities and aptitudes to the fullest extent possible.

The Association endorses and supports the concepts embodied in the Individuals with Disabilities Education Act and Section 504 of the Rehabilitation Act of 1973, with emphasis in early identification beginning at birth, guaranteeing that all youngsters, irrespective of handicapping and/or health conditions, are entitled to a free, appropriate education in the least restrictive environment.

NAESP supports inclusion of special education students, as appropriate, in regular classrooms with their peers in their neighborhood schools. To facilitate the successful inclusion of special education students, NAESP recognizes that appropriate financial resources, staff development, and support services must follow the child with disabilities.

The Association also recognizes that compliance with legal mandates presents additional managerial and administrative duties that impede the orderly and efficient delivery of educational services to all students.

NAESP supports continuation and expansion of related services to local districts by appropriate state and community service agencies. Additional state and federal financial support is imperative for local school districts to comply with the provisions of these laws.

Courtesy of the National Association of Elementary School Principals, Alexandria, Virginia.

National Association of School Psychologists Position Statement: Inclusive Programs for Students with Disabilities (1993)

The Individuals with Disabilities Education Act (IDEA) created significant educational opportunities for students with disabilities and established important safeguards that ensure the provision of a free, appropriate education to students with special needs. NASP strongly supports the continuation and strengthening of this mandate. NASP also recognizes the need to continually evaluate the effectiveness of all aspects of our educational system and to promote reform when needed.

PROBLEMS WITH THE CURRENT SYSTEM

NASP also recognizes that the special education system that evolved under this mandate includes a number of problems that create unintended negative outcomes for some students. These include:

- A referral and evaluation system that does not function as originally intended. Some of the weaknesses of this system include: (1) an inability to reliably differentiate among categories of students with disabilities; (2) a lack of evidence that students grouped by category learn differently or are taught differently; and (3) a classification system that lacks reliability, utility, and acceptance by many parents and professionals.
- Inequities in implementation of the least restrictive environment provisions of IDEA. Data suggests that the restrictiveness of many special education placements is not based upon the severity of students' disabilities, but may instead result from the configuration of the service delivery system that is available in the community.

- Concerns that traditional special education programs are not effective in terms of learner outcomes.
- Overly restrictive special education programs housed in separate schools or "cluster" sites that result in social segregation and disproportionate numbers of students with disabilities being grouped together. For example, some students, especially those with more severe disabilities, must attend separate schools to receive appropriate special services. Many parents and professionals feel that it is inherently inequitable that some students must leave their neighborhood schools and communities to receive appropriate services.

A CALL FOR INCLUSIVE SCHOOLS

NASP, in its continuing commitment to promote more effective educational programs for ALL students, advocates the development of inclusive programs for students with disabilities. Inclusive programs are those in which students, regardless of the severity of their disability, receive appropriate specialized instruction and related services within an age-appropriate general education classroom in the school that they would attend if they did not have a disability.

NASP believes that carefully designed inclusive programs represent a viable and legitimate alternative on the special education continuum that must be examined for any student who requires special education.

POTENTIAL BENEFITS

Some of the benefits of inclusive programs include:

- typical peers serving as models for students with disabilities

Courtesy of the National Association of School Psychologists, Bethesda, Maryland.

- the development of natural friendships within the child's home community
- learning new skills within natural environments, facilitating generalization of skills
- students with disabilities existing in "natural" proportions within the school community
- all students learning to value diversity
- general education classrooms that are better able to meet the needs of all students as a result of additional instructional resources, a more flexible curriculum, and adapted instructional delivery systems

DEVELOPING INCLUSIVE PROGRAMS

In advocating for the development of these programs, NASP takes the position that:

- Inclusive programs must provide all the services needed to ensure that students make consistent social and academic gains.
- General education teachers, special education teachers, school psychologists, other related service providers, and parents must collaborate to ensure appropriate services for all students and to ensure that all programs are based upon a careful analysis of each student's needs.
- Outcome-based data on inclusive programs must be collected to ensure that students with and without disabilities are making consistent educational progress.
- All educators involved in implementing inclusive programs must participate in planning and training activities. Knowledge and skills in effective collaboration, curriculum adaptation, developing supportive social relationships, and restructuring special services are but a few of the areas in which skills are needed. Training based upon the needs of the staff involved in planning these programs is essential.

THE ROLE OF THE SCHOOL PSYCHOLOGIST

School psychologists can provide effective leadership in the development of inclusive programs. School psychologists have training and experience in collaborative consultation, disabilities, intervention design and curriculum adaptation, modification of learning environments, program evaluation, and other issues critical to effective inclusive programs. Because of this expertise, school psychologists are in a unique position to assist schools in assessing student needs, reallocating existing resources, and restructuring service delivery systems to better meet the educational and mental health needs of all students. School psychologists can foster the development of inclusive schools by:

- providing meaningful support and consultation to teachers and other educators implementing inclusive programs
- distributing articles and research to fellow educators and district committees responsible for educational restructuring
- leading or serving as members of groups that are evaluating or restructuring education programs
- planning and conducting staff development programs that support inclusion
- providing information on needed changes to legislators and state and federal policy makers
- collecting and analyzing program evaluation and outcome-based student data

CHANGING OUR SCHOOLS

NASP recognizes that the current framework of special education policies and regulations is often incompatible with inclusive programs. Consequently, NASP joins with the National Association of State Boards of Education in calling for a fundamental shift in the policies that drive our compensatory education system. Changes are required in:

- *The system used to identify and evaluate students with special needs.* Categorical labeling systems are not only unreliable and stigmatizing, they are unnecessary in an inclusive system.
- *The current special education funding system.* The link between funding and placements must be severed. Many aspects of the funding system are driven by labels and program locations rather than by student needs.

NASP recognizes that the shift toward more inclusive schools will require profound changes in the ways in which schools are organized. We are committed to working with parents, other professional groups, and state and national policy makers in creating new funding and regulatory mechanisms that promote effective programs within neighborhood schools and ensure that students with special needs continue to receive appropriate resources. We endorse a process of planned change that involves all stakeholders in research, planning, and training to ensure that our nation's schools can attain excellence for *all* of our children.

National Association of State Boards of Education Resolution on Students with Special Needs

RESOLUTION

1. To ensure equal educational opportunities, services should be provided for special student needs. Learning programs should identify and address the individual needs and learning styles of all students, including those who are disabled, disadvantaged, migrant, gifted or talented, parenting or pregnant, minority, or of limited English proficiency.

2. State boards should ensure that policies are developed and implemented that guarantee that all students are educated in school environments that include rather than exclude them. School environments encompass all curricular, cocurricular, and extracurricular programs and activities. Inclusion means that all children must be educated in supported, heterogeneous, age-appropriate, natural, child-focused school environments for the purpose of preparing them for full participation in our diverse and integrated society.

WHAT DOES NASBE MEAN BY INCLUSION AND INCLUSIVE EDUCATION?*

At its core, inclusion means that students attend their home school along with their age and grade peers. A truly inclusive schooling environment is one in which students with the full range of abilities and disabilities receive their in-school educational services in the general education classroom with appropriate in-class support. In an inclusive education system, the proportion of students labeled for special services is relatively uniform for the schools within a particular school district and reflects the proportion of people with disabilities in society at large.

Inclusion, as defined by the NASBE, is based on a presumption of starting with the "norm" and then making adaptations as needed, rather than focusing on the "abnormal" and trying to "fix" disabilities to make students fit into a preconceived notion of what is normal.

In short, inclusion is not a place or a method of delivering instruction; it is a philosophy of supporting children in their learning that undergirds the entire system. It is part of the very culture of a school or school district and defines how students, teachers, administrators, and others view the potential of children. The inclusive philosophy of supported education espoused is truly grounded in the belief that all children *can* learn and *achieve*.

*From *System-wide Education Reform for All Students*, NASBE *Issues in Brief*, September 1995, Vol. 15, No. 2.

Courtesy of the National Association of State Boards of Education.

National Center for Learning Disabilities Statement on Inclusion (1994)

INCLUSION: CAN IT WORK FOR THE LEARNING DISABLED?

It is abundantly clear that every child deserves not only the right but the opportunity to receive the most appropriate education given his or her characteristics, needs, and potential to learn and contribute to society. This statement not only reflects common sense, but is also codified in federal law.

While parents, teachers, policy makers, and other educational professionals agree with the above-stated theme, there exists substantial disagreement among educators and policy makers about how to achieve the provision of an appropriate education for all. Recently, major conflicts have arisen about the educational concept of *inclusion* and its actual benefits for children with learning disabilities.

By most recent accounts, the concept of inclusion refers to an administrative arrangement within schools and classrooms whereby all children, regardless of handicap, receive educational services within a "regular" classroom environment. Inclusion, therefore, refers to an educational concept where children receive even specialized services within the context of the general classroom.

FORCES PROPELLING THE INCLUSION MODEL

Historically, the concept of educating children with handicaps within the regular classroom setting had its roots in the "normalization" movement of the late 1960s and early 1970s. The concept of normalization primarily emerged from observations that youngsters and adults with severe to moderate handicaps who were being educated in segregated institutional settings were not benefitting from their isolation from the larger society. The logic underlying normalization was that individuals with limitations in cognitive and behavioral skills could clearly acquire more appropriate *social and behavioral repertoires* if their education occurred in an environment where "typical" or "normal" behaviors and social interactions could be observed, modeled, taught, and reinforced. The benefits appear to accrue primarily in the social/affective domains, not necessarily the cognitive and academic domains.

During the past decade, and in particular, during the past five years, the educational establishment has promoted the concept of *inclusion* as an alternative to traditional special education primarily on the basis of the results achieved in the social domain via the normalization movement. Another important factor, though, is the perceived failure of special education for many children. Data obtained from studies relating to the efficacy of special education classrooms (i.e., resource rooms, self-contained classrooms, etc.) did not demonstrate any clear benefit of removing any child from the regular class environment. It is important to keep in mind that the lack of efficacy of special education for some children is due to factors that have not been fully explored. Consider also, that children with learning disabilities who did receive services in special education classrooms and did benefit from such services, did not continue to demonstrate gains once placed back in the regular classroom—primarily because the special educators and regular educators did not communicate with a common language about what might work and what did not work for an individual child—thus, there was no generalization and maintenance of skills learned in special education classes.

It is possible also that the current move towards inclusion is driven partly by expectation of cost savings and

All references supporting this statement are available from the NCLD office.

Courtesy of the National Center for Learning Disabilities, Inc., New York, New York.

many school systems may have seized on the idea to do that in times of budget crisis.

In adopting the concept of inclusion, enhancement of social development of children may be fostered, but it is not clear that the cognitive needs of children with learning disabilities will be addressed. Where, then, will the cost savings be? Many educators and administrators have already embraced inclusion with too little thought or planning.

Given that inclusion, as an educational policy, will be paramount in our children's educational experience, success, and outcomes, a number of critical conditions must be in place in schools and classrooms to ensure its effectiveness.

A brief overview of some of the most critical conditions is provided below. The status of each condition in our classrooms of today is evaluated and analyzed with respect to the most current information available.

The analysis of the status of critical conditions necessary for the effective implementation of inclusion as an educational policy reveals discouraging results. Simply put, the essential elements of teacher preparation, teaching practices, and teacher collaboration are clearly absent.

This is unfortunate. In the very best sense, inclusion seeks to provide for all children an opportunity to gain a respectful and profound knowledge of each other. It is a concept born of a desire to see children treated with equality and dignity. It epitomizes values that are worthy and consequential.

However, the ideal and the implementation are likely to be at odds with each other unless serious attention is paid to the true individual needs of all children. In the opinion of the National Center for Learning Disabilities, insufficient attention has been paid to this important issue. Enough data now exist that children with LD demonstrate a variety of unique learning needs. These needs are complex and require careful strategies in order to be effectively met. Given the present state of the art, vis-à-vis inclusion, children with LD and their parents have good reason to be concerned.

National Education Association Policy Statement on Appropriate Inclusion (1994)

The National Education Association is committed to equal educational opportunity, the highest quality education, and a safe learning environment for all students. The association supports and encourages appropriate inclusion. *Appropriate inclusion* is characterized by practices and programs that provide for the following on a sustained basis:

- A full continuum of placement options and services within each option. Placement and services must be determined for each student by a team that includes all stakeholders and must be specified in the individualized education program (IEP).

Courtesy of the National Education Association, Washington, D.C.

- Appropriate professional development, as part of normal work activity, of all educators and support staff associated with such programs. Appropriate training must also be provided for administrators, parents, and other stakeholders.
- Adequate time, as part of the normal school day, to engage in coordinated and collaborative planning on behalf of all students.
- Class sizes that are responsive to student needs.
- Staff and technical assistance that is specifically appropriate to student and teacher needs.

Inclusion practices and programs that lack these fundamental characteristics are inappropriate and must end.

National Joint Committee on Learning Disabilities Reaction to Full Inclusion: A Reaffirmation of the Right of Students with Learning Disabilities to a Continuum of Services (1993)

This January 1993 statement of the National Joint Committee on Learning Disabilities (NJCLD) was developed and approved by representatives of the member organizations only. Current members of the NJCLD are: the American Speech-Language-Hearing Association; the Association on Higher Education and Disability; the Council for Learning Disabilities; the Division for Children with Communication Disorders, a division of the Council for Exceptional Children; the International Reading Association; the Learning Disabilities Association of America; the National Association of School Psychologists; the National Center for Learning Disabilities; and the Orton Dyslexia Society.

The National Joint Committee on Learning Disabilities (NJCLD) supports many aspects of school reform. However, one aspect of school reform that the NJCLD cannot support is the idea that *all* students with learning disabilities must be served only in regular education classrooms, frequently referred to as *full inclusion*. The committee believes that *full inclusion*, when defined this way, violates the rights of parents and students with disabilities as mandated by the Individuals with Disabilities Education Act (IDEA).

Because each student with learning disabilities has unique needs, an individualized program must be tailored to meet those needs. For one student, the program may be provided in the regular classroom; yet for another student, the regular classroom may be an inappropriate placement. Therefore, the NJCLD supports the use of a continuum of services and rejects the arbitrary placement of all students in any one setting.

Courtesy of the National Joint Committee on Learning Disabilities.

In *Issues in the Delivery of Educational Services to Individuals with Learning Disabilities*, the NJCLD stated its support and commitment to "a continuum of education placements, including the regular education classroom that must be available to all students with learning disabilities and must be flexible enough to meet their changing needs." This was reaffirmed in 1991 in *Providing Appropriate Education for Students with Learning Disabilities in Regular Education Classrooms*, which recommended that public and private education agencies should "establish system-wide and state-based plans for educating students with learning disabilities in the regular education classroom when such placement is appropriate. The responsibility for developing plans must be shared by regular and special educators, parents, and student consumers of the services. Once developed, a plan must be supported at all levels of the educational system."

In summary, the NJCLD supports educational reform and efforts to restructure schools. As stated in *School Reform: Opportunities for Excellence and Equity for Individuals with Learning Disabilities*, "NJCLD demonstrates a deep concern and desire that parents, professionals, and policy makers work cooperatively in planning and implementing reforms. We strongly urge that strategies be developed within the reform movement to improve education for students with learning disabilities." As these strategies are developed, it is necessary to ensure that each student with a learning disability is provided a continuum of service options that will guarantee a free, appropriate public education based on the student's individual needs.

Orton Dyslexia Society Position Statement on Inclusion

As an international organization of and for a variety of professionals in partnership with individuals with dyslexia and their families, the Orton Dyslexia Society is concerned with the complex issues of dyslexia. The society promotes effective teaching approaches that include systematic multisensory instruction in reading, writing, and spelling that emphasizes phonemic awareness and the structure of the language, and related clinical educational intervention strategies for individuals with dyslexia. The Orton Dyslexia Society also supports and encourages interdisciplinary study and research while facilitating the exploration of the causes and early identification of dyslexia. The Orton Dyslexia Society is committed to the responsible and wide dissemination of research-based knowledge regarding dyslexia and related disorders.

CONTINUUM OF ALTERNATIVE PLACEMENT OPTIONS

All children and youths with specific learning disabilities, including dyslexia, can and do learn and are entitled to a free and appropriate education in the least restrictive environment as defined by *The Individuals with Disabilities Education Act and Section 504 of the Vocational Rehabilitation Act of 1973*. To this end, there must be available to each student with a specific learning disability a continuum of alternative placement options. These must include instruction in regular education classes, special classes, special schools, hospitals and institutions, and at home. Necessary modifications, accommodations, and supplementary aids and services must be provided on an individual basis to provide equal

Courtesy of the Orton Dyslexia Society, Baltimore, Maryland.

access to all educational programs and placement in the least restrictive environment.

INCLUSION

Inclusion is the opportunity for all students with disabilities to have access to and participate in all activities of the school environment in neighborhood schools. Inclusion allows some or all of a student's special education and related services to be provided in regular education classes. An appropriate goal is the education of students with specific learning disabilities in regular education classrooms within neighborhood schools in community settings. However, no single type of placement option will meet the needs of all students with specific learning disabilities. Thus, full inclusion, where all students receive all services including specialized services within the context of the regular education classroom, must not be the only placement option for the provision of services.

INDIVIDUALIZED INSTRUCTION

Students with specific learning disabilities require individualized and/or differential instruction that includes systematic multisensory instruction in reading, writing, and spelling that emphasizes phonemic awareness and the structure of the language. These students must be provided services that will match the severity and intensity of their disability. Each student's individual educational program defines the services needed. The decision as to where these services are provided must be based upon the specific needs of the individual. These services must be student centered and provided in the least restrictive environment that includes regular education classes, special classes, or a combination of the two. Additionally, these services must not be based upon a particular program model/option, the availability of personnel, and/or budgetary concerns.

TRAINING

Intensive prior and continuing inservice and staff development at the school level are critical components to ensure the success of inclusion. Regular and special education staff, administrators, support personnel, and families must be provided with information, pre- and post-planning opportunities, and skill development. These will assist all in the understanding of what a specific learning disability is, how it affects the ways in which the student processes information and learns, and which teaching techniques and interventions (e.g., academic, social, and behavioral) are appropriate and effective. These teaching techniques need to include systematic multisensory instruction.

Essential to the preparation of individuals pursuing a career in education is the curricula of colleges and universities that must stress a collaborative interdisciplinary effort to meet the educational needs of all students. As a result, the curricula must provide these future educators with an understanding of what a specific learning disability is; how it affects a student in the educational environment; effective teaching techniques and interventions that include systematic multisensory instruction, language development, and the structure of the language; and collaborative techniques to ensure cooperation between regular and special education staff. Such curricula are critical if schools are to provide an appropriate education to all students in the least restrictive and most inclusive environment.

ADMINISTRATIVE SUPPORT

With the full support and participation of a knowledgeable school administration and school board, inclusion can be successfully implemented as one way to provide services to individuals with specific learning disabilities. This support and participation are essential to ensure staff motivation, reasonable classroom size and staff caseloads, effective scheduling, consultation/planning time, necessary modifications and accommodations, supplementary aids and services, effective teaching techniques that include systematic multisensory instruction, ongoing staff development, and the provision of adequate human and physical resources.

SUMMARY

The Orton Dyslexia Society supports the provision of services to individuals with specific learning disabilities in the least restrictive environment that includes a continuum of alternative placement options including inclusion. Thus, full inclusion must not be the only placement option for the provision of services since it does not address the cognitive, academic, and social-emotional needs of all students with specific learning disabilities. However, the use of an inclusive placement option requires a collaborative interdisciplinary effort, teacher preparation, availability of effective teaching practices, students and parental involvement, administrative support, and the availability of alternative placement options to ensure the welfare and educational growth of all students as individuals.

The Association for Severe Handicaps Resolution on Inclusive Education (1993/1994)

PREAMBLE

The United States Congress, in passing the Americans with Disabilities Act (ADA) in 1990, found that there were approximately 43 million Americans with disabilities and found that these individuals had been isolated and segregated, faced restrictions and limitations, occupied an inferior status, and had been seriously disadvantaged. The implications of this situation have been evident in the field of education.

RESOLUTION

WHEREAS the democratic ideals of American society can be best served and protected when diversity is highly valued and seen as the norm in all schools; when *all* students are viewed as active, fully participating members of the school community; and when the reciprocal benefits of full inclusion for all students is understood and celebrated;

BE IT RESOLVED that TASH reaffirms a definition of inclusion that begins with the educational and moral imperatives that students with disabilities belong in general education classrooms and that they receive the supports and services necessary to benefit from their education in the general education setting. Inclusion proceeds to and is fully defined by a new way of thinking based upon current understandings about how *all* children and young people are educated—a new way of thinking that embraces a sociology of acceptance of *all* children into the school community as active, fully participating members; that views diversity as the norm and maintains a high-quality education for each student by assuring effective teaching, powerful pedago-

gies, and necessary supports to each child in the general education setting.

BE IT FURTHER RESOLVED that TASH calls upon local, state, provincial, regional, and federal governments, as well as all related organizations, to stand accountable for the development and maintenance of educational opportunities for *all* students that are fully inclusive and ultimately effective; and that the United States government be urged to vigorously enforce, at all levels, legislation *already enacted* that assures such accountability, development, and maintenance.

BE IT FURTHER RESOLVED that TASH recognizes the many highly successful inclusionary practices already in place in classrooms, schools, and school districts across the nation and beyond, and calls upon all those who can make a difference to combine their efforts in a cooperative manner to support and celebrate these efforts and at the same time continue to work as agents of change to bring inclusion to all those who have not yet experienced this new way of thinking.

Research findings and documented experience offer overwhelming support for the following components as essential to the creation of fully inclusive schools:

- General
  - teaching that uses heterogeneous groupings and a variety of age-appropriate instructional strategies based upon students' learning needs and that emphasize active learning strategies
  - high expectations for all students and teachers who treat each student as a uniquely important individual
  - program philosophy that emphasizes the value of diversity, multiculturalism, social inclusion, and belonging for everyone
  - access for all students to campuses and classrooms, including cocurricular and extracurricular

Courtesy of The Association for Persons with Severe Handicaps, Baltimore, Maryland.

activities that are free from prejudice and other physical and psychological barriers

- comprehensive, sensible, and culturally competent curricula that are effective for the full range of learners
- opportunities for all secondary school students to participate in work study or their community and/or job skill development programs that will not negatively impact participation and full membership in the high school community

• Assessment
- thorough analysis of the learning needs of *all* students
- broad use of unbiased and culturally sensitive assessment procedures that enhance students' strengths and assist in the identification of their needs
- accountability for achievement that is based on each student's personal potential and educational experience

• Communication
- emphasis on the importance of family involvement and home-school communication structures that are culturally responsive and that empower families
- conscious creation of a strong sense of community and fostering of mutual respect and support among education staff, parents, and students

- collaboration among teachers, other personnel, family members, students, and peers to plan and deliver educational services
- well-delineated process for problem solving as defined by the family, student, and classmates

• Staff development
- teacher training programs that are inclusive and collaborative of general and special education teachers so that all teachers will be prepared to teach all students effectively
- necessary and appropriate staff development programs for teachers and related services staff that will develop the necessary new understanding, beliefs, skills, and behaviors

• Supports
- the necessary and appropriate supports and services to provide *all* students with opportunity for success
- a broad range of support services (e.g., speech, reading, occupational therapy, assistive technology) that are closely coordinated with the general education classroom's goals and activities and that are provided in general education settings
- creative ways to allocate special and general education resources, with funding obstacles removed

Appendix B

Legal Concerns

Kathe Klare

The Individuals with Disabilities Education Act As Amended through January 1996

The IDEA (20 U.S.C. § 1400 *et seq.*), previously known as the EHA, is reproduced here in part as amended by Congress through January 1996.

(C) Purpose

It is the purpose of this chapter to assure that all children with disabilities have available to them, within the time periods specified in section 1412(2)(B) of this title, a free appropriate public education which emphasizes special education and related services designed to meet their unique needs, to assure that the rights of children with disabilities and their parents or guardians are protected, to assist States and localities to provide for the education of all children with disabilities, and to assess and assure the effectiveness of efforts to educate children with disabilities.

§ 1401. Definitions

(a) As used in this chapter—

(1)(A) The term "children with disabilities" means children—

(i) with mental retardation, hearing impairments including deafness, speech or language impairments, visual impairments including blindness, serious emotional disturbance, orthopedic impairments, autism, traumatic brain injury, other health impairments, or special learning disabilities; and

(ii) who, by reason thereof, need special education and related services.

(B) The term "children with disabilities" for children aged 3 to 5, inclusive, may, at a State's discretion, include children—

(i) experiencing developmental delays, as defined by the State and as measured by appropriate diagnostic instruments and procedures, in one or more of the following areas: physical development, cognitive development, communication development, social or emotional development, or adaptive development; and

(ii) who, by reason thereof, need special education and related services.

(16) The term "special education" means specially designed instruction, at no cost to parents or guardians, to meet the unique needs of a child with a disability, including—

(A) instruction conducted in the classroom, in the home, in hospitals and institutions, and in other settings; and

(B) instruction in physical education.

(17) The term "related services" means transportation, and such developmental, corrective, and other supportive services (including speech pathology and audiology, psychological services, physical and occupational therapy, recreation, including therapeutic recreation, social work services, counseling services including rehabilitation counseling, and medical services, except that such medical services shall be for diagnostic and evaluation purposes only) as may be required to assist a child with a disability to benefit from special education, and includes the early identification and assessment of disabling conditions in children.

(18) The term "free appropriate public education" means special education and related services that—

(A) have been provided at public expense, under public supervision and direction, and without charge,

(B) meet the standards of the State educational agency,

(C) include an appropriate preschool, elementary, or secondary school education in the State involved, and

(D) are provided in conformity with the individualized education program required under section 1414(a)(5) of this title.

Source: Reprinted from the Individuals with Disabilities Act as amended through January 1996.

(19) The term "transition services" means a coordinated set of activities for a student, designed within an outcome-oriented process, which promises movement from school to post-school activities, including post-secondary education, vocational training, integrated employment (including supported employment), continuing and adult education, adult services, independent living, or community participation. The coordinated set of activities shall be based upon the individual student's needs, taking into account the student's preferences and interests and shall include instruction, community experiences, the development of employment and other post-school adult living objectives, and, when appropriate, acquisition of daily living skills and functional vocational evaluation.

(20) The term "individualized education program" means a written statement for each child with a disability developed in any meeting by a representative of the local educational agency or an intermediate educational unit who shall be qualified to provide, or supervise the provision of, specially designed instruction to meet the unique needs of children with disabilities, the teacher, the parents or guardian of such child, and whenever appropriate, such child, which statement shall include—

(A) a statement of the present levels of educational performance of such child,

(B) a statement of annual goals, including short-term instructional objectives,

(C) a statement of the specific educational services to be provided to such child, and the extent to which such child will be able to participate in regular educational programs,

(D) a statement of the needed transition services for students beginning no later than age 16 and annually thereafter (and, when determined appropriate for the individual, beginning at age 14 or younger), including, when appropriate, a statement of the interagency responsibilities or linkages (or both) before the student leaves the school setting,

(E) the projected date for initiation and anticipated duration of such services, and

(F) appropriate objective criteria and evaluation procedures and schedules for determining, on at least an annual basis, whether instructional objectives are being achieved.

In the case where a participating agency, other than the educational agency, fails to provide agreed-upon services, the educational agency shall reconvene the IEP team to identify alternative strategies to meet the transition objectives.

§ 1415. Procedural Safeguards

(a) Establishment and maintenance

Any State educational agency, and local educational agency, and any intermediate educational unit which receives assistance under this subchapter shall establish and maintain procedures in accordance with subsection (b) through subsection (e) of this section to assure that children with disabilities and their parents or guardians are guaranteed procedural safeguards with respect to the provision of free appropriate public education by such agencies and units.

(b) Required procedures; hearing

(1) The procedures required by this section shall include, but shall not be limited to—

(A) an opportunity for the parents or guardian of a child with a disability to examine all relevant records with respect to the identification, evaluation, and educational placement of the child, and the provision of a free appropriate public education to such child, and to obtain an independent educational evaluation of the child;

(B) procedures to protect the rights of the child whenever the parents or guardian of the child are not known, unavailable, or the child is a ward of the State, including the assignment of an individual (who shall not be an employee of the State educational agency, local educational agency, or intermediate educational unit involved in the education or care of the child) to act as a surrogate for the parents or guardian;

(C) written prior notice to the parents or guardian of the child whenever such agency or unit—

(i) proposes to initiate or change, or

(ii) refuses to initiate or change, the identification, evaluation, or educational placement of the child or the provision of a free appropriate public education to the child;

(D) procedures designed to assure that the notice required by clause (C) fully informs the parents or guardian, in the parents' or guardian's native language, unless it clearly is not feasible to do so, of all procedures available pursuant to this section; and

(E) an opportunity to present complaints with respect to any matter relating to the identification, evaluation, or educational placement of the child, or the provision of a free appropriate public education to such child.

(2) Whenever a complaint has been received under paragraph (1) of this subsection, the parents or guardian shall have an opportunity for an impartial due process hearing, which shall be conducted by the State educational agency or by the local educational agency or intermediate educational unit, as determined by State law or by the State educational agency. No hearing conducted pursuant to the requirements of this paragraph shall be conducted by an employee of such agency or unit involved in the education or care of the child.

(c) Review of local decision by State education agency

If the hearing required in paragraph (2) of subsection (b) of this section is conducted by a local educational agency or an intermediate education unit, any party aggrieved by the findings and decision rendered in such a hearing may appeal to the State educational agency, which shall conduct an impartial review of such hearing. The officer conducting such review shall make an independent decision upon completion of such review.

(d) Enumeration of rights accorded parties to hearings

Any party to any hearing conducted pursuant to subsections (b) and (c) of this section shall be accorded—

(1) the right to be accompanied and advised by counsel and by individuals with special knowledge or training with respect to the problems of children with disabilities,

(2) the right to present evidence and confront, cross-examine, and compel the attendance of witnesses,

(3) the right to a written or electronic verbatim record of such hearing, and

(4) the right to written findings of fact and decisions (which findings and decisions shall be made available to the public consistent with the requirements of section 1417(c) of this title and shall also be transmitted to the advisory panel established pursuant to section 1413(a)(12) of this title).

Subchapter VIII—Infants and Toddlers with Disabilities

§ 1472. Definitions

As used in this subchapter—

(1) The term "infants and toddlers with disabilities" means individuals from birth to age 2, inclusive, who need early intervention services because they—

(A) are experiencing developmental delays, as measured by appropriate diagnostic instruments and procedures in one or more of the following areas: cognitive development (hereafter in this subchapter referred to as "communication development"), psychosocial development (hereafter in this subchapter referred to as "social or emotional development"), or self-help skills (hereafter in this subchapter referred to as "adaptive development"), or

(B) have a diagnosed physical or mental condition which has a high probability of resulting in developmental delay.

Such term may also include, at a State's discretion, individuals from birth to age 2, inclusive, who are at risk of having substantial developmental delays if early intervention services are not provided.

(2) The term "early intervention services" are developmental services which—

(A) are provided under public supervision,

(B) are provided at no cost except where Federal or State law provides for a system of payments; by families, including a schedule of sliding fees,

(C) are designed to meet the developmental needs of an infant or toddler with a disability in one or more of the following areas:

(i) physical development,

(ii) cognitive development,

(iii) communication development,

(iv) social or emotional development, or

(v) adaptive development.

(D) meet the standards of the state, including the requirements of this subchapter,

(E) include—

(i) family training, counseling, and home visits,

(ii) special instruction,

(iii) speech pathology and audiology,

(iv) occupational therapy,

(v) physical therapy,

(vi) psychological services,

(vii) case management services (hereafter in this subchapter referred to as "service coordination services"),

(viii) medical services only for diagnostic or evaluation purposes,

(ix) early identification, screening, and assessment services,

(x) health services necessary to enable the infant or toddler to benefit from the other early intervention services,

(xi) social work services,

(xii) vision services,

(xiii) assistive technology devices and assistive technology services, and

(xiv) transportation and related costs that are necessary to enable an infant or toddler or the infant's or toddler's family to receive early intervention services,

(F) are provided by qualified personnel, including—

(i) special educators,

(ii) speech and language pathologists and audiologists,

(iii) occupational therapists,

(iv) physical therapists,

(v) psychologists,

(vi) social workers,

(vii) nurses,

(viii) nutritionists,

(ix) family therapists,

(x) orientation and mobility specialists, and

(xi) pediatricians and other physicians,

(G) to the maximum extent appropriate, are provided in natural environments, including the home, and community settings in which children without disabilities participate, and

(H) are provided in conformity with an individualized family service plan adopted in accordance with section 1477 of this title.

(3) The term "developmental delay" has the meaning given such term by a State under section 1476(b)(1) of this title.

(4) The term "Council" means the State Interagency Coordinating Council established under section 1482 of this title.

§ 1477. Individualized family service plan

(a) Assessment and program development

Each infant or toddler with a disability and the infant's or toddler's family shall receive—

(1) a multidisciplinary assessment of the unique strengths and needs of the infant or toddler and the identification of services appropriate to meet such needs,

(2) a family-directed assessment of the resources, priorities, and concerns of the family and the identification of the supports and services necessary to enhance the family's capacity to meet the developmental needs of their infant or their infant or toddler with a disability, and

(3) a written individualized family service plan developed by a multidisciplinary team, including the parent or guardian, as required by subsection (d) of this section.

(b) Periodic review

The individualized family service plan shall be evaluated once a year and the family shall be provided a review of the plan at 6-month intervals (or more often where appropriate based on infant or toddler and family needs).

(c) Promptness after assessment

The individualized family service plan shall be developed within a reasonable time after the assessment required by subsection (a)(1) of this section is completed. With the parent's consent, early intervention services may commence prior to the completion of such assessment.

(d) Content of plan

The individualized family service plan shall be in writing and contain—

(1) a statement of the infant's or toddler's present levels of physical development, cognitive development, communication development, social or emotional development, and adaptive development, based on acceptable objective criteria,

(2) a statement of the family's resources, priorities, and concerns relating to enhancing the development of the family's infant or toddler with a disability,

(3) a statement of the major outcomes expected to be achieved for the infant or toddler and the family, and the criteria, procedures, and timelines used to determine the degree to which progress toward achieving the outcomes is being made and whether modifications or revisions of the outcomes or services are necessary,

(4) a statement of specific early intervention services necessary to meet the unique needs of the infant or toddler and the family, including the frequency, intensity, and the method of delivering services,

(5) a statement of the natural environments in which early intervention services shall appropriately be provided,

(6) the projected dates for initiation of services and the anticipated duration of such services,

(7) the name of the case manager (hereafter in this subchapter referred to as the "service coordinator") from the profession most immediately relevant to the infant's or toddler's or family's needs (or who is otherwise qualified to carry out all applicable responsibilities under this subchapter) who will be responsible for the implementation of the plan and coordination with other agencies and persons, and

(8) the steps to be taken supporting the transition of the toddler with a disability to services provided under subchapter II of this chapter to the extent such services are considered appropriate.

(e) Parental consent

The contents of the individualized family service plan shall be fully explained to the parents or guardian, and informed written consent from such parents or guardian shall be obtained prior to the provision of early intervention services described in such plan. If such parents or guardian do not provide such consent with respect to a particular early intervention service, then the early intervention services to which such consent is obtained shall be provided.

Federal Regulations and Amendments through July 1995: IDEA Regulations (Part 300)

[The most important federal regulations and amendments affecting the education of children with disabilities are Parts 300 and 104 of Title 34 of the Code of Federal Regulations. *Part 300 has been reproduced here in part as promulgated by the U.S. Department of Education.]*

§300.8 Free appropriate public education.

As used in this part, the term "free appropriate public education" means special education and related services that—

(a) Are provided at public expense, under public supervision and direction, and without charge;

(b) Meet the standards of the SEA, including the requirements of this part;

(c) Include preschool, elementary school, or secondary school education in the State involved; and

(d) Are provided in conformity with an IEP that meets the requirements of §§300.340–300.350. (Authority: 20 U.S.C. 1401(a)(18))

§ 300.17 Special education.

(a)(1) As used in this part, the term "special education" means specially designed instruction, at no cost to the parents, to meet the unique needs of a child with a disability, including—

(i) Instruction conducted in the classroom, in the home, in hospitals and institutions, and in other settings; and

(ii) Instruction in physical education.

(2) The term includes speech pathology, or any other related service, if the service consists of specially designed instruction, at no cost to the parents, to meet the unique needs of a child with a disability, and is considered special education rather than a related service under State standards.

_____

Source: Reprinted from Federal Regulation and Amendments through July 1995: IDEA Regulations (Part 300).

(3) The term also includes vocational education if it consists of specially designed instruction, at no cost to the parents, to meet the unique needs of a child with a disability.

(b) The terms in this definition are defined as follows:

(1) "At no cost" means that all specially designed instruction is provided without charge, but does not preclude incidental fees that are normally charged to nondisabled students or their parents as a part of the regular education program.

(2) "Physical education" is defined as follows:

(i) The term means the development of—

(A) Physical and motor fitness;

(B) Fundamental motor skills and patterns: and

(C) Skills in aquatics, dance, and individual and group games and sports (including intramural and lifetime sports).

(ii) The term includes special physical education, adaptive physical education, movement education, and motor development.

(Authority: 20 U.S.C. 1401(a)(16))

(3) "Vocational education" means organized educational programs which are directly related to the preparation of individuals for paid or unpaid employment, or for additional preparation for a career requiring other than a baccalaureate or advanced degree.

(Authority: 20 U.S.C. 1401(16))

Note 1: The definition of special education is a particularly important one under these regulations, since a child does not have a disability under this part unless he or she needs special education. (See the definition of children with disabilities in §300.7.) The definition of related services (§300.16) also depends on this definition, since a related service must be necessary for a child to benefit from special education. Therefore, if a child does not need special education, there can be no related services, and the child is not a child with a disability and is therefore not covered under the Act.

Note 2: The above definition of vocational education is taken from the Vocational Education Act of 1963, as amended by Pub. L. 94-482. Under that Act, "vocational education" includes industrial arts and consumer and home-making education programs. [57 FR 44798, Sept. 29, 1992: 57 FR 48694, Oct. 27, 1992]

300.18 Transition services.

(a) As used in this part, "transition services" means a coordinated set of activities for a student, designed within an outcome-oriented process, that promotes movement from school to post-school activities, including postsecondary education, vocational training, integrated employment (including supported employment), continuing and adult education, adult services, independent living, or community participation.

(b) The coordinated set of activities described in paragraph (a) of this section must—

(1) Be based on the individual student's needs, taking into account the student's preferences and interests; and

(2) Include—

(i) Instruction;

(ii) Community experiences;

(iii) The development of employment and other post-school adult living objectives; and

(iv) If appropriate, acquisition of daily living skills and functional vocational evaluation.

(Authority: 20 U.S.C. 1401(1)(19))

Note: Transition services for students with disabilities may be special education, if they are provided as specially designed instruction, or related services, if they are required to assist a student with a disability to benefit from special education. The list of activities in paragraph (b) is not intended to be exhaustive.

§300.342 When individualized education programs must be in effect.

(a) At the beginning of each school year, each public agency shall have in effect an IEP for every child with a disability who is receiving special education from that agency.

(b) An IEP must—

(1) Be in effect before special education and related services are provided to a child; and

(2) Be implemented as soon as possible following the meetings under §300.343.

(Authority: 20 U.S.C. 1412(2)(B), (4), (6); 1414(a)(5); Pub. L. 94-142, Sec 8(c)(1975))

Note: Under paragraph (b)(2) of this section, it is expected that the IEP of a child with a disability will be implemented immediately following the meetings under §300.343. An exception to this would be (1) when the meetings occur during the summer or a vacation period, or (2) where there are circumstances that require a short delay

(e.g., working out transportation arrangements). However, there can be no undue delay in providing special education and related services to the child.

§300.346 Content of individualized education program.

(a) *General.* The IEP for each child must include:

(1) A statement of the child's present levels of educational performance;

(2) A statement of annual goals, including short-term instructional objectives;

(3) A statement of the specific special education and related services to be provided to the child and the extent to which the child will be able to participate in regular educational programs;

(4) The projected dates for initiation of services and the anticipated duration of the services; and

(5) Appropriate objective criteria and evaluation procedures and schedules for determining, on at least an annual basis, whether the short-term instructional objectives are being achieved.

(b) *Transition services.* (1) The IEP for each student, beginning no later than age 16 (and at a younger age, if determined appropriate), must include a statement of the needed transition services as defined in §300.18 including, if appropriate, a statement of each public agency's and each participating agency's responsibilities or linkages, or both, before the student leaves the school setting.

(2) If the IEP team determines that services are not needed in one or more of the areas specified in §300.18 (b)(2)(i) through (b)(2)(iii), the IEP must include a statement to that effect and the basis upon which the determination was made.

(Authority: 20 U.S.C. 1401(a)(19), (a)(20); 1412(2)(B), (4), (6); 1414(a)(5))

Note 1: The legislative history of the transition services provisions of the Act suggests that the statement of needed transition services referred to in paragraph (b) of this section should include a commitment by any participating agency to meet any financial responsibility it may have in the provision of transition services. See House Report No. 101-544, p. 11 (1990).

Note 2: With respect to the provisions of paragraph (b) of this section, it is generally expected that the statement of needed transition services will include the areas listed in §300.18(b)(2)(i) through (b)(2)(iii). If the IEP team determines that services are not needed in one of those areas, the public agency must implement the requirements in paragraph (b)(2) of this section. Since it is a part of the IEP, the IEP team must reconsider its determination at least annually.

Note 3: Section 602(a)(20) of the Act provides that IEPs must include a statement of needed transition services for students beginning no later than age 16, but permits transition services to students below age 16 (i.e. " . . . and, when determined appropriate for the individual, beginning at age 14 or younger."). Although the statute does not mandate transition services to students beginning at age 14 or younger, the provision of these services could have a significantly positive effect on the employment and independent living outcomes for many of these students in the future, especially for students who are likely to drop out before age 16. With respect to the provision of transition services to students below age 16, the Report of the House Committee on Education and Labor on Public Law 101-476 includes the following statement:

> Although this language leaves the final determination of when to initiate transition services for students under age 16 to the IEP process, it nevertheless makes clear that Congress expects consideration to be given to the need for transition services for some students by age 14 or younger. The Committee encourages that approach because of their concern that age 16 may be too late for many students, particularly those at risk of dropping out of school and those with the most severe disabilities. Even for those students who stay in school until age 18, many will need more than two years of transitional services. Students with disabilities are now dropping out of school before age 16, feeling that the education system has little to offer them. Initiating services at a younger age will be critical. (House Report No. 101-555,10 (1990)).

Least Restrictive Environment [LRE]

§300.550 General.

(a) Each SEA shall ensure that each public agency establishes and implements procedures which meet the requirements of §§300.550–300.556.

(b) Each public agency shall ensure—

(1) That to the maximum extent appropriate, children with disabilities, including children in public or private institutions or other care facilities, are educated with children who are nondisabled; and

(2) That special classes, separate schooling, or other removal of children with disabilities from the regular educational environment occurs only when the nature or severity of the disability is such that education in regular classes with the use of supplementary aids and services cannot be achieved satisfactorily.

(Authority: 20 U.S.C. 1412(5)(B)); 1414(a)(1)(C)(iv))

§300.551 Continuum of alternative placements.

(a) Each public agency shall ensure that a continuum of alternative placements is available to meet the needs of children with disabilities for special education and related services.

(b) The continuum required under paragraph (a) of this section must—

(1) Include the alternative placements listed in the definition of special education under §300.17 (instruction in regular classes, special classes, special schools, home instruction, and instruction in hospitals and institutions); and

(2) Make provisions for supplementary services (such as resource room or itinerant instruction) to be provided in conjunction with regular class placement.

(Authority: 20 U.S.C. 1412(5)(B))

§300.552 Placements.

Each public agency shall ensure that;

(a) The educational placement of each child with a disability—

(1) Is determined at least annually;

(2) Is based on his or her IEP; and

(3) Is as close as possible to the child's home.

(b) The various alternative placements included at §300.551 are available to the extent necessary to implement the IEP for each child with a disability.

(c) Unless the IEP of a child with a disability requires some other arrangement, the child is educated in the school which he or she would attend if nondisabled.

(d) In selecting the LRE, consideration is given to any potential harmful effect on the child or on the quality of services that he or she needs.

(Authority: 20 U.S.C. 1414(5)(B))

Note: Section 300.552 includes some of the main factors which must be considered in determining the extent to which a child with a disability can be educated with children who are nondisabled. The overriding rule in this section is that placement decisions must be made on an individual basis. The section also requires each agency to have various alternative placements available in order to ensure that each child with a disability receives an education that is appropriate to his or her individual needs.

The requirements of §300.552, as well as the other requirements of §300.550–300.556, apply to all preschool children with disabilities who are entitled to receive FAPE. Public agencies that provide preschool programs for nondisabled preschool children must ensure that the requirements of §300.552(c) are met. Public agencies that do not operate programs for nondisabled preschool children are not required to initiate such programs solely to satisfy the requirements regarding placement in the LRE embodied in §§300.550–300.556. For these public agencies, some alternative methods for meeting the requirements of §§300.550–300.556 include:

(1) Providing opportunities for the participation (even part-time) of preschool children with disabilities in other preschool programs operated by public agencies (such as Head Start);

(2) Placing children with disabilities in private school programs for nondisabled preschool children or private school preschool programs that integrate children with disabilities and nondisabled children; and

(3) Locating classes for preschool children with disabilities in regular elementary schools.

In each case the public agency must ensure that each child's placement is in the LRE in which the unique needs of the child can be met, based upon the child's IEP, and meets all of the other requirements of §§300.340–300.350 and §§300.550-300.556.

The analysis of the regulations for Section 504 of the Rehabilitation Act of 1973 (34 CFR Part 104—Appendix, Paragraph 24) includes several points regarding educational placements of children with disabilities which are pertinent to this section:

(1) With respect to determining proper placements, analysis states: ". . . it should be stressed that, where a handicapped child is so disruptive in a regular classroom that the education of other students is significantly impaired, the needs of the handicapped child cannot be met in that environment. Therefore, regular placement would not be appropriate to his or her needs. . . .

(2) With respect to placing a child with a disability in an alternative setting, the analysis states that among the factors to be considered in placing a child is the need to place the child as close to home as possible. Recipients are required to take this factor into account in making placement decisions. The parents' right to challenge the placement of their child extends not only to placement in special classes or separate schools, but also to placement in a distant school, particularly in a residential program. An equally appropriate education program may exist closer to home; and this issue may be raised by the parent under the due process provisions of this subpart.

§300.553 Nonacademic settings.

In providing or arranging for the provision of nonacademic and extracurricular services and activities, including meals, recess periods, and the services and activities set forth in §300.306, each public agency shall ensure that each child with a disability participates with nondisabled children in those services and activities to the maximum extent appropriate to the needs of that child.
(Authority: 20 U.S.C. 1412(5)(B))

Note: Section 300.553 is taken from a requirement in the final regulations for Section 504 of the Rehabilitation Act of 1973. With respect to this requirement, the analysis of the Section 504 Regulations includes the following statement: "[This paragraph] specifies that [children with disabilities] must also be provided nonacademic services in as integrated a setting as possible. This requirement is especially important for children whose educational needs necessitate their being solely with other handicapped children during most of each day. To the maximum extent appropriate, children in residential settings are also to be provided opportunities for participation with other children." (34 CFR Part 104—Appendix, Paragraph 24)

§300.554 Children in public or private institutions.

Each SEA shall make arrangements with public and private institutions (such as a memorandum of agreement or special implementation procedures) as may be necessary to ensure that §300.550 is effectively implemented.
(Authority: 20 U.S.C. 1412(5)(B))

Note: Under section 612(5)(B) of the statute, the requirement to educate children with disabilities with nondisabled children also applies to children in public and private institutions or other care facilities. Each SEA must ensure that each applicable agency and institution in the State implements this requirement. Regardless of other reasons for institutional placement, no child in an institution who is capable of education in a regular public school setting may be denied access to an education in that setting.

Section 504 of the Rehabilitation Act of 1973 (Revised July 1, 1995): Part 104— Nondiscrimination on the Basis of Handicap in Programs and Activities Receiving Federal Financial Assistance

Subpart A—General Provisions

§104.1 Purpose.

The purpose of this part is to effectuate section 504 of the Rehabilitation Act of 1973, which is designed to eliminate discrimination of the basis of handicap in any program or activity receiving Federal financial assistance.

§104.3 Definitions.

As used in this part, the term:

(a) *The Act* means the Rehabilitation Act of 1973, Pub. L. 93-112, as amended by the Rehabilitation Act Amendments of 1974, Pub. L. 93-516, 29 U.S.C. 794.

(b) *Section 504* means section 504 of the Act.

(c) *Education of the Handicapped Act* means that statute as amended by the Education for all Handicapped Children Act of 1975, Pub. L. 94-142, 20 U.S.C. 1401 et seq.

(d) *Department* means the Department of Education.

(j) *Handicapped person.* (1) "Handicapped persons" means any person who (i) has a physical or mental impairment, which substantially limits one or more major life activities, (ii) has a record of such an impairment, or (iii) is regarded as having such an impairment.

(2) As used in paragraph (j)(1) of this section, the phrase:

(i) *Physical or mental impairment* means (A) any physiological disorder or condition, cosmetic disfigurement, or anatomical loss affecting one or more of the following body systems: neurological; musculoskeletal; special sense organs; respiratory, including speech organs; cardiovascular; reproductive, digestive, genitourinary; hemic and lymphatic; skin; and endocrine; or (B) any mental or psychological disorder,

such as mental retardation, organic brain syndrome, emotional or mental illness, and specific learning disabilities.

(ii) *Major life activities* means functions such as caring for one's self, performing manual tasks, walking, seeing, hearing, speaking, breathing, learning, and working.

(iii) *Has a record of such an impairment* means has a history of, or has been misclassified as having, a mental or physical impairment that substantially limits one or more major life activities.

(iv) *Is regarded as having an impairment* means (A) has a physical or mental impairment that does not substantially limit major life activities but that is treated by a recipient as constituting such a limitation; (B) has a physical or mental impairment that substantially limits major life activities only as a result of the attitudes of others toward such impairment; or (C) has none of the impairments defined in paragraph (j)(2)(i) of this section but is treated by a recipient as having such an impairment.

(k) *Qualified handicapped person* means:

(2) With respect to public preschool elementary, secondary, or adult educational services, a handicapped person (i) of an age during which nonhandicapped persons are provided such services, (ii) of any age during which it is mandatory under state law to provide such services to handicapped persons, or (iii) to whom a state is required to provide a free appropriate public education under section 612 of the Education of the Handicapped Act; and

(3) With respect to postsecondary and vocational education services, a handicapped person who meets the academic and technical standards requisite to admission or participation in the recipient's education program or activity;

(l) *Handicap* means any condition or characteristic that renders a person a handicapped person as defined in paragraph (j) of this section.

Source: Reprinted from Section 504 of the Rehabilitation Act of 1973 (Revised July 1, 1995): Part 104—Nondiscrimination on the Basis of Handicap in Programs and Activities Receiving Financial Assistance.

§104.4 Discrimination prohibited.

(a) *General.* No qualified handicapped person shall, on the basis of handicap, be excluded from participation in, be denied the benefits of, or otherwise be subjected to discrimination under any program or activity which receives or benefits from federal financial assistance.

Subpart D—Preschool, Elementary, and Secondary Education

§104.31 Application of this subpart.

Subpart D applies to preschool, elementary, secondary, and adult education programs and activities that receive or benefit from Federal financial assistance and to recipients that operate, or that receive or benefit from Federal financial assistance from the operation of, such programs or activities.

104.32 Location and notification.

A recipient that operates a public elementary or secondary education program shall annually:

(a) Undertake to identify and locate every qualified handicapped person residing in the recipient's jurisdiction who is not receiving a public education; and

(b) Take appropriate steps to notify handicapped persons and their parents or guardians of the recipient's duty under this subpart.

§104.33 Free, appropriate public education.

(a) *General.* A recipient that operates a public elementary or secondary education program shall provide a free, appropriate public education to each qualified handicapped person who is in the recipient's jurisdiction, regardless of the nature or severity of the person's handicap.

(b) *Appropriate education.* (1) For the purpose of this subpart, the provision of an appropriate education is the provision of regular or special education and related aids and services that (i) are designed to meet individual educational needs of handicapped persons as adequately as the needs of nonhandicapped persons are met and (ii) are based upon adherence to procedures that satisfy the requirements of §§104.34, 104.35, and 104.36.

(2) Implementation of an individualized education program developed in accordance with the Education of the Handicapped Act is one means of meeting the standard established in paragraph (b)(1)(i) of this section.

(3) A recipient may place a handicapped person in or refer such person to a program other than the one that it operates as its means of carrying out the requirements of this subpart. If so, the recipient remains responsible for ensuring that the requirements of this subpart are met with respect to any handicapped person so placed or referred.

(C) *Free education.* (1) *General.* For the purpose of this section, the provision of a free education is the provision of educational and related services without cost to the handicapped person or to his or her parents or guardian, except for those fees that are imposed on non-handicapped persons or their parents or guardian. It may consist either of the provision of free services or, if a recipient places a handicapped persons in or refers such person to a program not operated by the recipient as its means of carrying out the requirements of this subpart, of payment for the costs of the program. Funds available from any public or private agency may be used to meet the requirements of this subpart. Nothing in this section shall be construed to relieve an insurer or similar third party from an otherwise valid obligation to provide or pay for services provided to a handicapped person.

(3) *Residential placement.* If placement in a public or private residential program is necessary to provide a free appropriate public education to a handicapped person because of his or her handicap, the program, including nonmedical care and room and board, shall be provided at no costs to the person or his or her parents or guardian.

(4) *Placement of handicapped persons by parents.* If a recipient has made available, in conformance with the requirements of this section and §104.34, a free appropriate public education to a handicapped person and the person's parents or guardian choose to place the person in a private school, the recipient is not required to pay for the person's education in the private school. Disagreements between a parent or guardian and a recipient regarding whether the recipient has made such a program available or otherwise regarding the question of financial responsibility are subject to the due process procedures of §104.36.

§104.34 Educational setting.

(a) *Academic setting.* A recipient to which this subpart applies shall educate, or shall provide for the education of, each qualified handicapped person in its jurisdiction with persons who are not handicapped to the maximum extent appropriate to the needs of the handicapped person. A recipient shall place a handicapped person in the regular educational environment operated by the recipient unless it is demonstrated by the recipient that the education of the person in the regular environment with the use of supplementary aids and services cannot be achieved satisfactorily. Whenever a recipient places a person in a setting other than the regular educational environment pursuant to this paragraph, it shall take into account the proximity of the alternate setting to the person's home.

(b) *Nonacademic settings.* In providing or arranging for the provision of nonacademic and extracurricular services and activities, including meals, recess periods, and the services and activities set forth in §104.37(a)(2), a recipient shall ensure that handicapped persons participate with non-handicapped persons in such activities and services to the maximum extent appropriate to the needs of the handicapped person in question.

(c) *Comparable facilities.* If a recipient, in compliance with paragraph (a) of this section, operates a facility that is identifiable as being for handicapped persons, the recipient shall ensure that the facility and the services and activities provided therein are comparable to the other facilities, services, and activities of the recipient.

§104.35 Evaluation and placement.

(3) Tests are selected and administered so as best to ensure that, when a test is administered to a student with impaired sensory, manual, or speaking skills, the test results accurately reflect the student's aptitude or achievement level or whatever other factor the test purports to measure, rather than reflecting the student's impaired sensory, manual, or speaking skills (except where those skills are the factors that the test purports to measure).

§104.36 Procedural safeguards.

A recipient that operates a public elementary or secondary education program shall establish and implement, with respect to actions regarding the identification, evaluation, or educational placement of persons who, because of handicap, need or are believed to need special instruction or related services, a system of procedural safeguards that includes notice, an opportunity for the parents or guardian of the person to examine relevant records, an impartial hearing with opportunity for participation by the person's parents or guardian and representation by counsel, and a review procedure. Compliance with the procedural safeguards of Section 615 of the Education of the Handicapped Act is one means of meeting this requirement.

§104.37 Nonacademic services.

(c) *Physical education and athletics.* (1) In providing physical education courses and athletics and similar programs and activities to any of its students, a recipient to which this subpart applies may not discriminate on the basis of handicap. A recipient that offers physical education courses or that operates or sponsors interscholastic, club, or intramural athletics shall provide to qualified handicapped students an equal opportunity for participation in these activities.

(2) A recipient may offer to handicapped students physical education and athletic activities that are separate or different from those offered to nonhandicapped students only if separation or differentiation is consistent with the requirements of §104.34 and only if no qualified handicapped student is denied the opportunity to compete for teams or to participate in courses that are not separate or different.

Case Materials

Kathe Klare

DANIEL R.R. V. STATE BOARD OF EDUCATION (1989)

In this case, the parents of a six-year-old child with Down syndrome and a developmental age of two to three years, requested a placement for one-half day in an early childhood class and one-half day in a prekindergarten class. Although the child was not dangerous, he required almost constant supervision. The school wanted the child placed in a separate school attended only by children with disabilities. While the proceedings were going on, the child was placed in a regular public school, where he was mainstreamed for lunch, gym, and recess.[1] The school's position was that any minimal benefits that the child would receive would be greatly outweighed by the benefits from the services that could not reasonably be provided in a nonsegregated environment. Daniel was placed in the prekindergarten class and, according to school personnel, problems developed. These problems included Daniel's lack of participation in class unless he was constantly provided with individual attention of the teacher or aide. In addition, he was unable to master the skills in the prekindergarten class. The school argued that, based on his placement in this class, the necessary modifications to the curriculum would mean that Daniel would not be taught the same skills that were being taught to the other students in the class.

After Daniel was in the prekindergarten placement for about a month, the school convened a meeting to discuss an appropriate placement. The school district recommended placement in the early childhood class with mainstreaming for recess and for lunch, three times per week, if Daniel's mother supervised Daniel for the lunch period. The parents disagreed with the recommended placement and requested a review. The hearing officer found that having Daniel in the prekindergarten class was disruptive because Daniel absorbed too much of the teacher's time. In addition, the curriculum was modified so that Daniel was not required to learn any of the skills that were being taught in the regular classroom. The court, in applying its two-part test, found that mainstreaming for Daniel did not include inclusion in a regular education environment for academic subjects.

GREER V. ROME CITY SCHOOL DISTRICT (1991)

In *Greer*, the court applied the *Daniel R.R.* test. Christy was placed in kindergarten at her parents' request. The school district testified that, while in kindergarten, Christy required more attention than other children in the class and that she was not keeping up with the curriculum. The school also testified that Christy required repeated rehearsal and practice of basic skills in an individualized setting.[2] Although there was testimony that Christy could possibly make some progress in the regular curriculum, it was the opinion of the school that Christy would make more progress in a self-contained class. She would be mainstreamed for physical education, music, and lunch.

The parents disagreed with the school's assessment and decided to have Christy evaluated independently. The parents' psychologist expressed concern over placement in a self-contained class. Specifically, the psychologist stated that he believed that "if Christy was placed in the self-contained class, Christy would not have those peer models to imitate and therefore would not be intellectually stimulated and would be cheated of the opportunity to cognitively stretch herself to the limits."[3]

The only two options considered by the school for placement were the regular education placement with no special education services or the regular education class with speech services as the parents requested. The school's proposed placement was special education services in a self-contained class with speech-language services and mainstreaming for physical education, lunch, music, and assembly, increasing the mainstreaming where and when Christy could be successful.[4]

The evidence did not indicate that the school considered placing Christy in the regular class with the use of any supplementary aids and services such as a resource room, itinerant instruction, or curriculum adjustment.[5] Because of the length of these proceedings, Christy remained in a regular education class for three years. The court ultimately decided that the school district had failed to consider an individualized education program that would allow Christy to remain in the regular kindergarten with supplemental aids and services. Thus, no further inquiry was needed by the court.

OBERTI V. BOARD OF EDUCATION OF THE BOROUGH OF CLEMENTON SCHOOL DISTRICT (1993)

This disagreement began when the school recommended that Rafael be placed in a segregated special education class. The parents refused this placement. The parents requested "full inclusion" in a regular education class. The parties reached compromise to this proposal that permitted placement of Rafael into a developmental kindergarten in the mornings and a special education class in another district in the afternoons, as indicated on his IEP. Rafael received his academic subjects in the special class; when he was in the regular class, his educational goals included observing, modeling, and socializing with his nondisabled peers. When he was placed in the developmental kindergarten, it was without a curriculum plan or a behavior management plan. In addition, there was not sufficient support or consultation to the teacher.[6]

Rafael made progress academically, socially, and emotionally with respect to language development while in the developmental kindergarten. Rafael also exhibited some "serious" behavior problems such as temper tantrums, spitting, and hitting other children and the teachers. As a result of the behaviors, some attempts were made to modify the curriculum, but the IEP did not address the behavioral issues, nor was the special education teacher consulted. The behaviors were absent in the special education class.

Although another aide was added to the regular class, the behavior problems continued. The school recommended that Rafael be placed in a segregated class for the next school year. They based this decision on their opinions that he did not benefit from the regular placement. The parents and school agreed to a special education class for the "multiple handicapped" in a placement other than his neighbor-

hood school. The school was to continue to explore mainstreaming options during this time. Although Rafael made progress in this program, he had no meaningful contact with his nondisabled peers.

At the hearing, the parents' exhibits testified that a number of commonly applied strategies could have been used in the regular classroom. These included (1) modifying some of the curriculum for all students to accommodate Rafael's different ability; (2) modifying only Rafael's program so that he would perform a similar activity as the rest of the class, but at his level of ability; (3) having Rafael work separately within the class on an activity that he could benefit from while the rest of the class worked on an activity that he could not benefit from (parallel instruction); and (4) removing him from class to receive some special instruction in a resource room.

The school's experts testified that Rafael's behavior could not be managed in the regular class, that a regular teacher would not be able to communicate with him, and that it would be difficult, if not impossible, to adapt a curriculum without adversely affecting the education of the other children. This court, in making its decision, applied the articulated standards and found that the school district did not meet its burden of proving that Rafael could not be educated satisfactorily with the use of supplementary aides and services and ordered the more inclusive plan.

TARAH P. V. BOARD OF EDUCATION OF FREMONT SCHOOL DISTRICT 79 (1995)

In Tarah P., the school considered four options and decided on a cooperative school outside the school district that housed a fully integrated kindergarten.[7] This school was located four miles from Tarah's home. The class had 23 regular education students, 3 special education students, a full-time classroom teacher, a special education teacher, and an aide. This placement was recommended by the school to assist Tarah in using an augmentative communication device called the Macaw. The special education teacher would be available to modify the curriculum immediately at this school.[8] This placement was not in the neighborhood school. The parents placed Tarah in a Montessori school and initiated a due process review. The court believed that the availability of a special education teacher involved methodology and was, therefore, an administrative decision left to the schools. Thus, the court found that mainstreaming was not equal to placement in a neighborhood school, specifically when the issue turned on the question of methodology.

NOTES

1. *Daniel R.R. v. State Board of Education*, 874 F.2d 1036, 1039 (5th Cir. 1989).

2. *Greer v. Rome City School District*, 950 F.2d 688 (11th Cir. 1991).

3. *Id.* at 692.

4. *Id.* at 692.

5. *Id.*

6. *Oberti v. Board of Education of the Borough of Clementon School District*, 995 F.2d 1204, 1208 (3rd Cir. 1993).

7. *Tarah P. v. Board of Education of Fremont School District 79*, No. 94C3896, 1995 U.S. Dist. LEXIS 1845. (N.D. Ill. Feb. 14, 1995).

8. *Id.* at 4.

Index

C

D

T